A LINCOLN DIALOGUE

...W CITIZENS OF THE UNITED ... IN COMPLIANCE WITH A CUSTOM AS OLD AS THE GOVERNMENT ... ... BEFORE YOU T
...SS YOU BRIEFLY, AND TO TAK... ... PRESENCE, THE OATH PRESCRIBED BY THE CONSTITUTION ... ...ATES, TO BE TAKE...
...E PRESIDENT "BEFORE HE E... ...THE EXECUTION OF HIS OFFICE." I DO NOT CONSIDER IT ...NE... ...ENT, FOR ME T...
...SS THOSE MATTERS OF ADMIN... ...N ABOUT WHICH THERE IS NO SPECIAL ANXIETY, OR EXCITEM... ... SEEMS TO EXIS...
... THE PEOPLE OF THE SOUTH... ...TES, THAT BY THE ACCESSION OF A REPUBLICAN ADMINIST... ...TY, AND THE...
..., AND PERSONAL SECURITY, AR... ...ENDANGERED. THERE HAS NEVER BEEN ANY REASONABLE ... ...SION. INDEE...
...MOST AMPLE EVIDENCE TO TH... ...RY HAS ALL THE WHILE EXISTED, AND BEEN OPEN ... ...ND IN NEAR...
...HE PUBLISHED SPEECHES OF ... ...NOW ADDR... ... DO BUT QUOTE FR... ...LARE THAT
...NO PURPOSE, DIRECTLY OR IN... ...O TO IN... ... ... CLAUSE... I BELIE
...E NO LAWFUL RIGHT TO DO... ...HAVE N... ...SO. ... ...O WILL FU
...LEDGE THAT I HAD MADE T... ...ANY ST... ...AND ... THIS, TH...
...D IN THE PLATFORM, FOR M... ...CE ... VES, AN... ...TION WHICH
...READ: RESOLVED, THAT THE MAINTEN...NCE I... VIOLATE OF ... RIGHTS OF TH... ...ACH STATE ...
...R AND CONTROL ITS OWN DOMESTIC ...STITUTIONS ACCORDING TO ITS OWN ... ...HAT BALAN...
...WER ON WHICH THE PERFECTION A... ...NDURANCE OF OUR POLITICAL FABRIC... ...NO... ... INVASION
...D FORCE OF THE SOIL OF ANY STA... ...R TERRITORY, NO MATTER UNDER WHA... ...EXT IS... ...ONG ...CRIMES. I N...
...RATE THESE SENTIMENTS: AND IN ...NG SO, I ONLY PRESS UPON THE PUBLIC ...TION THE MOS... ...ENCE OF WHI...
...CASE IS SUSCEPTIBLE, THAT THE PRO...TY, PEACE AND SECURITY OF NO SEC... ...RE TO BE IN... ...RED BY THE N...
...MING ADMINISTRATION. I ADD TOO, TH... ...LL THE PROTECTION WHICH, CONSIS... ...WITH TH... ...THE LAWS, CAN...
...,WILL BE CHEERFULLY GIVEN TO ALL TH... ...TES WHEN LAWFULLY DEMANDED ... ...VER ... ...AL TO ONE SECTI...
...ANOTHER. THERE IS MUCH CONTROVER... ...THE DELIVER...NG U... ... ... CLAUSE I NOW RE
...PLAINLY WRITTEN IN THE CONSTITUTION... ...OTHER ...TS PRO... ...OR LABOR IN ONE STAT...
...R THE LAWS THEREFORE, ESCAPING INT... ...SHALL IN CONSEQU... ...THEREIN, BE DISCHARG...
...SUCH SERVICE OR LABOR, BUT SHALL BE DE... ...UP... CLAIM OF TH...PA... ...LABOR MAY BE DUE. IT...
...ELY QUESTIONED THAT THIS PROVISION WA... ...THOSE WHO MADE IT... ...WE CALL FUGITIVE SLAV...
...HE INTENTION OF THE LAW-GIVER IS THE ... ...EMB... OF C... ...HOLE CONSTITUTION –
...PROVISION AS MUCH AS TO ANY OTHER. TO ... ...TI... THEN, THAT SLAV... ...HE TERMS OF THIS CLAU...
...L BE DELIVERED UP," THEIR OATHS ARE UN... ...OU... IF THEY WOULD ... ...AR, COULD THEY NOT, WI...
...Y EQUAL UNANIMITY, FRAME AND PASS A LA... ...WHICH ... ...HERE IS SOME DIFFEREN...
...NION WHETHER THIS CLAUSE SHOULD BE E... ...THAT DIFFERENCE IS NO...
...MATERIAL ONE. IF THE SLAVE IS TO BE SURR... ... ...M, OR TO OTHERS, BY WH...
...ORITY IT IS DONE. AND SHOULD ANY ONE, IN A... ...ON A MERELY UNSUBSTANT...
...ROVERSY AS TO HOW IT SHALL BE KEPT? AGAIN... ...EGUARDS OF LIBERTY KNO...
...VILIZED AND HUMANE JURISPRUDENCE TO BE IN... ...RRENDERED AS A SLAVE? B...
...T IT NOT BE WELL, AT THE SAME TIME, TO PROV... ...US... IN THE CONSTITUTION WH...
...RANTIES THAT "THE CITIZENS OF EACH STATE SHAL... ...NITIE... OF CITIZENS IN THE SEVE...
...S?" I TAKE THE OFFICIAL OATH TO-DAY, WITH NO ME... ...SE TO CO...RUE THE CONSTITUTION ...
...BY ANY HYPERCRITICAL RULES. AND WHILE I DO ...OT ... ...S OF CONG...S PROPER TO BE ENFORC...
...SUGGEST, THAT IT WILL BE MUCH SAFER FOR ... BOT... ...TIONS, TO CONF... ...ND ABIDE BY, ALL TH...
...WHICH STAND UNREPEALED, THAN TO V... ...TE ANY ... ...TO FIND IMPUNIT... ...G THEM HELD TO...
...CONSTITUTIONAL. IT IS SEVENTY-TWO YEAR... ...CE THE F... ...N OF A PRESIDENT UN... ...NAL CONSTITUTI...
...NG THAT PERIOD FIFTEEN DIFFERENT AN... ...EATLY DISTINGUISHED CITIZEN... ... SUCCES... ...THE EXECUT...
...CH OF THE GOVERNMENT. THEY HAVE ... ...TED IT THROUGH MANY PERIL... ... ...WITH...
...SCOPE FOR PRECEDENT, I NOW ENTE... ...THE SA... ...AL ...
...IAR DIFFICULTY. A DISRUPTION... ...AL ...
...NTEMPLATION OF UNIVERS... ...
...XPRESSED, IN THE FU... ...
...PROVISION IN ITS ...
...ITUTION, AND ...
...E INSTRU... ...VER – ...
...NT... ...STAT...
... ...E PE...
...K; B... ...LAWFUL...
...HA... ...ON, THE UNION IS...
...THAT IT...TITUTION. IT WAS FORMED IN ...
...CLARATION OF INDEPENDENCE IN 1776. IT WA...
...AND ENGAGED THAT IT SHOULD BE PERPET...
...OBJECTS FOR ORDAINING AND ESTABLISH...
...ON, BY ONE, OR BY A PART ONLY, OF THE...
...HAVING LOST THE VITAL ELEMENT OF P...
...ULLY GET OUT OF THE UNION, – THAT...
...HIN ANY STATE OR STATES, AGAIN...
...TO CIRCUMSTANCES. I THEREFORE...
...XTENT OF MY ABILITY, I SHALL...
...FAITHFULLY EXECUTED IN AL...
...PRACTICABLE, UNLESS MY RIG...
...MANNER, DIRECT THE CONT...
...HAT IT WILL CONSTITUTIO...
...SHALL BE NONE, UNLES...
...OSSESS THE PROPERTY...
...ECESSARY FOR THES...
...TILITY TO THE UNI...
...ITIZENS FROM HOL...
...ECT. WHILE TH...
...WOULD BE SO...
...OFFICES. T...
...WHERE S...
...DICATED...
...VERY C...
...AND...
...HA...

A LINCOLN DIALOGUE

JAMES A. RAWLEY

Edited and with a foreword
by William G. Thomas

University of Nebraska Press
Lincoln and London

Library of Congress
Cataloging-in-Publication Data
Rawley, James A.
A Lincoln dialogue / James A. Rawley; edited
and with a foreword by William G. Thomas.
pages   cm
Includes bibliographical references and index.
ISBN 978-0-8032-4996-7 (cloth: alk. paper)
1. Lincoln, Abraham, 1809–1865. 2. United
States—Politics and government—1861–1865.
3. United States—History—Civil War, 1861–1865.
I. Thomas, William G., 1964– editor. II. Title.
E458.R26 2014
973.7092—dc23
2014002873

Set in Garamond Premier Pro
by Renni Johnson.
Designed by N. Putens.

CONTENTS

FOREWORD

I met James A. Rawley in 2005 when I joined the faculty at the University of Nebraska. Then eighty-nine years old, Rawley was still working in the office every day, and he invited me to lunch to welcome me to the department and to hear about my research. Needless to say, I was honored. I knew his work well and was aware of the breadth of his influence on southern history, the history of the American Civil War, and the history of the transatlantic slave trade. Though I later discovered that he issued a similar invitation to every new faculty member in the department, I believe I was the last new colleague James Rawley welcomed in this way. I remain grateful for his immense generosity and his boundless collegiality. And I continue to be impressed by the example of his scholarship—brilliant, penetrating, and thorough.

What I did not know then was that James Rawley was nearly finished with a major manuscript that he was calling "A Lincoln Dialogue." He had sent it—thirty-six chapters and well over a thousand pages of text—to the University of Nebraska Press earlier in the year. The press's history acquisitions editor, Heather Lundine, sent the manuscript out to two distinguished Civil War reviewers. Each recommended publication. They considered the book a unique contribution to the existing literature on Lincoln and a valuable addition to Civil War history. Though they suggested revisions, both reviewers concluded that the manuscript was well organized and the book would appeal to the educated reader interested in Lincoln and the war as well as to anyone teaching the Civil War.

James A. Rawley died on November 29, 2005. The manuscript and its readers' reports were filed in the offices of the University of Nebraska Press.

Born in Terre Haute, Indiana, Rawley earned his BA and MA at the

University of Michigan. He served in the navy in World War II and after the war began PhD studies at Columbia University under Allan Nevins, David Donald, and Merle Curti. He received his PhD in 1949, taught briefly at Hunter College, then moved to Sweet Briar College in Virginia. He published his first book in 1955, *Edwin D. Morgan: Merchant in Politics, 1811–1883*. At Sweet Briar he served as chair of the history department and as chair of the Division of Social Studies before moving to the University of Nebraska in 1964. At Nebraska Rawley entered a particularly productive phase of his long and distinguished career. He wrote important books on the Civil War era, focusing on race, slavery, and emancipation. In 1966 he published *Turning Points of the Civil War*, a brief, highly readable account of seven key episodes in the war. Rawley's book explicitly included social, economic, and diplomatic events, asserting that "the turning points in this book are not, contrary to what one might expect, 'decisive' battles—or, indeed, military events alone." The book is still in print almost fifty years later.

In 1969 Rawley published what became one of his best known works, *Race and Politics: 'Bleeding Kansas' and the Coming of the Civil War*. There he put the territorial issue at the center of the sectional crisis and argued forcefully for the critical importance of race in the formulation of political responses. Rawley's thesis was heavily influenced by the broader social forces at work in the 1960s, especially the civil rights movement. In *Race and Politics* he offered a stark reassessment of racial prejudice in American politics. In contrast to the prevailing assumptions of many white readers at the time, Rawley noted that "the ordeal of the Union was among other matters a racial ordeal" and that Northerners of all parties were as infected with racism as was everyone else in American society. His revisionist conclusion still bears significance today. Rawley wrote: "Because the Negro was emancipated and did receive civil rights at Republican hands, historians have perpetrated the error of supposing the party intended these things in the 1850s. They have labored to discover humanitarianism toward blacks in a party largely dedicated to the rights of whites."

If Rawley's evidence for *Race and Politics* came mainly from political speeches, pamphlets, newspapers, and personal papers, then his sources for his 1981 book *The Transatlantic Slave Trade* could not have been more different. Weaving together ship logs, first-hand accounts, and quantitative data, Rawley attempted to situate the trade in world history and elucidate the implications of the trade for American readers. He called the transatlantic slave trade "a significant theme in the history of the modern world" and was one of the first scholars to explore the "paradox" of the slave trade and its association with "the making of the modern era."

In *A Lincoln Dialogue* Rawley carries forward many of these same concerns and themes. He writes in a style favored by his mentor Allan Nevins, who believed that historians should write for wide readership by an engaged and informed general public. Rawley uncovers the complex world of Lincoln's rise and his presidency. No other work juxtaposes Lincoln's writing and speeches with contemporary commentaries and criticisms of him. Rawley's careful selection of these documents and his judicious interweaving of his historical analysis and background come together to create a powerful dialogue with the reader as well. The book is an extraordinary and compelling account of Abraham Lincoln and his presidency.

Who could guide us better through the vast collection of Lincoln's writings and the newspapers, speeches, letters, diaries, and pamphlets of his times? Rawley's previous books on the rise of the Republican Party, the sectional crisis, the Civil War, and Lincoln provided him with a deep working knowledge of the historical record. But Rawley clearly intended his readers to come along with him into these archives and to maintain an independent perspective on them. He wanted us to draw our own conclusions from these important selections. We hear directly from Lincoln and his adversaries and friends. We hear from the historian too, surveying and assessing these words, and placing them in context for us. We also hear our own assessment of them take shape. This is the dialogue Rawley so powerfully sets up in the following pages.

A few comments are in order about the editorial process for *A Lincoln Dialogue*. I have striven where possible to maintain the style of Rawley's intertextual commentary but made changes to it where I considered this appropriate and where the reviewers indicated that elaboration would be beneficial. The original documents are quoted as in the sources used, including original spelling and punctuation and bracketed asides, with only an occasional comma or dash added, apostrophe or word space dropped, or bracketed letter adjusted. I have consolidated parts of the manuscript, again at the suggestion of the anonymous reviewers and in consultation with Bridget Barry, who became history acquisitions editor at the press after the project was in process. Rawley included a long bibliography, which we decided not to publish as Civil War bibliographies are numerous. Endnotes indicate sources used for the documents quoted and discussed. To avoid an overload of source notes, brief quotes within intertextual discussion are not all sourced. When questions arose about Rawley's notes, we attempted to reconstruct the sources he used based on the text in the manuscript, a task made more accurate by the emergence of various online editions in recent years, including Google Books.

It is natural to ask why this manuscript took so long to be published. The reasons are twofold. First, after Rawley's death neither the press nor the family had a plan for its eventual publication, and second, complications surrounded the computer files he used to write *A Lincoln Dialogue*. In 2010 we decided to reexamine the possibility of publication, and a single copy of the original manuscript was discovered in the press's files along with the readers' reports. We enlisted the support of the University of Nebraska Foundation to have the typescript keyboarded into digital files for editing, and the press agreed to bring out the book in 2014.

We have many individuals to thank and recognize. Members of the Department of History have advised us and supported the work all along. We are grateful for the patience and backing of the editorial staff of the University of Nebraska Press, especially Heather Lundine, who believed in this project at the beginning, and Bridget Barry, who believed in it at the end. We graciously thank the University of Nebraska Foundation for financial support. Several graduate students worked on the project as interns at the press. Mikal Brotnov, Meghan Benson, and Paul Strauss worked with us to finalize images, edit the text, and track down sources. And we are all conscious that this book would not have been possible without the support and dedication of Ann Rawley, James Rawley's spouse. Her constant interest in and encouragement of the Department of History at the University of Nebraska has inspired faculty and students alike.

DDRESS YOU BRIEFLY, AND TO TAKE, IN YOUR PRESENCE, THE OATH PRESCRIBED BY THE CONSTITUTION OF THE UNITED STATES, TO BE
Y THE PRESIDENT "BEFORE HE ENTERS ON THE EXECUTION OF HIS OFFICE." I DO NOT CONSIDER IT NECESSARY, AT PRESENT, FOR
ISCUSS THOSE MATTERS OF ADMINISTRATION ABOUT WHICH THERE IS NO SPECIAL ANXIETY, OR EXCITEMENT. APPREHENSION SEEMS TO
MONG THE PEOPLE OF THE SOUTHERN STATES. THAT BY THE ACCESSION OF A REPUBLICAN ADMINISTRATION, THEIR PROPERTY, AND
EACE, AND PERSONAL SECURITY, ARE TO BE ENDANGERED. THERE HAS NEVER BEEN ANY REASONABLE CAUSE FOR SUCH APPREHENSION. IN
HE MOST AMPLE EVIDENCE TO THE CONTRARY HAS ALL THE WHILE EXISTED, AND BEEN OPEN TO THEIR INSPECTION. IT IS FOUND IN N
L THE PUBLISHED SPEECHES OF HIM WHO NOW ADDRESSES YOU. I DO BUT QUOTE FROM ONE OF THOSE SPEECHES WHEN I DECLARE, I
AVE NO PURPOSE, DIRECTLY OR INDIRECTLY, TO INTERFERE WITH THE INSTITUTION OF SLAVERY IN THE STATES WHERE IT EXISTS. I B
HAVE NO LAWFUL RIGHT TO DO SO, AND I HAVE NO INCLINATION TO DO SO. THOSE WHO NOMINATED AND ELECTED ME DID SO WIL
NOWLEDGE THAT I HAD MADE THIS, AND MANY SIMILAR DECLARATIONS, AND HAD NEVER RECANTED THEM. AND MORE THAN THIS
ACED IN THE PLATFORM, FOR MY ACCEPTANCE, AND AS A LAW TO THEMSELVES, AND TO ME, THE CLEAR AND EMPHATIC RESOLUTION W
OW READ: RESOLVED, THAT THE MAINTENANCE INVIOLATE OF THE RIGHTS OF THE STATES, AND ESPECIALLY THE RIGHT OF EACH ST
RDER AND CONTROL ITS OWN DOMESTIC INSTITUTIONS ACCORDING TO ITS OWN JUDGMENT EXCLUSIVELY, IS ESSENTIAL TO THAT BA
POWER ON WHICH THE PERFECTION AND ENDURANCE OF OUR POLITICAL FABRIC DEPEND; AND WE DENOUNCE THE LAWLESS INVAS
MED FORCE OF THE SOIL OF ANY STATE OR TERRITORY, NO MATTER UNDER WHAT PRETEXT, AS AMONG THE GRAVEST OF CRIMES.
ITERATE THESE SENTIMENTS; AND IN DOING SO, I ONLY PRESS UPON THE PUBLIC ATTENTION THE MOST CONCLUSIVE EVIDENCE OF
HE CASE IS SUSCEPTIBLE, THAT THE PROPERTY, PEACE AND SECURITY OF NO SECTION ARE TO BE IN ANYWISE ENDANGERED BY TH
COMING ADMINISTRATION. I ADD TOO, THAT ALL THE PROTECTION WHICH, CONSISTENTLY WITH THE CONSTITUTION AND THE LAWS, C
VEN, WILL BE CHEERFULLY GIVEN TO ALL THE STATES WHEN LAWFULLY DEMANDED, FOR WHATEVER CAUSE — AS CHEERFULLY TO ONE SE
TO ANOTHER. THERE IS MUCH CONTROVERSY ABOUT THE DELIVERING UP OF FUGITIVES FROM SERVICE OR LABOR. THE CLAUSE I NOW
AS PLAINLY WRITTEN IN THE CONSTITUTION AS ANY OTHER OF ITS PROVISIONS: NO PERSON HELD TO SERVICE OR LABOR IN ONE
JDER THE LAWS THEREOF, ESCAPING INTO ANOTHER, SHALL, IN CONSEQUENCE OF ANY LAW OR REGULATION THEREIN, BE DISCH
OM SUCH SERVICE OR LABOR, BUT SHALL BE DELIVERED UP ON CLAIM OF THE PARTY TO WHOM SUCH SERVICE OR LABOR MAY BE DUE
ARCELY QUESTIONED THAT THIS PROVISION WAS INTENDED BY THOSE WHO MADE IT, FOR THE RECLAIMING OF WHAT WE CALL FUGITIVE S
D THE INTENTION OF THE LAW-GIVER IS THE LAW.

A LINCOLN DIALOGUE

ALL MEMBERS OF CONGRESS SWEAR THEIR SUPPORT T
HOLE CONSTITUTION — TO THIS PROVISION AS MUCH AS TO ANY OTHER. TO THE PROPOSITION, THEN, THAT SLAVES WHOSE CASES COME IN
E TERMS OF THIS CLAUSE, "SHALL BE DELIVERED UP," THEIR OATHS ARE UNANIMOUS. NOW, IF THEY WOULD MAKE THE EFFORT IN
MPER, COULD THEY NOT, WITH NEARLY EQUAL UNANIMITY, FRAME AND PASS A LAW, BY MEANS OF WHICH TO KEEP GOOD THAT UNAN
TH? THERE IS SOME DIFFERENCE OF OPINION WHETHER THIS CLAUSE SHOULD BE ENFORCED BY NATIONAL OR BY STATE AUTHORIT
RELY THAT DIFFERENCE IS NOT A VERY MATERIAL ONE. IF THE SLAVE IS TO BE SURRENDERED, IT CAN BE OF BUT LITTLE CONSEQUE
M. OR TO OTHERS, BY WHICH AUTHORITY IT IS DONE. AND SHOULD ANY ONE, IN ANY CASE, BE CONTENT THAT HIS OATH SHALL GO U
A MERELY UNSUBSTANTIAL CONTROVERSY AS TO HOW IT SHALL BE KEPT? AGAIN, IN ANY LAW UPON THIS SUBJECT, OUGHT NOT A
EGUARDS OF LIBERTY KNOWN IN CIVILIZED AND HUMANE JURISPRUDENCE TO BE INTRODUCED, SO THAT A FREE MAN BE NOT, IN AN
RRENDERED AS A SLAVE? AND MIGHT IT NOT BE WELL, AT THE SAME TIME, TO PROVIDE BY LAW FOR THE ENFORCEMENT OF THAT CLA
E CONSTITUTION WHICH GUARRANTIES THAT "THE CITIZENS OF EACH STATE SHALL BE ENTITLED TO ALL PREVILEGES AND IMMUNIT
IZENS IN THE SEVERAL STATES?" I TAKE THE OFFICIAL OATH TO-DAY, WITH NO MENTAL RESERVATIONS, AND WITH NO PURPOSE TO CON
E CONSTITUTION OR LAWS, BY ANY HYPERCRITICAL RULES. AND WHILE I DO NOT CHOOSE NOW TO SPECIFY PARTICULAR ACTS OF CON
PROPER TO BE ENFORCED, I DO SUGGEST, THAT IT WILL BE MUCH SAFER FOR ALL, BOTH IN OFFICIAL AND PRIVATE STATIONS, TO CO
AND ABIDE BY, ALL THOSE ACTS WHICH STAND UNREPEALED, THAN TO VIOLATE ANY OF THEM, TRUSTING TO FIND IMPUNITY IN HAVING
LD TO BE UNCONSTITUTIONAL. IT IS SEVENTY-TWO YEARS SINCE THE FIRST INAUGURATION OF A PRESIDENT UNDER OUR NAT
NSTITUTION. DURING THAT PERIOD FIFTEEN DIFFERENT AND GREATLY DISTINGUISHED CITIZENS, HAVE, IN SUCCESSION, ADMINIS
E EXECUTIVE BRANCH OF THE GOVERNMENT. THEY HAVE CONDUCTED IT THROUGH MANY PERILS; AND, GENERALLY, WITH GREAT SU
", WITH ALL THESE SCOPE FOR PRECEDENT. I NOW ENTER UPON THE SAME TASK FOR THE BRIEF CONSTITUTIONAL TERM OF FOUR
DER GREAT AND PECULIAR DIFFICULTY. A DISRUPTION OF THE FEDERAL UNION HERETOFORE ONLY MENACED, IS NOW FORMIDABLY ATTEMP
LD. THAT IN CONTEMPLATION OF UNIVERSAL LAW, AND OF THE CONSTITUTION, THE UNION OF THESE STATES IS PERPETUAL. PERPE
IMPLIED. IF NOT EXPRESSED, IN THE FUNDAMENTAL LAW OF ALL NATIONAL GOVERNMENTS. IT IS SAFE TO ASSERT THAT NO GOVERN
PER, EVER HAD A PROVISION IN ITS ORGANIC LAW FOR ITS OWN TERMINATION. CONTINUE TO EXECUTE ALL THE EXPRESS PROVISIO
R NATIONAL CONSTITUTION, AND THE UNION WILL ENDURE FOREVER — IT BEING IMPOSSIBLE TO DESTROY IT, EXCEPT BY SOME ACTIO
VIDED FOR IN THE INSTRUMENT ITSELF. AGAIN, IF THE UNITED STATES BE NOT A GOVERNMENT PROPER, BUT AN ASSOCIATION OF
THE NATURE OF CONTRACT MERELY, CAN IT, AS A CONTRACT, BE PEACEABLY UNMADE, BY LESS THAN ALL THE PARTIES WHO MADE I
TY TO A CONTRACT MAY VIOLATE IT — BREAK IT, SO TO SPEAK; BUT DOES IT NOT REQUIRE ALL TO LAWFULLY RESCIND IT? DESCE
M THESE GENERAL PRINCIPLES, WE FIND THE PROPOSITION THAT, IN LEGAL CONTEMPLATION, THE UNION IS PERPETUAL. CONFIRA
HISTORY OF THE UNION ITSELF. THE UNION IS MUCH OLDER THAT THE CONSTITUTION. IT WAS FORMED IN FACT BY THE ARTIC
OCIATION IN 1774. IT WAS MATURED AND CONTINUED BY THE DECLARATION OF INDEPENDENCE IN 1776. IT WAS FURTHER MATURE
FAITH OF ALL THE THEN THIRTEEN STATES EXPRESSLY PLIGHTED AND ENGAGED THAT IT SHOULD BE PERPETUAL, BY THE ARTIC
FEDERATION IN 1778. AND FINALLY, IN 1787, ONE OF THE DECLARED OBJECTS FOR ORDAINING AND ESTABLISHING THE CONSTIT
"TO FORM A MORE PERFECT UNION." BUT IF DESTRUCTION OF THE UNION, BY ONE, OR BY A PART ONLY, OF THE STATES, BE LAW
SIBLE, THE UNION IS LESS PERFECT THAN BEFORE'S THE CONSTITUTION, HAVING LOST THE VITAL ELEMENT OF PERPETUITY. IT FO
M THESE VIEWS THAT NO STATE, UPON ITS OWN MERE MOTION, CAN LAWFULLY GET OUT OF THE UNION, — THAT RESOLVES AND ORDIN
THAT EFFECT ARE LEGALLY VOID; AND THAT ACTS OF VIOLENCE, WITHIN ANY STATE OR STATES, AGAINST THE AUTHORITY OF THE U
YES, ARE INSURRECTIONARY OR REVOLUTIONARY, ACCORDING TO CIRCUMSTANCES. I THEREFORE CONSIDER THAT, IN VIEW O
NSTITUTION AND THE LAWS, THE UNION IS UNBROKEN; AND, TO THE EXTENT OF MY ABILITY, I SHALL TAKE CARE, AS THE CONSTIT
LF EXPRESSLY ENJOINS UPON ME, THAT THE LAWS OF THE UNION BE FAITHFULLY EXECUTED IN ALL THE STATES. DOING THIS I DE
ONLY A SIMPLE DUTY ON MY PART; AND I SHALL PERFORM IT, SO FAR AS PRACTICABLE, UNLESS MY RIGHTFUL MASTERS, THE AME
PLE, SHALL WITHHOLD THE REQUISITE MEANS, OR, IN SOME AUTHORITATIVE MANNER, DIRECT THE CONTRARY. I TRUST THIS WILL
ARDED AS A MENACE, BUT ONLY AS THE DECLARED PURPOSE OF THE UNION THAT IT WILL CONSTITUTIONALLY DEFEND, AND MA
LF. IN DOING THIS THERE NEEDS TO BE NO BLOODSHED OR VIOLENCE; AND THERE SHALL BE NONE, UNLESS IT BE FORCED UPO
IONAL AUTHORITY. THE POWER CONFIDED TO ME, WILL BE USED TO HOLD, OCCUPY, AND POSSESS THE PROPERTY, AND PLACES BELO
HE GOVERNMENT, AND TO COLLECT THE DUTIES AND IMPOSTS; BUT BEYOND WHAT MAY BE NECESSARY FOR THESE OBJECTS, THER
NO INVASION — NO USING OF FORCE AGAINST, OR AMONG THE PEOPLE ANYWHERE. WHERE HOSTILITY TO THE UNITED STATES, A
ERIOR LOCALITY, SHALL BE SO GREAT AND SO UNIVERSAL, AS TO PREVENT COMPETENT RESIDENT CITIZENS FROM HOLDING THE FE
CES. THERE WILL BE NO ATTEMPT TO FORCE OBNOXIOUS STRANGERS AMONG THE PEOPLE FOR THAT OBJECT. WHILE THE STRICT
IT MAY EXIST IN THE GOVERNMENT TO ENFORCE THE EXERCISE OF THESE OFFICES. THE ATTEMPT TO DO SO WOULD BE SO IRRITATIN
JEARLY IMPRACTICABLE WITH ALL, THAT I DEEM IT BETTER TO FOREGO, FOR THE TIME, THE USES OF SUCH OFFICES. THE MAILS, U
ELLED, WILL CONTINUE TO BE FURNISHED IN ALL PARTS OF THE UNION, SO FAR AS POSSIBLE. THE PEOPLE EVERYWHERE SHALL HAV
E OF PERFECT SECURITY WHICH IS MOST FAVORABLE TO CALM THOUGHT AND REFLECTION. THE COURSE HERE INDICATED WILL BE FOL
ESS CURRENT EVENTS, AND EXPERIENCE, SHALL SHOW A MODIFICATION, OR CHANGE, TO BE PROPER; AND IN EVERY CASE AND EXI
EST DISCRETION WILL BE EXERCISED, ACCORDING TO CIRCUMSTANCES ACTUALLY EXISTING, AND WITH A VIEW AND A HOPE OF A PE
JTION OF THE NATIONAL TROUBLES, AND THE RESTORATION OF FRATERNAL SYMPATHIES AND AFFECTIONS. THAT THERE ARE PERS
SECTION, OR ANOTHER WHO SEEK TO DESTROY THE UNION AT ALL EVENTS, AND ARE GLAD OF ANY PRETEXT TO DO IT, I WILL N
RM OR DENY: BUT IF THERE BE SUCH, I NEED ADDRESS NO WORD TO THEM. TO THOSE, HOWEVER, WHO REALLY LOVE THE UNION, MA
K? BEFORE ENTERING UPON SO GRAVE A MATTER AS THE DESTRUCTION OF OUR NATIONAL FABRIC, WITH ALL ITS BENEFITS, ITS MEM
ITS HOPES, WOULD IT NOT BE WISE TO ASCERTAIN PRECISELY WHY WE DO IT? WILL YOU HAZARD SO DESPERATE A STEP, WHILE THERE
IBILITY THAT ANY PORTION OF THE ILLS YOU FLY FROM, HAVE NO REAL EXISTENCE? WILL YOU, WHILE THE CERTAIN ILLS YOU FLY
TER THAN ALL THE REAL ONES YOU FLY FROM? WILL YOU RISK THE COMMISSION OF SO FEARFUL A MISTAKE? ALL PROFESS TO BE EC
HE UNION, IF ALL CONSTITUTIONAL RIGHTS CAN BE MAINTAINED. IS IT TRUE, THEN, THAT ANY RIGHT, PLAINLY WRITTEN IN
TITUTION, HAS BEEN DENIED? I THINK NOT. HAPPILY THE HUMAN MIND IS SO CONSTITUTED, THAT NO PARTY CAN REACH TO THE AU

INTRODUCING
ABRAHAM LINCOLN

On the eve of the presidential election year 1860, Abraham Lincoln appeared to have little chance of becoming the Republican Party's nominee for president. Standing to the fore was William H. Seward, twice elected governor of New York. Seward had been a United States Senator since 1849 and was an articulate antislavery spokesman, representing the state with the largest electoral vote and enjoying the backing of the wily political boss Thurlow Weed.

Nearly as prominent was Salmon P. Chase, Free Soil leader turned Republican, co-author of an eloquent manifesto against repeal of the prohibition on slavery expansion known as the Missouri Compromise; Chase was an ardent foe of slavery, a former U.S. senator, and governor of Ohio, the third most populous state. Other conspicuous Republicans included Simon Cameron of the pivotal second largest state of Pennsylvania, once a Democrat, a former U.S. senator and machine politician handicapped by a soiled reputation; and Edward Bates, who was a Whig party leader in the border slave state of Missouri and who enjoyed favor among former Whigs and conservatives. All four of these candidates found themselves in Lincoln's cabinet in 1861.

Child of "undistinguished families," as he phrased it, Lincoln was born in 1809 in the young slave state of Kentucky and at the age of seven was taken by his migratory father to the just admitted free state of Indiana, and thence in 1830 to Illinois, twelve years a state: Lincoln was a product of the frontier.

His formal education was sparse. "I went to A B C schools by littles," he quaintly said, and "the aggregate of all my schooling did not amount to one year." Until the age of twenty-one he performed hard farm labor. His mother, Nancy Hanks, died when he was nine; and it was his loving stepmother, the widow Sally Johnston, not his distant father, Thomas, who encouraged Abraham to learn to read, write, and as he put it, to "cipher to the rule of three."

A striking trait Lincoln possessed was his ability to teach himself. His ability to read rose to a fervent appreciation of the Bible and Shakespeare; his ability to write soared to composing the Gettysburg Address; and his ability to cipher led him to learn surveying. He became a lawyer, later remarking he "did not read [the law] with any one."

Before he turned forty he "studied and nearly mastered the Six-books of Euclid." As president he became proficient in military strategy, prompting more than one authority to call him a military genius.

His reading embraced *Aesop's Fables, Pilgrim's Progress, Robinson Crusoe,* and Robert Burns, and he devoured newspapers. He read reflectively and somewhat narrowly, showing little interest in fiction, philosophy, or abstract literature. All the while he relished the popular humor of Petroleum V. Nasby and Artemus Ward.

In 1830 he made a flatboat voyage to New Orleans—his second visit to that great port city in the deep South; and in 1831, being of age and free from his father's charge, he established himself in the tiny village of New Salem, Illinois. During six years spent there he tried several trades, served as a captain in the Black Hawk War, studied law, and in 1834 was elected to the state legislature.

Serving for four two-year terms, he became familiar with the politics of campaigning, lawmaking, and what was then called logrolling—the strategic trading of votes. A Whig whose "beau ideal," as he said, was Henry Clay, he endorsed federal government support of internal improvements, a protective tariff, and a national bank. Government stimulation of the economy, not the states' rights of Andrew Jackson and the Democrats, marked his political thought.

As a state legislator he promoted moving the state capital from Vandalia to Springfield. That accomplished, in 1837 he moved there, practiced law, and in 1844 formed a partnership with the youthful William H. Herndon, who later became his biographer. In 1842 he married Mary Todd of Lexington, Kentucky, a well-educated aristocrat, suggesting a rise in his social status. The couple had four sons, only one of whom survived to maturity.

An aspiring politician, Lincoln was elected to the United States House of Representatives in 1846. His term in Congress was notable for several reasons: his challenge of President James K. Polk's assertion that the Mexican government had provoked the war with Mexico by shedding blood on U.S. soil; his support of the Wilmot Proviso to prohibit expansion of slavery to any territory acquired from Mexico; and his unsuccessful effort to provide compensated emancipation of slaves in the District of Columbia, with approval of the district's voters.

Holding office for but one term, as part of a gentlemen's agreement with other aspirants, Lincoln resumed law practice in Springfield. He displayed little interest in politics until 1854, when his fellow Illinoisan Stephen A. Douglas reopened the slavery controversy by introducing the Kansas-Nebraska bill to repeal the long-standing prohibition on slavery in the northern part of the Louisiana Territory.

Aroused as he had "never been before," he said, Lincoln returned to active politics. Speaking in Peoria in October 1854, Lincoln denounced the prospect of the spread of slavery. "I hate it because of the monstrous injustice of slavery itself. I hate it because it deprives our republican example of its just influence in the world . . . and especially because it forces so many really good men amongst ourselves into an open war with the very fundamental principles of civil liberty—criticizing the Declaration of Independence." Hammering at another cardinal theme of national unity, he charged that the bill aggravated "the only one thing which ever endangers the Union."

In these words Lincoln voiced bedrock views: the immorality of slavery, the worth of the republican form of government, the value of civil liberty, the centrality of the Declaration of Independence in his thought, and his fear of disunion.

The Kansas-Nebraska Act ominously led to the realignment of political parties. Many northern Democrats defected from their party, a Know Nothing movement surfaced and sank, the Whig Party waned, and the

Republican Party emerged as a new national party in 1856. Abraham Lincoln became a Republican in that year and made more than fifty speeches in favor of the party's presidential nominee, John C. Frémont. At the state convention he delivered the "lost speech"—so called because reporters were so enthralled that they neglected to write it down. A brief report of the speech, discovered in 1930, disclosed that Lincoln the nationalist emphasized that the "Union must be preserved in the purity of its principles as well as in the integrity of its territorial parts." At the party's national convention he won 110 votes for vice president, more than half of them from Indiana and Illinois, states where he had lived.

A year later in the Dred Scott decision the Supreme Court ruled that the Missouri Compromise was unconstitutional. In a speech at Springfield, Lincoln sharply attacked the decision, saying it was erroneous, and the Republicans would do what they could to overrule it. He went out of his way to deny Chief Justice Roger B. Taney's notorious assertion that Negroes were not part of the people for whom the Declaration of Independence and the Constitution were made.

Responding to a statement by Douglas that the Declaration referred only to the white race, Lincoln claimed that the great document was intended to embrace "*all* men." At the same time he repudiated racial amalgamation and endorsed separation of the black and white races by colonization—a position to which he clung until the end of 1862.

Nominated by his party for United States senator in 1858, in accepting Lincoln reaffirmed his apprehension for the nation's future. "A house divided against itself cannot stand. I believe the government cannot endure, permanently half *slave* and half *free*. . . . It will become *all* one thing, or *all* the other."

In his celebrated debates with Douglas that year Lincoln amplified his views on slavery policy. As to the Republican Party position on restricting the spread of slavery in the territories, he declared that he favored seeing the territories "as an outlet for *free white people everywhere,* the world over."

Though he shared in part the white racism of his time, he forthrightly stated his view of the wrongfulness of slavery. "The real issue in this controversy . . . is the sentiment on the part of one class that looks upon the institution of slavery *as a wrong,* and of another class that *does not* look upon it as a wrong." In his first debate he said: "I believe that we shall not have peace upon the question until the opponents of slavery arrest the further spread of it.... The crisis would be past and the institution might be let alone for a hundred years, yet it would be going out of existence in the way best for both the black and the white races." The statement evoked "great cheering."

The debates, though failing to place Lincoln in the Senate, enhanced his recognition in the North. Throughout the following year Lincoln traveled widely, speaking in Ohio, Wisconsin, Indiana, and Kansas; he declined an invitation to speak in Boston. His speeches continued his attack on Douglas and appealed to laborers, before whom he exalted a system in which "a *hired* laborer is [not] fatally fixed in that condition for life." Reaching for ethnic voters, Lincoln in May 1858 purchased a German language newspaper in Springfield. He told the editor that if the newspaper refrained from printing anything opposed to the Republican Party until after the presidential election, the editor would become owner of the press. Although Lincoln served just one term in Congress, he had become a well-known and respected political figure after his 1858 Senate campaign against Douglas. And like Douglas, he was a potential candidate for his party's nomination for president in 1860.

CHAPTER ONE

LINCOLN IS NOMINATED

Though Lincoln seemed to be preparing for consideration for his party's presidential nomination, the prospect held little promise. He had neither the prestige of the first generation of presidents, the Founding Fathers, nor the military luster worn by Andrew Jackson (Old Hickory), William Henry Harrison (Tippecanoe), Zachary Taylor (Old Rough and Ready), or even Franklin Pierce (Young Hickory). Lincoln's backers attempted to make up the difference by conferring upon him the sobriquets "Honest Abe," thrusting at corruption in the Buchanan administration, and "the rail splitter," recollecting the Whigs' success in the log cabin campaign of 1840.

Nor did he have much experience in national politics, unlike Martin Van Buren and even James K. Polk, the so-called dark horse, who in fact had served in the House of Representatives from 1825 to 1839, the last four years as speaker. No president had been as obscure before nomination; press references often called him Abram Lincoln.

As the presidential election year opened, Lincoln made a long stride toward his nomination. He had accepted an invitation to speak in New York. Behind it lurked sponsorship by prominent New Yorkers opposed to Seward. Recognizing the importance of the opportunity, Lincoln prepared carefully. He used Jonathan Elliott's six volumes of *Debates . . . on the Federal Constitution* and other writings to construct a landmark address. In good part it contained his debates with Douglas, who the year before had aired his views in *Harper's Magazine* and again in Columbus, Ohio, just before Lincoln's arrival. Douglas, replying to critics, argued that Congress had established territorial governments with power that the federal government itself did not have. Here, he claimed, lay the dividing line between federal and state power. Douglas's views, instead of quieting his critics, provoked lively discussion both within and outside his party.

Speaking to an audience that included eminent and influential easterners, Lincoln carefully presented his case for the Republican Party and, as the applause attested, for himself as its standard bearer.

The tale of Abraham Lincoln's rise to his party's nomination for president held within it his self doubts. "I am not fit for the presidency," he remarked in July 1859. William H. Seward, the front-runner, clearly agreed with the man he derisively called that "prairie statesman." Reminiscing in a letter to Seward's biographer, Joseph Medill recalled Seward's angry reaction to an editorial he wrote in February 1860 for the *Chicago Press and Tribune:*

Senator Seward was very anxious to be nominated for President in 1860, and had set his friends actively to work to promote the object of his ambition. I became acquainted with him when I lived in Ohio, as early as 1848, and corresponded frequently with him. In some respects he was my political mentor and *beau ideal* of a statesman.

I spent the winter of 1859–60 in Washington, and saw him there several times, but never promised or told him that I would urge or favor his nomination for President in 1860. My first belief was that he could not carry either Illinois, Indiana, or Pennsylvania, and without their electoral votes he could come no nearer being elected than was Fremont four years previously. He was regarded as too radical on the slavery question, with his "irrepressible" doctrine, for the conservative Whigs of those three states; but I believed that Lincoln—a Kentuckian by birth—could carry all of them in addition to the states which cast their electoral votes for Fremont, and that would suffice to elect him. Feeling in this way about it, I wrote to the Chicago *Tribune,* in the latter part of February, 1860, as strong an editorial letter as I was capable of, showing that Lincoln could be elected President that year and that Seward could not.

The article irritated Seward when he read it, and he took occasion to see me immediately thereafter, and "blew me up" tremendously for having disappointed him—"gone back on him"—and preferring that "prairie statesman," as he called Lincoln. He then proceeded to declare, with much heat of temper and expression, that if he was not nominated as the Republican candidate for President at the ensuing convention, he would shake the dust off his shoes, and retire from the service of an ungrateful party for the remainder of his days. He gave me to understand that he was the chief teacher of the principles of the Republican party before Lincoln was known other than as a country lawyer of Illinois. He considered himself as the logical candidate of the party for the presidency, and, if rejected for that position, would devote the residue of his life to his private affairs, which he had too long neglected in order to propagate the principles of freedom and the rights of man.

He dismissed me from his presence, saying that thereafter he and I would no longer be friends, but each would go his own way in the future. What I replied is of no consequence, but it had none of the tendency of oil poured on stormy water.

I do not claim to have repeated his exact words at this long lapse of time—thirty-six years—but I have condensed into as few words as possible the substance of his lecture and threat to retire from public life if not made the party's standard-bearer.[1]

Lincoln acknowledged his interest by late April, responding to a query from Lyman Trumbull, whose election to the U.S. Senate he had made possible by withdrawing his own name:

As you request, I will be entirely frank. The taste *is* in my mouth a little; and this, no doubt, disqualifies me, to some extent, to form correct opinions. You may confidently rely, however, that by no advice or consent of mine, shall my pretentions be pressed to the point of endangering our common cause.

Now, as to my opinions about the chances of others in Illinois. I think neither Seward nor Bates can carry Illinois if Douglas shall be on the track; and that either of them can, if he shall not be. I rather think McLean could carry it with D. on or off—in other words, I think McLean is stronger in Illinois, taking all sections of it, than either S. or B.; and I think S. the weakest of the three. I hear no objection to McLean, except his age; but that objection seems to occur to every one; and it is possible it might leave him no stronger than the others. By the way, if we should nominate him, how would we save to ourselves the chance of filling his vacancy in the Court? Have him hold on up to the moment of his inauguration? Would that course be no draw-back upon us in the canvass?

Recurring in Illinois, we want something here quite as much as, and which is harder to get than, the electoral vote—the Legislature. And it is exactly in this point that Seward's nomination would be hard upon us. Suppose he should gain us a thousand votes in Winnebago, it would not compensate for the loss of fifty in Edgar.

A word now for your own special benefit. You better write no letters which can possibly be distorted into opposition, or quasi opposition to me. There are men on the constant watch for such things out of which to prejudice my peculiar friends against you. While I have no more suspicion of you than I have of my best friend living, I am kept in a constant struggle against suggestions of this sort. I have hesitated some to write this paragraph, lest you should suspect I do it for my own benefit, and not for yours; but on reflection I conclude you will not suspect me.

Let no eye but your own see this—not that there is anything wrong, or even ungenerous, in it; but it would be misconstrued. Your friend as ever, A. Lincoln.[2]

Lincoln began considering his prospects. Richard M. Corwine wrote to him that he preferred Lincoln to other candidates. He continued, "we can not elect extreme men. Moderation in their past life & and their present views, must mark them." Lincoln replied:

Yours of the 30th ult. is just received. After what you have said, it is perhaps proper I should post you, so far as I am able, as to the "lay of the land." First then, I think the Illinois delegation will be unanimous for me at the start; and no other delegation will. A few individuals in other delegations would like to go for me at the start, but may be restrained by their colleagues. It is represented to me, by men who ought to know, that the whole of Indiana might not be difficult to get. You know how it is in Ohio. I am certainly not the first choice there; and yet I have not heard that any one makes any positive objection to me. It is just so everywhere so far as I can perceive. Everywhere, except in Illinois, and possibly Indiana, one or another is preferred to me, but there is no positive objection. This is the ground as it now appears. I believe you personally know C. M. Allen, of Vincennes, Ia. He is a delegate, and has notified me that the entire Ia. delegation will be in Chicago the same day as you name—Saturday the 12th. My friends Jesse K. Dubois, our Auditor, & Judge David Davis, will probably be there ready to confer with friends from other States. Let me hear from you again when anything occurs.[3]

A week before the Republican national convention Lincoln unwittingly contributed to a stereotype that promoted his political fortunes. When his cousin John Hanks brought to the floor of the state convention hall two rails inscribed "ABRAHAM LINCOLN. The Rail Candidate For President in 1860," he rose to respond:

He stated that, some thirty years ago, then just emigrating to the State, he stopped with his mother's family, for one season, in what is now Macon County; that he built a cabin, *split rails,* and cultivated a small farm down on the Sangamon River, some six or eight miles from Decatur. These, he was informed, were taken from that fence; but, whether they were or not, he had mauled many and many better ones since he had grown to manhood. The cheers were renewed with the same vigor when he concluded his remarks.[4]

The Republicans held their convention in Lincoln's home state, where a vast structure called the Wigwam had been erected in Chicago. Lincoln's Illinois sponsors made the most of the barnlike hall in their state. They packed the Wigwam with the candidate's partisans.

The delegates framed a platform in which the cardinal policies included these:

2. That the maintenance of the principles promulgated in the Declaration of Independence and embodied in the Federal Constitution, "That all men are created equal; that they are endowed by their Creator with certain inalienable rights; that among these are life, liberty and the pursuit of happiness; that, to secure these rights, governments are instituted among men, deriving their just powers from the consent of the governed," is essential to the preservation of our Republican institutions; and that the Federal Constitution, the Rights of the States, and the Union of the States, must and shall be preserved.

3. That to the Union of the States this nation owes its unprecedented increase in population, its surprising development of material resources, its rapid augmentation of wealth, its happiness at home and its honor abroad; and we hold in abhorrence all schemes for Disunion, come from whatever source they may; And we congratulate the country that no Republican member of Congress has uttered or countenanced the threats of Disunion so often made by Democratic members, without rebuke and with applause from their political associates; and we denounce those threats of Disunion, in case of a popular overthrow of their ascendency, as denying the vital principles of a free government, and as an avowal of contemplated treason, which it is the imperative duty of an indignant People sternly to rebuke and forever silence.

4. That the maintenance inviolate of the rights of the States, and especially the right of each State to order and control its own domestic institutions according to its own judgment exclusively, is essential to that balance of

powers on which the perfection and endurance of our political fabric depends; and we denounce the lawless invasion by armed force of the soil of any State or Territory, no matter under what pretext, as among the gravest of crimes. . . .

7. That the new dogma that the Constitution, of its own force, carries Slavery into any or all of the Territories of the United States, is a dangerous political heresy, at variance with the explicit provisions of that instrument itself, with contemporaneous exposition, and with legislative and judicial precedent; is revolutionary in its tendency, and subversive of the peace and harmony of the country.

8. That the normal condition of all the territory of the United States is that of freedom; That as our Republican fathers, when they had abolished slavery in all our national territory, ordained that "no person should be deprived of life, liberty, or property, without due process of law," it becomes our duty, by legislation, whenever such legislation is necessary, to maintain this provision of the Constitution against all attempts to violate it; and we deny the authority of the Congress, of a territorial legislature, or of any individuals, to give legal existence to Slavery in any Territory of the United States.

12. That, while providing revenue for the support of the General Government by duties upon imports, sound policy requires such an adjustment of these imposts as to encourage the development of the industrial interests of the whole country; and we commend that policy of national exchanges which secures to the working men liberal wages, to agriculture remunerating prices, to mechanics and manufacturers an adequate reward for their skill, labor, and enterprise, and to the nation commercial prosperity and independence.

13. That we protest against any sale or alienation to others of the Public Lands held by actual settlers, and against any view of the Homestead policy which regards the settlers as paupers or supplicants for public bounty; and we demand the passage by Congress of the complete and satisfactory Homestead measure which has already passed the house.

14. That the Republican Party is opposed to any change in our Naturalization Laws or any State legislation by which the rights of our citizenship hitherto accorded to immigrants from foreign lands shall be abridged or impaired; and in favor of giving a full and efficient protection of the rights of all classes of citizens, whether native or naturalized, both at home and abroad.

15. That appropriations by Congress for River and Harbor improvements of a National character, required for the accommodation and security of an

existing commerce, are authorized by the Constitution, and justified by the obligations of Government to protect the lives and property of its citizens.[5]

Many onlookers as well as delegates believed Seward's nomination was a foregone conclusion. The political reporter Murat Halstead penned a vivid account of the procedure:

> After adjournment on Thursday (the second day), there were few men in Chicago who believed it possible to prevent the nomination of Seward....
>
> But there was much done after midnight and before the Convention assembled on Friday morning. There were hundreds of Pennsylvanians, Indianians, and Illinoisans, who never closed their eyes that night....
>
> The Seward men generally abounded in confidence Friday morning. The air was full of rumors of the caucusing the night before, but the opposition of the doubtful States to Seward was an old story; and after the distress of Pennsylvania, Indiana & Co., on the subject of Seward's availability, had been so freely and ineffectually expressed from the start, it was not imagined their protests would suddenly become effective....
>
> When the Convention was called to order, breathless attention was given the proceedings. There was not a space a foot square in the wigwam unoccupied. There were tens of thousands still outside, and torrents of men had rushed in at the three broad doors until not another one could squeeze in....
>
> The applause, when Mr. Evarts named Seward, was enthusiastic. When Mr. Judd named Lincoln, the response was prodigious, rising and raging far beyond the Seward shriek. Presently, upon Caleb B. Smith seconding the nomination of Lincoln, the response was absolutely terrific. It now became the Seward men to make another effort, and when Blair of Michigan seconded his nomination,
>
> > At once there rose so wild a yell,
> > Within that dark and narrow dell;
> > As all the fiends from heaven that fell,
> > Had pealed the banner cry of hell.
>
> The effect was startling. Hundreds of persons stopped their ears in pain. The shouting was absolutely frantic, shrill and wild. No Camanches, no panthers ever struck a higher note, or gave screams with more infernal intensity. Looking from the stage over the vast amphitheatre, nothing was

to be seen below but thousands of hats—a black, mighty swarm of hats—flying with the velocity of hornets over a mass of human heads, most of the mouths of which were open. Above, all around the galleries, hats and handkerchiefs were flying in the tempest together. The wonder of the thing was, that the Seward outside pressure should, so far from New York, be so powerful.

Now the Lincoln men had to try it again, and as Mr. Delano of Ohio, on behalf 'of a portion of the delegation of the State,' seconded the nomination of Lincoln, the uproar was beyond description. . . . I thought the Seward yell could not be surpassed; but the Lincoln boys were clearly ahead, and feeling their victory, as there was a lull in the storm, took deep breaths all round, and gave a concentrated shriek that was positively awful, and accompanied it with stamping that made every plank and pillar in the building quiver. . . .

The Division of the first vote caused a fall in Seward stock. It was seen that Lincoln, Cameron and Bates had the strength to defeat Seward, and it was known that the greater part of the Chase votes would go for Lincoln. . . .

The Convention proceeded to a second ballot. . . . The first gain for Lincoln was in New Hampshire. The Chase and Fremont vote from that State were given to him. His next gain was the whole vote of Vermont. This was a blighting blow upon the Seward interest. The New Yorkers started as if an Orsini bomb had exploded. And presently the Cameron vote of Pennsylvania was thrown for Lincoln, increasing his strength forty-four votes. The fate of the day was now determined. New York saw 'checkmate' next move, and sullenly proceeded with the game, assuming unconsciousness of her inevitable doom. On this ballot Lincoln gained seventy-nine votes! Seward had 184½ votes, Lincoln, 181. . . .

While this [the third] ballot was taken amid excitement that tested the nerves, the fatal defection from Seward in New England still further appeared—four votes going over from Seward to Lincoln in Massachusetts. The latter received four additional votes from Pennsylvania and fifteen additional votes from Ohio. . . . The number of votes necessary to a choice were two hundred and thirty-three, and I saw under my pencil, as the Lincoln column was completed, the figures 231½–one vote and a half to give him the nomination. In a moment the fact was whispered about. A hundred pencils had told the same story. The news went over the house wonderfully, and there was a pause. There are always men anxious to distinguish themselves on such occasions. There is nothing that politicians like better than a crisis. I looked up to see who would be the man to give the decisive vote. . . . In about ten ticks of a watch, Cartter of Ohio was up. I had imagined Ohio would be slippery enough for the crisis. And sure enough! Every eye was on Cartter, and every body who understood the matter at all, knew what he was about to do. . . . He said, 'I rise (eh), Mr. Chairman (eh), to announce the change of four votes of Ohio from Mr. Chase to Mr. Lincoln.' The deed was done. There was a moment's silence. The nerves of the thousands, which through the hours of suspense had been subjected to terrible tension, relaxed, and as deep breaths of relief were taken, there was a noise in the wigwam like the rush of a great wind, in the van of a storm—and in another breath, the storm was there. There were thousands cheering with the energy of insanity.

A man who had been on the roof, and was engaged in communicating the results of the ballotings to the mighty mass of outsiders, now demanded by gestures at the sky-light over the stage, to know what had happened. One of the secretaries, with a tally sheet in his hands, shouted–'Fire the salute! Abe Lincoln is nominated!' As the cheering inside the wigwam subsided, we could hear that outside, where the news of the nomination had just been announced. And the roar, like the breaking up of the fountains of the great deep, that was heard, gave a new impulse to the enthusiasm inside. Then the thunder of the salute rose above the din, and shouting was repeated with such tremendous fury that some discharges of the cannon were absolutely not heard by those on the stage. Puffs of smoke, drifting by the open doors, and the smell of gunpowder, told what was going on.

The moment that half a dozen men who were on their chairs making motions at the President could be heard, they changed the votes of their States to Mr. Lincoln. . . .

While these votes were being given, the applause continued, and a photograph of Abe Lincoln which had hung in one of the side rooms was brought in, and held up before the surging and screaming masses. The places of the various delegations were indicated by staffs, to which were attached the names of the States, printed in large black letters on pasteboard. As the Lincoln enthusiasm increased, delegates tore these standards of the States from their places and swung them about their heads. A rush was made to get the New York standard and swing it with the rest, but the New Yorkers would not allow it to be moved, and were wrathful at the suggestion.

When the vote was declared, Mr. Evarts, the New York spokesman, mounted the Secretaries' table and handsomely and impressively expressed his grief at the failure of the Convention to nominate Seward—and in melancholy tones, moved that the nomination be made unanimous. . . .[6]

When on the following Saturday evening the notifying committee arrived in Springfield to make official notification to the nominee, the town was ablaze with bonfires and fireworks. To the formal notice Lincoln replied, making the platform policy his:

> Sir, I accept the nomination tendered me by the Convention over which you presided, and of which I am formally apprized in the letter of yourself and others, acting as a committee of the convention, for that purpose.
>
> The declaration of principles and sentiments, which accompanies your letter, meets my approval; and it shall be my care not to violate, or disregard it, in any part.
>
> Imploring the assistance of Divine Providence, and with due regard to the views and feelings of all who were represented in the convention; to the rights of all the states, and territories, and people of the nation; to the inviolability of the constitution, and the perpetual union, harmony, and prosperity of all, I am most happy to co-operate for the practical success of the principles declared by the convention.[7]

Edward Bates, unsuccessful candidate for the nomination and destined to become Lincoln's attorney general, mused in his diary:

> *May 19. The Chicago Republican Convention* is over. That party, will henceforth, subside into weakness and then break into pieces, its fragments seeking, each its own safety, in new affiliations and organizations....
>
> At the beginning it was generally thought that the contest would be between Mr. Seward and me, and that the Convention would take the one or the other, as it might determine the question whether the party should act independently upon its own internal strength, both as regards numbers locality and moral support, or modify its platform and mollify its tone, in order to win a broader foundation and gather new strength, both numerical and oral, from outside—i.e. the Whig and American opposition. The shew in favor of other candidates was understood to be complimentary only, to the respective local favorites. But all calculations based upon these views were, as the event proves, signally erroneous.[8]

The hostile *New York Herald* cried of the nomination, "It is the triumph of radicalism."[9] Wendell Phillips, the nation's foremost abolitionist orator, passionate if not fanatical, was interrupted in a speech with the question, "Was he [Lincoln] nominated because he was a better man than Mr. Seward?" Phillips replied:

No, not because he was a better; for he never had said, he never had even condescended to consider whether there is an "irrepressible conflict." William H. Seward's name is irremediably associated with that great philosophic principle. Mr. Lincoln is known merely as the antagonist of Douglas. He is claimed, here, by his defenders, as not up to the level even of the Whigs of 1844. Webster may gather his dust together in his grave, and ask of the North, "Why blame me, if pattern Anti-Slavery can select a man not worthy to unloose the latchet of my shoes as its standard-bearer in 1860?" (Applause) For every blow that Abraham Lincoln ever struck against the system of slavery, the martyr of Marshfield may claim that he has struck a hundred (applause;) and yet we say, and say it justly, that Webster was a traitor to the Northern States, and when Massachusetts put his statue on the Statehouse green, she wrote herself down recreant. We say, and say truly, that he sacrificed the North, and that God will probably hold him, more than any other single man, accountable for the wasted twenty years of political anti-slavery. But who is this huckster in politics? who is this county court advocate? who is this who does not know whether he has got any opinions? Why, he is like the tutor at Cambridge, of whom the students said, that "his mind was full of all manner of emptiness." (Great merriment) What is his recommendation? Is it that nobody knows bad or good of him? His recommendation is, that out of the unknown things in his past life, journals may make for him what character they please. His recommendation is, that his past is a blank; and the statesman of New York, who had done (for so it may be said, to the honor of William H. Seward) as much as any man in politics has done, to marshal the North on the political anti-slavery platform, is unavailable because of those efforts—nothing else.[10]

CHAPTER TWO

THE CAMPAIGN OF 1860

The strong endorsement given Lincoln at the Wigwam was offset during the campaign by vigorous and diverse criticism. The Democratic Party divided into two factions; a largely northern faction nominated Douglas, supporting popular sovereignty, and a largely southern wing nominated John C. Breckinridge, the vice president of the United States, demanding Federal protection, if needed, of slavery in the territories. The Constitutional Union Party, a haven for Whigs and conservatives, nominated John Bell of Tennessee on a bland platform upholding the Union, the Constitution, and enforcement of the laws.

Wendell Phillips, continuing his verbal assault, denounced Lincoln as the "slave-hound of Illinois," a stab at Lincoln's willingness to enforce the fugitive slave law, albeit moderated. The editor of the *Liberator* refused to publish Phillips's extremist letter unless Phillips signed it. Here is Phillips's original:

> We gibbet a Northern hound to-day, side by side with the infamous Mason of Virginia. Mason's Slave Bill is based on that clause of the United States Constitution, which provides for the surrender of slaves escaping from one *State* into another *State* of the Union.
>
> The Supreme Court of the United States has decided that the District of Columbia is not a *State* within the meaning of the Constitution. See Hepburn *vs.* Ellzey, 2 Cranch 445. The District of Columbia is not, therefore, included in the terms of the Fugitive Slave clause. Whoever tries to extend the dominion of that clause over the District of Columbia, exhibits only his own voluntary baseness, out-Mason's Mason, and stamps himself a hound of special "alacrity."
>
> This deed Abraham Lincoln, Republican candidate for President, has done! Here are the facts: Extract of a Bill introduced by Hon. ABRAHAM

LINCOLN, in the U.S. House of Representatives, Jan. 10, 1849. (See Congressional Globe, appendix, 2d Session 30th Congress, p. 212.)

Section 5. That the municipal authorities of Washington and Georgetown, within their respective jurisdictional limits, are hereby *empowered* and REQUIRED to provide *active and efficient means to arrest and deliver up to their owners,* ALL FUGITIVE SLAVES *escaping into said District.*

Mr. Lincoln, in order to introduce this Bill, requested the House to reconsider the vote, instructing the Committee on the District of Columbia to report a Bill for abolishing the Slave Trade therein. To this request, Bingham, Dickenson, Giddings, Greeley, Horace Mann, Palfrey, Hudson, Wentworth, Wilmot, voted NAY. While Albert G. Brown, (now the slave-code and slave-trading Senator,) Butler, (of Bully Brooks infamy,) Howell Cobb, Goggin, Rhett, Iverson, LINCOLN, Toombs, voted YEA.

Mr. Lincoln, in urging his request, said he had submitted his proposition to various leading citizens of the District of Columbia, who gave it their *unanimous* approval.

No wonder Mr. Lincoln is unwilling to make any opposition to the Fugitive Slave Bill! No wonder the Chicago Convention omitted that point in their Resolutions! Their standard-bearer has a worse Bill to answer for than even Mr. Mason.[1]

On the Fourth of July a twenty-eight-year-old black abolitionist, H. Ford Douglas, bitterly assailed his fellow Illinoisan:

Take Abraham Lincoln. I want to know if any man can tell me the difference between the anti-slavery of Abraham Lincoln, and the anti-slavery of the old Whig party or the anti-slavery of Henry Clay? Why, there is no difference between them. Abraham Lincoln is simply a Henry Clay Whig, and he believes just as Henry Clay believed in regard to this question. And Henry Clay was just as odious to the anti-slavery cause and anti-slavery men as ever was John C. Calhoun. In fact, he did as much to perpetuate negro slavery in this country as any other man who has ever lived. Henry Clay once said, "That is property which the law declares to be property," and that "two hundred years of legislation have sanctioned and sanctified property in slaves"! Wherever Henry Clay is to-day in the universe of God, that atheistic lie is with him, with all its tormenting memories. (Applause.)

I know Abraham Lincoln, and I know something about his anti-slavery. I know the Republicans do not like this kind of talk, because, while they are willing to steal our thunder, they are unwilling to submit to the conditions imposed upon that party that assumes to be anti-slavery. They say that they cannot go as fast as you anti-slavery men go in this matter; that they cannot afford to be uncompromisingly honest, or so radical as you Garrisonians; that they want to take time; that they want to do the work gradually. They say, "We must not be in too great a hurry to overthrow slavery; at least, we must take half a loaf, if we cannot get the whole." Now, my friends, I believe that the very best way to overthrow slavery in this country is to occupy the highest possible anti-slavery ground. Washington Irving tells a story of a Dutchman, who wanted to jump over a ditch, and he went back three miles in order to get a good start, and when he got up to the ditch, he had to sit down on the wrong side to get his breath. So it is with these political parties; they are compelled, they say, when they get up to the ditch of slavery, to stop and take a breath.

I do not believe in the anti-slavery of Abraham Lincoln, because he is on the side of this Slave Power of which I am speaking, that has possession of the Federal Government. What does he propose to do? Simple—to let the people and the Territories regulate their domestic institutions in their own way. . . .

Then, there is another item which I want to bring out in this connection. I am a colored man; I am an American citizen; and I think that I am entitled to exercise the elective franchise. I am about twenty-eight years old, and I would like to vote very much. I think I am old enough to vote, and I think that, if I had a vote to give, I should know enough to place it on the side of freedom. (Applause.) No party, it seems to me, is entitled to the sympathy of anti-slavery men, unless that party is willing to extend to the black man all the rights of a citizen. I care nothing about that anti-slavery which wants to make the Territories free, while it is unwilling to extend to me, as a man, in the free States, all the rights of a man. (Applause.) In the State of Illinois, where I live—my adopted State—I have been laboring to make it a place fit for a decent man to live in. In that State, we have a code of black laws that would disgrace any Barbary State, or any uncivilized people in the far-off islands of the sea. Men of my complexion are not allowed to testify in a court of justice, where a white man is a party. If a white man happens to owe me anything, unless I can prove it; by the testimony of a white man, I cannot collect the debt. Now, two years ago, I went through the State of Illinois for the purpose of getting signers to a petition, asking the Legislature to repeal the "Testimony Law," so as to permit colored men to testify against white men. I went to prominent Republicans, and among others, to Abraham Lincoln and Lyman Trumbull, and neither of them dared to sign that petition, to give me the right to testify in a court of justice! ("Hear, hear.") In the State of Illinois, they tax the colored people for every conceivable purpose. They tax the negro's property to support schools for the education of the white man's children, but the colored people are not permitted to enjoy any of the benefits resulting from that taxation. We are compelled to impose upon ourselves additional taxes, in order to educate our children. The State lays its iron hand upon the Negro, holds him down, and puts the other hand into his pocket and steals his hard earnings, to educate the children of white men: and if we sent our children to school, Abraham Lincoln would kick them out, in the name of Republicanism and anti-slavery.[2]

In South Carolina, the boundaries of which reverberated with threats of secession, the *Charleston Mercury,* guided by the fire-eater R. B. Rhett, branded Lincoln a Black Republican and exhorted South Carolinians to vote for Breckinridge.

The Presidential election turns upon a single fact. If the Northern people, believe that the Southern people will dissolve their connections with them, should the Black Republican party succeed in electing LINCOLN to the Presidency—LINCOLN *will be defeated.* Should they, on the contrary, believe, that the Southern people will submit to Black Republican domination by the election of LINCOLN to the Presidency—LINCOLN *will be elected.*

There is but one way, by which the people of the North can be convinced, that the people of the South will not submit to Black Republican domination by the election of LINCOLN; and that is, *by their union against him.* Everything, therefore, which tends to disunite the South, aids the election of LINCOLN.[3]

The widely read *Springfield Republican,* edited by the antislavery Samuel Bowles, retorted to southern secessionists:

The South, through the mouth of many of its leading politicians and journals, defies the North to elect Abraham Lincoln to the presidency. It threatens secession in case he shall be elected. It arrogantly declares that he shall never take his seat. It passes resolutions of the most outrageous and insolent character, insulting every man who dares to vote for what they call a "Black Republican." To make a long matter very short and plain, they claim the privilege of conducting the government in all the future, as they have in all the past, for their own benefit and in their own way, with the alternative of dissolving the Union of the States. Now, if the non-slaveholding people have any spirit at all, they will settle this question at once and forever. Look at the history of the last two administrations, in which the slave interest has had undisputed sway. This sway, the most disgraceful and shameless of anything in the history of the government, must not be thrown off or else the Union will be dissolved. Let's try it! Are we forever to be governed by a slaveholding minority? Will the passage of four years more of misrule make it any easier for the majority to assume its functions?

There are many reasons why we desire to see this experiment tried this fall. If the majority cannot rule the country without the secession of the minority, it is time the country knew it. If the country can only exist under the rule of an oligarchy, let the fact be demonstrated at once, and let us change our institutions. We desire to see the experiment tried, because we wish to have the Southern people, who have been blinded and cheated by the politicians, learn that a "Black Republican" respects the requirements of the Constitution and will protect their interests. Harmony between the two sections of this country can never be secured until the South has learned that the North is not its enemy, but its best friend. We desire to see it tried, that the whole horde of corrupt officials at Washington may be swept by the board, and something of decency and purity introduced there. We desire to see it, that the government may be restored to its original integrity. And any Northern man who has not the pluck enough to stand up and help do this thing is a poltroon. It will be tried, and our minority friends may make up their mind to it.[4]

Unlike Lincoln, who supervised his campaign from Springfield, Stephen A. Douglas took the extraordinary step of taking his campaign to the voters, South as well as North. In Norfolk, Virginia, a questioner asked, "If Abraham Lincoln be elected president of the United States, will the Southern States be justified in seceding from the Union?"

Douglas replied, "To this I emphatically answer No. The election of a man to the presidency by the American people in conformity with the constitution of the United States, would not justify any attempt at dissolving this glorious confederacy."

The questioner continued: "If they (the Southern States) secede from the Union upon the inauguration of Abraham Lincoln, before he commits an overt act against their constitutional rights, will you advise or vindicate resistance by force to the decision?"

Douglas responded: "I answer emphatically that it is the duty of the president of the United States, and all others in authority under him to enforce the laws of the United States passed by Congress, and as the courts expound them."[5]

Abolitionists meeting in Syracuse nominated for president Gerrit Smith, upstate New York reformer and philanthropist, who in 1859 had assured John Brown of support. They adopted a resolution reading:

> That for Abolitionists to vote for a candidate like Abraham Lincoln, who stands ready to execute the accursed Fugitive Slave Law, to suppress insurrections among slaves, to admit new slave States, and to support the ostracism, socially and politically, of the black man of the North, is to give the lie to their professions, to expose their hypocrisy to the world, and to do what they can to put far off the day of the slave's deliverance.[6]

The *Washington Constitution,* a pro-Breckinridge paper, sympathized with anxious voters throughout the nation:

> Nor can it be said that any inclination has been shown since the Chicago nomination to hold the extremists in check. The opposite has been the case. The nomination of Lincoln has invested them with an influence which they are not backward in using in several of the States. True, we hear comparatively little of their stump orators in the East. Mr. Douglas is doing their work too skillfully to allow of their being anxious about accredited orators whilst he is upon the stump. But where they do put in appearances, you meet champions worthy of the candidate and the cause: here a Sumner, there a Lovejoy, there, again, a Giddings—out-and-out creatures, whom the leaders have heretofore chained in the background to save the credit of the party during the progress of a canvass. The Lincoln nomination has reversed matters—how completely the recent gubernatorial nomination in Massachusetts sufficiently attests. Driven from the stage by the preponderance of the radical element, Mr. Banks sees the abolitionist Andrew nominated as his successor; the nomination being heralded forth as a concession to those who hold with Lincoln that "this Union cannot stand half slave, half free," and would act accordingly if once installed in Washington.

> We contend, then, that the anxiety, the alarm with which the contest is viewed in the South, and by national men everywhere, is not only defensible,

but rational and just. Although four candidates are in the field, the struggle is really between two principles, of which Mr. Breckinridge and Mr. Lincoln are the respective champions. Were it limited personally to these candidates, we should not dread the result. The patriotic sentiment of the country would rise in its might and crush the party whose progress must render the maintenance of the Union impossible. The danger springs from the aid and comfort which the black-republicans are enabled to derive "from the apostles of squatter sovereignty on the one hand, and the remnants of know-nothingism on the other."[7]

The pro-Douglas *Pittsburgh Post* declared apprehensively: "If Lincoln were elected President . . . the Union would be endangered from that hour."

All the while Douglas was endeavoring to assure voters that Lincoln's election should not be a cause for secession, abolitionists were deploring Lincoln's election, and editors of newspapers opposing Lincoln were expressing apprehension that he might be elected. Lincoln himself kept silent.

Many urged him to speak out. George D. Prentice, editor of the *Louisville Journal,* wrote to him on October 26:

> There is evidently a very strong possibility of your being elected to the Presidency by the popular vote. Whilst I have the strongest confidence in both your personal and political integrity, and have at no time hesitated to express it in my paper, I have warmly opposed your election because I greatly fear its influence upon the power of the country.
>
> You undoubtedly know the condition of public sentiment in the far South as well as I do. I dread lest, almost as soon as the fact of you election shall be proclaimed, a desperate blow will be struck for the dismemberment of the Union. Under these circumstances I take the liberty of suggesting to you whether it will not be advisable for you to prepare a letter to some friend, which, in the event of your election, shall be published at once a letter setting forth your conservative views and intentions and therefore calculated to assure all the good citizens of the South and to take from the disunionists every excuse or pretext for treason.
>
> I hope I am not pressuring too far in thus addressing you. If I am, pardon me.
>
> Very respectfully,
> Geo. D. Prentice[8]

In reply Lincoln said:

Your suggestion that I, in a certain event, shall write a letter, setting forth my conservative views and intentions, is certainly a very worthy one. But would it do any good? If I were to labor a month, I could not express my conservative views and intentions more clearly and strongly, than they are expressed in our plat-form, and in my many speeches already in print, and before the public. And yet even you, who do occasionally speak of me in terms of personal kindness, give no prominence to these oft-repeated expressions of conservative views and intentions; but busy yourself with appeals to all conservative men, to vote for Douglas—to vote any way which can possibly defeat me—thus impressing your readers that you think, I am the very worst man living. If what I have already said has failed to convince you, no repetition of it would convince you.[9]

On November 6, election day, the *New York Herald,* edited by James Gordon Bennett, urged northern workingmen to vote Democratic:

If Lincoln is elected today, you will have to compete with the labor of four million emancipated Negroes. . . . The North will be flooded with free negroes, and the labor of the white man will be depreciated and degraded.[10]

With only two of every five voters voting for him, and none in ten slave states that joined the Confederate States of America, and only a handful in the eleventh slave state completing that new government, the balloting revealed a divided Union.

Undismayed, the *Herald,* describing itself as "an independent organ of the public," urged the president-elect to take conciliatory steps:

As an independent organ of public opinion, having nothing to ask and nothing to fear from parties or politicians, in or out of power, this journal is free to say that if the President elect shall measure his steps by the landmarks of the constitution, and for the harmony of the country, we expect to stand by him. On the contrary, should he be led astray by the false lights of the "irrepressible conflict," we shall stick to him as we stuck to poor Pierce from the day of his departure from the line of his duty until the day of his banishment from Washington. To Abraham Lincoln now belongs the power of restoring or destroying the happy relations of peace and fraternity between the North and the South, and let us hope that he may prove equal to the crisis and responsibility.

Let the new President make a clean discharge of the present batch of officeholders, if he will, but let not their places be supplied by scurvy politicians, but by honest and capable men. In this way he may do a great and good work for the country; but, above all, let him specifically and promptly proclaim his adhesion to the federal constitution, for only upon that platform can the Union be saved.[11]

CHAPTER THREE

INTERREGNUM

Although appeals for Lincoln to speak out continued, Gideon Welles, a Connecticut newspaper editor, advised Lincoln:

> [T]he southern mind has become demoralized and perverted. They will not tolerate republican papers—they will not listen to republican speakers—they know not the truth and will not receive it. How then is the southern mind to be disabused? I confess I know of no way but by practical experience. When they shall have witnessed and felt a republican administration, they will be convinced their fears were groundless. . . .
>
> Any disavowal of yours or your friends would be misconstrued and only aggravate existing evils.[1]

Lincoln's election in November precipitated a national crisis of dimensions heretofore unknown. The *Liberator,* proclaiming that "for the first time in our history, the *slave* has chosen a President of the United States," described "Southern Desperation":

> Never has the truth of the ancient proverb, "Whom the gods intend to destroy, they first make mad," been more signally illustrated than in the present condition of the Southern slaveholders. They are insane from their fears, their guilty forebodings, their lust of power and rule, their hatred of free institutions, their consciousness of merited judgments; so that they may be properly classed with the inmates of a lunatic asylum. Their dread of Mr. Lincoln, of his administration, of the Republican party, demonstrates their insanity. In vain does Mr. Lincoln tell them, "I do not now, nor ever did, stand in favor of the unconditional repeal of the Fugitive Slave Law"—"I do not now, nor ever did, stand pledged against the admission of any more Slave States into the Union"—"I do not stand pledged to the abolition of slavery in the District of Columbia"—"I do not stand pledged to the prohibition

27

of the slave trade between the different States"—they rave just as fiercely as though he were another John Brown, armed for Southern invasion and universal emancipation! In vain does the Republican party present but one point of antagonism to slavery—to wit, no more territorial expansion—and exhibit the utmost cautiousness not to give offence in any other direction— and make itself hoarse in uttering professions of loyalty to the Constitution and the Union—still, they protest that its designs are infernal, and for them there is "sleep no more"! Are not these the signs of a demented people?

Nevertheless, there is "method" in their madness. In their wildest paroxysms, they know precisely how far to proceed. "Will they secede from the Union?" Will they jump into the Atlantic? Will they conflagrate their own dwellings, cut their own throats, and enable their slaves to rise in successful insurrection? Perhaps they will—probably they will not! By their bullying and raving, they have many times frightened the North into a base submission to their demands—and they expect to do it again! Shall they succeed?"[2]

South Carolina promptly threatened to withdraw from the Union and prepared for speedy secession. The *Charleston Courier,* voice of South Carolina extremism, rang the tocsin of dissolution. T. R. R. Cobb, a highly regarded constitutional lawyer who became a Confederate general and was killed at the battle of Fredericksburg, spoke on November 12 at the Georgia secession convention in favor of "immediate, unconditional secession."

In the North influential voices accepted severance of the Union. In his widely circulated *New York Tribune,* only two days after the election, Greeley published an editorial with the theme: let the Cotton States "go in peace." Asked whether the South would secede, Henry Ward Beecher, perhaps the North's most influential preacher and brother of Harriet Beecher Stowe, replied in late November, "I don't believe they will; and I don't care if they do." Frederick Douglass, born a slave and now an eloquent abolitionist, cried, "I am for a dissolution of the Union—decidedly for a dissolution of the Union."[3]

An alarmed Winfield Scott, hero of the Mexican War and general-in-chief of the army, sent Lincoln a copy of a memorandum titled "Views suggested by the imminent danger of a disruption of the Union by the secession of one or more Southern States." He called for moderation and firmness to prevent secession. Scott urged President Buchanan and the pro-southern secretary of war, John B. Floyd, to strengthen the federal forts in the principal southern cities.

Lincoln continued to preserve a public silence, though aware of business interests' uneasiness and besought by various people to speak out. Nathaniel P. Paschall, editor of the *Missouri Republican,* warned that if his border slave state was to be kept in the Union, Lincoln would have to make a statement. Lincoln answered:

> Mr. Ridgely showed me a letter of yours in which you manifest some anxiety that I should make some public declaration with a view to favorably affect the business of the country. I said to Mr. Ridgely I would write you to-day, which I now do.
>
> I could say nothing which I have not already said, and which is in print and accessible to the public. Please pardon me for suggesting that if the papers, like yours, which heretofore have persistently garbled, and misrepresented what I have said, will now fully and fairly place it before their readers, there can be no further misunderstanding. I beg you to believe me sincere when I declare I do not say this in a spirit of complaint or resentment; but that I urge it as the true cure for any real uneasiness in the country that my course may be other than conservative. The Republican newspapers now, and for some time past, are and have been republishing copious extracts from my many published speeches, which would at once reach the whole public if your class of papers would also publish them.
>
> I am not at liberty to shift my ground—that is out of the question. If I thought a *repetition* would do any good I would make it. But my judgment is it would do positive harm. The secessionists, *per se* believing they had alarmed me, would clamor all the louder.[4]

As the year closed General Scott anxiously asked the president for permission to reinforce Fort Sumter, encompassed by hostile Charleston. Buchanan refused. He had earlier asked Attorney General Jeremiah S. Black for an opinion upon the powers of the president. The opinion upheld the president's duty to enforce the laws but severely limited his options with respect to secession and use of force. Black wrote:

> If one of the States should declare her independence, your action cannot depend upon the rightfulness of the cause upon which such declaration is

based. Whether the retirement of a State from the Union be the exercise of a right reserved in the Constitution, or a revolutionary movement, it is certain that you have not in either case the authority to recognize her independence or to absolve her from her Federal obligations. Congress or the other States in convention assembled must take such measures as may be necessary and proper. . . . There was undoubtedly a strong and universal conviction among the men who framed and ratified the Constitution, that military force would not only be useless, but pernicious as a means of holding the States together.[5]

Two weeks later, in his final annual message to Congress, Buchanan echoed these views, telling Congress:

What, in the meantime, is the responsibility and true position of the Executive? He is bound by solemn oath, before God and country, "to take care that the laws be faithfully executed," and from this obligation he cannot be absolved by any human power. But what if the performance of this duty, in whole or in part, has been rendered impracticable by events over which he could have exercised no control? Such, at the present moment, is the case throughout the State of South Carolina, so far as the laws of the United States to secure the administration of justice by means of the federal judiciary are concerned. All the federal officers within its limits, through whose agency alone these laws can be carried into execution, have already resigned. We no longer have a district judge, a district attorney, or a marshal in South Carolina. In fact, the whole machinery of the federal government necessary for the distribution of remedial justice among the people has been demolished, and it would be difficult, if not impossible, to replace it. . . .

Apart from the execution of the laws, so far as this may be practicable, the Executive has no authority to decide what shall be the relations between the federal government and South Carolina. He has been invested with no such discretion. He possesses no power to change the relations heretofore existing between them, much less to acknowledge the independence of that State. This would be to invest a mere executive officer with the power to recognize the dissolution of the Confederacy among our thirty-three sovereign States. . . .

The question fairly stated is: Has the Constitution delegated to Congress the power to coerce a State into submission which is attempting to withdraw or has actually withdrawn from the Confederacy? If answered in the affirmative, it must be on the principle that the power has been conferred upon Congress to declare and to make war against a State. After much serious reflection I have arrived at the conclusion that no such power has been delegated to Congress or to any other department of the federal government.[6]

In contrast to this circumscribed outlook, Lincoln, days after his election, had confided to a private secretary a startlingly different outlook:

> My own impression is at present (leaving myself room to modify the opinion if upon further investigation I should see fit to do so) that this government possesses both the authority and the power to maintain its own integrity.[7]

In confidential and private correspondence the president-elect repeatedly told influential members of Congress that he opposed extension of slavery—the lower South's demand. His reasons for opposing it varied. Responding to a letter from Senator Lyman Trumbull of Illinois, Lincoln on December 10 wrote:

> Let there be no compromise on the question of *extending* slavery. If there be, all our labor is lost, and, ere long, must be done again. The dangerous ground—that into which some of our friends have a hankering to run—is Pop. Sov. Have none of it. Stand firm. The tug has come, & better now, than any time hereafter.[8]

Though unwilling to issue a public declaration, Lincoln quietly made known his views to key persons. Reading that a former respected Whig colleague in Congress, Alexander H. Stephens, had made a speech on secession before the Georgia Assembly, Lincoln wrote for a copy, prudently marking his letter, "For your own eye only."

> Your obliging answer to my short note is just received, and for which please accept my thanks. I fully appreciate the present peril the country is in, and the weight of responsibility on me.
>
> Do the people of the South really entertain fears that a Republican administration would, *directly,* or *indirectly,* interfere with their slaves, or with them, about their slaves? If they do, I wish to assure you, as once a friend, and still, I hope, not an enemy, that there is no cause for such fears.
>
> The South would be in no more danger in this respect, than it was in the days of Washington. I suppose, however, this does not meet the case.

You think slavery is *right* and ought to be extended; while we think it is *wrong* and ought to be restricted. That I suppose is the rub. It certainly is the only substantial difference between us.[9]

On December 30 Stephens replied:

Personally, I am not your enemy—far from it; and however widely we may differ politically, yet I trust we both have an earnest desire to preserve and maintain the Union. . . . When men come under the influence of fanaticism, there is no telling where their impulses or passions may drive them. This is what creates our discontent and apprehensions, not unreasonable when we see . . . such reckless exhibition of madness as the John Brown raid into Virginia, which has received so much sympathy from many, and no open condemnation from any of the leading members of the dominant party. . . . In addressing you thus, I would have you understand me as being not a personal enemy, but as one who would have you do what you can to save our common country. A word fitly spoken by you now would be like "apples of gold in pictures of silver."[10]

Meanwhile, on December 11, when a member of the congressional compromise committee, William Kellogg of Illinois, asked Lincoln for suggestions about what the committee might do "in relation to the present difficulties," Lincoln had responded:

Entertain no proposition for a compromise in regard to the extension of slavery. The instant you do, they have us under again; all our labor is lost, and sooner or later must be done over. Douglas is sure to be again trying to bring in his "Pop. Sov." Have none of it. The tug has to come & better now than later.

You know I think the fugitive slave clause of the constitution ought to be enforced—to put it on the mildest form, ought not to be resisted.[11]

To apprehensive Congressman Elihu Washburne of Illinois—fearing that Buchanan might abandon the Charleston fort by not dispatching military forces, that Republicans in Congress might refrain from debate in Congress, and that the committee formed in Congress to consider compromise would do little good—Lincoln replied:

Your long letter received. Prevent, as far as possible, any of our friends from demoralizing themselves, and our cause, by entertaining propositions for compromise of any sort, on "slavery extention." There is no possible compromise upon it, but which puts us under again, and leaves all our work to do over again. Whether it be a Mo. Line, or Eli Thayer's Pop. Sov. it is all the same. Let either be undone, & immediately filibustering and extending slavery recommences. On that point hold firm, as with a chain of steel.[12]

John D. Defrees, chairman of the Indiana State Republican Committee, had learned while in Washington that secessionist threats were more real than westerners realized. Some Republicans were willing "to secure genuine popular sovereignty to the people of our Territories," he told the president-elect. Lincoln in reply reaffirmed on December 18 his opposition to popular sovereignty by describing his grounds for opposing it.

If congressional compromise had become a threat to Republican policy and, as Lincoln saw it, to the Union's future, there was a threat from another quarter as well—southern conquest of federal forts in the South. Elihu Washburne conveyed to Lincoln the results of an interview between himself and General Scott, unfolding the policy of Buchanan and the secretary of war, their neglect of Scott's advice, and the dire peril to Fort Sumter.[13]

Scott described his plight in 1864 in his *Memoirs:*

By appointment, the Secretary accompanied me to the President, December 15, when the same topics, secessionism, etc., were again pretty fully discussed. There being, at the moment, in the opinion of the President, no danger of an early secession, beyond South Carolina, the President, in reply to my arguments for immediately reinforcing Fort Moultrie, and sending a garrison to Fort Sumter, said, in substance, the time had not arrived for doing so; that he would wait the action of the Convention of South Carolina, in the expectation that a commission would be appointed and sent to negotiate with him and Congress, respecting the secession of the State and the property of the United States held within its limits; and that, if Congress should decide against the secession, then he would send reinforcement, and telegraph the commanding officer (Major Anderson) of Fort Moultrie, to hold the forts (Moultrie and Sumter) against attack.

And the Secretary, with animation, added: "We have a vessel of war (the Brooklyn) held in readiness at Norfolk, and he would then send three hundred men, in her, from Fort Monroe, to Charleston." To which I replied, first, "That so many men could not be withdrawn from that garrison, but could be taken from New York. Next, that it would then be too late, as the

South Carolina Commissioners would have the game in their hands—first by using, and then cutting the wires; that, as there was not a soldier in Fort Sumter, any handful of armed secessionists might seize and occupy it," etc. etc.

Here the remark may be permitted, that, if the Secretary's three hundred men had then (or some time later) been sent to Forts Moultrie and Sumter, *both* would now have been in the possession of the United States, and not a battery, below them, could have been erected by the Secessionists. Consequently, the access to those forts from the sea would now (the end of March, 1861) be unobstructed and *free.*"[14]

Taking a far different position from that of Buchanan, Lincoln transmitted a confidential message to Washburne:

> Last night I received your letter giving an account of your interview with Gen. Scott, and for which I thank you. Please present my respects to the General, and tell him, confidentially, I shall be obliged to him to be as well prepared as he can to either hold, or retake, the forts, as the case may require, at, and after the inauguration.[15]

On December 20 South Carolina took the fateful step of seceding from the Union, the first of seven states that with great speed formed a so-called separate union, the Confederate States of America. Buchanan sent Duff Green, a political veteran who exalted states' rights above the federal government, to ascertain Lincoln's views toward secession. After a secret meeting Lincoln contrived a letter that he sent to Green, recognizing those state rights made secure in the Constitution and at the same time calling on six states in the deep South not to secede unless the new administration should violate their rights. Lincoln sent a copy of his letter, which did not become public, to Senator Lyman Trumbull:

> I do not desire any amendment of the Constitution. Recognizing, however, that questions of such amendment rightfully belong to the American People, I should not feel justified, nor inclined, to withhold from them, if I co[u]ld, a fair opportunity of expressing their will thereon, through either of the modes prescribed in the instrument.
>
> In addition I declare that the maintainance inviolate of the rights of States, and especially the right of each state to order and control its own domestic institutions according to its own judgment exclusively, is essential to that balance of powers on which the perfection and

endurance of our political fabric depends—and I denounce the lawless invasion, by armed force, of the soil of any State or Territory, no matter under what pretext, as the gravest of crimes.

I am greatly averse to writing anything for the public at this time; and I consent to the publication of this, only upon the condition that six of the twelve United States Senators for the States of Georgia, Alabama, Mississippi, Louisiana, Florida, and Texas shall sign their names to what is written on this sheet below my name, and allow the whole to be published together.

Yours truly A. Lincoln.

We recommend to the people of the States we represent respectively, to suspend all action for dismemberment of the Union, at least, until some act, deemed to be violative of our rights, shall be done by the incoming administration.[16]

As the crisis of the Union deepened, Lincoln went beyond advising individual congressmen in confidence to drafting a set of resolutions to guide the action of the Republican members of the Senate Committee of Thirteen named to consider compromise. His document read:

Resolved: That the fugitive clause of the Constitution ought to be enforced by a law of Congress, with efficient provisions for that object, not obliging private persons to assist in its execution, but punishing all who resist it, and with the usual safeguards to liberty, securing free men against being surrendered as slaves—

That all state laws, if there be such, or apparantly, in conflict with such law of Congress, ought to be repealed; and no opposition to the execution of such law of Congress ought to be made—

That the Federal Union must be preserved.[17]

Seward, to whom Lincoln had offered the post of secretary of state, described the course he had followed in presenting Lincoln's resolution:

This evening the Republican members of the committee, with Judge Trumbull and Mr. Fessenden, met at my house, to consider your written suggestion, and determine whether it shall be offered. While we think the ground has been already covered, we find that, in the form you give it, it would divide our friends, not only in the committee, but in Congress, a portion being unwilling to give up their old opinion, that the duty of executing the constitutional provisions, concerning fugitives from service, belongs to the states, and not at all to Congress.[18]

With the crisis worsening, compromise failing, and seven slave states forming the Confederate States of America, Lincoln made his views plain in a letter to Seward:

On the 21st ult. Hon. W. Kellogg, a Republican M.C. of this state whom you probably know, was here, in a good deal of anxiety, seeking to ascertain to what extent I would be consenting for our friends to go in the way of compromise on the now vexed question. While he was with me I received a dispatch from Senator Trumbull, at Washington, alluding to the same question, and telling me to await letters. I thereupon told Mr. Kellogg that when I should receive these letters, posting me as to the state of affairs at Washington, I would write you, requesting you to let him see my letter. To my surprise when the letters mentioned by Judge Trumbull came, they made no allusion to the "vexed question." The[y] baffled me so much that I was near not writing you at all, in compliance with what I had said to Judge Kellogg.

I say now, however, as I have all the while said, that on the territorial question—that is, the question of extending slavery under the national auspices,—I am inflexible. I am for no compromise which *assists* or *permits* the extension of the institution on soil owned by the nation. And any trick by which the nation is to acquire territory, and then allow some local authority to spread slavery over it, is as obnoxious as any other.

I take it that to effect some such result as this, and to put us again on the high-road to a slave empire is the object of all these proposed compromises. I am against it.

As to fugitive slaves, District of Columbia, slave trade among the slave states, and whatever springs of necessity from the fact that the institution is amongst us, I care but little, so that what is done be comely, and not altogether outrageous. Nor do I care much about New-Mexico, if further extension were hedged against it.[19]

CHAPTER FOUR

FROM SPRINGFIELD
TO WASHINGTON

Abraham Lincoln with his wife Mary and their three sons, Robert, Willie, and Tad, began their journey from Springfield to Washington on February 11, 1861. Henry Villard, a reporter who accompanied the special train most of the way, estimated that Lincoln made fifty speeches en route.

In these speeches he affirmed earlier views: "I am not at liberty to shift my ground," he remarked. He foretold in part the policy he would announce in his First Inaugural. The historian James Ford Rhodes observed that his journey, with his appearances in many communities, frequent speeches, and extensive publicity in the nation's press, laid a foundation for his popularity among the plain people.

If Lincoln seemed to have little novel to say, aware that he must speak prudently and not prematurely, he nevertheless made some speeches and stops that were notable. At the Springfield railroad station a crowd of a thousand gathered early on a Monday morning to say goodbye. In a moving impromptu speech the president-elect said:

> My friends—No one, not in my situation, can appreciate my feeling of sadness at this parting. To this place, and the kindness of these people, I owe every thing. Here I have lived a quarter of a century, and have passed from a young to an old man. Here my children have been born, and one is buried. I now leave, not knowing when, or whether ever, I may return, with a task before me greater than that which rested upon Washington. Without the assistance of that Divine Being, who ever attended him, I cannot succeed. With that assistance I cannot fail. Trusting in Him, who

can go with me, and remain with you and be every where for good, let us confidently hope that all will yet be well. To His care commending you, as I hope in your prayers you will commend me, I bid you an affectionate farewell.[1]

As the train traveled eastward across the prairie it made its first stop in Indianapolis. Speaking from the balcony of the Bates House, Lincoln said:

The words "coercion" and "invasion" are in great use about these days. Suppose we were simply to try if we can, and ascertain what, is the meaning of these words. Let us get, if we can, the exact definitions of these words—not from dictionaries, but from the men who constantly repeat them—what things they mean to express by the words. What, then, is "coercion"? What is "invasion"? Would the marching of an army into South Carolina, for instance, be coercion or invasion? I very frankly say, I think it would be an invasion, and it would be coercion too, if the people of that country were forced to submit. But if the Government, for instance, but simply insists upon holding its own forts, or retaking those forts which belong to it,—[cheers,]—or even the withdrawal of the mails from those portions of the country where the mails themselves are habitually violated; would any or all of these things be coercion? Do the lovers of the Union contend that they will resist coercion or invasion of any State, understanding that any or all of these would be coercing or invading a State? If they do, then it occurs to me that the means for the preservation of the Union they so greatly love, in their own estimation, is of a very thin and airy character. [Applause.] If sick, they would consider the little pills of the homoepathist as already too large for them to swallow. In their view, the Union, as a family relation, would not be anything like a regular marriage at all, but only as a sort of free-love arrangement,—[laughter,]—to be maintained on what that sect calls passionate attraction. [Continued laughter.] But, my friends, enough of this.

What is the particular sacredness of a State? I speak not of that position which is given to a State in and by the Constitution of the United States, for that all of us agree to—we abide by; but that position assumed, that a State can carry with it out of the Union that which it holds in sacredness by virtue of its connection with the Union. I am speaking of that assumed right of a State, as a primary principle, that the Constitution should rule all that is less than itself, and ruin all that is bigger than itself. [Laughter.] But, I ask, wherein does consist that right? If a State, in one instance, and a county in another, should be equal in extent of territory, and equal in the number of people, wherein is that State any better than the county? Can a change of name change the right? By what principle of original right is it that one-fiftieth or one-ninetieth of a great nation, by calling themselves a State, have the right to break up and ruin that nation as a matter of original principle? Now, I ask the question—I am not deciding anything—[laughter,]—and with the request that you will think somewhat upon that subject and decide for yourselves, if you choose, when you get ready,—where is the mysterious, original right, from principle, for a certain district of country with inhabitants, by merely being called a State, to play tyrant over all its own citizens, and deny the authority of everything greater than itself. [Laughter.] I say I am deciding nothing, but simply giving something for you to reflect upon; and, with having said this much, and having declared, in the start, that I will make no long speeches, I thank you again for this magnificent welcome, and bid you an affectionate farewell. [Cheers.][2]

Lincoln's frank disclosure of his policy toward secession startled many people. He would hold the nation's forts, retake those claimed by the new Confederacy, enforce the tariff laws, and withdraw the mails from rebel areas. His remark that those who merely professed a love for the Union viewed it "only as a sort of free-love arrangement" brought laughter from his audience but concern to his distant targets.

A startled Virginia congressman, Muscoe R. H. Garnett, who had recently signed an appeal to the people of Virginia to try to avert an impending civil war, rose in the House of Representatives to say: "After the recent declaration of war by the President elect of the United States, I deem it my duty to interpose every obstacle to the tyrannical and military despotism now about to be inaugurated."[3]

Proceeding to Cincinnati, Lincoln sought to reassure his audience by quoting from a speech he had made in 1859 to Kentuckians, just across the Ohio River. "We mean to leave you alone.... There is no difference between us, other than the difference of circumstances." He added his hope "that we shall again be brethren, forgetting all parties."[4]

Heading north to Columbus, he spoke to the state legislature. There he used words that troubled contemporaries as well as future writers. With the nation split in twain, he said, "there is nothing that really hurts anybody ...

nobody is suffering anything."[5] The *Daily Missouri Republican* scored the speeches made in Indianapolis and Columbus:

> The speeches of Mr. LINCOLN, since the commencement of his *progress* to Washington, have been looked for with great interest, in the hope that they might give some inkling of his Administrative policy, and present, also, some insight into the character of the man. So far as his *policy* is concerned, it may be said that he did not use too strong terms to his Kentucky visitor, when, after being told that the Kentucky Legislature had, by nearly an unanimous vote, passed resolutions against Coercion of the Seceding States, he told Kentucky to "prepare for war." His speech at Indianapolis is in perfect consonance with this idea. The forts, arsenals, mint and customhouses, in possession of the Seceding States must be *retaken,* according to the President, and to do this the army must be called into requisition, as well as the navy, and so civil war begins—the North against the South, and the latter to be subjugated at all hazards.
>
> Mr. LINCOLN may begin this war if he likes it, but the end of his term will see him further than ever from the object in view, or can he ever bring back the slave States into the Union by the employment of force; and if coercion be attempted—if war be made in the territory of the Border States, he will meet an army at the threshold quite powerful enough to destroy him.
>
> At Columbus, Ohio, the President *improvised* a little—and [it] certainly is the most remarkable speech on record. The burden of it is that "nobody is hurt"—"nobody is suffering" from the present condition of affairs, pecuniary and political. Was the like of that ever heard? What could he have meant? With a perfect knowledge that the Union has been virtually dissolved—that six of the States have renounced this confederacy and formed a new government; with official information that the government was bankrupt, and that on the 4th of March not a dollar will be found in the Treasury, but pressing demands for at least eight millions, acknowledged to be due, but without the means of payment; with a knowledge that the Secretary of the Treasury had asked of any kind to meet the necessities of the office, and that even the indorsement of States had been solicited to give character to the national credit; with a congressional appropriation of the credit of the United States for from fifty to sixty-five millions of dollars, authorized for the ordinary wants of the Government; with communications before him, stating that not a dollar of money could be obtained by him for carrying on his government until all difficulties between the States

are settled—he proceeds to tell us, that "nobody is hurt," and "nobody is suffering," from the present condition of the country.[6]

A touching scene took place in Westfield, New York. Months before, an eleven-year-old girl had written to him:

Dear Sir My Father has just home from the fair and brought home your picture and Mr. Hamlin's. I am a little girl only eleven years old, but want you should be President of the United States very much so I hope you wont think me very bold to write to such a great man as you are. Have you any little girls about as large as I am if so give them my love and tell her to write to me if you cannot answer this letter. I have got 4 brother's and part of them will vote for you any way and if you will let your whiskers grow I will try and get the rest of them to vote for you you would look a great deal better for your face is so thin. All the ladies like whiskers and they would tease their husband's to vote for you and then you would be President. My father is a going to vote for you and if I was a man I would vote for you to but I will try and get every one to vote for you that I can I think that rail fence around your picture makes it look very pretty I have got a little baby sister she is nine weeks old and is just as cunning as can be. When you direct your letter dir[e]ct to Grace Bedell Westfield Chatauque County New York I must not write any more answer this letter right off Good bye Grace Bedell[7]

Lincoln had promptly replied:

My dear little Miss. Your very agreeable letter of the 15th is received.
    I regret the necessity of saying I have no daughters. I have three sons—one seventeen, one nine, and one seven, years of age. They, with their mother, constitute my whole family.
    As to the whiskers, having never worn any, do you not think people would call it a piece of silly affection if I were to begin it now? Your very sincere well-wisher A. Lincoln.[8]

A Philadelphia reporter described what happened when Lincoln's train reached the girl's hometown:

At Westfield, Mr. LINCOLN greeted a large crowd of ladies, and several thousand of the sterner sex. Addressing the ladies, he said, 'I am glad to see you; I suppose you are to see me; but I certainly think I have the best of the bargain. [Applause.] Some three months ago, I received a letter from a young lady here; it was a very pretty letter, and she advised me to let my whiskers grow, as it would improve my personal appearance; acting partly upon her suggestion, I have done so; and now, if she is here, I would like to see her; I think her name was Miss BARLLY.' A small boy, mounted on a post, with his mouth and eyes both wide open, cried out, 'there she is, Mr. LINCOLN,' pointing to a beautiful girl, with black eyes, who was blushing all over her fair face. The President left the car, and the crowd making way for him, he reached her, and gave her several hearty kisses, and amid the yells of delight from the excited crowd, he bade her good-bye, and on we rushed.[9]

On February 22, keenly aware of the day and the place and "visibly moved and affected," his secretaries noted, he spoke in Independence Hall, Philadelphia. Here he disclosed the wellspring of his political philosophy:

I can say in return, sir, that all the political sentiments I entertain have been drawn, so far as I have been able to draw them, from the sentiments which originated, and were given to the world from this hall in which we stand. I have never had a feeling politically that did not spring from the sentiments embodied in the Declaration of Independence.[10]

In his final speech of the journey, at Harrisburg, he described the experience:

Allusion has been made to the fact—the interesting fact, perhaps we should say—that I for the first time appear at the Capitol of the great Commonwealth of Pennsylvania, upon the birthday of the Father of his Country. In connection with that beloved anniversary connected with the history of this country, I have already gone through one exceedingly interesting scene this morning in the ceremonies at Philadelphia. Under the conduct of gentlemen there, I was for the first time allowed the privilege of standing in the old Independence Hall, [enthusiastic cheering], to have a few words addressed to me there and opening up to me an opportunity of expressing with much regret that I had not more time to express something of my own feelings, excited by the occasion—somewhat to harmonize and give shape to the feelings that had been really the feelings of my whole life.

Besides this, our friends there had provided a magnificent flag of the country. The[y] had arranged it so that I was given the honor of raising it to the head of its staff [applause]; and when it went up, I was pleased that it went to its place by the strength of my own feeble arm. When, according to the arrangement, the cord was pulled and it flaunted gloriously to the wind without an accident, in the light glowing sunshine of the morning, I could not help hoping that there was in the entire success of that beautiful ceremony, at least something of an omen of what is to come. [Loud applause] Nor could I help, feeling then as I often have felt, that in the whole of that proceeding I was a very humble instrument. I had not provided the flag; I had not made the arrangements for elevating it to its place; I had applied but a very small portion of my feeble strength in raising it. In the whole transaction, I was in the hands of the people who had arranged it, and if I can have the same generous co-operation of the people of this nation, I think the flag of our country may yet be kept flaunting gloriously. [Enthusiastic, long continued cheering.]

I recur for a moment but to repeat some words uttered at the hotel in regard to what has been said about the military support which the general government may expect from the Commonwealth of Pennsylvania, in a proper emergency. To guard against any possible mistake do I recur to this. It is not with any pleasure that I contemplate the possibility that a necessity may arise in this country for the use of the military arm. [Applause.] While I am exceedingly gratified to see the manifestation upon your streets of your military force here, and exceedingly gratified at your promise to use that force upon a proper emergency, while I make these acknowledgments, I desire to repeat, in order to preclude any possible misconstruction, that I do most sincerely hope that we shall have no use for them—[loud applause]—that it will never become their duty to shed blood, and most especially never to shed fraternal blood. I promise that (in so far as I may have wisdom to direct,) if so painful a result shall in any wise be brought about, it shall be through no fault of mine. [Cheers]

Allusion has also been made, by one of your honored Speakers, to some remarks recently made by myself at Pittsburgh, in regard to what is supposed to be the especial interest of this great Commonwealth of Pennsylvania. I now wish only to say, in regard to that matter, that the few remarks which I uttered on that occasion were rather carefully worded. I took great pains that they should be so. I have seen no occasion since to add to them or subtract from them. I leave them precisely as they stand; [applause] adding only now that I am pleased to have an expression from you, gentlemen of Pennsylvania, significant that they are satisfactory to you.

And now, gentlemen of the General Assembly of the Commonwealth of Pennsylvania, allow me again to return to you my most sincere thanks.[11]

43

Lincoln's presidency was preceded by a presumed plot against his life and he was repeatedly warned en route to Washington, especially by Pinkerton detectives, that his life was in danger. He received a warning from William H. Seward, forwarded by General Scott, that read:

> My Dear Sir: My son goes express to you. He will show you a report made by our detective to General Scott, and by him communicated to me this morning. I deem it so important as to dispatch my son to meet you wherever he may find you.
>
> I concur with General Scott in thinking it best for you to reconsider your arrangement. No one here but General Scott, myself, and the bearer is aware of this communication.
>
> I should have gone with it myself, but for the peculiar sensitiveness about my attendance at the Senate at this crisis. Very truly yours, William H. Seward.
>
> A New York detective officer who has been on duty in Baltimore for three weeks past reports this morning that there is serious danger of violence to, and the assassination of, Mr. Lincoln in his passage through that city, should the time of that passage be known. He states that there are banded rowdies holding secret meetings, and that he has heard threats of mobbing and violence, and has himself heard men declare that if Mr. Lincoln was to be assassinated they would like to be the men.[12]

Lincoln heeded the report and stole into the nation's capital at night, arriving at six in the morning on February 23. The secret arrival of the president-elect occasioned caustic criticism. The *Baltimore Sun* charged:

> We do not believe the Presidency can ever be more degraded by any of his successors, than it has been by him, even before his inauguration; and so, for aught we care, he may go to the full extent of his wretched comicalities. We have only too much cause to fear that such a man, and such advisers as he has, may prove capable of infinitely more mischief than folly when invested with power. A lunatic is only dangerous when armed and turned loose; but only imagine a lunatic invested with authority over a sane people and armed with weapons of offense and defence. What sort of a fate can we reflect that fanaticism is infested with like fears, suspicions, impulses, follies, flights of daring and flights of cowardice common to lunacy itself, and to which it is akin, what sort of a future can we anticipate under the presidency of Abraham Lincoln?[13]

Later a journalist accompanied by Lincoln's close friend Congressman I. N. Arnold extracted from Lincoln a detailed account of the affair:

I arrived at Philadelphia on the 21st. I agreed to stop over night, and on the following morning hoist the flag over Independence Hall. In the evening there was a great crowd where I received my friends, at the Continental Hotel. Mr. Judd, a warm personal friend from Chicago, sent for me to come to his room. I went, and found there Mr. Pinkerton, a skillful police detective, also from Chicago, who had been employed for some days in Baltimore, watching or searching for suspicious persons there. Pinkerton informed me that a plan had been laid for my assassination, the exact time when I expected to go through Baltimore being publicly known. He was well informed as to the plan, but did not know that the conspirators would have pluck enough to execute it. He urged me to go right through with him to Washington that night. I didn't like that. I had made engagements to visit Harrisburg, and go from there to Baltimore, and I resolved to do so. I could not believe that there was a plot to murder me. I made arrangements, however, with Mr. Judd for my return to Philadelphia the next night, if I should be convinced that there was a danger in going through Baltimore, I told him that if I should meet at Harrisburg, as I had at other places, a delegation to go with me to the next place (then Baltimore), I should feel safe, and go on.

When I was making my way back to my room, through crowds of people, I met Frederick Seward. We went together to my room, when he told me that he had been sent, at the instance of his father and General Scott, to inform me that their detectives in Baltimore had discovered a plot there to assassinate me. They knew nothing of Pinkerton's movements. I now believed such a plot to be in existence.

The next morning I raised the flag over Independence Hall, and then went on to Harrisburg with Mr. Sumner, Major (now General) Hunter, Mr. Judd, Mr. Lamon, and others. There I met the Legislature and people, dined, and waited until the time appointed for me to leave. In the meantime, Mr. Judd had so secured the telegraph that no communication could pass to Baltimore and give the conspirators knowledge of a change in my plans.

In New York some friend had given me a new beaver hat in a box, and in it had placed a soft wool hat. I had never worn one of the latter in my life. I had this box in my room. Having informed a very few friends of the secret of my new movements, and the cause, I put on an old overcoat that I had with me, and putting the soft hat in my pocket, I walked out of the house at the back door, bareheaded, without exciting any special curiosity. Then I put on the soft hat and joined my friends without being recognized by strangers, for I was not the same man. Sumner and Hunter wished to accompany me. I said no; you are known, and your presence might betray me. I will only take Lamon (Now Marshal of this District), whom nobody knew, and Mr. Judd. Sumner and Hunter felt hurt.

We went back to Philadelphia and found a message there from Pinkerton (who had returned to Baltimore), that the conspirators had held their final meeting that evening, and it was doubtful they had the nerve to attempt the execution of their purpose. I went on, however, as the arrangement had been made, in a special train. We were a long time in the station at Baltimore. I heard people talking around, but no one particularly observed me. At an early hour on Saturday morning, at about the time I was expected to leave Harrisburg, I arrived at Washington.[14]

On balance, however, his long journey had served to assure audiences of his intention, as he said in New Jersey, "to perpetuate the Constitution, the Union, and the liberties of the people."

CHAPTER FIVE

LINCOLN FRAMES A CABINET

On the November 1860 night when he left the Springfield telegraph office after learning he had been elected president, Lincoln remarked, "When I finally bade my friends good-night, I had substantially completed the framework of my Cabinet as it now exists."

The task proved daunting, however. His was a new party, a coalition never having held the presidency with the unifying effect that high office could bring. He needed to take cognizance of party leaders, their former party affiliation, and geographical representation including New York, Pennsylvania, and Ohio (the three largest states), New England, and the border slave states. Not long after he took up the task South Carolina seceded, and a little more than a month before he assumed office the Confederate States of America had been formed.

On the day South Carolina seceded—an event that Lincoln is said to have taken calmly—Thurlow Weed, maker of presidents, who, however, had failed to make William H. Seward the Republican nominee, was in Springfield. The two men discussed the developing crisis, and Lincoln drew up three resolutions for Republican senators to consider. In his autobiography Weed related their conversation about crafting the cabinet:

> Mr. Lincoln observed that "the making of a cabinet, now that he had it to do, was by no means as easy as he had supposed; that he had, even before the result of the election was known, assuming the probability of success, fixed upon the two leading members of his cabinet, but that in looking about for suitable men to fill the other departments, he had been much embarrassed, partly from his want of acquaintance with the prominent men of the day, and partly, he believed, that while the population of the country

47

had immensely increased, really great men were scarcer than they used to be." ... [I]n my judgment it was desirable that at least two members of his cabinet should be selected from slave-holding States. ... I remarked that there were Union men in Maryland, Virginia, North Carolina, and Tennessee, for whose loyalty, under the most trying circumstances and in any event, I would vouch. "Would you rely on such men if their States secede?" "Yes, sir; the men whom I have in my mind can always be relied on." ...

On naming Gideon Welles as the gentleman he thought of as the representative of New England in the cabinet, I remarked that I thought he could find several New England gentlemen whose selection for a place in his cabinet would be more acceptable to the people of New England. ...

"But," said Mr. Lincoln, "Pennsylvania, any more than New York of Ohio, cannot be overlooked. Her strong Republican vote, not less than her numerical importance, entitles her to a representative in the cabinet. Who is stronger or better than General Cameron?" ...

"Very well," said Mr. Lincoln, "I will now give you the name of a gentleman who not only resides in a slave State, but who is emphatically a representative man. What objection have you to Edward Bates of Missouri?" ...

It was now settled that Governor Seward was to be Secretary of State, Governor Chase, Secretary of the Treasury, and Mr. Bates the Attorney General. I was satisfied that Mr. Lincoln intended to give Mr. Welles one of the other places in the cabinet; that he was strongly inclined to give another place to Mr. Blair, and that his mind was not quite clear in regard to General Cameron.[1]

The choice of Seward as secretary of state, the top cabinet post, was inevitable. Acknowledged leader of the party until Lincoln toppled him at the Chicago convention, senator from New York, the Empire State, he enjoyed a wide following. Standing five feet four, under his tousled hair, once red, he had a striking face, with large ears, long nose, and receding chin. Scholarly in outlook, he had the capacity to make speeches that reverberated throughout the nation. On December 8, 1860, Lincoln penned two letters to him, one notifying Seward that he would be nominated as secretary of state, the other marked "Private & Confidential":

My dear Sir: With your permission, I shall, at the proper time, nominate you to the Senate, for confirmation, as Secretary of State, for the United States.

48

Please let me hear from you at your earliest convenience. Your friend and obedient servant. A. Lincoln.

My dear Sir: In addition to the accompanying, and more formal note, inviting you to take charge of the State Department, I deem it proper to address you this. Rumors have got into the newspapers to the effect that the Department, named above, would be tendered you, as a compliment, and with the expectation that you would decline it. I beg you to be assured that I have said nothing to justify these rumors. On the contrary, it has been my purpose, from the day of the nomination at Chicago, to assign you, by your leave, this place in the administration. I have delayed so long to communicate that purpose, in deference to what appeared to me to be a proper caution in the case. Nothing has been developed to change my view in the premises; and I now offer you the place, in the hope that you will accept it, and with the belief that your position in the public eye, your integrity, ability, learning, and great experience, all combine to render it an appointment pre-eminently fit to be made.

One word more. In regard to the patronage, sought with so much eagerness and jealousy, I have prescribed for myself the maxim, "Justice to all"; and I earnestly beseech your co-operation in keeping the maxim good. Your friend, and obedient servant A. Lincoln[2]

On the same day Lincoln replied to a letter he had received from Senator Lyman Trumbull of Illinois, whose election he had helped effect. Trumbull's letter said that William Cullen Bryant, poet and editor of the *New York Evening Post,* and a committee had visited him. They related reports of corruption in the New York legislature, implicating Seward's friends and endangering Republican success in the state elections if not repudiated. Bryant, who preferred to see Salmon P. Chase as secretary of state, told Trumbull that the committee "did not think it advisable for Gov. S. to go into the cabinet, lest his going should bring with it a set of dishonest men."[3]

Seward put off acceptance, writing on December 13:

It would be a violation of my own feelings, as well as a great injustice to you, if I were to leave occasion for any doubt on your part that I appreciate as highly as I ought the distinction which, as chief Magistrate of the Republic, you propose to confer upon me, and that I am fully, perfectly, and entirely satisfied with the sincerity and kindness of your sentiments and wishes in regard to my acceptance of it.

You will readily believe that, coming to the consideration of so grave a subject all at once, I need a little time to consider whether I possess the qualifications and temper of a minister, and whether it is in such a capacity that my friends would wish that I should act if I am to continue at all in the public service. These questions are, moreover, to be considered in view of a very anomalous condition of public affairs. I wish, indeed, that a conference with you upon them were possible. But I do not see how it could prudently be held under existing circumstances. Without publishing the fact of your invitation, I will, with your leave, reflect upon it a few days, and then give you my definite answer, which, if I know myself, will be made under the influence of the most earnest desire for the success of your Administration, and through it for the safety, honor, and welfare of the Union.

Whatever may be my conclusion, you may rest assured of my hearty concurrence in your views in regard to the distribution of the public offices as you have communicated them.

Believe me, my dear sir, most respectfully and most faithfully your friend and humble servant, William H. Seward.[4]

Meanwhile Bryant approached Lincoln directly, mentioning the cabinet, praising Lincoln's efforts to include Republicans who had been Democrats, and expressing his apprehension that Weed might try to influence Lincoln to accept compromise on slavery expansion. Bryant's letter said:

The rumor having got abroad that you have been visited by a well known politician of New York who has a good deal to do with the stock market and who took with him a plan of compromise manufactured in Wall Street, it has occurred to me that you might like to be assured of the manner in which those Republicans who have no connection with Wall Street regard a compromise of the slavery question. The feeling of decided aversion to the least concession was never stronger than it is now. The people have given their verdict and they do not expect that either their representatives in Congress or their politicians out of Congress will attempt to change or modify it in any degree. The restoration of the Missouri Compromise would disband the Republican party. Any other concession recognizing the right of slavery to protection or even existence in the territories would disgust and discourage the large majority of Republicans in this state and cool their interest in the incoming administration down to the freezing point. Whatever else be done the slavery question, so far as it is a federal question must remain as it is or the Republican party is annihilated. Nor will any concession of the sort proposed satisfy the South. South Carolina cannot be hired to return to the Union by any thing short of the removal of all restraints on the African slave trade. To do that would convert at once into friends of the Union, a class of the southern politicians who are doing a great deal to foment the discontents of the South and might effect what the Wall Street managers hope to bring about by restoring the Missouri line, and giving protection to slavery south of it.

You will excuse me if I say a word concerning the formation of the Cabinet. I am glad to hear that it is decided to have regard in its composition to that part of the Republican party which is derived from the old democratic party. It would be most unfortunate if the Cabinet were to be constituted as to turn the policy of the administration into the old whig channels. To instance a single branch of that policy—the policy of restraints upon trade for the advantage of the manufacturers. We of the old democratic party who are the friends of free trade are perfectly willing that this should be regarded as an open question, but we shall be placed in immediate antagonism to the administration, the moment this is made a part of its governing policy. A bigot to protection placed at the head of the Treasury department would at once open a controversy on that question which would be carried on with zeal, perhaps with heat.

You will I know excuse these suggestions. If not wise they are at least disinterested. I have not, that I know of the remotest interest in politics except that our country should be governed with wisdom and justice, and with the allowance of the largest liberty in all things consistent with good order. You will receive perhaps from me letters in favor of persons desiring some office under the federal government or see my signature to recommendations got up by them or their friends. I pray you, in all these cases to believe, that no personal favor will be conferred on me, in any possible instance by bestowing the desired office on the person whom I may recommend. What I say for them should be taken as my opinion of their fitness and nothing more.[5]

Lincoln answered:

Yours of the 25th is duly received. The "well-known politician" to whom I understand you to allude did write me, but not press upon me any such compromise as you seem to suppose, or, in fact, any compromise at all.

As to the matter of the cabinet, mentioned by you, I can only say I shall have a great deal of trouble, do the best I can.

I promise you that I shall unselfishly try to deal fairly with all men and all shades of opinion among our friends.[6]

Before the year was out Seward officially accepted. Lincoln wrote to him:

Your selection for the State Department having become public, I am happy to find scarcely any objection to it. I shall have trouble with every other Northern cabinet appointment—so much so that I shall have to defer them as long as possible, to avoid being teased to insanity to make changes.[7]

In February, however, strong anti-Seward criticism developed. At the same time Seward's friends came to fear the potential influence in the new cabinet of Salmon Chase, Lincoln's choice as secretary of the treasury, offsetting the dominance they anticipated for Seward. Two days before the inauguration Seward wrote Lincoln: "Circumstances which have occurred since I expressed to you in December last my willingness to accept the office of Secretary of State seem to me to render it my duty to ask leave to withdraw that consent."[8]

The loss of Seward, upsetting the balance between Chase and Seward extremes as well as losing the strength Seward represented, was intolerable. On Inauguration Day Lincoln responded:

Your note of the 2nd. inst. asking to withdraw your acceptance of my invitation to take charge of the State Department, was duly received.

It is the subject of most painful solicitude with me; and I feel constrained to beg that you will countermand the withdrawal. The public interest, I think, demands that you should; and my personal feelings are deeply inlisted in the same direction. Please consider, and answer by 9 o'clock, A.M. to-morrow.[9]

Seward yielded to Lincoln's appeal.

Sixty-seven-year-old Edward Bates was a man Lincoln had known for years. A Missouri Whig, he had served in Congress, declined appointment as secretary of war in 1850, and presided over the Whig national convention in 1856. Esteemed as a lawyer, he had received an honorary degree from Harvard University in 1858.

In April 1860, as noted in chapter 1, Lincoln had said, "I think neither Seward nor Bates can carry Illinois if Douglas shall be on the track; and that either of them can, if he shall not be." Slight in build, white bearded, and possessing piercing eyes, Bates was the father of seventeen children. He was conservative in his politics. He disliked slavery but believed blacks to be an inferior race. He opposed repeal of the Missouri Compromise and admission of Kansas under the pro-slavery Lecompton constitution.

In Mid-December 1860 Bates set down in his diary:

Last Thursday I recd. a message from Mr. Lincoln to the effect that he would come down the next day to St Louis, to see and consult me, about some points connected with the formation of his Cabinet. I thought I saw an unfitness in *his coming to me,* and that I *ought to go to him,* as soon as his wish to see me was known. Accordingly, I had him telegraphed that I would wait on him saturday.

Went up friday night. Saturday morning called on him at his room in the Capitol, and had a free conversation—till interrupted by a crowd of visiters—and then, at his suggestion, and for greater privacy, it was arranged that we should meet again at my room, at 3 p.m.

I found him free in his communications and candid in his manner. He assured me that from the time of his nomination, his determination was, in case of success, to invite me into the Cabinet—and, in fact, was so complimentary as to say that my participation in the administration, he considered necessary to its complete success.

He did not attempt to disguise the difficulties in the way of forming a Cabinet, so as at once to be satisfactory to himself, acceptable to his party and not specially offensive to the more conservative of his party adversaries. He is troubled about Mr. Seward; feeling he is under moral, at least party, duress, to tender to Mr. S.(eward) the *first* place in the Cabinet. *By position* he seems to be entitled to it, and if refused, that would excite bad feeling, and lead to a dangerous if not fatal rupture of the party. And the actual appointment of Mr. S.(eward) to be secretary of State would be dangerous in two ways—1. It would exasperate the feelings of the South, and make conciliation impossible, because they consider Mr. S.(eward) the embodiment of all that they hold odious in the Republican party—and 2. That it would alarm and dissatisfy that large section of the Party which opposed Mr. S.(eward)'s nomination, and now think that they have reason to fear that, if armed with the powers of that high place, he would treat them as enemies. Either the one or the other of these would tend greatly to weaken the Administration.

(These particular arguments, as set down, are my own, but they were all glanced at in the conversation.)

He said that if this difficulty were out of the way, he would at once offer me the State Department—but, failing that, he would offer me the Att.y. generalship, and urge my acceptance.

He did not state, and I did not choose to press him to state, who would probably fill the other Departments, or any of them. Inde(e)d, I suppose he does not yet know—so much depends on Mr. Seward's position, and upon the daily-changing phases of political affairs.

He assured me however, that I am the only man that he desired in the Cabinet, to whom he has yet spoken a (or) written a word, about their own appointments(.)

I told Mr. L.(incoln) with all frankness, that if peace and order prevailed in the country, and the Government could now be carried on quietly, I would decline a place in the Cabinet, as I did in 1850—and for the same reasons. But *now,* I am not at liberty to consult my own interests and wishes, and must subordinate them to my convictions of public duty, and to the necessity in which I find myself, to sustain my own personal character, by acting out, in good faith, the principles to which I stand pledged. And that, therefore, and as a matter of duty, I accepted his invitation, and in that view, would take their office in which he might think I would be most useful. That as a matter personal to myself, and in regard to my private affairs, the Att.y. Genl.'s place is most desirable.

He replied that he never intended to offer me either of the Departments deemed laborious, as involving a great many details of administrative business—That, in short, I must be either Sec.y. of State or Att.y. Genl.

I suggested that my visit to Springfield could hardly escape the vigilance of the press and probably the truth would lead out—He said he didn't care if it did, and for his mind his mind was fully made up as to me. And further, if I thought, after consultation with friends, that it would be best to let his offer be known, and would write him so, he would stop conjectures, by letting it be known.

(*Marginal Note.*) On the 18th. Decr: I wrote Mr. L(incoln) that friends here thought it advisable that the fact of my connection with the adm(inistratio)n. should be made public. On the 20th I recd. a note from him, dra(f)ting a publication to the effect that he had offered and I had accepted a place in the Cabinet, but what particular place not yet determined.

Feeling under necessity to offer the *State* Dept. to Mr. S.(eward) and having some reason (hope at last) to beli(e)ve that he wd. decline it, he is anxious to *know* the fact; and I must try the best methods I can to ascertain it for him, without committing him."[10]

Lincoln promptly responded in a "Confidential" letter:

My dear sir: Yours of to-day is just received. Let a little editorial appear in the Missouri Democrat, in about these words:

We have the permission of both Mr. Lincoln and Mr. Bates to say that the latter will be offered, and will accept, a place in the new Cabinet, subject of course to the action of the Senate. It is not yet definitely settled which Department will be assigned to Mr. Bates.

Let it go just as above, or with any modification which may seem proper to you.[11]

Although as yet semi-official, it was the first announcement of a cabinet appointment. A border slave state would be in the new cabinet, represented by a prominent conservative ex-Whig.

Salmon Portland Chase was the resounding name of a tall man, with massive shoulders and firm jaw, who perhaps looked more like a president to his contemporaries than any member of Lincoln's cabinet. Born in New Hampshire, he was brought up from the age of nine, after his father's death, by his uncle, the Episcopal bishop of Ohio. Religion, reform, and antislavery zeal, combined with political ambition, marked his life. After graduating from Dartmouth in 1826 he became known as an "attorney for runaway Negroes." In 1849 he was elected U.S. Senator from Ohio through the support of the Free Soil Party. As senator he attained national fame with his assault on the Kansas-Nebraska bill that reopened the question of slavery expansion. Becoming a Republican, he served as governor of Ohio until he was reelected senator in 1860. His bid for the presidential nomination that year garnered only 49 of 465 votes on the first ballot. His hope for the office was not snuffed out, however, and continued to burn for the rest of his career.

Chase campaigned for Lincoln and wrote to him the day after his victory:

You are President elect. I congratulate you, and thank God. The great object of my wishes and labors for nineteen years is accomplished in the overthrow of the slave power. The space is now clear for the establishment of the policy of freedom on safe and firm grounds. The lead is yours. The responsibility is great. May God strengthen you for your great duties.[12]

On the last day of the year Lincoln wrote to Simon Cameron:

I think fit to notify you now, that by your permission, I shall, at the proper time, nominate you to the U.S. Senate, for confirmation as Secretary of the Treasury, or as Secretary of War—which of the two, I have not yet definitely decided. Please answer at your earliest convenience.

But Lincoln on the same day wrote to Chase:

My dear Sir: In these troublous times, I would [much] like a conference with you. Please visit me here at once.[13]

Chase described the next step toward a cabinet post in a letter to his friend John T. Trowbridge.

After his election he invited me to Springfield to confer with me as to the selection of his Cabinet. He said that he had felt bound to offer the position of Secretary of State to Mr. Seward as the generally recognized leader of the Republican party, intending, if he should decline it, to offer it to me. He did not wish that Mr. Seward should decline it, and was glad that he had accepted, and now desired to have me take the place of Secretary of the Treasury. He had feared there might be some objections to this in Pennsylvania, but had been assured none would be urged. I replied that I did not wish and was not prepared to say that I would accept that place if offered. A good deal of conversation followed in reference to other possible members of the Cabinet, but every thing was left open when we parted, and I returned to Columbus.

Shortly after this, in December, South Carolina seceded and every thing indicated great irresolution and timidity on the part of the administration. I wrote a very earnest letter to General Scott, entreating him as head of the army to take the necessary measures to secure the public safety and rely upon the country for its sanction and support. The general replied very kindly, but did not evince a disposition to assume the responsibility of the crisis. In February, Virginia invited a conference of the States at Washington, and appointed commissioners on her part. This conference, doubtless, was intended as a means of extorting new concessions to the slave interest from Congress. To prevent injurious results it seemed necessary that there should be a general representation from all the States—from free as well as from the slave States which had not become involved in secession. I was one of the commissioners selected by the governor to represent Ohio. Unfortunately I was the only one who was prepared to resist the purchase of peace by undue concessions. I was quite willing to give to the slave States the strongest assurances that no aggression upon their rights or real interests were meditated, but I was not at all willing to disguise from them the fact that the further extension of slavery could not be allowed. The death of Judge Wright and the appointment of Mr. Wolcott in his place, gave me one resolute and like-minded associate in the commission; but we were a minority. The vote of Ohio in the conference was steadily on the side of submission. The commissioners whose general views agreed with mine, finally determined to propose to refer all matters of difference to a national convention, and in the meantime to arrest the progress of disunion by assurance that no invasion of State rights over the subject of slavery or over any other subject, was mediated or would be attempted. In support of this proposition, I addressed the conference with great earnestness with great plainness. I warned them of the consequences which must follow secession, and implored them not to reject the only proposition which, in my judgment, was likely to save the country from a civil war. The proposition was, nevertheless, rejected, and the vote of Ohio was cast for its rejection. Instead of it, a proposed amendment to the constitution making large concessions to the slave interest was forced through the convention in disregard to its rules, and submitted to Congress. There, as I had predicted, it received little favor. I am not certain that any thing which the conference could have done would have saved the country from the insurrection which has since assumed such fearful proportions of civil war. It is only certain that nothing which was done had the slightest salutary effect upon the disastrous course of events. The convention was an abortion.[14]

Chase's appointment became entangled with naming Simon Cameron to a cabinet position. On January 11, 1861, Chase wrote to Lincoln:

Your nomination over Mr. Seward was due in great part, as you are well aware, to the belief that you would give the country a pure financial administration, whereas serious apprehension was felt of a different result from the influences supposed to surround him. It is as absolutely indispensable that this belief be realized as it is that the expectation of substantial advantage to the cause of freedom from your election be not disappointed.

Permit me to suggest the expediency of confidential consultation in respect to gentlemen whom you may think of inviting into your administration with such of your friends as you most rely on, through whom, either from their own knowledge or by their confidential correspondence or personal enquiries, you can easily obtain the full information essential to safe conclusions.

You know my feelings for I expressed them frankly when with you. God grant that we may see the old integrity & wisdom of Washington & Jefferson restored & that you may be the honored instrument of the blessed restoration.

With unfeigned respect & esteem. Yours most truly S: P: Chase[15]

Lincoln failed to answer and five days later Chase described his dilemma to another friend, John Jay:

Would you be willing to take charge of a broken down department, as a member of a cabinet with which you could not be sure of six months agreement and enslave yourself to the most toilsome drudging almost without respite for four years, exchanging a position from which you could speak freely to the country during half the year and during the other half retire to books, travel and friends for one you could speak in at all except through report and where no leisure is expected? Answer that.[16]

On the day after the inauguration, still a senator, Chase learned he had been nominated for the Treasury Department and confirmed. He sped to the White House, lectured the beleaguered president, and resigned. It was the first of several Chase resignations, and Lincoln patiently talked him out it.

Caleb Smith, born in Boston in 1808, moved west and hung out his shingle as a lawyer in 1828. A Whig, he served in Congress simultaneously with Lincoln, joining in opposing the Mexican War. As a Republican delegate to the 1860 Chicago convention, he seconded Lincoln's nomination and helped deliver Indiana's vote to the nominee. In return, some said, Lincoln's campaign manager promised him a cabinet position. On December 11 two visitors called on Lincoln to urge Smith's claims to a cabinet seat. Lincoln responded that he saw no insuperable obstacle but otherwise remained noncommittal. He later appointed Smith as secretary of interior. A better local politician and orator than cabinet officer, Smith believed the cabinet meetings were useless and Lincoln himself made the major decisions. Smith resigned in 1862, and Lincoln appointed him judge of the U.S. District Court for Indiana.

Simon Cameron, born in Pennsylvania in 1799, was a political chameleon, who in successive shifts of party allegiance gained a seat in the U.S. Senate in 1845 by a coalition of parties and again in 1857 by Republican and Democratic support. He had forever stained his reputation when as commissioner to settle Indian claims he made dubious arrangements that branded him with the sobriquet "The Great Winnebago Chief." In the Chicago convention on the first ballot he stood in third place, next after Lincoln. His supporters switched to Lincoln and later claimed that in exchange their man had been promised a cabinet post.

Lincoln found the matter a nettlesome affair. Letters in support of Cameron were mixed with those charging corruption. On December 31 Lincoln drafted a memorandum on the appointment, listing the names of those who had written to him.

The following day Lincoln telegraphed Alexander K. McClure, an influential Pennsylvania politician, to come to Springfield. What transpired there McClure did not disclose in his memoirs. But on January 3, 1861, Lincoln sent a "Private" letter to Cameron:

> Since seeing you things have developed which make it impossible for me to take you into the cabinet. . . . And now I suggest that you write me declining the appointment, in which case I do not object to its being known that it was tendered you. Better do this at once, before things so change, that you can not honorably decline, and I be compelled to openly recall the tender. No person living knows, or has an intimation that I write this letter. Yours truly A. Lincoln
>
> P.S. Telegraph, me instantly, on receipt of this, saying "All right"[17]

Lincoln later sent Cameron a conciliatory letter, but the Pennsylvanian's backers would not budge. A delegation representing the Republican Club of Philadelphia arrived in Springfield to press Cameron's candidacy. Lincoln frankly told the members:

Gentlemen, in the formation of my Cabinet, I shall aim as nearly as possible at perfection. Any man whom I may appoint to such a position,
must be, as far as possible, like Caesar's wife, pure and above suspicion, of
unblemished reputation, and undoubted integrity. I have already appointed
Senator SEWARD and Mr. BATES, of Missouri, and they are men whose
characters I think the breath of calumny cannot impeach. In regard to
Gen. CAMERON, I have received assurances without limit from gentlemen
whose word is entitled to credit, that he is eminently fitted for the position
which his friends desire him to fill, and that his appointment would give
great satisfaction to Pennsylvania. I have a great desire to appoint Gen.
CAMERON, for the reason that he was formerly a Democrat, and I wish to
give that element a fair representation in the distribution of offices. Both
Mr. SEWARD and Mr. BATES were formerly old line Whigs, and, for this
reason, I feel a disposition to appoint Gen. CAMERON. But on the other
hand, there is a strong opposition to him; not from his own State, it is
true, for the opposition to him there is so slight that it is scarcely worth
mentioning. The feeling against him appears to come from Ohio, and one
or two other Western States. His opponents charge him with corruption
in obtaining contracts, and contend that if he is appointed he will use the
patronage of his office for his own private gain. I have no knowledge of
the acts charged against him, but I intend to make an investigation of the
whole matter, by allowing his opponents to submit their proof, and I shall
give him an opportunity of explaining any part he may have had in the
transactions alleged against him. . . . I shall deal fairly with him, but I say
to you, gentlemen, frankly, that if the charges against him are proven, he
cannot have a seat in my Cabinet, as I will not have any man associated with
me whose character is impeached. I will say further, that if he vindicates
himself, I have the strongest desire to place him in the position you wish
him to fill, and which you think the interests of your State demand. If, after
he has been appointed, I should be deceived by subsequent transactions of
a disreputable character, the *responsibility will rest upon you gentlemen of
Pennsylvania who have so strongly presented his claims to my consideration.*
But this is supposing a state of things which may never occur.[18]

Finding no clear evidence against Cameron, Lincoln sent his name to the
Senate on March 5, 1861, for approval as secretary of war. Within months he
would rue the recommendation. It ranks as one of his worst appointments.

Montgomery Blair was a member of a clan that figured prominently in
American politics for two generations. Francis P. Blair Sr. was a close adviser

to Andrew Jackson and a journalist who edited that president's official newspaper. A former Democrat, he helped organize the Republican Party in 1856 and, together with his sons, Francis Jr. and Montgomery, promoted party fortunes during the ensuing years. Montgomery, after graduating from the United States Military Academy and serving in the Seminole War, settled in St. Louis, where he practiced law. In 1853 he moved to Washington, living in Blair House near the White House before moving to Silver Spring, Maryland. He won fame as counsel to Dred Scott, whose case for freedom failed but firmly established Montgomery Blair's reputation for upholding the Republican Party claim that Congress could outlaw slavery in the territories. His brother, known as Frank, remained in Missouri; the Blairs thus held influence in two border slave states.

Tall and slender, Montgomery Blair was an able constitutional lawyer often called "the Judge"; one reporter considered him the best-read man in the cabinet. Knowledgeable about military matters, he would have been well suited to be secretary of war. He presided over the Republican state convention in Maryland and served as a delegate to the Chicago convention. Frank stumped for Lincoln and wrote letters to the victor after his election.

Blair's claim to a cabinet post competed with that of young Henry Winter Davis, an impressive orator and congressman from Maryland, favored by Weed. Lincoln had to choose between Whig and ex-Democrat, and when Weed spoke about the presence of four ex-Democrats and three ex-Whigs as his advisers, Lincoln roguishly remarked: "You seem to forget that I expect to be there." Lincoln appointed Montgomery postmaster general, whereby he sat in Lincoln's cabinet until 1864, the same year that Davis launched a vigorous attack on Lincoln.

Gideon Welles, born in Connecticut in 1802, graduated from Norwich University and became a newspaper editor and state legislator. From 1846 to 1849 he served as chief of the Bureau of Provisions and Clothing in the navy, a useful experience for his future cabinet position. A Democrat, he abandoned the party in 1855 and helped organize the Republican Party in his state. From 1856 to 1864 he served on the party's national executive committee. Favoring the ex-Democrat Chase for president in 1860, he headed Connecticut's delegation to Chicago.

Lincoln and Welles had held an hour's conversation in Hartford when Lincoln made a speaking tour following his Cooper Union address. Welles wrote in his newspaper:

This orator and lawyer has been caricatured. He is not Apollo, but he is not Caliban. He was made where the material for strong men is plenty; and his loose, tall frame is loosely thrown together. He is in every way large—brain included, but his countenance shows intellect, generosity, great good nature, and keen discrimination. . . . He is an effective speaker, because he is earnest, strong, honest, simple in style, and clear as crystal in his logic.[19]

Ambitious to rise in politics, and armed with an extraordinary memory and a keen interest in people, Welles made sharp judgments in his voluminous diary. Wearing abundant white whiskers, he concealed his baldness under a gray wig. On December 24, 1860, Lincoln wrote to vice president-elect Hannibal Hamlin: "I need a man of Democratic antecedents from New England. I cannot get a fair share of that element in. . . . Which of them do the New England delegation prefer? Or shall I decide for myself?" Hamlin, himself a man of Democratic antecedents, responded that of various possibilities, "Welles is the better man for New England."[20]

Thurlow Weed and his Albany clique and the Massachusetts congressional delegation opposed a Welles appointment. In their interview in December when Lincoln said he was considering Welles as the representative of New England in the cabinet, Weed hid his hostility to Welles by remarking, as he later wrote, "I thought he could find several New England gentlemen whose selection for the place in his cabinet would be more acceptable in New England." Governor Edwin D. Morgan of New York spoke privately with Lincoln en route to Washington, in behalf of Welles. He informed Welles, brother-in-law of his cousin and business partner George Morgan, that Lincoln "intends to offer you the appointment." Welles remained uncertain until as late as the morning of Inauguration Day.[21]

In crafting his composite cabinet Lincoln hoped also to reach into the South for a member. An opportunity seemed to present itself when in early December he received a letter from John A. Gilmer, a North Carolina congressman who advocated compromise. But at the end of the month Gilmer refused Lincoln's invitation to come to Springfield. The ironic outcome was that Gilmer was elected to the North Carolina secession convention and in 1863 to the Confederate Congress.

By the time Lincoln sent his list of nominees to the Senate for confirmation, he had built a cabinet notable for its inclusiveness. He had named the leaders of his party—some said he had named all those who had competed with him for the presidential nomination. The cabinet nominees included representatives of factions within his party, geographical sections of slave states, and members of former parties—Whig, Free Soil, and Know Nothing as well as Democrat and Republican. The populous and pivotal states were included, although he had failed to lure a member from the South, from below the Potomac. The slave state of Maryland, a threat to the nation's capital, was represented—how firmly remained to be seen.

CHAPTER SIX

THE FIRST INAUGURAL

The fourth of March, 1861, Inauguration Day, began cloudy, brightening later in the day. General Winfield Scott, mindful of the threats to Lincoln's life, made the city safe by placing horse artillery, cavalry, and infantry as guards. In his memoirs he wrote:

> In concert with Congressional Committees of arrangements, the President was escorted to and from the Capitol by volunteers—the regulars, with whom I marched, flanking the movement in parallel streets,—only I claimed the place immediately in front of the President for the fine company of Sappers and Miners under Captain Duane of the Engineers. To this choice body of men it was only necessary to say: *The honor of our country is in your hands.*
>
> With a view to freedom of movement, I remained just outside of the Capitol Square with the light batteries. The procession returned to the President's mansion in the same order, and happily the Government was saved.[1]

Charles Francis Adams Jr. observed an atmosphere of "nervous expectancy." Adams later wrote:

> The following day was clear and, as I remember it, somewhat blustery. Any one who has ever encountered on Pennsylvania Avenue a March dust borne on a March wind is not likely even in the Washington of to-day to covet a repetition of the experience; and fifty years ago the streets of Washington, as yet unpaved, were always either impassable from mud or ankle-deep in dust. On the day of Lincoln's first inaugural a rasping wind was dust-ladened. None the less for that, from an early hour the whole town seemed to gather towards the Capitol. . . .
>
> As a spectacle, it was not heartening. The Capitol, it must be remembered, was at that time in a wholly unfinished condition, and derricks

rose from the great dome as well as from the Senate and Representative wings. On the staging front I saw a tall, ungainly man addressing a motley gathering,—some thousands in number,—with a voice elevated to its highest pitch; but his delivery, as I remember it, was good—quiet, accompanied by little gesture and with small pretence at oratory. The grounds at the east front are so large that it is difficult ever to compute correctly an audience there gathered. I should say, however, that the mob of citizens on that occasion did not exceed four or five thousand. Probably there were many more. It was a very ordinary gathering, with a somewhat noticeable absence of pomp, state, ceremony, or even of constabulary. As I remember, not a uniform was to be seen. I recall it as a species of mass meeting evincing little enthusiasm; but silent, attentive, appreciative, and wonderfully respectable and orderly.

Throughout, however, a curious sense of uneasiness prevailed,—a sort of nervous expectancy. The thought was ever present in my mind, as I fancy in that of every individual there, of something not on the programme about to occur. I did not myself really fear, much less expect it; but, none the less, I very distinctly recall the latent mental suggestion,—what if some Southern fire-eater or fanatical secessionist should now bring this ceremony to a sudden close by a deed of violence,—by a pistol bullet from near at hand, or a rifle shot from some more distant window yonder? There was, however, no crazed and theatrical John Wilkes Booth in that gathering, or at least, if there, he did not put himself in evidence; and so the tragic outcome of four years later was not then forestalled.[2]

That day Lincoln received the stark message, "You will be shot."

Speaking in a penetrating voice to a throng of ten thousand, Lincoln made it clear he was addressing not the North alone but an entire nation. He devoted the address to the dilemma facing him. He assured his audience not only that he did not intend to interfere with slavery in the states but, astonishingly, that he had no objection to a proposed constitutional amendment that the federal government shall never interfere with slavery in the states. Return of fugitive slaves, mandated by the Constitution, would be done, but free blacks should be protected from being apprehended as slaves.

Moving on to a second source of sectional tension, he branded secession as "the essence of anarchy." He argued strongly for the principle of nationalism, knitting together the Union. He asserted that it had originated in 1774, not 1776 nor 1787, making the Union older than the Constitution. It was also perpetual, and though separated by different views of the morality of slavery, North and South could not physically separate. The American people should have recourse not to secession but to democracy, their power to change the laws, elect representatives, and amend the Constitution. The controversial Supreme Court decision in the Dred Scott case could be overruled.

He pointed out he had taken an oath prescribed by the Constitution to preserve, protect, and defend the Constitution; and the president derives all his authority from the people. The entire address warrants close reading:

Fellow citizens of the United States:

In compliance with a custom as old as the government itself, I appear before you to address you briefly, and to take, in your presence, the oath prescribed by the Constitution of the United States, to be taken by the President "before he enters on the execution of his office."

I do not consider it necessary, at present, for me to discuss those matters of administration about which there is no special anxiety, or excitement.

Apprehension seems to exist among the people of the Southern States, that by the accession of a Republican Administration, their property, and their peace, and personal security, are to be endangered. There has never been any reasonable cause for such apprehension. Indeed, the most ample evidence to the contrary has all the while existed, and been open to their inspection. It is found in nearly all the published speeches of him who now addresses you.

I do but quote from one of those speeches when I declare that "I have no purpose, directly or indirectly, to interfere with the institution of slavery in the States where it exists. I believe I have no lawful right to do so, and I have no inclination to do so." Those who nominated and elected me did so with full knowledge that I had made this, and many similar declarations, and had never recanted them. And more than this, they placed in the platform, for my acceptance, and as a law to themselves, and to me, the clear and emphatic resolution which I now read:

Resolved, That the maintenance inviolate of the rights of the States, and especially the right of each State to order and control its own domestic institutions according to its own judgment exclusively, is essential to that balance of power on which the perfection and endurance of our political fabric depend; and we denounce the lawless invasion by armed force of the soil of any State or Territory, no matter under what pretext, as among the gravest of crimes.

I now reiterate these sentiments: and in doing so, I only press upon the public attention the most conclusive evidence of which the case is susceptible, that the property, peace and security of no section are to be in anywise endangered by the now incoming Administration. I add too, that all the protection which, consistently with the Constitution and the laws, can be given, will be cheerfully given to all the States when lawfully demanded, for whatever cause—as cheerfully to one section, as to another.

There is much controversy about the delivering up of fugitives from service or labor. The clause I now read is as plainly written in the Constitution as any other of its provisions:

No person held to service or labor in one State, under the laws therefore, escaping into another, shall, in consequence of any law or regulation therein, be discharged from such service or labor, but shall be delivered up on claim of the party to whom such service or labor may be due.

It is scarcely questioned that this provision was intended by those who made it, for the reclaiming of what we call fugitive slaves; and the intention of the law-giver is the law. All members of Congress swear their support to the whole Constitution—to this provision as much as to any other. To the proposition, then, that slaves whose cases come within the terms of this clause, "shall be delivered up," their oaths are unanimous. Now, if they would make the effort in good temper, could they not, with nearly equal unanimity, frame and pass a law, by means of which to keep good that unanimous oath?

There is some difference of opinion whether this clause should be enforced by national or by state authority; but surely that difference is not a very material one. If the slave is to be surrendered, it can be of but little consequence to him, or to others, by which authority it is done. And should any one, in any case, be content that his oath shall go unkept, on a merely unsubstantial controversy as to how it shall be kept?

Again, in any law upon this subject, ought not all the safeguards of liberty known in civilized and humane jurisprudence to be introduced, so that a free man be not, in any case, surrendered as a slave? And might it not be well, at the same time, to provide by law for the enforcement of that clause in the Constitution which guarranties that "The citizens of each State shall be entitled to all previleges and immunities of citizens in the several States?"

I take the official oath to-day, with no mental reservations, and with no purpose to construe the Constitution or laws, by any hypercritical rules.

And while I do not choose now to specify particular acts of Congress as proper to be enforced, I do suggest, that it will be much safer for all, both in official and private stations, to conform to, and abide by, all those acts which stand unrepealed, than to violate any of them, trusting to find impunity in having them held to be unconstitutional.

It is seventy-two years since the first inauguration of a President under our national Constitution. During that period fifteen different and greatly distinguished citizens, have, in succession, administered the executive branch of the government. They have conducted it through many perils; and, generally, with great success. Yet, with all this scope for precedent, I now enter upon the same task for the brief constitutional term of four years, under great and peculiar difficulty. A disruption of the Federal Union heretofore only menaced, is now formidably attempted.

I hold, that in contemplation of universal law, and of the Constitution, the Union of these States is perpetual. Perpetuity is implied, if not expressed, in the fundamental law of all national governments. It is safe to assert that no government proper, ever had a provision in its organic law for its own termination. Continue to execute all the express provisions of our national Constitution, and the Union will endure forever—it being impossible to destroy it, except by some action not provided for in the instrument itself.

Again, if the United States be not a government proper, but an association of States in the nature of contract merely, can it, as a contract, be peaceably unmade, by less than all the parties who made it? One party to a contract may violate it—break it, so to speak; but does it not require all to lawfully rescind it?

Descending from these general principles, we find the proposition that, in legal contemplation, the Union is perpetual, confirmed by the history of the Union itself. The Union is much older that the Constitution. It was formed in fact, by the Articles of Association in 1774. It was matured and continued by the Declaration of Independence in 1776. It was further matured and the faith of all the then thirteen States expressly plighted and engaged that it should be perpetual, by the Articles of Confederation in 1778. And finally, in 1787, one of the declared objects for ordaining and establishing the Constitution, was *to form a more perfect union.*

But if destruction of the Union, by one, or by a part only, of the States, be lawfully possible, the union is *less* perfect than before the Constitution, having lost the vital element of perpetuity.

It follows from these views that no State, upon its own mere motion, can lawfully get out of the Union,—that *resolves* and *ordinances* to that effect are legally void; and that acts of violence, within any State or States, against the authority of the United States, are insurrectionary or revolutionary, according to circumstances.

I therefore consider that, in view of the Constitution and the laws, the Union is unbroken; and, to the extent of my ability, I shall take care, as the Constitution itself expressly enjoins upon me, that the laws of the Union be faithfully executed in all the States. Doing this I deem to be only a simple duty on my part; and I shall perform it, so far as practicable, unless my rightful masters, the American people, shall withhold the requisite means, or, in some authoritative manner, direct the contrary. I trust this will not be regarded as a menace, but only as the declared purpose of the Union that it *will* constitutionally defend, and maintain itself.

In doing this there needs to be no bloodshed or violence; and there shall be none, unless it be forced upon the national authority. The power confided to me, will be used to hold, occupy, and possess the property, and places belonging to the government, and to collect the duties and imposts; but beyond what may be necessary for these objects, there will be no invasion—no using of force against, or among the people anywhere. Where hostility to the United States, in any interior locality, shall be so great and so universal, as to prevent competent resident citizens from holding the Federal offices, there will be no attempt to force obnoxious strangers among the people for that object. While the strict legal right may exist in the government to enforce the exercise of these offices, the attempt to do so would be so irritating, and so nearly impracticable with all, that I deem it better to forego, for the time, the uses of such offices.

The mails, unless repelled, will continue to be furnished in all parts of the Union. So far as possible, the people everywhere shall have that sense of perfect security which is most favorable to calm thought and reflection. The course here indicated will be followed, unless current events, and experience, shall show a modification, or change, to be proper; and in every case and exigency, my best discretion will be exercised, according to circumstances actually existing, and with a view and a hope of a peaceful solution of the national troubles, and the restoration of fraternal sympathies and affections.

That there are persons in one section, or another who seek to destroy the Union at all events, and are glad of any pretext to do it, I will neither affirm or deny; but if there be such, I need address no word to them. To those, however, who really love the Union, may I not speak?

Before entering upon so grave a matter as the destruction of our national fabric, with all its benefits, its memories, and its hopes, would it not be wise to ascertain precisely why we do it? Will you hazard so desperate a step, while there is any possibility that any portion of the ills you fly from, have no real existence? Will you, while the certain ills you fly to, are greater than all the real ones you fly from? Will you risk the commission of so fearful a mistake?

All profess to be content in the Union, if all constitutional rights can be maintained. Is it true, then, that any right, plainly written in the Constitution, has been denied? I think not. Happily the human mind is so constituted, that no party can reach to the audacity of doing this. Think, if you can, of a single instance in which a plainly written provision of the Constitution has ever been denied. If, by the mere force of numbers, a majority should deprive a minority of any clearly written constitutional right, it might, in a moral point of view, justify revolution—certainly would, if such right were a vital one. But such is not our case. All the vital rights of minorities, and of individuals, are so plainly assured to them, by affirmations and negations, guarranties and prohibitions, in the Constitution, that controversies never arise concerning them. But no organic law can ever be framed with a provision specifically applicable to every question which may occur in practical administration. No foresight can anticipate, nor any document of reasonable length contain express provisions for all possible questions. Shall fugitives from labor be surrendered by national or by State authority? The Constitution does not expressly say. *May* Congress prohibit slavery in the territories? The Constitution does not expressly say. *Must* Congress protect slavery in the territories? The Constitution does not expressly say.

From questions of this class spring all our constitutional controversies, and we divide upon them into majorities and minorities. If the minority will not acquiesce, the majority must, or the government must cease. There is no other alternative; for continuing the government, is acquiescence on one side or the other. If a minority, in such case, will secede rather than acquiesce, they make a precedent which, in turn, will divide and ruin them; for a minority of their own will secede from them, whenever a majority refuses to be controlled by such minority. For instance why may not any portion of a new confederacy, a year or two hence, arbitrarily secede again, precisely as portions of the present Union now claim to secede from it. All who cherish disunion sentiments, are now being educated to the exact temper of doing this. Is there such perfect identity of interests among the States to compose a new Union, as to produce harmony only, and prevent renewed secession?

Plainly, the central idea of secession, is the essence of anarchy. A majority, held in restraint by constitutional checks, and limitations, and always

changing easily, with deliberate changes of popular opinions and sentiments, is the only true sovereign of a free people. Whoever rejects it, does,
of necessity, fly to anarchy or to despotism. Unanimity is impossible; the
rule of a minority, as a permanent arrangement, is wholly inadmissible; so
that, rejecting the majority principle, anarchy, or despotism in some form,
is all that is left.

I do not forget the position assumed by some, that constitutional questions are to be decided by the Supreme Court; nor do I deny that such
decisions must be binding in any case, upon the parties to a suit, as to the
object of that suit, while they are also entitled to very high respect and consideration, in all parallel cases, by all other departments of the government.
And while it is obviously possible that such decision may be erroneous in any
given case, still the evil effect following it, being limited to that particular
case, with the chance that it may be over-ruled, and never become a precedent
for other cases, can better be borne than could the evils of a different practice.
At the same time the candid citizen must confess that if the policy of the
government, upon vital questions, affecting the whole people, is to be irrevocably fixed by decisions of the Supreme Court, the instant they are made,
in ordinary litigation between parties, in personal actions, the people will
have ceased, to be their own rulers, having, to that extent, practically resigned
their government, into the hands of that eminent tribunal. Nor is there, in
this view, any assault upon the court, or the judges. It is a duty, from which
they may not shrink, to decide cases properly brought before them; and it is
no fault of theirs, if others seek to turn their decisions to political purposes.

One section of our country believes slavery is *right,* and ought to be
extended, while the other believes it is *wrong,* and ought not to be extended.
This is the only substantial dispute. The fugitive slave clause of the Constitution, and the law for the suppression of the foreign slave trade, are each as
well enforced, perhaps, as any law can ever be in a community where the
moral sense of the people imperfectly supports the law itself. The great
body of the people abide by the dry legal obligation in both cases, and a few
break over in each. This, I think, cannot be perfectly cured; and it would
be worse in both cases *after* the separation of the sections, than before. The
foreign slave trade, now imperfectly suppressed, would be ultimately revived
without restriction, in one section; while fugitive slaves, now only partially
surrendered, would not be surrendered at all, by the other.

Physically speaking, we cannot separate. We cannot remove our respective
sections from each other, nor build an impassable wall between them. A
husband and wife may be divorced, and go out of the presence, and beyond

the reach of each other; but the different parts of our country cannot do this. They cannot but remain face to face; and intercourse, either amicable or hostile, must continue between them. Is it possible then to make that intercourse more advantageous, or more satisfactory, *after* separation than *before*? Can aliens make treaties easier than friends can make laws? Can treaties be more faithfully enforced between aliens, than laws can among friends? Suppose you go to war, you cannot fight always; and when, after much loss on both sides, and no gain on either, you cease fighting, the identical old questions, as to terms of intercourse, are again upon you.

This country, with its institutions, belongs to the people who inhabit it. Whenever they shall grow weary of the existing government, they can exercise their *constitutional* right of amending it, or their *revolutionary* right to dismember, or overthrow it. I can not be ignorant of the fact that many worthy, and patriotic citizens are desirous of having the national constitution amended. While I make no recommendation of amendments, I fully recognize the rightful authority of the people over the whole subject, to be exercised in either of the modes prescribed in the instrument itself; and I should, under existing circumstances, favor, rather than oppose, a fair opportunity being afforded the people to act upon it.

I will venture to add that, to me, the convention mode seems preferable, in that it allows amendments to originate with the people themselves, instead of only permitting them to take, or reject, propositions, originated by others, not especially chosen for the purpose, and which might not be precisely such, as they would wish to either accept or refuse. I understand a proposed amendment to the Constitution—which amendment, however, I have not seen, has passed Congress, to the effect that the federal government, shall never interfere with the domestic institutions of the States, including that of persons held to service. To avoid misconstruction of what I have said, I depart from my purpose not to speak of particular amendments, so far as to say that, holding such a provision to now be implied constitutional law, I have no objection to its being made express, and irrevocable.

The Chief Magistrate derives all his authority from the people, and they have conferred none upon him to fix terms for the separation of the States. The people themselves can do this also if they choose; but the executive, as such, has nothing to do with it. His duty is to administer the present government, as it came to his hands, and to transmit it, unimpaired by him, to his successor.

Why should there not be a patient confidence in the ultimate justice of the people? Is there any better, or equal hope, in the world? In our present differences, is either party without faith of being in the right? If the Almighty Ruler of nations, with his eternal truth and justice, be on your side of the North, or on yours of the South, that truth, and that justice, will surely prevail, by the judgment of this great tribunal, the American people.

By the frame of the government under which we live, this same people have wisely given their public servants but little power for mischief; and have, with equal wisdom, provided for the return of that little to their own hands at very short intervals.

While the people retain their virtue, and vigilance, no administration, by any extreme of wickedness or folly, can very seriously injure the government, in the short space of four years.

My countrymen, one and all, think calmly and *well,* upon this whole subject. Nothing valuable can be lost by taking time. If there be an object to *hurry* any of you, in hot haste, to a step which you would never take *deliberately,* that object will be frustrated by taking time; but no good object can be frustrated by it. Such of you as are now dissatisfied, still have the old Constitution unimpaired, and, on the sensitive point, the laws of your own framing under it; while the new administration will have no immediate power, if it would, to change either. If it were admitted that you who are dissatisfied, hold the right side in the dispute, there still is no single good reason for precipitate action. Intelligence, patriotism, Christianity, and a firm reliance on Him, who has never yet forsaken this favored land, are still competent to adjust, in the best way, all our present difficulty.

In *your* hands, my dissatisfied fellow countrymen, and not in *mine,* is the momentous issue of civil war. The government will not assail *you.* You can have no conflict, without being yourselves the aggressors. *You* have no oath registered in Heaven to destroy the government, while *I* shall have the most solemn one to "preserve, protect and defend" it.

I am loth to close. We are not enemies, but friends. We must not be enemies. Though passion may have strained, it must not break our bonds of affection. The mystic chords of memory, stretching from every battle-field, and patriot grave, to every living heart and hearthstone, all over this broad land, will yet swell the chorus of the Union, when again touched, as surely they will be, by the better angels of our nature.[3]

Influenced in some degree by party and section, readers of the address found differing interpretations of the president's purposes. The *Albany Atlas and Argus* dismissed the address as ineffectual and misguided and discerned in it an intention to restore the seceded states to the Union:

It is useless to criticize the style of the President's Inaugural when the policy it declares is fraught with consequences so momentous. Still this rambling, discursive, questioning, loose-jointed stump speech, is itself a symptom of the pending revolution and of its downward tendencies. There is as wide a difference between the State papers of a JEFFERSON or a JACKSON, and this feeble rhetorical stuff, as there is between the policy of those great Statesmen, and the rash, crude views which Mr. LINCOLN has determined to foist upon the government.

Mr. LINCOLN assumes the responsibility of revolutionizing the Federal Government and making it an instrument of force, instead of opinion. True, he asserts that the responsibility of civil war will rest with the dissatisfied States. But how? He will undertake, with the Army and Navy, to capture forts, and collect revenues, in those States; and if the people resist, they will be treated as insurgents, and will be regarded as commencing civil war!

Two monstrous propositions precede this conclusion. MR. LINCOLN assumes to represent the majority of the people; and quotes the undigested resolutions of a disreputable party gathering at Chicago, as his instructions, confirmed by the voice of the people. He was not the free choice of a majority of that body; nor in any sense, the original choice of the party it represented. And that party was itself in a minority of two to one—concentrating the votes of only one-third of the electors of the Union. This, we admit, does not impair his constitutional right to office; but it should have admonished Mr. LINCOLN to the duty of forbearance. He should have said, on accepting office: "The voice of two-thirds of the American people must be regarded as an instruction to me to maintain the Constitution, as they understand it; as it has stood heretofore; and as the Supreme Court have expounded it; and I must surrender my personal views to such a requisition."

On the contrary, he declares: "The minority have given me power, and I will use it against the majority. I deny the authority of the Supreme Court to bind me by their decision. I will disregard it. I will use military force against the dissatisfied States; and the responsibility of Civil War will rest upon the insurgents who resist."

It is he that is the nullifier. It is he that defies the will of the majority. It is he that initiates Civil War.

Never was a man so little competent for such a task. Never were means devised so inadequate to the proposed ends.—Never did the head of a State challenge a trial to bloody conclusions, who was destined to so ignominious a retreat.

But we will not anticipate the future.—The bewildered man had the path of peace before him, and yet has chosen to take the bloody warpath whose end he knows not, but which all men know, can never be tread with honor, or even retraced, by footsteps so unsteady as his. We see the evil beginning; but we fear we shall not have long to wait to behold the inglorious ending.[4]

Its rival, Thurlow Weed's *Albany Evening Journal,* considered the speech evidence of Lincoln's conciliatory nature and the possibility of a peaceful future:

No document was ever looked for with more intense interest than the Inaugural Message of President LINCOLN. And no Message was ever received with greater favor. It is universally conceded to be alike clear, compact and impressive—equally firm and conciliatory. Every sentence bears the impress of a pure and exalted patriotism, and affords unmistakable evidence of his purpose to go to the very verge of his constitutional duty to reconcile conflicting interests, to restore harmony to the Union and to bring back the Seceding States to their allegiance to the Republic.

He could have said no less than he has said in vindication of his own position and of the principles which, in his election, have received the endorsement of the people. Nor could he have said more, without subjecting himself to the charge of cowardice and hypocrisy, to manifest his desire for a peaceful adjustment of all questions at issue between the North and the South. He commends the conciliatory action of Congress, as embodied in the proposed amendment of the Constitution, guaranteeing to every State supreme control over its own domestic institutions; and approves the suggestion of a Convention of the People to revise and amend the Constitution so as, if possible, to remove all future sectional conflicts. He thus, as well as in the general tone of his address, foreshadows the conciliatory spirit which will govern his administration, and presents solid ground upon which to base the hope that, ere long, the dark war clouds which hang over the Republic will be dispersed by the rising sun of fraternal fellowship and peace.[5]

The *New York Herald* sharply attacked the message as "it abound[ed] in traits of craft and cunning":

It would have been almost as instructive if President Lincoln had contented himself with telling his audience yesterday a funny story and let them go. His inaugural is but a paraphrase of the vague generalities contained in his pilgrimage speeches, and shows clearly either that he has not made up his mind respecting his future course, or else that he desires, for the present, to keep his intentions to himself. The stupendous questions of the last month have been whether the incoming Administration would adopt a coercive or a conciliatory policy towards the Southern States; whether it would propose satisfactory amendments to the Constitution, convening an extra session of Congress for the purpose of considering them; and whether, with the spirit of the statesmen who laid the cornerstone of the institutions of the republic, it would rise to the dignity of the occasion, and meet as was fitting the terrible crisis through which the country is passing. The inaugural gives no satisfaction on any of these points. Parts of it contradict those that precede them, and where the adoption of any course is hinted at, a studious disavowal of its being a recommendation is appended. Not a small portion of the columns of our paper, in which the document is amplified, look as though they were thrown in as a mere make-weight. A resolve to procrastinate, before committing himself, is apparent throughout. Indeed, Mr. Lincoln closes by saying that "there is no object in being in a hurry," and that "nothing valuable can be lost by taking time." Filled with careless *bonhomie* as this first proclamation to the country of the new President, is, it will give but small contentment to those who believe that not only its prosperity, but its very existence is at stake.

The inaugural opens by deliberately ignoring the true issue between the Southern and Northern States. It declares that the slaveholding members of the confederation have no grievances; that "nobody is hurt," or will have a right to imagine himself hurt, until the peculiar institution is actively invaded when it exists. "Apprehension," he says, "seems to exist among the people of the Southern States, that their property, and their peace and personal security, are to be endangered. There has never been any reasonable cause for apprehension. Indeed, the most ample evidence to the contrary has all the while existed, and been open to their inspection." The same spirit runs through the whole speech. He quotes the Chicago platform resolution against John Brown, as though that were an all-sufficient reply to his objections, and elsewhere exclaims:—"Is it true that any right written in the Constitution has been denied? I think not." Yet, in the line and a half which is all that he thinks proper to devote to the momentous question of the common Territories, out of which has grown the sectional strife which convulses the Union, he virtually kicks to pieces the whole groundwork of Republican aggressions, and confesses the untenableness of their past claims. "Must Congress," he says, "protect slavery in the Territories? The Constitution does not expressly say."

A couple of paragraphs devoted to the Fugitive Slave law contain acknowledgment of his duty to enforce it, but while emphatically promising to do so, the President quibbles respecting the manner of carrying out the law, and interpolates for the benefit of his abolitionist friends a query respecting free negroes which is completely out of place. "Might it not be well," he asks, in their behalf, "to provide by law for the enforcement of that clause in the Constitution which 'guarantees that the citizens of each State shall be entitled to all the privileges and immunities of citizens in the several States?'" This is a covert fling, of course, at South Carolina, whose recent legislation on the subject of free negroes is thus held up for reprobation. . . .

In a word, the inaugural is not a crude performance—it abounds in traits of craft and cunning. It bears marks of indecision, and yet of strong coercive proclivities, with serious doubts whether the government will be able to gratify them. It is so clearly intended to admit of a double, or even of any possible interpretation, that many will content themselves with waiting for the progress of events, in the meanwhile seeking in it for no meaning at all. It is neither candid nor statesmanlike; nor does it possess any essential of dignity or patriotism. It would have caused a Washington to mourn and would have inspired Jefferson, Madison, or Jackson with contempt. With regard to the ultimate projects of Mr. Lincoln, the public is no wiser than before. It is sincerely to be trusted that he is yet ignorant of them himself.[6]

The Baltimore press divided in appraising the message. The *Baltimore Sun* denounced the address as "sectional and mischievous," adding that "if it means what it says, it is the knell and the requiem of the Union, and the death of hope." The *Baltimore Exchange* said, "the measures of Mr. Lincoln mean war." The *Baltimore Patriot* believed, with the *American*, that Mr. Lincoln meant to avoid aggression, and added:

The reasoning and expositions of the Inaugural, in the virtues of patience, forbearance, &c., apply as well to Mr. Lincoln as to the people of the several States, and as he expects the people to expect that he will apply the counsel to himself, as well as to them. In this there is *another assurance of pacificatory purposes, and of the intention to enforce the laws, as nearly as possible, in conformity with the will of the whole people.* This position is greatly strengthened by the appeal to the Almighty Ruler of Nations, with his eternal truth and justice, as the great appellate tribunal of the American people. We make this observation in reference to Mr. Lincoln as an enlightened and conscientious fanatic. In the character of the statesman, he will wisely and judiciously apply the law he is obliged to enforce as a sufficient instrument for the accomplishment of its purposes, without any appeal to the higher law of the fanatics, which is subversive of all human law and government, and impels the submission of all human thought and consideration and action to the whim or notion of an individual man.[7]

Frederick Douglass, the black leader, was disappointed in the address, and considered it insufficiently forceful, "casting pearls before swine." Struck more by its evidence of cowardice than its efforts at conciliation, he wrote an extensive critique in his *Douglass's Monthly* in April:

Elsewhere in the columns of our present monthly, our readers will find the Inaugural Address of Mr. Abraham Lincoln, delivered on the occasion of his induction to the office of President of the United States. The circumstances under which the Address was delivered, were the most extraordinary and portentous that ever attended any similar occasion in the history of the country. Threats of riot, rebellion, violence and assassination had been freely, though darkly circulated, as among the probable events to occur on that memorable day. The life of Mr. Lincoln was believed, even by his least timid friends, to be in most imminent danger." No mean courage was required to face the probabilities of the hour. He stood up before the pistol or dagger of the sworn assassin, to meet death from an unknown hand, while upon the very threshold of the office to which the suffrages of the nation had elected him. The outgoing Administration, either by its treachery or weakness, or both, had allowed the Government to float to the very verge of destruction. A fear, amounting to agony in some minds, existed that the great American Republic would expire in the arms of its newly elected guardian upon the very moment of his inauguration. For weeks and months previously to the fourth of March, under the wise direction and management of General Scott, elaborate military preparations were made with a view to prevent the much apprehended outbreak of violence and bloodshed, and secure the peaceful inauguration of the President elect. How much the nation is indebted to General Scott for its present existence, it is impossible to tell. No doubt exists that to him, rather than to any forbearance of the rebels, Washington owes its salvation from blood[y] streets on the fourth of March. The manner in which Mr. Lincoln entered the Capital was in keeping with the menacing and troubled state of the times. He reached the Capital as the poor, hunted fugitive slave reaches the North, in disguise, seeking concealment, evading pursuers, by the underground railroad, between two days, not during the sunlight, but crawling and dodging under the sable wing of night. He changed his programme, took another route, started at another hour, travelled in other company, and arrived at another time in Washington. We have no censure for the President at this point. He only did what braver men have done. It was, doubtless, galling to his very soul to be compelled to avail himself of the methods of a fugitive slave, with a nation howling on his track. The great party that elected him fairly wilted under it. The act, in some sense, was an indication of the policy of the new Government—more cunning than bold, evading rather than facing danger, outwitting rather than bravely conquering and putting down the enemy. The whole thing looked bad, but it was not adopted without reason. Circumstances gave to an act which, upon its face, was cowardly and mean, the merit of wisdom, forethought and discretion.

Once in Washington, Mr. Lincoln found himself in the thick atmosphere of treason on the one hand, and a cowardly, sentimental and deceitful profession of peace on the other. With such surroundings, he went to work upon his Inaugural Address, and the influence of those surroundings may be traced in the whole character of his performance. Making all allowance for circumstances, we must declare the address to be but little better than ... we hoped it might be. It is a double-tongued document, capable of two constructions, and conceals rather than declares a definite policy. No man reading it could say whether Mr. Lincoln was for peace or war, whether he abandons or maintains the principles of the Chicago Convention upon which he was elected. The occasion required the utmost frankness and decision. Overlooking the whole field of disturbing elements, he should have boldly rebuked them. He saw seven States in open rebellion, the Constitution set at naught, the national flag insulted, and his own life murderously sought by slave-holding assassins. Does he expose and rebuke the enemies of his country, the men who are bent upon ruling or ruining the country? Not a bit of it. But at the very start he seeks to court their favor, to explain himself where nobody misunderstands him, and to deny intentions of which nobody had accused him. He turns away from his armed enemy, deals his blows on the head of an innocent bystander. He knew, full well, that the grand objection to him and his party respected the one great question of slavery extension. The South want to extend slavery, and the North want to confine it where it is, "where the public mind shall rest in the belief of its ultimate extinction." This was the question which carried the North and defeated the South in the election which made Mr. Abraham Lincoln President. Mr. Lincoln knew this, and the South has known it all along; and yet this subject only gets the faintest allusion, while others, never seriously in dispute, are dwelt upon at length.

Mr. Lincoln opens his address by announcing his complete loyalty to slavery in the slave States, and quotes from the Chicago platform a resolution affirming the rights of property in slaves, in the slave States. He is not content with declaring that he has no lawful power to interfere with slavery in the States, but he also denies having the least "*inclination*" to interfere with slavery in the States. This denial of all feeling against slavery, at such a time and in such circumstances, is wholly discreditable to the head and heart of Mr. Lincoln. Aside from the inhuman coldness of the sentiment, it was a weak and inappropriate utterance to such an audience, since it could neither appease nor check the wild fury of the rebel Slave Power. Any but a blind man can see that the disunion sentiment of the South does not arise from any misapprehension of the disposition of the party represented by Mr. Lincoln. The very opposite is the fact. The difficulty is, the slaveholders understand the position of the Republican party too well. Whatever may be the honied phrases employed by Mr. Lincoln when confronted by actual disunion; however silvery and beautiful may be the subtle rhetoric of his long-headed Secretary of State, when wishing to hold the Government together until its management should fall into other hands; all know that the masses at the North (the power behind the throne) had determined to take and keep this Government out of the hands of the slave-holding oligarchy, and administer it hereafter to the advantage of free labor as against slave labor. The slaveholders knew full well that they were hereafter to change the condition of rulers to that of being ruled; they knew that the mighty North is outstripping the South in numbers, and in all the elements of power, and that from being superior, they were to be doomed to hopeless inferiority. This is what galled them. They are not afraid that Lincoln will send out a proclamation over the slave States declaring all the slaves free, nor that Congress will pass a law to that effect. They are no such fools as to believe any such thing; but they do think, and not without reason, that the power of slavery is broken, and that its prestige is gone whenever the people have made up their minds that Liberty is safer in the hands of freemen than in those of slaveholders. To those sagacious and crafty men, schooled into mastery over bondmen on the plantation, and thus the better able to assume the airs of superiority over Northern doughfaces, Mr. Lincoln's disclaimer of any power, right or inclination to interfere with slavery in the States, does not amount to more than a broken shoe-string! They knew it all before, and while they do not accept it as a satisfaction, they do look upon such declarations as the evidence of cowardly baseness, upon which they may safely presume.

The slaveholders, the parties especially addressed, may well inquire if you, Mr. Lincoln, and the great party that elected you, honestly entertain this very high respect for the rights of slave property in the States, how happens it that you treat the same rights of property with scorn and contempt when they are set up in the Territories of the United States?—If slaves are property, and our rights of property in them are to be so sacredly guarded in the States, by what rule of law, justice or reason does that property part with the attributes of property, upon entering into a Territory owned in part by that same State? The fact is, the slaveholders have the argument all their own way, the moment that the right of property in their slaves is conceded under the Constitution. It was, therefore, weak, uncalled for and useless for Mr. Lincoln to begin his Inaugural Address by thus at the outset prostrating himself before the foul and withering curse of slavery. The time and the occasion called for a very different attitude. Weakness, timidity and conciliation towards the tyrants and traitors had emboldened them to a pitch of insolence which demanded an instant check. Mr. Lincoln was in a position that enabled him to wither at a single blast their high blown pride. The occasion was one for honest rebuke, not for palliations and apologies. The slaveholders should have been told that their barbarous system of robbery is contrary to the spirit of the age, and to the principles of Liberty in which the Federal Government was founded, and that they should be ashamed to be everlastingly pressing that scandalous crime into notice. Some thought we had in Mr. Lincoln the nerve and decision of an Oliver Cromwell; but the result shows that we merely have a continuation of the Pierces and Buchanans, and that the Republican President bends the knee to slavery as readily as any of his infamous predecessors. Not content with the broadest recognition of the right of property in the souls and bodies of men in the slave States, Mr. Lincoln next proceeds, with nerves of steel, to tell the slaveholders what an excellent slave hound he is, and how he regards the right to recapture fugitive slaves a constitutional duty; and lest the poor bondman should escape being returned to the hell of slavery by the application of certain well known rules of legal interpretation, which any and every white man may claim in his own case, Mr. Lincoln proceeds to cut off the poor, trembling Negro who had escaped from bondage from all advantages from such rules. He will have the pound of flesh, blood or no blood, be it more or less, a just pound or not. The Shylocks of the South, had they been after such game, might have exclaimed, in joy, an Abraham come to judgment! But they were not to be caught with such fodder. The hunting down a few slaves, the sending back of a few Lucy Bagleys, young and beautiful though they be, to the lust and brutality of the slavebreeders of the Border States, is to the rapacity of the rebels only as a drop of water upon a house in flames. The value of the thing was wholly in its quality. "Mr. Lincoln, you will catch and return our slaves if they run away from us, and will help us hold them where they are"; what cause, then, since you have descended to this depth of wickedness, withholds you from coming down to us entirely? Indeed, in what respect are you better than ourselves, or our overseers and drivers who hunt and flog our Negroes into obedience?— Again, the slaveholders have a decided advantage over Mr. Lincoln, and over his party. He stands upon the same moral level with them, and is in no respect better than they. If we held the Constitution, as held by Mr. Lincoln, no earthly power could induce us to swear to support it. The fact is, (following the lead of the Dred Scott decision, and all the Southern slaveholding politicians, with all the doughfaces of the North who have been engaged in making a Constitution, for years, outside of the Constitution of 1789,) Mr. Lincoln has taken everything at this point in favor of slavery for granted. He is like the great mass of his countrymen, indebted to the South for both law and gospel.

But the Inaugural does not admit of entire and indiscriminate condemnation. It has at least one or two features which evince the presence or something like a heart as well as a head. Horrible as is Mr. Lincoln's admission of the constitutional duty of surrendering persons claimed as slaves, and heartily as he seems determined that that revolting work shall be performed, he has sent along with his revolting declaration a timid suggestion which, tame and spiritless as it is, must prove as unpalatable as gall to the taste of slaveholders. He says: "In any law on this subject, ought not all the safeguards of liberty known in humane and civilized jurisprudence be introduced, so that a free man be not in any case surrendered as a slave." For so much, little as it is, let the friends of freedom thank Mr. Lincoln. This saves his Address from the gulf of infamy into which the Dred Scott decision sunk the Supreme Court of the United States. Two ideas are embraced in this suggestion: First, a black man's rights should be guarded by all the safeguards known to liberty and to humane jurisprudence; secondly, that slavery is an inhuman condition from which a free man ought by all lawful means to be saved. When we remember the prevailing contempt for the rights of all persons of African descent, who are mostly exposed to the operation of these slave catching laws, and the strenuous efforts of the American

Church and clergy to make slavery a divine relation, and especially blissful to our much hated variety of the human family, we are disposed to magnify and rejoice over even this slight recognition of rights, and this implied acknowledgment of the hatefulness of slavery. One of the safeguards of liberty is trial in open court. Another is the right of bringing evidence in one's own favor, and of confronting and questioning opposing witnesses. Another is the trial by a jury of our peers. Another is that juries are judges both of the law and the evidence in the case. There are other safeguards of liberty which we might specify, any one of which, faithfully applied, would not only make it difficult to surrender a free man as a slave, but would make it almost impossible to surrender any man as such. Thanking Mr. Lincoln for even so much, we yet hold him to be the most dangerous advocate of slavehunting and slave-catching in the land.

He has laid down a general rule of legal interpretation which, like most, if not all general rules, may be stretched to cover almost every conceivable villainy. "*The intention of the law-giver is the law,*" says Mr. Lincoln. But we say that this depends upon whether the *intention* itself is lawful. If law were merely an arbitrary rule, destitute of all idea of right and wrong, the intention of the lawgiver might indeed be taken as the law, provided that intention were certainly known. But the very idea of law carries with it ideas of right, justice and humanity. Law, according to Blackstone, commands that which is right and forbids that which is wrong. A law authorizing murder is not law, because it is an outrage upon all the elements out of which laws originate. Any man called to administer and execute such a law is bound to treat such an edict as a nullity, having no binding authority over his action or over his conscience. He would have a right to say, upon the authority of the Supreme Court, that "laws against fundamental morality are void"; that a law for murder is an absurdity, and not only from the purpose of all law and government, but wholly at war with every principle of law. It would be no avail in such a case to say that the "intention of law-makers is the law." To prove such an intention is only to destroy the validity of the law.

But the case is not murder, but simply the surrendering of a person to slavery who has made his or her escape from slavery into a free State. But what better is an act of this kind than murder? Would not Mr. Lincoln himself prefer to see a dagger plunged to the hilt into the heart of his own daughter, than to see that daughter given up to the lust and brutality of the slaveholders of Virginia, as was poor, trembling Lucy Bagley given up a few weeks ago by the Republicans of Cleveland? What is slavery but a slow process of soul murder? What but murder is its chief reliance? How do slaveholders hold their slaves except by asserting their right and power to murder their slaves if they do not submit to slavery? Does not the whole slave system rest upon a basis of murder? Your money or your life, says the pirate; your liberty or your life, says the slaveholder. And where is the difference between the pirate and the slaveholder?

But the "intention of the law is the law." Well, suppose we grant it in the present case, that the intention of the law-maker is the law, and two very important questions arise—first, as to who were the makers, and, secondly, by what means are we required to learn their intentions? Who made the Constitution? The preamble to the Constitution answers that question. "We, the people, do ordain and establish this Constitution." The people, then, made the law. How stood their intention as to the surrender of fugitive slaves? Were they all agreed in this intention to send slaves to bondage who might escape from it? Or were only a part? and if a part, how many? Surely, if a minority only were of the intention, that intention could not be the law, especially as the law itself expresses no such intention. The fact is, there is no evidence whatever that any considerable part of the people who made and adopted the American Constitution intended to make that instrument a slave-hunting or a slaveholding instrument, while there is much evidence to prove the very reverse. Daniel Webster, even in his famous 7th of March speech, was sufficiently true to the letter of the Constitution, and to the history of the times in which the Constitution was framed and adopted, to deny that the Constitution required slaves to be given up, and quoted Mr. James Madison in corroboration of his statement. This is Mr. Webster's language: "It may not be important here to allude to that—I had almost said celebrated—opinion of Mr. Madison. You observe, sir, that the term slavery is not used in the Constitution. The Constitution does not require that fugitive slaves shall be delivered up; it requires that persons bound to service in one State escaping into another, shall be delivered up. Mr. Madison opposed the introduction of the term slave, or slavery, into the Constitution; for he said he did not wish to see it recognized by the Constitution of the United States of America, that there could be property in men."

How sadly have the times changed, not only since the days of Madison— the days of the Constitution—but since the days even of Daniel Webster. Cold and dead as that great bad man was to the claims of humanity, he was not sufficiently removed from the better days of the Republic to claim, as Mr. Lincoln does, that the surrender of fugitive slaves is a plain requirement of the Constitution. But there comes along a slight gleam of relief.

Mr. Lincoln tremblingly ventures to *inquire* (for he is too inoffensive to the slaveholders to assert and declare, except when the rights of the black men are asserted and declared away) if it "might not be well to provide by law for the enforcement of that clause in the Constitution which guarantees that the citizens of each State shall be entitled to all the privileges and immunities of citizens in the several States."

Again we thank Mr. Lincoln. He has, however, ventured upon a hazardous suggestion. The man has not quite learned his lesson. He had not been long enough in Washington to learn that Northern citizens, like persons of African descent, have no rights, privileges or immunities that slaveholders are bound to respect. To break open a man's trunk, to read the letters from his wife and daughters, to tar and feather him, to ride him on a rail and give him the alternative of being hanged or of leaving town the same hour, simply because he resides in a free State, is a privilege and immunity which our Southern brethren will not give up, though the requirement were made in every line of the Constitution. Yet, we say, we are thankful. It is something even to have a sickly intimation that other American citizens, not belonging to the privileged slaveholding class, have rights which it *"might be well"* to secure by law, and that the mere fact of living in a free State ought not to subject the unfortunate traveler either to being whipped, hanged or shot. Yes, this is something to be thankful for and is more than any other American President has ever ventured to say, either in his Inaugural Speech or Annual Message. It is, perhaps, this latter fact that gives Mr. Lincoln's casual remark its chief importance.—Hitherto our Presidents had pictured the South as the innocent lamb, and the greedy north as the hungry wolf, ever ready to tear and devour.

From slave-catching, Mr. Lincoln proceeds to give a very lucid exposition of the nature of the Federal Union, and shows very conclusively that this Government from its own nature and the nature of all Governments, was intended to be perpetual, and that it is revolutionary, insurrectionary and treasonable to break it up. His argument is excellent; but the difficulty is that the argument comes too late. When men deliberately arm themselves with the avowed intention of breaking up the Government; when they openly insult its flag, capture its forts, seize its munitions of war, and organize a hostile Government, and boastfully declare that they will fight before they will submit, it would seem of little use to argue with them. If the argument was merely for the loyal citizen, it was unnecessary. If it was for those already in rebellion, it was as casting pearls before swine. No class of men in the country understood better than the rebels themselves the nature of the business on which they are engaged.—They tell us this in the thousands of pounds of powder they have been buying, and the millions of money and arms they have been stealing. They know that unless the Government is a miserable and contemptible failure, destitute of every attribute of a Government except the name, that that Government must meet them on the field and put them down, or be itself put down. To parley with traitors is but to increase their insolence and audacity.

It remains to be seen whether the Federal Government is really able to do more than hand over some John Brown to be hanged, suppress a slave insurrection, or catch a runaway slave—whether it is powerless for liberty, and only powerful for slavery. Mr. Lincoln says, "I shall take care that the laws of the Union shall be faithfully executed in all the States"—that is, he will do so as "*as far as practicable,*" and *unless* the American people, his masters, shall, in some authoritative manner direct the contrary. To us, both these provisions had better have been omitted. They imply a want of confidence in the ability of the Government to execute its own laws, and open its doors to all that border tribe who have nothing but smiles for the rebels and peace lectures for the Government. The American people have placed the Government in the hands of Abraham Lincoln for the next four years, and his instructions are in the Constitution. He had no right to suppose that they will reverse those instructions in a manner to give immunity to traitors; and it was a mistake to admit such a possibility, especially in the presence of the very traitors themselves. But we are dwelling longer upon Mr. Lincoln's speech than we had intended, and longer than we are warranted either by the patience of our readers, or the extent of our space. The perusal of it has left no very hopeful impression upon our mind for the cause of our down-trodden and heart-broken countrymen. Mr. Lincoln has avowed himself ready to catch them if they run away, to shoot them down if they rise against their oppressors, and to prohibit the Federal Government *irrevocably* from interfering for their deliverance. With such declarations before them, coming from our first modern anti-slavery President, the Abolitionists must know what to expect during the next four years, (should Mr. Lincoln not be, as he is likely to be, driven out of Washington by his rival, Mr. Jeff. Davis, who has already given out that should Mr. Lincoln attempt to do, what he has sworn to do—namely, execute the laws, fifty thousand soldiers will march directly upon Washington!) This might be taken as an empty threat on the part of the President of the Confederated States, if we did not see with what steadiness, promptness and certainty the rebels have from the first executed all their designs and fulfilled all their promises. A thousand things are less probable than that Mr. Lincoln and his Cabinet will be driven out of Washington, and made to go out, as they came in, by the Underground Railroad. The game is completely in the hands of Mr. Jefferson Davis, and no doubt he will avail himself of every advantage.[8]

Douglass's perceptive and powerful conclusions were vindicated in a matter of weeks. He judged the temper of the Confederate men well. Writing from Washington DC, a Confederate correspondent told the Confederacy's secretary of war:

> The inaugural undoubtedly means war, and that right off. I have never doubted as to Lincoln's views, and nothing would have changed them but the secession of the border States, who have not acted.
>
> Mr. Crawford is here, and will proceed to execute the duties of his mission as soon as the new Secretary of State is installed. This will be, I suppose, tomorrow morning at furthest.
>
> I was present last evening at a consultation of Southern gentlemen, at which Messrs. Crawford, Garnett, Pryor, De Jarnette, of Virginia, and Wigfall, of Texas, were present. We all put the same construction on the inaugural, which we carefully went over together. We agreed that it was Lincoln's purpose at once to attempt the collection of the revenue, to re-enforce and hold Fort Sumter and Pickens, and to retake the other places. He is a man of will and firmness. His Cabinet will yield to him with alacrity, I think. Seward has, of course, agreed to the inaugural, and the pretenses of his conservatism are idle.[9]

The *Richmond Enquirer,* on March 5, with Virginia yet unseceded but seeing war clearly on the horizon, asked and answered a question:

> Mr. Lincoln's Inaugural Address is before our readers—couched in the cool, unimpassioned, deliberate language of the fanatic, with the purpose of pursuing the promptings of fanaticism even to the dismemberment of the Government with the horrors of civil war. Virginia has the long looked for and promised peace offering before her—and she has more, she has the denial of all hope of peace. Civil war must now come. Sectional war, declared by Mr. Lincoln, awaits only the signal gun from the insulted Southern Confederacy, to light its horrid fires all along the borders of Virginia. . . .
>
> The question, "where shall Virginia go?" is answered by Mr. Lincoln. She must go *to war*—and she must decide with whom she wars—whether

with those who have suffered her wrongs, or with those who have inflicted her injuries.

Our ultimate destruction pales before the present emergency. To war! to arms! is now the cry, and when peace is declared, if ever, in our day, Virginia may decide where she will finally rest. But for the present she has no choice left; war with Lincoln or with Davis is the choice left us. Read the inaugural carefully, and then let every reader demand of his delegate in the Convention the prompt measures of defense which it is now apparent we must make.[10]

A New Yorker wrote reassuringly to Lincoln that the address was well received by "the honest portion of the American people":

I read your Inaugural approving every argument it contains, and my heart responded "Amen" to every patriotic sentiment therein expressed—I took it home and read it to my wife, and she seemed delighted with it—This morning I called on a Breckenridge Democrat and put the question "How do you like the Inaugural?" "First rate, It is short and full of pith, was the reply"—I then called on a "Silver Gray" [a supporter of the defunct Whig Party—Ed.] friend and asked him. "How do you like the Inaugural"? ["] Splendid It could not be bettered" he answered.

I then stepped into the office of a staunch Douglass [sic] man and inquired "How do you like the Inaugural?" "All right & if Mr Lincoln will stand firm to his position I am with him heart and hand" was his answer—It being about lunch time I dropped into the restaurant of the black man across the street and says, "Well Mr Ray how do you like the Inaugural ["] "I think he has hit the nail on the head, our folks will all stand by him" said he— Lastly I called on a stock broker and asked the same question, and added "how does the Inaugural effect the stock market" "We are afraid there is too much fight in it, the market is feverish" was his answer—From these indications I think the honest portion of the American people are with you and will hold themselves subject to your direction whether it be storm or sunshine that may follow.[11]

In the Senate two days after the inaugural, Thomas Clingman, senator from North Carolina and a supporter of the right to secede, attacked the speech and Lincoln's policy:

If I understand it aright, all that is direct in it, I mean, at least, that purpose which seems to stand out clearly and directly, is one which I think must lead to war against the confederate or seceding States; and, as I think that policy will be very unwise for the United States, I must say frankly to gentlemen on the other side that I do not see, if we adopt the principles of the inaugural, how that is to be avoided.

The President declares expressly, in the inaugural, that he intends to treat those States as though they were still members of the Union; as though the acts of secession were mere nullities; and, as they claim to be independent, there can be no result except a collision. In plain, unmistakable language, he declares that it is his purpose to hold, occupy, and possess the forts and arsenals in those States. We all know that he can hold them only by dispossessing the State authorities. He says, further, that it is his purpose to collect the revenue from those States. Surely, [I] need not argue to any Senator that this must lead to a collision of arms. After we declared independence from Great Britain, nobody supposed that the colonies were willing still to pay taxes or duties to the British Government. In point of fact, they refused to pay them even before the declaration of independence. If that policy be carried out, it is, therefore, unmistakably war. I will not argue it; I merely throw in this protest. I do not see how we are to escape a collision of arms the moment the President attempts to carry out that policy. I have merely said this, in order that, if I should assent to the printing of the message, I may not be misunderstood.[12]

Stephen A. Douglas immediately rose to contradict his fellow Democrat:

Mr. President, I cannot assent to the construction which the Senator from North Carolina [Mr. CLINGMAN] has placed upon the President's inaugural. I have read it carefully, with a view of ascertaining distinctly what the policy of the Administration is to be. The inaugural is characterized by ability, and by directness on certain points; but with such reservations and qualifications as require a critical analysis to arrive at its true construction on other points. I have made such an analysis, and come to the conclusion that it is a peace-offering rather than a war message. Having examined it critically, I think I can demonstrate that there is no foundation for the apprehension which has been spread through the country, that this message is equivalent to a declaration of war; that it commits the President of the United States to recapture the forts in the seceded States, and to hold them at all hazards; to collect the revenue under all circumstances; and to execute the laws in all the States, no matter what may be the circumstances that surround him. I do not understand that to be the character of the message. On the contrary, I understand it to contain a distinct pledge that the policy of the

Administration shall be conducted with exclusive reference to a peaceful solution of our national difficulties. True, the President indicates a certain line of policy which he intends to pursue, so far as it may be consistent with the peace of the country; but he assures us that this policy will be modified and changed whenever necessary to a peaceful solution of these difficulties.

The address is not as explicit as I could desire on certain points; on certain other points it is explicit. The message is explicit and certain upon the point that the President will not, directly or indirectly, interfere with the institution of slavery within the States; is specific upon the point that he will do everything in his power to give a faithful execution to the Constitution and the laws for the return of fugitive slaves; is explicit upon the point that he will not oppose such amendments to the Constitution as may be deemed necessary to settle the slavery question and restore peace to the country. Then, it proceeds to indicate a line of policy for his administration. He declares that, in view of the Constitution and laws, the Union remains unbroken. I do not suppose any man can deny the proposition, that in contemplation of law, the Union remains intact, no matter what the fact may be. There may be a separation *de facto,* temporary or permanent, as the sequal may prove; but, in contemplation of the Constitution and the laws, the Union does remain unbroken. I think no one can deny the correctness of the proposition, as a constitutional principle. Let us go further and see what there is in the address that is supposed to pledge the President to a coercive policy. He says:

I shall take care, as the Constitution itself expressly enjoins upon me, that the laws of the Union be faithfully executed in all the States.

This declaration is relied upon as conclusive evidence that coercion is to be used in the seceding States; but take the next sentence:

Doing this I deem to be only a simple duty on my part. I shall perform it, so far as Is practicable, unless—

Unless what? Let us see what the condition is on the happening of which he will not enforce the laws—

unless my rightful masters, the American people, shall withhold the requisite means, or in some other authoritative manner direct the contrary.

This condition, on which he will not enforce the laws in the seceding States, is not as explicit as I could desire. When he alludes to his "rightful masters, the American people," I suppose he means the action of Congress in withholding the requisite means. Query: does he wish to be understood as saying that the existing laws confer upon him "the requisite means?" or, does he mean to say that, inasmuch as the existing laws do not confer the requisite means, he cannot execute the laws in the seceding States unless those means shall be conferred by Congress? The language employed would seem to imply that the President was referring to the future action of Congress as necessary to give him the requisite means to enforce obedience to the laws in the seceding States.[13]

Whose interpretation or prediction was right? In the inaugural Lincoln had said "in your hands, my dissatisfied fellow countrymen, and not in mine, is the momentous issue of civil war." We know, of course, that the outcome was momentous beyond imagining; his contemporaries would very soon know it too.

CHAPTER SEVEN

FORT SUMTER CRISIS

In his post-election correspondence Lincoln had stated he intended to keep or retake the federal forts in the states that seceded. His inaugural oath required him to preserve, protect, and defend the Union. The test of his intention arrived on his desk the day after he took the oath. A letter from General Winfield Scott read in part:

[I]t is evident that the officers of the fort have changed their opinions, with the great change of circumstances, & now see no alternative but a surrender, in some weeks, more or less, as they well know that we cannot send the third of the men (regulars) in several months (weeks) ... necessary to give them relief beyond a few weeks, if for a day. Evacuation seems almost inevitable, & in this view, our distinguished Chief Engineer (Brigadier Totten) concurs—if, indeed, the worn out garrison be not assaulted & carried in the present week.[1]

On March 9 Lincoln requested Scott to respond to three questions specifically about Fort Sumter, and Scott did:

The President has done me the honor to address to me certain professional questions, to which he desires answers. I proceed with them categorically.

1. To what point of time can Major Anderson maintain his position, at Fort Sumter, without fresh supplies or reinforcement?
Answer. In respect to subsistence, for the garrison, he has hard bread, flour & rice for about 26 days, & salt meat (pork) for about 48 days; but how long he could hold out against the whole means of attack which the South Carolinians have in, & about the city of Charleston & its Harbour, is a question that cannot be answered with absolute accuracy. Reckoning the (batteries) troops at 3,500 (now somewhat disciplined)

the batteries at 4 powerfull land, & at least one floating—all mounting guns & mortars of large caliber, & of the best patterns;–& supposing those means to be skillfully & vigorously employed—Fort Sumter with its less than 100 men—including common laborers & musicians—ought to be taken by a single assault, & easily, if harassed perseveringly for several previous days & nights by threats & false attacks, with the ability, from the force of overwhelming numbers, of converting one out of every three or four of those, into a real attack.

2. Can you with all the means now in your control, supply or reinforce Fort Sumter within that time?

Answer. No: Not within many months. See answer to No. 3.

3. If not, what amount of means, & of what description in addition to that already at your control, would enable you to supply & reinforce that fortress within the time?

Answer: A fleet of war vessels & transports, 5,000 additional regular troops & 20,000 volunteers, in order to take all the batteries in the Harbor of Charleston (including Ft. Moultrie) after capture of all the batteries in the approach or outer Bay. And to raise, organize & discipline such an army, would require new acts of Congress & from six to eight months.[2]

On the same day Scott composed a draft order for evacuation of the fort:

Sir: The time having been allowed to pass by when it was practicable to fit out an expedition adequate to the succor of your garrison, before the exhaustion of its means of subsistence—you will, after communicating your purpose to His Excellency, the Governor of So. Carolina,—engage suitable water transportation, & peacefully evacuate Fort Sumter so long gallantly held—& with your entire command embark for New York;— your officers and men taking with them their small arms, accoutrements & private effects.[3]

On March 15 Lincoln asked his cabinet to give him their opinions in writing on this question: "Assuming it to be possible to now provision Fort Sumter, under all circumstances is it wise to attempt it?"

Lincoln's phrase "under all circumstances," comprehended the fact that the decision was many sided: political, military, financial, and involving the welfare of the beleaguered men at Fort Sumter. Seward, the politician, favored conciliation: "I would not provoke war in any way now. I would resort to force to protect the collection of the revenue, because this is a necessary as well as a legitimate Union object. Even then it should be only a naval force that I would employ for that necessary purpose, while I would defer military action on land until a case should arise when we would hold the defense. In that case, we should have the spirit of the country and the approval of mankind on our side."[4]

Chase, perhaps second only to Seward among cabinet members in party standing, advised:

Sir, The following question was submitted to my consideration by our note of yesterday:

Assuming it to be possible to now provision Fort Sumter, under all the circumstances is it wise to attempt it?

I have given to this question all the reflection which the engrossing duties of this Department has allowed.

A correct solution must depend, in my judgment, on the degree of possibility; on the combination of reinforcement with provisioning; and on the probable effects of the measure upon the relations of the disaffected States to the National Government.

I shall assume, what the statements of the distinguished officers consulted seem to warrant, that the possibility of success amounts to a reasonable degree of probability; and, also, that the attempt to provision is to include an attempt to reinforce, for it seems to be generally agreed that provisioning without reinforcement, notwithstanding hostile resistance, will accomplish no substantially beneficial purpose.

The probable political effects of the measure allow room for much fair difference of opinion; and I have not reached my own conclusion without serious difficulty.

If the attempt will so inflame civil war as to involve an immediate necessity for the enlistment of armies and the expenditure of millions I cannot advise it, in the existing circumstances of the country and in the present condition of the National Finances.

But it seems to me highly improbable that the attempt, especially if accompanied or immediately followed by a Proclamation setting forth a liberal & generous yet firm policy towards the disaffected States, in harmony with the principles of the Inaugural Address, will produce such consequences; while it cannot be doubted that in maintaining a post belonging to the United States and in supporting the officers and men engaged, in the regular course of service, in its defence, the Federal Government exercises a clear right and under all ordinary circumstances, performs a plain duty. I return, therefore, an affirmative answer to the question submitted to me.[5]

Only Blair agreed with Chase that the president should proceed to provision Fort Sumter. The cabinet, in fact, stood five to two against the action. The five included the two war ministers, Cameron and Welles.

Meanwhile, Seward was surreptitiously meeting with Confederate representatives. Supreme Court Justice John A. Campbell, an Alabamian, was acting as an intermediary between Confederates and Seward. After conferences with Seward, on March 21 Campbell reported to Confederate commissioners:

> My confidence in the two facts stated in my note of 15th, to wit: that Fort Sumter is to be evacuated, and that provisions have been made for that purpose and will be completed without any delay or any disposition for delay, is unabated. 2d. That no prejudicial movement to the South is contemplated as respects Fort Pickens. I shall speak positively to-morrow afternoon.[6]

The next day he gained reassurance of his view. While cabinet members and Confederates talked, other voices also suggested conciliation as the best means to avoid all-out war. Stephen A. Douglas on March 15 urged the Senate to adopt a policy he described as "*The Restoration and Preservation of the Union* by such amendments to the Constitution as will insure the domestic tranquility, safety, and equality of all the States, and thus restore peace, unity, and fraternity, to the whole country." The *Washington Daily National Intelligencer* on March 21 declared:

> In view of the difficulties which surround an adjustment of the questions raised by the dismemberment of the Union, we have come to the conclusion that no authority less final and comprehensive than a General Convention of the States still remaining loyal to their Federal allegiance can be successfully invoked in the premises.[7]

On the night of March 28, following a state dinner in the Executive Mansion, Lincoln asked cabinet members to remain. He told them General Scott had recommended evacuation not only of Fort Sumter but also of Fort Pickens off the Florida coast, in the hope that withdrawal would effect recovery of the seceded states and retention of the unseceded slave states. Not only was Scott was proposing concession beyond Sumter; he was quite clearly mixing political with military advice.

At noon next day when the cabinet met it was clear that the mood had shifted. Chase, Welles, Blair, and Bates favored action, while Seward and Smith still favored evacuation of Fort Sumter; Cameron was apparently not present. That day Lincoln arranged for an expedition by sea to be ready as early as April 6. Before then he would encounter further hampering from Seward.

Supported by France, Spain had recently reacquired Santo Domingo. On April 1, April Fool's Day, still striving for supremacy in the administration, Seward presented an extraordinary memorandum to the president. He titled it "Some Thoughts for the President's Consideration":

First. We are at the end of a month's administration, and yet without a policy, either domestic or foreign.

Second. This, however, is not culpable, and it has even been unavoidable. The presence of the Senate, with the need to meet applications for patronage, have prevented attention to the other and more grave matters.

Third. But further delay to adopt and prosecute our policies for both domestic and foreign affairs would not only bring scandal on the Administration, but danger upon the country.

Fourth. To do this we must dismiss the applicants for office. But how? I suggest that we make the local appointments forthwith, leaving foreign or general ones for ulterior and occasional action.

Fifth. The policy at home. I am aware that my views are singular, and perhaps not sufficiently explained. My system is built upon this *idea* as a ruling one, namely, that we must

CHANGE THE QUESTION BEFORE THE PUBLIC FROM ONE UPON SLAVERY, or about slavery, for a question upon UNION OR DISUNION.

In other words, from what would be regarded as a party question, to one of *Patriotism or Union.*

The occupation or evacuation of Fort Sumter, although not in fact a slavery or party question, is so *regarded.* Witness the temper manifested by the Republicans in the free States, and even by the Union men in the South.

I would therefore terminate it as a safe means for changing the issue. I deem it fortunate that the last Administration created the necessity.

For the rest I would simultaneously defend and reenforce all the forts in the Gulf, and have the navy recalled from foreign stations to be prepared for a blockade. Put the island of Key West under martial law.

This will raise distinctly the question of *Union* or *Disunion*. I would maintain every fort and possession in the South.

FOR FOREIGN NATIONS.

I would demand explanations from Spain and France, categorically, at once.

I would seek explanations from Great Britain and Russia, and send agents into Canada, Mexico, and Central America, to rouse a vigorous continental spirit of independence on this continent against European intervention.

And, if satisfactory explanations are not received from Spain and France, Would convene Congress and declare war against them.

But whatever policy we adopt, there must be an energetic prosecution of it.

For this purpose it must be somebody's business to pursue and direct it incessantly.

Either the President must do it himself, and be all the while active in it, or

Devolve it on some member of his Cabinet. Once adopted, debates on it must end, and all agree and abide.

It is not in my especial province.

But I neither seek to evade nor assume responsibility.[8]

Without delay the president replied:

Since parting with you I have been considering your paper dated this day, and entitled "Some thoughts for the President's consideration." The first proposition in it is,

> *First,* We are at the end of a month's administration, and yet without a policy, either domestic or foreign.

At the beginning of that month, in the inaugural, I said, The power confided to me will be used to hold, occupy, and possess the property and places belonging to the Government, and to collect the duties and imposts.

This had your distinct approval at the time; and, taken in connection with the order I immediately gave General Scott, directing him to employ every means in his power to strengthen and hold the forts, comprises the exact domestic policy you now urge, with the single exception that it does not propose to abandon fort Sumter.

Again, I do not perceive how the reinforcement of Fort Sumter would be done on a slavery or party issue, while that of Fort Pickens would be on a more national and patriotic one.

The news received yesterday in regard to St. Domingo certainly brings a new item within the range of our foreign policy; but up to that time we have been preparing circulars and instructions to ministers and the like, all in perfect harmony, without even a suggestion that we had no foreign policy.

Upon your closing propositions, that whatever policy we adopt, there must be an energetic prosecution of it,

For this purpose it must be somebody's business to pursue and direct it incessantly,

Either the President must do it himself, and be all the while active in it, or

Devolve it on some member of his Cabinet. Once adopted, debates on it must end, and all agree and abide,

I remark that if this must be done, *I* must do it. When a general line of policy is adopted, I apprehend there is no danger of its being changed without good reason or continuing to be a subject of unnecessary debate; still, upon points arising in its progress I wish, and suppose I am entitled to have, the advice of all the Cabinet.[9]

Lincoln proceeded with his plans to retain Fort Sumter. He drafted a letter to Major Robert Anderson, commanding the fort, which carried Cameron's signature:

Your letter of the 1st inst. occasions some anxiety to the President.

On the information of Capt. Fox, he had supposed you could hold out till the 15th. inst. without any great inconvenience; and had prepared an expedition to relieve you before that period.

Hoping still that you will be able to sustain yourself till the 11th. or 12th. inst. the expedition will go forward; and, finding your flag flying, will attempt to provision you, and, in case the effort is resisted, will endeavor also to reinforce you.

You will therefore hold out if possible till the arrival of the expedition.

It is not, however, the intention of the President to subject your command to any danger or hardship beyond what, in your judgment, would be usual in military life; and he has entire confidence that you will act as becomes a patriot and a soldier, under all circumstances.

Whenever, if at all, in your judgment, to save yourself and command, a capitulation becomes a necessity, you are authorized to make it.[10]

Lincoln's decision to hold firm and repossess the forts grew ever clearer and more purposeful. Not surprisingly, the rankly partisan *New York Herald* on April 9 savagely attacked the Lincoln administration:

Nine out of ten of the people of the Northern and Central States repudiate the coercive policy which is hurrying the republic to destruction, and contemplate with terror and dismay the prospect before us. Oceans of blood and millions of treasure are about to be expended, in order to carry out, ostensibly, an impracticable theory, with no other conceivable end than to leave the country exhausted, impoverished and wretched. The *ultimo ratio* which Mr. Lincoln and his advisers have appealed to, will result, before the lapse of many months, in the overthrow of the prosperity which it has required over three-quarters of a century of industry and energy to create, and in exhausting the means which it has cost so much toil and labor to accumulate. The last act of the tragedy will be, either that the North and South, after having drained the land of its resources, burdened it with an immense debt, and expended the lives of tens of thousands of useful citizens, will find themselves compelled to negotiate a peace from the very same basis that exists at present; or that some Western Napoleon will bind the disunited fragments of the confederacy together under one common yoke; or else that petty generals will extend through the United States the direful scenes that have been witnessed through Mexico for over twenty-five years, and that utter anarchy will be the consequence of the collision which the republican party has so suicidally provoked.[11]

On April 12 the long suspense over peace or war ended when the Confederates opened fire on Fort Sumter. The *New York Times,* reporting that the Confederacy had opened fire, urged Lincoln to maintain the fort:

For no other offence than that of trying to relieve its soldiers from starvation, the batteries of the Southern Confederacy have opened upon the Government of the United States. The flag of the Republic is to be lowered in disgrace—or the issue of war is to be met.

The President of the United States must not hesitate an instant as to the policy he will pursue, nor must he spare anything of vigor and energy in the manner of putting it into execution. He has command of the Army and Navy of the United States, and has full power to summon the militia of the Republic, for the protection of the Government and in defence of the Constitution. He must instantly put forth every power at his command to maintain the authority which he represents. *Fort Sumter must not be surrendered, if there is force enough in the United States to hold it.* That point is the head of the rebellion, and it is precisely there that a stand must be made. The people of this country will feel humiliated and disgraced if that fort is ever surrendered to the traitors who have commenced the war by firing upon it. It must be reinforced at every hazard—and if the forces already sent thither are not sufficient for that purpose, they must be promptly followed by others.[12]

Responding the same day to a committee from the Virginia secession convention anxious about the president's policy toward the seceded states, Lincoln remarked: "I scarcely need to say that I consider the Military posts and property situated within the states, which claim to have seceded, as yet belonging to the Government of the United States, as much as they did before the supposed secession." The next day the fort, symbol of federal power and the Union, surrendered. On April 15, with the approval of his cabinet, Lincoln took the giant step of issuing a proclamation calling up 75,000 militia and convening Congress in special session. The proclamation read:

Whereas the laws of the United States have been for some time past, and now are opposed, and the execution thereof obstructed, in the States of South Carolina, Georgia, Alabama, Florida, Mississippi, Louisiana, and Texas, by combinations too powerful to be suppressed by the ordinary course of judicial proceedings, or by the powers vested in the Marshals by law,

Now, therefore, I, Abraham Lincoln, President of the United States, in virtue of the power in me vested by the Constitution, and the laws, have thought fit to call forth, and hereby do call forth, the militia of the several States of the Union, to aggregate number of seventy-five thousand, in order to suppress said combinations, and to cause the laws to be duly executed. The details, for this object, will be immediately communicated to the State authorities through the War Department.

I appeal to all loyal citizens to favor, facilitate and aid this effort to maintain the honor, the integrity, and the existence of our National Union, and the perpetuity of popular government; and to redress wrongs already long enough endured.

I deem it proper to say that the first service assigned to the forces hereby called forth will probably be to re-possess the forts, places, and property which have been seized from the Union; and in every event, the utmost care will be observed, consistently with the objects aforesaid, to avoid any devastation, any destruction of, or interference with, property, or any disturbance of peaceful citizens in any part of the country.

And I hereby command the persons composing the combinations aforesaid to disperse, and retire peaceably to their respective abodes within twenty days from this date.

Deeming that the present condition of public affairs presents an extraordinary occasion, I do hereby, in virtue of the power in me vested by the Constitution, convene both Houses of Congress. Senators and Representatives are therefore summoned to assemble at their respective chambers, at 12 o'clock, noon, on Thursday, the fourth day of July, next, then and there to consider and determine, such measures, as, in their wisdom, the public safety, and interest may seem to demand.[13]

Response from the free states was enthusiastic; indeed, the volunteers overwhelmed the number called and the nation's capacity to arm. The president of the University of Michigan, Henry Tappan, wrote:

My heart impels me at the risk of appearing impertinent to write you a few words. The heart of the great West—the heart of the entire North is with you in the defense of our beloved country. You cannot ask of us too much. We are ready to give ourselves and all that we have to this great work. The 700 young men committed to my charge are ready to march in a body if need be, & I am ready to march at their head. The country will give you 750,000 instead of 75000 if you ask it. Men and money without limit are at your disposal.

The long repressed enthusiasm breaks forth like a volcano. We are no longer democrats and Republicans—We are under one flag—the flag of our glorious Union. We feel that the stronger the demonstration, the more rapid the movement, the more mighty & decisive the action, the better. Let the traitors see, let the whole world see that we are strong enough to make our cause good, to preserve the integrity of the Union without the loss of a single inch of our domain. We are ready to blockade every Southern port, to protect Washington, to retake Sumpter, to scatter the enemy at Pensacola, to send an army to Texas, to send another down the Mississippi. Why should not five great armies of 100,000 each—move to the grand points and finish the work?

Honored President!

As if the God of our fathers spoke to me, I feel constrained to say that our God & our Country are with you in the mightiest effort you can make. The more we put forth our strength, the more united and stronger we would be. Thus, all true patriots will be stirred up to the highest zeal; all the vacillating will become decided; the timid will become strong; those who are looking for the strongest side will know where to go; the Union men in the Border States will dare to put their hand to the work; and the overawed patriots in the Seceding states will be called forth to speak and to act. I may add to that according to Napoleonic tactics one great battle won is worth a thousand skirmishes—

Pardon me this letter—my apology is that it gushes from my heart.

Without being accounted presumptuous may I not say these few words while I subscribe myself with sincere and profound respect and earnest love.[14]

Governors of yet unseceded slave states differed sharply from their northern counterparts in the way they responded to Lincoln's call for troops, the governor of North Carolina replying:

> Your dispatch is received, and, if genuine—which its extraordinary character leads me to doubt—I have to say in my reply that I regard the levy of troops made by the Administration, for the purpose of subjugating the States of the South, as in violation of the Constitution and a usurpation of power. I can be no party to this wicked violation of the laws of the country, and to this war upon the liberties of a free people. You can get no troops from North Carolina.[15]

Undeterred, Lincoln followed this levy on state militias with a series of proclamations of extraordinary character, all while Congress was not in session. Infringing on legislative authority, he justified his actions under a theory that the president held the "war power." He added men to the regular army and navy, blockaded the Confederate coast, entrusted (in effect appropriated) federal money to private citizens, and—notably, and to some persons notoriously—suspended the privilege of the writ of habeas corpus in certain places.

Lincoln's proclamation of May 3 calling for 42,034 volunteers to be added to the regular army and navy for a period of three years, unlike the ninety days of his call for militia, outraged Ohio congressman Clement L. Vallandigham. The spirited and eloquent states'-righter, who would be a thorn in Lincoln's flesh throughout the war, angrily addressed his constituents:

> Sir, the history of the world does not fail to condemn *the folly, weakness, and wickedness of that Government which drew its sword upon its own people when they demanded guarantees for their rights.* This cry, that we must have a Government, is merely following the example of the besotted Bourbon, who never learned anything by misfortune, never forgave an injury, never forgot an affront. Must we demonstrate that we have got a Government, and coerce obedience without reference to the justice or injustice of the complaints? Sir, whenever ten million people proclaim to you, with one unanimous voice, that they apprehend their rights, their firesides, and their family altars are in danger, it becomes a wise Government to listen to the appeal and to remove the apprehension. *History does not record an example where any human Government has been strong enough to crush ten millions of people into subjection when they believed their rights and liberties were imperiled, without first converting the Government itself into a despotism, and destroying the last vestige of freedom.* . . .
>
> Waiving the question of the doubtful legality of the first proclamation of April 15th, calling on the militia for "three months," under the Act of 1795, I will yet vote to pay them, because *they* had no motive but supposed duty and patriotism to move them; and, moreover, they will have rendered almost the entire service required of them before Congress shall meet. But the audacious usurpation of President Lincoln, for which he deserves impeachment, in daring, against the very letter of the Constitution, and without a shadow of law, to "raise and support armies," and to "provide and maintain a navy," for three or five years, by *mere executive proclamation,* I will not vote to sustain or ratify—NEVER! Millions for defence; not a dollar or a man for aggressive and offensive civil war. . . . A public debt of hundreds of millions weighing us and our posterity down for generations, we cannot escape. Fortunate shall we be if we escape with our liberties. Indeed, it is no longer so much a question of war with the South as whether we ourselves are to have constitutions and a republican form of government hereafter in the North and West.
>
> In brief: I am for the CONSTITUTION first, and at all hazards; for whatever can now be saved of the Union next; and for peace always as essential to the preservation of either. But whatever any one may think of the war, one thing at least every lover of liberty ought to demand inexorably: *that it shall be carried on strictly subject to the Constitution.*[16]

After rowdies in Baltimore assaulted Massachusetts troops marching from one railroad station to another and before the convening of the Maryland legislature suspected of being secessionist, Lincoln authorized General Winfield Scott "in the extremist necessity" to suspend the writ. The privilege of the writ, bringing a prisoner before a court and saying why he was arrested, was a time-honored defense against arbitrary government. Lincoln's policy of suspension, which continued throughout the war and was proclaimed without congressional approval, provoked controversy within and without the president's party.

On May 26 a Baltimore citizen, John Merryman, was arrested on various charges and imprisoned in a federal fort. He petitioned Chief Justice Roger B. Taney, acting as circuit court judge, for the writ, which Taney issued. But the federal marshal was not permitted to enter the prison gate to serve the writ. In the celebrated case of *Ex parte Merryman,* Taney wrote:

> The case, then, is simply this: A military officer residing in Pennsylvania issues an order to arrest a citizen of Maryland, upon vague and indefinite charges, without any proof, so far as appears. Under this order his house is entered in the night; he is seized as a prisoner, and conveyed to Fort McHenry, and there kept in close confinement. And when a *habeas corpus* is served on the commanding officer, requiring him to produce the prisoner before a Justice of the Supreme Court, in order that he may examine into the legality of the imprisonment, the answer of the officer is that he is authorized by the President to suspend the writ of *habeas corpus* at his discretion, and, in the exercise of that discretion, suspends it in this case, and on that ground refuses obedience to the writ.
>
> As the case comes before me, therefore, I understand that the President not only claims the right to suspend the writ of *habeas corpus* himself, at his discretion, but to delegate that discretionary power to a military officer, and to leave it to him to determine whether he will or will not obey judicial process that may be served upon him.
>
> No official notice has been given to the courts of justice, or to the public, by proclamation or otherwise, that the President claimed this power, and had exercised it with some surprise, for I had supposed it to be one of those points of constitutional law upon which there was no difference of opinion, and that it was admitted on all hands that the privilege of the writ could not be suspended except by an act of Congress. . . .

The clause in the Constitution which authorizes the suspension of the privilege of the writ of *habeas corpus* is in the ninth section of the first article.

This article is devoted to the Legislative Department of the United States, and has not the slightest reference to the Executive Department. . . .

It is the second article of the Constitution that provides for the organization of the Executive Department, and enumerates the powers conferred on it, and prescribes its duties. . . . But there is not a word in it that can furnish the slightest ground to justify the exercise of the power. . . .

The Constitution expressly provides . . . that "no person shall be deprived of life, liberty, or property, without due process of law." It declares that

the right of the people to be secure in their persons, houses, papers, and effects against unreasonable searches and seizures shall not be violated, and no warrant shall issue but upon probable cause, supported by oath or affirmation, and particularly describing the place to be searched and the persons or things to be seized.

It provides that the party accused shall be entitled to a speedy trial in a court of justice.

And these great and fundamental laws, which Congress itself could not suspend, have been disregarded and suspended, like the writ of *habeas corpus,* by a military order, supported by force of arms. Such is the case now before me; and I can only say that if the authority which the Constitution has confided to the judiciary department and judicial officers may thus upon any pretext or under any circumstances be usurped by the military power at its discretion, the people of the United States are no longer living under a Government of laws, but every citizen holds life, liberty, and property at the will and pleasure of the army officer in whose military district he may happen to be found.

In such a case my duty was too plain to be mistaken. I have exercised all the power which the Constitution and laws confer on me, but that power has been resisted by a force too strong for me to overcome. It is possible that the officer who had incurred this grave responsibility may have misunderstood his instructions, and exceeded the authority intended to be given him. I shall, therefore, order all the proceedings in this case, with my opinion, to be filed and recorded in the Circuit Court of the United States for the District of Maryland, and direct the clerk to transmit a copy, under seal, to the President of the United States. It will then remain for that high officer, in fulfillment of his constitutional obligation to "take care that the laws will be faithfully executed," to determine what measures he will take to cause the civil process of the United States to be respected and enforced.[17]

To the Court's severe language Lincoln made no immediate reply. Instead he cleverly called upon an eminent Baltimore lawyer and former attorney general of the United States to respond. Taney's fellow Marylander Reverdy Johnson, a political moderate, stoutly supported the president's action:

> Several States of the Union having renounced their allegiance and that of their citizens to the Government of the United States, and asserted their right to do so, and organized a Government of their own, were in arms to maintain the rebellion. The laws of the United States were forcibly resisted; their officers, either voluntarily or through violence, were abandoning their duty and resigning their commissions, and a determination announced by the rebels to continue the rebellion until its success was achieved, and the usurped Government recognized by that of the United States. In this treasonable effort it was believed that there were misguided citizens in Maryland and elsewhere, whose States were yet loyal, who participated in the treason, aided it secretly, and designed to involve their States in the rebellion. In this state of things the President, under his sworn duty to "take care that the laws be faithfully executed," . . . [t]herefore decided, as he was bound to do, "to call forth" such of the militia as he deemed necessary to suppress the combination, and to employ to the same end the land and naval forces of the United States. Of his duty to see to the execution of the laws he could have had no doubt, as that is in words imposed by the Constitution itself. Nor could he have had any doubt of his authority and obligation to resort for that purpose to the powers conferred on him by the laws referred to. The meaning of these laws is free from all question, and the constitutionality of the first was long since sanctioned by a unanimous decision of the Supreme Court in the case of Martin and Mott, 12 Wheat. 19, whilst the validity of the last was never drawn into doubt. In that case it was also decided that the President was the sole judge of the facts which would authorize his use of the means provided by these laws, and that his decision was conclusive not only upon the citizens, but upon every branch of the Government, whether Federal or State. In the language of the Court, "the authority to decide whether the exigency has arisen belongs exclusively to the President, and that his decision is conclusive upon all other persons." . . .
>
> A state of quasi war exists. The President, under the authority of Congress, the war power, is in the field to put down the rebellion, aimed, avowedly, at the very existence of the Government. States and their people are in arms, with the declared design to wage the war until that object, the destruction of the Government, is accomplished. In this state of things what are the

powers and the duty of the President? His sworn obligation is to suppress the rebellion, in order "that the laws be faithfully executed." In the use of the force placed by Congress under his command as the Constitutional commander-in-chief, has he not all powers directly or indirectly belonging to a state of war, and necessary to accomplish its end? . . .

The paper has been made the more elaborate because of the justly high character of the Chief-Justice of the United States, and because of a desire to satisfy the judgment of the people of the country upon the point in issue between that functionary and the President; a people whom the President is faithfully serving with all the ability he possesses in this crisis of their Government, and whom he hopes to be able, when he retires from the elevated office in which their confidence has placed him, to leave in the peaceful and happy enjoyment of an unbroken Union, and the undisturbed and faithful execution of the laws.[18]

The *New York Herald,* a Democratic paper that during the war would heap criticism on the president, supported waging war to sustain the national government and predicted that Wall Street would find the money necessary to win the war.

On one point, so far as we have been able to ascertain, perfect unanimity exists among our moneyed men—the Government must be sustained. Every one deplores the terrible calamity which has befallen the Republic. But there is no desire among the merchants or capitalists of New York to shirk the issue, or to evade the responsibilities of the contest. Upon New York will devolve the chief burden of providing ways and means for the war; our financial community accept the duty, and will perform it. This view we find to be universal among moneyed men, including many whose sympathies have heretofore been with the South. If the Government prove true to the country, it need not feel any uneasiness about money. . . . If for the purpose of bringing the war to an end, and settling this controversy of ours forever, a further sum be requisite, it will be forthcoming. Wall street, so far as we can judge, is ready to sustain the Government heartily and liberally.[19]

Nationalism burst forth from other sources across the North. Poet Phoebe Cary, described as one of "the eminent women of the age," wrote "Voice of the Northern Women," lyrically proclaiming their loyalty to the Union cause:

Rouse, freemen, the foe has arisen,
    His hosts are abroad on the plain;
And, under the stars of your banner,
    Swear never to strike again!

O, fathers, who sit with your children,
    Would you leave them a land that is free?
Turn now from their tender caresses,
    And put them away from your knee.

O, brothers, we played with in childhood,
    On hills where the clover bloomed sweet;
See to it, that never a traitor
    Shall trample them under his feet.

O, lovers, awake to your duty
    From visions that fancy has nursed;
Look not in the eyes that would keep you;
    Our country has need of you first.

And we, whom your lives have made blessed,
    Will pray for your souls in the fight;
That you may be strong to do battle
    For Freedom, for God, and the Right

We are daughters of men who were heroes;
    We can smile as we bid you depart;
But never a coward or traitor
    Shall have room for a place in our heart.

Then quit you like men in conflict,
    Who fight for their home and their land;
Smite deep, in the name of Jehovah,
    And conquer, or die where you stand.[20]

Events of March and early April had impelled the president to take vigorous action in fulfillment of his oath of office. He had received conflicting advice from the sage and experienced senior general Scott, and from his cabinet advisors, and he had weathered a reach for power from his most prominent advisor. All this turbulence complicated Lincoln's coming to a decision. But the Confederate attack on the federal fort brought on war.

In his handling of the intricate Sumter crisis, Lincoln had gone a long way in establishing himself as leader of his party, over Seward; as president, over Buchanan's acquiescence in secession; and as commander in chief, over Scott.

CHAPTER EIGHT

THE FIRST CIVIL
WAR CONGRESS

Lincoln faced a political backlash over his actions while Congress was not in session. No act was more controversial than his suspension of the writ of habeas corpus, even though he had done so in a limited fashion, only along the railroad "military line" between Philadelphia and Washington. On the Fourth of July—a significant date designated by Lincoln for convening a special session of Congress—lawmakers gathered in the unfinished Capitol building, symbolic of an incomplete nation. Shrunken in numbers by the secession of eleven states, the Senate was composed of 31 Republicans, 10 Democrats, and 8 Unionists. The House of Representatives held 105 Republicans, 43 Democrats, and 30 Unionists. Secessionists had given the infant Republican Party control of the Congress.

The newly fledged Republican president had carefully prepared his message to Congress. The night before Congress met Lincoln read it aloud to his friend Orville Hickman Browning, successor in the Senate to the recently deceased Stephen A. Douglas. Browning, an inveterate diarist, observed: "It is a most admirable history of our present difficulties, and a conclusive and unanswerable argument against the abominable heresy of secession. It is an able state paper and will fully meet the expectations of the Country."[1]

In his message Lincoln described the condition confronting him when he took office. He went on to explain his action on Fort Sumter, his call to arms and responses to it, and other executive measures. He branded secession as "an ingenious sophism," and laid out his concept of nationalism and his purpose. In the course of his state message he claimed, astoundingly, that he had done "nothing beyond the constitutional competence of Congress." A long defense of his suspension of the privilege of habeas corpus was followed by an appeal to maintaining the guarantee clause of the Constitution assuring every state of a republican form of government. Very significantly for the past as well as the future of the presidency, he claimed his duty was to exercise the war power of the executive:

Fellow-citizens of the Senate and House of Representatives:

Having been convened on an extraordinary occasion, as authorized by the Constitution, your attention is not called to any ordinary subject of legislation.

At the beginning of the present Presidential term, four months ago, the functions of the Federal Government were found to be generally suspended within the several States of South Carolina, Georgia, Alabama, Mississippi, Louisiana, and Florida, excepting only those of the Post Office Department.

Within these States, all the Forts, Arsenals, Dock-yards, Customhouses, and the like, including the movable and stationary property in, and about them, had been seized, and were held in open hostility to this Government, excepting only Forts Pickens, Taylor, and Jefferson, on, and near the Florida coast, and Fort Sumter, in Charleston harbor, South Carolina. The Forts thus seized had been put in improved condition; new ones had been built; and armed forces had been organized, and were organizing, all avowedly with the same hostile purpose.

The Forts remaining in the possession of the Federal government, in, and near, these States, were either besieged or menaced by warlike preparations; and especially Fort Sumter was nearly surrounded by well-protected hostile batteries, with guns equal in quality to the best of its own, and outnumbering the latter as perhaps ten to one. . . .

Finding this condition of things, and believing it to be an imperative duty upon the incoming Executive, to prevent, if possible, the consummation of such attempt to destroy the Federal Union, a choice of means to that end became indispensable. This choice was made; and was declared in the Inaugural address. The policy chosen looked to the exhaustion of all peaceful measures, before a resort to any stronger ones. It sought only to hold the public places and property, not already wrested from the Government, and to collect the revenue; relying for the rest, on time, discussion, and the ballot-box. It promised a continuance of the mails, at government expense, to the very people who were resisting the government; and it gave repeated pledges against any disturbance to any of the people, or any of their rights. Of all that which a president might constitutionally, and justifiably, do in such a case, everything was foreborne, without which, it was believed possible to keep the government on foot.

On the 5th of March, (the present incumbent's first full day in office) a letter of Major Anderson, commanding at Fort Sumter, written on the 28th of February, and received at the War Department on the 4th of March, was, by that Department, placed in his hands. This letter expressed the professional opinion of the writer, that re-inforcements could not be thrown into that Fort within the time for his relief, rendered necessary by the limited supply of provisions, and with a view of holding possession of the same, with a force of less than twenty thousand good, and well-disciplined men. This opinion was concurred in by all the officers of his command; and their *memoranda* on the subject, were made enclosures of Major Anderson's letter. The whole was immediately laid before Lieutenant General Scott who at once concurred with Major Anderson in opinion. . . .

It was believed, however, that to so abandon that position, under the circumstances, would be utterly ruinous; that the *necessity* under which it was to be done, would not be fully understood—that, by many, it would be construed as a part of a *voluntary* policy—that, at home, it would discourage the friends of the Union, embolden its adversaries, and go far to insure to the latter, a recognition abroad—that, in fact, it would be our national destruction consummated. This could not be allowed. Starvation was not yet upon the garrison; and ere it would be reached, *Fort Pickens* might be reinforced. This last, would be a clear indication of *policy,* and would better enable the country to accept the evacuation of Fort Sumter, as a military *necessity.* An order was at once directed to be sent for the landing of the troops from the Steamship Brooklyn, into Fort Pickens. . . . [T]he officer commanding the Sabine, to which vessel the troops had been transferred from the Brooklyn, . . . had refused to land the troops. To now re-inforce Fort Pickens, before a crisis would be reached at Fort Sumter was impossible— rendered so by the near exhaustion of provisions in the latter-named Fort. In precaution against such a conjuncture, the government had, a few days before, commenced preparing an expedition, as well adapted as might be, to relieve Fort Sumter, which expedition was intended to be ultimately used, or not, according to circumstances. The strongest anticipated case, for using it, was now presented; and it was resolved to send it forward. As had been intended, in this contingency, it was also resolved to notify the Governor of South Carolina, that he might expect an attempt would be made to provision the Fort; and that, if the attempt should not be resisted, there would be no effort to throw in men, arms, or ammunition, without further notice, or in case of an attack upon the Fort. This notice was accordingly given; whereupon the Fort was attacked, and bombarded to its fall, without even awaiting the arrival of the provisioning expedition.

It is thus seen that the assault upon, and reduction of, Fort Sumter, was, in no sense, a matter of self defence on the part of the assailants. They well knew that the garrison in the Fort could, by no possibility, commit aggression upon them. They knew—they were expressly notified—that the giving of bread to the few brave and hungry men of the garrison, was all which would on that occasion be attempted, unless themselves, by resisting so much, should provoke more. They knew that this Government desired to keep the garrison in the Fort, not to assail them, but merely to maintain visible possession, and thus to preserve the Union from actual, and immediate dissolution—trusting, as herein-before stated, to time, discussion, and the ballot-box, for final adjustment; and they assailed, and reduced the Fort, for precisely the reverse object—to drive out the visible authority of the Federal Union, and thus force it to immediate dissolution.

That this was their object, the Executive well understood; and having said to them in the inaugural address, "You can have no conflict without being yourselves the aggressors," he took pains, not only to keep this declaration good, but also to keep the case so free from the power of ingenious sophistry, as that the world should not be able to misunderstand it. By the affair at Fort Sumter, with its surrounding circumstances, that point was reached. Then, and thereby, the assailants of the Government, began the conflict of arms, without a gun in sight, or in expectancy, to return their fire, save only the few in the Fort, sent to that harbor, years before, for their own protection, and still ready to give that protection, in whatever was lawful. In this act, discarding all else, they have forced upon the country, the distinct issue: "Immediate dissolution, or blood."

And this issue embraces more than the fate of these United States. It presents to the whole family of man, the question, whether a constitutional republic, or a democracy—a government of the people, by the same people—can, or cannot, maintain its territorial integrity, against its own domestic foes. It presents the question, whether discontented individuals, too few in numbers to control administration, according to organic law, in any case, can always, upon the pretences made in this case, or on any other pretences, or arbitrarily, without any pretence, break up their Government, and thus practically put an end to free government upon the earth. It forces us to ask: "Is there, in all republics, this inherent, and fatal weakness?" "Must a government, of necessity, be too *strong* for the liberties of its own people, or too *weak* to maintain its own existence?"

So viewing the issue, no choice was left but to call out the war power of the Government; and so to resist force, employed for its destruction, by force, for its preservation.

The call was made; and the response of the country was most gratifying; surpassing, in unanimity and spirit, the most sanguine expectation. Yet none of the States commonly called Slave States, except Delaware, gave a Regiment through regular State organization. . . .

Recurring to the action of the government, it may be stated that, at first, a call was made for seventy-five thousand militia; and rapidly following this, a proclamation was issued for closing the ports of the insurrectionary districts by proceedings in the nature of Blockade. So far all was believed to be strictly legal. At this point the insurrectionists announced their purpose to enter upon the practice of privateering.

Other calls were made for volunteers, to serve three years, unless sooner discharged; and also for large additions to the regular Army and Navy. These measures, whether strictly legal or not, were ventured upon, under what appeared to be a popular demand, and a public necessity; trusting, then as now, that Congress would readily ratify them. It is believed that nothing has been done beyond the constitutional competency of Congress.

Soon after the first call for militia, it was considered a duty to authorize the Commanding General, in proper cases, according to his discretion, to suspend the privilege of the writ of habeas corpus; or, in other words, to arrest, and detain, without resort to the ordinary processes and forms of law, such individuals as he might deem dangerous to the public safety. This authority has purposely been exercised but very sparingly. Nevertheless, the legality and propriety of what has been done under it, are questioned; and the attention of the country has been called to the proposition that one who is sworn to "take care that the laws be faithfully executed," should not himself violate them. Of course some consideration was given to the questions of power, and propriety, before this matter was acted upon. The whole of the laws which were required to be faithfully executed, were being resisted, and failing of execution, in nearly one-third of the States. Must they be allowed to finally fail of execution, even had it been perfectly clear, that by the use of the means necessary to their execution, some single law, made in such extreme tenderness of the citizen's liberty, that practically, it relieves more of the guilty, than of the innocent, should, to a very limited extent, be violated? To state the question more directly, are all the laws, *but one,* to go unexecuted, and the government itself go to pieces, lest that one be violated? Even in such a case, would not the official oath be broken, if the government should be overthrown, when it was believed that disregarding the single law, would tend to preserve it? But it was not believed that this question was presented. It was not believed that any law was violated. The provision of the Constitution that "The privilege of the writ of habeas corpus, shall not be suspended unless when, in cases of rebellion or invasion, the public safety may require it," is equivalent to a provision—is a provision—that such privilege may be suspended when, in cases of rebellion, or invasion, the public safety does require it. It was decided that we have a case of rebellion, and that the public safety does require the qualified suspension of the privilege of the writ which was authorized to be made. Now it is insisted that Congress, and not the Executive, is vested with this power. But the Constitution itself, is silent as to which, or who, is to exercise the power; and as the provision was plainly made for a dangerous emergency, it cannot be believed the framers of the instrument intended, that in every case, the danger should run its course, until Congress could be called together; the very assembling of which might be prevented, as was intended in this case, by the rebellion. . . .

It is now recommended that you give the legal means for making this contest a short, and a decisive one; that you place at the control of the government, for the work, at least four hundred thousand men, and four hundred millions of dollars. That number of men is about one tenth of those of proper ages within the regions where, apparently, all are willing to engage; and the sum is less than a twentythird part of the money value owned by the men who seem ready to devote the whole. A debt of six hundred millions of dollars *now,* is a less sum per head, than was the debt of our revolution, when we came out of that struggle; and the money value in the country now, bears even a greater proportion to what it was *then,* than does the population. Surely each man has as strong a motive *now,* to *preserve* our liberties, as each had *then,* to *establish* them.

A right result, at this time, will be worth more to the world, then ten times the men, and ten times the money. The evidence reaching us from the country, leaves no doubt, that the material for the work is abundant; and that it needs only the hand of legislation to give it legal sanction, and the hand of the Executive to give it practical shape and efficiency. One of the greatest perplexities of the government, is to avoid receiving troops faster than it can provide for them. In a word, the people will save their government, if the government itself, will do its part, only indifferently well.

It might seem, at first thought, to be of little difference whether the present movement at the South be called "secession" or "rebellion." The movers, however, well understand the difference. At the beginning, they knew they could never raise their treason to any respectable magnitude, by any name which implies *violation* of law. They knew their people possessed as much of moral sense, as much of devotion to law and order, and as much pride in, and reverence for, the history, and government, of their common country, as any other civilized, and patriotic people. They knew they could make no advancement directly in the teeth of these strong and noble sentiments. Accordingly they commenced by an insidious debauching of the public mind. They invented an ingenious sophism, which, if conceded, was followed by perfectly logical steps, through all the incidents, to the complete destruction of the Union. The sophism itself is, that any state of the Union may, *consistently* with the national Constitution, and therefore *lawfully,* and *peacefully,* withdraw from the Union, without the consent of the Union, or of any other state. The little disguise that the supposed right is to be exercised only for just cause, themselves to be the sole judge of its justice, is too thin to merit any notice....

Unquestionably the States have the powers, and rights, reserved to them in, and by the National Constitution; but among these, surely, are not included all conceivable powers, however mischievous, or destructive, but, at most, such only, as were known in the world, at the time, as governmental powers; and certainly, a power to destroy the government itself, had never been known as a governmental—as a merely administrative power. This relative matter of National power, and State rights, as a principle, is no other than the principle of *generality,* and *locality.* Whatever concerns the whole, should be confided to the whole—to the general government; while, whatever concerns *only* the State, should be left exclusively, to the State. This is all there is of original principle about it. Whether the National Constitution, in defining boundaries between the two, has applied the principle with exact accuracy, is not to be questioned. We are all bound by that defining, without question.

What is now combated, is the position that secession is *consistent* with the Constitution—is *lawful,* and *peaceful.* It is not contended that there is any express law for it; and nothing should ever be implied as law, which leads to unjust, or absurd consequences....

It may be affirmed, without extravagance, that the free institutions we enjoy, have developed the powers, and improved the condition, of our whole people, beyond any example in the world. Of this we now have a striking, and an impressive illustration. So large an army as the government has now on foot, was never before known, without a soldier in it, but who had taken his place there, of his own free choice. . . .

This is essentially a People's contest. On the side of the Union, it is a struggle for maintaining in the world, that form, and substance of government, whose leading object is, to elevate the condition of men—to lift artificial weights from all shoulders—to clear the paths of laudable pursuit for all—to afford all, an unfettered start, and a fair chance, in the race of life. Yielding to partial, and temporary departures, from necessity, this is the leading object of the government for whose existence we contend. . . .

Great honor is due to those officers who remain true, despite the example of their treacherous associates; but the greatest honor, and most important fact of all, is the unanimous firmness of the common soldiers, and common sailors. To the last man, so far as known, they have successfully resisted the traitorous efforts of those, whose commands, but an hour before, they obeyed as absolute law. This is the patriotic instinct of the plain people. They understand, without an argument, that destroying the government, which was made by Washington, means no good to them.

Our popular government has often been called an experiment. Two points in it, our people have already settled—the successful *establishing,* and the successful *administering* of it. One still remains—its successful *maintenance* against a formidable [internal] attempt to overthrow it. It is now for them to demonstrate to the world, that those who can fairly carry an election, can also suppress a rebellion—that ballots are the rightful, and peaceful, successors of bullets; and that when ballots have fairly, and constitutionally, decided, there can be no successful appeal, back to bullets; that there can be no successful appeal, except to ballots themselves, at succeeding elections. Such will be a great lesson of peace; teaching men that what they cannot take by an election, neither can they take it by a war—teaching all, the folly of being the beginners of a war.

Lest there be some uneasiness in the minds of candid men, as to what is to be the course of the government, towards the Southern States, *after* the rebellion shall have been suppressed, the Executive deems it proper to say, it will be his purpose then, as ever to be guided by the Constitution, and the laws; and that he probably will have no different understanding of the powers, and duties of the Federal government, relatively to the rights of the States, and the people, under the Constitution, than that expressed in the inaugural address.

He desires to preserve the government, that it may be administered for all, as it was administered by the men who made it. Loyal citizens everywhere, have the right to claim this of their government; and the government has no right to withhold, or neglect it. It is not perceived that, in giving it, there is any coercion, any conquest, or any subjugation, in any just sense of those terms.

The Constitution provides, and all the States have accepted the provision, that "The United States shall guarantee to every State in this Union a republican form of government." But, if a State may lawfully go out of the Union, having done so, it may also discard the republican form of government; so that to prevent its going out, is an indispensable *means,* to the *end,* of maintaining the guaranty mentioned; and when an end is lawful and obligatory, the indispensable means to it, are also lawful, and obligatory.

It was with the deepest regret that the Executive found the duty of employing the war-power, in defence of the government, forced upon him. He could but perform this duty, or surrender the existence of the government. No compromise, by public servants, could, in this case, be a cure; not that compromises are not often proper, but that no popular government can long survive a marked precedent, that those who carry an election, can only save the government from immediate destruction, by giving up the main point, upon which the people gave the election. The people themselves, and not their servants, can safely reverse their own deliberate decisions. As a private citizen, the Executive could not have consented that these institutions shall perish; much less could he, in betrayal of so vast, and so sacred a trust, as these free people had confided to him. He felt that he had no moral right to shrink; nor even to count the chances of his own life, in what might follow. In full view of his great responsibility, he has, so far, done what he has deemed his duty. You will now, according to your own judgment, perform yours. He sincerely hopes that your views, and your action, may so accord with his, as to assure all faithful citizens, who have been disturbed in their rights, of a certain, and speedy restoration to them, under the Constitution, and the laws.

And having thus chosen our course, without guile, and with pure purpose, let us renew our trust in God, and go forward without fear, and with manly hearts.[2]

Against the backdrop of a war begun under the maneuvers of a new, untried president, and with ports blockaded, habeas corpus suspended, money appropriated, and the regular army and navy increased, what would the Congress do? The Constitution gave the legislators authority over these matters. For eighty days the president alone had run the war without Congress in session.

The special session, which lasted just over one month, accomplished much. Restricting itself to war matters, it gave the president more men than he requested and allowed enlistment for three years, unlike the ninety-day limit in the old militia law. It made provision for financing the war and authorized the president by proclamation to close rebel ports.

Six days after the session began Senator Henry Wilson of Massachusetts, once a cobbler and now chairman of the Senate's Committee on Military Affairs, introduced a joint resolution to approve the acts of the president, hoping to smooth over the matter of Lincoln's "extraordinary acts":

Whereas, since the adjournment of Congress, on the 4th day of March last, a formidable insurrection in certain States of the Union has arrayed itself in armed hostility to the Government of the United States, constitutionally administered; and whereas the President of the United States did, under the extraordinary exigencies thus presented, exercise certain powers and adopt certain measures for the preservation of this Government—that is to say: First. He did, on the 15th day of April last, issue his proclamation calling upon the several States for seventy-five thousand men to suppress such insurrectionary combinations, and to cause the laws to be faithfully executed. Secondly. He did, on the 19th day of April last, issue a proclamation setting on foot a blockade of ports within the States of South Carolina, Georgia, Alabama, Florida, Mississippi, Louisiana, and Texas. Thirdly. He did, on the 17th day of April last, issue a proclamation establishing a blockade of the ports within the States of Virginia and North Carolina. Fourthly. He did, by the order of the 27th day of April last, addressed to the Commanding General of the Army of the United States, authorize that officer to suspend the writ of *habeas corpus* at any point on or in the vicinity of any military line between the city of Philadelphia and the city of Washington. Fifthly. He did on the 3d day of May last, issue a proclamation calling into the service of the United States forty-two thousand and thirty-four volunteers, increasing the regular Army by the addition of twenty-two thousand seven hundred and fourteen men, and the Navy by an addition of eighteen thousand seamen. Sixthly. He did, on the 10th day of May last, issue a proclamation authorizing the commander of the forces of the United States on the coast of Florida to suspend the writ of *habeas corpus,* if necessary. All of which proclamations and orders have been submitted to Congress. Now, therefore,

Be it resolved by the Senate and the House of Representatives of the United States of America in Congress assembled, That all of the extraordinary acts, proclamations, and orders, hereinbefore mentioned, be, and the same are hereby, approved and declared to be in all respects legal and valid, to the same intent, and with the same effect, as if they had been issued and done under the previous express authority and direction of the Congress of the United States.[3]

The rub came, however, over executive suspension of habeas corpus—an act many considered an open road to dictatorship. Republicans as well as Democrats were concerned.

Senator Edward Baker was an early defender of the president. He was a close friend of Lincoln, so close in fact that Lincoln had named his son Eddie for the brilliant English-born orator, lawyer, and soldier. Baker on July 10 told the Senate:

Mr. President, as a member of the Military Committee, agreeing heartily in the reports of its chairman of the bills now upon your table, I deem it proper to seize this early opportunity to state the principles by which I propose to be governed during what I hope will be this very short session of the Senate.

I approve, as a personal and political friend of the President, of every measure of his administration in relation to the rebellion at present raging in this country. I propose to ratify whatever needs ratification. I propose to render my clear and distinct approval not only of the measure, but of the motive which prompted it. I propose to lend the whole power of the country, arms, men, money, and place them in his hands, with authority almost unlimited, until the conclusion of this struggle. He has asked for $400,000,000. We propose to give him $500,000,000. He has asked for four hundred thousand men. We propose to give him half a million; and for my part, if, as I do not apprehend, the emergency should be still greater, I will cheerfully add a cipher to either of these figures.

But, sir, while I do that, I desire, by my word and by my vote, to have it clearly understood that I do that as a measure of war. As I had occasion to say, in a very early discussion of this question, I want sudden, bold, forward, determined war; and I do not think anybody can conduct war of that kind as well as a dictator. . . .

My honored friend from Maine (Mr. FESSENDEN) will bear me witness that I was perhaps the last man in the Senate to give up the hope that something might be done by conciliation and compromise—words I never propose to use again. I hoped, I sympathized, I struggled to the last. Now I hope to be among the last of all men willing to lay down arms at all. I will never vote to do it till, without treaty, the flag of the United States waves over every portion of its territory, and over a population either enthusiastically rallying beneath its shadow, or else abjectly subject to its sway. Till then, give the President a million men; till then, give him, not only the whole revenue of the Government, but the whole property of the people; do not refuse a single regiment; do not furl a single sail; do not abate a single jot of all your embattled vigor, till that hour shall come; but when peace returns, resume the condition and the arts of peace. Do not make peace until the glory of the American flag shall be its own defense.[4]

Later in the session, after the First Battle of Bull Run, appearing in uniform and absenting himself from the troops he was commanding, Baker made a celebrated reply to Senator John Breckinridge of Kentucky, who suggested that Union could not continue and the war effort was doomed. Breckinridge, until March vice president of the United States, rose to condemn Lincoln on August 1:

The Constitution declares that Congress alone shall have power "to declare war." The President has made war. Congress alone shall have power "to raise and support armies." The President has raised and supported armies on his own authority. Congress shall have power "to provide and maintain a navy." The President has provided an immense Navy, and maintains it without authority of law. The Constitution declares that no money shall be taken from the Treasury except in pursuance of appropriations made by law. The President has taken money from the Treasury without appropriations made by law for the purpose of carrying out the preceding unconstitutional acts. . . .

The Executive of the United States has assumed judicial powers. The executive power belongs to him by the Constitution. He has, therefore, concentrated in his own hands executive, legislative, and judicial powers, which, in every age of the world, has been the very definition of despotism, and exercises them today, while we sit in the Senate Chamber, and the other branch of the legislative authority at the other end of the Capitol. . . .

[Mr. Baker] is a constitutional lawyer; he knows what the Constitution of his country is—no man better. He declared, in the presence of the Senate and the country, that he meant direct war, and that for that purpose nothing was so good as a dictator; he therefore was for conferring upon the President of the United States almost unlimited powers. I give his words. Nobody so good as a dictator to conduct this sort of war we were in, and of which he is in favor! Is anything necessary more than to state this to show that, at least so far as that Senator is concerned, he proposes to conduct it without regard to the Constitution? I heard no rebuke administered to that eminent gentleman. Upon the contrary, I saw warm congratulations from more than one Senator, apparently upon the sentiments and the character of the address.[5]

As Breckinridge spoke, Baker entered the chamber in his blue uniform, placed his sword on his Senate desk, and took his seat. When Breckinridge finished, Baker stood and in a dramatic speech castigated Breckinridge's remarks as "words of brilliant, polished treason." On October 22 Baker was killed in action at the Battle of Ball's Bluff; on December 4 Breckinridge was expelled from the Senate; since November he had vacated his seat and joined the Confederate Army.

In the House William Steele Holman of Indiana, a states'-righter turned War Democrat, responded to a denunciatory speech by Peace Democrat Clement Vallandigham, who had accused the president of "a glaring usurpation of power." Holman declared:

> I am not here, sir, to defend the Administration or to assault it. The time will come when its measures of policy will be dispassionately considered, and scrutinized as a people of their freedom will ever scrutinize the acts of their public servants. But, while an enemy almost threatens your capital, and the ear that listens to your deliberations can almost hear the thunder of his artillery, and the eye, as it glances westward, from the very portals of this Hall, can almost see the light flash from his bayonets, and liberty itself is in danger, the public safety may well demand the undivided wisdom and energy of Congress, while patriotism silences the clamor of the party strife.
>
> When the patriotic masses—who know better than philosophers or statesmen have ever known, that every interest that clusters around the firesides of freemen is involved in this effort to maintain the Union—are rallying in countless numbers to the flag of the Republic, the type and symbol of Union and liberty, and ready to pour out their blood in torrents in its defense, they may well demand that their Representatives shall not, by dividing the public councils, sharpen the bayonet that would strike them

down. I have said, sir, that I am not here to defend the Administration; I am no champion of its cause; I had no part or lot in its triumph; I resisted, as an American citizen might resist, its elevation to power; I do not indorse one principle of its original policy. But, sir, so help me God, I will not desert my country or give encouragement to its enemies, because the judgment of the people has been pronounced against the principles I have cherished. I will not desert the old ship because I do not approve of the helmsman. And, sir, when, for any cause or from any provocation, bitter and unjust it may be, I shall fail or forget to defend the flag of my country against its enemies at home or abroad, in the language of the old Hebrew king, "May my right hand forget its cunning."

But in defense of the public policy, I will say, sir, that if the President had abandoned Fort Sumter on the insolent demand of the public enemy, except as the result of an absolute physical necessity; had he surrendered the forts on the coasts of Florida, erected by the whole nation for the protection of the national commerce, to the men who, in the insolence and madness of ambition, had forgotten gratitude and public faith, I tell you, sir, the fiery wrath of the people, whose trust he would have betrayed, would have driven him with irresistible fury from your capital.

Sir, the gentleman from Kentucky, (Mr. BURNETT,) and especially the gentleman from Ohio, (Mr. VALLANDIGHAM,) who addressed the House with so much ability a few days since, misapprehended the spirit which pervaded the country prior to the 12th of April. The people acquiesce in the breaking to pieces of the Union! The eye of the gentleman from Ohio did not pierce beyond the surface. He misconceived the spirit of the popular forbearance. The people consent to disunion!"[6]

As debate continued until almost the close of the session, Senator John Sherman, brother of the general and at an early stage of a long, distinguished political life, offered a striking view:

Mr. President, it was my purpose quietly to vote against this resolution [Joint resolution to approve and confirm certain acts of the President of the United States for suppressing insurrection and rebellion] without expressing any opinion about it; but the attitude in which the question is now presented makes it necessary for me to submit simply the results of my judgment, made without passion or prejudice.

The first three acts enumerated in the preamble of this resolution, I would vote heartily to approve. I believe they were right and proper—strictly legal, and strictly constitutional. I believe that the President had the right, and that it was his duty, to issue the proclamation of April last. I believe he had a right, it was a part of the power of suppressing an insurrection, to blockade the ports of the United States, or any of them. I do not believe the President of the United States has the power to suspend the writ of *habeas corpus,* because that power is expressly given to Congress, and to Congress alone. I do not believe the President of the United States has the power to increase the regular Army, because that power is expressly given by the Constitution to Congress alone; and therefore I cannot vote for either of the last three propositions—the fourth, the fifth, or the sixth. Still I approve of the action of the President. I believe the President did right. He did precisely what I would have done if I had been in his place—no more, nor less; but I cannot here, in my place, as a Senator, under oath, declare what he did do was legal. I may say it was proper, and was justified by the necessity of the case; but I cannot here in my place, under oath, declare that it was strictly legal, and in consonance with the provisions of the Constitution. I shall therefore be compelled to vote against the resolution, although I indorse and ratify and approve, as a matter of public necessity, every act of the Administration.[7]

Sherman was immediately followed on the floor by an outright endorsement of the president's course from Wisconsin's Timothy Howe, a believer in a strong federal government:

I am going to vote for the resolution, and I am going to vote for it upon the assumption that the different acts of the Administration recited in this preamble were illegal, and not upon the assumption that they were legal and valid. I "approve" of the doing of them, and therefore vote for that portion of the resolution. I am willing to make them as "legal and valid" as if they had previous express sanction of Congress; and therefore I vote for that clause of the resolution. The resolution does not affirm that they were legal; that they were sanctioned by the legislative power of the United States; but it declares that they shall be as legal and valid as if they had had the previous express authority and direction of the Congress of the United States.[8]

On the day before adjournment Wilson knew his joint resolution could not pass. He thereupon introduced a bill to legalize some of the measures in the resolution, omitting the section on habeas corpus, a point of obvious disagreement even among Republicans. Wilson's resolution, added to a bill to increase the pay of army privates, sailed through the Senate with only five border slave state members voting in the negative. After an unsuccessful effort by House Democrats to remove the ratifying section, the bill passed without a division.

In the debate over suspension of habeas corpus, close friends of the president, loyal and maverick Republicans, Peace and War Democrats had joined the issues and had been essentially unable to agree. Authorization for executive suspension would be withheld for nearly two years; meanwhile the president gradually expanded the scope of the suspension, eventually denying habeas corpus to more than nine hundred persons who were arbitrarily arrested in the first eighteen months of the war.

Irony lay in the fact that the Congress passed a resolution stating that war was waged to maintain the Constitution and preserve the Union and not to interfere with established institutions of the southern states; and yet almost in the same breath Congress passed a bill allowing for the confiscation of any slaves put to labor or service against the United States. Congress's unwillingness to sanction Lincoln's suspension of habeas corpus ominously and precariously came with its simultaneous passage of the confiscation bill that Lincoln only reluctantly signed. Together these actions prefigured a rift between legislative and executive.

CHAPTER NINE

THE LOYALTY QUESTION
IN BORDER SLAVE STATES

Before Lincoln took office, seven slave states in the lower South had seceded and formed their own government styled the Confederate States of America. After Lincoln called forth the militia in April, four more slave states joined the Confederacy. From Virginia through Texas the nation had been severed, leaving four slave states in the Union—Delaware, Maryland, Kentucky, and Missouri. The fault line that emerged between the Confederacy and the Union centered on racial slavery—those states with high proportions of slaves seceded first, those with lesser but substantial proportions departed next, and those with small proportions hesitantly, except for Delaware, adhered to the old Union.

The census of 1860 reported a national population of 23,191,876. The Confederacy contained 9,037,172 persons, of whom 3,521,110 were enslaved. The unseceded slave states, termed border states, held 3,136,824 persons, of whom 429,401 were enslaved. Subtract these border state numbers from the Union numbers, and the scales change their balance rather substantially—from a Union majority of 14 million, with 9 million in the Confederacy, to a Union minority of 11 million against 12 million in the South.

Yet numbers alone do not fully signify the importance of the border states to the waging of the war. Delaware was of minor importance, except in Congress. Maryland, Kentucky, and Missouri, however, hesitated in 1861 between loyalty and secession. Maryland included the nation's capital, sited within its former boundaries and separated from slaveholding Virginia only by the Potomac River. A seceded Maryland would have surrounded Washington with hostile states and had portentous consequences for its security and existence as the nation's capital. Kentucky—stretching west from Virginia to Missouri, bounded on the north by the Ohio River with its crucial western commerce flowing south to New Orleans, and confronting the states of Ohio, Indiana, and Illinois—possessed economic and strategic importance that affected the strategy and course of the Civil War. Moreover, a seceded Kentucky might have weakened Unionist sentiment in western Virginia.

Tiny Delaware, tucked off to the northeast of Washington DC, incorporated only 1,798 slaves, 1.6 percent of its population. In 1860 its voters had overwhelmingly supported Breckinridge, the favorite of the deep South, for president. However, when courted by a commissioner from Mississippi, the Delaware legislature rejected the invitation to join the Confederacy. Upon Lincoln's appeal to arms, Governor William Burton, a Democrat, faced with the fact that the state had no militia, successfully encouraged volunteering, enlisting about 775 men. Even so, many citizens doubted that the North could win the war; some favored conciliation and peace, and many feared the prospect of emancipation. But Delaware did not pose a serious threat of secession.

Maryland was another matter. Slaves numbering 87,189 formed one eighth of the population. The state had awarded Breckinridge its electoral vote. Governor Thomas Hicks, elected as a member of the American (Know Nothing) Party, had voted for Breckinridge. As we have seen, on his passage from Springfield to Washington, Lincoln had been warned of a plot to assassinate him in Baltimore. When a commissioner from Mississippi came to Maryland, urging "prompt and decisive action," Hicks had replied, "I do not doubt the people of Maryland are ready to go with the people of those States (the Border States) for weal or woe." For months he staved off appeals to summon the legislature by persons who hoped it would affect secession. In January he issued an address against secession. In the anxious month of April he followed an uncertain course of cooperation with the federal government.

Two days after Lincoln's call to arms Virginia secretly seceded. Word quickly leaked out. Delegates from western Virginia, apparently told Lincoln the next day of eastern Virginia's secession. Former governor of Virginia Henry A. Wise lamented the "blindness which had prevented Virginia from seizing Washington before the Republican hordes got possession of it." The nation's capital now appeared surrounded by slave states—one, the old Dominion, cynosure of Southern eyes, seceding; the other, renowned for its role in the American Revolution and known as the Old Line State, teetering on the brink of secession.

On April 18 at Lincoln's request, Francis Preston Blair Sr. offered Robert E. Lee command of the Union forces. Lee initially opposed secession. Had he accepted this offer, which he did not, the course of the Civil War would have shifted. The event-filled day had not ended before Hicks issued a proclamation stating, among other things, that his powers would be employed to maintain the honor of Maryland. Ominously, Philadelphia volunteers en route through Baltimore for Washington heard jeers as well as cheers as they passed through Baltimore. Secretary of War Cameron telegraphed to let Hicks know "the president is informed that threats are made and measures taken by unlawful combinations of misguided citizens of Maryland." As dusk was falling the "Frontier Guards," led by colorful senator-elect Jim Lane, spent the night in the White House. Speaking to the men, Lincoln said:

> I have desired as sincerely as any man—I sometimes think more than any other man—that our present difficulties might be settled without the shedding of blood. I will not say that all hope is yet gone. But if the alternative is presented, whether the Union is to be broken in fragments and the liberties of the people lost, or blood be shed, you will probably make the choice, with which I shall not be dissatisfied.[1]

The next day inaugurated days of fear in the capital. Rail connections between Washington and the North ran through Baltimore. Mayor George W. Brown warned on April 18 in a letter to be carried to Lincoln: "The people are exasperated . . . by the passage of troops." On the April 19—anniversary of the battle of Lexington and Concord—a Baltimore mob assaulted the Sixth Massachusetts Regiment marching between rail connections, killing about four soldiers and nine citizens. Mayor Brown promptly telegraphed the news to Lincoln, urging that no more troops pass though Baltimore. At four in the afternoon Governor Hicks avowed to a crowd in Baltimore's Monument Square: "I am a Marylander, and I love my State, and I love the Union; but I will suffer my right arm to be torn from my body before I will raise it to strike a sister State."[2]

Lincoln learned that on Hicks's advice the heads of railroads leading to Washington had determined to transport no more troops. Meeting with his cabinet and General Scott, Lincoln instructed the adjutant general to inform Samuel M. Felton, president of the Philadelphia, Wilmington & Baltimore Railroad: "Governor Hicks has neither right nor authority to stop troops coming into Washington. Send them on, prepared to fight their way through, if necessary."[3] This was followed by the decision of Brown and apparently Hicks to burn the railroad bridges between Baltimore and Philadelphia and Harrisburg.

On April 20 Lincoln replied to Brown and by separate communication summoned the mayor and governor to Washington. He is reported to have told them essentially what he wrote in his letter of April 20, responding to Brown's monitory letter of April 18:

Your letter by Messrs. Bond, Dobbin & Brune, is received. I tender you both my sincere thanks for your efforts to keep the peace in the trying situation in which you are placed. For the future, troops must be brought here, but I make no point of bringing them *through* Baltimore. Without any military knowledge myself, of course I must leave the details to Gen. Scott. He hastily said, this morning, in presence of these gentlemen, "March them *around* Baltimore, and not through it." I sincerely hope the General, on fuller reflection, will consider this practical and proper, and that you will not object to it. By this, a collision of the people of Baltimore with the troops will be avoided, unless they go out of their way to seek it. I hope you will exert your influence to prevent this.

Now, and ever, I shall do all in my power for peace, consistently with the maintenance of government.[4]

Also on April 20 Governor Hicks declined to furnish troops in response to Lincoln's call:

Up to yesterday there appeared promise, but the outbreak came; the turbulent passions of the riotous element prevailed; fear for safety became a reality; what they had endeavored to conceal, but what was known to us, was no longer concealed, but made manifest; the rebellious element had the control of things. We were arranging and organizing forces to protect the city and preserve order, but want of organization and of arms prevented success. They had arms; they had the principal part of the organized military forces with them; and for us to have made the effort, under the circumstances, would have had the effect to aid the disorderly element. They took possession of the armories, have the arms and ammunition, and I therefore think it prudent to decline (for the present) responding affirmatively to the requisition made by President Lincoln for four regiments of infantry.[5]

A committee of fifty from Baltimore's Young Men's Christian Associations waited on the president on April 22. Lincoln responded:

You, gentlemen, come here to me and ask for peace on any terms, and yet have no word of condemnation for those who are making war on us. You express great horror of bloodshed, and yet would not lay a straw in the way of those who are organizing in Virginia and elsewhere to capture this city. The rebels attack Fort Sumter, and your citizens attack troops sent to the defense of the Government, and the lives and property in Washington, and yet you would have me break my oath and surrender the Government without a blow. There is no Washington in that—no Jackson in that—no manhood nor honor in that. I have no desire to invade the South; but I must have troops to defend this Capital. Geographically it lies surrounded by the soil of Maryland; and mathematically the necessity exists that they should come over her territory. Our men are not moles, and can't dig under the earth; they are not birds, and can't fly through the air. There is no way but to march across, and that they must do. But in doing this there is no need of collision. Keep your rowdies in Baltimore, and there will be no bloodshed. Go home and tell your people that if they will not attack us, we will not attack them; but if they do attack us, we will return it, and that severely.[6]

Lincoln's resolve was tested. "Maryland is the object of chief anxiety with the North and the Administration," Supreme Court justice John A. Campbell, an Alabamian soon to join the Confederate cause, informed Confederate President Jefferson Davis. Anxiety overcame the normally stout-hearted president, who was awaiting arrival of troops from the North. Pacing what he thought was his deserted office, he was overheard to exclaim: "Why don't they come! Why don't they come!" Still dispirited the following day, he remarked to wounded soldiers of the Sixth Massachusetts, "I begin to believe that there is no North. The Seventh Regiment is a myth. Rhode Island is another. You are the only real thing."

While in Washington on April 24 Reverdy Johnson, the same eminent Marylander who had been U.S. senator and attorney general under President Taylor and who supported Lincoln regarding habeas corpus, wrote to Lincoln saying:

> The existing excitement and alarm ... of my own State and of Virginia are owing ... to an apprehension that it is your purpose to use the military force you are assembling in the District for the invasion of ... these States.

In reply Lincoln wrote:

> Your note of this morning is just received. I forebear to answer yours of the 22d because of my aversion (which I thought you understood,) to getting on paper, and furnishing new grounds for misunderstanding.
>
> I *do* say the sole purpose of bringing troops *here* is to defend this capital.
>
> I *do* say I have no purpose to *invade* Virginia, with them or any other troops, as I understand the word *invasion*. But suppose Virginia sends her troops, or admits others through her borders, to assail this capital, am I not to repel them, even to the crossing of the Potomac if I can?
>
> Suppose Virginia erects, or permits to be erected, batteries on the opposite shore, to bombard the city, are we to stand still and see it done? In a word, if Virginia strikes us, are we not to strike back, and as effectively as we can?
>
> Again, are we not to hold Fort Monroe (for instance) if we can? I have no objection to declare a thousand times that I have no purpose to *invade* Virginia or any other State, but I do not mean to let them invade us without striking back.[7]

April 25 was a day of rejoicing in Washington as the New York Seventh arrived and proudly marched down Pennsylvania Avenue. It was also a day of worrying, as the Maryland legislature, at last called by Governor Hicks, was to meet the next day. Some advised Lincoln to arrest the Maryland legislators. Rejecting the idea of preventing the meeting, Lincoln instructed General Scott:

> The Maryland Legislature assembles to-morrow at Anapolis; and, not improbably, will take action to arm the people of that State against the United States. The question has been submitted to, and considered by me,

whether it would not be justifiable, upon the ground of necessary defence, for you, as commander in Chief of the United States Army, to arrest, or disperse the members of that body. I think it would not be justifiable; nor, efficient for the desired object.

First, they have a clearly legal right to assemble; and, we can not know in advance, that their action will not be lawful, and peaceful. And if we wait until they shall have acted, their arrest, or dispersion, will not lessen the effect of their action.

Secondly, we can not permanently prevent their action. If we arrest them, we can not long hold them as prisoners; and when liberated, they will immediately re-assemble, and take their action. And, precisely the same if we simply disperse them. They will immediately re-assemble in some other place.

I therefore conclude that it is only left to the commanding General to watch, and wait their action, which, if it shall be to arm their people against the United States, he is to adopt the most prompt, and efficient means to counteract, even, if necessary, to the bombardment of their cities—and in the extremest necessity, the suspension of the writ of habeas corpus.[8]

Two days later he authorized the general to suspend the writ along certain military lines from Philadelphia and New York to Washington. Arrival of the New York Seventh did not end the danger to Washington, General Scott warned the president. On April 29 Lincoln wrote to the secretary of the navy:

You will please to have as strong a War Steamer as you can conveniently put on that duty, to cruise upon the Potomac, and to look in upon, and, if practicable, examine the Bluff and vicinity, at what is called the White House, once or twice per day; and, in case of any attempt to erect a battery there, to drive away the party attempting it, if practicable; and, in every event to report daily to your Department, and to me. . . . *Private note.* The above order I make at the suggestion of General Scott, though the execution of it, I believe is substantially what you are already doing.[9]

The Maryland Legislature, sitting at Frederick amidst a loyal population, refused 13–53 to pass an ordinance of secession. The House, however, by a 43–12 vote, passed resolutions condemning the war and military occupation of the state. General Benjamin Butler, a strong-minded and controversial politician, a War Democrat, and commander of the Eighth Massachusetts, had assumed authority of the Department of Annapolis. His forces began repairing the railroads and occupied Annapolis. The Maryland lawmakers appointed a committee to wait upon the president's next act. The committee carried a resolution directing it:

> . . . to communicate immediately, in person, with the President of the United States in regard to the present and any proposed prospective Military use or occupation of the soil and property of the state by the General Government.

Lincoln in response said:

> On presenting me the resolution of the Legislature of your State, and addressing me verbally, two days ago, you had the kindness to say you did not expect an immediate answer. Appreciating what you said orally, I, however, attempt no answer except to what is written in the resolution.
>
> The resolution is as follows (Here insert it)
>
> To the question "in regard to the present and any proposed prospective Military use or occupation of the soil and property of the State, by the General Government &c" the answer must necessarily be contingent.[10]

After the committee's return to Maryland without the assurance that the members wanted, the legislature resolved on May 10:

> That Maryland implores the President . . . to cease this unholy war, at least until Congress assembles; that Maryland desires and consents to the recognition of the independence of the Confederate States. (That) the military occupation of Maryland is unconstitutional, and she protests against it, though the violent interference with the transit of Federal troops is discountenanced; that the vindication of her rights be left to time and reason, and that a Convention, under existing circumstances, is expedient.[11]

The preceding day John Pendleton Kennedy, secretary of the navy under President Millard Fillmore, made a speech, "The Great Drama: An Appeal to Maryland." His appeal was to support the Union cause, not Lincoln, and he noted that "we censure the policy of the Administration." Kennedy's concern extended across the other border slave states. Maryland's "example may influence the course of the other Border States which are now on the verge of secession," he hoped.

The pro-Union speech was reported to have exerted great influence on Baltimore's businessmen and citizens, thirteen hundred of whom signed a memorial supporting Governor Hicks's policy of remaining in the Union.

The Merryman decision in early June condemning Lincoln's suspension of the writ of habeas corpus muddled matters but failed in the end to stop Maryland voters on June 13 from electing pro-Union candidates to the U.S. House of Representatives. A week later Reverdy Johnson, the noted Maryland constitutional lawyer, published his stout defense of Lincoln's suspension of habeas corpus in the *National Intelligencer*:

> The obligation on the President being to suppress the revolt and to "cause the laws to be duly executed," the military authority vested in him for that purpose is to be exercised until the end is attained. The sole limitation is one of time, and that regards only the militia whom he can use but from the period of their call into service till the expiration of thirty days after the commencement of the next session of Congress. It thus appears that the militia and army and navy of the United States, now being used by the President to suppress the rebellion, are in the field by the authority of Congress, in whom the war power is vested, and to whom is also delegated the authority, and consequently in such cases the duty, "to provide for calling forth the militia to execute the laws of the Union, suppress insurrections, and repel invasions." The entire force has consequently now been "called into the actual service of the United States," and, by the very words of the Constitution, is under the direction of the President as commander-in-chief....
>
> [T]he only question in the case is, whether the power which the President is exercising is in its nature an Executive one. That it is, has been, it is believed, satisfactorily shown; and under the rule stated by Hamilton, impliedly sanctioned by Madison, and expressly adopted by Jackson, it is in the President by force of the general delegation to him of *the Executive power*.[12]

So siding with the president, Johnson labored in the Maryland House of Delegates to keep the state in the Union. In the following year he was elected U.S. senator. Like many Maryland Democrats, he later opposed the Emancipation Proclamation, and in 1864 deplored Lincoln's interference in elections in Maryland and Kentucky and favored McClellan for president, but ultimately voted for the Thirteenth Amendment.

Believing secession not yet laid to rest, General Winfield Scott on June 24 had ordered the arrest of the police commissioners of Baltimore for secession activities. Congress on July 24 passed a resolution that read:

Resolved, That the President be requested immediately to communicate to this House, if in his judgment not incompatible with the public interest, the grounds, reason, and evidence upon which the police commissioners of Baltimore were arrested, and are now detained as prisoners at Fort McHenry.[13]

Lincoln replied:

In answer to the resolution of the House of Representatives of the 24th instant, asking the grounds, reason, and evidence upon which the police commissioners of Baltimore were arrested and are now detained as prisoners at Fort McHenry, I have to state that it is judged to be incompatible with the public interest at this time to furnish the information called for by the resolution.[14]

The situation in Maryland changed little in the following months, as the line to Washington became ever more vital to protect. In September Secretary of War Cameron and General McClellan ordered the arrest of twenty-seven members of the Maryland legislature on suspicion of secessionist tendencies. Lincoln's views of this extraordinary interference with a state legislature were believed to be:

The public safety renders it necessary that the grounds of these arrests should at present be withheld, but at the proper time they will be made public. Of one thing the people of Maryland may rest assured: that no arrest has been made, or will be made, not based on substantial and unmistakable complicity with those in armed rebellion against the Government of the United States. In no case has an arrest been made on mere suspicion, or through personal or partisan animosities, but in all cases the Government is in possession of tangible and unmistakable evidence, which will, when made public, be satisfactory to every loyal citizen.[15]

A widely watched pivotal event, therefore, became the election in Maryland for state offices. Troops were furloughed to return home and vote. Union soldiers under Generals Nathaniel P. Banks and John A. Dix maintained a federal presence. Provost marshals stood at the polls. Augustus Bradford, a staunch Unionist, handily garnered more than twice as many votes for governor as the states' rights candidate. Large Unionist majorities elected other state officers. By forceful measures, it appeared, the possible secession of Maryland had been put down.

Filling a vacancy created by a death, Hicks became a U.S. senator in 1862; in his first major speech the ex-governor strongly commended suspension of habeas corpus in Maryland. Reverdy Johnson was elected to the U.S. Senate in 1863, replacing Anthony Kennedy, a sharp critic of Lincoln's "implied powers."

Responding to a letter from Reverdy Johnson, who had been sent to make an investigation in Louisiana, Lincoln wrote to him in July 1862:

> You are ready to say I apply to friends what is due only to enemies. I distrust the wisdom if not the sincerity of friends, who would hold my hands while my enemies stab me. This appeal of professed friends has paralyzed me more in this struggle than any other one thing. You remember telling me the day after the Baltimore mob in April 1861, that it would crush all Union feeling in Maryland for me to attempt bringing troops over Maryland soil to Washington. I brought the troops notwithstanding, and yet there was Union feeling enough left to elect a Legislature the next autumn which in turn elected a very excellent Union U.S. Senator![16]

In mid-November 1861 a delegation from Baltimore appeared at the White House, lamenting the hard times that had overtaken the city. Lincoln responded:

> I thank you for the address you have presented to me in behalf of the people of Baltimore. I have deplored the calamities which the sympathies of some misguided citizens of Maryland had brought down upon that patriotic and heretofore flourishing State. The prosperity of Baltimore up to the 19th of April last, was one of the wonders produced by the American Union. He who strangles himself, for whatever motive, is not more unreasonable than were those citizens of Baltimore who, in a single night, destroyed the Baltimore and Ohio Railroad, the Northern Pennsylvania Railroad, and the railroad from Baltimore to Philadelphia. From the day when that mad transaction occurred, the Government of the United States has been diligently engaged in endeavoring to restore those great avenues to their former

usefulness, and, at the same time, to save Baltimore and Maryland from the danger of complete ruin through an unnecessary and unnatural rebellion.

I congratulate you upon the declaration which the people of Baltimore and Maryland have made in the recent election, of their recent approbation of the Federal Government, and of their enduring loyalty to the Union. I regard the results of these elections as auspicious of returning loyalty throughout all the insurrectionary States.

Your wishes for a fair participation by the mechanics and laboring men of Baltimore in the benefits of supplying the Government with materials and provisions are reasonable and just. They have deserved that participation. Loyalty has involved them in some danger, and has demanded of them some sacrifices. Their wishes, as you have communicated them, shall be referred to the proper Departments, and I am sure that every member of the Administration will cheerfully lend his aid to carry them out so far as it can be done consistently with the prudence and economy which ought always to regulate the public service.[17]

As the year closed strong measures, including suspension of the privilege of habeas corpus, arrest of public officials, and presence of federal troops, had saved Maryland for the Union. The progress of events during the war would drastically change the state's attitude toward Lincoln and emancipation. Looking back on the crisis of April 1861 and what he had done, Lincoln told the Congress:

The insurrection which is yet existing in the United States, and aims at the overthrow of the federal Constitution and the Union, was clandestinely prepared during the winter of 1860 and 1861, and assumed an open organization in the form of a treasonable provisional government at Montgomery, in Alabama, on the 18th day of February, 1861. On the 12th day of April, 1861, the insurgents committed the flagrant act of civil war by the bombardment and capture of Fort Sumter, which cut off the hope of immediate conciliation. Immediately afterwards all the roads and avenues to this city were obstructed, and the capital was put into the condition of a siege. The mails in every direction were stopped, and the lines of telegraph cut off by the insurgents, and military and naval forces, which had been called out by the government for the defence of Washington, were prevented from reaching the city by organized and combined treasonable resistance in the State of Maryland. There was no adequate and effective organization for the public defence. Congress had indefinitely adjourned. There was no time to convene them. It became necessary for me to choose whether, using only the existing means, agencies, and processes which Congress had provided, I should let the government fall at once into ruin, or whether, availing myself of the broader powers conferred by the Constitution in cases of insurrection, I would make an effort to save it with all its blessings for the present age and for posterity.[18]

Kentucky, Lincoln's native state, bridged between Missouri and western Virginia, bordered on the north by the Ohio River and on the west by the Mississippi, held the largest slave population proportion of the loyal border states—one fifth of its residents. Of great commercial significance, Kentucky potentially barred enemy access to Ohio, Indiana, and Illinois.

In the 1860 presidential election Kentucky had awarded its electoral votes to John Bell of Tennessee and not to either of its native sons, Breckinridge and Lincoln. The latter polled just 1,364 votes, Breckinridge 53,143.

Governor Beriah Magoffin, a leader of the Breckenridge Democrats, strove to save the Union, opposing the breakup of his party and favoring the aborted Crittenden Compromise. Even so he believed in the right of secession and held strong sympathy for the slave states. Lincoln's call for militia on April 15 evoked an immediate response from Magoffin to Secretary of War Cameron: "Your dispatch is received. In answer, I say, emphatically, Kentucky will furnish no troops, for the wicked purpose of subduing her sister Southern States."

The *Louisville Democrat* thundered:

Depend upon it, Messrs. Lincoln & Co., you're wasting treasure and blood to no purpose. All your professions of peace will count nothing. You talk like enemies and act like them. Even these border Slave states, who have stood by their government, who feel a patriotic attachment to the Union their fathers made, are unheeded. Their advice disregarded, and their wise counsels spurned. They ask for peace most earnestly, as essential to a restoration of confidence and salvation of the Union; and Lincoln & Co. call for troops, and are mustering armies, when all the effect will be to their own resentment and make a breach incurable. They mistake altogether our government and people. No power can restore a State to the Union but its people.[19]

At a meeting in Louisville attended by five thousand conservative Unionists, Kentucky's U.S. senator Archibald Dixon, a Whig who was Henry Clay's successor, described the national crisis and urged neutrality:

We do not mean to submit to Lincoln. He has commanded us to send troops. We send word that Kentucky will not do it. Will he compel us? Let him not dare it! Let him not rouse the sleeping lions of the Border States. She sleeps now—still and quiet, but it is not from lack of strength, courage, or power. She waits for the assault. Let it come, and, roused, she will crush the power that assails, and drag Mr. Lincoln from his high place. Can he make Kentucky help him kill? He has a right to demand troops, and he did. . . . No, they will never lend themselves to such a cause. But, Kentucky will stand firm with her sister Border States in the centre of the Republic, to calm the distracted sections. This is her true position, and in it she saves the Union and frowns down Secession. Let us wait for reason to resume her seat. Let us not fight the North or South, but firm in our position tell our sister Border States that with them we will stand to maintain the Union, to preserve the peace, and uphold our honor, and our flag, which they would trail in the dust. . . . If we give up the Union, all is lost. There will then be no breakwater, but instead, Kentucky will be the battle-ground—the scene of a conflict between brethren—such a conflict as no country has yet witnessed. But if we take the true stand, the tide of war and desolation will be rolled back on both sides. If we must fight, let us fight Lincoln and not our Government. To go out of the Union is to raise a new issue with the North and turn the whole country against you. The ship of state is one in which we *all* sail, and when thus launched into the ocean, and about to founder because part of the crew rebel against the commander, it is the duty of all, unhesitatingly, to aid and save. Safely demands that we stand by the flag, by the Government, by the Constitution! In the distance you hear the shouts of men and the roaring of cannon. The foemen are gathering for the dreadful conflict, and when you cut loose from the union it is to take a part. But you are secure from both as long as you remain neutral.[20]

During these tense days Magoffin was secretly dealing with the Confederacy. Yet, believing in democratic procedures, he called the legislature into special session, to meet on May 6. In his message to the legislature he appealed for a constitutional convention to determine Kentucky's status. The legislators refused to authorize a sovereign convention, and by a vote of

69 to 26 resolved in favor of neutrality; and at the same time they endorsed the governor's refusal to furnish troops to the Union cause. Petitions from women across the state had urged the lawmakers to "guard them from the direful calamities of civil war." Bowing to legislative will, Magoffin on May 20 proclaimed Kentucky a neutral. It was the act of a sovereign nation, declaring neutrality in another nation's war.[21]

Meanwhile Lincoln was carefully attempting to draw Kentucky into the fold. On May 7, the day after the legislature met, he sent an order to Major Robert Anderson, the Kentuckian who had commanded at Fort Sumter. Now a national hero, he vaulted to brigadier general on June 17. The order read:

> To all who shall see these presents greeting:
> Know Ye, That reposing special trust and confidence in the patriotism, valor, fidelity, and abilities of Colonel Robert Anderson, U.S. Army, I have empowered him and do hereby empower him to receive into the Service of the United States, as many regiments of volunteer troops from the State of Kentucky and from the Western part of the State of Virginia, as shall be willing to engage in the service of the United States for the period of three years, upon the terms and according to the plan proposed by the Proclamation of May 3, 1861, and General Order, No. 15, from the War Department of May 4, 1861.
> The troops whom he may receive shall be on the same footing in every respect as those of the like kind called for in the proclamation above cited, except that the officers thereof shall be commissioned by the United States.
> He is, therefore, carefully and diligently to discharge the duty hereby devolved upon him by doing and performing all manner of things thereunto belonging.[22]

Lincoln took a step beyond encouraging enlistment of Kentuckians. On May 14 he again wrote to Anderson:

> Some time ago, and before it was arranged for you to go West, as now, the question was upon us how arms sent to Cincinnati for Kentuckians, could surely be put in the hands of friends, and not of enemies; and, for this purpose, and without their knowledge, Messrs Crittenden, Guthrie, and Joshua F. Speed, bearer of this, or any one of them, were designated to distribute the arms, in their discretion. After you left here last week it

occurred to us that you could perform this service as safely, and perhaps more expeditiously, by reason that you will be on the spot, and will not have to wait for the co-operation of any one; and a direction was accordingly sent to the parties forwarding the arms to Cincinnati. It now occurs further that the kind assistance of these gentlemen may still be valuable to you in this, and perhaps other matters; and when it shall so appear to you it is hoped you will avail yourself of it. Mr. Speed, though less well known to the world than the other gentlemen, is far better known to me than either of them; and I have the utmost confidence in his loyalty and integrity, and also in his judgment on any subject which he professes to understand. I think you will find him a most agreeable companion, and at the same time a most valuable assistant in our common cause.[23]

The next day the president wrote to General Simon Bolivar Buckner, who had been dispatched by Governor Magoffin to secure Lincoln's approval of Kentucky's neutrality policy:

It is my duty, as I conceive, to suppress an insurrection existing within the United States. I wish to do this with the least possible disturbance, or annoyance to well disposed people anywhere. So far I have not sent an armed force into Kentucky; nor have I any present purpose to do so. I sincerely desire that no necessity for it may be presented; but I mean to say nothing which shall hereafter embarrass me in the performance of what may seem to be my duty.[24]

Before the year was out Buckner, after refusing Lincoln's offer of a commission as brigadier general of volunteers in the Union Army, had become a brigadier general in the Confederate Army. Months later Buckner suffered a humiliating defeat and surrendered his Confederate forces to his friend General Ulysses S. Grant at Fort Donelson.

Still prudent but encouraged by the state elections, which had sent nine Unionists to Congress, Lincoln on July 29 wrote to the Kentucky delegation in Congress:

Gentlemen of the Kentucky delegation, who are for the Union—I somewhat wish to authorize my friend Jesse Bayles to raise a Kentucky Regiment; but I do not wish to do it without your consent. If you consent, please write so, at the bottom of this.[25]

The delegates agreed with Lincoln, and on August 5 the Fourth Kentucky Cavalry was formed in Louisville.

Vigorously protesting any organization of Union troops in Kentucky, Magoffin on August 19 wrote to Lincoln:

> In a word, an army is now being organized and quartered in this State, supplied with all the appliances of war, without the consent or advice of the authorities of the State, and without consultation with those most prominently known and recognized as loyal citizens. This movement now imperils that peace and tranquility which from the beginning of our pending difficulties have been the paramount desire of this people, and which, up to this time, they have so secured to the State.
>
> Within Kentucky there has been, and is likely to be, no occasion for the presence of military force. The people are quiet and tranquil, feeling no apprehension of any occasion arising to invoke protection from the Federal arm. They have asked that their territory be left free from military occupation, and the present tranquility of their communication left uninvaded by soldiers. They do not desire that Kentucky shall be required to supply the battle-field for the contending armies, or become the theatre of the war.
>
> Now, therefore, as Governor of the State of Kentucky, and in the name of the people I have the honor to represent, and with the single and earnest desire to avert from their peaceful homes the horrors of war, I urge the removal from the limits of Kentucky of the military force now organized and in camp within the State. If such action as is hereby urged be promptly taken, I firmly believe the peace of the people of Kentucky will be preserved, and the horrors of a bloody war will be averted from a people now peaceful and tranquil.[26]

Having secured permission once, Lincoln would not back down or ask again. He firmly rejected Magoffin's request to remove Union troops from Kentucky:

> Your letter of the 19th. Inst. in which you "urge the removal from the limits of Kentucky of the military force now organized, and in camp within said State" is received.
>
> I may not possess full and precisely accurate knowledge upon this subject; but I believe it is true that there is a military force in camp within Kentucky, acting by authority of the United States, which force is not very large, and is not now being augmented.

I also believe that some arms have been furnished to this force by the United States.

I also believe this force consists exclusively of Kentuckians, having their camp in the immediate vicinity of their own homes, and not assailing, or menacing, any of the good people of Kentucky.

While I have conversed on this subject with many eminent men of Kentucky, including a large majority of her Members of Congress, I do not remember that any one of them, or any other person, except your Excellency and the bearers of your Excellency's letter, has urged me to remove the military force from Kentucky, or to disband it. One other very worthy citizen of Kentucky did solicit me to have the augmenting of the force suspended for a time.

Taking all the means within my reach to form a judgment, I do not believe it is the popular wish of Kentucky that this force shall be removed beyond her limits; and, with this impression, I must respectfully decline to so remove it.

I most cordially sympathize with your Excellency, in the wish to preserve the peace of my own native State, Kentucky; but it is with regret I search, and can not find, in your not very short letter, any declaration, or intimation, that you entertain any desire for the preservation of the Federal Union.[27]

The Kentucky Legislature learned on September 5 that Confederate forces had occupied and fortified Hickman and Columbus, Kentucky. After instructing Magoffin to proclaim that Kentucky expected the Confederacy to withdraw the troops, the lawmakers invited Major Robert Anderson to take command of Kentucky forces. Overriding the governor's veto, the lawmakers further resolved that "the invaders must be expelled." On October 1 the legislature asked the pro-Southern senators, John Breckinridge and Lazarus W. Powell, to resign from the U.S. Senate. Kentucky, it appeared, would not secede and would safely remain in the Union.

CHAPTER TEN

MISSOURI, AN UNRULY
UNION PARTNER

Missouri, made a slave state by the heated Compromise of 1820, entrenching slavery, was the only border slave state west of the Mississippi River. With a population of 1,182,012—nearly 10 percent being slaves—together with Kentucky it guarded the middle reaches of the great north-south artery of western commerce. Missouri's loyalty to the Union held strategic and commercial implications for Kentucky, Illinois, and Iowa—all loyal—and Arkansas, a Confederate state. The only significant battle west of the river would occur at Wilson's Creek, Missouri, in August 1861, where federal forces defeated secessionist forces and placed Missouri under Unionist sway. St. Louis, a large commercial center and home to many German Americans who were loyal to the Union, was the site of an important federal arsenal.

The state was well connected to Lincoln's administration. The president had appointed his attorney general, Bates, from Missouri; his postmaster general, Montgomery Blair, had been mayor of St. Louis, and in 1860 Blair's brother, Frank Jr., had been elected to the House of Representatives from Missouri. In Washington the Blairs owned Blair House across the street from the White House.

Missouri in 1860 had awarded its electoral votes to Douglas, who enjoyed a small margin over Bell, with Lincoln trailing in fourth place. Claiborne Jackson, a pro-slavery Democrat, was elected governor in 1860. In his inaugural address he declared that in the event the Union was dissolved, Missouri must join the South. His zeal for secession was compounded by his conspiratorial correspondence with Jefferson Davis. But neither prevented loyalists from gaining the majority in a state sovereignty convention, called on his recommendation. The delegates on the one hand rejected immediate secession and, on the other hand, opposed coercion of the seceded states. When Lincoln called out the militia Jackson blasted in angry reply, "Your requisition is illegal, unconstitutional, revolutionary, inhuman, diabolical, and cannot be complied with."

Less than a fortnight later he confided to the editor of a secessionist newspaper in St. Louis, "I do not think Missouri should secede to-day or to-morrow, but I do not think it good policy that I should so openly declare. I want a little time to arm the State, and I am assuming every responsibility to do it with all possible despatch. . . . That she [Missouri] ought to go, and will go, at the proper time, I have no doubt."[1] Jackson and Magoffin, if given their way, might have tipped the scales in the Civil War.

More than any of the border slave states, Missouri was the scene of internal strife throughout the war. At the beginning control of the federal arsenal became a crucial issue. Captain Nathaniel Lyon, who had worked with Frank Blair Jr. to organize a home guard, became commander of the arsenal. The city itself became an armed camp, with many restless elements in it. Lyon was subordinate to General William S. Harney, headquartered in St. Louis. Rivals established Camp Jackson in St. Louis.

Antagonism developed between the impetuous Lyon and the conciliatory Harney, making it difficult to incorporate the home guards into the federal service and to dispatch arms to Illinois. On April 20 Lincoln relieved Harney of his command and called him to Washington.

A friend of Bates, C. Gibson, described the scene and the secessionists' attitude toward the president:

The secessionists here have changed their tactics completely. Such is the excitement created here by the calling out of the militia, that they are confident the people of this State will vote her out of the Union, and they have good grounds to think so. They are, therefore, for leaving everything to the people, and committing no violence. They have substituted the false charge that Mr. Lincoln intends to subjugate the South in lieu of their own lawless acts, and have suddenly become the most law-abiding citizens. If the State goes out, they expect the public property belonging to the United States to pass *ipso facto* to them. This is my own inference as to their plans, but I think it is correct.

Captain Lyon agrees with me that both the arsenal and barracks are untenable as military positions. It therefore requires a large force to maintain the rights of the Government. To send the militia from any non-slaveholding State would be in my opinion most injudicious. It would inflame the popular mind to a very dangerous degree. What I propose and earnestly recommend is to enroll volunteers from this State, purging them all with an oath, to the number of three, four, or five thousand men. This number can be easily obtained if it be understood they are not to leave the State. It would place Saint Louis in the hands of Union men, and thus give them courage, which they now lack, and it could excite but little jealousy. It would also show that there were Union men in Missouri, which is important at this time. The Government would lose nothing in permitting them to remain here, for I think they should be kept here at all events. They would not lose their citizenship by being enrolled. There is much talk in certain quarters of "superseding" the convention, and we may need all our citizens here.

Permit me also to suggest that it would be well to quietly remove a great portion of the arms and munitions of war now at the barracks to Cairo, with the avowed purpose of arming the troops to be there mustered into the service. One great point to be gained by the secessionists in capturing the arsenal is to get the arms for the State, which is now almost wholly without arms of any kind. I will be here ten days or perhaps two weeks, and any service I can render the Government will be cheerfully done.[2]

The growing conspiracy caused Lincoln on April 30 to have the secretary of war order Lyon to enlist ten thousand men and proclaim martial law in St. Louis:

The President of the United States directs that you enroll in the military service of the United States the loyal citizens of St. Louis and vicinity, not exceeding, with those heretofore enlisted, ten thousand in number, for the purpose of maintaining the authority of the United States for the protection of the peaceable inhabitants of Missouri; and you will, if deemed necessary for that purpose by yourself and by Messrs. Oliver T. Filley, John How, James O. Broadhead, Samuel T. Glover, J. Witzig, and Francis P. Blair, Jr., proclaim martial law in the city of Saint Louis.[3]

All the while Governor Jackson carried on a clandestine correspondence with President Davis and the Confederate secretary of war, Leroy P. Walker. In response to their question whether he could furnish an infantry regiment to serve the Confederate cause in Virginia, Jackson replied:

> Sir: Yours of 26th ultimo via Louisville is received. I have no legal authority to furnish the men you desire. Missouri, you know, is yet under the tyranny of Lincoln's Government, so far, at least, as forms go. We are woefully deficient here in arms, and cannot furnish them at present; but so far as men are concerned, we have plenty of them, ready, willing, and anxious to march at any moment to the defense of the South. Our legislature has just met, and I doubt not will give me all necessary authority over the matter. If you can arm the men they will go whenever wanted, and to any point where they may be most needed. I send this to Memphis by private hand, being afraid to trust our mails or telegraphs. Let me hear from you by the same means. Missouri can and will put one hundred thousand men in the field, if required. We are using every means to arm our people, and, until we are better prepared, must move cautiously. I write this in confidence.
>
> With my prayers for your success, I remain, very respectfully, your obedient servant, C.F. Jackson, *Governor of Missouri.*[4]

In early May arms from the Confederacy arrived. Lyon peacefully took control of Camp Jackson, but the surrender, watched by a mob, ignited a large-scale riot in the city. That night secessionists in the legislature, meeting in Jefferson City, gave the governor dictatorial powers by legislation Harney described as "an indirect secession ordinance."

Former governor Sterling Price became major general of the state troops. Price and Harney, who had resumed command, made an agreement, Price pledging to maintain order, Harney declaring he had no intention of making military moves that might create excitement and jealousies.

Disorder, however, persisted. Within a week Lincoln instructed his adjutant general to send an order:

> The President observes with concern that, notwithstanding the pledge of the State authorities to co-operate in preserving peace in Missouri, loyal citizens in great numbers continue to be driven from their homes. It is immaterial whether these outrages continue from inability or indisposition on the part of the State authorities to prevent them. It is enough that they

continue to devolve on you the duty of putting a stop to them summarily by the force under your command, to be aided by such troops as you may require from Kansas, Iowa, and Illinois. The professions of loyalty to the Union by the State authorities of Missouri are not to be relied upon. They have already falsified their professions too often, and are too far committed to secession to be entitled to your confidence, and you can only be sure of their desisting from their wicked purposes when it is out of their power to prosecute them. You will therefore be unceasingly watchful of their movements, and not permit the clamors of their partisans and opponents of the wise measures already taken to prevent you from checking every movement against the Government, however disguised, under the pretended State authority. The authority of the United States is paramount, and whenever it is apparent that a movement, whether by color of State authority or not, is hostile, you will not hesitate to put it down.[5]

For some time Frank Blair Jr. had been carrying an order from the War Department giving him discretionary authority to relieve Harney from command. Lincoln had written to Blair privately on May 18:

We have had a good deal of anxiety here about St. Louis. I understand an order has gone from the War Department to you, to be delivered or withheld in your discretion, relieving Gen. Harney from his command. I was not quite satisfied with the order when it was made, though on the whole I thought it best to make it; but since then I have become more doubtful of its propriety. I do not write now to countermand it; but to say I wish you would withhold it, unless in your judgment the necessity to the contrary is very urgent.

There are several reasons for this. We have better have him a *friend* than an *enemy*. It will dissatisfy a good many who otherwise would be quiet. More than all, we first relieved him, then restored him, & now if we relieve him again, the public will ask, "why all this vacillation."

Still if, in your judgment, it is *indispensable* let it be so.[6]

On May 30 Blair notified Lincoln:

I have to-day delivered to General Harney the order of the 16th of May above mentioned relieving him, feeling that the progress of events and condition of affairs in this State make it incumbent upon me to assume the grave responsibility of this act, the discretionary power in the premises having been given me by the President.[7]

Following an unsuccessful four-hour meeting between Blair and Lyon on one side and Price and Jackson on the other, Jackson issued a proclamation summoning fifty thousand into service. The proclamation in part read:

> In issuing this proclamation I hold it to be my solemn duty to remind you that Missouri is still one of the United States; that the Executive Department of the State government does not arrogate to itself the power to disturb that relation; that that power has been wisely vested in a convention which will at the proper time express your sovereign will; and that meanwhile it is your duty to obey all constitutional requirements of the Federal Government.
>
> But it is equally my duty to advise you that your first allegiance is due to your own State, and that you are under no obligation whatever to obey the unconstitutional edicts of the military despotism which has enthroned itself at Washington, nor to submit to the infamous and degrading sway of its wicked minions in this State. No brave and true-hearted Missourian will obey one or submit to the other. Rise, then, and drive out ignominiously the invaders who have dared to desecrate the soil which your labors have made fruitful, and which is consecrated by your homes.[8]

Three days later Lyon took possession of the state capital, Jefferson City, and raised the Union flag over the State house. Pursuing disloyal state forces, Lyon lost his life at Wilson's Creek. Price remained in southwestern Missouri, where he and his men joined the Confederate Army.

Meanwhile in an extraordinary move, the Missouri State Convention, first called to consider secession and acting as sovereign of the state, deposed Jackson as governor and in June appointed Hamilton R. Gamble governor. He had earlier declared that "going out of the Union would be the most ruinous thing Missouri could do."[9] He now announced his unalloyed loyalty to the Union. Gamble's appointment quelled Lincoln's concern about Missouri's loyalty but by no means stilled the internal strife that characterized this border state.

Not only did adherence of the four border states seem assured by the end of 1861, but also there appeared the prospect of gaining Union strength from a divided Virginia. Separated from the eastern part of the state by the Allegheny Mountains, western Virginia had only a small slave population, was connected to the west by the bordering Ohio River, and had east-west connections by the Baltimore and Ohio Railroad. Western Virginians from twenty-five counties had met at Wheeling on May 13, 1861. With the Union flag flying above the custom house, the delegates repudiated secession and arranged for a convention to meet on June 11. Before that date Union forces under General George B. McClellan had defeated rebel forces at Phillippi. The convention, grown to about forty counties, met in June, created a provisional government that it called Virginia, and appointed Francis H. Pierpont governor. He promptly appealed to Washington for help to suppress rebellion and protect his people. Answering for Lincoln, Secretary of War Cameron sent assurance that a substantial military force would be dispatched. In a letter dated September 3 Pierpont wrote to Lincoln about the need to call out eight or ten volunteer regiments in western Virginia. Lincoln responded in a one-sentence note to Cameron, "Will War Department please consider the within request of Gov. Pierpont?"[10]

Pursuing their extra-constitutional course, the western Virginia legislators, deeming themselves the legislature of Virginia, sent two U.S. senators to the special session of Congress. In a lively debate over whether these senators should be seated, Breckinridge of Kentucky cried:

[S]o far as I have witnessed the action of the Executive, and, I regret to say, some of the acts of this body, it does not seem to me that the Constitution is much regarded. This proceeding is, in my judgment, an overthrow of the Constitution and the forms of our government.[11]

In his first annual message in December 1861, Lincoln summed up the encouraging situation in the border slave states:

The insurgents confidently claimed a strong support from north of Mason and Dixon's line; and the friends of the Union were not free from apprehension on that point. This, however, was soon settled definitely and on the right side. South of the line, noble little Delaware led off right from the first. Maryland was made to *seem* against the Union. Our soldiers were assaulted, bridges were burned, and railroads torn up, within her limits; and we were many days, at one time, without the ability to bring a single regiment over her soil to the capital. Now, her bridges and railroads are repaired and open to the government; she already gives seven regiments to the cause of the Union and none to the enemy; and her people, at a regular election, have sustained the Union, by a larger majority, and a larger aggregate vote than they ever before gave to any candidate, or any question. Kentucky, too, for some time in doubt, is now decidedly, and, I think, unchangeably, ranged on the side of the Union. Missouri is comparatively quiet; and I believe cannot again be overrun by the insurrectionists. These three States of Maryland, Kentucky, and Missouri, neither of which would promise a single soldier at first, have now an aggregate of not less than forty thousand in the field, for the Union; while, of their citizens, certainly not more than a third of that number, and they of doubtful whereabouts, and doubtful existence, are in arms against it. After a somewhat bloody struggle of months, winter closes on the Union people of western Virginia, leaving them masters of their own country.[12]

Lincoln had secured a significant strategic advantage through the division of Virginia and the defection of secessionists in Maryland and Kentucky. But in Missouri Lincoln was perhaps too rosy in his assessment. In that state a civil war within the Civil War developed, and it would not be "quiet" for long.

CHAPTER ELEVEN

FRÉMONT PROCLAIMS
FREEDOM IN MISSOURI

An English friend of Nathaniel Hawthorne, F. Bennoch, writing from London on August 1, 1861, described his uncertainty about the war's ultimate purpose—reunion or abolition. "I have failed to discover the precise grounds on which or principles for which they [Northern statesmen] are fighting." Bennoch questioned whether the Lincoln administration and the North were really fighting to end slavery. The war appeared to "imitate the blood-spilling propensities of despots" rather than to aim at some higher moral purpose. Could it be that the war would cost millions of dollars and thousands of lives and yet not free a single slave?[1]

The dilemma was central to the first year of the war. The cardinal stand of the Republican Party was not abolition but prohibition of the expansion of slavery into the territories. In his inaugural address Lincoln had acknowledged his willingness to have the Constitution amended to prohibit the federal government from ever interfering with slavery in the states. He had also pledged to uphold the constitutional pledge to return fugitive slaves to their owners.

The war against the seceded slave states nourished the sentiment that slavery should be rooted out. The military and the Congress were moving beyond Lincoln and the party's 1860 stand. General Benjamin F. Butler, addressing the problem of fugitive slaves escaping into Union lines, declared them contraband of war and retained them. Congress in the Confiscation Act had imposed on the president the duty of confiscating slaves employed in the rebellion but did not specify their ultimate status, free or enslaved.

John Charles Frémont, famed as "the Pathfinder," had been the Republican Party's nominee for the presidency in 1856. Shunted aside in 1860, he was made major general in July 1861 and given charge of the Department of the West, headquartered in St. Louis, where he confronted guerrilla warfare and disloyalty in the state.

Beset with the disorder in the state and inept in politics, Frémont on August 30 issued a proclamation that reverberated in the North and roiled the border slave states:

> Circumstances, in my judgment of sufficient urgency, render it necessary that the commanding general of this department should assume the administrative powers of the State. . . . In order, thereof, to suppress disorder, to maintain as far as now practicable the public peace, and to give security and protection to the persons and property of loyal citizens, I do hereby extend and declare established martial law throughout the State of Missouri. . . . All persons who shall be taken with arms in their hands within these lines shall be tried by court-martial, and if found guilty will be shot. The property, real and personal, of all persons in the State of Missouri who shall take up arms against the United States, or who shall be directly proven to have taken an active part with their enemies in the field, is declared to be confiscated to the public use, and their slaves, if any they have, are hereby declared freemen. . . . The object of this declaration is to place in the hands of the military authorities the power to give instantaneous effect to existing laws, and to supply such deficiencies as the conditions of war demand. But this is not intended to suspend the ordinary tribunals of the country, where the law will be administered by the civil officers in the usual manner, and with their customary authority, while the same can be peaceably exercised.[2]

With little delay Lincoln on September 2 wrote the general a "private and confidential" letter that did not conceal his anxiety:

> Two points in your proclamation of August 30th give me some anxiety. First, should you shoot a man, according to the proclamation, the Confederates would very certainly shoot our best man in their hands in retaliation; and so, man for man, indefinitely. It is therefore my order that you allow no man to be shot, under the proclamation, without first having my approbation or consent.
>
> Secondly, I think there is a greater danger that the closing paragraph, in relation to the confiscation of property, and the liberating slaves of traitorous

owners, will alarm our Southern Union friends, and turn them against us—perhaps ruin our rather fair prospect for Kentucky. Allow me therefore to ask, that you will as of your own motion, modify that paragraph so as to conform to the *first* and *fourth* sections of the act of Congress, entitled, "An act to confiscate property used for insurrectionary purposes," approved August, 6th, 1861, and a copy of which act I herewith send you. This letter is written in a spirit of caution and not of censure.

I send it by special messenger, in order that it may certainly and speedily reach you.[3]

In a letter dated September 8 Frémont defended his proclamation, made without consultation with anyone and deemed by him "as much a movement in the war as a battle." In so doing he threw upon the president the responsibility to order him to change the language. Frémont wrote:

Trusting to have your confidence, I have been leaving it to events themselves to show you whether or not I was shaping affairs here according to your ideas. The shortest communication between Washington and St. Louis generally involves two days, and the employment of two days in time of war goes largely towards success or disaster. I therefore went along according to my own judgment, leaving the result of my movements to justify me with you. And so in regard to my proclamation of the 30th. Between the rebel armies, the Provisional Government, and home traitors, I felt the position bad and saw danger. In the night I decided upon the proclamation and the form of it. I wrote it the next morning and printed it the same day. I did it without consultation or advice with any one, acting solely with my best judgment to serve the country and yourself, and perfectly willing to receive the amount of censure which should be thought due if I had made a false movement. This is as much a movement in the war as a battle, and in going into these I shall have to act according to my judgment of the ground before me, as I did on this occasion. If, upon reflection, your better judgment still decides that I am wrong in the article respecting the liberation of slaves, I have to ask that you will openly direct me to make the correction. The implied censure will be received as a soldier always should the reprimand of his chief. If I were to retract of my own accord, it would imply that I myself thought it was wrong, and that I had acted without the reflection which the gravity of the point demanded. But I did not. I acted with full deliberation, and upon the certain conviction that it was a measure right and necessary, and I think so still. In regard to the other point of the proclamation to which you refer, I desire to say that I do not think the enemy can either misconstrue or urge anything against it, or undertake to make unusual retaliation. The shooting of men who shall rise in arms against an army in the military occupation of a country is merely a necessary measure of defense, and entirely according to the usages of civilized warfare. The article does not at all refer to prisoners of war, and certainly our enemies have no ground for requiring that we should waive in their benefit any of the ordinary advantages which the usages of war allow us.[4]

Frémont gave the letter for delivery to the president to his wife Jesse, the daughter of former senator Thomas Hart Benton. Weary after sitting up for two nights in a crowded train, Jesse on the night of her arrival, wearing a dusty dress, walked from her hotel to the nearby White House. She received an instant reply to her note asking when she could see the president: "A Lincoln. Now."

Accompanied by a New York lawyer, Judge Cowles, she took her place in the red room of the White House. Her account of the tense meeting reads:

It was some time before he came in, though it was an appointment of his own making and the "now" had indicated I was to hasten. When he did enter it was from the far door of the dining room which he pushed to, but it was gently set open again from the other side. The President did not speak, only bowed slightly, and I introduced Judge Co(w)les as a member of the New York bar, and as the President still said nothing, I gave him the letter, telling him General Fremont felt the subject to be of so much importance, that he had sent me to answer any points on which the President might want more information. At this he smiled with an expression that was not agreeable, then moving nearer the chandelier to see better, read the letter standing. Judge Co(w)les had withdrawn to the door way of the blue parlor where he walked up and down like a sentinel. I had not been offered a seat though I was looking as tired as I felt. The President's unusual manner was a reversal of the old order of things. As he remained standing to read the letter, I drew out one of the row of chairs and sat down for I was trembling from fatigue and recent illness and instinct told me the President intended to discourage me, and I did not intend to appear nervous.

At length the President drew up a chair and sat down near me with the letter, saying, "I have written to the General and he knows what I want done." I answered the General thought it would be an advantage for him if I came to explain more fully what he wished him to know, for, I said "the General feels he is at the great disadvantage of being perhaps opposed by people in whom you have every confidence."

"Who do you mean?" he said, "Persons of differing views?" I answered; "the General's conviction is that it will be long and dreadful work to conquer by arms alone, that there must be other consideration to get us the support of foreign countries—that he *knew* the English feeling for gradual emancipation and the strong wish to meet it on the part of important men in the South" (*note:* *General Wm. Preston, John Breckenridge and others): that as the President knew we were on the eve of England, France and Spain recognizing the South: they were anxious for a pretext to do so; England on account of her cotton interests, and France because the Emperor dislikes us." The President said "You are quite the female politician."

I felt the sneering tone and saw there was a foregone decision against all listening. Then the President spoke more rapidly and unrestrainedly: "The General ought not to have done it; he never would have done it if he had consulted Frank Blair; I sent Frank there to advise him and keep me advised about the work, the true condition of things then, and how they were going." The President went on almost angrily–"Frank never would have let him do it—the General should have never dragged the Negro into the war. It is a war for a great national object and the Negro has nothing to do with it."

"Then," I answered, "there is no use to say more, except that we were not aware that Frank Blair represented you—he did not do so openly."

I asked when I could have the answer? "Maybe by tomorrow," said the President, "I have a great deal to do—to-morrow if possible, or the next day." To my saying I could come for it—"No, I will send it to you, to-morrow or the day after." He asked where I was staying, and was answered at Willard's—and we came away.[5]

Lincoln wrote to Frémont on September 11:

Yours of the 8th. in answer to mine of the 2nd. Inst. is just received. Assuming that you, upon the ground, could better judge of the necessities of your position than I could at this distance, on seeing your proclamation of August 30th. I perceived no general objection to it. The particular clause, however, in relation to the confiscation of property and the liberation of slaves, appeared to me to be objectionable, in its non-conformity to the Act of Congress passed the 6th. of last August upon the same subjects; and hence I wrote you expressing my wish that that clause should be modified accordingly. Your answer, just received, expresses the preference on your part, that I should make an open order for the modification, which I very cheerfully do. It is therefore ordered that the said clause of said proclamation be so modified, held, and construed, as to conform to, and not to transcend, the provisions on the same subject contained in the act of Congress entitled "An Act to confiscate property used for insurrectionary purposes" Approved, August 6, 1861; and that said act be published at length with this order.[6]

Lincoln apparently ended his correspondence with Jesse and the general over the impetuous proclamation with a note to her:

My dear Madam—Your two notes of to-day are before me. I answered the letter you bore me from Gen. Fremont, on yesterday; and not hearing from you during the day, I sent the answer to him by mail.

I do not exactly correct, as you say you were told by the elder Mr. Blair, to say that I sent Post-Master-General Blair to St. Louis to examine into that Department, and report. Post-Master-General Blair did go, with my approbation, to see and converse with Gen. Fremont as a friend.

I do not feel authorized to furnish you with copies of letters in my possession without the consent of the writers.

No impression has been made on my mind against the honor or integrity of Gen. Fremont; and now I enter my protest against being understood as acting in any hostility towards him.[7]

A Kentucky War Democrat, Joseph Holt, laboring to nudge his state from neutrality, wrote to Lincoln, defining the legal reasons for repudiation of Frémont's proclamation and expressing Kentucky's concern about emancipation:

The late act of Congress providing for the confiscation of the estates of persons in open rebellion against the Government was, as a necessary war measure, accepted and fully approved by the loyal men of the country. It limited the penalty of confiscation to property actually employed in the service of the rebellion with the knowledge and consent of its owners and, instead of emancipating slaves thus employed, left their status to be determined either by the Courts of the United States or by subsequent legislation. The proclamation, however, of General Fremont, under date of the 30th of August transcends, and, of course, violates the law in both these particulars, and declares that the property of rebels, whether used in support of the rebellion or not, shall be confiscated, and if consisting in slaves, that they shall be at once manumitted. The act of Congress referred to was believed to embody the conservative policy of your Administration upon this delicate and perplexing question, and hence the loyal men of the Border Slave States have felt relieved of all fears of any attempt on the part of the Government of the United States to liberate suddenly in their midst a population unprepared for freedom, and whose presence could not fail to prove a painful apprehension if not a terror to the homes and families of all. You may, therefore, well judge of the alarm and condemnation with which the Union-loving citizens of Kentucky—the State with whose popular sentiment I am best acquainted—have read this proclamation.

The hope is earnestly indulged by them as it is by myself that this paper was issued under the pressure of military necessity which Gen. Fremont believed justified the step, but that in the particulars specified it has not your approbation and will to be enforced in derogation of law. The magnitude of the interest at stake, and my extreme desire that by no misapprehension of your sentiments or purposes shall the power and fervor of the loyalty of Kentucky be at this moment abated or chilled, must be my apology for the frankness with which I have addressed you, and for the request I venture to make of an expression of your views upon the points of General Fremont's proclamation on which I have commented.[8]

Lincoln replied:

Yours of this day, in relation to the late proclamation of Gen. Fremont, is received. Yesterday I addressed a letter to him by mail, on the same subject, and which is intended to be made public when he receives it. I herewith send you a copy of that letter, which, perhaps, shows my position as distinctly as any new one I could write. I will thank you to not make it public, until Gen. Fremont shall have had time to receive the original.[9]

Holt, after serving Lincoln in various capacities, became judge advocate general of the army in September 1862.

It was at this time that Holt's fellow Kentuckian Simon Bolivar Buckner abandoned the Union and became a Confederate general. Buckner issued a flamboyant address to the "freeman of Kentucky," assailing the president and announcing, "I will enter the lists of freedom," meaning the Confederacy:

The condition of the country renders it unnecessary that I should offer any apology for addressing you. An issue has been forced upon every citizen of Kentucky by the edict of Abraham Lincoln. We are told that we must be for or against him. We must give our active support to his arbitrary acts, or we must oppose them. We must aid him in overthrowing the Constitution of the United States, or we must oppose his usurpations. We must aid him in building upon the ruins of the fair fabric of constitutional liberty a despotic authority as arbitrary as that of an Oriental despot, or we must battle like men for the preservation of the principles of liberty guaranteed by the Constitution. We must be his instruments to drag from their houses, and immure in his numerous dungeons, all who have enough of independence in their natures to express disapprobation of his policy, or we must oppose that policy. We must consent, in order that his imperial will shall have undisputed sway, that the judicial ermine shall be trampled beneath his unhallowed feet, or we must determine to maintain the principles of liberty as expounded by the judicial tribunals.

We must aid him in reviving the *letter de cachet,* that instrument of tyranny which banishes his political victims to the prisons of his numerous Bastiles; or, like the men of another day, we must wipe away these relics of barbarism which the advocate of free speech has revived as a means of enslaving us. We must sustain an usurped tyranny which has no affiliation with the Constitution or with justice, or we must resist the application of the fetters with which he seeks to bind us. We must lay our lives, our fortunes, our honor, our liberty at his feet, in order that he may consent to be the master of willing slaves, or, like men who at least are descended from freemen, we must with our own arms make good our claim to a legitimate parentage. These, freemen of Kentucky, are the issues which have been forced upon us.

Hitherto Kentucky has been, to a great extent, exempt from the evils with which the President has sought to afflict our sister Southern States. We have been lulled with the syren song of peace into a lethargy from which it was hoped we would not awake. We have been told that the armies of despotism which are to encamp upon our soil will not crush a petal of the most delicate flower, or bruise a blade of grass that decorates our fields; yet wherever they have gone, though in some instances commanded by soldiers unsurpassed in the best qualities of men, their course is marked by desolation, and lighted by the flames of burning fields and houses. It might rather be said of them, as of the host of Attila, that where they once pass the grass never grows. The President promised peace to our mother, Virginia;

he promised peace to our daughter, Missouri; he now sings in our ears the delusive sound. It is the peace which reigns in his water-girt Bastiles; it is the peace which is found in the graves of his victims.

Freemen of Kentucky! We have been slow to oppose the usurpations of Abraham Lincoln. We have heard his promises that he would observe the neutrality of Kentucky, and we have heard the echoed reassurances of his chosen instruments. We have seen the lawless military organizations which for months he has been engaged in introducing among us to over-awe the true sentiment of Kentucky. We have witnessed the clandestine introduction among us of arms and munitions, and the establishment, in defiance of the Constitution, of his military camps to subjugate us to the will of a Northern fanaticism. We have seen a portion of our own people, while preaching peace and good-will toward ourselves and our brethren of the South, drawing from beneath the cloak of neutrality the assassin dagger, which is aimed to pierce our hearts. When its point is already at our breast, this mask is at last thrown aside, and we suddenly find a son of Kentucky, a gentleman distinguished in history, but now a willing ser-vant to execute the will of his master, coming among us to direct the blow which other slaves have prepared. When our own Legislature, disregard-ing every obligation imposed upon them by justice, humanity, and the Constitution, have stripped us of the defences which they were bound to throw around us; when the gold of Philip has opened the gates of Athens; when her guardians, equally influenced by craven fear and by venal avarice, have, as they think, exposed the fair form of Kentucky an easy prey to the ravisher, this gentleman now steps forward from his chosen place in his-tory to rivet the chains which are intended to make her the victim and the slave of lustful ambition.

Men of Kentucky! are we indeed slaves, that we are thus to be dragged in chains at the feet of despotic power? Are the virtues of our ancestors buried with them in their graves? Must our loyalty to constitutional liberty be measured only by our servility to the tools of acknowledged enemies? Shall we bend our trembling knees before this modern Gesler, and bow to the tyrant's cap, which is held up as the object of our worship? Were our liberties given us but to be trampled beneath the feet of Abraham Lincoln? Has God so stamped his ignoble brow and meagre intellect with his special seal, that we are fit for no higher uses than to obey his mandates and to fill his dungeons?

Let us rise, freemen of Kentucky! and show that we are worthy of our sires.[10]

Lincoln's countermanding of Frémont's proclamation stirred an extraordinary controversy. It revealed a stronger public sentiment for emancipation than might have been supposed, particularly as measured against the congressional caution expressed in the Crittenden-Johnson resolution passed by Congress on July 25, 1861, purporting to limit the aim of the war strictly to "preserve the Union" and explicitly not to interfere with "the rights or established institutions of the states"—that is, slavery. Senator James W. Grimes of Iowa wrote to Senator Fessenden of Maine:

> Of course, you are so terribly oppressed with the great affairs of the finance department of this Government as to be wholly unable to write a letter to one of the outside barbarians in Iowa. I would not disturb your labors or your repose, if I did not deem important to glorify myself a little over the result of the "circulation Treasury—notes" measures, about the success of which those learned financial pundits, Fessenden and Chase, expressed so many doubts. You learn, of course, as I do, that at least one hundred thousand dollars of them can be floated to the manifest advantage of the Government, and to the immense advantage of this poor and benighted region. If that pure patriot and model of a public officer, whom you feel called on to defend when aspersed, would call some Pennsylvanians into the field, instead of keeping them all at home to fill army contracts, and let some of the army contracts and supplies be furnished here, business would once more assume a hopeful condition in the West. But we ought not to complain. We ought to console ourselves with the reflection that Pennsylvania furnishes one-third of all the officers to the army, and of course this draw upon her resources must impair her ability to furnish privates.
>
> When it was reported that Fremont was suspended, cold chills began to run up and down people's backs, they bit their lips, said nothing, *but refused to enlist.* I know nothing of the merits of the controversy, but it is as evident as the noonday sun that the *people* are all with Fremont, and will uphold him "through thick and thin." My wife says, and I regard her as a sort of moral thermometer for my guidance, that the only real noble and true thing done during this war has been his proclamation. Everybody of every sect, party, sex, and color, approves it in the Northwest, and it will not do for the Administration to causelessly tamper with the man who had the sublime moral courage to issue it.
>
> I wish you to understand that I do not intend by this letter to impose upon you the labor of answering it. I had nothing to write about, but I had

not heard from you, and the spirit said, "write," and I have written as the spirit moved. If my wife knew that I was writing, she would send her love; as it is, you must content yourself with mine.[11]

A startling attack came from conservative Illinois senator Orville Hickman Browning, a frequent visitor to the White House. A letter from Browning asserted that Frémont's proclamation enjoyed favor from all loyal citizens, and the government should support the general. Browning protested in part: "We must strike them [traitors and rebels] terrible blows, and strike them hard and quick, or the government will go hopelessly to pieces."[12]

Lincoln in acknowledgment told his friend he was astonished at the views "coming from you" and continued lucidly to defend his action:

Yours of the 17th is just received; and coming from you, I confess it astonishes me. That you should object to my adhering to a law, which you had assisted in making, and presenting to me, less than a month before, is odd enough. But this is a very small part. Genl. Fremont's proclamation, as to confiscation of property, and the liberation of slaves, is purely political, and not within the range of military law, or necessity. If a commanding General finds a necessity to seize the farm of a private owner, for a pasture, an encampment, or a fortification, he has the right to do so, and to so hold it, as long as the necessity lasts; and this is within military law, because within military necessity. But to say the farm shall no longer belong to the owner, or his heirs forever; and this as well when the farm is not needed for military purposes as when it is, is purely political, without the savor of military law about it. And the same is true of slaves. If the General needs them, he can seize them, and use them; but when the need is past, it is not for him to fix their permanent future condition. That must be settled according to laws made by law-makers, and not by military proclamations. The proclamation in the point in question, is simply "dictatorship." It assumes that the general may do anything he pleases—confiscate the lands and free the slaves of loyal people, as well as of disloyal ones. And going the whole figure I have no doubt would be more popular with some thoughtless people, than that which has been done! But I cannot assume this reckless position; nor allow others to assume it on my responsibility. You speak of it as being the only means of saving the government. On the contrary it is itself the surrender of the government. Can it be pretended that it is any longer the government of the U.S.—any government of Constitution and laws,—wherein a General, or a President, may make permanent rules of property by proclamation?

I do not say Congress might not with propriety pass a law, on the point, just such as General Fremont proclaimed. I do not say I might not, as a member of Congress, vote for it. What I object to, is, that I as President, shall expressly or impliedly seize and exercise the permanent legislative functions of the government.

So much as to principle. Now as to policy. No doubt the thing was popular in some quarters, and would have been more so if it had been a general declaration of emancipation. The Kentucky Legislature would not budge till that proclamation was modified; and Gen. Anderson telegraphed me that on the news of Gen. Fremont having actually issued deeds of manumission, a whole company of our Volunteers threw down their arms and disbanded. I was so assured, as to think it probable, that the very arms we had furnished Kentucky would be turned against us. I think to lose Kentucky is nearly the same as to lose the whole game. Kentucky gone, we can not hold Missouri, nor, as I think, Maryland. These all against us, and the job on our hands is too large for us. We would as well consent to separation at once, including the surrender of this capitol. On the contrary, if you will give up your restlessness for new positions, and back me manfully on the grounds upon which you and other kind friends gave me the election, and have approved in my public documents, we shall go through triumphantly.

You must not understand I took my course on the proclamation because of Kentucky. I took the same ground in a private letter to General Fremont before I heard from Kentucky.

You think I am inconsistent because I did not also forbid Gen. Fremont to shoot men under the proclamation. I understand that part to be within military law; but I also think, and so privately wrote Gen. Fremont, that it is impolitic in this, that our adversaries have the power, and will certainly exercise it, to shoot as many of our men as we shoot of theirs. I did not say this in the public letter, because it is a subject I prefer not to discuss in the hearing of our enemies.

There has been no thought of removing Gen. Fremont on any ground connected with his proclamation; and if there has been any wish for his removal on any ground, our mutual friend Sam. Glover can probably tell you what it was. I hope no real necessity for it exists on any ground.[13]

Apart from the matter of Frémont's emancipation proclamation, Lincoln had to consider reports of the general's mismanagement and incompetence.

These reports were substantive enough for Lincoln to send none other than the secretary of war to deliver a letter and to interrogate General Samuel R. Curtis, in charge of a camp near St. Louis:

> Without prejudice, and looking to nothing but justice, and the public interest, I am greatly perplexed about Gen: Fremont: In your position, you can not but have a correct judgment in the case; and I beseech you to answer Gen. Cameron, when he hands you this, "Ought Gen: Fremont to be relieved from, or retained in his present command?" It shall be entirely confidential; but you can perceive how indispensable it is to justice & the public service, that I should have, an intelligent unprejudiced, and judicious opinion from some professional Military man on the spot, to assist me in the case.[14]

By October 24, 1861, Lincoln had concluded that Frémont had to be removed unless he won a battle. He authorized Curtis to deliver a removal order and replace Frémont with General David Hunter. Word of the removal in early November swept the North like a storm. The outraged editor of the *Cincinnati Gazette,* Richard Smith, poured out his wrath to Secretary of the Treasury Salmon P. Chase:

> Could you have been among the people yesterday and witnessed the excitement, could you have seen sober citizens pulling from their walls and trampling under foot the portrait of the President, and could you hear to-day the expressions of all classes of men, of all political parties, you would, I think, feel as I feel, and as every sincere friend of the government must feel, alarmed. What meaneth this burning of the President in effigy, by citizens who have hitherto sincerely and enthusiastically supported the war? What mean these boisterous outbursts of indignation, and these low mutterings favorable to the Western confederacy that we hear? Why this sudden check to enlistments? Why this rejection of Treasury notes by German citizens? Why is it that on the 6th of November, 1861, not one dollar was subscribed here to the national loan? Why is it that it would not be safe to go into places where the Germans resort, and publicly express an opinion favorable to the President? Why this sudden, this extraordinary, this startling change in public sentiment, on change, in the street, in the banking-house, in the palace and the cottage, in country and city? Is it not time for the President to stop and consider whether, as this is a government of the people, it is not unsafe to disregard and overrule public sentiment,

as has been done in the case of General Fremont? The public consider that Fremont has been made a martyr of. . . . Consequently he is now, so far as the West is concerned, the most popular man in the country. He is to the West what Napoleon was to France; while the President has lost the confidence of the people.[15]

The relationship between Frémont and Lincoln continued to be bothersome throughout the war, but Lincoln had clarified that he, as commander in chief, would control the timing and scope of emancipation orders. The reaction to Frémont's controversial order, and Lincoln's countermanding it in the first few months of the war, indicated how volatile the politics of emancipation would be. The issue would be clarified on the battlefield.

CHAPTER TWELVE

FIRST BULL RUN

Lincoln was ill prepared to meet the high responsibility of commander in chief of the army and navy. Unlike a number of his predecessors who had been generals, he had briefly served as captain in the Black Hawk War. In a congressional speech he took aim at the 1848 Democratic presidential nominee General Lewis Cass. Lincoln made fun of Cass's and his own military records, saying, "If he saw any live, fighting Indians, it was more than I did; but I had a good many blood struggles with the mosquitoes."[1]

Confronted with civil war at the start of his of presidency, he exerted extraordinary authority as commander in chief, broadcasting one proclamation after another. He suffered from having appointed an incompetent machine politician as secretary of war, Simon Cameron, and from inheriting an aging military hero, wise in military matters but less responsive than he to political considerations, Winfield Scott. Lincoln learned as the war progressed, however, so much so that one historian described him as a "military genius."[2]

After the surrender of Fort Sumter and the summons of militia, public pressure to fight built up. A letter to Lincoln on May 6 from Wisconsin's governor Alexander Randall, who as early as January had urged preparedness, exemplified public impatience. Speaking for several northwestern governors, he said:

> We see a necessity now, not only for the safety of the Government, but for the safety of the free border States, for immediate action. There is no occasion for the Government to delay, because the States themselves are willing to act vigorously and efficiently. I must be permitted to say it, because it is a fact, there is a spirit evoked by this rebellion among the liberty-loving

people of the country that is driving them to action, and if the Government will not permit them to action, and if the Government will not permit them to act for it, they will act for themselves. It is better for the Government to direct this current than to let it run wild. So far as possible we have attempted to allay this excess of spirit, but there is a moral element and a reasoning element in this uprising that cannot be met in the ordinary way. There is a conviction of great wrongs to be redressed, and that the Government is to be preserved by them. The Government must provide an outlet for this feeling or it will find one for itself. If the Government does not at once shoulder this difficulty and direct its current there will come something more than a war to put down rebellion—it will be a war between border States, which will lose sight, for the time, of the Government.[3]

On June 1 Confederate general Pierre Gustave Toutant Beauregard, to whom Fort Sumter surrendered, assumed command of forces assembled at Manassas, Virginia, near Bull Run Creek, just twenty-five miles from Washington. Edwin Stanton, who had served in Buchanan's cabinet and within months would serve in Lincoln's cabinet, on June 11 wrote to his fellow Democrat John A. Dix, who three days later would be appointed a major general, a letter sharply critical of Lincoln and his policies:

No one can imagine the deplorable condition of this city [Washington, D.C.], and the hazard of the Government, who did not witness the weakness and panic of the administration, and the painful imbecility of Lincoln.[4]

To gather military information into his own hands, on June 22 Lincoln wrote to the heads of the federal military bureaus:

You will please, under the direction of my private Secretary, make to me such abstract reports, as will show the number of men now enlisted as soldiers or seamen in the service of the United States, or mustered into the service as State Militia or Volunteers, the state of their equipment and drill, the time of their probable readiness for active service, and the place of rendezvous or present station. Also (if practicable) like information in regard to the organization of military forces in the Free States, under State authority. Also the number and kind of arms and ammunition furnished, and yet on hand, and being manufactured. Also the number and description of War vessels and transports at present owned or chartered by the government, where and on what service at present stationed and the number description and time of probable readiness for service of those being prepared.[5]

Readers of the *New York Tribune* beginning on June 26 daily saw in bold, hortatory headlines: "Forward to Richmond! Forward to Richmond! The rebel Congress must not be allowed to meet there on the 20th of July. By that date the place must be held by the national army!"

General Scott developed a long-term plan, usually called the "Anaconda policy," named for the large snake that crushes its victim. Addressing General G. B. McClellan, Scott explained:

It is the design of the Government to raise 25,000 additional regular troops, and 60,000 volunteers, for three years. . . .

We rely greatly on the sure operation of a complete blockade of the Atlantic and Gulf ports soon to commence. In connection with such blockade we propose a powerful movement down the Mississippi to the ocean, with a cordon of posts at proper points, . . . the object being to clear out and keep open this great line of communication in connection with the strict blockade of the seaboard, so as to envelop the insurgent States and bring them to terms with less bloodshed than by any other plan. I suppose there will be needed from twelve to twenty steam gun-boats, and a sufficient number of steam transports (say forty) to carry all the *personnel* (say 60,000 men) and *material* of the expedition; most of the gun-boats to be in advance to open the way; and the remainder to follow and protect the rear of the expedition, etc. This army, in which it is not improbable you may be invited to take an important part, should be composed of our best regulars for the advance, and of three years' volunteers, all well officered, and with four and a half months of instruction in camp prior to (say) November 10. In the progress down the river all the enemy's batteries on its banks we of course would turn and capture, leaving a sufficient number of posts with complete garrisons to keep the river open behind the expedition. Finally, it will be necessary that New Orleans should be strongly occupied and securely held until present difficulties are composed.[6]

I propose to organize an army of regulars and volunteers on the Ohio River, of say 80,000 men, to be divided into two unequal columns, the smaller to proceed by water on the first autumnal swell in the rivers, headed and flanked by gun-boats (propellers of great speed and strength), and the other column to proceed as nearly abreast as practicable by land—of course without the benefit of rail transportation—and receiving at certain points on the river its heavier articles of consumption from the freight boats of the first column. By this means the wagon train of the land column may no doubt be much diminished, but would still remain, I fear, so large as to constitute a great impediment to the movement. Would 80,000 men be sufficient to conquer its way to New Orleans and clear out the Mississippi to the Gulf? What should be the relative numbers of the two columns, and at how many points besides Louisville, Paducah, Columbus, Hickman, Memphis, Vicksburg, and New Orleans would the two columns be able to hold a close communication with each other? Of course much would depend upon the relations to the United States of Kentucky, Tennessee, and Missouri. I ask your views not only on the foregoing points, but also as to the form, drought, tonnage, and armament of the gun-boats or tugs. Cincinnati abounds in the best information on all these heads.[7]

A word now as to the greatest obstacle in the way of this plan—the great danger now pressing upon us—the impatience of our patriotic and loyal Union friends. They will urge instant and vigorous action, regardless, I fear, of consequences—that i[s], unwilling to wait for the slow instruction of (say) twelve or fifteen camps, for the rise of rivers, and the return of frost to kill the virus of the malignant fevers below Memphis. I fear this; but impress right views, on every proper occasion, upon the brave men who are hastening to the support of their Government. Lose no time, while necessary preparations for the great expedition are in progress, in organizing, drilling, and disciplining your three months' men, many of whom, it is hoped, will be ultimately found enrolled under the call for three years' volunteers. Should an urgent and immediate occasion arise meantime for their services, they will be the more effective. I commend these views to your consideration and shall be happy to hear the result.[8]

Lincoln on June 29 called a council of his cabinet, Scott, and others to discuss a move against Manassas. Scott opposed the move but, overruled by Lincoln and the cabinet, he produced a plan drawn up by Irvin McDowell, recently appointed brigadier general and favored by Scott. McDowell was summoned to the meeting. His plan was excellent, resting, however, upon Union general Robert Patterson to prevent nearby Confederate forces from joining Beauregard at Bull Run. Patterson failed to do this, and McDowell's forces, confronted by the enlarged Confederate army on July 21, lost the battle and hastily retreated. Months later McDowell gave an account of the circumstances to a congressional committee. He said:

> Now, in regard to my plan, I had, in the first place, to assume what the enemy had in front of me. I next assumed that there would be no secret of my preparing to go against them. They would know it, and as a consequence of that they would bring up whatever disposable force they had. Therefore, it was not so much what they had here, but what they would bring here, that I was to go against. I assumed that if General Butler would keep them engaged below, and General Patterson would keep Johnson engaged above, I would then have so much to go against. To do that I asked for a certain force. They agreed to it, and gave me the force, but very late in the day. But they did not fulfil the condition with me so far as General Johnson was concerned. I had a part to play in the matter. It was but a part in a whole; it was a large part, still only a part. I had no control over the whole; that was controlled by General Scott. On several occasions I mentioned to the general that I felt tender on the subject of General Patterson and General Johnson. In reply to some suggestion once made about bringing Patterson over to Leesburg, I said if he went there Johnson might escape and join Beauregard, and I was not in a condition to meet all their forces combined. I said that I went over there with everything green. I said that the chances of accident were much more with green troops than with veterans, and I could not undertake to meet all their forces together. General Scott assured me—I use his own words–"if Johnson joins Beauregard he shall have Patterson on his heels." He gave me this assurance that there should be no question in regard to keeping Johnson's troops engaged in the valley of Virginia. I estimated to go from Vienna with the largest force, and get in behind Fairfax Court-House; go with one force down the Little River turnpike upon Fairfax Court-House; go with one force by way of Anandale, and then go off to the south by the old Braddock road, as it is called, and then have the fourth column go south of the railroad. . . . The largest part of the 30,000 men were in front. I moved down Tuesday evening. When General Scott was called upon, or when the question was asked in the cabinet, when he would be ready to carry out this plan, General Scott fixed for me that day week. Up to that time General Scott never wished anything done on the other side of the river further than to merely fortify Arlington Heights. General Scott was exceedingly displeased that I should go over there. He had other plans in view, and personal plans, so far as I was concerned. And he was piqued and irritated

that I was sent over there, and the more so that General Sandford was here in somewhat an equivocal position. He was here for three months, a major general of troops in New York. General Scott did not wish to give him the command here in Washington; at least I infer so because he did not put him in command, and he put him in command on the other side of the river. But General Scott was told that he must put either General Mansfield or myself over there. He wished to keep General Mansfield here, and he put me over there. The general had opposed my somewhat rapid promotion, because he thought it was doing a hurt to General Mansfield, and when I was promoted he insisted that General Mansfield should also be promoted, and date back a week before my own promotion. . . . I was on the other side a long while without anything. No additions were made to the force at all. With difficulty could I get any officers. I had begged of the Secretary of War and the Secretary of the Treasury, who at that time was connected with the Secretary of War in many of the plans and organizations going forward, that I should not be obliged to organize and discipline and march and fight all at the same time. I said that it was too much for any person to do. But they could not help it, or did not help it, and the thing went on until this project was broached. . . . I went over the river, as I have told you. . . . I got everything with great difficulty. Some of my regiments came over very late; some of them not till the very day I was to move the army. I had difficulty in getting transportation. . . . But there is one thing clear beyond any doubt. If the movements which had been ordered had been carried out, we should have had no difficult[y] at all. My plan was simply this: It was to move out this force upon these four lines. I had to move them on four lines that had no communication with each other from the very nature of the country. But I thought I made each column strong enough to hold its own. If it could not penetrate it could stand still, and if attacked it could hold its own, while the other columns were pressing forward and trying to get behind the enemy. . . . At Fairfax Court-House was the South Carolina brigade. And I do not suppose anything would have had a greater cheering effect upon the troops, and perhaps upon the country, than the capture of that brigade. And if General Tyler could have got down there any time in the forenoon instead of in the afternoon the capture of that brigade was beyond question. It was but 5,000 or 6,000 men, and Tyler had 12,000, at the same time that we were pressing on in front. He did not get down there until in the afternoon; none of us got forward in time. . . . General Tyler was late, and General Hunter was slow in getting around; still, we substantially carried out the plan. We got over there and met the enemy; and there I found that, in addition to General Beauregard, I had General Johnston—how much of him I did not know. I learned afterwards that some 7,000 or 8,000, the bulk of his force, had arrived. Still, we were successful against both until about 3 o'clock in the afternoon, when the remainder of his force came upon us upon our right when our men were tired and exhausted, and that caused the day to turn against us.[9]

The loss at the first major battle of the war weighed heavily on the Union commanders. At a meeting with Lincoln General Scott said:

Sir, I am the greatest coward in America. I will prove it. I have fought this battle, sir, against my judgment; I think the President ought to remove me today for doing it. As God is my judge, after my superiors had determined to fight it, I did all in my power to make the army efficient. I deserve removal because I did not stand up, when my army was not in condition for fighting, and resist to the last.[10]

Lincoln responded, "Your conversation seems to imply that I forced you to fight this battle." The old soldier replied, "I have never served a President who has been kinder to me than you have been."[11]

The day after the battle Lincoln ordered General George B. McClellan, his reputation inflated by the battle of Phillipi, to report to Washington to assume command of the Division of the Potomac, which incorporated McDowell's forces.

Lincoln began to become a strategist of the war and to take a more explicit role in directing the Union armies. On July 23 he composed a memorandum of military policy suggested by the Bull Run defeat, and four days later another. They read:

July 23, 1861.
  1. Let the plan for making the Blockade effective be pushed forward with all possible dispatch.
  2. Let the volunteer forces at Fort-Monroe & vicinity under Genl. Butler—be constantly drilled, disciplined, and instructed without more for the present.
  3. Let Baltimore be held, as now, with a gentle, but firm, and certain hand.

4. Let the force now under Patterson, or Banks, be strengthened, and made secure in its position.

5. Let the forces in Western Virginia act, till further orders, according to instructions, or orders from Gen. McClellan.

6. (Let) Gen. Fremont push forward his organization, and operations in the West as rapidly as possible, giving rather special attention to Missouri.

7. Let the forces late before Manassas, except the three months men, be reorganized as rapidly as possible, in their camps here and about Arlington

8. Let the three months forces, who decline to enter the longer service, be discharged as rapidly as circumstances will permit.

9. Let the new volunteer forces be brought forward as fast as possible; and especially into the camps on the two sides of the river here.

July 27, 1861.

When the foregoing shall have been substantially attended to—

1. Let Manassas junction, (or some point on one or other of the railroads near it;); and Strasburg, be seized, and permanently held, with an open line from Washington to Manassas; and and (sic) open line from Harper's Ferry to Strasburg—the military men to find the way of doing these.

2. This done, a joint movement from Cairo on Memphis; and from Cincinnati on East Tennessee.[12]

The irrepressible and sometimes irresponsible Horace Greeley, whose newspaper's cry had helped bring on the big battle, wrote to Lincoln on July 29. His letter read:

This is my seventh sleepless night—yours, too, doubtless—yet I think I shall not die, because I have no right to die. I must struggle to live, however bitterly. But to business. You are not considered a great man, and I am a hopelessly broken one. You are now undergoing a terrible ordeal, and God has thrown the gravest responsibilities upon you. Do not fear to meet them. Can the rebels be beaten after all that has occurred, and in view of the actual state of feeling caused by our late, awful disaster? If they can,—and it is your business to ascertain and decide,—write me that such is your judgment, so that I may know and do my duty. And if they *cannot* be beaten,—if our recent disaster is fatal,—do not fear to sacrifice yourself to your country. If the rebels are not to be beaten,—if that is your judgment in view of all the light you can get,—then every drop of blood henceforth shed in this quarrel will be wantonly, wickedly shed, and the guilt will rest heavily on the soul of every promoter of the crime. I pray you to decide quickly and let me know my duty.

If the Union is irrevocably gone, an armistice for thirty, sixty, ninety, one hundred and twenty days—better still for a year—ought at once to be proposed, with a view to a peaceful adjustment. Then Congress should call a National Convention, to meet at the earliest possible day. And there should be an immediate and mutual exchange or release of prisoners and a disbandment of forces. I do not consider myself at present a judge of anything but the public sentiment. That seems to me everywhere gathering and deepening against a prosecution of the war. The gloom in this city is funereal—for our dead at Bull Run were many, and they lie unburied yet. On every brow sits sullen, scorching, black despair. It would be easy to have Mr. Crittenden move any proposition that ought to be adopted, or to have it come from any proper quarter. The first point is to ascertain what is best that can be done,—which is the measure of our duty,—and do that very thing at the earliest moment.

This letter is written in the strictest of confidence, and is for your eye alone. But you are at liberty to say to members of your Cabinet that you know I will second any move you may see fit to make. But to do nothing timidly nor by halves. Send me word what to do. I will live till I can hear it at all events. If it is best for the country and for mankind that we make peace with the rebels at once and on their own terms, do not shrink even from that. But bear in mind the greatest truth: "Whoso would lose his life for my sake shall save it." Do the thing that is the highest right, and tell me how I am to second you.

Yours, in the depths of bitterness, Horace Greeley.[13]

Nearly three years later, appearing one night in a room occupied by John Hay and John Nicolay, Lincoln showed Hay the letter written in Greeley's cramped hand. Hay recorded in his diary:

The President came loafing in as it grew late and . . . gave to me to decipher Greeley's letter to him of the 29th July, 1861. This most remarkable letter still retains for me its wonderful interest as the most insane specimen of pusillanimity that I have ever read. When I had finished reading Nicolay said

"That wd. be nuts to the Herald. Bennett wd. willingly give $10,000.00 for that." To which the Prest., tying the red tape round the package, answered, "I need $10,000 very much but he could not have it for many times that."[14]

Lincoln was unmoved by Greeley's panicked response to the defeat at Bull Run and his suggestion to propose an armistice. Instead, he called up a new commander for the Division of the Potomac and began to take a more direct role in military policy. For his part Lincoln "pushed forward."

CHAPTER THIRTEEN

ENTER MCCLELLAN

George B. McClellan, Philadelphia aristocrat, graduated second in his class from West Point in 1846 and served in the army until he resigned in 1857 to become a railroad executive. On the outbreak of the war he returned to military duty and won recognition with a victory in western Virginia, securing the region for the Union. Called to duty in Washington, he found citizens fearful about their security and soldiers dispirited after Bull Run. He plunged into his work, training and reorganizing the Division of the Potomac, lifting his army's morale.

Letters intended only for his wife's eyes reveal both the deference shown him as well as the serious flaws in his character. A letter written the day after his arrival read in part: "I find myself in a new and strange position here—by some strange operation of magic I seem to have become *the* power of the land." Days later he wrote: "I went to the Senate ... and was quite overwhelmed by the congratulations I received and the respect with which I was treated. . . . All tell me that I am held responsible for the fate of the nation, and that all its resources shall be placed at my disposal."

A subsequent letter told his wife Ellen: "I handed the President to-night a carefully considered plan for conducting the war on a large scale. . . . I shall carry this thing on *en grand* and crush the rebels in one campaign." Another letter reported: "I dined at the president's yesterday. I suppose some forty were present—Prince Napoleon and his staff, French minister, English ditto, cabinet, some senators, Gen. Scott, and myself. The dinner was not especially interesting; rather long, and rather tedious, as such things generally are." Still another letter informed Ellen:

I receive letter after letter, have conversation after conversation, calling on me to save the nation, alluding to the presidency, dictatorship, etc . . . I would cheerfully take the dictatorship, and agree to lay down my life when the country is saved. I am not spoiled by my new unexpected position.

The letters reveal Washington's state of mind and also McClellan's arrogance, ego, and egregious misunderstanding of the magnitude of the war to be won.[1]

Beyond these matters the letters shockingly disclosed his attitude toward Lincoln, his commander in chief. In mid-August he told Ellen: "I am here in a terrible place—the enemy have from 3 to 4 times my force—the Presdt is an idiot, the old General in his dotage—they cannot or will not see the true state of affairs." Weeks later Ellen read:

I can't tell you how disgusted I am becoming with these wretched politicians—they are a most despicable set of men & I think Seward is the meanest of them all—a meddling, officious, incompetent little puppy. . . . The Presdt is nothing more than a well meaning baboon.

A month later Ellen learned, "I went to the White House shortly after tea where I found 'the *original gorilla*,' about as intelligent as ever. What a specimen to be at the head of our affairs!"[2]

In mid-December an incident occurred that, in the case of another president, might have terminated McClellan's military career. One night Lincoln and others went to call on the general. Told he was not in, they spent about an hour until he returned and was informed by a servant that the president was waiting to see him. The general walked past the door where Lincoln, Seward, and Hay were waiting. Half an hour later the servant was asked to tell the general the president was there. The servant returned to say the general had gone to bed.

Hay penned in his diary:

I merely record this unparalleled insolence of epaulettes without comment. . . . Coming home I spoke to the president about the matter but he seemed not to have noticed it specially, saying it was better at this time not to be making points of etiquette & personal dignity.[3]

The general's summary treatment of visitors was likewise experienced by William H. Russell, American correspondent of the *Times* of London. He recorded an episode in his diary and went on to describe a beleaguered president:

This poor President! He is to be pitied; surrounded by such scenes, and trying with all his might to understand strategy, naval warfare, big guns, the movements of troops, military maps, reconnoissances, occupations, interior and exterior lines, and all the technical details of the art of slaying. He runs form one house to another, armed with plans, papers, reports, recommendations, sometimes good-humored, never angry, occasionally dejected, and always a little fussy. The other night, as I was sitting in the parlor at head-quarters, with an English friend who had come to see his old acquaintance the General, walked in a tall man with a navvy's cap, and an illmade shooting-suit, from the pockets of which protruded paper and bundles. "Well," said he to Brigadier Van Vliet, who rose to receive him, "is George in?"

"Yes, sir. He's come back, but is lying down, very much fatigued. I'll send up, sir, and inform him you wish to see him."

"O, no, I can wait. I think I'll take supper with him. Well, and what are you now,—I forget your name—are you a major, or a colonel, or a general?"

"Whatever you like to make me, sir."

Seeing that General McClellan was occupied, I walked out with my friend, who asked me when I got into the street why I stood up when that tall fellow came into the room. "Because it was the President."

"The President of what?"

"Of the United States."

"Oh! Come, now you're humbugging me. Let me have another look at him."

He came back more incredulous than ever, but when I assured him I was quite serious, he exclaimed, "I give up the United States after this."[4]

Meanwhile McClellan aspired to succeed Scott as general-in-chief. At 1:15 a.m. on October 30 he wrote to Ellen: "For the last three hours I have been at Montgomery Blair's, talking with Senators Wade, Trumbull, Chandler about war matters. They will make a desperate effort tomorrow to have Gen. Scott retired at once . . . he is ever in my way."[5] On the last day of October the old general, feeling insulted by a letter from McClellan and aware of his physical infirmity, requested retirement.

The following day Lincoln issued an order retiring Scott and stating:

On the 1st day of November, A.D. 1861, upon his own application to the President of the United States, Brevet Lieutenant General Winfield Scott is ordered to be placed, and hereby is placed, upon the list of retired officers of the Army of the United States, without reduction in his current pay, subsistence, or allowances.

The American people will hear with sadness and deep emotion that General Scott has withdrawn from the active control of the army, while the President and a unanimous Cabinet express their own and the nation's sympathy in his personal affliction and their profound sense of the important public services rendered by him to his country during his long and brilliant career, among which will ever be gratefully distinguished his faithful devotion to the Constitution, the Union, and the Flag, when assailed by parricidal rebellion.[6]

On the same day he wrote a private letter to McClellan:

Lieut. Genl. Scott having been, upon his own application, placed on the list of retired officers, with his advice, and the concurrence of the entire cabinet, I have designated you to command the whole Army. You will, therefore, assume this enlarged duty at once, conferring with me so far as necessary.[7]

As weeks passed without McClellan engaging the enemy, and as troops drilled and marched in review, public patience wore thin. On October 26 Hay had recorded in his diary:

This evening the Jacobin club [Republican radicals], represented by Trumbull Chandler and Wade, came up to worry the administration into a battle. The agitation of the summer is to be renewed. The President defended McClellan's deliberateness. We then went over to the General's Headquarters. We found Col Key there. He was talking also about the grand necessity of an immediate battle to clean out the enemy, at once. He seemed to think we were ruined if we did not fight. The President asked what McC. thot about it. Key answered, "The General is troubled in his mind. I think he is much embarrassed by the radical differences between his views and those of General Scott.

Here McC. came in—Key went out—the President began to talk about his wonderful new repeating battery of rifled gun, shooting 50 balls a minute. The President is delighted with it and has ordered ten and asks McC.

to go down and see it, and if proper, detail a corps of men to work it. He further told the General that Reverdy Johnson wants the Maryland Vols in Maryld to vote in November. All right.

They then talked about the Jacobins. McC said that Wade preferred an unsuccessful battle to delay. He said a defeat could be easily repaired, by the swarming recruits. McClellan answered, "that he would rather have a few recruits before a victory—than a good many after a defeat."

The President deprecated this new manifestation of popular impatience but at the same time said it was a reality and should be taken into account. "At the same time General you must not fight till you are ready."

"I have everything at stake," said the General. "If I fail I will not see you again or anybody."

"I have a notion to go out with you and stand or fall with the battle."

The President has written a letter to St. Louis giving plan of campaign as suggestion [to] the officer in Command, probably Hunter. It is to halt the pursuit of Price, go back in two columns to Rolla and Sedalia, and there *observe* taking the surplus for active operation in the South. The plan though entirely original with the President seemed a good one both to Scott and McC. and will probably be followed.[8]

On another occasion Lincoln planned a conference involving McClellan, a governor, and a general. McClellan did not come, and after a long wait, Lincoln remarked: "Never mind; I will hold McClellan's horse if he will only bring us success." A few days later Lincoln paid the general a call. Hay recorded in his diary:

> The night of the 1st November we went over to McClellans. The General was there and read us his general order in regard to Scotts resignation & his own assumption of command. The President thanked him for it and said it greatly relieved him. He added, "I should be perfectly satisfied if I thought that this vast increase of responsibility would not embarrass you."
>
> "It is a great relief, sir. I feel as if several tons were taken from my shoulders today. I am now in contact with you, and the Secretary. I am not embarrassed by intervention."
>
> "Well" says the President, "Draw on me for all the sense I have, and all the information. In addition to your present command, the supreme command of the army will entail a vast labor upon you."
>
> "I can do it all," McC said quietly.

Going to Sewards he talked long and earnestly about the matter. He had been giving a grave and fatherly lecture to McC. which was taken in good part, advising him to enlarge the sphere of his thoughts and feel the weight of the occasion.[9]

Public impatience grew in intensity as the year progressed, rising to demands from Republican radicals that McClellan move against the enemy. The general was accused of unnecessary delay and secrecy about his plans. On December 10 Congress created a Joint Committee on the Conduct of the War. Radical Republican Benjamin F. Wade, "Bluff Ben Wade," given to violent speeches, became chairman. At an early interrogation Wade declared:

This nation is making an extraordinary effort. Next march we shall be 600,000,000 in debt for what we have already done . . . nothing has yet been done . . . everybody knows that our finances are not in a condition to keep this up eternally. All this is hanging on one man who keeps his counsels entirely to himself.[10]

At this critical juncture, McClellan fell ill. Concerned about him and the rumors circulating about the committee, Lincoln on January 1 wrote him a reassuring letter. A few days later he followed the first with another:

Jany. 1. 1862.

I hear that the doings of an Investigating Committee, give you some uneasiness. You may be entirely relieved on this point. The gentlemen of the Committee were with me an hour and a half last night; and I found them in a perfectly good mood.

As their investigation brings them acquainted with facts, they are rapidly coming to think of the whole case as all sensible men would.

Jan. 9. 1862

I think you better go before the Congressional Committee the earliest moment your health will permit—to-day, if possible.[11]

Still inertia prevailed. Distressed by the lack of action by both the general and the president, Attorney General Bates recorded in his diary:

For months past (and lately more pressingly) I have urged upon the President to have some military organization about his own person—appoint suitable aid(e)s—2–3 or 4—to write and carry his orders, to collect information, to keep the needful papers and records always at hand, and to do his bidding generally, in all Military and Naval affairs. I insisted that, being "Commander in chief" by law, he must command—especially in such a war as this. The Nation requires it, and History will hold him responsible.

In this connexion, it is lamentable that Gen McClellan—the *General in chief,* so called—is, and for some time has been incapacitated by a severe spell of illness (and Genl. Marcy, his chief of Staff—and father in law, is sick also). It now appears that the Genl. in chief has been very reticent— kept his plans absolutely to himself, so that the strange and dangerous fact exists, that the Sec of War and the Prest. are ignorant of the condition of the army and its intended operations!

I see no reason for having a Genl. in chief at all. It was well enough to call the veteran Lieut. Genl. Scott so, when we had no enemies *in the field,* and no army but a little nucleus of 15,000 men. But now that we have several mighty armies and active operations spreading over half a continent, there seems to me no good sense in confiding to one general the command of the whole; and especially, as we have no general who has any experience in the handling of large armies—not one of them ever commanded 10,000 under fire, or has any personal knowledge of the complicated movements of a great army.

If I were President, I *would* command *in chief*—not *in detail,* certainly— and I *would* know what army I had, and what the high generals (my Lieutenants) were doing with that army.[12]

In the midst of this early crisis, Lincoln descended into despair. On January 10, seeking counsel, he appeared at the door of his Quartermaster General Montgomery C. Meigs. Meigs wrote about the visit:

On Friday, January 10th, 1862, the President, in great distress, entered my office. He took a chair in front of the open fire and said, "General, what shall I do? The people are impatient; Chase has no money and he tells me he can raise no more; the General of the Army has typhoid fever. The bottom is out of the tub. What shall I do?"

I said, "If General McClellan has typhoid fever, that is an affair of six weeks at least; he will not be able sooner to command. In the meantime, if the enemy in our front is as strong as he believes, they may attack on any day, and I think you should see some of those upon whom in such case, or in case any forward movement becomes necessary, the control must fall.

Send for them to meet you soon and consult with them; perhaps you may select the responsible commander for such an event."

The council was called. On Sunday, January 12th, McDowell and Franklin called on me with a summons to the White House for one P.M. These officers, and Messrs. Seward, Chase and Blair of the Cabinet attended. The President announced that he had called this meeting in consequence of the sickness of General McClellan, but he had that morning heard from him that he was better, and would be able to be present the next day; and that, on this promise, he adjourned the discussion for twenty four hours.[13]

Later that evening Lincoln met with Generals McDowell and Franklin and some members of his cabinet. Discussion centered on getting McClellan to move his army. A worried Lincoln remarked: "If something were not soon done, and if General McClellan did not want to use the army he would like to borrow it, provided he could see how it could be made to do something."[14]

The next afternoon Lincoln sat down with a war council attended by Generals McClellan, McDowell, Franklin, and Meigs as well as Chase, Seward, and Montgomery Blair. Meigs was a captain when the war broke out, was commissioned a colonel on May 14, and later became the next brigadier general at the same time as he was appointed quartermaster general of the army. He left a vivid account:

The next day, Jany. 13th, the same persons and General McClellan appeared at the rendezvous. The President opened the proceedings by making a statement of the cause of his calling the Council. Mr. Chase, and Mr. Blair, if memory is accurate, both spoke. All looked to McClellan, who sat still with his head hanging down, and mute. The situation grew awkward. The President spoke again a few words. One of the Generals said something; McClellan said something which evidently did not please the speaker, and again was mute.

I move[d] my chair to the side of McClellan's and urged him, saying, "The President evidently expects you to speak; can you not promise some movement towards Manassas? You are strong." He replied, "I cannot move on them with as great a force as they have." "Why, you have near 200,000 men, how many have they?" "Not less than 175,000 according to my advices." I said, "Do you think so?, and the President expects something of you."

He replied, "If I tell him my plans they will be in the New York Herald tomorrow morning. He can't keep a secret, he will tell them to Todd." I said: "That is a pity, but he is the President,—the Commander-in-Chief; he has a right to know; it is not respectful to sit mute when he so clearly requires you to speak. He is superior to all."

After some further urging, McClellan moved, and seemed to prepare to speak. He declined to give his plans in detail, but thought it best to press the movement of Buell's troops the central line of operation. After a few words that brought out nothing more, Mr. Lincoln said, "Well, on this assurance of the General that he will press the advance in Kentucky, I will be satisfied, and will adjourn this Council."[15]

McClellan's unresponsiveness was compounded for Lincoln by the apparent corruption in his cabinet. Secretary of War Cameron had become an embarrassment to Lincoln. On January 11 Lincoln wrote Cameron two letters, one a brief official notice, making him minister to Russia, the other personal and explanatory:

My dear Sir. As you have, more than once, expressed a desire for a change of position, I can now gratify you, consistently with my view of the public interest. I therefore propose nominating you to the Senate, next Monday, as minister to Russia.[16]

Though I have said nothing hitherto in response to your wish, expressed long since, to resign your seat in the cabinet, I have not been unmindful of it. I have been only unwilling to consent to a change at a time, and under circumstances which might give occasion to misconstruction, and unable, till now to see how such misconstruction could be avoided.

But the desire of Mr. Clay to return home and to offer his services to his country in the field enables me now to gratify your wish, and at the same time evince my personal regard for you, and my confidence in your ability, patriotism, and fidelity to public trust.

I therefore tender your acceptance, if you still desire to resign your current position, the post of Minister to Russia. Should you accept it, you will bear with you the assurance of my undiminished confidence, of my affectionate esteem, and of my sure expectations that, near the great sovereign whose personal and hereditary friendship for the United States, so much endears him to Americans, you will be able to render services to your country, not less important than those you could render at home.[17]

Cameron promptly replied:

I have devoted myself, without intermission, to my official duties; I have given them all my energies; I have done my best. It was impossible, in the direction of operations so extensive, but that some mistakes happen, and some complications and complaints arise. In view of these recollections, I thank you from a full heart, for the expression of your "confidence in my ability, patriotism, and fidelity to public trust." Thus my own conscientious sense of doing my duty to the Executive and by my Country, is approved by the acknowledged head of the Government himself. . . .

In retiring from the War Department, I feel that the mighty Army of the United States, is ready to do battle for the Constitution—that it is marshaled by gallant and experienced leaders—that it is fired with the greatest enthusiasm for the good cause; and also, that my successor, in this department, is my personal friend, who unites to wonderful intellect and vigor, the grand essential of being in earnest in the present struggle, and of being resolved upon a speedy and overwhelming triumph of our arms. I therefore gratefully accept the new distinction you have conferred upon me, and as soon as important and long neglected private business has been arranged, I will enter upon the important duties of the mission to which you have called me.[18]

Edwin Stanton, Cameron's successor in the War Department, had snubbed Lincoln in the 1850s as the prairie lawyer and had secretly criticized him later; a Democrat, Stanton had served in the discredited Buchanan administration. He was, however, from the politically crucial state of Pennsylvania (Cameron's state) and was supported by members of Lincoln's cabinet. The appointment proved to be shrewd and successful in its results. The new secretary quickly began to try to stir McClellan to act.

But McClellan would not move. Sensitive to the widespread criticism from press and politicians, Lincoln on January 27 issued an extraordinary order, forceful if perhaps amateurish, in his role as commander in chief. Four days later he issued another:

27 January 1862. President's General War Order No. 1. Ordered that the 22nd. day of February 1862, be the day for a general movement of the Land and Naval forces of the United States against the insurgent forces.

That especially–

The Army at & about, Fortress Monroe.

The Army of the Potomac.

The Army of Western Virginia.

The Army near Munfordsville, Ky.

The Army and Flotilla at Cairo.

And a Naval force in the Gulf of Mexico, be ready for a movement on that day.

That all other forces, both Land and Naval, with their respective commanders, obey existing orders, for the time, and be ready to obey additional orders when duly given.

That the Heads of Departments, and especially the Secretaries of War and of the Navy, with all their subordinates; and the General-in-Chief, with all other commanders and subordinates, of Land and Naval forces, will severally be held to their strict and full responsibilities, for the prompt execution of this order.

January 31, 1862. Presidents special War Order, No. 1. Ordered that all the disposable force of the Army of the Potomac, after providing safely for the defense of Washington, be formed into an expedition, for the immediate object of seizing and occupying a point upon the Rail Road South Westward of what is known of Manassas Junction, all details to be in the discretion of the general-in-chief, and the expedition to move before, or on, the 22nd. day of February next.[19]

In a communication to Stanton dated January 31, but perhaps submitted on February 3, McClellan explained why he believed he could not move on February 22 and presented a plan of operations. On February 3 McClellan wrote to Stanton:

I ask you indulgence for the following paper, rendered necessary by circumstances.

I assumed command of the troops in the vicinity of Washington on Saturday July 27 1861, 6 days after the battle of Bull Run.

I found no army to command, a mere collection of regiments cowering on the banks of the Potomac, some perfectly raw, others dispirited by their recent defeat.

Nothing of any consequence had then been done to secure the southern approaches to the Capital by means of defensive works; nothing whatever had been undertaken to defend the avenues to the city on the northern side of the Potomac. . . .

Many weeks, I may say many months, ago this Army of the Potomac was fully in condition to repel any attack;—but there is a vast difference between that & the efficiency required to enable troops to attack successfully an Army elated by victory, and entrenched in a position long since selected, studied, & fortified. In the earliest papers I submitted to the Presdt I asked for an effective movable force far exceeding the aggregate now on the banks of the Potomac—I have not the force I asked for. Even when in a subordinate position I always looked beyond the operations of the Army of the Potomac; I was never satisfied in my own mind with a barren victory, but looked to combine & decisive operations....

I have ever regarded our true policy as being that of fully preparing ourselves & then seeking for the most decisive results;—I do not wish to waste life in useless battles, but prefer to strike at the heart....

In this latitude the weather will for a considerable period be very uncertain, & a movement commenced in force on roads in tolerably firm condition will be liable, almost certain, to be much delayed by rains & snow. It will therefore be next to impossible to surprise the enemy, or take him at a disadvantage by rapid manoeuvres;—our slow progress will enable him to divine our purposes & take his measures accordingly....

If at the expense of 30 days delay we can gain a decisive victory which will probably end the war, it is far cheaper than to gain a battle tomorrow that produces no final results, & may require years of warfare & expenditure to follow up....

I know that his Excellency the President, you & I all agree in our wishes—& that our desire is to bring this war to as prompt a close as the means in our possession will permit. I believe that the mass of the people have entire confidence in us—I am sure of it—let us then look only to the great result to be accomplished, & disregard everything else.

In conclusion I would respectfully, but firmly, advise that I may be authorized to undertake at once the movement by Urbana....

I will stake my life, my reputation on the result—more than that, I will stake upon it the success of our cause.[20]

On February 3 Lincoln wrote to McClellan:

My dear Sir: You and I have distinct, and different plans for a movement of the Army of the Potomac—yours to be down the Chesapeake, up the Rappahannock to Urbana, and across land to the terminus of the Railroad on the York River—, mine to move directly to a point on the Railroad South West of Manassas.

If you will give me satisfactory answers to the following questions, I shall gladly yield my plan to yours.

1st. Does not your plan involve a greatly larger expenditure of *time,* and *money* than mine?

2nd. Wherein is a victory *more certain* by your plan that mine?

3rd. Wherein is a victory *more valuable* by your plan than mine?

4th. In fact, would it not be *less* valuable, in this, that it would break no great line of the enemie's communications, while mine would?

5th. In the case of disaster, would not a safe retreat be more difficult by your plan than by mine? Yours truly A. Lincoln

(Memorandum accompanying Letter of President to General McClellan, dated February 3, 1862)

1. Suppose the enemy should attack us in force before we reach the Ocoquan, what? In view of the possibility of this, might it not be safest to have our entire force to move together from above the Ocoquan.

2. Suppose the enemy, in force, shall dispute the crossing of the Ocoquan, what? In view of this, might it not be safest for us to cross the Ocoquan at Colchester rather than at the village of Ocoquan? This would cost the enemy two miles mor[e] of travel to meet us, but would, on the contrary, leave us two miles further from our ultimate destination.

3. Suppose we reach Maple valley without an attack, will we not be attacked there, in force, by the enemy marching by the several roads from Manassas? And if so, what?[21]

McClellan called a council of war with his generals, who voted on whether to adopt Lincoln's plan to move against the Confederate force at Manassas or McClellan's to move the Army of the Potomac to the peninsula formed by the York and James rivers as a route to the enemy capital at Richmond. The council voted seven in favor of McClellan's plan, four against it, and one gave conditional support to McClellan's plan, wanting the army first to clear and remove the Confederate batteries on the Potomac.

It was a sore point between the president and the general, but Lincoln yielded. He, however, issued a general war order intended to protect the city of Washington:

President's General War Order No. 3. Ordered that no change of the base of operations of the Army of the Potomac shall be made without leaving in, and about Washington, such a force as, in the opinion of the General-in-chief, and the commanders of all the Army corps, shall leave said City entirely secure.

That not more than two Army corps, (about fifty thousand troops) of said Army of the Potomac, shall be moved en route for a new base of operations until the navigation of the Potomac, from Washington to the Chesapeake bay shall be freed from enemies batteries and other obstructions, or, until the President shall hereafter give express permission.

That any movement, as aforesaid, en route for a new base of operations, which may be ordered by the General-in-chief, & which may be intended to move upon the Chesapeake-bay, shall begin to move upon the bay as early as the 18th. day of March Inst.; and the General-in-chief shall be responsible that it so move as early as that day.

Ordered that the Army and Navy co-operate in an immediate effort to capture the enemies batteries upon the Potomac between Washington and the Chesapeak-bay.[22]

The next day, hearing reports that the Confederates were abandoning their positions on the Potomac and perhaps Manassas, McClellan ordered his huge army of 120,000 to march toward Manassas "to push the retreat of rebels," he said.[23] When the expedition arrived it found a deserted camp protected by logs painted black to simulate cannon. In any case McClellan had moved too late to carry out Lincoln's plan.

Two days later Lincoln removed McClellan from command of all departments except the Department of the Potomac. In effect Lincoln, commander in chief, now assumed the role of general in chief, assisted by Stanton and a newly formed War Board. On April 1, five weeks after Lincoln had ordered him to move, McClellan and his army set sail for the peninsula.[24]

George B. McClellan had assumed supreme command of Union armies November 1, 1861. He quickly displayed skill in training and in enhancing morale. At the same time he had evinced traits suggesting unsuitability for his post. By early March he had not moved his large forces, causing Lincoln to intervene with general orders to move and also causing Lincoln to restrict his field of command. How the general would conduct actual military operations with his large army remained to be seen.

CHAPTER FOURTEEN

THIRTY-SEVENTH CONGRESS, SECOND SESSION

In its first regular session the Thirty-Seventh Congress gathered on December 2, 1861. The war no longer promised to be brief. Union Army forces had suffered a series of reverses in addition to Bull Run; only the navy was finding success on the southern coast. Congress itself wore a different demeanor, soon expelling three senators and two representatives. On the next day the lawmakers heard the president's first annual message on the state of the Union.

He evinced particular concern about relations with foreign nations, financing the war, and Indian policy, and he reported progress in curtailing the illegal participation of Americans in the Atlantic slave trade. He suggested gradual, compensated emancipation by states; colonization of slaves forfeited under the confiscation act or by state emancipation; and the colonization of previously free colored people. His focus was not on executive emancipation.

Instead, Lincoln developed a geographical case for maintaining national unity. Cautiously he assumed, perhaps with an eye on radical Republicans, "I have been careful [that the war] shall not degenerate into a violent and remorseless war." Condemning the insurrection as "a war upon the first principle of popular government," he entered into a paean of labor's superiority over capital and concluded with broad vision: "The struggle for today, is not altogether for today—it is for a vast future also."

In his first annual message to Congress, on December 3, 1861, Lincoln stated:

In the midst of unprecedented political troubles, we have cause of great gratitude to God for unusual good health, and most abundant harvests.

You will not be surprised to learn that, in the peculiar exigencies of the times, our intercourse with foreign nations has been attended with profound solicitude, chiefly turning upon our own domestic affairs.

A disloyal portion of the American people have, during the whole year, been engaged in an attempt to divide and destroy the Union. A nation which endures factious domestic division, is exposed to disrespect abroad; and one party, if not both, is sure, sooner or later, to invoke foreign intervention.

Nations, thus tempted to interfere, are not always able to resist the counsels of seeming expediency, and ungenerous ambition, although measures adopted under such influences seldom fail to be unfortunate and injurious to those adopting them.

The disloyal citizens of the United States who have offered the ruin of our country, in return for the aid and comfort which they have invoked abroad, have received less patronage and encouragement than they probably expected. If it were just to suppose, as the insurgents have seemed to assume, that foreign nations, in this case, discarding all moral, social, and treaty obligations, would act, solely, and selfishly, for the most speedy restoration of commerce, including, especially, the acquisition of cotton, those nations appear, as yet, not to have seen their way to their object more directly, or clearly, through the destruction, than through the preservation, of the Union. If we could dare to believe that foreign nations are actuated by no higher principle than this, I am quite sure a sound argument could be made to show them that they can reach their aim more readily, and easily, by aiding to crush this rebellion, than by giving encouragement to it.

The principal lever relied on by the insurgents for exciting foreign nations to hostility against us, as already intimated, is the embarrassment of commerce. Those nations, however, not improbably, saw from the first, that it was the Union which made as well our foreign, as our domestic, commerce. They can scarcely have failed to perceive that the effort for disunion produces the existing difficulty; and that one strong nation promises more durable peace, and a more extensive, valuable and reliable commerce, than can the same nation broken into hostile fragments.

It is not my purpose to review our discussions with foreign states, because whatever might be their wishes, or dispositions, the integrity of our country, and the stability of our government, mainly depend, not upon them, but on the loyalty, virtue, patriotism, and intelligence of the American people. The correspondence itself, with the usual reservations, is herewith submitted.

I venture to hope it will appear that we have practiced prudence, and liberality towards foreign powers, averting causes of irritation; and with firmness, maintaining our own rights and honor. . . .

[I]t is apparent that here, as in every other state, foreign dangers necessarily attend domestic difficulties, I recommend that adequate and ample measures be adopted for maintaining the public defences on every side. . . .

The operations of the treasury during the period which has elapsed since your adjournment have been conducted with signal success. The patriotism of the people has placed at the disposal of the government the large means demanded by the public exigencies. Much of the national loan has been taken by citizens of the industrial classes, whose confidence in their country's faith, and zeal for their country's deliverance from present peril, have induced them to contribute to the support of the government the whole of their limited acquisitions. This fact imposes peculiar obligations to economy in disbursement and energy in action. . . .

I respectfully refer to the report of the Secretary of War for information respecting the numerical strength of the army, and for recommendations having in view an increase of its efficiency and the well being of the various branches of the service intrusted to his care. It is gratifying to know that the patriotism of the people has proved equal to the occasion, and that the number of troops tendered greatly exceeds the force which Congress authorized me to call into the field. . . .

There are three vacancies on the bench of the Supreme Court—two by the decease of Justices Daniel and McLean, and one by the resignation of Justice Campbell. I have so far forborne making nominations to fill these vacancies for reasons which I will now state. Two of the outgoing judges resided within the States now overrun by revolt; so that if successors were appointed in the same localities, they could not now serve upon their circuits; and many of the most competent men there, probably would not take the personal hazard of accepting to serve, even here, upon the supreme bench. I have been unwilling to throw all the appointments northward, thus disabling myself from doing justice to the south on the return of peace; although I may remark that to transfer to the north one which has heretofore been in the south, would not, with reference to territory and population, be unjust. . . .

Three modifications occur to me either of which, I think, would be an improvement upon our present system. Let the Supreme Court be of convenient number in every event. Then, first, let the whole country be divided into circuits of convenient size, the supreme judges to serve in a number of them corresponding to their own number, and independent circuit judges be provided for all the rest. Or, secondly, let the supreme judges be relieved from circuit duties, and circuit judges provided for all the circuits. Or, thirdly, dispense with circuit courts altogether, leaving the judicial functions wholly to the district courts and an independent Supreme Court. . . .

The relations of the government with the Indian tribes have been greatly disturbed by the insurrection, especially in the southern superintendency and in that of New Mexico. The Indian country south of Kansas is in the possession of insurgents from Texas and Arkansas. The agents of the United States appointed since the 4th. of March for this superintendency have been unable to reach their posts, while the most of those who were in office before that time have espoused the insurrectionary cause, and assume to exercise the powers of agents by virtue of commissions from the insurrectionists. It has been stated in the public press that a portion of those Indians have been organized as a military force, and are attached to the army of the insurgents. Although the government has no official information upon this subject, letters have been written to the Commissioner of Indian Affairs by several prominent chiefs, giving assurance of their loyalty to the United States, and expressing a wish for the presence of federal troops to protect them. It is believed that upon the repossession of the country by the federal forces the Indians will readily cease all hostile demonstrations, and resume their former relations to the government.

Agriculture, confessedly the largest interest of the nation, has, not a department, nor a bureau, but a clerkship only, assigned to it in the government. While it is fortunate that this great interest is so independent in its nature as to not have demanded and extorted more from the government, I respectfully ask Congress to consider whether something more cannot be given voluntarily with general advantage. . . .

Under and by virtue of the act of Congress entitled "An act to confiscate property used for insurrectionary purposes," approved August, 6, 1861, the legal claims of certain persons to the labor and service of certain other persons have become forfeited; and numbers of the latter, thus liberated, are already dependent on the United States, and must be provided for in some way. Besides this, it is not impossible that some of the States will pass similar enactments for their own benefit respectively, and by operation of which persons of the same class will be thrown upon them for disposal. In such case I recommend that Congress provide for accepting such persons from such States, according to some mode of valuation, in lieu, *pro tanto*, of direct taxes, or upon some other plan to be agreed on with such States respectively; that such persons, on such acceptance by the general government, be at once deemed free; and that, in any event, steps be taken for colonizing both classes, (or the one first mentioned, if the other shall not be brought into existence,) at some place, or places, in a climate congenial to them. It might be well to consider, too,—whether the free colored people already in the United States could not, so far as individuals may desire, be included in such colonization. . . .

Labor is prior to, and independent of, capital. Capital is only the fruit of labor, and could never have existed if labor had not first existed. Labor is the superior of capital, and deserves much the higher consideration. Capital has its rights, which are as worthy of protection as any other rights. Nor is it denied that there is, and probably always will be a relation between labor and capital, producing mutual benefits. . . .

From the first taking of our national census to the last are seventy years; and we find our population at the end of the period eight times as great as it was at the beginning. The increase of those other things which men deem desirable has been even greater. We thus have at one view, what the popular principle applied to government, through the machinery of the States and the Union, has produced in a given time; and also what, if firmly maintained, it promises for the future. There are already among us those, who, if the Union be preserved, will live to see it contain two hundred and fifty millions. The struggle of today, is not altogether for today—it is for a vast future also. With a reliance on Providence, all the more firm and earnest, let us proceed in the great task which events have devolved upon us.[1]

The House of Representatives refused to reaffirm the conservative Crittenden-Johnson resolution limiting the war's purposes to restoring the Union and the Constitution. The following day radical senator Zachariah Chandler of Michigan moved to create a committee to investigate the Union losses at Ball's Bluff and Bull Run. The upshot was the establishment of a Joint Committee on the Conduct of the War, which alarmed those who deemed that it encroached on the president's role as commander in chief.

This session of Congress has been celebrated by historians as forming a conspicuous part in the so-called Second American Revolution. Free from the restraint of southern members, the Congress enacted a notable series of laws distributing the public lands among homesteaders, railroads, and land grant colleges. Much of this legislation represented the Republican

Party platform. The Congress also passed laws abolishing slavery in the District of Columbia and in the territories. In all this Lincoln played a small role, in keeping with his purpose to leave "all questions which are not of vital military importance to the more deliberate action of the legislature." Congress all the while continued to provide ample support in money and men for the armed services.

Throughout the session, however, there flowed a strong undercurrent of opposition to Lincoln, formed by Republicans as well as Democrats. Several sources contributed to the opposition to executive authority: the war power, confiscation, the suspension of habeas corpus, and emancipation of slaves. The sources often intermingled, as president and Congress vied for a power not specifically mentioned in the Constitution. That organic document assigned to Congress the authority to declare war, raise armies, provide a navy, and appropriate money to wage war. It made the president commander in chief of the army and navy and of the militia when called into national service. It also required of the president, but not of members of Congress, the obligation to "preserve, protect and defend the Constitution of the United States." Both branches of government grasped for the undefined war power. In his first message to Congress Lincoln described the fall of Fort Sumter and observed that "no choice was left but to call out the war power." He would return to the phrase and use his role as commander in chief to justify executive suspension of habeas corpus, emancipation of slaves, and reconstruction of the Union—all matters not purely within a military orbit.

As early as January 22 Republican congressman Alexander S. Diven of New York, a staunch Lincoln supporter, who had voted against tabling the Crittenden-Johnson resolution, cried:

Mr. Chairman, I suppose I need not state to this House that since the assemblage of this Congress at the extra session a principle has been gathering strength that has divided the councils of this House, and that has divided the sentiments of this country. One side of the question has been strongly represented upon this floor. If the other side has remained quiet, I apprehend it has not been because they have not been as firmly rooted in their principles as the side that has been more active. If we were to judge from the debates which have occurred in this House, it might be supposed that the Executive of this country had no support from the party that elevated him to power. All the attacks which have been made upon the Administration have come from the Republican side of the House, and all the replies which have been made to those attacks have come either from the Democratic side of the House, which opposed his elevation to power, or from those who represent the border States, and who really were neither for or against him in the election.

Now, Mr. Chairman, I regret that this division has been made; I regret that I feel obliged to recognize it; and I regret that I feel a necessity for speaking in defense of the Executive of this country, and in opposition to men who have professed, and who still profess, to be his friends. I regret it, because there is one set of opinions here that favor the prosecution of this war for the paramount purpose of abolishing slavery throughout the land. Somebody says, 'Oh, no;' but that gentleman is mistaken. I say there are such principles avowed and advocated here.

There is another set of men here, among whom I rank myself, who are in favor of prosecuting this war in the spirit in which it was commenced— for the purpose of restoring this Union to its original position, and leaving all these States in the possession of the same constitutional power that they possessed before this rebellion. That is the division that exists, and I regret that it has not been made now. Those men who want to prosecute this war for the paramount purpose of abolishing slavery, must know, if they know anything, that they cannot attain their end until they anni-hilate the rebel army that stands between them and the slaves. We, also, who want to prosecute this war for the restoration of the Union, know equally well that we never can attain our end until we annihilate that same army. Thus far we are traveling upon the same road. The same force is to be overcome for the attainment of either end. Why, then, should we not unite all our energies[,] why, then, should we introduce any disturbing element to divide our councils or distract our aims? Why should we not employ those whole energies in obtaining a victory over this common foe, and when that shall have been attained, then determine what use we will make of that victory? . . .

I was surprised the other day, at hearing the gentleman from Maine (Mr. Fessenden) quoting Abraham Lincoln in favor of the abolition of slavery, and appealing to know whether Mr. Lincoln or this Congress would establish another rule on that point, different from that which was disseminated over the plains of Illinois in 1858. No, sir, I am for the same rule which Abraham Lincoln disseminated emphatically in 1858. I am for the same rule that was disseminated when the Republican party was inaugurated in Philadelphia. I am in favor of adhering to the same rule that was more explicitly avowed at Chicago, when Mr. Lincoln was put in nomination. I am for adhering to the same rule on which I stumped my State and district in favor of Abraham Lincoln. That doctrine emphatically is, that Congress has no power over the institution, of slavery in the States where it exists."[2]

Testy about Lincoln's exercise of executive authority, Congress entered a dispute over presidential control of railroads during the war:

Mr. Wade: I move to take up Senate bill No. 169, to authorize the President of the United States, in certain cases, to take possession of railroad and telegraph lines, and for other purposes....

Mr. Pearce: I [desire] to know whether ... it was necessary to apply this rule to those regions of country which are notoriously not in insurrection, but in which armies are stationed....

It seems to me that this bill is a very extraordinary one. It has taken me by surprise. I believe it was only laid on our tables yesterday. If it were confined to the States in secession I should make no objection; but I confess I am appalled with the idea of giving the Executive such an enormous power as this over States which are not in insurrection, which may not be in insurrection, and in which there is not a fortieth part of the people who desired it ever should get into insurrection....

But further, sir—it may be a minor objection with some, but it is a great objection in my opinion—you authorize them to place under military control all the officers, agents, and employés belonging to the telegraphs and railroads thus taken possession of the by the Government, so that they shall be considered a part of the military forces of the United States, subject to all the liabilities imposed by the rules and articles of war. Where do you get the authority to make these civil employés of these railroads subject to the rules and articles of war? They are only military men who are subject to them. These persons have not made themselves subject to them by enlisting in the military service of the United States, or by volunteering into its service, or by being drafted into the militia; and yet you take these pure civilians, the whole business of whose lives is railroad transportation for passengers and freight, and make them subjects of military law. I think you have no more power to do it, sir, than you have to "pluck bright honor from the pale-faced moon." If the bill can be amended so as to make it apply within the limits of the seceded States, I have no sort of objection to it; but if it is not, I would soon have my head cut off as to vote for it. . . .

Mr. Wade: We believe, however, it is better to have the power under the regulation of law, so that there may be no dispute about the extent of their powers; and also that the compensation for damages that they shall receive, and all these things, shall be known beforehand, and not leave it to the arbitrary exercise of the executive branch of the Government, without restraint or restriction. Then the idea that we have conferred a dangerous power on the Executive falls to the ground. We have conferred no power upon him, as I understand it. . . .

Mr. Davis: I think that the other exception taken to the bill by the Senator from Maryland is well taken. He objects to that portion of it which proposes "to place under military control all the officers, agents, and employés belonging to the telegraph and railroad lines thus taken possession of by the President." I say that that is wholly an unauthorized power. Congress, the law-making power of the United States, cannot invest the President with that authority. He has no right to assume that persons who are in civil employment, either in a State or in a State corporation, or in their own private and individual capacity, can be seized by authority of a law of Congress, and appropriated to and made part of the military power of the United States, and subjected to the military law. I utterly deny that that is constitutional. . . .

Mr. Sherman: In my judgment, the President of the United States has exercised many powers that are not conferred upon him either by the Constitution or the laws. I have maintained and do now maintain them; but why? Simply because Congress has uniformly failed to legislate on the subject and give the power that ought to have been given. Congress ought to place itself in a more intimate and close connection with the Executive; ought to place itself and place its rules in such condition that it may act more efficiently with these measures; and therefore it was that I desired very much the adoption of the proposition of my colleague yesterday, so that on this bill we might have gone into secret session, confined the debate to the subject-matter, to the pending amendments, and short speeches, and disposed of this bill; correcting all its inaccuracies, if there were any in it.

Upon the question of the war power of the President, the Constitution is very plain and simple.

The Constitution declares that—

The President shall be Commander-in-Chief of the Army and Navy of the United States, and of the militia of the several States, when called into the actual service of the United States.

It also provides that

He shall take care that the laws be faithfully executed, and shall commission all officers of the United States.

These are the only powers conferred by the Constitution on the President, which touch this question. On the other hand, Congress has the following powers:

To declare war, grant letters of marque and reprisal, and make rules concerning captures on land and water.

To raise and support armies.

To provide and maintain a navy.

To make rules for the government and regulation of the land and naval forces.

To provide for calling forth the militia to execute the laws of the Union, suppress insurrections, and repel invasions.

To provide for organizing, arming, and disciplining the militia, and for governing such part of them as may be employed in the service of the United States.

In the absence of a law by Congress, if Congress fails to exercise these powers conferred upon it, then, as the President is required to see that the laws are faithfully executed, he must usurp, seize all the necessary powers to carry into execution his duty. But it is the duty of Congress to make rules and regulations, to prescribe the limitations, to say how far he shall go, what power he shall use, what kind of force he shall use, how it shall be governed; in short to prescribe all the rules and regulations relating to the Army and the Navy of the United States. The President has no other duty to perform except simply to carry out the powers conferred on him by Congress. As a matter of course if Congress fails to do its duty, if Congress fails to give him the power to seize railroad and telegraph lines, he ought to seize the railroad railroads and telegraph lines; but it is the duty of Congress, it seems to me, to prescribe the limitations of that power, to prescribe the mode and manner in which it is to be done, the mode and manner of compensation, and all the various details necessary in the exercise of such a power. . . .

Mr. Cowan: When Congress declares war, and provides an army and a navy for the President to achieve a particular thing, it confers upon him at the same time all the powers necessary to attain the desired end; and among other things it confers on him power, as has been well said, to impress horses, railroads, telegraph lines, men, teams, everything of that kind into his service, and compel them to work according to his plan and pattern. It is not necessary that Congress should interfere at all; and if Congress does attempt to interfere, their influence is a restraining rather than an enlarging influence. Put the case: to-day it is said that this is an emergency, it is said that the President ought to have this power immediately; well, if he waits until he gets it from Congress, a body of this size, moving as we move, with this want of celerity, the emergency may pass away. But the Constitution and the laws have wisely clothed him with it himself; it is not necessary that he should wait for our action. . . .

Mr. Bayard: I do not rise for the purpose of opposing this bill. I shall vote against it. I consider it a plain and palpable violation of the Constitution of the United States. I know of no power, executive or legislative, to establish martial law within the United States. I therefore have no comments to make upon this bill. The provisions of it speak for themselves. It assumes the power to compel citizens of the United States to act under military law without their consent, and subjects them to the penalties of military law. Though the Constitution says that private property shall not be taken for public purposes without compensation, it assumes the power, not to seize private property, but the power to use it temporarily for Government purposes without compensation for the value of the property. . . .

Mr. Powell: Believing this bill to be a violation of the Constitution of the United States, I shall vote against its passage.

The question being taken by yeas and nays, resulted—yeas 23, nays 12; as follows:

YEAS—Messrs. Carlile, Chandler, Clark, Dixon, Doolittle, Foot, Hale, Howard, Howe, Johnson, King, Lane, of Indiana, Latham, Pomeroy, Rice, Sherman, Sumner, Ten Eyck, Wade, Wilkinson, Wilmot, Wilson of Massachusetts, and Wilson of Missouri–23.

NAYS—Messrs. Browning, Cowan, Davis, Fessenden, Foster, Grimes Harris, McDougall, Powell, Saulsbury, Trumbul, and Willey–12.

So the bill was passed.[3]

Despite Congress's approval of the railroad measure, the administration saw continued opposition. Every member of the cabinet confronted a degree of opposition. Attorney General Edward Bates noted on February 2, 1862:

There is a feverish excitement in both Houses: In the senate there were strong indications of opposition to the admn. and Mr. *Hale* led off very plainly in that direction, but recoiled, as to oppose the admn. *now* is to oppose the *War* and the nation. But, as the steam is up, it must find a vent, and so is let off against individuals—Cameron is driven out, and exiled to Russia, and now they are battering away upon Welles, and many think that he must yield to the storm. I will not decide that injustice was done to Cameron—I do not judge his case. But I think that Welles gets hard measure for his faults. He is not strong or quick, but I believe him an honest and faithful man.

Out of doors, there is a formidable clique organized against Mr. Seward, who, fearing his adroitness, work very privily against him. Their object (at least *friend* Newton thinks so) is to compel his retirement and put senator Harris in his place. It is said that some of them have approached Mrs. Lincoln and not without success, making her believe that Mr. Seward is laboring with persistent effort, to override the Prest. and make himself the chief man of the admn.[4]

Some of the opposition was pure partisanship, some personal. Much of it stemmed from legitimate concerns about constitutionality. At issue throughout, it seemed, was whether the president and his party had assumed too much power when Congress was not in session and what to do about his actions *ex post facto*. From the session's opening, moderate senator Jacob Collamer of Vermont strongly believed in presidential conduct of the war:

> It was not the function of Congress, insisted Lincoln's supporters, to define the purposes of the war. Senator Collamer, veteran Vermont Republican, summed up their views in an interview at Boston on his way to Washington: War is not a business Congress can engineer. It is properly *executive business,* and the moment Congress passes beyond the line of providing for the wants of the government, and deciding the purposes of the war, to say how it shall be conducted, the whole thing will prove a failure."[5]

A week later Chicago newspaper editor Joseph Medill warned the president that "our nation is on the brink of ruin. Mr. Lincoln, for God's sake and your Country's sake rise to the realization . . . that this is a slaveholder rebellion."[6]

Radical Republican Thaddeus Stevens in a flaming speech on January 22 claimed that congressional power extended even to declaring a dictatorship:

This Government is empowered to suppress insurrection: its Executive is enjoined, "to see all the laws faithfully executed;" Congress is granted power to pass all laws necessary to that end. If no other means were left to save the Republic from destruction, I believe we have no power, *under the Constitution and according to its express provision,* to declare a dictator, without confining the choice to any officer of the Government. Rather than the nation should perish, I would do it; rather than see a nation dishonored by compromise, concession; rather than see the Union disserved; nay, rather than see one star stricken from its banner, all other things failing, I would do it now. Oh, for six months' resurrection in the flesh of stern old Jackson! Give him power, and he would handle this rebellion with iron gloves.... A three months' campaign, and one hundred thousand soldiers, would suffice him for this; when he would resign his power, and the people would gladly return him to his honored resting-place.

I think I have shown that we possess all the power now claimed to be under the Constitution, even the tremendous power of dictatorship. Nothing certainly would justify its exercise but its necessity to snatch the nation from the jaws of death.

Our object should be not only to end this terrible war now, but to prevent its recurrence. All must admit that slavery is the cause of it. Without slavery we should this day be a united and happy people. So long as it exists we cannot have a solid Union. Patch up a compromise now and leave this germ of evil, it would soon again overrun the whole South, even if you freed three fourths of the slaves, and your peace would be a curse. You would have expended countless treasures and untold lives in vain. The principles of our Republic are wholly incompatible with slavery. They cannot live together. While you are quelling this insurrection at such fearful cost, remove the cause, that future generations may live in peace.[7]

Orville H. Browning, Republican senator from Illinois, a frequent visitor to what he called the President's House, on March 10 vigorously denied that the war power belonged to Congress. Early in his speech he quoted Senator William P. Fessenden of Maine as saying:

"There is no limit on the power of Congress; but it is invested with the absolute powers of war. The civil functions of Government are, for the time being, in abeyance when in conflict, and all State and national authority subordinated to the extreme authority of Congress, as the supreme power in the peril of external or internal hostilities. The ordinary provisions of the Constitution, peculiar to a state of peace, and all laws and municipal regulations must yield to the force of martial law, as resolved by Congress."[8]

To this claim, shutting out the president from holding war powers, Browning rejoined:

The functions of Congress are civil and legislative only. It can exercise no war powers, properly so called. They belong to another department of the Government. This question has been considered and I think fully passed upon by the supreme judicial department of this Government. . . .

The Supreme Court . . . said: "It is said that this power (the war power) in the President is dangerous to liberty, and may be abused. All power may be abused, if placed in unworthy hands. But it would be difficult, we think, to point out any other hands in which this power would be more safe, and at the same time equally effectual."

But, sir, if Congress, on the contrary, should assume the exercise of war powers, should usurp them, and should use them for the purposes of tyranny, there is absolutely no remedy to be found anywhere.[9]

Arguments flew back and forth as members of congress debated the locus of the war power. Scholarly Senator Charles Sumner on May 19 extolled Congress's possession of the war power and the right to confiscate property including slaves and to declare them free:

I cannot doubt that Senators are in earnest, that they mean what they say, and that they intend to do all in their power, by all proper legislation, to carry the war to a final close. But if this be their purpose, they will not hesitate to employ all the acknowledged rights of war calculated to promote this end. Two transcendent powers have already been exercised without a murmur: first, to raise armies, and secondly, to raise money. These were essential to the end. But there is another power without which, I fear, the end will escape us. It is that of confiscation and liberation, and this power is just as constitutional as the other two. The occasion for its exercise is found in the same terrible necessity. An army is not a *posse comitatus;* nor is it, when in actual war, face to face with the enemy, amenable to the ordinary provisions of the Constitution. It takes life without a jury trial or any other process of law, and, we have already seen, it is by virtue of the same right of war that the property of enemies may be taken and freedom be given to their slaves. Of course on the exercise of these rights there can be no check or limitation in the Constitution. Any such check or limitation would be irrational. War cannot be conducted *in vinculis*. In seeking to fasten upon it the restraints of the Constitution you repeat the ancient tyranny which compelled its victims to fight in chains. Glorious as it is that the citizen is surrounded by the safeguards of the Constitution, yet this rule is super-seded by war, which brings into being other rights which know no master. An Italian publicist has said that there is no right which does not, in some measure, impinge upon some other right. But this is not correct. Rights, when properly understood, harmonize with each other. The rights of war can never impinge upon any rights under the Constitution, nor can any rights under the Constitution impinge upon the rights of war.

Assuming, then, what has been so amply demonstrated, that the rights of war are ours without abridgement, and assuming also that you will not allow our present cause, which has enlisted such mighty energies, to be thwarted through any failure on your part, I ask you to exercise these rights in such a way as to assure promptly and surely that permanent peace in which all that we desire is contained. . . .

Nor is it to be forgotten that these rights are without any of these limita-tions which modern times have adopted with regard to the private property of enemies in an international war, and that, on reason and principle, which are the foundations of all public law, *every rebel who voluntarily becomes an enemy is as completely responsible in all his property, whether real or personal, as a hostile Government or prince,* whose responsibility to this extent is unquestioned. . . .

In declaring the slaves free, you will at once do more than in any other way, whether to conquer, to pacify, to punish, or to bless. You will take from the rebellion its mainspring of activity and strength; you will stop its chief source of provisions and supplies; you will remove a motive and temptation to prolonged resistance, and you will destroy forever that disturbing influ-ence which, so long as it is allowed to exist, will keep this land a volcano ever ready to break forth anew.[10]

In a carefully prepared and lengthy speech on June 25, Browning directly challenged Sumner:

A very important part of the Senator's speech, and which appears to me to be among the most heterodox, and dangerous, and indefensible doctrines he puts forward, are ranged under the inquiry, 'what are the rights against enemies which Congress may exercise in war?' To this inquiry the Con-stitution gives a very explicit answer. They have already been enumerated.

Congress may declare war, grant letters of marque and reprisal, and make rules concerning captures on land and water.' It may 'raise and support armies;' 'provide and maintain a navy;' It 'may make rules for the government and regulation of the land and naval forces;' 'provide for calling forth the militia to execute the laws of the Union, suppress insurrections, and repel invasions;' and 'provide for organizing, arming, and disciplining the militia, and for governing such part of them as may be employed in the service of the United States.' There is the answer, and there is the whole of it. . . .

It is not true that Congress may assume and exercise all the active war powers in the actual prosecution of war. The Constitution invests it with no such prerogative. It is not true that Congress may decide upon the measures demanded by military necessities and order them to be enforced. If it can do so in one instance, it can do so in every instance. If it can grasp and wield this power in one case, it can do so in all cases. I deny that the right exists, in any case, to pass in judgment upon what is properly called a military necessity. . . .

These necessities can be determined only by the military commander, and to him the Constitution has intrusted the prerogative of judging of them. When the Constitution made the President 'Commander-in-Chief of the Army and Navy of the United States,' it clothed him with all the incidental powers necessary to a full, faithful, and efficient performance of the duties of that high office; and to decide what are military necessities, and to devise and execute the requisite measures to meet them, is one of these incidents. It is not a legislative, but an executive function, and Congress has nothing to do with it. Congress can 'raise and support,' but cannot command armies. That duty the Constitution has devolved upon the President. It has made him Commander-in-Chief, and therefore Congress cannot be. Nor can Congress control him in the command of the Army, for, if it can, then he is not Commander-in-Chief, and the assertion of the Constitution to that effect is a falsehood. And whenever Congress assumes the control of the Army in the field, it usurps the powers of a coordinate department of the Government, destroys the checks and balances provided for the safety of the people, and subverts the Constitution. Legislative encroachment upon the prerogatives of the other departments thus boldly once begun, where will it end? It will go on increasing in strength, and pushing its conquests, till it subordinates the Constitution itself to its will, and becomes as omnipotent as the British Parliament. It is from the legislative department of the Government that danger is to be apprehended, not the executive or judicial. . . .

The fathers of the Constitution, whose long experience of the imperfections of existing systems had taught them all the necessities to be provided for by organic laws, distributed the powers of Government to different departments, and to prevent conflicts and collisions, preserve order, and secure harmony in the working of the system, they erected barriers to keep them separate, and to confine each department to its appropriate sphere, and restrain it from encroachments upon another.

The honorable Senator recognizes no such barriers, no such separation of powers, but claims that all executive powers which the President may exercise in the prosecution of the war are held by him in subordination to the will of Congress, subject to its control and direction, and all of which Congress may exercise concurrently with the President if it so chooses.[11]

Browning continued the debate:

I stated and I reiterate that the President is under the constraints of the Constitution and the restraints of the Constitution. So is Congress. Congress has no more power to undertake to control the President in the discharge of the duties that are devolved upon him by the Constitution, to control him in the exercise of the authority with which the Constitution has clothed him, than he has to undertake to control Congress in the discharge of its duty. He is independent in his sphere of Congress, and Congress is independent of him in its sphere.[12]

The same day, Benjamin Wade, Ohio radical, claimed full power for the Senate:

Sir, it is as I said before, and I cannot speak of it in any other terms than a most slavish and un-American doctrine, to contend for this irresponsible power of the Chief Magistrate in time of war. I have as much respect for our Chief Magistrate as has the gentleman from Illinois. I would be as loth to interfere with him in any of his constitutional rights; but when it is set up for him or anybody else that he may be a tyrant, not only trampling upon the people, but their representatives in Congress, overriding all they can do, and endeavoring to prevent their making such laws with regard to the prosecution of this war as in their judgment are right and proper, that this chief is armed with irresponsible power, I, with all my disposition to remain at rest and not talk here, feel that I should be aside from my duty if I saw such doctrines as these, more Asiatic than American, proclaimed in an American Senate and allowed them to pass unchallenged.

Sir, they savor of the absolute despotism of the eastern continent, rather than of the stock from which we sprang that go for limited government everywhere. I hope that such doctrines will not ever gain a foothold in America. . . .

Now, sir, what are the rights of war? They are just precisely such as Congress see fit to confer on the Chief Magistrate. . . .

Why, then, in order to resist this confiscation bill, talk of the enormous overpowering despotic authority of the President of the United States? Sir, it has no relevancy to the case. We have full power over the question. This is the proper place where the power should be lodged. In my judgment, it should be promptly executed. While I am up I will say—for I do not intend to argue this confiscation bill over again—I want the people to understand that I am in favor of the bill, and had I the power of Congress, I would take all the property of rebels, and I would appropriate it to the discharge of the enormous debt that we are incurring in defense of this glorious Constitution of ours.[13]

Sumner on June 27 retorted:

Under the present bill there can be no title which is not founded on the terms of the bill, and the bill starts with declaring that certain property shall be the subject of seizure, prize, and capture wherever found, and capture means taking.

The Senator must be very hardy who denies the power of Congress, in the exercise of belligerent rights, to pass such a bill; and he must be equally hardy when he insists that belligerent rights are impaired by any limitations of the Constitution.

If the enemies against whom we are now waging war were not our own fellow-citizens—if they were aliens unhappily established for the time on our territory—there would be no fine-spun question of constitutional immunities. Such immunities are essentially municipal in their character; but a public enemy can claim nothing merely municipal. The immunities which he enjoys are such only as are conceded by the rights of war; nor more, nor less. As a public enemy, he seeks to subvert our Government, its laws, and its Constitution; and in this warfare he proceeds according to the rights of war, indifferent to any mere local law. . . .

And yet, sir, the Constitution is cited as a limitation on these rights. As well cite the Constitution on the field of battle to check the bayonet charge of our armies, or at the bombardment of a fortress to restrain the fiery rain of shells. Or, to adopt the examples with which I began, as well cite the Constitution to prevent the occupation of churches here in Washington as hospitals for our soldiers, or to save the house of General Lee in Virginia from a similar dedication. The Constitution is entirely inapplicable. Sacred and inviolable, the Constitution is made for friends who acknowledge it, and not for enemies who disavow it; and it is made for a state of peace, and not for the fearful exigencies of war. War, as it comes, treads down within its sphere all rights except the rights of war. . . .

But there are Senators who claim these vast war powers for the President, and deny them to Congress. The President, it is said, as Commander-in-Chief, may seize, confiscate, and liberate under the rights of war; but Congress cannot direct these things to be done. Pray, sir, where is the limitation on Congress? Read the text of the Constitution, and you will find its powers vast as all the requirements of war. There is nothing which may be done anywhere under the rights of war, which may not be done by Congress. I do not mean to question the powers of the President in his sphere, or of any military commander within his department. But I claim for Congress all that belongs to any Government in the exercise of the rights of war. And when I speak of Congress, let it be understood that I mean *an act of Congress,* passed, according to the requirements of the Constitution by both Houses and approved by the President.[14]

As the session was closing and the long debate over confiscating ended, Lincoln, who had reluctantly signed the first confiscation act, learned details of a proposed second confiscation act. Troubled by some of its provisions, he made known his objections, including an *ex post facto* provision making the law apply to acts performed before its passage, and a provision involving "a forfeiture of the real estate of the offender beyond his natural life," which he believed contrary to the Constitution. Eager to get the bill approved, Congress revised it to satisfy Lincoln's objections. Republican congressmen had thus avoided a break with the president, but they were reminded of presidential authority when in an unprecedented act he appended to his approval the veto message he had intended to use before the revision to the bill:

> Fellow-Citizens of the Senate, and House of Representatives, Considering the bill for "An act to suppress insurrection, to punish treason, and rebellion, to seize and confiscate the property of rebels, and for other purposes,"

and the Joint Resolution as being substantially one, I have approved and signed both.

Before I was informed of the passage of the Resolution, I had prepared the draft of a Message, stating objections to the bill becoming a law, a copy of which draft is herewith transmitted.

Fellow citizens of the House of Representatives. I herewith return to your honorable body, in which it originated, the bill for an act entitled "An act to suppress treason and rebellion, to seize and confiscate the property of rebels, and for other purposes" together with my objections to its becoming a law.

There is much in the bill to which I perceive no objection. It is wholly prospective; and it touches neither person nor property, of any loyal citizen; in which particulars, it is just and proper. The first and second sections provide for the conviction and punishment of persons who shall be guilty of treason, and persons who shall "incite, set on foot, assist, or engage in any rebellion, or insurrection, against the authority of the United States, or the laws thereof, or shall give aid or comfort thereto, or shall engage in, or give aid and comfort to any such existing rebellion, or insurrection." By fair construction, persons within these sections are not to be punished without regular trials, in duly constituted courts, under the forms, and all the substantial provisions of law, and of the constitution, applicable to their several cases. To this I perceive no objection; especially as such persons would be within the general pardoning power, and also the special provision for pardon and amnesty, contained in this act. It is also provided, that the slaves of persons convicted under these sections shall be free. I think there is an unfortunate form of expression, rather than a substantial objection, in this. It is startling to say that Congress can free a slave within a State; and yet if it were said the ownership of the slave had first been transferred to the nation, and that Congress had then liberated, him, the difficulty would at once vanish. And this is the real case. The traitor against the general government forfeits his slave, at least as justly as he does any other property; and he forfeits both to the government against which he offends. The government, so far as there can be ownership, thus owns the forfeited slaves; and the question for Congress, in regard to them is, "Shall they be made free, or be sold to new masters?" I perceive no objection to Congress deciding in advance that they shall be free. To the high honor of Kentucky, as I am informed, she has been the owner of some slaves by *escheat,* and that she sold none, but liberated all. I hope the same is true of some other states. Indeed, I do not believe it would be physically possible, for the General government, to return persons, so circumstanced, to actual slavery. I believe there would be physical resistance to it, which could neither be turned aside by argument, nor driven away by force. In this view I have no objection to this feature of the bill. Another matter involved in these two sections, and running through other parts of the act, will be noticed hereafter. . . . The severest justice may not always be the best policy. The principle of seizing, and appropriating the property of the persons embraced within these sections is certainly not very objectionable; but a justly discriminating application of it, would be very difficult, and, to a great extent, impossible. And would it not be wise to place a power of remission somewhere, so that these persons may know they have something to lose by persisting, and something to save by desisting? I am not sure whether such power of remission is or is not within section Thirteen. . . .

What I have said in regard to slaves, while commenting on the first and second sections, is applicable to the ninth, with the difference, that no provision is made in the whole act for determining whether a particular individual slave does or does not fall within the classes defined in that section. He is to be free upon certain conditions; but whether those conditions do, or do not pertain to him, no mode of ascertaining is provided. This could be easily supplied. . . .

The eleventh section simply assumes to confer discretionary powers upon the executive. Without this law I have no hesitation to go as far in the direction indicated, as I may at any time deem expedient. And I am ready to say now I think it is proper for our military commanders to employ, as laborers, as many persons of African de[s]cent, as can be used to advantage. . . .

That to which I chiefly object, pervades most parts of the act, but more distinctly appears in the first, second, seventh and eighth sections. It is the sum of those provisions which results in the divesting of title forever. For the causes of treason, and the ingredients of treason, not amounting to the full crime, it declares forfeiture, extending beyond the lives of the guilty parties; whereas the Constitution of the United States declares that "no attainder of treason shall work corruption of blood, or forfeiture, except during the life of the person attainted." True, there is to be no formal attainder in this case; still I think the greater punishment can not be constitutionally inflicted, in a different form, for the same offence. With great respect, I am constrained to say I think this feature of the act is unconstitutional. It would not be difficult to modify it. . . .

Again, this act, by proceedings *in rem* forfeits property, for the ingredients of treason, without a conviction of the supposed criminal, or a personal hearing given him in any proceeding. That we may not touch property lying within our reach, because we can not give personal notice to an owner who is absent endeavoring to destroy the government is certainly not very satisfactory; still the owner may not be thus engaged, and I think a reasonable time should be provided for such parties to appear and have personal hearings. Similar provisions are not uncommon in connection with proceedings *in rem*.

For the reasons stated I return the bill to the House in which it originated.[15]

The long, often acrimonious session that had bristled over the president's wielding of the war power ended with the president still ascendant. Congress had not curtailed his employment of the war power to suspend habeas corpus, to reconstruct the Union as he had begun to do by appointing military governors in southern states, or to command the army. It had conformed to his view of the confiscation bill, and had refrained from congressional emancipation, which he believed lacked constitutional authority. And he had withstood a Senate challenge to his employment of the cabinet.

In the course of the war an influential voice spoke in favor of Lincoln's view of the war power. William Whiting, solicitor of the War Department, made speeches and wrote a book on the subject. Published in 1863 and running through more than forty editions, *War Powers under the Constitution* asserted:

> Whatever any commander-in-chief, in accordance with the usual practice of carrying on war among civilized nations, may order his army and navy to do, is within the *power* of the President to order and to execute, because the constitution, in express terms, gives him the supreme command of both. If he makes war upon a foreign nation, he should be governed by the law of nations; if lawfully engaged in civil war, he may treat his enemies as subjects and as belligerents.
>
> The constitution provides that the government and regulation of the land and naval forces, and the treatment of captures, should be according to law; but it imposes, in express terms, no other qualification of the war power of the President. . . . It requires the President, as an executive magistrate, in time of peace to see that the laws existing in time of peace are faithfully executed- and as commander-in-chief, in time of war, to see that the laws of war are executed. In doing both duties he is strictly obeying the constitution.[16]

The first regular session of the Thirty-Seventh Congress, then, saw a straining of relations between Lincoln and the legislators. As the president invoked vast authority under the war power, a phrase not found in the Constitution, some in Congress challenged his claim and claimed the power for themselves.

"The steam is up," noted the attorney general. In particular, members of Congress were steamed up over presidential suspension of the privilege of habeas corpus. Not until early 1863 would an accommodation be reached. On the theoretical side and over time, Lincoln's claim derived substantial strength from the published work of William Whiting, which went through many editions.

CHAPTER FIFTEEN

GRANT AND THE WAR
IN THE WEST

While McClellan dawdled and Congress passed significant economic measures and quarreled over who held the war power, military operations in the West brought both success and joy to the Union cause. Major General Henry Wager Halleck—Phi Beta Kappa, author of the standard military treatise *Elements of Military Art and Science,* third in his West Point class of 1839, and sometimes known as "Old Brains"—succeeded Frémont in command of the Department of Missouri. His department extended beyond Missouri and included the command of Brigadier General Ulysses S. Grant at Cairo. Not far distant were Confederate forces under General Albert Sidney Johnston and Confederate Forts Henry on the Tennessee River and Donelson on the Cumberland River. These positions controlled the rivers and governed their access to Tennessee and its capital on the Cumberland.

Lincoln had long been alert to military matters in the West. When Indiana's governor Oliver Morton requested guns, remarking of his state, "the war is now upon her borders," and voicing concern about Kentucky, Lincoln wrote to him:

> As to Kentucky, you do not estimate that state as more important than I do; but I am compelled to watch all points. While I write this I am, if not in *range,* at least in *hearing* of cannon-shot, from an army of enemies more than a hundred thousand strong. I do not expect them to capture this city; but I *know* they would, if I were to send the men and arms from here, to defend Louisville, of which there is not a single hostile armed soldier within forty miles, nor any force known to be moving upon it from any distance.[1]

About the first of October, continuing to become a military strategist, Lincoln wrote a "Memorandum for a Plan of Campaign":

On, or about the 5th. of October, (the exact day to be determined hereafter) I wish a movement made to seize and hold a point on the Railroad connecting Virginia and Tennesse, near the Mountain pass called Cumberland Gap.

That point is now guarded against us by Zolicoffer, with 6000 or 8000, rebels at Barboursville, Kentucky, say twentyfive miles from the Gap towards Lexington.

We have a force of 5000 or 6000, under General Tomas, at Camp Dick Robinson, about twentyfive miles from Lexington, and seventyfive from Zollicoffer's camp on the road between the two, which is not a Railroad, anywhere between Lexington and the point to be seized—and along the whole length of which the Union sentiment among the people largely predominates.

We have military possession of the Railroads from Cincinnati to Lexington, and from Louisville to Lexington, and some Home Guards under General Crittenden are on the latter line.

We have possession of the Railroad from Louisville to Nashville, Tenn, so far as Muldrough's Hill, about forty miles, and the rebels have possession of that road all South of there. At the Hill we have a force of 8000 under Gen. Sherman; and about an equal force of rebels is a very short distance South, under under [sic] Gen. Buckner.

We have a large force at Paducah, and a smaller at Fort Holt, both on the Kentucky side, with some at Bird's Point, Cairo, Mound City, Evansville, & New Albany, all on the other side; and all which, with the Gun Boats on the River, are, perhaps, sufficient to guard the Ohio from Louisville to its mouth.

About supplies of troops, my general idea is that all from Wisconsin, Minesota, Iowa, Illinois, Missouri, and Kansas, not now elsewhere, be left to *Fremont.*

All from Indiana and Michigan, not now elsewhere, be sent to Anderson at Louisville.

All from Ohio, needed in Western Virginia be sent there; and any remainder, be sent to Mitchell at Cincinnati, for Anderson.

All East of the Mountains be appropriated to McClellan, and to the coast.

As to movements, my idea is that the one for the coast, and that on Cumberland Gap be simultaneous; and that, in the mean time, preparation, vigilant watching, and the defensive only be acted upon (this however, not to apply to Fremonts operations in Northern and middle Missouri) that before these movements, Thomas and Sherman shall respectively watch, but not attack Zollicoffer, and Buckner.

That when the coast and Gap movements shall be ready, Sherman is merely to stand fast; while all at Cincincinnati [sic], and all at Louisville with all on the lines, concentrate rapidly at Lexington, and thence to Thomas' camp joining him, and the whole thence upon the Gap.

It is for the Military men to decide whether they can find a pass through the mountains at or near the Gap, which can not be defended by the enemy, with a greatly inferior force, and what is to be done in regard to this.

The Coast and Gap movements made, Generals McClellan and Fremont, in their respective Departments, will avail themselves of any advantages the diversions may present.[2]

In his annual message of 1861 Lincoln had evinced his concern about the loyalists of eastern Tennessee as well as those of western North Carolina. In twenty-nine eastern Tennessee counties, voters had cast more than twice as many ballots against secession as for it. Residents complained of persecution by the courts in the counties, and loyalist U.S. Senator Andrew Johnson pleaded the Tennessee Unionists' case.

At the turn of the year Lincoln began to press for action in eastern Tennessee. He found himself caught between the commanders Halleck in St. Louis and General Don Carlos Buell in Louisville, head of the Army of the Ohio, who was charged to invade and liberate east Tennessee. Lincoln also was confronted with inaction, delay, and conflict of strategic ideas between himself and his generals. Action seemed particularly needed because in Virginia McClellan was not only persisting in his habit of inaction but also lingering in his illness.

On December 31 Lincoln telegraphed Halleck; he sent a similar letter to Buell: "General McClellan is sick. Are General Buell and yourself in concert? When he moves on Bowling Green, what hinders it being re-enforced from Columbus? A simultaneous movement by you on Columbus might prevent it."[3] Their replies dismayed Lincoln, revealing a complete lack of cooperation. Buell wrote on January 1:

There is no arrangement between General Halleck and myself. I have been informed by General McClellan that he would make suitable disposition for concerted action. There is nothing to prevent Bowling Green being re-enforced from Columbus if a military force is not brought to bear on the latter place.

And Halleck wrote Lincoln on the same day:

I have never received a word from General Buell. I am not ready to cooperate with him. Hope to do so in few weeks. Have written fully on this subject to Major-General McClellan. Too much haste will ruin everything.[4]

In quick response Lincoln sent identically worded messages to the two generals:

General McClellan should not yet be disturbed with business. I think you better get in concert with General Halleck at once. I write you to-night. I also telegraph and write Halleck.

Gen. McClellan should not yet be disturbed with business. I think Gen. Buell and yourself should be in communication and concert at once. I write you to-night, and also Telegraph and write him.[5]

In a separate wire to Halleck, saying he was very anxious, Lincoln urged Halleck and Buell to act in concert with each other:

General McClellan is not dangerously ill, as I hope, but would better not to be disturbed with business. I am very anxious that, in case of General Buell's moving toward Nashville, the enemy shall not be greatly re-enforced, and I think there is danger he will be from Columbus. It seems to me that a real or feigned attack upon Columbus from up-river at the same time would either prevent this or compensate for it by throwing Columbus into our hands. I wrote General Buell a letter similar to this, meaning that he and you shall communicate and act in concert, unless it be your judgment and his that there is no necessity for it. You and he will understand much better than I how to do it. Please do not lose time in this matter.[6]

Halleck's reply was reassuring:

I immediately communicated with Genl Buell and have since sent him all the information I could obtain of the enemy's movements about Columbus and Camp Beauregard. No considerable force has been sent from those places to Bowling Green. They have about 22,000 men at Columbus. . . .

I have at Cairo, Fort Holt & Paducah only about 15,000. . . . I cannot . . . withdraw any from Missouri.[7]

Three days later, his anxiety unallayed, Lincoln asked Buell: "Have arms gone forward for East-Tennessee? Please tell me the progress and condition of the movement, in that direction. Answer."[8]

Buell in reply pled a reason for not going forward and at the same time proposed Nashville, not east Tennessee, as his target:

Arms can only go forward for East Tennessee under the protection of an army. My organization of the troops has had in view two columns with reference to that movement. . . . But it was necessary also to have regard to contingencies which . . . might require a modification. . . . I will confess . . . I have been bound to it more by . . . sympathy for the people of Eastern Tennessee, and the anxiety with which yourself and the General in Chief have desired it, than by my opinion of its wisdom.[9]

Adding to his discouragement, Lincoln on the sixth heard the following from Halleck:

I have delayed writing to you for several days in hopes of getting some favorable news from the Southwest. The news received to-day, however, is unfavorable, it being stated that Price is making a stand near Springfield, and that all our available forces will be required to dislodge and drive him out. My advices from Columbus represent that the enemy has about 22 000 men there. I have only about 15,000 at Cairo, Fort Holt, and Paducah, and after leaving guards at these places I could not send into the field over 10,000 or 11,000. Moreover, many of these are very imperfectly armed. Under these circumstances it would be madness for me to attempt any serious operation against Camp Beauregard or Columbus. Probably in the course of a few weeks I will be able to send additional troops to Cairo and Paducah to co-operate with you, but at present it is impossible; and it seems to me that if you deem such co-operation necessary to your success your movement on Bowling Green should be delayed. I know nothing of the plan of campaign, never having received any information on the subject; but it strikes me that to operate from Louisville and Paducah or Cairo against an enemy at Bowling Green is a plain case of exterior lines, like that of McDowell and Patterson, which, unless each of the exterior columns is superior to the enemy, leads to disaster ninety-nine times in a hundred.[10]

Lincoln sighed: "The within is a copy of a letter just received from General Halleck. It is exceedingly discouraging. As everywhere else, nothing can be done."[11]

Confessing that Buell's response "distresses me," Lincoln on the sixth responded:

> Your despatch of yesterday has been received, and it disappoints and distresses me. I have shown it to Gen. McClellan, who says he will write you to-day. I am not competent to criticize your views; and therefore what I offer is merely in justification of myself. Of the two, I would rather have a point on the Railroad south of Cumberland Gap, than Nashville, first, because it cuts a great artery of the enemies' communication, which Nashville does not, and secondly because it is in the midst of loyal people, who would rally around it, while Nashville is not. Again, I cannot see why the movement on East Tennessee would not be a diversion in your favor, rather than a disadvantage, assuming that a movement towards Nashville is the main object.
>
> But my distress is that our friends in East Tennessee are being hanged and driven to despair, and even now I fear, are thinking of taking rebel arms for the sake of personal protection. In this we lose the most valuable stake we have in the South. My despatch, to which yours is an answer, was sent with the knowledge of Senator Johnson and Representative Maynard of East Tennessee, and they will be upon me to know the answer, which I cannot safely show them. They would despair—possibly resign to go and save their families somehow, or die with them.
>
> I do not intend this to be an order in any sense, but merely, as intimated before, to show you the grounds of my anxiety.[12]

The following day, remarking "Delay is ruining us," Lincoln sent an urgent request:

> Please name as early a day as you safely can, on, or before which you can be ready to move Southward in concert with Gen. Halleck. Delay is ruining us; and it is indispensable for me to have something definite. I send a like despatch to Halleck.[13]

Yet, on the ninth Lincoln received a dismaying letter from Buell:

> [U]ndoubtedly there ought to be more and better artillery and better cavalry, but I shall work with what I have, and as soon as possible. Concert of action by which the enemy may be prevented from concentrating his

whole force from Columbus to Bowling Green . . . would have the same and better effect than more troops.[14]

"Exceedingly" discouraged, Lincoln on January 10 sent Secretary Cameron a copy of a letter from Halleck: "The within is a copy of a letter just receid from General Halleck. It is exceedingly discouraging. As everywhere else, nothing can be done."[15]

Meanwhile finding time to dismiss Cameron and appoint Stanton, Lincoln on the thirteenth returned to the Buell problem, writing to him and sending a copy to Halleck. The difficulty with Buell prompted Lincoln, the emerging strategist, to assume a more confident strategic posture. He gave the generals his "general idea of this war," suggesting a clear course of action and revealing that the Tennessee line was a "matter of no small anxiety to me." Lincoln explained:

Your despatch of yesterday is received, in which you say "I have received your letter and Gen. McClellan's; and will, at once devote all my efforts to your views, and his." In the midst of my many cares, I have not seen, or asked to see, Gen. McClellan's letter to you. For my own views, I have not offered, and do not now offer them as orders; and while I am glad to have them respectfully considered, I would blame you to follow them contrary to your own clear judgment—unless I should put them in the form of orders. As to Gen. McClellan's views, you understand your duty in regard to them better than I do. With this preliminary, I state my general idea of this war to be that we have the *greater* numbers, and the enemy has the *greater* facility of concentrating forces upon points of collision; that we must fail, unless we can find some way of making *our* advantage an over-match for *his;* and that this can only be done by menacing him with superior forces at *different* points, at the *same* time; so that we can safely attack, one, or both, if he makes no change; and if he *weakens* one to *strengthen* the other, forbear to attack the strengthened one, but seize, and hold the weakened one, gaining so much. To illustrate, suppose last summer, when Winchester ran away to re-inforce Mannassas, we had forborne to attack Mannassas, but had seized and held Winchester. I mention this to illustrate, and not to criticise. I did not lose confidence in McDowell, and I think less harshly of Patterson than some others seem to. In application of the general rule I am suggesting, every particular case will have its modifying circumstances, among which the most constantly present, and most difficult to meet, will be the want of perfect knowledge of the enemies' movements. This had its part in the Bull-Run case; but worse, in that case, was the expiration of the terms of the three months men. Applying the principle to your case, my idea is that Halleck shall menace Columbus, and 'down river' generally; while you menace Bowling Green, and East Tennessee. If the enemy shall concentrate at Bowling Green, do not retire from his front; yet do not fight him there, either, but seize Columbus and East Tennessee, one or both, left exposed by the concentration at Bowling Green. It is matter of no small anxiety to me and one which I am sure you will not over-look, that the East Tennessee line, is so long, and over so bad a road.[16]

In late January the energetic Grant, directing attention to western Tennessee, made repeated pleas to Halleck for permission to attack Fort Henry. Only after Grant presented a plan for an amphibious assault, his troops to be accompanied by river gunboats, and Halleck learned that General Beauregard was coming to Kentucky or Tennessee, did Halleck on January 29 give permission.

Grant sprang into action. On February 6 Halleck received Grant's triumphant telegram, "Fort Henry is ours." And he coolly announced, "I shall take Fort Donelson on the 8th." Grant's prediction was premature. Donelson was a harder nut to crack than Henry. Worried, Halleck asked Buell for reinforcements and offered to transfer Grant. Buell refused. Though many officers and officials were nervous, Lincoln now seemed unalarmed, though warning Halleck to be cautious. Asked by a friend whether the warning was necessary, Lincoln responded that he did not know, but there was too much at stake on the battle, and "no hazard must run which could be avoided."[17]

On Sunday morning February 16 the Confederate commander of Fort Donelson asked Grant for terms of capitulation. Grant's response overjoyed a northern public weary of delays and reverses: "No terms except unconditional and immediate surrender. I propose to move immediately upon your works." The night of capitulation Stanton brought the nomination of Grant as major general of volunteers to Lincoln, who signed it.

Twice defeated, the Confederate forces abandoned Kentucky and western and middle Tennessee and dropped south to the rail junction at Corinth, Mississippi, near the Tennessee border. Grant pursued and encamped at

Pittsburgh Landing, where, perhaps overconfident, he failed to prepare for an attack. With superior numbers the Confederates early on the morning of April 6 struck Grant's army at Shiloh Church, which gave a name to the ensuing struggle. By skilled assistance of General William T. Sherman, Grant's army stood firm against the surprise assault. Refusing advice to retreat, Grant the next day hit back hard, helped by the timely arrival of 25,000 troops. The Confederates retreated; their commander, General Albert Sidney Johnston, was killed. Mary Todd Lincoln's half-brother Sam was mortally wounded. The slaughter at Shiloh cost each side more than 1,700 killed and 8,000 wounded. The historian James M. McPherson wrote: "Shiloh was the most ghastly bloodbath in the history of the Western Hemisphere thus far."[18]

The northern outcry over the bloodshed was loud, and calls for Grant's removal were numerous. Rumors of his drunkenness circulated. Senator James Harlan of Iowa bluntly said to the Senate, "From all I can learn on the subject I do not think General Grant is fit to command a great army in the field." He quoted from a letter from a constituent:

> Although our victory on Monday was complete, and the rebels utterly routed, yet it was too dearly purchased. The criminal carelessness, or something worse, on the part of General Grant, whereby so many brave soldiers were slaughtered, admits of no palliation or excuse. Newspaper correspondents may write as they please, but the united voice of every soldier in Grant's army condemns him, and it is now time that the Government should do likewise.[19]

John Sherman wrote to his brother, the general, "there is much feeling against Grant, and I try to defend him, but with little success."[20]

The Pennsylvania politician and editor Alexander K. McClure, a defender of Lincoln, later wrote of the outcry and its outcome:

> It was not until after the battle of Shiloh, fought on the 6th and 7th of April, 1862, that Lincoln was placed in a position to exercise a controlling influence in shaping the destiny of Grant. The first day's battle at Shiloh was a serious disaster to the Union army commanded by Grant, who was driven from his position, which seems to have been selected without any special reference to resisting an attack from the enemy, and, although his

army fought most gallantly in various separate encounters, the day closed with the field in possession of the enemy and Grant's army driven back to the river. Fortunately, the advance of Buell's army formed a junction with Grant late in the evening, and that night all of Buell's army arrived, consisting of three divisions. The two generals arranged their plans for an offensive movement early the next morning, and, after another stubborn battle, the lost field was regained and the enemy compelled to retreat with the loss of their commander, General Albert Sidney Johnston, who had fallen early in the first day's action, and with a larger aggregate loss of killed, wounded, and missing than Grant suffered. The first reports from the Shiloh battle field created profound alarm throughout the entire country, and the wildest exaggerations were spread in a floodtide of vituperation against Grant. It was freely charged that he had neglected his command because of dissipation, that his army had been surprised and defeated, and that it was saved from annihilation only by the timely arrival of Buell.

The few of to-day who can recall the inflamed condition of public sentiment against Grant caused by the disastrous first day's battle at Shiloh will remember that he was denounced as incompetent for his command by the public journals of all parties in the North, and with almost entire unanimity by Senators and Congressmen without regard to political faith. Not only in Washington, but throughout the loyal States, public sentiment seemed to crystallize into an earnest demand for Grant's dismissal from the army....

So much was I impressed with the importance of prompt action on the part of the President after spending a day and evening in Washington that I called on Lincoln at eleven o'clock at night and sat with him alone until after one o'clock in the morning. He was, as usual, worn out with the day's exacting duties, but he did not permit me to depart until the Grant matter had been gone over and many other things relating to the war that he wished to discuss. I pressed upon him with all the earnestness I could command the immediate removal of Grant as an imperious necessity to sustain himself. As was his custom, he said but little, only enough to make me continue the discussion until it was exhausted. He sat before the open fire in the old Cabinet room, most of the time with his feet up on the high marble mantel, and exhibited unusual distress at the complicated condition of military affairs. Nearly every day brought some new and perplexing military complication. He had gone through a long winter of terrible strain with McClellan and the Army of the Potomac; and from the day that Grant started on his Southern expedition until the battle of Shiloh he had had little else than jarring and confusion among his generals in the West.

He knew that I had no ends to serve in urging Grant's removal, beyond the single desire to make him be just to himself, and he listened patiently.

I appealed to Lincoln for his own sake to remove Grant at once, and in giving my reasons for it I simply voiced the admittedly overwhelming protest from the loyal people of the land against Grant's continuance in command. I could form no judgment during the conversation as to what effect my arguments had upon him beyond the fact that he was greatly distressed at this new complication. When I had said everything that could be said from my standpoint, we lapsed into silence. Lincoln remained silent for what seemed a very long time. He then gathered himself up in his chair and said in a tone of earnestness that I shall never forget: "I can't spare this man; he fights." That was all he said, but I knew that it was enough, and that Grant was safe in Lincoln's hands against his countless hosts of enemies. The only man in all the nation who had the power to save Grant was Lincoln, and he had decided to do it. He was not influenced by any personal partiality for Grant, for they had never met, but he believed just what he said—"I can't spare this man; he fights."[21]

More than a year later, an officer in Grant's army, fresh from the victory at Vicksburg in 1863, visited Lincoln. The president asked for details of the battle. When the officer had finished his account Lincoln mused: "I guess I was right in standing by Grant, although there was great pressure made after Pittsburgh Landing to have him removed. I thought I saw enough in Grant to convince me that he was the one on whom the country could depend."[22]

As head of the Department of the Missouri, Halleck took command of Grant's forces, with the objective of capturing Corinth, the Confederate rail junction and stronghold twenty-five miles distant, considered by some Confederates crucial to the West. Halleck slowly organized his battered forces and asked for more men. On April 26 he assured Stanton, "We are now at the enemy's throat."[23]

The throat must have been distant; nearly a month later on May 26 Lincoln telegraphed Halleck to inquire of his progress:

Several despatches from Assistant Secretary Scott, and one from Gov. Morton, asking re-inforcements for you have been received. I beg you to be assured we do the best we can. I mean to cast no blame when I tell you each of our commanders along our line from Richmond to Corinth sup-poses himself to be confronted by numbers superior to his own. Under this pressure we thinned the line on the upper Potomac until yesterday it was broken, at heavy loss to us, and Gen. Banks put in great peril, out of which he is not yet extricated, and may be actually captured. We need men to repair this breach, and have them not at hand.

My dear general, I feel justified to rely very much on you. I believe you and the brave officers and men with you, can and will get the victory at Corinth.[24]

Halleck replied through Stanton: "Permit me to remark that we are operating upon too many points. Richmond and Corinth are now the great strategical points of war, and our success at these points should be insured at all hazards."[25]

Beauregard's Confederates had abundant opportunity to make plans, as Halleck took thirty-seven days to advance twenty miles from Shiloh to Corinth. When on May 29 his army attained Corinth, he found that Beauregard had evacuated the city, choosing to fight elsewhere.

Meanwhile McClellan, campaigning against Richmond, was asking for men too. In the ensuing correspondence these strategic objectives col-lided: McClellan's purpose to take Richmond, Lincoln's to gain eastern Tennessee, and Halleck's to hold western Tennessee. Stanton on June 28 ordered Halleck to send 25,000 men east to assist McClellan. However, Stanton qualified his order: "But in detaching your force, the president directs that it be done in such a way as to enable you to hold your ground and not interfere with the movement against Chattanooga and East Ten-nessee."[26] Halleck speedily replied that compliance would endanger the ground won in western Tennessee and force abandonment of the east Tennessee expedition under Buell.

Lincoln then took a direct hand in the matter. He sent a telegram acqui-escing in Halleck's desire to withhold troops at the expense of east Tennessee policy and at the same time reinforced his opinion of the significance of Buell's objective:

Would be very glad of twenty five thousand Infantry—no artillery, or cavalry—but please do not send a man if it endangers any place you deem important to hold, or if it forces you to give up, or weaken, or delay the expedition against Chattanooga. To take and hold the Rail-road at, or East of, Cleveland in East Tennessee, I think fully as important as the taking and holding of Richmond.[27]

As July opened, Lincoln's objective since the beginning of the year—eastern Tennessee—had not been secured, and Richmond had not fallen. For months Lincoln had been acting as general in chief. He now believed he needed a military expert to coordinate the Union armies and counsel him. On July 11 he made Halleck general in chief of the land forces.

Historians, fascinated by the war in the East where Lee and McClellan were active, have emphasized operations there. Lincoln, a westerner, knew the importance of the West and its rivers and its loyalist element. In 1862 he often spoke of the importance of the region. He was delighted to discover a winning general, defended him against critics, and maintained him in authority until a time came when he could be elevated to a higher command.

CHAPTER SIXTEEN

EXIT MCCLELLAN, ENTER POPE,
AND ANOTHER BULL RUN

Just as he was pressing for action to secure eastern Tennessee, Lincoln also was pressing for action in Virginia. Given command of the Army of the Potomac in late July 1861, the "young Napoleon," as George McClellan came to be called, had displayed merits as well as weaknesses in the extended span of time before he arrived at Fort Monroe on April 2, 1862, the beginning point of his Peninsula Campaign. His skills in training troops, in lifting morale, in applying energy to his tasks were manifest. His ambition bolstered by a high opinion of himself, his disdain if not contempt for others, a streak of paranoia, and his failure to comprehend the civil-military relationship in the American system were also manifest.

The day after his arrival he told his wife Ellen with characteristic optimism, "I hope to get possession of Yorktown day after tomorrow." Almost immediately the quarrel over numbers began. Advised that McClellan had failed to leave behind enough troops to assure the safety of Washington, Lincoln had detached McDowell's 30,000 men from McClellan's command and kept them in northern Virginia to protect the capital.

On April 5 McClellan telegraphed Lincoln:

The Enemy are in large force along our front and, apparently, intend making a determined resistance. A reconnaissance just made by Genl. Barnard, shows that their line of works extends across the entire Peninsula from Yorktown and Warwick river. Many of these are formidable. Deserters say that they are being reinforced daily from Richmond, and from Norfolk.

Under these circumstances I beg that you will reconsider the order detaching the first Corps from my Command. In my deliberate judgment that success of our cause will be imperiled when it is actually under the fire of the enemy, and active operations have commenced. Two or three of my Divisions have been under fire of Artillery most of the day. I am now of the opinion that I shall have to fight all of the available force of the Rebels not far from here. Do not force me to do so with diminished numbers. But whatever your decision may be, I will leave nothing undone to obtain success. If you cannot leave me the whole of the first Corps, I urgently ask that I may not lose Franklin and his Division.[1]

The next day he exclaimed to Ellen:

I find the enemy in strong force & in a very strong position but will drive him out. Fitz John is in the advance on the right, Baldy on the left—they are doing splendidly. Their Divisions have been under fire all the afternoon [April 5]—have lost only about 5 killed in each & have punished secesh badly. Thus far it has been altogether an artillery affair. While listening this pm. to the sound of the guns, I received the order detaching McDowell's Corps from my command—it is the most infamous thing that history has recorded. I have made such representations as will probably induce a revocation of the order—or at least save Franklin to me. The idea of depriving a General of 35,000 troops when actually under fire! Tomorrow night I can tell you exactly what I intend doing.

We have no baggage tonight—our wagons being detained by the bad roads. Have taken possession of a *hut* in a deserted secesh camp—found a table therein—& sleep on a horse blanket if I find time to "retire." Colburn is copying a long letter—Seth, standing by the fire, looking *very* sleepy! He wakes up & sends his kindest regards, in which Colburn asks to participate—I am sorry to say that your Father is snoring loudly in a corner.[2]

On the same day he again appealed to Lincoln for more men:

The order forming new Departments, if rigidly enforced deprives me of the power of ordering up wagons and troops absolutely necessary to enable me to advance to Richmond. I have by no means the transportation I must have to move my army even a few miles. I respectfully request I may not be placed in this position, but that my orders for wagons—trains, ammunition and other material that I have prepared & necessarily left behind, as well as Woodbury's brigade, may at once be complied with. The Enemy is strong in my front, & I have a most serious task before me, in the fulfillment of which I need all the aid the Government can give me. I again repeat the urgent request that Genl Franklin & his division be restored to my command.[3]

Lincoln replied the same day, providing Washington's account of McClellan's manpower strength and urging action:

> Yours of 11 A.M. to-day received. Sec. of War informs me that the forwarding of transportation, ammunition, & Woodbury's, brigade, under your orders, is not, and will not be interfered with. You now have over one hundred thousand troops, with you independent of Gen. Wool's command. I think you better break the enemies' line from York- town to Warwick River, at once. They will probably use *time,* as advantageously as you can.[4]

McClellan persisted in his dissatisfaction and paid little attention to Lincoln's direction. In a letter to Ellen he wrote: "I have raised an awful row about McDowell's Corps—& have I think rather seared the authorities that be. The Presdt very coolly telegraphed me yesterday that he thought I had better break the enemy's lines at once! I was much tempted to reply that he had better come & do it himself."[5]

The correspondence temporarily climaxed in a long letter in which Lincoln described why McDowell had been retained, questioned the discrepancy in numbers between McClellan and the secretary of war, and spoke of the danger of delay and of the public's opinion.

> Your despatches complaining that you are not properly sustained, while they do not offend me, do pain me very much.
>
> Blencker's Division was withdrawn from you before you left here; and you knew the pressure under which I did it, and, as I thought, acquiesced in it—certainly not without reluctance.
>
> After you left, I ascertained that less than twenty thousand unorganized men, without a single field battery, were all you designed to be left for the defence of Washington, and Manassas Junction; and part of this even, was to go to Gen. Hooker's old position. Gen. Banks' corps, once designed for Manassas Junction, was diverted, and tied up on the line of Winchester and Strausburg, and could not leave it without again exposing the upper Potomac, and the Baltimore and Ohio Railroad. This presented, (or would present, when McDowell and Sumner should be gone) a great temptation to the enemy to turn back from the Rappahanock, and sack Washington.

My explicit order that Washington should, by the judgment of *all* the commanders of Army corps, be left entirely secure, had been neglected. It was precisely this that drove me to detain McDowell.

I do not forget that I was satisfied with your arrangement to leave Banks at Mannassas Junction; but when that arrangement was broken up, and *nothing was* substituted for it, of course I was not satisfied. I was constrained to substitute something for it myself. And now allow me to ask "Do you really think I should permit the line from Richmond, via Mannassas Junction, to this city to be entirely open, except what resistance could be presented by less than twenty thousand unorganized troops?" This is a question which the country will not allow me to evade.

There is a curious mystery about the number of the troops now with you. When I telegraphed you on the 6th. saying you had over a hundred thousand with you, I had just obtained from the Secretary of War, a statement, taken as he said, from your own returns, making 108,000 then with you, and en route to you. You now say you will have but 85,000, when all en route to you shall have reached you. How can the discrepancy of 23,000 be accounted for?

As to Gen. Wool's command, I understand it is doing for you precisely what a like number of your own would have to do, if that command was away.

I suppose the whole force which has gone forward for you, is with you by this time; and if so, I think it is the precise time for you to strike a blow. By delay the enemy will relatively gain upon you—that is, he will gain faster, by *fortifications* and *re-inforcements,* than you can by re-inforcements alone.

And, once more let me tell you, it is indispensable to you that you strike a blow. I am powerless to help this. You will do me the justice to remember I always insisted, that going down the Bay in search of a field, instead of fighting at or near Mannassas, was only shifting, and not surmounting, a difficulty—that we would find the same enemy, and the same, or equal, intrenchments, at either place. The country will not fail to note—is now noting—that the present hesitation to move upon an intrenched enemy, is but the story of Manassas repeated.

I beg to assure you that I have never written you, or spoken to you, in greater kindness of feeling than now, nor with a fuller purpose to sustain you, so far as in my most anxious judgment, I consistently can. *But you must act.*[6]

On April 23 the general wrote to the president referring to his "apparent inaction," and describing his activities, which seemed to look not to offensive warfare but to defensive actions against those he was sent to conquer:

I am well aware of the firm friendship & confidence you have evinced for me, & instead of again thanking you for it will endeavor to assure you that it is not misplaced.

Do not misunderstand the apparent inaction here—not a day, not an hour has been lost, works have been constructed that may almost be called gigantic—roads built through swamps & difficult ravines, material brought up, batteries built. I have tonight in battery & ready for action 5 100 pdr Parrott guns, 10 4½" Ordnance guns, 18 20 pdr Parrotts, 6 Napoleon guns & 6 10 pdr Parrotts—this not counting the batteries in front of Smith & on his left—45 guns. I will add to it tomorrow night 5 30 pdr Parrotts, 6 20 pdr Parrotts, from 5 to 10 13" mortars, & (if it arrives in time) 1 200 pdr Parrott. Before sundown tomorrow I will essentially complete the redoubts necessary to strengthen the left of the 1st Parallel; & will construct that Parallel as far as Wormley's Creek from the left, & probably all the way to York River tomorrow night. I will then be secure against sorties. It has become necessary to make tomorrow morning early a 'forced reconnaissance' to gain some information as to the ground on the left flank of the proposed 1st Parallel—this ground is strongly held by the enemy's pickets, is swampy & covered with thick brush & timber—I cannot now tell what facilities they possess for crossing the stream in force—to gain this information I have ordered Col Gove to move with his Regt, the 22nd Massachusetts, early in the morning—I have taken all possible precautions, so that the object may be gained without loss— yet it is possible that many lives may be lost—there is no other way of accomplishing the object, & I merely wish to state beforehand what the purpose is, in order that the result may be understood. I do not propose to open fire at present unless the enemy attempt to interfere with the construction of the 1st Parallel & the new batteries which will be commenced at once. If he will permit it I will at once build a battery at close range for 5 more 100 pdrs & another 200 pdr rifle, batteries for the 10 & 8 inch mortars, 8" howitzers, & additional 30 & 20 pounder Parrotts, in the mean time pushing the approaches forward as rapidly as possible. I still hope that we will not be seriously interfered with until I can open an overwhelming fire & give the assault from a reasonable distance under its cover. My course must necessarily depend to a great extent upon that of the enemy—but I see the way clear to success & hope to make it brilliant, although with but little loss of life. I expect great aid from the Galena— Franklin will probably land as soon as she arrives—his preparations ought to be completed tomorrow.[7]

A week later the president replied to the general's request for 30-pounder Parrott guns: "Your call for Parrott guns from Washington alarms me—chiefly because it argues indefinite procrastination. Is anything to be done?"[8]

McClellan had vigorously protested about the reorganization of the Army Corps. Deferring to McClellan as battle impended, Lincoln drafted an authorization for the general to suspend the reorganization. Separately sent, a letter describing the origins of the reorganization disclosed the opposition to McClellan's preferred scheme, reminded the general of the importance of congressional support, challenged his strength to deal with his generals, and succinctly combined McClellan's task with the greater "cause of the country."

After advancing beyond Williamsburg, McClellan telegraphed Lincoln, complaining about the secretary of war, underestimating the strength of his forces and overestimating that of his foes, and begging for more men in order to strike "a fatal blow."[9]

In response Lincoln on May 15 said:

Your long despatch of yesterday is just received. I will answer more fully soon. Will say now that all your despatches to the Secretary of War have been promptly shown to me. Have done, and shall do, all I could and can to sustain you—hoped that the opening of James River, and putting Wool and Burnside in communication, with an open road to Richmond, or to you, had effected something in that direction. I am still unwilling to take all our force off the direct line between Richmond and here.[10]

Lincoln followed this immediately with a communication sent through the War Department:

I left Gen. McDowell's camp at dark last evening. Shield's command is there, but it is so worn that he cannot move before Monday morning, the twenty-sixth (26th). We have so thinned our line to get troops for other places that it was broken yesterday at Front Royal, with a probable loss to us of one (1) regiment infantry, two (2) companies cavalry, putting Gen. Banks in some peril.

The enemy's forces, under Gen. Anderson, now opposing Gen. McDowell's advance have, as their line of supply and retreat, the road to Richmond.

If, in conjunction with McDowell's movement against Anderson, you could send a force from your right to cut off the enemy's supplies from Richmond, preserve the railroad bridges across the two (2) forks of the Pamunkey, and intercept the enemy's retreat, you will prevent the army now opposed to you from receiving an accession of numbers of nearly fifteen thousand (15,000) men; and if you succeed in saving the bridges you will secure a line of railroad for supplies in addition to the one you now have. Can you not do this almost as well as not while you are building the Chickahominy bridges? McDowell and Shields both say they can, and positively will, move Monday morning. I wish you to move cautiously and safely.

You will have command of McDowell, after he joins you, precisely as you indicated in your long despatch to us of the twenty-first (21st).[11]

Meanwhile "Stonewall" Jackson was rapidly moving down the Shenandoah Valley toward Harper's Ferry. Lincoln changed McDowell's march from joining McClellan to meeting Jackson. He explained to McClellan: "In consequence of Gen. Banks' critical position I have been compelled to suspend Gen. McDowell's movement to join you. The enemy are making a desperate push upon Harper's Ferry, and we are trying to throw Fremont's force & part of McDowell's in their rear."[12]

Throughout the Peninsula Campaign McClellan maintained a steady drumbeat of criticism and complaint. His self-revealing letters included a remark on April 21 that he had received "a letter yesterday from Francis Cutting, of New York, hoping that I would not allow these treacherous hounds to drive me from my path." On May 1 he complained, "I know that my enemies are pursuing me more remorselessly than ever, and 'kind friends' are constantly making themselves agreeable by informing me of the pleasant predicament in which I am—the rebels on one side, and the abolitionists and other scoundrels on the other." On May 3 he wrote, "I feel that the fate of a nation depends on me, and I feel that I have not one single friend at the seat of government. Any day may bring a letter relieving me from command." A month after he had expected to take Yorktown, he notified Stanton, "The enemy [had] abandoned Yorktown."[13]

As Jackson's forces marched north, Lincoln on May 25 telegraphed McClellan, delivering a virtual ultimatum:

The enemy is moving North in sufficient force to drive Banks before him in precisely what force we can not tell. He is also threatening Leesburgh and Geary on the Manassas Gap Rail Road from both north and south in precisely what force we can not tell. I think the movement is a general and concerted one, such as could not be if he was acting upon the purpose of a very desperate defence of Richmond. I think the time is near when you must either attack Richmond or give up the job and come to the defence of Washington. Let me hear from you instantly.[14]

Before informing the president he would comply, McClellan began dashing off another blistering letter to Ellen:

I have this moment received a dispatch from the Presdt who is terribly scared about Washington–& talks about the necessity of my returning in order to save it! Heaven save a country governed by such counsels! I must reply to his telegram & finish this by & by![15]

An hour and half later he continued the letter:

Have just finished my reply to his Excellency! It is perfectly sickening to deal with such people & you may rest assured that I will lose as little time as possible in breaking off all connection with them—I get more sick of them every day—for every day brings with it only additional proofs of their hypocrisy, knavery & folly—well, well, I ought not to write in this way, for they may be right & I entirely wrong, so I will drop the subject.[16]

The general's calls for more men and his complaints about Lincoln and his administration continued. On June 25 McClellan telegraphed Stanton:

I have just returned from the field and find your dispatch in regard to Jackson.
Several contrabands just in give information confirming supposition that Jackson's advance is at or near Hanover CH & that Beauregard arrived with strong reinforcements in Richmond yesterday. I incline to think that Jackson will attack my right & rear. The rebel force is stated at (200,000) two hundred thousand including Jackson & Beauregard. I shall have to contend against vastly superior odds if these reports be true. But this Army will do all in the power of men to hold their position & repulse any attack.
I regret my great inferiority in numbers but feel that I am in no way responsible for it as I have not failed to represent repeatedly the necessity of reinforcements, that this was the decisive point, & that all the available means of the Govt should be concentrated here. I will do all that a General

can do with the splendid Army I have the honor to command & if it is destroyed by overwhelming numbers can at least die with it & share its fate.

But if the result of the action which will probably occur tomorrow or within a short time is a disaster the responsibility cannot be thrown on my shoulders—it must rest where it belongs.

Since I commenced this I have received additional intelligence confirming the supposition in regard to Jackson's movements & Beauregard's arrival. I shall probably be attacked tomorrow—& now go to the other side of the Chickahominy to arrange for the defense on that side.

I feel that there is no use in my again asking for reinforcements.[17]

Lincoln himself replied:

Your three dispatches of yesterday in relation to the affair, ending with the statement that you completely succeeded in making your point, are very gratifying. The later one of 6:15 p.m., suggesting the probability of your being overwhelmed by 200,000, and talking of where the responsibility will belong, pains me very much. I give you all I can, and act on the presumption that you will do the best you can with what you have, while you continue, ungenerously I think, to assume that I could give you more if I would. I have omitted and shall omit no opportunity to send you reenforcements whenever I possibly can.[18]

After a Confederate assault at Gaines's Mill, McClellan on June 28 wrote a long letter to Stanton, rehearsing yet again his request for more troops and absolving himself yet again of any responsibility if defeated:

I now know the full history of the day [June 27]. On this side of the river— the right bank—we repulsed several very strong attacks. On the left bank our men did all that men could do, all that soldiers could accomplish—but they were overwhelmed by vastly superior numbers even after I brought my last reserves into action. The loss on both sides is terrible—I believe it will prove to be the most desperate battle of the war. The sad remnants of my men behave as men—those battalions who fought most bravely & suffered most are still in the best order. My regulars were superb & I count upon what are left to turn another battle in company with their gallant comrades of the Volunteers. Had I (20,000) twenty thousand or even (10,000) ten thousand fresh troops to use tomorrow I could take Richmond, but I have not a man in reserve & shall be glad to cover my retreat & save the material & personnel of the Army.

If we have lost the day we have yet preserved our honor & no one need blush for the Army of the Potomac. I have lost this battle because my force was too small. I again repeat that I am not responsible for this & I say it with the earnestness of a General who feels in his heart the loss of every brave man who has been needlessly sacrificed today. I still hope to retrieve our fortunes, but to do this the Govt must view the matter in the same earnest light that I do—you must send me very large reinforcements, & send them at once.

I shall draw back to this side of the Chickahominy & think I can withdraw all our material. Please understand that in this battle we have lost nothing but men & those the best we have.

In addition to what I have already said I only wish to say to the Presdt that I think he is wrong, in regarding me as ungenerous when I said that my force was too weak. I merely reiterated a truth which today has been too plainly proved. I should have gained this battle with (10,000) ten thousand fresh men. If at this instant I could dispose of (10,000) ten thousand fresh men I could gain the victory tomorrow.

I know that a few thousand men more would have changed this battle from a defeat to a victory—as it is the Govt must not & cannot hold me responsible for the result.

I feel too earnestly tonight—I have seen too many dead & wounded comrades to feel otherwise than that the Govt has not sustained this Army. If you do not do so now the game is lost.

If I save this Army now I tell you plainly that I owe no thanks to you or any other persons in Washington—you have done your best to sacrifice this Army.[19]

McClellan's claim that his men "were overwhelmed by vastly superior numbers" flew in the face of the fact that he held numerical superiority. The War Department telegraph office withheld the last extraordinary sentence before sending the message to Stanton.

Lincoln, not having seen the final accusatory sentence, said in return:

Save your Army at all events. Will send re-inforcements as fast as we can. Of course they can not reach you to-day, to-morrow, or next day. I have not said you were ungenerous for saying you needed reinforcement. I thought you were ungenerous in assuming that I did not send them as fast as I could. I feel any misfortune to you and your Army quite as keenly as you feel it yourself. If you have had a drawn battle, or a repulse, it is the price we pay for the enemy not being in Washington. We protected Washington, and the enemy concentrated on you; had we stripped Washington, he would have been upon us before the troops sent could have got to you. Less than a week ago you notified us that reinforcements were leaving Richmond to come in front of us. It is the nature of the case, and neither you or the government that is to blame. Please tell at once the present condition and aspect of things.[20]

On that same day, surveying the several fields of war, Lincoln wrote to Seward:

My view of the present condition of the War is about as follows:

The evacuation of Corinth, and our delay by the flood in the Chicahominy, has enabled the enemy to concentrate too much force in Richmond for McClellan to successfully attack. In fact there soon will be no substantial rebel force any where else. But if we send all the force from here to McClellan, the enemy will, before we can know of it, send a force from Richmond and take Washington. Or, if a large part of the Western Army be brought here to McClellan, they will let us have Richmond, and retake Tennessee, Kentucky, Missouri &c. What should be done is to hold what we have in the West, open the Mississippi, and, take Chatanooga & East Tennessee, without more—a reasonable force should, in every event, be kept about Washington for its protection. Then let the country give us a hundred thousand new troops in the shortest possible time, which added to McClellan, directly or indirectly, will take Richmond, without endangering any other place which we now hold—and will substantially end the war. I expect to maintain this contest until successful, or till I die, or am conquered, or my term expires, or Congress or the country forsakes me; and I would publicly appeal to the country for this new force, were it not that I fear a general panic and stampede would follow—so hard is it to have a thing understood as it really is. I think the new force should be all, or nearly all infantry, principally because such can be raised most cheaply and quickly.[21]

Using the letter Seward arranged to have the northern governors request the president to call for more troops. Their memorial read:

The undersigned, Governors of States of the Union, impressed with the belief that the citizens of the States which they respectively represent are of one accord in the hearty desire that the recent successes of the Federal

arms may be followed up by measures which must insure the speedy restoration of the Union; and believing that in view of the present state of the
important military movement now in progress and the reduced condition
of our effective forces in the field, resulting from the usual and unavoidable
casualties of the service, that the time has arrived for prompt and vigorous
measures to be adopted by the people in support of the great interests committed to your charge, we respectfully request, if it meets with your entire
approval, that you at once call upon the several States for such number
of men as may be required to fill up all military organizations now in the
field, and add to the armies heretofore organized such additional number
of men as may in your judgment be necessary to garrison and hold all of
the numerous cities and military positions that have been captured by our
armies, and to speedily crush the rebellion that still exists in several of the
Southern States, thus practically restoring to the civilized world our great
and good Government. All believe that the decisive moment is near at
hand, and to that end the people of the United States are desirous to aid
promptly in furnishing all re-enforcements that you may deem needful to
sustain our Government."[22]

Coming from the governors, the memorial avoided the appearance of
panic in Washington. The president issued the call for 300,000 volunteers,
prompting the patriotic song: "We are Coming, Father Abraham, Three
Hundred Thousand More." On the same day he replied to a wire from
McClellan that read: "You must send me very large reinforcements . . .
and they must come very promptly."[23]

At length Lincoln decided to visit McClellan in the field, where he had
retired to Harrison's Landing on the James River, after a series of battles
over seven days culminated at Malvern Hill on July 1. Upon the president's
arrival, the general handed him a letter marked "confidential." The letter
trespassed into highly political recommendations and commentary, and
when later revealed, it furnished fuel to McClellan's critics. Saying the time
had come to "determine upon a civil and military policy," he gave his views
on how the president and Congress should conduct the war. He opposed
confiscation of property, war against the population, and military arrests
except where hostilities existed, and he warned against "a declaration of
radical views on slavery." He suggested his willingness to become commander in chief of the army.

The president made no comment, but he soon acted. Profoundly troubled by the unhappy course of events, he made a quiet trip to the venerable General Winfield Scott. The president's secretaries conjectured about this unrecorded conversation that Scott advised the appointment of Halleck as general in chief. The president made the appointment on July 11 and three days later telegraphed Halleck, still in Corinth, Mississippi: "I am very anxious—almost impatient—to have you here."[24]

The day after Halleck arrived in Washington he paid a visit to McClellan. Differences in strategy separated the generals. On August 3 Halleck notified McClellan: "It is determined to withdraw your army from the Peninsula." When McClellan protested, Halleck telegraphed: "The president expects that the instructions which were sent you yesterday, with his approval, will be carried out with all possible despatch and caution."[25]

On August 9, believing Confederate forces were planning to advance to the Potomac, Halleck telegraphed: "You must send reinforcements instantly to Acquia Creek." A week later McClellan sent the message, "Movement has commenced." August 24, three weeks after he had been informed it had been determined he was to withdraw his forces to Aquia Creek, McClellan arrived there.

Meanwhile a new figure had appeared in the eastern theater. The son of an Illinois judge in whose court Lincoln had practiced, and a graduate of West Point, John Pope had distinguished himself early in the war by action in the West and had counseled Lincoln during McClellan's failing Peninsula Campaign. His influence could be seen in Lincoln's letter of June 28 to McClellan. In early July Pope testified before the Joint Committee on the Conduct of the War, outlining a strategy different from McClellan's. He gave assurances of favoring a policy aimed at securing the protection of Washington, approaching Richmond over land rather than by the peninsula. He believed that McClellan's army stood in danger of having supplies cut off, and he suggested to the committee that the success experienced in the West could be attributed to "a harmonious endeavor on the part of the officers there."[26] Pope had interviews with Lincoln and the cabinet. On June 26 Lincoln issued an order constituting the Army of Virginia, General John Pope commanding, charged with protecting western Virginia and Washington and at the appropriate time cooperating with the Army of the Potomac.

Pope soon faced a challenge to his generalship. Learning that McClellan was withdrawing his troops, Confederate General Robert E. Lee dispatched some of his forces north under Jackson and General James Longstreet. As Jackson advanced toward Manassas, General N. P. Banks, commanding a corps in Pope's army, tried to execute Pope's rash order, "Attack him immediately." Outnumbered four to one at the Battle of Cedar Mountain, Banks pushed Jackson back at a heavy cost in casualties. Hay wrote to a friend:

> You will have seen by the papers that Pope has been running his head into a hornet's nest. He fought a desperate battle the other day—or rather Banks did—Pope coming up at the end of it. He stands now in good position eager for another fight and confident of licking the enemy. The Tycoon [Lincoln] has given orders that he shan't fight unless there is a first rate chance of cleaning them out. The Tycoon thinks a defeat then would be a greater nuisance than several victories would abate.[27]

Chase recorded a cabinet meeting on August 19: "President's uneasy about Pope. He sent to the War Department for telegrams." Confederates and Pope clashed at Bull Run in late August. An anxious Lincoln on August 27 telegraphed McClellan, "What news from the front?" Receiving no answer, two days later while the battle was being fought Lincoln again asked him, "What news from direction of Manassas Junction?"

McClellan's reply dismayed the president:

> The last news I recd from the direction of Manassas was from stragglers to the effect that the enemy were evacuating Centreville & retiring towards Thorofare Gap this by no means reliable. I am clear that one of two courses should be adopted. First to concentrate all our available forces to open communication with Pope. Second to leave Pope to get out of his scrape & [a]t once use all our means to make the capital perfectly safe. No middle course will now answer. Tell me what you wish me to do & I will do all in my power to accomplish it. I wish to know what my orders & authority are. I ask for nothing but will obey whatever orders you give. I only ask a prompt decision that I may at once give the necessary orders. It will not do to delay longer.[28]

The president's young secretary John Hay and the president, on Saturday morning, August 30, while the battle was still raging, rode their horses to the White House from the Soldiers' Home, where Lincoln spent much of the summer to escape the heat of the city. Hay recorded in his diary:

We talked about the state of things by Bull Run and Pope's prospect. The President was very outspoken in regard to McClellan's present conduct. He said it really seemed to him that McC wanted Pope defeated. He mentioned to me a despatch of McC.s in which he proposed, as one plan of action, to "leave Pope to get out of his own scrape, and devote ourselves to securing Washington." He spoke also of McCs dreadful panic in the matter of Chain Bridge, which he had ordered blown up the night before, but which order had been countermanded; and also of his incomprehensible interference with Franklin's corps which he recalled once, and then when they had been sent ahead by Halleck's order, begged permission to recall them again & only desisted after Hallecks sharp injunction to push them ahead till they whipped something or got whipped themselves. The President seemed to think him a little crazy. Envy jealousy and spite are probably a better explanation of his present conduct. He is constantly sending despatches to the President and Halleck asking what is his real position and command. He acts as chief alarmist and grand marplot of the Army.

The President, on my asking if Halleck had any prejudices, rejoined "No! Halleck is wholly for the service. He does not care who succeeds or who fails so the service is benefited."

Later in the day we were in Halleck's room. H. was at dinner & Stanton came in while we were waiting for him and carried us off to dinner. A pleasant little dinner and a pretty wife as white and cold and motionless as marble, whose rare smiles seemed to pain her. Stanton was loud about the McC. business. He was unqualifiedly severe upon McClellan. He said that after these battles, there should be one Court Martial, if never any more. He said that nothing but foul play could lose us this battle & that it rested with McC. and his friends. Stanton seemed to believe very strongly in Pope. So did the President for that matter.

We went back to the Headquarters and found General Halleck. He seemed quiet and somewhat confident. He said the greatest battle of the Century was now being fought. He said he had sent every man that could go, to the field. At the War Department we found that Mr. Stanton had sent a vast army of Volunteer Nurses out to the field, probably utterly useless, over which he gave Genl. Wadsworth command.[29]

That night Hay recorded:

> Every thing seemed to be going well and hilarious on Saturday & we went to
> bed expecting glad tidings at sunrise. But about Eight oclock the President
> came to my room as I was dressing and calling me out said, "Well John we
> are whipped again, I am afraid. The enemy reinforced on Pope and drove
> back his left wing and he has retired to Centerville where he says he will be
> able to hold his men. I don't like that expression. I don't like to hear him
> admit that his men need holding."[30]

The second battle of Manassas culminated on August 30 when Jackson,
reinforced by Longstreet, destroyed a large part of Pope's army. Union
casualties from the battle reached 14,462, while Confederate losses were
9,474. Pope reassembled his army at Centerville, but the Confederates
commanded by Robert E. Lee had positioned a powerful force in northern
Virginia on the outskirts of Washington, D.C., poised either to threaten the
capital or to move north across the Potomac River. For all of his confidence,
John Pope had mismanaged his generals and utterly failed to defeat, much
less deter, the Confederate thrust.

That day McClellan received the War Department order describing
the duties of Union commanders in Virginia. The order stated: "General
McClellan commands the Army of Virginia that has not been sent forward
to Gen. Pope's command." He wailed to Ellen: "They have taken all my
troops from me! . . . I am left in command of *nothing!*"

Lincoln's response was recorded in a conversation reported by Welles:

> The President called on me . . . He expressed himself very decidedly concern-
> ing the management or mismanagement of the army. Said, "We had the
> enemy in the hollow of our hands on Friday if our generals, who are vexed
> with Pope had done their duty. All of our present difficulties and reverses
> have been brought upon us by these quarrels of the generals." These were, I
> think his very words. While we were conversing, Collector Barney of New
> York came in. The President . . . went on, freely commenting and repeating
> some things said before B. joined us. Of Pope he spoke in complimentary
> terms as brave, patriotic, and as having done his duty in every respect in
> Virginia, to the entire satisfaction of himself and Halleck, who both knew
> and watched, day and night, every movement. On only one point had Hal-
> leck doubted any order P. had given, that was, in directing one division, I

think Heintzelman's, to march for the Chain Bridge, by which the flanks of that division were exposed. . . . Pope said the President, did well, but there was here an army prejudice against him, and it was necessary he should leave. He had gone off very angry.[31]

On September 1 McClellan took command of troops for the defense of Washington; five days later Pope was relieved of his army and sent to command the Department of the Northwest.

On the last day of Second Bull Run the eloquent abolitionist Wendell Phillips loosed oratorical volleys at both McClellan and Lincoln. He had earlier in the month called Lincoln "a first rate second rate man." He now said:

I think the present purpose of the government, so far as it has now a purpose, is to end the war and save slavery. I believe Mr. Lincoln is conducting this war, at present, with the purpose of saving slavery. That is his present line of policy, so far as trustworthy indications of any policy reach us. The Abolitionists are charged with a desire to make this a political war. All civil wars are necessarily political wars,—they can hardly be anything else. Mr. Lincoln is intentionally waging a *political* war. He knows as well as we do at this moment as well as every man this side of a lunatic hospital knows that, if he wants to save lives and money, the way to end this war is to strike at slavery. I do not believe that McClellan himself is mad or idiotic enough to have avoided that idea, even if he has tried to do so. But General McClellan is waging a political war; so is Mr. Lincoln. When General Butler ordered the women and children to be turned out of the camps at New Orleans, and one of the colonels of the Northwest remonstrated and hid himself in his tent, rather than witness the misery which the order occasioned,— when the slaveholders came to receive the women and children who were to be turned out of the camps, and the troops actually charged upon them with bayonets to keep them out of the line,—General Butler knew what he was doing. It was not to save rations, it was not to get rid of individuals; it was to conciliate New Orleans. It was a political move. When Mr. Lincoln, by an equivocal declaration, nullifies General Hunter, he does not do it because he doubts either the justice or the efficiency of Hunter's proclamation; he does it because he is afraid of Kentucky on the right hand, and the Daily Advertiser on the left. [Laughter.] He has not taken one step since he entered the Presidency that has been a purely military step, and he could not. A civil war can hardly be anything but a political war. That is, all civil wars are a struggle between opposite ideas, and armies are but the tools. If Mr. Lincoln believed in the North and in Liberty, he would let our army act on the principles of Liberty. He does not. He believes in the South as the most efficient and vital instrumentality at the present moment, therefore defers to it. . . .

When I was here a year ago, I said I thought the President needed the advice of great bodies of prominent men. That has taken a year. The New York Chamber of Commerce, the Common Council, and the Defence Committee, have just led the way. Some of the Western Councils have followed, it is said. Let us hope that they may have decisive effect at Washington; but I do not believe they will. I do not believe there is in that Cabinet— Seward, Chase, Stanton, Wells, or the President of the country—enough to make a leader. . . .

I never did believe in the capacity of Abraham Lincoln, but I do believe in the pride of Davis, in the vanity of the South, in the desperate determination of those fourteen States; and I believe in a sunny future, because God has driven them mad; and their madness is our safety. They will never consent to anything that the North can grant; and you must whip them, because, unless you do, they will grind you to powder.

This war is to go on. There will be drafting in three months or six. The hunker, when he is obliged to go to war, will be like the man of whom Mr. Conway told us, who was willing to sit by a negro in the cars rather than stand all night,—he will be willing that the negro shall fight, with him or without him. That is a part of the logic of events which will be very effective; but even that will not make Lincoln declare for emancipation. We shall wait one year or two, if we wait for him, before we get it.

The most serious charge I have against the President, the only thing that makes a film upon his honesty,—for I believe him as honest as the measure of his intellect and circumstances of his life allow,—is this: that, while I do not believe that in his heart he trusts McClellan a whit more than I do, from fear of the Border States and Northern conservatism he keeps him at the head of the army, which loses two thousand men by disease every week, and spends from sixty to seventy thousand dollars a day; and if, twenty years hence, he renders up an account of his stewardship to his country, you that live, mark me I will see him confess that this whole winter he never believed in McClellan's ability. That is the sore spot in the character of an otherwise honest officer, and that is where his fear of conservatism sends him.[32]

In military affairs the year opened with a dawdling McClellan. Months after assuming command, after prevailing over the president about strategy, he at last faced the enemy troops. Inconclusive battles on the peninsula, petulant missives to his wife, failure to take an aggressive stand, and a seeming willingness to take charge of war policies marked McClellan's tenure in the field.

The Union saw a second Bull Run, and a second defeat. Abolitionists grew increasingly restless about Lincoln's conduct of the war. Confronted with Lee's invasion of the North, Lincoln again turned to McClellan.

CHAPTER SEVENTEEN

ANTIETAM AND ANOTHER

MCCLELLAN EXIT

Members of Lincoln's cabinet were uneasy about restoring McClellan to any command in the army. Stanton, Bates, Chase, and Smith joined in signing a remonstrance against McClellan. Welles agreed but, unwilling to sign, said he would speak in the cabinet meeting. Seward was out of the city. While McClellan was at breakfast on September 2 Lincoln, accompanied by Halleck, called on him and asked him to resume command of Washington troops returning from Second Bull Run.

Later that day the cabinet began to discuss the matter before Lincoln arrived. Welles recorded the meeting's events:

> The President was called out for a short time and while he was absent Stanton said he was informed McClellan had been ordered to take command of the forces in Washington. General surprise was expressed. When the President came in, he said he had done what seemed to him best. Halleck had proposed it. McClellan knows this whole ground—his specialty is to defend—he is a good engineer, all admit—there is no better organizer. He can be trusted to act on the defensive, but having "slows" he is good for nothing for an onward movement. Much was said. There was a more disturbed and desponding feeling than I have ever witnessed in council and the President was extremely distressed. There was a general conversation as regarded the infirmities of McClellan, but it was claimed he had beyond any officer the confidence of the army. Though deficient in the positive qualities which are necessary for an energetic commander, his organizing powers could be temporarily available till the troops could rally.

This, the President said, was General Halleck's view as well as his own, and some who were dissatisfied with his action had thought H. was the man for General-in-Chief, "felt that there was nothing to do but to acquiesce, yet Chase earnestly and emphatically stated his conviction that it would prove a national calamity."[1]

Days later, while Lincoln and Hay were walking to the telegraph office in the War Department, the president remarked of McClellan's appointment: "They were all ready to denounce me for it, except Blair. . . . We must use the tools we have. There is no man in the Army who can man these fortifications and lick these troops of ours into shape half as well as he."[2]

Halleck on September 5 informed Pope that the armies of the Potomac and Virginia had been consolidated. McClellan was again in charge. Pope's army, in fact, had disintegrated, and its members were still coming into Washington. On September 8 after seeing Lincoln at the War Department, Chase observed: "The president said he had felt badly all day. [General] Wadsworth said there was no danger of an attack on Washington, and that the man ought to be severely punished who intimated the possibility of its surrender. The president spoke of the great number of stragglers he had seen coming in to town this morning; and of the immense losses by desertion."[3]

Lee on September 4, exploiting his defeat of Pope, began to invade Maryland. He hoped Marylanders would rise to his aid, victories would ensue, Great Britain and France would recognize the Confederacy, and a weary defeated North would acquiesce to peace. An anxious president, on September 8, 10, and 12 sent identical telegrams to McClellan, who was moving his forces toward Lee's invaders: "How does it look now?"

Lee's Army of Northern Virginia and McClellan's Army of the Potomac clashed from daybreak to dark on September 17 at Antietam, Maryland. Lee lost one-fourth of his army, McClellan one-sixth on this bloodiest day of the Civil War. Holding an advantage, McClellan ignored Lincoln's earlier urgings: "Please do not let him get off without being hurt" and "Destroy the rebel army, if possible."[4] But McClellan would not move.

Lincoln busied himself with the preliminary Emancipation Proclamation and his blanket suspension of habeas corpus. From October 1 to 5 he

visited McClellan in camp. The general described the visit in McClellan's
Own Story:

> On the first day of October his Excellency the President honored the Army
> of the Potomac with a visit, and remained several days, during which he
> went through the different encampments, reviewed the troops, and went
> over the battle-fields of South Mountain and Antietam. I had the oppor-
> tunity during this visit to describe to him the operations of the army since
> the time it left Washington, and gave him my reasons for not following the
> enemy after he crossed the Potomac.
>
> He was accompanied by Gen. McClernand, John W. Garrett, the Sec-
> retary of State of Illinois, and others whom I have forgotten. During the
> visit we had many and long consultations alone. I urged him to follow a
> conservative course, and supposed from the tenor of his conversation that
> he would do so. He more than once assured me that he was fully satisfied
> with my whole course from the beginning; that the only fault he could
> possibly find was that I was perhaps too prone to be sure that everything
> was ready before acting, but that my actions were all right when I started. I
> said to him that I thought a few experiments with those who acted before
> they were ready would probably convince him that in the end I consumed
> less time than they did. He told me that he regarded me as the only general
> in the service capable of organizing and commanding a large army, and
> that he would stand by me. We parted on the field of South Mountain,
> whither I had accompanied him. He said there that he did not see how we
> ever gained that field, and that he was sure that, if I had defended it, Lee
> could never have carried it.
>
> We spent some time on the battle-field and conversed fully on the state
> of affairs. He told me that he was entirely satisfied with me and with all
> that I had done; that he would stand by me against "all comers"; that he
> wished me to continue my preparations for a new campaign, not to stir
> an inch until fully ready, and when ready to do what I thought best. He
> repeated that he was entirely satisfied with me; that I should be let alone;
> that he would stand by me. I have no doubt that he meant exactly what he
> said. He parted from me with the utmost cordiality. We never met again
> on this earth.[5]

However pleasant Lincoln's manner seemed to McClellan, the president
wanted action. Three weeks after Antietam he ordered McClellan to move.
On October 6 the general received a telegram from Halleck:

I am instructed to telegraph you as follows: The President directs that you cross the Potomac and give battle to the enemy or drive him south. Your army must move now while the roads are good. If you cross the river between the enemy and Washington, and cover the latter by your operation, you can be reinforced with 30,000 men. If you move up the valley of the Shenandoah not more than 12,000 or 15,000 can be sent to you. The President advises the interior line between Washington and the enemy, but does not order it. He is very desirous that your army move as soon as possible. You will immediately report what line you adopt and when you intend to cross the river; also to what point the reinforcements are to be sent. It is necessary that the plan of your operations be positively determined on before orders are given for building bridges and repairing railroads. I am directed to add that the Secretary of War and the general-in-chief fully concur with the President in these instructions.[6]

A week later, with McClellan still inert, Lincoln himself wrote a long letter to the general, chiding him for being overcautious, giving a lesson in military science, and suggesting a strategy around the sentence: "If we can not beat the enemy where he now is, we never can."[7]

As McClellan procrastinated, Lincoln's patience grew thin. He received a report from McClellan that read:

I have in camp 267 horses . . . of these, 128 are positively and absolutely unable to leave the camp, from the following causes, viz, sore-tongue, grease, and consequent lameness, and sore backs. . . . The horses, which are still sound, are absolutely broken down from fatigue and want of flesh. . . .

In reply to your telegram of this date, I have the honor to state, from the time this army left Washington, on the 7th of September, my cavalry has been constantly employed in making reconnaissances, scouting, and picketing. Since the battle of Antietam, six regiments have made a trip of 200 miles, marching 55 miles in one day, while endeavoring to reach Stuart's cavalry.

General Pleasonton, in his official report, states that he, with the remainder of our available cavalry, while on Stuart's track, marched 78 miles in twenty-four hours.

Besides these two remarkable expeditions, our cavalry has been engaged in picketing and scouting 150 miles of river front ever since the battle of Antietam, and has made repeated reconnaissances since that time, engaging the enemy on every occasion, and, indeed, it has performed harder service since the battle than before. I beg that you will also consider that this same cavalry was brought from the Peninsula, where it encountered most laborious service, and was, at the commencement of this campaign, in low condition, and from that time to the present has had no time to recruit.

If any instance can be found where overworked cavalry has performed more labor than mine since the battle of Antietam, I am not conscious of it.[7]

To this the president made an unaccustomedly acerbic reply: "I have just read your despatch about sore tongued and fatiegued [sic] horses. Will you pardon me for asking what the horses of your army have done since the battle of Antietam that fatigue anything?"[8]

More than a month after Antietam, McClellan began to move his army. In a letter to Ellen he said:

I move a respectable number of troops across the Potomac today—the beginning of the general movement, which will however require several days to accomplish—for the cavalry is still terribly off. I was mad as a 'march hare' yesterday at a telegram received from the Presdt asking what my "cavalry had done since the battle of Antietam to fatigue anything"–it was one of those dirty little flings that I can't get used to when they are not merited.[9]

On their nightly ride to the Soldiers' Home, Lincoln and Hay talked about McClellan. The president said McClellan "was doing nothing to make himself either respected or feared." Hay penned in his diary:

Last night, September 25, the President and I were riding [to] the Soldiers Home; he said he had heard of an officer who had said they did not mean to gain any decisive victory but to keep things running on so that they, the Army, might manage things to suit themselves. He said he should have the matter examined and if any such language had been used, his head should go off.

I talked a great deal about the McClellan conspiracy but he would make no answer to anything. He merely said that McC. was doing nothing to make himself either respected or feared.[10]

Lincoln later confided to Hay:

After the battle of Antietam, I went up to the field to try to get him to move & came back thinking he would move at once. But when I got home he began to argue why he ought not to move. I peremptorily ordered him to advance. It was 19 days before he put a man over the river. It was 9 days longer before he got his army across and then he stopped again, delaying on little pretexts of wanting this and that. I began to fear he was playing false—that he did not want to hurt the enemy. I saw how he could intercept the enemy on the way to Richmond. I determined to make that the test. If he let them get away I would remove him. He did so & I relieved him."[11]

Lincoln instructed Halleck to relieve the man critics were calling "tardy George" and turn over his command to General Ambrose Burnside.

McClellan's military career ended, but he had laid the foundations of a political career. A Kentucky correspondent, Leslie Combs, veteran of the War of 1812, wrote a sympathetic letter to McClellan. Combs said the order to withdraw from the peninsula was "military madness," and "I think your battle of Antietam, the most remarkable in history, certainly our history." Responding, McClellan not only concurred in spirit with Combs but also appraised the roles of Lincoln and Stanton, whom Combs had termed an "ass." Three days later in a letter to August Belmont, national chairman of the Democratic Party, McClellan wrote, "I fear that Mr L is busily engaged in breaking the rest of the eggs in the basket! Is this the blackest hour which precedes the dawn?"[12]

CHAPTER EIGHTEEN

EMANCIPATION

Lincoln is an icon in world history—best known as "the Great Emancipator." His early record on emancipation, however, did not always appear to live up to the phrase; not until 1865 did he fully earn the accolade. Black freedom and racial equality were not his foremost priorities. Lincoln's record as an antislavery politician starts early in his career. At age twenty-eight he and another state legislator, lonely voices in the assembly, made clear their views on slavery and emancipation. He held these views until the Civil War:

> The following protest was presented to the House, which was read and ordered to be spread on the journals, to wit:
>
> Resolutions upon the subject of domestic slavery having passed both branches of the General Assembly at its present session, the undersigned hereby protest against the passage of the same.
>
> They believe that the institution of slavery is founded on both injustice and bad policy; but that the promulgation of abolition doctrines tends rather to increase than to abate its evils.
>
> They believe that the Congress of the United States has no power, under the constitution, to interfere with the institution of slavery in the different States.
>
> They believe that the Congress of the United States has the power, under the constitution, to abolish slavery in the District of Columbia; but that that power ought not to be exercised unless at the request of the people of said District.
>
> The difference between these opinions and those contained in the said resolutions, is their reason for entering this protest.
>
> DAN STONE,
> A. LINCOLN,
> Representatives from the county of Sangamon.[1]

At the close of his single term in Congress he introduced a measure to abolish slavery in the District of Columbia with the consent of the slave owners and compensation to them. The effort failed. In his debates with Stephen A. Douglas in 1858 he denounced slavery as immoral and urged its ultimate extinction. The Republican platform in 1860 upheld the right of states to control slavery and the right of Congress to prohibit slavery in the territories. In his inaugural address he declared he had no objection to a pending amendment that the federal government should never interfere with slavery in the states.

Within weeks war erupted. General Benjamin Butler, commanding at Fort Monroe, Virginia, soon found that slaves were streaming within his lines. The adroit politician, unlike McClellan, discovered a way to ignore the fugitive slave law by calling the fugitives contrabands and retaining them. Lincoln quietly acquiesced.

General Butler and Congress advanced the cause while Lincoln quietly watched. In its first confiscation act Congress included slaves used or employed in aiding the rebellion, authorizing the president to seize, confiscate, and condemn such "property." When General John C. Frémont proclaimed free those slaves belonging to enemies, Lincoln required him to modify the proclamation to bring it within the confiscation act. In reversing the proclamation Lincoln asked his critic, Senator O. H. Browning: "Can it be pretended that it is any longer the government of the U.S.—any government of Constitution and laws,—wherein a General, or a President, may make permanent rules of property by proclamation?" He was disclaiming his authority to emancipate by proclamation.

All the while influential political leaders were urging him to act. The day following Bull Run, Vice President Hamlin and radical Republican senators Zachariah Chandler of Michigan and Charles Sumner of Massachusetts came to the White House to urge Lincoln to use his full war powers both to free and to arm the slaves. Lincoln complained to Senator John B. Henderson of Missouri, "Stevens, Sumner and Wilson simply haunt me with their importunities for a Proclamation of Emancipation."

When Lincoln to his surprise read in Secretary of War Cameron's annual report that fugitive or abandoned slaves should be armed and incorporated in the military service, he ordered the report recalled, even though many copies were already printed and in the post offices.

Days earlier, however, Lincoln himself had taken a significant step toward an emancipation plan, not to be undertaken by the president, nor by the Congress, but by the border slave states. For most of the year he had been concerned about keeping these states in the Union, which, as in the case of Kentucky's response to Frémont's proclamation, required retention of slavery.

By late November the loyalty of these states seemed assured, as Lincoln informed Congress early the next month. In mid-November he received a letter from George Bancroft, an eminent historian and Democratic politician, which enclosed a clipping about a New York meeting to aid suffering loyalists in North Carolina and closed with a paragraph anticipating emancipation as an outcome of the war:

> Your administration has fallen upon times, which will be remembered as long as human events find a record. I sincerely wish to you the glory of perfect success. Civil war is the instrument of Divine Providence to root out social slavery; posterity will not be satisfied with the result, unless the consequences of the war shall effect an increase of free states. This is the universal expectation and hope of men of all parties.[2]

In response on November 18 Lincoln wrote:

> I esteem it a high honor to have received a note from Mr. Bancroft, inclosing the report of proceedings of a New York meeting, taking measures for the relief of Union people of North Carolina. I thank you, and all others participating, for this benevolent and patriotic movement.
>
> The main thought in the closing paragraph of your letter is one which does not escape my attention, and with which I must deal in all due caution, and with the best judgment I can bring to it.[3]

Employing due caution and his best judgment, in late November Lincoln drafted a bill that disclosed a shift in attitude toward the border states. Adhering to his fixed aim to restore the Union, he would pursue the aim, refraining from federal interference in slavery but encouraging the states themselves to free their slaves. To this end he drafted two versions of a bill to be enacted by a state legislature. He chose Delaware, the loyalty of which had been least in doubt and which held only 1,798 slaves. The provisions of the second version, which he preferred, were revelatory of Lincoln's thinking about the process of emancipation. State action, federal compensation, and gradualism marked the process. At the end of the second version he summed up its salient points:

> Be it enacted by the State of Delaware that on condition the United States of America will, at the present session of Congress, engage by law to pay, and thereafter faithfully pay to the said State of Delaware, in the six per cent bonds of said United States, the sum of seven hundred and nineteen thousand, and two hundred dollars, in thirty one equal annual instalments, there shall be neither slavery nor involuntary servitude, at any time after the first day of January in the year of our Lord one thousand eight hundred and ninety three, within the said State of Delaware, except in the punishment of crime, whereof the party shall have been duly convicted; nor, except in the punishment of crime as aforesaid, shall any person who shall be born after the passage of this act, nor any person above the age of thirty five years, be held in slavery, or to involuntary servitude, within said State of Delaware, at any time after the passage of this act.
>
> And be it further enacted that said State shall, in good faith prevent, so far as possible, the carrying of any person out of said state, into involuntary servitude, beyond the limits of said State, at any time after the passage of this act.
>
> And be it further enacted that said State may make provision of apprenticeship, not to extend beyond the age of twentyone years for males, nor eighteen for females, for all minors whose mothers were not free at the respective births of such minors.

On reflection, I like No. 2 the better. By it the Nation would pay the State $23,200 per annum for thirtyone years—and

All born after the passage of the act would be born free—and
    All slaves above the age of 35 years would become free on the passage of the act—and
    All others would become free on arriving at the age of 35 years, until January 1893—when
    All remaining of all ages would become free, subject to apprenticeship for minors born of slave mothers, up to the respective ages of 21 and 18.

If the State would desire to have the money sooner, let the bill be altered only in fixing the time of final emancipation earlier, and making the annual instalments correspondingly fewer in number; by which they would also be correspondingly larger in amount. For instance, strike out "1893," and insert "1872"; and strike out "thirtyone" annual instalments, and insert "ten" annual instalments. The instalments would then be $71,920 instead of $23,200 as now. In all other particulars let the bill stand precisely as it is.[4]

The bill was never introduced. A condemnatory joint resolution won a majority vote in the Delaware house and deadlocked in the state senate. Lincoln's compensated emancipation plan could have been a starting point, emulated by other border states, strengthening the unionism of the North and weakening hopes of the South for allies in spirit if not in fact.

Congress in the session that began in December exhibited a new militancy against slavery. On opening day Representative Thomas Eliot of Massachusetts introduced a resolution stating that the president as commander in chief had the right to emancipate in any military district in insurrection. Representative Thaddeus Stevens promptly rose to introduce a resolution asking the president to free every slave who aided in the rebellion, with compensation for their masters.

On January 15, 1862, radical Senator Lyman Trumbull introduced a second confiscation bill that included freeing rebels' slaves. Less than a month later abolitionist Senator Charles Sumner introduced a resolution stating that by seceding, the southern states had committed state "suicide." Slavery, resting on state law, no longer existed in those states, he claimed. Unlike his predecessors, Lincoln himself in February refused appeals to spare the life of Captain Nathaniel Gordon, convicted of engaging in the Atlantic slave trade, and ordered his execution, the first time in American history.

Lincoln persevered in his plan to initiate state-compensated emancipation. As early as December 1861 he confided to Browning and Sumner that he was preparing a document on compensated emancipation, this time for federal action. On March 6, 1862, he sent a special message to Congress. He recommended adoption of a joint resolution containing the principles of state-compensated, gradual emancipation. State emancipation, he argued, would dissipate southern hope that the North might recognize the independence "of the disaffected region." In a burst of hyperbole, he said, "To deprive them [the southern states] of this hope, substantially ends the rebellion." He couched the policy as a means to preserve the Union rather than a moral matter. "A practical re-acknowledgment of the national authority would render the war unnecessary, and it would at once cease."

Response was mixed. Radical Republican Thaddeus Stevens spoke for many radicals and abolitionists when he branded the plan "the most diluted, milk and water gruel proposition that was ever given to the American nation." Much of the New York press praised the proposal. Lincoln responded to a *New York Times* account by writing to the editor, Henry J. Raymond, himself a conspicuous Republican politician:

> I am grateful to the New-York Journals, and not less so to the Times than to others, for their kind notices of the late special Message to Congress. Your paper, however, intimates that the proposition, though well-intentioned, must fail on the score of expense. I do hope you will reconsider this. Have you noticed the facts that less than one half-day's cost of this war would pay for all the slaves in Delaware, at four hundred dollars per head?–that eighty-seven days cost of this war would pay for all in Delaware, Maryland, District of Columbia, Kentucky, and Missouri at the same price? Were those states to take the step, do you doubt that it would shorten the war more than eighty seven days, and thus be an actual saving of expense. Please look at these things, and consider whether there should not be another article in the Times?[5]

On the same day Lincoln requested the representatives of the border slave states to meet with him the next day. John W. Crisfield of Maryland made notes of the meeting:

> After the usual salutations and we were seated, the President said, in substance, that he had invited us to meet him to have some conversation with us in explanation of his message of the 6th; that since he had sent it in several of the gentlemen then present had visited him, but had avoided any allusion to the message, and he therefore inferred that the import of the message had been misunderstood, and was regarded as inimical to the interests we represented; and he had resolved he would talk with us, and disabuse our minds of that erroneous opinion.

The President then disclaimed any intent to injure the interests or wound the sensibilities of the slave States. On the contrary, his purpose was to protect the one and respect the other; that we were engaged in a terrible wasting, and tedious war; immense armies were in the field, and must continue in the field as long as the war lasts; that these armies must, of necessity, be brought into contact with slaves in the States we represented and in other States as they advanced; that slaves would come to the camps and continual irritation was kept up; that he was constantly annoyed by conflicting and antagonistic complaints; on the one side, a certain class complained if the slave was not protected by the army; persons were frequently found who, participating in these views, acted in a way unfriendly to the slaveholder; on the other hand, slaveholders complained that their rights were interfered with, their slaves induced to abscond and protected within the lines; these complaints were numerous, loud, and deep; were a serious annoyance to him and embarrassing to the progress of the war; that it kept alive a spirit hostile to the Government in the States we represented; strengthened the hopes of the confederates that, at some day the border States would unite with them, and thus tend to prolong the war; and he was of opinion, if this resolution should be adopted by Congress and accepted by our States, these causes of irritation and these hopes would be removed, and more would be accomplished towards shortening the war than could be hoped from the greatest victory achieved by Union armies; that he made this proposition in good faith, and desired it to be accepted, if at all, voluntarily, and in the same patriotic spirit in which it was made; that emancipation was a subject exclusively under the control of the States, and must be adopted or rejected by each for itself; that he did not claim nor had this Government any right to coerce them for that purpose; that such was no part of his purpose in making this proposition, and he wished it to be clearly understood; that he did not expect us there to be prepared to give him an answer, but he hoped we would take the subject into serious consideration; confer with one another, and then take such course as we felt our duty and the interests of our constituents required of us.

Mr. Noell, of Missouri, said that in his State slavery was not considered a permanent institution; that natural causes were there in operation which would, at no distant day, extinguish it, and he did not think that this proposition was necessary for that; and, besides that, he and his friends felt solicitous as to the message on account of the different constructions which the resolution and message had received. The *New York Tribune* was for it, and understood it to mean that we must accept gradual emancipation according to the plan suggested, or get something worse.

The PRESIDENT replied, he must not be expected to quarrel with the *New York Tribune* before the right time; he hoped never to have to do it; he would not anticipate events. In respect to emancipation in Missouri, he said that what had been observed by Mr. Noell was probably true, but the operation of these natural causes had not prevented the irritating conduct to which he had referred, or destroyed hopes of the Confederates that Missouri would at some time range herself alongside of them, which, in his judgment, the passage of this resolution by Congress and its acceptance by Missouri would accomplish.

Mr. CRISFIELD, of Maryland, risked what would be the effect of the refusal of the State to accept this proposal, and desired to know if the President looked to any policy beyond the acceptance or rejection of this scheme.

The PRESIDENT replied that he had no designs beyond the action of the States on this particular subject. He should lament their refusal to accept it, but he had no designs beyond their refusal of it.

Mr. Menzies, of Kentucky, inquired if the President thought there was any power except in the States themselves to carry out his scheme of emancipation.

The PRESIDENT replied, he thought there could not be. He then went off into a course of remarks not qualifying the foregoing declaration nor material to be repeated to a just understanding of his meaning.

Mr. CRISFIELD said he did not think the people of Maryland looked upon slavery as a permanent institution; and he did not know that they would be very reluctant to give it up if provision was made to meet the loss, and they could be rid of the race; but they did not like to be coerced into emancipation, either by the direct action of the Government or by indirection, as though the emancipation of slaves in this District, or the confiscation of southern property as now threatened; and he thought before they would consent to consider this proposition they would require to be informed on these points.

The PRESIDENT replied that, "unless he was expelled by the act of God or the Confederate armies, he should occupy that house for three years, and as long as he remained there Maryland had nothing to fear, either for her institutions or her interests, on the points referred to."

Mr. CRISFIELD immediately added: "Mr. President, if what you now say could be heard by the people of Maryland they would consider your proposition with a much better feeling than I fear without it they will be inclined to do."

The PRESIDENT. "That (meaning a publication of what he said) will not do; it would force me into a quarrel before the proper time;" and, again intimating, as he had before done, that a quarrel with the "Greeley faction" was impending, he said "he did not wish to encounter it before the proper time, nor at all if it could be avoided."

Governor WICKLIFFE, of Ky., then asked him respecting the constitutionality of his scheme.

The PRESIDENT replied: "As you may suppose, I have considered that; and the proposition now submitted does not encounter any constitutional difficulty. It proposes simply to co-operate with any State by giving such State pecuniary aid; and he thought that the resolution, as proposed by him, would be considered rather as the expression of a sentiment than as involving any constitutional question."

Mr. HALL, of Mo., thought that if this proposition was adopted at all it should be by the votes of the free States, and come as a proposition from them to the slave States, affording them an inducement to put aside this subject of discord; that it ought not to be expected that members representing slaveholding constituencies should declare at once, and in advance of any proposition to them, for the emancipation of slavery.

The PRESIDENT said he saw and felt the force of the objection; it was a fearful responsibility, and every gentleman must do as he thought best; that he did not know how this scheme was received by the members from the free States; some of them had spoken to him and received it kindly; but for the most part they were as reserved and chary as we had been, and he could not tell how they would vote. And in reply to some expression of Mr. Hall as to his own opinion regarding slavery, he said he did not pretend to disguise his anti-slavery feeling; that he thought it was wrong and should continue to think so; but that was not the question we had to deal with now. Slavery existed, and that, too, as well by the act of the North as of the South; and in any scheme to get rid of it, the North, as well as the South, was morally bound to do its full and equal share. He thought the institution wrong, and ought never to have existed; but yet he recognized the rights of property which had grown out of it, and would respect those rights as fully as similar rights in any other property; that property can exist, and does legally exist. He thought such a law wrong, but the rights of property resulting must be respected; he would get rid of the odious law, not by violating the right, but by encouraging the proposition and offering inducements to give it up.

Here the interview, so far as this subject is concerned, terminated by Mr. Crittenden's assuring the President that, whatever might be our final action, we all thought him solely moved by a high patriotism and sincere devotion to the happiness and glory of his country; and with that conviction we should consider respectfully the important suggestions he had made.

After some conversation on the current war news, we retired, and I immediately proceeded to my room and wrote out this paper.[6]

California's Senator James McDougall stoutly opposed the scheme. Lincoln on March 14 addressed to him a letter, replete with statistics supplied by the superintendent of the census:

As to the expensiveness of the plan of gradual emancipation with compensation, proposed in the late Message, please allow me one or two brief suggestions.

Less than one half-day's cost of this war would pay for all the slaves in Delaware at four hundred dollars per head:

Thus, all the slaves in Delaware,

by the Census of 1860, are	[...]	1798
		[x]400
Cost of the slaves	[...]	$ 719,200
One day's cost of the war	[...]	" 2,000,000.

Again, less than eighty seven days cost of this war would, at the same price, pay for all in Delaware, Maryland, District of Columbia, Kentucky, and Missouri.

Thus, slaves in Delaware	[...]	1798
" " Maryland	[...]	87,188
" " Dis. of Col	[...]	3,481
" " Kentucky	[...]	225,490
" " Missouri	[...]	114,965
		432,622
		[x]400
Cost of the slaves	[...]	$173,048,800
Eightyseven days' cost of the war	[...]	" 174,000,000.

Do you doubt that taking the initiatory steps on the part of those states and this District, would shorten the war more than eightyseven days, and thus be an actual saving of expense?

A word as to the *time* and *manner* of incurring the expence. Suppose, for instance, a State devises and adopts a system by which the institution absolutely ceases therein by a named day—say January 1st. 1882. Then, let the sum to be paid to such state by the United States, be ascertained by taking from the Census of 1860, the number of slaves within the state, and multiplying that number by four hundred—the United States to pay such sum to the state in twenty equal annual instalments, in six per cent. bonds of the United States.

The sum thus given, as to time and manner, I think would not be half as onerous, as would be an equal sum, raised now, for the indefinite prossecution of the war; but of this you can judge as well as I.

I inclose a Census-table for your convenience.[7]

After wide-ranging debate Congress approved the resolution for federal support of any gradual, compensated emancipation by the states. As the session continued the lawmakers added to the antislavery legislation. A second confiscation act extended confiscation to the slaves of traitors and rebels. Particularly pleasing to the president was a bill abolishing slavery in the District of Columbia, with compensation and colonization provisions. Instead of merely signing the bill Lincoln sent a message to Congress, expressing his gratification and suggesting amendments:

Fellow citizens of the State, and House of Representatives.

The Act entitled "An Act for the release of certain persons held to service, or labor in the District of Columbia" has this day been approved, and signed.

I have never doubted the constitutional authority of congress to abolish slavery in this District; and I have ever desired to see the national capital freed from the institution in some satisfactory way. Hence there has never been, in my mind, any question upon the subject, except the one of expediency, arising in view of all the circumstances. If there be matters within and about this act, which might have taken a course or shape, more satisfactory to my jud[g]ment, I do not attempt to specify them. I am gratified that the two principles of compensation, and colonization, are both recognized, and practically applied in the act.

In the matter of compensation, it is provided that claims may be presented within ninety days from the passage of the act "but not thereafter"; and there is no saving for minors, femes-covert, insane, or absent persons. I presume this is an omission by mere over-sight, and I recommend that it be supplied by an amendatory or supplemental act.[8]

While Congress was in session, Lincoln with surprise tardily learned from New York newspapers that General David Hunter, whom he knew well, had proclaimed freedom for slaves in the Department of the South, comprising three states in the southeast. Pleased to hear of Hunter's proclamation, Chase sent a note to Lincoln saying that "it seems to me of the highest importance . . . that this order be not revoked." Lincoln quickly and firmly replied: "No commanding general shall do such a thing, upon *my* responsibility, without consulting me."[9]

In consultation with Stanton, Lincoln issued a proclamation voiding Hunter's proclamation; reserving to himself, the commander in chief, the power to declare slaves free; and lecturing the border states that had not moved to accept the policy of state emancipation:

By the President of The United States of America.
A Proclamation.
Whereas there appears in the public prints, what purports to be a proclamation, of Major General Hunter, in the words and figures following, twit:

Headquarters Department of the South,
Hilton Head, S.C., May 9, 1862.
General Orders No. 11.—The three States of Georgia, Florida and South Carolina, comprising the military department of the south, having deliberately declared themselves no longer under the protection of the United States of America, and having taken up arms against the said United States, it becomes a military necessity to declare them under martial law. This was accordingly done on the 25th day of April, 1862. Slavery and martial law in a free country are altogether incompatible; the persons in these three States—Georgia, Florida and South Carolina—heretofore held as slaves, are therefore declared for ever free.
DAVID HUNTER,
(Official)   Major General Commanding.
ED. W. SMITH, Acting Assistant Adjutant General.

And whereas the same is producing some excitement, and misunderstanding: therefore

I, Abraham Lincoln, president of the United States, proclaim and declare, that the government of the United States, had no knowledge, information, or belief, of an intention on the part of General Hunter to issue such a proclamation; nor has it yet, any authentic information that the document is genuine. And further, that neither General Hunter, nor any other commander, or person, has been authorized by the Government of the United States, to make proclamations declaring the slaves of any State free; and that the supposed proclamation, now in question, whether genuine or false, is altogether void, so far as respects such declaration.

I further make known that whether it be competent for me, as Commander-in-Chief of the Army and Navy, to declare the Slaves of any state or states, free, and whether at any time, in any case, it shall have become a necessity indispensable to the maintainance of the government, to exercise such supposed power, are questions which, under my responsibility, I reserve to myself, and which I can not feel justified in leaving to the decision of commanders in the field. These are totally different questions from those of police regulations in armies and camps.

On the sixth day of March last, by a special message, I recommended to Congress the adoption of a joint resolution to be substantially as follows:

Resolved, That the United States ought to co-operate with any State which may adopt a gradual abolishment of slavery, giving to such State pecuniary aid, to be used by such State in its discretion to compensate for the inconveniences, public and private, produced by such change of system.

The resolution, in the language above quoted, was adopted by large majorities in both branches of Congress, and now stands an authentic, definite, and solemn proposal of the nation to the States and people most immediately interested in the subject matter. To the people of those states I now earnestly appeal. I do not argue. I beseech you to make the arguments for yourselves. You can not if you would, be blind to the signs of the times. I beg of you a calm and enlarged consideration of them, ranging, if it may be, far above personal and partisan politics. This proposal makes common cause for a common object, casting no reproaches upon any. It acts not the pharisee. The change it contemplates would come gently as the dews of heaven, not rending or wrecking anything. Will you not embrace it? So much good has not been done, by one effort, in all past time, as, in the providence of God, it is now your high privilege to do. May the vast future not have to lament that you have neglected it.

In witness whereof, I have hereunto set my hand, and caused the seal of the United States to be affixed.

Done at the City of Washington this nineteenth day of May, in the year of our

[L.S.] Lord one thousand eight hundred and sixty-two, and of the Independence of the United States the eighty-sixth.

ABRAHAM LINCOLN.

By the President:

WILLIAM H. SEWARD, Secretary of State.[10]

A disappointed Chase, not above working behind Lincoln's back, wrote to Hunter, regretting the president's proclamation and enclosing a copy of the note he had sent Lincoln:

It seems to me not improper to enclose to you a copy of a letter which I addressed to the President at the very moment of starting for Philadelphia, after reading your proclamation.

Of course I need not say that I greatly regret the proclamation which the President has seen fit to make.

It did not seem to me that it was worth while to enquire whether your proclamation was authorized or not, or even whether it was such as I or any other member of the Administration would or would not have issued. It was enough, I thought, that you, the Commanding General of the Department [had seen] fit to issue it and the only question remaining was whether or not it should be modified or nullified or allowed to stand.

On this question I had no doubt. I believed the proclamation merely recognized an inevitable necessity; that, at any rate, your calm judgment and upright intelligence might be safely trusted; & that the safest course at all events was to wait until you could be fully heard in exposition of your action.

I trust now you will not think of resigning your command or of leaving your department. You have begun a great & necessary work. It may be checked, but it will be accomplished &, I hope, by you.[11]

On the eve of the session's expiration Lincoln again called the border state congressmen to the White House. He read them an appeal to favor compensated emancipation by the border states:

Gentlemen. After the adjournment of Congress, now very near, I shall have no opportunity of seeing you for several months. Believing that you of the border-states hold more power for good than any other equal number of members, I feel it a duty which I can not justifiably waive, to make this appeal to you. I intend no reproach or complaint when I assure you that in my opinion, if you all had voted for the resolution in the gradual emancipation message of last March, the war would now be substantially ended. And the plan therein proposed is yet one of the most potent, and swift means of ending it. Let the states which are in rebellion see, definitely and certainly, that, in no event, will the states you represent ever join their proposed Confederacy, and they can not, much longer maintain the contest. But you can not divest them of their hope to ultimately have you with them so long as you show a determination to perpetuate the institution within your own states. Beat them at elections, as you have overwhelmingly done, and, nothing daunted, they still claim you as their own. You and I know what the lever of their power is. Break that lever before their faces, and they can shake you no more forever.

Most of you have treated me with kindness and consideration; and I trust you will not now think I improperly touch what is exclusively your own, when, for the sake of the whole country I ask "Can you, for your states, do better than to take the course I urge?["] Discarding *punctillio,* and maxims adapted to more manageable times, and looking only to the unprecedentedly stern facts of our case, can you do better in any possible event? You prefer that the constitutional relation of the states to the nation shall be practically restored, without disturbance of the institution; and if this were done, my whole duty, in this respect, under the constitution, and my oath of office, would be performed. But it is not done, and we are trying to accomplish it by war. The incidents of the war can not be avoided. If the war continue long, as it must, if the object be not sooner attained, the institution in your states will be extinguished by mere friction and abrasion—by the mere incidents of the war. It will be gone, and you will have nothing valuable in lieu of it. Much of its value is gone already. How much better for you, and for your people, to take the step which, at once, shortens the war, and secures substantial compensation for that which is sure to be wholly lost in any other event. How much better to thus save the money which else we sink forever in the war. How much better to do it while we can, lest the war ere long render us pecuniarily unable to do it. How much better for you, as seller, and the nation as buyer, to sell out, and buy out, that without which the war could never have been, than to sink both the thing to be sold, and the price of it, in cutting one another's throats.

I do not speak of emancipation *at once,* but of a *decision* at once to emancipate *gradually.* Room in South America for colonization can be obtained cheaply, and in abundance; and when numbers shall be large enough to be company and encouragement for one another, the freed people will not be so reluctant to go.

I am pressed with a difficulty not yet mentioned—one which threatens division among those who, united are none too strong. An instance of it is known to you. Gen. Hunter is an honest man. He was, and I hope, still is, my friend. I valued him none the less for his agreeing with me in the general wish that all men everywhere, could be free. He proclaimed all men free within certain states, and I repudiated the proclamation. He expected more good, and less harm from the measure, than I could believe would follow. Yet in repudiating it, I gave dissatisfaction, if not offence, to many whose support the country can not afford to lose. And this is not the end of it. The pressure, in this direction, is still upon me, and is increasing. By conceding what I now ask, you can relieve me, and much more, can relieve the country, in this important point. Upon these considerations I have again begged your attention to the message of March last. Before leaving the Capital, consider and discuss it among yourselves. You are patriots and statesmen; and, as such, I pray you, consider this proposition; and, at the least, commend it to the consideration of your states and people. As you would perpetuate popular government for the best people in the world, I beseech you that you do in no wise omit this. Our common country is in great peril, demanding the loftiest views, and boldest action to bring it speedy relief. Once relieved, its form of government is saved to the world; its beloved history, and cherished memories, are vindicated; and its happy future fully assured, and rendered inconceivably grand. To you, more than to any others, the previlege is given, to assure that happiness, and dwell that grandeur, and to link your own names therewith forever.[12]

Two days later twenty congressmen, a majority, rejected the appeal. Their reply acknowledged that a few of their members had voted for the resolution of March 6, but now all concurred in saying that it seemed like federal interference with a question belonging to the states, it would vastly add to the government debt, and it would not substantially end the war, as Lincoln had claimed. "Confine yourself to your constitutional authority," they adjured. They concluded that if Congress appropriated the enabling money (which the Congress failed to do), "then will our State and people take this proposition into careful consideration."

A minority of seven, three of whom were from the rump state of Virginia (West Virginia), pledged that they would ask their people to consider the president's recommendations. A representative from Tennessee, Horace Maynard, and a senator from Missouri, John B. Henderson, wrote similar responses, the first being Maynard's:

SIR: The magnitude and gravity of the proposition submitted by you to Representatives from the Slave States would naturally occasion diversity, if not contrariety, of opinion. You will not, therefore, be surprised that I have not been able to concur in view with the majority of them. This is attributable, possibly, to the fact that my State is not a border State, properly so called, and that my immediate constituents are not yet disenthralled from the hostile arms of the rebellion. This fact is a physical obstacle in the way of my now submitting to their consideration this or any other proposition looking to political action, especially such as, in this case, would require a change fit the organized law of the State.

But do not infer that I am insensible to your appeal. I am not. You are surrounded with difficulties far greater than have embarrassed any of your predecessors. You need the support of every American citizen, and you ought to have it—active, zealous, and honest. The union of every Union man to aid you in preserving the Union is the duty of the time. Differences as to policy and methods must be subordinated to the common purpose.

In looking for the cause of this rebellion, it is natural that each section and each party should ascribe as little blame as possible to itself, and as much as possible to its opponent section and party. Possibly you and I might not agree on a comparison of our views. That there should be differences of opinion as to the best mode of conducting our military operations, find the best men to lead our armies, is equally natural. Contests on such questions weaken ourselves and strengthen our enemies. They are unprofitable, and possibly unpatriotic. Somebody must yield, or we waste our strength in a contemptible struggle among ourselves.

You appeal to the loyal men of the slave States to sacrifice something of feeling and a great deal of interest. The sacrifices they have already made and the sufferings they have endured give the best assurance that the appeal will not have been made in vain. He who is not ready to yield all his material interests, and to forego his most cherished sentiments and opinions for the preservation of his country, although he may have periled his life on the battle-field in her defence, is but half a patriot. Among the loyal people that I represent there are no half patriots.

Already the rebellion has cost us much, even to our undoing; we are content, if need be, to give up the rest to suppress it. We have stood by you from the beginning of this struggle, and we mean to stand by you, God willing, till the end of it.

I did not vote for the resolution to which you allude, solely for the reason that at the time I was absent at the capital of my own State. It is right.

Should any of the slave States think proper to terminate that institution, as several of them, I understand, or at least some of their citizens propose, justice and a generous comity require that the country should interpose to aid it in lessening the burden, politic and private, occasioned by so radical a change in its social and industrial relations.

I will not now speculate upon the effect, at home or abroad, of the adoption of your policy, nor inquire what action of the rebel leaders has rendered something of the kind important. Your whole administration gives the highest assurance that you are moved, not so much from a desire to see all men everywhere made free, as from a higher desire to preserve free institutions for the benefit of men already free; not to make slaves freemen, but to prevent freemen from being made slaves; not to destroy an institution, which a portion of us only consider bad, but to save institutions which we all alike consider good. I am satisfied you would not ask from any of your fellow-citizens a sacrifice not, in your judgment, imperatively required by the safety of the country.

This is the spirit of your appeal, and I respond to it in the same spirit.

MR. PRESIDENT: The pressure of business in the Senate during the last few days of the session prevented my attendance at the meeting of the border State members, called to consider your proposition in reference to gradual emancipation in our States.

... The border States, so far, are the chief sufferers by this war, and the true Union men of those States have made the greatest sacrifices for the preservation of the Government. This fact does not proceed from mismanagement on the part of the Union authorities, or a want of regard for our people, but it is the necessary result of the war that is upon us. Our States are the battle-fields. Our people, divided among themselves, maddened by the struggle and blinded by the smoke of battle, invited upon our soil contending armies—the one to destroy the Government, the other to maintain it. The consequence to us is plain. The shock of the contest upturns society and desolates the land. We have made sacrifices, but at last they were only the sacrifices demanded by duty, and unless we are willing to make others, indeed any that the good of the country, involved in the overthrow of treason, may exact at our hands, our title to patriotism is not complete.

When you submitted your proposition to Congress, in March last, "that the United States ought to co-operate with any State which may adopt a gradual abolishment of slavery, giving to such State pecuniary aid, to be used by such State in its discretion, to compensate for the inconveniences, public and private, produced by such change of system," I gave it a most cheerful support, and I am satisfied it would have received the approbation of a large majority of the border States delegations in both branches of Congress, if, in the first place, they had believed the war, with its continued evils—the most prominent of which, in a material point of view, is its injurious effect on the institution of slavery in our States—could possibly have been protracted for another twelve months; and if, in the second place, they had felt assured that the party having the majority in Congress would, like yourself, be equally prompt in practical action as in the expression of a sentiment. While scarcely any one doubted your own sincerity in your own promises, and your earnest wish speedily to terminate the war, you can readily conceive the grounds for difference of opinion where conclusions could only be based upon conjecture.

Believing, as I did, that the war was not so near its termination as some supposed, and feeling disposed to accord to others the same sincerity of purpose that I should claim for myself under similar circumstances, I voted for the proposition. I will suppose that others were actuated by no sinister motives.

In doing so, Mr. President, I desire to be distinctly understood by you and by my constituents. I did not suppose at the time that I was personally making any sacrifice by supporting the resolution, nor that the people of my State were called upon to make any sacrifice, either in considering or accepting the proposition, if they saw fit. I agreed with you at the remarks contained in the message accompanying the resolution, that "the Union must be preserved, and hence all indispensable means must be, employed. * * * War has been and continues to be an indispensable means to this call. A practical reacknowledgment of the national authority would render the war unnecessary, and it would at once cease. If, however, resistance continues, the war must also continue. . . .

Whatever may be the status of the border States in this respect, the war cannot be ended until the power of the Government is made manifest in the seceded States. They appealed to the sword; give them the sword. They asked for war; let them see its evils on their own soil. They have erected a

Government and they force obedience to its behests. This structure must be destroyed; this image, before which an unwilling people have been compelled to bow, must be broken. The authority of the Federal Government must be felt in the heart of the rebellious district. To do this let armies be marched upon them at once, and let them feel what they have inflicted on us is the border. Do not fear our States; we will stand by the Government in this work.

I ought not to disguise from you or the people of my State that personally I have fixed and unalterable opinions on the subject of your communication. Those opinions I shall communicate to the people in that spirit of frankness that should characterize the intercourse of the representative with his constituents. If I were to-day the owner of the lands and slaves of Missouri, your proposition, so far as that State is concerned, would be immediately accepted. Not a day would be lost. Aside from public considerations, which you suppose to be involved in the proposition, and which no patriot, I agree, should disregard at present, my own personal interest would prompt favorable and immediate action.

But having said this, it is proper that I say something more. The representative is the servant and not the master of the people. He has no authority to bind them to any course of action, or even to indicate what they will nor will not do when the subject is exclusively theirs and not his. I shall take occasion, I hope honestly, to give my views of existing troubles and impending dangers, and shall leave the rest to them, disposed as I am, rather to trust their judgment upon the case states than my own, and at the same time most cheerfully to acquiesce in their decision.

For you, personally, Mr. president, I think I can pledge the kindest considerations of the people of Missouri, and I shall not hesitate to express the belief that your recommendation will be considered by them in the same spirit of kindness manifested by you in its presentation to us, and that their decision will be such as is demanded "by their interests, their honor, and their duty to the whole country."[13]

The day after Lincoln confronted the border state congressmen he confided in two cabinet members that he himself was contemplating proclaiming freedom for slaves. On July 22 he read to the cabinet a draft of an emancipation proclamation. It exhibited three aspects of his thinking about the preeminence of the Union over slavery, his preferred means of emancipation, and the basis for presidential authority to emancipate:

rebels who returned to the Union could escape confiscation of their property (which included slaves), he would continue to urge adoption of his preferred policy of state emancipation with compensation, and an emancipation proclamation by him, which he intended to make on January 1, 1863, would be justified as a military measure to effect reunion of the states under his authority as commander in chief of the army and navy. On Seward's advice to delay promulgation until a military success, he put the document aside. Three days after the meeting, however, as required by the confiscation act, he issued a public warning of rebels' risk of having their property confiscated:

> In pursuance of the sixth section of the act of congress entitled "An act to suppress insurrection and to punish treason and rebellion, to seize and confiscate property of rebels, and for other purposes" Approved Jul 17. 1862, and which act, and the Joint Resolution explanatory thereof, are herewith published, I, Abraham Lincoln, President of the United States, do hereby proclaim to, and warn all persons within the contemplation of said sixth section to cease participating in, aiding, countenancing, or abetting the existing rebellion, or any rebellion against the government of the United States, and to return to their proper allegiance to the United States, on pain of the forfeitures and seizures, as within and by said sixth section provided.
>
> And I hereby make known that it is my purpose, upon the next meeting of congress, to again recommend the adoption of a practical measure for tendering pecuniary aid to the free choice or rejection, of any and all States which may then be recognizing and practically sustaining the authority of the United States, and which may then have voluntarily adopted, or thereafter may voluntarily adopt, gradual abolishment of slavery within such State or States—that the object is to practically restore, thenceforward to be maintain[ed], the constitutional relation between the general government, and each, and all the states, wherein that relation is now suspended, or disturbed; and that, for this object, the war, as it has been, will be, prosecuted. And, as a fit and necessary military measure for effecting this object, I, as Commander-in-Chief of the Army and Navy of the United States, do order and declare that the first day of January in the year of Our Lord one thousand, eight hundred and sixty-three, all persons held as slaves within any state or states, wherein the constitutional authority of the United States shall not then be practically recognized, submitted to, and maintained, shall then, thenceforward, and forever, be free.[14]

A deputation of black leaders, disturbed by the president's advocacy of colonization of freedmen, called on Lincoln in mid-August. It was an unfortunate meeting for the president. He relied on racist assumptions and asserted that African Americans by their very presence caused the war. In defense of his policy, the president said:

> This afternoon the President of the United States gave audience to a Committee of colored men at the White House. . . . Having all been seated, the President, after a few preliminary observations, informed them that a sum of money had been appropriated by Congress, and placed at his disposition for the purpose of aiding the colonization in some country of the people, or a portion of them, of African descent, thereby making it his duty, as it had for a long time been his inclination, to favor that cause; and why, he asked, should the people of your race be colonized, and where? Why should they leave this country? This is, perhaps, the first question for proper consideration. You and we are different races. We have between us a broader difference than exists between almost any other two races. Whether it is right or wrong I need not discuss, but this physical difference is a great disadvantage to us both, as I think your race suffer very greatly, many of them by living among us, while ours suffer from your presence. In a word we suffer on each side. If this is admitted, it affords a reason at least why we should be separated. You here are freemen I suppose.
>
> A VOICE: Yes, sir.
>
> The President—Perhaps you have long been free, or all your lives. Your race are suffering, in my judgment, the greatest wrong inflicted on any people. But even when you cease to be slaves, you are yet far removed from being placed on an equality with the white race. You are cut off from many of the advantages which the other race enjoys. The aspiration of men is to enjoy equality with the best when free, but on this broad continent, not a single man of your race is made the equal of a single man of ours. Go where you are treated the best, and the ban is still upon you.
>
> I do not propose to discuss this, but to present it as a fact with which we have to deal. I cannot alter it if I would. It is a fact, about which we all think and feel alike, I and you. We look to our condition, owing to the existence of the two races on this continent. I need not recount to you the effects upon white men, growing out of the institution of Slavery. I believe in its general evil effects on the white race. See our present condition—the country engaged in war!–our white men cutting one

another's throats, none knowing how far it will extend; and then consider what we know to be the truth. But for your race among us there could not be war, although many men engaged on either side do not care for you one way or the other. Nevertheless, I repeat, without the institution of Slavery and the colored race as a basis, the war could not have an existence.

It is better for us both, therefore, to be separated. I know that there are free men among you, who even if they could better their condition are not as much inclined to go out of the country as those, who being slaves could obtain their freedom on this condition. I suppose one of the principal difficulties in the way of colonization is that the free colored man cannot see that his comfort would be advanced by it. You may believe you can live in Washington or elsewhere in the United States the remainder of your life [as easily], perhaps more so than you can in any foreign country, and hence you may come to the conclusion that you have nothing to do with the idea of going to a foreign country. This is (I speak in no unkind sense) an extremely selfish view of the case.

But you ought to do something to help those who are not so fortunate as yourselves. There is an unwillingness on the part of our people, harsh as it may be, for you free colored people to remain with us. Now, if you could give a start to white people, you would open a wide door for many to be made free. If we deal with those who are not free at the beginning, and whose intellects are clouded by Slavery, we have very poor materials to start with. If intelligent colored men, such as are before me, would move in this matter, much might be accomplished. It is exceedingly important that we have men at the beginning capable of thinking as white men, and not those who have been systematically oppressed.

There is much to encourage you. For the sake of your race you should sacrifice something of your present comfort for the purpose of being as grand in that respect as the white people. It is a cheering thought throughout life that something can be done to ameliorate the condition of those who have been subject to the hard usage of the world. It is difficult to make a man miserable while he feels he is worthy of himself, and claims kindred to the great God who made him. In the American Revolutionary war sacrifices were made by men engaged in it; but they were cheered by the future. Gen. Washington himself endured greater physical hardships than if he had remained a British subject. Yet he was a happy man, because he was engaged in benefiting his race—something for the children of his neighbors, having none of his own. . . .

The place I am thinking about having for a colony is in Central America. It is nearer to us than Liberia—not much more than one-fourth as far as Liberia, and within seven days' run by steamers. Unlike Liberia it is on a great line of travel—it is a highway. The country is a very excellent one for any people, and with great natural resources and advantages, and especially because of the similarity of climate with your native land—thus being suited to your physical condition.

The particular place I have in view is to be a great highway from the Atlantic or Caribbean Sea to the Pacific Ocean, and this particular place has all the advantages for a colony. On both sides there are harbors among the finest in the world. Again, there is evidence of very rich coal mines. A certain amount of coal is valuable in any country, and there may be more than enough for the wants of the country. Why I attach so much importance to coal is, it will afford an opportunity to the inhabitants for immediate employment till they get ready to settle permanently in their homes.

If you take colonists where there is no good landing, there is a bad show; and so where there is nothing to cultivate, and of which to make a farm. But if something is started so that you can get your daily bread as soon as you reach there, it is a great advantage. Coal land is the best thing I know of with which to commence an enterprise. . . .

I shall, if I get a sufficient number of you engaged, have provisions made that you shall not be wronged. If you will engage in the enterprise I will spend some of the money intrusted to me. I am not sure you will succeed. The Government may lose the money, but we cannot succeed unless we try; but we think, with care, we can succeed.

The political affairs in Central America are not in quite as satisfactory condition as I wish. There are contending factions in that quarter; but it is true all the factions are agreed alike on the subject of colonization, and want it, and are more generous than we are here. To your colored race they have no objection. Besides, I would endeavor to have you made equals, and have the best assurance that you should be the equals of the best.

The practical thing I want to ascertain is whether I can get a number of ablebodied men, with their wives and children, who are willing to go, when I present evidence of encouragement and protection. Could I get a hundred tolerably intelligent men, with their wives and children, to "cut their own fodder," so to speak? Can I have fifty? If I could find twenty-five able-bodied men, with a mixture of women and children, good things in the family relation, I think I could make a successful commencement.

I want you to let me know whether this can be done or not. This is the practical part of my wish to see you. These are subjects of very great importance, worthy of a month's study, [instead] of a speech delivered in an hour. I ask you then to consider seriously not pertaining to yourselves merely, nor for your race, and ours, for the present time, but as one of the things, if successfully managed, for the good of mankind—not confined to the present generation, but as

"From age to age descends the lay,

To millions yet to be,

Till far its echoes roll away,

Into eternity."

The above is merely given as the substance of the President's remarks.

The Chairman of the delegation briefly replied that "they would hold a consultation and in a short time give an answer." The President said: "Take your full time—no hurry at all."

The delegation then withdrew.[15]

Lincoln had in fact invited the black delegation to meet in the White House and had met with African American leaders on several occasions previously. But he ended up lecturing them and used the meeting to defend his position on colonization. Horace Greeley, who blew hot and cold on Lincoln's policies, on August 20 published a long editorial pretentiously entitled "The Prayer of Twenty Millions," referring to the northern population. It read:

I do not intrude to tell you—for you must know already—that a great proportion of those who triumphed in your election, and of all who desire the unqualified suppression of the Rebellion now desolating our country, are sorely disappointed and deeply pained by the policy you seem to be pursuing with regard to the slaves of the Rebels. I write only to set succinctly and unmistakably before you what we require, what we think we have a right to expect, and of what we complain. . . .

VIII. On the face of this wide earth, Mr. President, there is not one disinterested, determined, intelligent champion of the Union cause who does not feel that all attempts to put down the Rebellion and at the same time uphold its inciting cause are preposterous and futile—that the Rebellion, if crushed out tomorrow, would be renewed within a year if Slavery were left in full vigor—that Army officers who remain to this day devoted to Slavery can at best be but half-way loyal to the Union—and that every hour of deference to Slavery is an hour of added and deepened peril to the Union. I appeal to the testimony of your Embassadors in Europe. It is freely at your service, not at mine. Ask them to tell you candidly whether the seeming subserviency of your policy to the slaveholding, slavery-upholding interest, is not the perplexity, the despair of statesmen of all parties, and be admonished by the general answer.[16]

So influential a statement could not be ignored. Three days later Lincoln replied in one of his most quoted statements of purpose about slavery:

I have just read yours of the 19th. addressed to myself through the New-York Tribune. If there be in it any statements, or assumptions of fact, which I may know to be erroneous, I do not, now and here, controvert them. If there be in it any inferences which I may believe to be falsely drawn, I do not now and here, argue against them. If there be perceptible in it an impatient and dictatorial tone, I waive it in deference to an old friend, whose heart I have always supposed to be right.

As to the policy I "seem to be pursuing" as you say, I have not meant to leave any one in doubt.

I would save the Union. I would save it the shortest way under the Constitution. The sooner the national authority can be restored; the nearer the Union will be "the Union as it was." If there be those who would not save the Union, unless they could at the same time *save* slavery, I do not agree with them. If there be those who would not save the Union unless they could at the same time *destroy* slavery, I do not agree with them. My paramount object in this struggle *is* to save the Union, and is *not* either to save or to destroy slavery. If I could save the Union without freeing *any* slave I would do it, and if I could save it by freeing *all* the slaves I would do it; and if I could save it by freeing some and leaving others alone I would also do that. What I do about slavery, and the colored race, I do because I believe it helps to save the Union; and what I forbear, I forbear because I do *not* believe it would help to save the Union. I shall do *less* whenever I shall believe what I am doing hurts the cause, and I shall do *more* whenever I shall believe doing more will help the cause. I shall try to correct errors when shown to be errors; and I shall adopt views so fast as they shall appear to be true views.

I have here stated my purpose according to my view of *official* duty; and I intend no modification of my oft-expressed *personal* wish that all men every where could be free.[17]

On the same day Lincoln wrote to Greeley, Lydia Maria Child, a New England abolitionist and writer, impatient that Lincoln had not made emancipation his foremost goal, penned a letter to the president, which he apparently did not answer. Child wrote:

> It may seem a violation of propriety for a woman to address the Chief Magistrate of the nation at a crisis so momentous as this. But if the Romans, ages ago, accorded to Hortensia the right of addressing the Senate on the subject of a tax unjustly levied on the wealthy ladies of Rome, surely an American woman of the nineteenth century need not apologize for pleading with the rulers of her country in behalf of the poor, the wronged, the cruelly oppressed. Surely the women of America have a right to inquire, nay, demand, whether their husbands, sons, and brothers are to be buried by thousands in Southern swamps, without obtaining thereby "indemnity for the past and security for the future."
>
> In your Appeal to the Border States, you have declared slavery to be "that without which the war could never have been," and you speak of emancipation as "the step which at once shortens the war." I would respectfully ask how much longer the nation is to wait for the decision of the Border States, paying, meanwhile $2,000,000 a day, and sending thousands of its best and bravest to be stabbed, shot, and hung by the rebels, whose property they are employed to guard. How much longer will pro-slavery officers be permitted to refuse obedience to the laws of Congress, saying, "We shall continue to send back fugitives to their masters until we receive orders form the *President* to the contrary." What fatal spell is cast over your honest mind, that you hesitate so long to give such orders? . . .
>
> President Lincoln, it is an awful responsibility before God to quench the moral enthusiasm of a generous people. It wastes thousands of precious lives, causes an unutterable amount of slow, consuming agony, and tarnishes our record on the pages of history. . . . Slavery is on trial, and the verdict is left to slaveholders in the Border States. The report of their majority shows them to be slaveholders in heart and spirit. The process of reasoning and entreaty has been very properly tried with them, and the people of the free States have waited long and patiently for some obvious good result. They are getting restive; very restive. Everywhere I hear men saying: "Our President is an honest, able man, but he appears to have no firmness of purpose. He is letting the country drift to ruin for want of earnest action and a consistent policy." . . .

I trust you will not deem me wanting in respect for yourself or your high position, if I say frankly that you seem to trust too much to diplomatic and selfish politicians, and far too little to the heart of the people. You do them wrong, irreparable wrong, by stifling their generous instincts, and putting an extinguisher on every scintillation of moral enthusiasm. Are you not aware that moral enthusiasm is the mightiest of all forces? It is the fire which produces the steam of energy and courage, and the motion of all the long train of crowded cars depends on its expansive power. In the name of our suffering country, for the sake of a world that needs enfranchisement, I beseech you not to check the popular enthusiasm for freedom! Would that you could realize what a mighty power there is in the *heart* of a free people! . . .

In thus entreating you to trust to the impulses of the people, I by no means overlook the extreme difficulties of your position. I know that the proslavery spirit of the land is a mighty giant, characterized by unscrupulous selfishness and exceeding obstinacy. But I also know that all the enthusiasm is on the side of freedom. . . .

That you sincerely wish to save the republic the people do not doubt for a moment; and your scruples about constitutional obligations have commanded their respect. But events have educated them rapidly, and they now deny that any constitutional obligation exists toward rebels who have thrown off the Constitution, spit upon it, and trampled it under their feet. . . . But it is urged that some slaveholders are loyal. I apprehend that their name is not legion, nor their loyalty always of a kind that will stand much wear and tear. . . .

Pardon me if, in my earnestness, I have said aught that seems disrespectful. I have not so intended. I have been impelled to write this because night and day the plaintive song of the bondmen resounds in my ears:

"Go down, Moses, go down to Egypt's land,
And say to Pharaoh: 'Let my people go.'"

That you may be guided by Him who has said: "First righteousness; and then peace," is the earnest prayer of

Yours, respectfully,
L. MARIA CHILD[18]

In addition to the pleas from Greeley and Child, importunities for a proclamation continued. A delegation of Chicago Christians of All Denominations on September 13 met for more than an hour with the president, bringing their memorial as well as one from German citizens of Chicago. The record of Lincoln's remarks and the delegation's ongoing responses reads:

> The subject presented in the memorial is one upon which I have thought much for weeks past, and I may even say for months. I am approached with the most opposite opinions and advice, and that by religious men, who are equally certain that they represent the Divine will. I am sure that either the one or the other class is mistaken in that belief, and perhaps in some respects both. I hope it will not be irreverent for me to say that if it is probable that God would reveal his will to others, on a point so connected with my duty, it might be supposed he would reveal it directly to me; for, unless I am more deceived in myself than I often am, it is my earnest desire to know the will of Providence in this matter. *And if I can learn what it is I will do it!* These are not, however, the days of miracle, and I suppose it will be granted that I am not to expect a direct revelation. I must study the plain physical facts of the case, ascertain what is possible and learn what appears to be wise and right. The subject is difficult, and good men do not agree....
>
> What *good* would a proclamation of emancipation from me do, especially as we are now situated? I do not want to issue a document that the whole world will see must necessarily be inoperative, like the Pope's bull against the comet! Would *my word* free the slaves when I cannot even enforce the Constitution in the rebel States? Is there a single court, or magistrate, or individual that would be influenced by it there? And what reason is there to think it would have any greater effect upon the slaves than the late law of Congress, which I approved, and which offers protection and freedom to the slaves of rebel masters who come within our lines? Yet I cannot learn that that law has caused a single slave to come over to us. And suppose they could be induced by a proclamation of freedom from me to throw themselves upon us, *what should we do with them?*[19]

Four days later the Union won the victory at Antietam that Seward had thought was needed to release the Emancipation Proclamation. On September 22 Lincoln convened his cabinet. Before reading the document to the members, he had set his face like flint, silencing opposition by saying, "I do not wish your advice about the main matter—for that I have determined for myself." Chase made an elaborate diary entry:

> "Gentlemen; I have, as you are aware, thought a great deal about the relation of this war to Slavery; and you all remember that, several weeks ago, I

read to you an Order I had prepared on this subject, which, on account of objections made by some of you, was not issued. Ever since then, my mind has been much occupied with this subject, and I have thought all along that the time for acting on it might very probably come. I think the time has come now. I wish it were a better time. I wish that we were in a better condition. The action of the army against the rebels has not been quite what I should have best liked. But they have been driven out of Maryland, and Pennsylvania is no longer in danger of invasion. When the rebel army was at Frederick, I determined, as soon as it should be driven out of Maryland, to issue a Proclamation of Emancipation such as I thought most likely to be useful. I said nothing to any one; but I made the promise to myself, and (hesitating a little)—to my Maker. The rebel army is now driven out, and I am going to fulfil that promise. I have got you together to hear what I have written down. I do not wish your advice about the main matter—for that I have determined for myself. This I say without intending any thing but respect for any one of you. But I already know the views of each on this question. They have been heretofore expressed, and I have considered them as thoroughly and carefully as I can. What I have written is that which my reflections have determined me to say. If there is anything in the expression I use, or in any other minor matter, which anyone of you thinks had best be changed, I shall be glad to receive the suggestions. One other observation I will make. I know very well that many others might, in this matter, as in others, do better than I can; and if I were satisfied that the public confidence was more fully possessed by any one of them than by me, and knew of any Constitutional way in which he could be put in my place, he should have it. I would gladly yield it to him. But though I believe that I have not so much of the confidence of the people as I had some time since, I do not know that, all things considered, any other person has more; and, however this may be, there is no way in which I can have any other man put where I am. I am here. I must do the best I can, and bear the responsibility of taking the course which I feel I ought to take."

The President then proceeded to read his Emancipation Proclamation, making remarks on the several parts as he went on, and showing that he had fully considered the whole subject, in all the lights under which it had been presented to him. . . .

I followed, saying: "What you have said, Mr. President, fully satisfies me that you have given to every proposition which has been made, a kind and candid consideration. And you have now expressed the conclusion to which you have arrived, clearly and distinctly. This it was your right, and under your oath of office your duty, to do. The Proclamation does not, indeed, mark out exactly the course I should myself prefer. But I am ready to take it just as it is written, and to stand by it with all my heart. I think, however, the suggestions of Gov. Seward very judicious, and shall be glad to have them adopted."

The President then asked us severally our opinions as to the modifications proposed, saying that he did not care much about the phrases he had used. Everyone favored the modification and it was adopted. Gov. Seward then proposed that in the passage relating to colonization, some language should be introduced to show that the colonization proposed was to be only with the consent of the colonists, and the consent of the States in which colonies might be attempted. This, too, was agreed to; and no other modification was proposed. Mr. Blair then said that the question having been decided, he would make no objection to issuing the Proclamation; but he would ask to have his paper, presented some days since, against the policy, filed with the Proclamation. The President consented to this readily. And then Mr. Blair went on to say that he was afraid of the influence of the Proclamation on the Border States and on the Army, and stated at some length the grounds of his apprehensions. He disclaimed most expressly, however, all objection to emancipation *per se,* saying he had always been personally in favor of it—always ready for immediate Emancipation in the midst of Slave States, rather than submit to the perpetuation of the system.[20]

Lincoln listened to comments, accepting Seward's suggestion "that the colonization was to be only with the consent of the colonists and the consent of the States in which colonies might be attempted," as Chase recorded in his diary. He brushed aside Blair's fear of the proclamation's influence on the border states and the army.

Failure of the loyal slave states to initiate voluntary, compensated, gradual emancipation had impelled the president to proclaim, as a military measure, federal uncompensated emancipation as the alternative to rejoining the Union within one hundred days. The two—voluntary loyal slave state emancipation and federal imposition of emancipation on rebel slave states on short notice to resume their loyal status—seem to present a dramatic contrast with one another. But each looked to the same end—restoration of the Union. The proclamation in fact gave an assurance the president would ask the Congress to provide compensation, accept gradual abolition, and promote colonization, with the freedmen's consent.

The next day the famous document was published in the press:

I, Abraham Lincoln, President of the United States of America, and Commander-in-chief of the Army and Navy thereof, do hereby proclaim and declare that hereafter, as heretofore, the war will be prossecuted for the object of practically restoring the constitutional relation between the United States, and each of the states, and the people thereof, in which states that relation is, or may be, suspended or disturbed.

That it is my purpose, upon the next meeting of Congress to again recommend the adoption of a practical measure tendering pecuniary aid to the free acceptance or rejection of all slave-states, so called, the people whereof may not then be in rebellion against the United States, and which states, may then have voluntarily adopted, or thereafter may voluntarily adopt, immediate, or gradual abolishment of slavery within their respective limits; and that the effort to colonize persons of African descent, with their consent, upon this continent, or elsewhere, with the previously obtained consent of the Governments existing there, will be continued.

That on the first day of January in the year of our Lord, one thousand eight hundred and sixty-three, all persons held as slaves within any state, or designated part of a state, the people whereof shall then be in rebellion against the United States shall be then, thenceforward, and forever free; and the executive government of the United States, including the military and naval authority thereof, will recognize and maintain the freedom of such persons, and will do no act or acts to repress such persons, or any of them, in any efforts they may make for their actual freedom.

That the executive will, on the first day of January aforesaid, by proclamation, designate the States, and parts of states, if any, in which the people thereof respectively, shall then be in rebellion against the United States; and the fact that any state, or the people thereof shall, on that day be, in good faith represented in the Congress of the United States, by members chosen thereto, at elections wherein a majority of the qualified voters of such state shall have participated, shall, in the absence of strong countervailing testimony, be deemed conclusive evidence that such state and the people thereof, are not then in rebellion against the United States.

That attention is hereby called to an act of Congress entitled "An act to make an additional Article of War" approved March 13, 1862, and which act is in the words and figure following:

Be it enacted by the Senate and House of Representatives of the United States of America in Congress assembled, That hereafter the following shall be promulgated as an additional article of war for the government of the army of the United States, and shall be obeyed and observed as such:

Article–. All officers or persons in the military or naval service of the United States are prohibited from employing any of the forces under their respective commands for the purpose of returning fugitives from service or labor, who may have escaped from any persons to whom such service or labor is claimed to be due, and any officer who shall be found guilty by a court-martial of violating this article shall be dismissed from the service.

SEC. 2. *And be it further enacted,* That this act shall take effect from and after its passage.

Also to the ninth and tenth sections of an act entitled "An Act to suppress Insurrection, to punish Treason and Rebellion, to seize and confiscate property of rebels, and for other purposes," approved July 17, 1862, and which sections are in the words and figures following;

SEC. 9. *And be it further enacted,* That all slaves of persons who shall hereafter be engaged in rebellion against the government of the United States, or who shall in any way give aid or comfort thereto, escaping from such persons and taking refuge within the lines of the army; and all slaves captured from such persons or deserted by them and coming under the control of the government of the United States; and all slaves of such persons found *on* (or) being within any place occupied by rebel forces and afterwards occupied by the forces of the United States, shall be deemed captives of war, and shall be forever free of their servitude and not again held as slaves.

SEC. 10. *And be it further enacted,* That no slave escaping into any State, Territory, or the District of Columbia, from any other State, shall be delivered up, or in any way impeded or hindered of his liberty, except for crime, or some offence against the laws, unless the person claiming said fugitive shall first make oath that the person to whom the labor or service of such fugitive is alleged to be due is his lawful owner, and has not borne arms against the United States in the present rebellion, nor in any way given aid and comfort thereto; and no person engaged in the military or naval service of the United States shall, under any pretence whatever, assume to decide on the validity of the claim of any person to the service or labor of any other person, or surrender up any such person to the claimant, on pain of being dismissed from the service.

And I do hereby enjoin upon and order all persons engaged in the military and naval service of the United States to observe, obey, and enforce, within their respective spheres of service, the act, and sections above recited.

And the executive will in due time recommend that all citizens of the United States who shall have remained loyal thereto throughout the rebellion, shall (upon the restoration of the constitutional relation between the United States, and their respective states, and people, if that relation shall have been suspended or disturbed) be compensated for all losses by acts of the United States, including the loss of slaves.

In witness whereof, I have hereunto set my hand, and caused the seal of the United States to be affixed.

Done at the City of Washington, this twenty second day of September, in the year of our

[L.S.] Lord, one thousand eight hundred and sixty two, and of the Independence of the United States, the eighty seventh.

By the President: ABRAHAM LINCOLN
WILLIAM H. SEWARD, Secretary of State.[21]

The proclamation quickly won the support of the governors of the free states. In a document they presented to the president on September 29 they said:

Adopted at a meeting of Governors Of loyal States, held to take measures for the more active support of the Government merit, at Altoona, Pennsylvania, on the 22d day of September, 1862.

After nearly one year and a half spent in contest with an armed and gigantic rebellion against the national Government of the United States, the duty and purpose of the loyal States and people continue, and must remain as they were at its origin—namely, to restore and perpetuate the authority of this Government and the life of the nation. No matter what consequences are involved in our fidelity, this work, of restoring the Republic, preserving the institutions of democratic liberty, and justifying the hopes and toils of our fathers shall not fail to be performed.

And we pledge without hesitation, to the President of the United States, the most loyal and cordial support, hereafter as heretofore, in the exercise of the functions of his great office. We recognize in him the Chief Executive Magistrate of the nation, the Commander-in-Chief of the Army and Navy of the United States, their responsible and constitutional head, whose rightful authority and power, as well as the constitutional powers of Congress, must be rigorously and religiously guarded and preserved, as the condition on which alone our form of Government and the constitutional rights and liberties of the people themselves can be saved from the wreck of anarchy or from the gulf of despotism.

In submission to the laws which may have been or which may be duty enacted, and to the lawful orders of the President, co-operating always in our own spheres with the national Government, we mean to continue in the most vigorous exercise of all our lawful and proper powers, contending against treason, rebellion, and the public enemies, and, whether in public life or in private station, supporting the arms of the Union, until its cause shall conquer, until final victory shall perch upon its standard, or the rebel foe shall yield a dutiful, rightful, and unconditional submission.

And, impressed with the conviction that an army of reserve ought, until the war shall end, to be constantly kept on foot, to be raised, armed, equipped, and trained at home, and ready for emergencies, we respectfully ask the President to call for such a force of volunteers for one year's service, of not less than one hundred thousand in the aggregate, the quota of each State to be raised after it shall have filled its quota of the requisitions already made, both for volunteers and militia. We believe that this would be a measure of military prudence, while it would greatly promote the military education of the people.

We hail with heartfelt gratitude and encouraged hope the proclamation of the President, issued on the 22d instant, declaring emancipated from their bondage all persons held to service or labor as slaves in the rebel States, whose rebellion shall last until the first day of January now next ensuing. The right of any person to retain authority to compel any portion of the subjects of the national Government to rebel against it, or to maintain its encodes, implies in those who are allowed possession of such authority the right to rebel themselves; and therefore the right to establish martial law or military government in a State or Territory in rebellion implies the right and the duty of the Government to liberate the minds of all men living therein by appropriate proclamations and assurances of protection, in order that all who are capable, intellectually and morally, of loyalty and obedience, may not be forced into treason as the unwilling tools of rebellion traitors. To have continued indefinitely the most efficient cause, support, and stay of the rebellion, would have been, in our judgment, unjust to the loyal people whose treasure and lives are made a willing sacrifice on the altar of patriotism—would have discriminated against the wife who is compelled to surrender her husband, against the parent who is to surrender his child to the hardships of the camp and the perils of battle, in favor of rebel masters permitted to retain their slaves. It would have been a final decision alike against humanity, justice, the rights and dignity of the Government, and against sound and wise national policy[.] The decision of the President to strike at the root of the rebellion will lend new vigor to the efforts and new life and hope to the hearts of the people. Cordially tendering to the President our respectful assurances of personal and official confidence, we trust and believe that the policy now inaugurated will be crowned with success, will give speedy and triumphant victories over our enemies, and secure to this nation and this people the blessing and favor of Almighty God. We believe that the blood of the heroes who have already fallen, and those who may yet give their lives to their country, will not have been shed in vain.

The splendid valor of our soldiers, their patient endurance, their manly patriotism, and their devotion to duty, demand from us and from all their countrymen the homage of the sincerest gratitude and the pledge of our constant reinforcement and support. A just regard for these brave men, whom we have contributed to place in the field, and for the importance of the duties which may lawfully pertain to us hereafter, has called us into friendly conference. And now, presenting to our national Chief Magistrate this conclusion of our deliberations, we devote ourselves to our country's service, and we will surround the President with our constant support, trusting that the fidelity and zeal of the loyal States and people will always assure him that he will be constantly maintained in pursuing with the utmost vigor this war for the preservation of the national life and this hope of humanity.

A. G. CURTIN,

JOHN A. ANDREW,

RICHARD YATES,

ISRAEL WASHBURNE JR.,

EDWARD SOLOMON,

SAMUEL J. KIRKWOOD,

O.P. MORTON,

BY D.G. ROSE, HIS REPRESENTATIVE,

WM. SPRAGUE.

F.H. PEIRPOINT,

DAVID TOD,

N.S. BERRY,

AUSTIN BLAIR.[22]

Republican newspapers generally approved the president's bold move. Greeley's *Tribune* shouted, "God bless Abraham Lincoln." The *National Intelligencer* wrote:

[W]here we expect no good, we shall be only too happy to find that no harm has been done by the present declaration of the Executive. . . . The proclamation may be said to open issues too tremendous and to be fraught with consequences too undeveloped, to admit of calculation or forecast by an intelligence we can command.[23]

The *Times* of London said:

Is LINCOLN yet a name not known to us as it will be known to posterity, and is it ultimately to be classed among that catalogue of monsters, the wholesale assassins and butchers of their kind? . . . [The Emancipation Proclamation] will not deprive Mr. LINCOLN of the distinctive affix which he will share with many, for the most part foolish and incompetent, Kings and Emperors, Caliphs and Doges, that of being LINCOLN.[24]

Responding to an enthusiastic letter from Vice President Hannibal Hamlin, who was at home in Maine, Lincoln said:

Your kind letter of the 25th is just received. It is known to some that while I hope something from the proclamation, my expectations are not as sanguine as are those of some friends. The time for its effect southward has not come; but northward the effect should be instantaneous.

It is six days old, and while commendation in newspapers and by distinguished individuals is all that a vain man could wish, the stocks have declined, and troops come forward more slowly than ever. This, looked soberly in the face, is not very satisfactory. We have fewer troops in the field at the end of six days than we had at the beginning—the attrition among the old outnumbering the addition by the new. The North responds to the proclamation sufficiently in breath; but breath alone kills no rebels.

I wish I could write more cheerfully; nor do I thank you the less for the kindness of your letter.[25]

For his part McClellan, long after the war, said:

My own view was that emancipation should be accomplished gradually, and that the negroes should be fitted for it by certain preparatory steps in the way of education, recognition of the rights of family and marriage, prohibition against selling them without their own consent, the freedom of those born after a certain date, etc. I was always prepared to make it one of the essential conditions of peace that slavery should be abolished within a fixed and reasonable period. Had the arrangements of the terms of peace been in my hands I should certainly have insisted on this.[26]

Two days after proclaiming freedom, Lincoln cast another thunder bolt. Congress so far had failed to legalize or ban his propensity to suspend the privilege of habeas corpus. Earlier in the year he had ameliorated relations with his critics by providing amnesty for many political prisoners and transferring the program from the unpopular Seward to the new secretary of war Edwin Stanton.

The Militia Act of July 17, 1862, in effect authorized the president, when necessary, to draft men. This step, extraordinary in American history, had provoked much resistance to drafting. Unconnected with the Emancipation Proclamation, though sometimes thought otherwise, the second thunder bolt breathtakingly by fiat suspended habeas corpus throughout the whole North.

CHAPTER NINETEEN

THE FALL OF 1862

The war did not pause while Lincoln pursued his emancipation policies. Indeed, in the West the Union Army lurched into Tennessee, and in the East after Antietam the army returned to the plains of northern Virginia, where Lee's army remained entrenched around the Rappahannock River.

Don Carlos Buell had distinguished himself at Shiloh. In early June 1862 he was given command of four divisions and ordered to repair the railroad to Chattanooga. He was a man of medium height, whose full beard failed to hide his stern appearance. Not given to hurrying or aggressive warfare, he moved slowly.

On July 8, 1862, Halleck telegraphed Buell:

It seems that the enemy at Tupelo and Okolona are moving, but what is to be their point of attack is doubtful. General Grant thinks it is Memphis, others Corinth or Tuscumbia, and others again your lines at Chattanooga. A few days more may reduce these doubts to a certainty, when our troops will operate accordingly.

The President telegraphs that your progress is not satisfactory and that you should move more rapidly. The long time taken by you to reach Chattanooga will enable the enemy to anticipate you by concentrating a large force to meet you.

I communicate his views, hoping that your movements hereafter may be so rapid as to remove all cause of complaint, whether well founded or not.[1]

Halleck was still relaying concerns on August 25, to Major General Horatio G. Wright, commander of the Department of the Ohio:

The Government, or rather I should say the President and Secretary of War, is greatly displeased with the slow movements of General Buell. Unless he does something very soon I think he will be removed. Indeed it would have been done before now if I had not begged to give him a little more time. There must be more energy and activity in Kentucky and Tennessee, and the one who first does something brilliant will get the entire command. I therefore hope to hear very soon of some success in your department. I can hardly describe to you the feeling of disappointment here in the want of activity in General Buell's large army.

The Government seems determined to apply the guillotine to all unsuccessful generals. It seems rather hard to do this where the general is not in fault, but perhaps with us now, as in the French Revolution, some harsh measures are required.

Keep me informed by telegraph of what you are doing, and I will help you all I can.[2]

To the first communication Buell replied, explaining his problems of securing supplies for his men and horses and concluding, "The dissatisfaction of the President pains me exceedingly."

In the course of time Buell learned that Confederate general Braxton Bragg was moving north. Uncertainty about Bragg's intentions and locations characterized both Buell and Lincoln. Between September 7 and 10 the following exchange took place: "Where is Gen. Bragg? What do you know on the subject?" Lincoln asked Jeremiah T. Boyle.[3] Boyle promptly responded: "I do not know . . . but believe he is in Tennessee threatening Genl Buell."[4] Lincoln then wrote to Buell: "What degree of certainty have you, that Bragg, with his command, is not now in the valley of the Shenandoah, Virginia?"[5]

On October 8 Buell found Bragg at Perryville, Kentucky. Their armies clashed inconclusively, and a concerned Lincoln sought news. On the eleventh he asked General Jeremiah Boyle, commanding at Louisville, for news, and the following day, receiving none, he wired Boyle: "We are very anxious to hear from Gen. Buell's Army." Boyle could furnish no details at the moment. Bragg withdrew into Tennessee. Buell failed to make a vigorous pursuit. In language presumably written by Lincoln, Halleck on October 19 telegraphed Buell:

Your telegram of the 17th was received this morning, and has been laid before the President, who concurs in the views expressed in my telegram to you yesterday. The capture of East Tennessee should be the main object of your campaign. You say it is the heart of the enemy's resources; make it the heart of yours. Your army can live there if the enemy's can. You must in a great measure live upon the country, paying for your supplies where proper and levying contributions where necessary. I am directed by the President to say to you that your army must enter East Tennessee this fall, and that it ought to move there while the roads are passable. Once between the enemy and Nashville there will be no serious difficulty in reopening your communications with that place. He does not understand why we cannot march as the enemy marches, live as he lives, and fight as he fights, unless we admit the inferiority of our troops and of our generals. Once hold the valley of the Upper Tennessee and the operations of guerrillas in that State and Kentucky will soon cease.[6]

Five days later Buell was relieved of his command. He was replaced by General William S. Rosecrans. "Old Rosy," as he was called by his soldiers, had graduated at West Point in 1842. During the early months of the war he had served under McClellan, then succeeded Pope in the West when that general was summoned to the East. Associated with Grant, on October 4 he had inflicted a severe victory upon Confederate forces at Corinth, checking a plan to invade west Tennessee. Now a major general of volunteers, he became commander of a reorganized Army of the Cumberland.

Rosecrans's behavior proved to annoy and perplex Lincoln. On October 26 Lincoln exclaimed to Stanton: "This, to my annoyance, shows that at half past two p.m. yesterday, Gen. Rosecrans was still at Corinth!"

Two months later Lincoln questioned Halleck:

I find on maps that Huntsville [Hartsville, Tennessee] is on the North bank of Cumberland river, sixteen miles directly east of Gallatin, and apparently on a turnpike road leading towards East Tennessee generally. What on earth an isolated Brigade was doing there I can not conceive.

The road is not a line between any two places in our possession.[7]

Rosecrans sent a long reply to Halleck, saying "the brigade was stationed at Hartsville . . . to cover the crossing of the Cumberland River against rebel cavalry." After spending a month at Nashville gathering supplies Rosecrans moved against General Bragg, who was at Stone River, Tennessee. There from December 31 to January 3, 1863, blue and gray waged a battle that ended when Bragg withdrew his exhausted men.

An elated Lincoln, amidst political troubles that we shall later examine, read Rosecrans's triumphant telegram: "We have fought one of the greatest battles of the war, and are victorious. . . . The last of their columns of cavalry left this morning. Their loss has been very heavy." Lincoln replied:

> Your despatch announcing retreat of enemy has just reached here. God bless you, and all with you! Please tender to all, and accept for yourself, the Nation's gratitude for yours, and their skill, endurance, and dauntless courage.[8]

In the East General Ambrose E. Burnside succeeded McClellan to command of the Army of the Potomac on November 5. A graduate of the U.S. Military Academy in 1847, Burnside looked the part of a general. Tall and possessed of a flashing eye and a sonorous voice, he is perhaps remembered almost as much for his side whiskers as for his Civil War activities. Needing to drop McClellan and unwilling to appoint the controversial and opinionated Joseph Hooker, Lincoln had asked Burnside to take the post, and he had declined, presciently admitting he was not the man for the job. On a raw November day Lincoln sent an emissary back to Burnside with an order for him to take command. After saying he was "shocked," protesting he "was not competent to command such a large army," and resisting for an hour, Burnside at last yielded to his commander in chief's order.

Within days he sent Lincoln his plan of operations. He would cross the Rappahannock River at Fredericksburg, using pontoon boats, and proceed to Richmond. Lincoln preferred instead that he pursue the Confederate army wherever it was to be found. He sent Halleck to talk with Burnside. On his return to Washington Halleck telegraphed the general: "The president has assented to your plan. He thinks it will succeed if you move rapidly, otherwise not." The pontoons proved to be unavailable, delaying Burnside's movement. Lincoln privately confided to a critical Carl Schurz, a Union general in Burnside's command, a well-known German-American, and a prominent Wisconsin Republican: "I certainly have been dissatisfied with the slowness of Buell and McClellan; but before I relieved them I had great fears I should not find successors to them who would do better; and I am sorry to add, that I have seen little since to relieve those fears. I do not clearly see the prospect of any more rapid movements."[9]

The next day Lincoln himself went to see Burnside at Aquia Creek, Virginia. On the steamer bearing him home he wrote to Halleck, describing his own plan of operations:

> I have just had a long conference with Gen. Burnside. He believes that Gen. Lees whole army, or nearly the whole of it is in front of him, at and near Fredericksburg. Gen. B. says he could take into battle now any day, about, one hundred and ten thousand men, that his army is in good spirit, good condition, good moral, and that in all respects he is satisfied with officers and men; that he does not want more men with him, because he could not handle them to advantage; that he thinks he can cross the river in face of the enemy and drive him away, but that, to use his own expression, it is somewhat risky. I wish the case to stand more favorable than this in two respects. First, I wish his crossing of the river to be nearly free from risk; and secondly, I wish the enemy to be prevented from falling back, accumulating strength as he goes, into his intrenchments at Richmond. I therefore propose that Gen. B. shall not move immediately; that we accumulate a force on the South bank of the Rappahanock—at, say, Port-Royal, under protection of one or two gun-boats, as nearly up to twenty-five thousand strong as we can. At the same time another force of about the same strength as high up the Pamunkey, as can be protected by gunboats. These being ready, let all three forces move simultaneously, Gen. B.'s force in its attempt to cross the river, the Rappahanock force moving directly up the South side of the river to his assistance, and ready, if found admissible, to deflect off to the turnpike bridge over the Mattapony in the direction of Richmond. The Pamunkey force to move as rapidly as possible up the North side of the Pamunkey, holding all the bridges, and especially the turnpike bridge immediately North of Hanover C.H; hurry North, and seize and hold the Mattapony bridge before mentioned, and also, if possible, press higher up the streams and destroy the railroad bridges. Then, if Gen. B. succeeds in driving the enemy from Fredericksburg, the enemy no longer has the road to Richmond, but we have it and can march into the city. Or, possibly, having forced the enemy from his line, we could move upon, and destroy his army. Gen. B.'s main army would have the same line of supply and retreat as he has now provided; the

Rappahanock force would have that river for supply, and gun-boats to fall back upon; and the Pamunkey force would have that river for supply, and a line between the two rivers—Pamunkey & Mattapony—along which to fall back upon it's gun-boats. I think the plan promises the best results, with the least hazard, of any now conceivable.

Note—The above plan, proposed by me, was rejected by Gen. Halleck & Gen. Burnside, on the ground that we could not raise and put in position, the Pamunkey force without too much waste of time.[10]

Three days later Burnside came to Washington and with Halleck's concurrence successfully pushed his plan. Meanwhile Lee had established forces on the heights of Fredericksburg. Burnside returned to Fredericksburg and initiated his army's movement to cross the river and move toward Richmond. With substantially larger numbers than Lee, Burnside hurled his forces against Lee's well-placed men at Fredericksburg, only to incur disaster. The battlefield was strewn with 12,600 Federal casualties and fewer than 5,000 Confederates. The day after the battle an anxious Lincoln sent four words to his secretary John Nicolay, whom he had dispatched to the scene: "What news have you?" On December 15 the Federals gave up the attack and recrossed the river, having been defeated and facing a despairing North. William O. Stoddard, one of Lincoln's secretaries, after the battle recorded not only the gloom in Washington but also what he termed Lincoln's "awful arithmetic" about the casualties:

> This odor of gunpowder and this whisper of grief have been here, floating around the house, ever since the battle of Fredericksburg was fought and was not won. Its cost was mournfully heavy. We lost fifty per cent, more men than did the enemy, and yet there is sense in the awful arithmetic propounded by Mr. Lincoln. He, says that if the same battle were to be fought over again, every day, through a week of days, with the same relative results, the army under Lee would be wiped out to its last man, the Army of the Potomac would still be a mighty host, the war would be over, the Confederacy gone, and peace would be won at a smaller cost of life than it will be if the week of lost battles must be dragged out through yet another year of camps and marches, and of deaths in hospitals rather than upon the field. No general yet found can face the arithmetic, but the end of the war will be at hand when he shall be discovered.[11]

LETTERS OF ACCEPTANCE
FROM ABRAHAM LINCOLN AND HANNIBAL HAMLIN,
INDORSING THE PLATFORM.

MR. LINCOLN'S LETTER.

SPRINGFIELD, Ill., May 23, 1860.

Hon. George Ashmun, President of the Republican National Convention:

SIR: I accept the nomination tendered me by the Convention over which you presided, and of which I am formally apprised in the letter of yourself and others, acting as a Committee of the Convention, for that purpose.

The declaration of principles and sentiments, which accompanies your letter, meets my approval; and it shall be my care not to violate, or disregard it, in any part.

Imploring the assistance of Divine Providence; and with due regard to the views and feelings of all who were represented in the Convention; to the rights of all the States, and Territories, and people of the nation; to the inviolability of the Constitution, and the perpetual union, harmony and prosperity of all, I am most happy to co-operate for the practical success of the principles declared by the Convention.

Your obliged friend and fellow-citizen,   ABRAHAM LINCOLN.

MR. HAMLIN'S LETTER.

WASHINGTON, May 30, 1860.

GENTLEMEN: Your official communication of the 18th instant, informing me that the representatives of the Republican Party of the United States, assembled at Chicago on that day, had, by a unanimous vote, selected me as their candidate for the office of Vice-President, has been received, together with the resolutions adopted by the Convention as its declaration of principles.

Those resolutions enunciate clearly and forcibly the principles which unite us and the objects proposed to be accomplished. They address themselves to all, and there is neither necessity nor propriety in my entering upon a discussion of any of them. They have the approval of my judgment, and in any action of mine will be faithfully and cordially sustained.

I am profoundly grateful to those with whom it is my pride and pleasure politically to co-operate, for the nomination so unexpectedly conferred; and I desire to tender through you, to the members of the Convention, my sincere thanks for the confidence thus reposed in me. Should the nomination, which I now accept, be ratified by the people, and the duties devolve upon me of presiding over the Senate of the United States, it will be my earnest endeavor faithfully to discharge them with a just regard for the rights of all.

It is to be observed, in connection with the doings of the Republican Convention, that a paramount object with us, is, to preserve the normal condition of our territorial domain as homes for free men. The able advocate and defender of Republican principles whom you have nominated for the highest place that can gratify the ambition of man, comes from a State which has been made what it is, by special action in that respect, of the wise and good men who founded our institutions. The rights of free labor have there been vindicated and maintained. The thrift and enterprise which so distinguished Illinois, one of the most flourishing States of the glorious West, we would see secured to all the Territories of the Union, and restore peace and harmony to the whole country by bringing back the Government to what it was under the wise and patriotic men who created it. If the Republicans shall succeed in that object, as they hope to, they will be held in grateful remembrance by the busy and teeming millions of future ages.   I am, very truly, yours,   H. HAMLIN.

Hon. GEORGE ASHMUN, President of the Convention, and others of the Committee.

MR. SEWARD'S INDORSEMENT OF THE CANDIDATES AND PLATFORM.

The following cordial indorsement of the Candidates and Platform of the Republican Party appeared in the Auburn Daily Advertiser on the day after the nomination, written by Senator Seward:

"We place the names of Lincoln and Hamlin at the head of our columns, with pride and satisfaction. No truer exposition of the Republican creed could be given, than the platform adopted by the Convention contains. No truer or firmer defenders of the Republican faith could have been found in the Union, than the distinguished and esteemed citizens on whom the honors of the nomination have fallen. Their election, we trust, by a decisive majority, will restore the Government of the United States to its constitutional and ancient course. Let the watchword of the Republican Party, then, be Union and Liberty, and onward to Victory."

(*previous page*) Lincoln's Letter of Acceptance and Platform Endorsement 1860. The Republican Party platform held "in abhorrence all schemes for Disunion, come from whatever source they may," and affirmed "the right of each State to order and control its own domestic institutions [meaning slavery] according to its own judgment exclusively." Rare Book and Special Collections Division, Library of Congress, Alfred Whital Stern Collection of Lincolniana.

(*right*) Broadside Image of the Lincoln Cabinet. Because he was the first Republican elected to the presidency, Lincoln's choice of cabinet officials was especially consequential. He included his principal rivals for the presidency as well as members from other parties: Democrat, Whig, Free Soil, and Know Nothing. He attempted to include southerners as well, without compromising his party's platform. Rare Book and Special Collections Division, Library of Congress, Alfred Whital Stern Collection of Lincolniana.

Hon. Simon Cameron, Secretary of War.|

Hon. S. P. Chase, Secretary of the Treasury.—Photographed by J. E. Ryder, of Cleveland, O.

Hon. William H. Seward, Secretary of State.
Hon. Gideon Welles, Secretary of the Navy.
Hon. Montgomery Blair, Postmaster-General.

Hon. Caleb B. Smith, Secretary of the Interior.
Hon. Edward Bates, Attorney-General.

THE MEMBERS OF PRESIDENT LINCOLN'S CABINET.

Lincoln's Pre-Inauguration Journey to Washington, Reaching Philadelphia, February 22, 1861. When he set out from Springfield on February 11, 1861, Lincoln remarked, "I am not at liberty to shift my ground." Prints and Photographs Division, Library of Congress, LC-USZ62-50817.

1861 Inauguration. Attempting to prevent disunion, Lincoln argued, "One section of our country believes slavery is *right,* and ought to be extended, while the other believes it is *wrong,* and ought not to be extended," and he asked, "Why should there not be a patient confidence in the ultimate justice of the people?" Prints and Photographs Division, Library of Congress, LC-DIG-ppmsca-07636.

Unfinished Capitol, Lincoln Inauguration, 1861. Lincoln's inaugural speech did not impress Frederick Douglass, who considered it "casting pearls before swine" and a cowardly response to the crisis of the nation. Prints and Photographs Division, Library of Congress, LC-USZ62-75795.

President Lincoln Seated, May 18, 1861. After the firing on Fort Sumter on April 12, 1861, and the secession of Virginia on April 17, 1861, Lincoln began to take war measures even though Congress was not in session. Brady Photograph, Prints and Photographs Division, Library of Congress, LC-USZ62-15178.

ARREST OF MARSHALL KANE, AT HIS HOUSE IN BALTIMORE, AT THREE O'CLOCK A. M., WEDNESDAY, JUNE 27, BY ORDER OF MAJOR-GENERAL BANKS ON A CHARGE OF TREASON.—AT 4½ A. M. A SKETCH BY OUR SPECIAL ARTIST ACCOMPANYING GENERAL BANKS' COMMAND.—SEE PAGE 118.

Arrest of Marshall Kane of Baltimore on June 27, 1861. One of the most controversial measures Lincoln took in April 1861 was the suspension of the writ of habeas corpus along the Baltimore and Ohio Railroad in Maryland. Union General Benjamin Butler declared martial law in Baltimore and arrested George P. Kane, marshal of police, for southern sympathies. From Frank Leslie's *Illustrated Newspaper*, July 6, 1861, Prints and Photographs Division, Library of Congress, LC-USZ62-133074.

LINCOLN—"*I'm sorry to have to drop you, Sambo, but this concern won't carry us both!*"

Frémont Proclamation. The Republican nominee for president in 1856 and major general in charge of the Department of the West in July 1861, John C. Frémont issued a proclamation on August 30, 1861, declaring martial law and that the confiscated slaves of all Confederates were "hereby declared freemen." Lincoln asked him to withdraw the proclamation. From Frank Leslie's *Illustrated Newspaper*, October 12, 1861, Prints and Photographs Division, Library of Congress, LC-USZ62-133077.

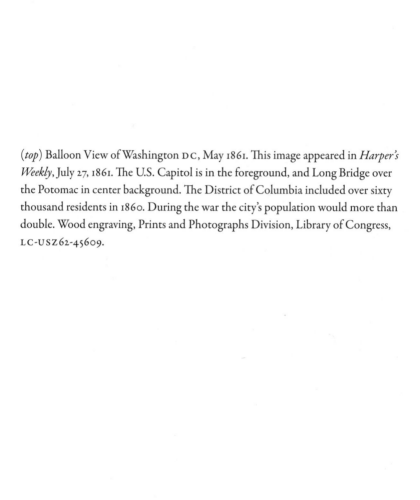

(*top*) Balloon View of Washington DC, May 1861. This image appeared in *Harper's Weekly*, July 27, 1861. The U.S. Capitol is in the foreground, and Long Bridge over the Potomac in center background. The District of Columbia included over sixty thousand residents in 1860. During the war the city's population would more than double. Wood engraving, Prints and Photographs Division, Library of Congress, LC-USZ62-45609.

(*bottom*) Batteries of Field Pieces in Arsenal, Washington DC. During the war the capital became a fortified base for the Union Army with dozens of hospitals, forts, and encampments. Russell photograph, Prints and Photographs Division, Library of Congress, LC-DIG-ppmsca-08296.

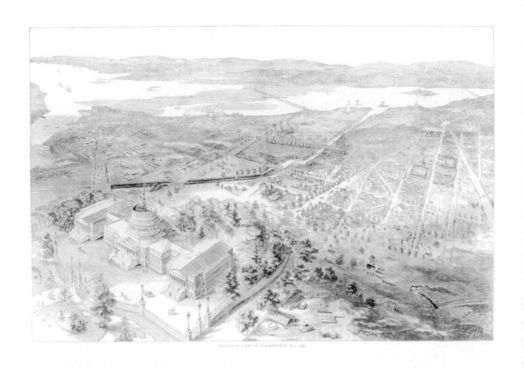

BALLOON VIEW OF WASHINGTON, MAY, 1861.

Hotel Entrance to the Long Bridge, Washington DC, ca. 1861–65. Long Bridge was rebuilt for railroads to cross the Potomac River and reach supply depots at Alexandria, Virginia. Bridges and railroads were strategic choke points in the war, often heavily fortified and protected. Prints and Photographs Division, Library of Congress, LC-DIG-ppmsca-08252.

Tent Life of the 31st Pennsylvania Infantry at Queen's Farm, near Fort Slocum. Fort Slocum was one of dozens of forts designed to encircle and protect Washington DC. This fort provided support for Fort Stevens and was named for Col. John Slocum of the 2nd Rhode Island, killed in action on July 21, 1861, at the First Battle of Manassas. Women and children occupied camps with soldiers, especially on the outskirts of Washington. Prints and Photographs Division, Civil War Photographs, Library of Congress, LC-DIG-cwpb-01663.

Citizen Volunteers Assisting the Wounded at Antietam. This drawing by Alfred Waud was in *Harper's Weekly*, October 11, 1862. After the Battle of Antietam Lincoln issued his preliminary Emancipation Proclamation on September 22, 1862, freeing slaves after January 1, 1863, in the Confederacy wherever the Union Army could reach. Prints and Photographs Division, Civil War Photographs, Library of Congress, LC-DIG-ppmsca-21468.

McClellan and Lincoln at Antietam. Lincoln struggled to find an effective leader of the Army of the Potomac throughout 1862 and 1863. Despite his popularity and his early victories in western Virginia, George B. McClellan favored a conservative and conciliatory policy toward the South. Prints and Photographs Division, Civil War Photographs, Library of Congress, LC-USZ62-2276.

Lincoln's Cabinet Discussing the Emancipation Proclamation. On September 22, 1862, Lincoln convened his cabinet. Before reading the document to the members, he had set his face like flint, silencing opposition by saying, "I do not wish your advice about the main matter—for that I have determined for myself." Rare Book and Special Collections Division, Library of Congress, Alfred Whital Stern Collection of Lincolniana.

Lincoln Writing the Proclamation of Freedom Printed in 1863. Library of Congress. The image of Lincoln as the Emancipator developed during the war with popular lithographs such as this one. Lincoln has a Bible and a copy of the Constitution nearby, and a bust of former president Andrew Jackson, a strong Unionist, looks on approvingly. Other symbols include the bust of his dithering predecessor, James Buchanan, hanging by a rope around its neck, and the railsplitter's hammer on the floor at Lincoln's feet. Lithograph by Ehrgott, Forbriger and Company, Pittsburgh PA, Prints and Photographs Division, Library of Congress, LC-DIG-ppmsca-18444.

657.   A Negro Family coming into the Union Lines.
[FOR DESCRIPTION OF THIS VIEW SEE THE OTHER SIDE OF THIS CARD.]

An Emancipated Family Coming into Union Lines. African American men and women took action during the war to claim freedom for themselves and their families. Loading their possessions into mule-drawn wagons or onto Union troop trains, many former slaves made their way to Union bases or to occupied cities, such as Memphis, Tennessee, or Alexandria, Virginia. Prints and Photographs Division, Civil War Photographs, Library of Congress, LC-DIG-stereo-1S02761.

(*top*) Lincoln Delivering the Gettysburg Address. Lincoln spoke at Gettysburg on November 19, 1863, at the dedication of the Soldiers' National Cemetery. Shortly thereafter, in December, the first session of the Thirty-Eighth Congress opened under a completed Capitol dome. Prints and Photographs Division, Civil War Photographs, Library of Congress, LC-DIG-cwpb-07639.

(*left*) Lincoln in 1863. The photograph was shot by Alexander Gardner on November 8, 1863, eleven days before the Gettysburg Address. Prints and Photographs Division, Library of Congress, LC-USZ62-13016.

(*top*) The Crowd at the Second Lincoln Inauguration. Lincoln spoke with uncommon humility on March 4, 1865 "The Almighty has His Own purposes," he said. Prints and Photographs Division, Library of Congress, LC-DIG-ppmsc-02927.

(*left*) Lincoln in 1864. The photograph was shot by Anthony Berger on February 9, 1864, as the reference for Lincoln's image on the five-dollar bill. Facing reelection in November 1864, Lincoln at one point in the campaign clarified his views for the public: "I am naturally anti-slavery. If slavery is not wrong, nothing is wrong. I can not remember when I did not so think, and feel. And yet I have never understood that the Presidency conferred upon me an unrestricted right to act officially upon this judgment and feeling." Prints and Photographs Division, Library of Congress, LC-DIG-ppmsca-19305.

PRESIDENT LINCOLN RIDING THROUGH RICHMOND, APRIL 4, AMID THE ENTHUSIASTIC CHEERS OF THE INHABITANTS.—FROM A SKETCH BY OUR SPECIAL ARTIST, J. BECKER.

Lincoln Riding through Richmond, April 4, 1865. When news of the fall of Richmond came into Washington DC, Lincoln decided to travel there. "I will take care of myself," he telegraphed his worried Secretary of War Edwin Stanton. Black Richmonders greeted Lincoln with unrestrained enthusiasm. Wood engraving, from Frank Leslie's *Illustrated Newspaper,* April 22, 1865, Prints and Photographs Division, Library of Congress, LC-USZ62-6931.

Burnside forthrightly shouldered responsibility and praised his men in his report, written four days after his loss, as Lincoln's secretaries John Nicolay and John Hay recorded:

> He gave generous praise to his officers and men, "For the failure in the attack I am responsible," he said, "as the extreme gallantry, courage, and endurance shown by them was never excelled and would have carried the points had it been possible. . . . The fact that I decided to move from Warrenton on to this line rather against the opinion of the President, Secretary, and yourself [General Halleck], and that you have left the whole management in my hands, without giving me orders, makes me the more responsible. . . . I will add here that the movement was made earlier than you expected, and after the President, Secretary, and yourself requested me not to be in haste, for the reason that we were supplied much sooner by the different Staff Departments than was anticipated when I last saw you."[12]

Upon reading the report, Lincoln sent his congratulations to the Army of the Potomac:

> I have just read your Commanding General's preliminary report of the battle of Fredericksburg. Although you were not successful, the attempt was not an error, nor the failure other than an accident. The courage with which you, in an open field, maintained the contest against an entrenched foe, and the consummate skill and success with which you crossed and re-crossed the river, in face of the enemy, show that you possess all the qualities of a great army, which will yet give victory to the cause of the country and of popular government. Condoling with the mourners for the dead, and sympathizing with the severely wounded, I congratulate you that the number of both is comparatively so small.
>
> I tender to you, officers and soldiers, the thanks of the nation.[13]

By this time a cabinet rupture had emerged in Lincoln's administration over the mounting challenges and setbacks in the war. Reflecting on the entire Washington scene, Benjamin B. French, commissioner of public buildings, moaned:

> The war! I have no heart to write about either it or the political aspect of affairs. Defeat at Fredericsburg—the Cabinet breaking up—our leading men fighting with each other! Unless something occurs very soon to

brighten up affairs, I shall begin to look upon our whole Nation as on its way to destruction.[14]

At month's end two of Burnside's generals, circumventing their commander, visited Lincoln to tell him the general was considering a forward movement that could only be disastrous, because the beaten army was demoralized. They suggested returning to the McClellan strategy of approaching the enemy by way of the peninsula. Lincoln rejected the proposal and dispatched a brief message to Burnside: "I have good reason for saying you must not make a general movement of the army without letting me know." Burnside replied he would be in Washington the next day and would see Lincon.[15] Following their interview Burnside wrote a letter to the president discussing his relations with Halleck and offering to resign his command.

In a sharply worded letter to Halleck, Lincoln asked for the general in chief's advice. Considering Lincoln's letter harsh, Halleck offered his resignation, the second that day from two of his principal military advisers. Lincoln's patience wore thin. He drafted this reply:

> Gen. Burnside wishes to cross the Rappahannock with his army, but his Grand Division commanders all oppose the movement. If in such a difficulty as this you do not help, you fail me precisely in the point for which I sought your assistance. You know what Gen. Burnside's plan is; and it is my wish that you go with him to the ground, examine it as far as practicable, confer with the officers, getting their judgment, and ascertaining their temper, in a word, gather all the elements for forming a judgment of your own; and then tell Gen. Burnside that you *do* approve, or that you do *not* approve his plan. Your military skill is useless to me, if you will not do this.[16]

Then Lincoln withdrew the letter. All this occurred on New Year's Day, when Lincoln held a long, tiring reception for the public and signed the Emancipation Proclamation.

Discord between Burnside and his officers continued. On January 5 Burnside wrote to Lincoln, acknowledging the disagreement, stating that he still favored crossing the Rappahannock, and again offering his resignation. Responding to Burnside's overall strategy, Halleck reminded the general that "our first object was, not Richmond, but the defeat or scattering of Lee's army." He authorized a movement against Lee on the Rappahannock.

Upon reading Halleck's letter Lincoln wrote to Burnside, rejecting the resignation and endorsing the movement:

> I understand Gen. Halleck has sent you a letter of which this is a copy. I approve the letter. I deplore the want of concurrence with you, in opinion by your general officers, but I do not see the remedy. Be cautious, and do not understand that the government, or country, is driving you. I do not yet see how I could profit by changing the command of the A.P. & if I did, I should not wish to do it by accepting the resignation of your commission.[17]

Burnside began his move on January 21, 1863. The rain fell and fell, quickly miring his men in what became known as "the mud march." Its ignominious failure and the constant disagreement in his high command impelled the general two days later to prepare an order, relieving from duty five of his generals and a lieutenant colonel, dismissing from the service the two officers who had visited Lincoln with their alternate plan. He began his list with a direct assault on General Joseph Hooker, dismissing him for making unjust criticisms, creating distrust, and disparaging other officers.

Burnside made a night trip to see the president. Lincoln refused to accept Burnside's proposed order, and relieved him from command, replacing him with General Hooker. Henry J. Raymond had been in Burnside's camp, where the general had told him of the contents of the order. Raymond accompanied the general to Washington, and at a president's levee, as he wrote in his journal, "found a great crowd surrounding Mr. Lincoln. I managed, however, in brief terms, to tell him that I had been with the army and that many things were occurring there which he ought to know. I told him of the obstacles thrown in Burnside's way by his subordinates, and especially of General Hooker's conversation. He put his hand on my shoulder and said in my ear, as if desirous of not being overheard, 'That is all true—Hooker does talk badly; but the trouble is, he is stronger with the country to-day than any other man.' I ventured to ask him how long he would retain that strength when his real conduct and character should be understood. 'The country,' he answered, 'would not believe it; they would say it is all a lie.'"[18] As January waned, the saga continued for the Army of the Potomac. Lincoln turned from a discredited general, Burnside, to one whose credibility was dubious, Hooker.

CHAPTER TWENTY

A WINTER OF DISCONTENT

Elections for Congress and state offices occurred in October and November. A uniform day of voting had not yet been fixed, and some elections followed in the spring. A cloud of circumstances darkened Republican fortunes. The preliminary Emancipation Proclamation was immediately followed by the suspension of habeas corpus throughout the entire North. Both of these administration policies generated considerable opposition. Dissatisfaction with the sluggish progress of the war deepened with Burnside's failure at Fredericksburg. The draft provoked violence in Wisconsin and Pennsylvania, and apprehension about northern migration of blacks and resulting labor competition produced race riots in Ohio. Arbitrary arrests under the suspension of habeas corpus included some notable citizens. An outbreak of violence in Minnesota between Dakota and white settlers threatened open warfare on the plains. All these events combined to turn many northerners away from Lincoln and the party in power.

Asked for advice on party strategy, Lincoln declined "to suggest any course of action, preferring to rely upon intelligence and patriotism of friends." New York, the most populous state in the nation, held the most important election. Two-term governor Edwin D. Morgan, who also served as national chairman of the Republican Party, declined a third term candidacy. The Democrats brought forth a former governor, Horatio Seymour, who at the nominating convention attacked the Emancipation Proclamation as "a proposal for the butchery of women and children, for scenes of lust and rapine, and of arson and murder, which would invoke the interference of civilized Europe."[1] When elected he moderated his rhetoric but not his resistance to Lincoln's policies.

The nation's leading Copperhead, Clement L. Vallandigham, a Democratic congressman, was defeated—with Lincoln's help, wittingly or unwittingly, by his promoting the Republican candidate to major general. Though Vallandigham lost his Capitol forum, he continued his forceful role as a Lincoln critic.

Just before the November polling, Harvard law professor Joel Parker penned a letter to the Boston *Courier,* inquiring of its readers, "Do you not perceive that the president is not only a monarch, but that his is a perfect military despotism."[2]

Accompanied by strong anti-Lincoln feeling, the election cost Lincoln's party seats, not only in New York but also in his home state of Illinois as well as in states that in 1860 had voted for Lincoln. The next House of Representatives, to meet in December 1863, would hold about 101 administration members and 77 anti-administration ones. State legislatures were yet to fill one third of the Senate seats.

The Thirty-seventh Congress meeting for its final session heard Lincoln's annual message on December 1, 1862. After referring to foreign affairs he made one of his rare recommendations about domestic affairs. The low condition of wartime finance caused him to recommend organization of a national banking system. Describing the Sioux rising in Minnesota for which three hundred Indians had been sentenced to death, he asked Congress to consider remodeling the Indian system.

A section on American nationalism led him to recommend a plan of gradual, compensated emancipation of slavery, a divisive institution, he said, without which "the rebellion could never have existed." State laws, not federal, could provide emancipation as late as January 1, 1900. The federal government would provide compensation to the states and also money to provide for colonizing consenting black freed persons. He justified compensatory pay with the observation that "in a certain sense the liberation of slaves is the destruction of property . . . the same as other property." He recognized that many persons would be dissatisfied, including northerners fearing an influx of free blacks. To this he queried, "Cannot the North decide for itself, whether to receive them?"[3]

The antislavery Lincoln of the second annual message, with its elements of state action, gradual emancipation over a third of a century, compensation of slaves as property, and colonization, starkly contrasts with the Lincoln of the Emancipation Proclamation issued a month later. His peroration, set against the mundane matters at the beginning of the message, soared to great heights. "We shall nobly save, or meanly lose, the last, best hope of earth."

As the Republican-led Congress took up its work in the aftermath of a difficult election season, Lincoln faced growing questions. He confronted the uncertainty of the lawmakers' attitude toward executive emancipation and his widened suspension of habeas corpus; the flagging draft under the 1862 Militia Act; skepticism about establishing a national banking system; conflicting constitutional theories about admitting West Virginia to the Union; and the usual political antagonism toward him in his own party.

Three days after hearing the annual message, Democratic Copperhead Clement L. Vallandigham of Ohio offered a series of resolutions in Congress imposing harsh penalties upon any person perverting the war from its purpose of restoring the Union and any person affirming that the House or any authority could establish a dictatorship. His thrust, aimed at Lincoln's administration, was parried by a 79-50 vote to table.

On December 8, 1862, Democratic congressman William A. Richardson of Illinois made a long speech scoring the president's annual message. He attacked the emancipation scheme, arbitrary arrests, military "intimidation" at the polls, and granting of immunity to persons who carried out the president's extreme policies. The Republican course of action, he concluded, "leads to the destruction of both the Constitution and the Union."[4]

Kentucky's George H. Yeaman on December 11 introduced resolutions reading:

> *Resolved by the House of Representatives,* (the Senate concurring,) That the proclamation of the President of the United States, of date the 22d of September, 1862, is not warranted by the Constitution.
> *Resolved,* That the policy of emancipation, as indicated in that proclamation, is not calculated to hasten the restoration of peace, was not well chosen as a war measure, and is an assumption of power dangerous to the rights of citizens and the perpetuity of a free people.[5]

Maine's Samuel C. Fessenden, a Lincoln Republican, the next day countered with resolutions reading:

> *Resolved,* That the proclamation of the President of the United States, of the date of 22d September, 1862, is warranted by the Constitution.
>
> *Resolved,* That the policy of emancipation, as indicated in that proclamation, is well adapted to hasten the restoration of peace, was well chosen as a war measure, and is an exercise of power with proper regard for the rights of the States, and the perpetuity of free government.[6]

Yeaman's resolutions were tabled over the protest of 47 mostly Democratic representatives. Fessenden's resolutions were opposed by 52 members but won a majority of 78 votes.

In mid-December, as the House went through these motions, gloom settled over Republican senators. After adjourning for the day many of them met and discussed "the present condition of the country." Moderates and radicals caucused in a room under the Capitol roof. William Pitt Fessenden recorded the meeting. "A Radical without the petulant and vicious fretfulness of many Radicals," as Lincoln described him, he would become Lincoln's secretary of the treasury. His account reads:

> On the 16th of December, 1862, during the session of the Senate, I was notified by the doorkeeper that there would be a meeting of Republican senators in the reception room immediately after the adjournment. Accordingly I attended, and in a few moments nearly all the Republican senators were assembled. I think Mr. Hale and Mr. Sherman were the only absentees.
>
> The meeting was called to order by Mr. Anthony, our chairman, who requested that the object of the meeting might be stated, as it had not been made known to him. Mr. Clark said he had requested that the meeting might be called, at the suggestion of several senators, but he was not precisely informed as to its object. After a short delay, Mr. Trumbull said he believed it was called to ascertain whether the Republican senators would deem it their duty to take any action, or advise any action by the Senate, with regard to the present condition of the country, that the recent repulse at Fredericksburg had occasioned great excitement, and it had been thought best to ascertain whether any steps could be taken to quiet the public mind and to produce a better condition of affairs.

Silence ensued for a few moments, when Mr. Wilkinson said that in his opinion the country was ruined and the cause was lost; that the Senate might save it but would not for the reason that Republican senators would not adopt any united and vigorous course; that there were senators who would not support the majority in any plan that might devise for the safety of the country at this crisis, and he thought no good would come of any action that might be proposed. In his judgment the source of all our difficulties and disasters was apparent. The Secretary of State, Mr. Seward, exercised a controlling influence upon the mind of the President. He, Mr. Seward, had never believed in the war—had been averse to it from the beginning, and so long as he remained in the Cabinet nothing but defeat and disaster could be expected. . . .

Mr. Foster said that he did . . . agree with Mr. Wilkinson in the opinion that no improvement could be expected in our affairs so long as Mr. Seward remained in the Cabinet.[7]

As the griping intensified, in late December a cabinet crisis occurred. Partly a measure of discontent about how the war was flagging, it was also a test of Lincoln's leadership. Secretary of the Navy Gideon Welles gave a substantial account:

Soon after reaching the Department this a.m., I received a note from Nicolay, the President's secretary, requesting me to attend a special Cabinet-meeting at half-past ten. All the members were punctually there except Seward.

The President desired that what he had to communicate should not be the subject of conversation elsewhere, and proceeded to inform us that on Wednesday evening, about six o'clock, Senator Preston King and F. W. Seward came into his room, each bearing a communication. That which Mr. King presented was the resignation of the Secretary of State, and Mr. F. W. Seward handed in his own. Mr. King then informed him that at a Republican caucus held that day a pointed and positive opposition had shown itself against the Secretary of State, which terminated in a unanimous expression, with one exception, against him and a wish for his removal. The feeling finally shaped itself into resolutions of a general character, and the appointment of a committee of nine to bear them to the President, and to communicate to him the sentiments of the Republican Senators. Mr. King, the former colleague and the friend of Mr. Seward, being also from the same State, felt it to be a duty to inform the Secretary at once of what had occurred. On receiving this information, Mr. Seward immediately

tendered his resignation. Mr. King suggested it would be well for the committee to wait upon the President at an early moment, and, . . . Mr. King
on Wednesday morning notified Judge Collamer, the chairman, who sent
word to the President that they would call at the Executive Mansion at any
hour after six that evening, and the President sent word he would receive
them at seven.

The committee came at the time specified, and the President says the
evening was spent in a pretty free discussion of animated conversation.
No opposition was manifested towards any other member of the Cabinet
than Mr. Seward. Some not very friendly feelings were shown towards one
or two others, but no wish that any one should leave but the Secretary of
State. Him they charged, if not with infidelity, with indifference, with want
of earnestness in the war, with want of sympathy with the country in this
great struggle, and with many things objectionable, and especially with a
too great ascendency and control of the President. This, he said, was the
point and pith of their complaint.

The President in reply to the committee stated how this movement
shocked and grieved him; that the Cabinet he had selected in view of
impending difficulties and of all the responsibilities upon him; that the
members and himself had gone on harmoniously; that there had never
been serious disagreements, though there had been differences; that in the
overwhelming troubles of the country, which had borne heavily upon him,
he had been sustained and consoled by the good feeling and the mutual
and unselfish confidence and zeal that pervaded the Cabinet.

He expressed a hope that there would be no combined movement on the
part of other members of the Cabinet to resist this assault, whatever might
be the termination. Said the movement was uncalled for, that there was no
such charge, admitting all that was said, as should break up or overthrow
a Cabinet, nor was it possible for him to go on with a total abandonment
of old friends. . . .

The President requested that we should, with him, meet the committee. . . .

At the meeting last evening there were present of the committee Senators Collamer, Fessenden, Harris, Trumbull, Grimes, Howard, Sumner, and
Pomeroy. Wade was absent. The President, and all the Cabinet but Seward
were present. The subject was opened by the President, who read the resolutions and stated the substance of his interviews with the committee,—their
object and purpose. He spoke of the unity of his Cabinet, and how, though
they could not be expected to think and speak alike on all subjects, all had
acquiesced in measures when once decided. The necessities of the times,

he said, had prevented frequent and long sessions of the Cabinet, and the submission of every question at the meetings.

Secretary Chase indorsed the President's statement fully and entirely, but regretted that there was not a more full and thorough consideration and canvass of every important measure in open Cabinet.

Senator Collamer, however, chairman of the committee, succeeded the President, and calmly and fairly presented the views of the committee and of those whom they represented. They wanted united counsels, combined wisdom, and energetic action. If there is truth in the maxim, that in a multitude of counselors there is safety, it might be well that those advisers who were near the President and selected by him, and all of whom were more or less responsible, should be consulted on the great questions which affected the national welfare, and that the ear of the Executive should be open to all and that he should have the minds of all. . . .

The President managed his own case, speaking freely, and showed great tact, and ability, provided such a subject were a proper one for such a meeting and discussion. I have no doubt he considered it most judicious to conciliate the Senators with respectful deference, whatever may have been his opinion of their interference. When he closed his remarks, he said it would be a gratification to him if each member of the committee would state whether he now thought it advisable to dismiss Mr. Seward, and whether his exclusion would strengthen or weaken the Administration, and the Union cause in their respective States. Grimes, Trumbull, and Sumner, who had expressed themselves decidedly against the continuance of Mr. Seward in the Cabinet indicated no change of opinion. Collamer and Fessenden declined committing themselves on the subject; were not prepared to answer the questions. Senator Harris felt it a duty to say that while many of the friends of the Administration would be gratified, others would feel deeply wounded, and the effect of Mr. Seward's retirement would, on the whole, be calamitous in the State of New York. Pomeroy of Kansas said, personally, he believed the withdrawal of Mr. Seward would be a good movement and he sincerely wished it might take place. Howard of Michigan declined answering the question. . . .

It was nearly midnight when we left the President; and it could not be otherwise than that all my wakeful moments should be absorbed with a subject which, time and circumstances considered, was of grave importance to the Administration and the country. A Senatorial combination to dictate to the President in regard to his political family in the height of a civil war which threatens the existence of the Republic cannot be permitted even if the person to whom they object is as obnoxious as they represent. After fully canvassing the subject in all its phases, my mind was clear as to the course which it was my duty to pursue, and what I believed was the President's duty also.

My first movement this morning was to call on the President as soon as I supposed he could have breakfasted. I informed the President I had pondered the events of yesterday and last evening, and felt it incumbent on me to advise him not to accept the resignation of Mr. Seward; that if there were objections, real or imaginary, against Mr. Seward, the time, manner, and circumstances—the occasion, and the method of presenting what the Senators considered objections—were all inappropriate and wrong; that no party or faction should be permitted to dictate to the President in regard to his Cabinet; it would be of evil example and fraught with incalculable injury to the Government and country; . . . that it devolved on him, and was his duty to assert and maintain the rights and independence of the Executive; that he ought not, against his own convictions, to yield one iota of the authority intrusted to him on the demand of either branch of Congress or both combined, or to any party, whatever might be its views and intentions. . . . In short, I considered it for the true interest of the country, now as in the future, that this scheme should be defeated; that, so believing, I had at the earliest moment given him my conclusions.

The President was much gratified; said the whole thing had struck him as it had me, and if carried out as the Senators prescribed, the whole Government must cave in. . . .

I added that, having expressed my wish that he would not accept Mr. Seward's resignation, I thought it equally important that Seward should not press its acceptance. In this he also concurred, and asked if I had seen Seward. I replied I had not, my first duty was with him, and, having ascertained that we agreed, I would now go over and see him. He earnestly desired me to do so.

I went immediately to Seward's house . . . and returned to the White House. . . .

When the President came in, which was in a few moments his first address was to me, asking if I "had seen the man." I replied that I had, and that he assented to my views. He then turned to Chase and said, "I sent for you, for this matter is giving me great trouble." At our first interview . . . he rang and directed that a message be sent to Mr. Chase.

Chase said he had been painfully affected by the meeting last evening, which was a total surprise to him, and, after some, not very explicit remarks as to how he was affected, informed the President he had prepared his resignation. "Where is it?", said the President quickly, his eye lighting up in a moment. "I brought it with me," said Chase, taking it from his pocket; "I wrote it this morning." "Let me have it," said the President, reaching his long arm and fingers towards C., who held on, seemingly reluctant to part with the letter, which was sealed, and which he apparently hesitated to surrender. Something further he wished to say, but the President was eager and did not perceive it, but took the letter.

"This," said he, looking towards me with a triumphal laugh, "cuts the Gordian knot." An air of satisfaction spread over his countenance such as I have not seen for some time. "I can dispose of this subject now," he added, as he turned on his chair and broke the seal. "I see my way clear."[8]

Lincoln had confronted the Republican caucus members head on and had faced them down. He had succeeded in retaining in his cabinet leaders of two factions of his party. After a cabinet meeting he told Senator Ira Harris of New York that when Chase followed Seward in tendering his resignation, he felt secure, using the language of a horseman. "Now I can ride; I have got a pumpkin in each end of my bag."

Months later he remarked with some satisfaction: "I do not see how it could have been done better. I am sure it was right. If I had yielded to that storm and dismissed Seward the thing would all have slumped over one way, and we should have been left with a scanty handful of supporters. When Chase gave in his resignation I saw that the same was in my hands, and I put it through."[9]

Chase's ambition was to be a candidate for the presidency in 1864 should Lincoln stumble. Indeed, he blamed Seward, his rival in the cabinet, for undue influence over Lincoln and told his own radical supporters in Congress that Seward controlled Lincoln. But Lincoln skillfully managed to disarm Chase by holding his letter of resignation and demonstrating to congressional radicals that Chase's depiction of a deeply divided cabinet was not entirely accurate.

As the days of December grew shorter, troubles continued to pile high for the president. Citizens in western Virginia framed a constitution and petitioned to be admitted to the Union. Article Four of the United States

Constitution states: "New States may be admitted into this Union; but no new State shall be formed or erected within the Jurisdiction of any other State . . . without the Consent of the legislatures of the States concerned as well as of the Congress." The rump legislature of what called itself the "restored Government of Virginia" at Wheeling, ignoring the Richmond legislature as well as the Constitution, gave its consent.

Congress inserted a requirement of gradual emancipation, and on December 10 passed the West Virginia bill by a vote of 96 yeas and 55 nays. The Senate had been previously approved the measure. Lincoln accordingly confronted a constitutional dilemma—to sign or not to sign. He asked his cabinet members to answer in writing two questions, each of a very different nature: "is the said Act constitutional?; and is the said Act expedient?"

The cabinet split evenly, three for admission, three against. Seward, in favor, wrote on the constitutional question: "It seems to me that the political body which has given consent in this case is really and incontestably the State of Virginia." On the question of expediency he believed the people of the new state would become safer from molestation and would promote the harmony and peace of the Union.

In a vigorously argued negative opinion, Attorney General Bates, presumably the best qualified cabinet officer to advise the president on these questions, argued that "the Legislature which pretends to give the consent of Virginia to her own dismemberment is (as far as I am credibly informed) composed chiefly if not entirely of men who represent those forty-eight counties which constitute the new State of West Virginia. The act of consent is less in the nature of a law than a contract. It is a grant of power, an agreement, and with whom?" he asked, his indignation rising. "The representatives of the forty-eight counties with themselves! Is that fair dealing? Is that honest legislation? Is that a legitimate exercise of a constitutional power by the Legislature of Virginia? It seems to me that it is a mere abuse, nothing less than attempted secession, hardly veiled under the flimsy forms of law."[10]

Lincoln the lawyer penned an ingenious answer to his question about constitutionality, and went on as Lincoln the politician to justify admission of West Virginia. The document that underlay his signing of the bill on December 31 reads:

The consent of the Legislature of Virginia is constitutionally necessary to the bill for the admission of West-Virginia becoming a law. A body claiming to be such Legislature has given its consent. We can not well deny that it is such, unless we do so upon the outside knowledge that the body was chosen at elections, in which a majority of the qualified voters of Virginia did not participate.

But it is a universal practice in the popular elections in all these states, to give no legal consideration whatever to those who do not choose to vote, as against the effect of the votes of those, *who do choose to vote.* Hence it is not the qualified voters, but the qualified voters who choose to vote, that constitute the political power of the state. Much less than to nonvoters, should any consideration be given to those who did not vote, *in this case:* because it is also matter of outside knowledge, that they were not merely neglectful of their rights under, and duty to, this government, but were also engaged in open rebellion against it. Doubtless among these non-voters were some Union men whose voices were smothered by the more numerous secessionists; but we know too little of their number to assign them any appreciable value. Can this government stand, if it indulges constitutional constructions by which men in open rebellion against it, are to be accounted, man for man, the equals of those who maintain their loyalty to it? Are they to be accounted even better citizens, and more worthy of consideration, than those who merely neglect to vote? If so, their treason against the constitution, enhances their constitutional value! Without braving these absurd conclusions, we can not deny that the body which consents to the admission of West-Virginia, is the Legislature of Virginia. I do not think the plural form of the words "Legislatures" and "States" in the phrase of the constitution "without the consent of the Legislatures of the States concerned et cetera" has any reference to the *new* State concerned. That plural form sprang from the contemplation of two or more old States contributing to form a new one. The idea that the new state was in danger of being admitted without its own consent, was not provided against, because it was not thought of, as I conceive. It is said, the devil takes care of his own. Much more should a good spirit—the spirit of the Constitution and the Union—take care of its own. I think it can not do less, and live.

But is the admission into the Union, of West-Virginia, expedient. This, in my general view, is more a question for Congress, than for the Executive. Still I do not evade it. More than on anything else, it depends on whether the admission or rejection of the new state would under all the circumstances tend the more strongly to the restoration of the national authority throughout the Union. That which helps most in this direction is the most expedient at this time. Doubtless those remaining in Virginia would return to the Union, so to speak, less reluctantly without the division of the old state than with it; but I think we could not save as much in this quarter by rejecting the new state, as we should lose by it in West-Virginia. We can scarcely dispense with the aid of West-Virginia in this struggle; much less can we afford to have her against us, in congress and in the field. Her brave and good men regard her admission into the Union as a matter of life and death. They have been true to the Union under very severe trials. We have so acted as to justify their hopes; and we can not fully retain their confidence, and co-operation, if we seem to break faith with them. In fact, they could not do much for us, if they would.

Again, the admission of the new state, turns that much slave soil to free; and thus, is a certain, and irrevocable encroachment upon the cause of the rebellion.

The division of a State is dreaded as a precedent. But a measure made expedient by a war, is no precedent for times of peace. It is said that the admission of West-Virginia, is secession, and tolerated only because it is our secession. Well, if we call it by that name, there is still difference enough between secession against the constitution, and secession in favor of the constitution.

I believe the admission of West-Virginia into the Union is expedient.[11]

The following day stood out as the time appointed by his preliminary proclamation to issue his formal proclamation. No seceded state had availed itself of the opportunity to return to the Union and avoid emancipation of its slaves. Congress had not passed the measures needed for the program of emancipation outlined in his second annual message.

Frederick Douglass, the black abolitionist, in October hailed the preliminary proclamation. "We shout for joy that we live to record this righteous decree," he exulted. Yet in November, worried about the outcome of the autumn elections, he voiced uncertainty:

We say three courses although in a radical point of view there are but two. One is the issuing, according to promise, of his proclamation abolishing slavery in all the States and parts of States which shall be in rebellion on the first of January and the second is, not to issue it at all. Any postponement, any apology—any plan of compromise which saves the guilty neck of slavery one hour beyond the first of January, will be in effect a suppression of the proclamation altogether. And now supposing that Mr. Lincoln shall fail, supposing that the hour comes and the man is missing, what will be the effect upon him? Thus far the loyal north has trusted him, less for his ability than his honesty. They have supported him with patience rather than enthusiasm. His word though clumsily uttered has been esteemed his bond, good for all, and more than all it has promised. But what, as we have already said, if the President fails in this trial hour, what if he now listens to the demon slavery—and rejects the entreaties of the Angel of Liberty? Suppose he cowers at last before the half loyal border Slave States, which have already nearly ruined his administration, and have been of more service to Richmond than to Washington from the beginning— withholds his proclamation of freedom—disappoints the just hopes of his true friends, dispels the fear and dismay of his enemies—and thus gives a new lease of life to the slaveholder's rebellion? Where then will stand Mr. Abraham Lincoln? We know not what will become of him. The North has been so often betrayed and trifled with that it has become unsafe to predicate anything spirited, resolute and decided on her part. But this we will say, if Mr. Lincoln shall thus trifle with the wounds of his bleeding country—thus fiddle, while the cold earth around Fredericksburg is wet with the warm blood of our patriot soldiers—every one of whom was slain by slaveholding rebels, he will be covered with execrations as bitter and as deep as any that ever settled upon the head of any perjured tyrant ancient or modern. His name would go down in history scarcely less loathsome than that of Nero. Such a course on the part of Mr. Lincoln would justly make him the distrust and scandal of his friends, the scorn of the world and the contempt of his enemies. Henceforth none but fools will believe in him and his protestations of honesty and patriotism will be hailed but as the deceitful utterances of another Iago.[12]

As 1863 opened, Lincoln received comments and advice from all quarters. An obscure poet in slaveholding Kentucky in December wrote "ABRAHAM LINCOLN" January First, Eighteen Hundred and Sixty-three:

> Stand like an anvil, when 'tis beaten
>> With the full vigor of the smith's right arm!
> Stand like the noble oak-tree, when 'tis eaten
>> By the Saperda and his ravenous swarm
> For many smiths will strike the ringing blows,

Ere the red drama now enacting close;
And human insects, gnawing at they fame,
Conspire to bring thy honored head to shame.

Stand like the firmament, upholden
    By an invisible but Almighty hand!
He whomsoever JUSTICE doth embolden,
    Unshaken, unseduced, unawed shall stand.
Invisible support is mightier far,
With noble aims, than walls of granite are;
And simple consciousness of justice gives
Strength to a purpose while that purpose lives.

Stand like the rock that looks defiant
    Far o'er the surging seas that lash its form!
Composed, determined, watchful, self-reliant,
    Be master of thyself, and rule the storm!
And thou shalt soon behold the bow of peace
Span the broad heavens, and the wild tumult cease,
And see the billows, with the clouds that meet,
Subdued and calm, come crouching to thy feet.[13]

Conservatives were less enthusiastic. Orville H. Browning was increasingly distancing himself from Lincoln's policies. In July he had counseled the president to veto the second confiscation bill. On the eve of the formal emancipation proclamation he sought through an intermediary to dissuade the president from issuing the famous document.[14]

To the relief of Frederick Douglass and like-minded persons and to the dismay of others, Lincoln kept his word and issued the formal Emancipation Proclamation. In a sense his various policies aimed at gradually ending slavery had failed: on state emancipation, colonization, and federal compensation. His words represented a vast change from his earlier thinking. He claimed authority, which he had earlier doubted, as commander in chief in time of rebellion, and he claimed justification "as a fit and necessary war measure," to free rebels' slaves. He spoke not of gradual emancipation but declared that those slaves "are, and henceforward shall be free." Nor did he speak of colonization; rather he urged freed persons to abstain from violence and to work, when allowed, for wages. And further overcoming earlier views, he announced that freedmen would be received in the armed service. On the suggestion of the pious Chase and softening the legalistic and martial tone of the document, Lincoln added the words, "And upon this act, sincerely believed to be an act of justice, warranted by the Constitution, upon military necessity, I invoke the considerate judgment of mankind, and the gracious favor of almighty God."[15]

Europeans with keen interest in American affairs watched the freeing of slaves by Lincoln's proclamation. Workingmen of Manchester, England, a center of cotton textile manufacturing, suffering from the cotton shortage occasioned by the war, sent the president an address of broad-ranging commendation. In response Lincoln reflected on his purpose, reviewed Anglo-American relations, and bespoke his sympathy for the hardship imposed on European workingmen:

I have the honor to acknowledge the receipt of the address and resolutions which you sent to me on the eve of the new year.

When I came, on the fourth day of March, 1861, through a free and constitutional election, to preside in the government of the United States, the country was found at the verge of civil war. Whatever might have been the cause, or whosoever the fault, one duty paramount to all others was before me, namely, to maintain and preserve at once the Constitution and the integrity of the federal republic. A conscientious purpose to perform this duty is a key to all the measures of administration which have been, and to all which will hereafter be pursued. Under our form of government, and my official oath, I could not depart from this purpose if I would. It is not always in the power of governments to enlarge or restrict the scope of moral results which follow the policies that they may deem it necessary for the public safety, from time to time, to adopt.

I have understood well that the duty of self-preservation rests solely with the American people. But I have at the same time been aware that favor or disfavor of foreign nations might have a material influence in enlarging and prolonging the struggle with disloyal men in which the country is engaged. A fair examination of history has seemed to authorize a belief that the past action and influences of the United States were generally regarded as having been beneficent towards mankind. I have therefore reckoned upon the forbearance of nations. Circumstances, to some of which you kindly allude, induced me especially to expect that if justice and good faith should be practiced by the United States, they would encounter no hostile influence on the part of Great Britain. It is now a pleasant duty to acknowledge the demonstration you have given of your desire that a spirit of peace and amity towards this country may prevail in the councils of your Queen, who is respected and esteemed in your own country only more than she is by the kindred nation which has its home on this side of the Atlantic.

I know and deeply deplore the sufferings which the workingmen at Manchester and in all Europe are called to endure in this crisis. It has been often and studiously represented that the attempt to overthrow this government, which was built upon the foundation of human rights, and to substitute for it one which should rest exclusively on the basis of human slavery, was likely to obtain the favor of Europe. Through the actions of our disloyal citizens the workingmen of Europe have been subjected to a severe trial, for the purpose of forcing their sanction to that attempt. Under these circumstances, I cannot but regard your decisive utterance upon the question as an instance of sublime Christian heroism which has not been surpassed in any age or in any country. It is, indeed, an energetic and reinspiring assurance of the inherent power of truth and of the ultimate and universal triumph of justice, humanity, and freedom. I do not doubt that the sentiments you have expressed will be sustained by your great nation, and, on the other hand, I have no hesitation in assuring you that they will excite admiration, esteem, and the most reciprocal feelings of friendship among the American people. I hail this interchange of sentiment, therefore, as an augury that, whatever else may happen, whatever misfortune may befall your country or my own, the peace and friendship which now exist between the two nations will be, as it shall be my desire to make them, perpetual.[16]

In the American North opposition to the proclamation came from many sources, including the legislature of Lincoln's home state. Democratic in its majority and containing many Copperheads, on January 7 it resolved:

That the emancipation proclamation of the President of the United States is as unwarrantable in military as in civil law; a gigantic usurpation, at once converting the war, professedly commenced by the administration for the vindication of the authority of the constitution, into the crusade for the sudden, unconditional and violent liberation of 3,000,000 negro slaves; a result which would not only be a total subversion of the Federal Union but a revolution in the social organization of the Southern States, the immediate and remote, the present and far-reaching consequences of which to both races cannot be contemplated without the most dismal foreboding of horror and dismay. The proclamation invites servile insurrection as an element in this emancipation crusade—a means of warfare, the inhumanity and diabolism of which are without example in civilized warfare, and which we denounce, and which the civilized world will denounce, as an uneffaceable disgrace to the American people.[17]

Lincoln in his annual message to the Congress had suggested "the organization of banking associations . . . under a general act of Congress." Six weeks later, viewing the wartime difficulties of raising money, he urged:

In order to raise money by way of loans most easily and cheaply, it is clearly necessary to give every possible support to the public credit. To that end, a uniform currency, in which taxes, subscriptions to loans, and all other ordinary public dues, as well as all private dues, may be paid, is almost if not quite indispensable. Such a currency can be furnished by banking associations, organized under a general act of Congress, as suggested in my message at the beginning of the present session. The securing of this circulation by the pledge of United States bonds, as therein suggested, would still further facilitate loans, by increasing the present and causing a future demand for such bonds.

In view of the actual financial embarrassments of the Government, and of the greater embarrassments sure to come if the necessary means of relief be not afforded, I feel that I should not perform my duty by a simple announcement of my approval of the joint resolution which proposes relief only by increasing circulation, without expressing my earnest desire that measures, such in substance as those I have just referred to, may receive the early sanction of Congress.

By such measures, in my opinion, will payment be most certainly secured, not only to the army and navy, but to all honest creditors of the Government, and satisfactory provision made for future demands on the Treasury.[18]

A week later Senator John Sherman of Ohio, identified with finance throughout his forty-year congressional career, introduced a bill "to provide a uniform national currency." The issues of a national bank and a national currency had been bitterly debated in the age of Andrew Jackson. Lincoln as a Clay Whig had vigorously, though unsuccessfully, favored a national bank. Proponents of state banking and states' rights forcefully resisted nationalization.

Jacob Collamer, the Republican senator from Vermont who had headed the delegation to ask Lincoln to dismiss Seward from the cabinet, led the Senate opposition to the banking bill. On February 11, 1863, he dismissed the need to establish a national banking system. His remarks included a thinly veiled reference to Lincoln's frequent justifications of measures on the ground of wartime necessity:

> In the first place, I would say that I do not regard this as a measure in any respect connected with the war. It is not a war measure. I am the more willing to put it in that light from this consideration: I have observed that almost everything that is asked for, especially if it is asked for with any degree of pertinacity, is put upon that ground; it is either a military necessity or a political necessity, or you cannot keep the Union together without it, or something of that kind by which we are appealed to let our conscience and our discernment go, and obey the dictates pressed upon us. I do not view this as of that character. I take it that this war will come to some end within the course of a year or so—not exceeding two years at most. It is not necessary for me now to predict what will be the form of that termination. I do not desire to make preparations for its continuing much longer than that, at any rate not at present. . . . I think that is the expression contained in his report. I will not trouble the Senate with reading the words; I have stated the substance. I believe he is correct in that. I have no occasion to take issue on that point. Then, if it is a thing from which we are to expect no practical effect for this year, and probably very little for another year afterward, we cannot call this a present war measure. If it be anything connected with the war, it is for a war to be continued some four, five, six, or ten years hence, to which view, I take it, we will not at present accede.
>
> I know it is not very easy for men who reside and have been brought up and educated in different sections of our country to understand the minute business relations of other distant sections. I suppose it is difficult to make a man at the West understand how it is in New England that all the ordinary affairs and business of the people are interwoven with the banks. The connection of the banks enters into all the filaments of our business; it is the warp and woof of it. Every little manufacturing village has its bank; large numbers of the owners of the various factories are also

stock holders in the bank; that bank counting-room is the place where the business of the factory is done, where all its family affairs, where all the business of the different mechanics and little tradesmen is done through the bank. Young men setting up in business have fathers out on farms who indorse for them. What will be the effect of this scheme now, to say nothing about the bank, exercising no care or concern about the bank—that is not the effect that we are to contemplate; but what is the result that will be produced on the condition of society by the winding up these banks, by undergoing this great process of transition which the bill demands? If we pass this bill, it lays the foundation for passing the next bill that comes up before us, that is the bill for raising money, in which is inserted a tax of two per cent. [O]n the circulation of the State banks, with a view to effect this object, and that must pass if this does; and if this does not pass, I take it that will not, unless it receives large modifications.[19]

Rightly predicting it would take two years to organize such a system, Collamer declared that not much could be expected for perhaps that long. A spokesman for eastern state-chartered banks, he correctly predicted the eventual termination of state bank money.

Senators were almost evenly divided; eastern members in particular saw little advantage in the proposal. Sherman and Secretary Chase visited wavering Rhode Island senator Henry B. Anthony. They persuaded him to vote for the measure. The next day it passed 23 to 21; without his affirmative vote the Senate would have deadlocked. Eight days later the House approved the bill 78 to 64, three Democrats joining the majority, twenty Republicans joining the minority. So narrowly begun, the national banking system lasted until the Federal Reserve system came into being.[20]

The divisive question of who held authority to suspend habeas corpus entered into its third legislative session. For nearly two years Lincoln had been withholding the privilege from thousands of persons. Soon after the session opened, radical Republican leader Thaddeus Stevens of Pennsylvania introduced a bill to validate the arrests and imprisonments Lincoln had made, and to invest him with the authority to continue to suspend habeas corpus during the war's existence. Some members thought it was too late for Congress to enter into a conflict with the president over the issue. Indiana congressman and speaker of the House of Representatives Schuyler Colfax rose to remark: "We have either to vindicate him as now proposed or leave him to be persecuted as soon as he retires from office by those whom he arrested."[21]

Impassioned oratory filled the legislative chambers throughout the session. The virulent Daniel W. Voorhees of Indiana, a leading Democrat who was called "the tall sycamore of the Wabash," assailed Lincoln mercilessly. Speaking on February 18, 1863, Voorhees held forth at length:

> Sir, the bill now before the House has no parallel in the history of this or any other free people. It is entitled "An act to indemnify the President and other persons for suspending the privilege of the writ of habeas corpus, and acts done in pursuance thereof." But it embraces even more than its startling title would indicate. It gives to the Executive and all his subordinates not merely security for crimes committed against the citizen in times past, but confers a license to continue in the future the same unlimited exercise of arbitrary power which has brought disgrace and danger to the country. . . .
>
> Mr. Speaker, on the 24th day of last September the President of the United States, in a few brief lines published in the newspapers, and styled a proclamation, declared that the people of this country were under martial law, and that all civil rights and remedies touching their personal liberties were suspended. The blow was sudden, quick, and radical. It was a piece of the inevitable logic of executive encroachment. . . . [T]his act of the President and his Cabinet is the unblushing assumption of power which has ceased to respect or fear the Constitution or laws which the people have made, and which these servants of the people have sworn to support. It throws aside all disguise, tears off its vail, and displays the horrible features of despotism to American citizens. . . .
>
> It will not be denied on this floor or elsewhere that the suspension of the writ of habeas corpus by proclamation, to which I have alluded, closed the civil courts of this country, from one ocean to the other, against the trial of any one arrested by the order of the President or his subordinates. It gave access to the vaults of the prison, but not to the bar of justice. . . .
>
> Sir, I challenge the worst ages of the most profligate and corrupt despots for a more intolerable picture of personal outrage than is here presented. In prisons, in dungeons, in cells, in solitude and desolation of heart, citizens of this free country are threatened with increased punishment if they

resort to the only possible mode of approaching those in power to obtain information or trial with a view to liberty. . . .

Let those who control the Administration now in power give over their wanderings into dangerous latitudes. Let them hastily retrace their steps, and take their stand within the limits of the law. Let them abandon their impious claim of power outside of the provisions of the Constitution. Let them purge their minds of that madness which dares to treat American citizens as slaves. Let this be done, and public confidence will once more brighten the face of the country, and a new strength will spring up from a sense of public security. . . .[22]

Immediately responding, and evoking applause in the galleries, Samuel G. Daily, delegate from Nebraska Territory, said:

[I]t is told us by gentlemen that it will not do, as is done by the bill under consideration, to indemnify the President for the suspension of the writ of habeas corpus; that it is against the Constitution; that it is against the law; that it is in contravention of the principles of liberty. Let us look at the thing. We have men on this floor who are continually out against the acts of this Administration. Especially do they cry out against the suspension of the writ of habeas corpus. Why, the Constitution itself gives us this privilege. The Constitution gives us the power when it says the privilege of the writ of habeas corpus shall not be suspended unless, in case of rebellion and invasion, the public safety may require it. Is not this a case in which the public safety required it?

What are the facts in the case? The facts in the case are that there is a party in this country and a party in this House which has been continually finding fault with the Administration; which is finding fault with the conduct of the war; which is all the time dissatisfied with the purposes of the war. And yet what do they give us in lieu of these things? While the gentleman from Indiana is crying out against the suspension of the writ of habeas corpus, what does he propose in lieu of it for dealing with those gentlemen who are in sympathy with this rebellion? There is nothing proposed. . . . We may talk of the glories of liberty, but how is liberty to be obtained and liberty sustained? We cannot do it by letting all those who are in sympathy with this rebellion and secession go unpunished.

I declare here that the great fault of the Administration has been, and the great fault of the Administration to-day is, that it has not and does not arrest enough, and has not punished severely enough. We have in this country to-day hundreds and thousands of men who sympathize with this rebellion; and the great mistake the Administration has committed is that it has not gone straight to work, arrested these men, and punished them as they deserve.[23]

Albert G. Riddle, bitter enemy of slavery and Republican from Ohio, rose to speak eloquently in defense of Lincoln. He fended off the Democrats' attacks as well as arguing that the extraordinary circumstances provided the necessary authority to suspend habeas corpus.

In a note in his recollections Riddle observed: "Very early there came to be a difference in the estimate of the President, his policy, capacity and intentions, between the distant northern public and the leading men of the two Houses, and he soon became the theme of criticism, reflection, reproach, and condemnation on the part of these gentlemen. . . . To such extent did this condemnation reach, that, at the end of the Thirty-seventh Congress, there were in the House but two men, capable of being heard, who openly and everywhere defended him—Mr. Arnold of Illinois, and Mr. Riddle of Ohio."[24]

Not until the day before adjournment did Congress pass the bill to suspend habeas corpus; the House voted 99 to 45. The Senate passed the bill without a record of the vote. Thirty-six Democrats united in entering a protest in the *Journal.* They objected to giving the president the congressional power to suspend, without geographical limits, the privilege of habeas corpus and to validate arrests and imprisonments not warranted by the Constitution.

The Militia Act of July 1862 had authorized the president to call forth the militia of the states for nine months, in contrast to the ninety-day period of service employed in his proclamation of April 1861. Within a short while Congress and the president found even the 1862 act inadequate to the imperious demands of the war. Volunteers and state militia had not raised enough numbers, and efforts to impose a draft under the act had provoked resistance. A national army serving for long terms seemed dictated by circumstances.

In an exchange with Democratic governor Horatio Seymour of New York, who in 1863 proposed that the constitutionality of conscription be judged in the courts, Lincoln replied:

Your communication of the 3rd. Inst. has been received, and attentively considered.

I can not consent to suspend the draft in New-York, as you request, because, among other reasons, *time* is too important.

By the figures you send, which I presume are correct, the twelve Districts represented fall into two classes of eight, and four respectively. The disparity of the quotas for the draft, in these two classes is certainly very striking, being the difference between an average of 2200 in one class, and 4864 in the other. Assuming that the Districts are equal, one to another, in entire population, as required by the plan on which they were made, this disparity is such as to require attention. Much of it, however, I suppose will be accounted for by the fact that so many more persons fit for soldiers, are in the city than are in the country, who have too recently arrived from other parts of the United States and from Europe to be either included in the Census of 1860, or to have voted in 1862. Still, making due allowance for this, I am yet unwilling to stand upon it as an entirely sufficient explanation of the great disparity.

I shall direct the draft to proceed in all the Districts, drawing however, at first, from each of the four Districts, to wit: the second, fourth, sixth, and eighth, only 2200, being the average quota of the other class. After this drawing, these four Districts, and also the seventeenth and twenty ninth, shall be carefully re-enrolled, and, if you please, agents of yours may witness every step of the process. Any deficiency which may appear by the new enrollment will be supplied by a special draft for that object, allowing due credit for volunteers who may be obtained from these Districts respectively, during the interval. And at all points, so far as consistent, with practical convenience, due credits will be given for volunteers; and your Excellency shall be notified of the time fixed for commencing a draft in each District.

I do not object to abide a decision of the United States Supreme Court, or of the judges thereof, on the constitutionality of the draft law. In fact, I should be willing to facilitate the obtaining of it; but I can not consent to lose the *time* while it is being obtained. We are contending with an enemy who, as I understand, drives every able bodied man he can reach, into his ranks, very much as a butcher drives bullocks into a slaughter-pen. No time is wasted, no argument is used. This produces an army which will soon turn upon our now victorious soldiers already in the field, if they shall not be sustained by recruits, as they should be. It produces an army with a rapidity not to be matched on our side, if we first waste time to re-experiment with the volunteer system, already deemed by congress, and palpably, in fact, so far exhausted, as to be inadequate; and then more time, to obtain a court decision, as to whether a law is constitutional, which requires a part of those not now in the service, to go to the aid of those who are already in it; and still more time, to determine with absolute certainty, that we get those, who are to go, in the precisely legal proportion, to those who are not to go.

My purpose is to be, in my action, just and constitutional; and yet practical, in performing the important duty, with which I am charged, of maintaining the unity, and the free principles of our common country.[25]

Henry Wilson, chairman of the Senate Committee on Military Affairs, possessed vast energy and dedication to winning the war. He recognized the need: "Volunteers we cannot obtain, and everything forbids that we should resort to the temporary expedient of calling out the militia." On February 16, 1863, he spoke to the Senate on behalf of a bill to draft soldiers into the national forces. Urging resort to conscription for the first time in the nation's history, he said:

If we accept peace, disunion, death, then we may speedily summon home again our armies; if we accept war, until the flag of the Republic waves over every foot of our united country, then we must see to it that the ranks of our armies, broken by toil, disease, and death, are filled again with the health and vigor of life. . . .

The Constitution of the United States confers upon Congress the absolute and complete power "to raise and support armies." . . .

Sir, this grant to Congress of power "to raise and support armies" carries with it the right to do it by voluntary enlistment or by compulsory process. If men cannot be raised by voluntary enlistment then the Government must raise men by involuntary means, or the power to raise and support armies for the public defense is a nullity. . . .

[T]he Committee of Military Affairs have reported this bill to enroll and draft the arms-bearing population of the country. Believing, too, with the same illustrious soldier and statesman, "that the conservation of a State is a duty paramount to all others," that "the Commonwealth has a right to the service of its citizens," we have framed this bill so as to comprehend the entire arms-bearing population between the ages of eighteen and forty-five. . . .

The passage of this great measure will clothe the President with ample authority to summon forth the sons of the Republic to the performance of the high and sacred duty of saving their country, now menaced, and the periled cause of civilization and freedom in America. . . .

I am confident the enactment of this bill, embodying so many provisions required by the exigencies of the public service, will weapon the hands of the nation, fire the drooping hearts of the people, thrill the wasting ranks of our legions in the field, carry dismay into the councils of treason, and give assurance to the nations that the American people have the sublime virtue of heroic constancy and endurance that will assure the unity and indivisibility of the Republic of the United States.[26]

The Senate promptly approved the proposal and dispatched it to the House. There the Democrats rose in anger against transforming the state militia system into a conscripted national army. Pennsylvania's Charles J. Biddle in fiery rhetoric attacked the bill with its enlarged powers conferred on the president:

This is part of a series of measures which, to my mind, seem materially to alter the structure of the Government under which we live. The bill to transfer to the President, without limitation of time or place, our power over the writ of habeas corpus; the bill of indemnity which, to use the words of the Senate's amendment, secures for all wrongs or trespasses committed by any officer of the Government full immunity if he pleads in the courts of justice the order of the President, and which also deprives State courts of their jurisdiction in such cases; the bank bill, which puts the purse strings in the same hands with the sword—these bills, to my mind, couple themselves with this bill, and they seem to me, taken together, to change the whole framework of this Government, and instead of the constitutional Government which was originally so carefully devised for this country, they leave us a system which does not materially differ, according to any definition I can frame, from the despotism of France or of Russia.

This particular bill, to sum it up in a word, for I shall not continue at any length these general objections, turns the militia of the United States into a regular army. That is its leading feature.

The Executive, empowered, as the very word shows, only to execute known laws, establishes "martial law," that is, "the will of a conqueror," over all the people of the North. I should think that gentlemen on the other side of the House would concur with us very heartily in condemnation of these measures; for I do believe that the trivial, wanton, fantastic, ridiculous acts of arbitrary power committed under this proclamation, did more to defeat many of the candidates of the Republican party in the recent elections than anything else that could be urged against them; yes, even more than their negro policy. But I do not wish to speak as a politician. I feel a personal interest, an interest as a citizen, that things should not go on thus; for I believe it is at the constant risk of lighting up the flame of social revolution around your hearthstones and mine. Let us be warned in time. Have you noted the significant circumstance of men fresh from unjust imprisonment in Federal dungeons being received with high public honors and elevated to high positions?[27]

The Ohio Copperhead Clement L. Vallandigham, on February 23, 1863, at length stoutly opposed not only the conscription bill but also a series of executive encroachments on his concept of constitutional liberty:

Sir, what are the bills which have passed, or are still before the House? The bill to give the President entire control of the currency—the purse—of the country. A tax bill to clothe him with power over the whole property of the country. A bill to put all power in his hands over the personal liberties of the people. A bill to indemnify him, and all under him, for every act of oppression and outrage already consummated. A bill to enable him to suspend the writ of habeas corpus in order to justify or protect him, and every minion of his, in the arrests which he or they may choose to make—arrests, too, for mere opinions' sake. . . .

And, as if that were not enough, a bill is introduced here, to-day, and pressed forward to a vote, with the right of debate, indeed—extorted from you by the minority—but without the right to amend, with no more than the mere privilege of protest—a bill which enables the President to bring under his power, as Commander-in-Chief, every man in the United States between the ages of twenty and forty-five—three millions of men. And, as if not satisfied with that, this bill provides, further, that every other citizen, man, woman, and child, under twenty years of age and over forty-five, including those that may be exempt between these ages, shall be also at the mercy—so far as his personal liberty is concerned—of some miserable "provost marshal" with the rank of a captain of cavalry, who is never to see service in the field; and every congressional district in the United States is to be governed yes, governed—by this petty satrap—this military eunuch—this Baba—and he even may be black—who is to do the bidding of your Sultan, or his Grand Vizier. Sir, you have but one step further to go—give him the symbols of his office—the Turkish bow-string and the sack.

What is it, sir, but a bill to abrogate the Constitution, to repeal all existing laws, to destroy all rights, to strike down the judiciary, and erect upon the ruins of civil and political liberty a stupendous superstructure of despotism. And for what? To enforce law? No, sir. It is admitted now by the legislation of Congress, and by the two proclamations of the President, it is admitted by common consent, that the war is for the abolition of negro slavery, to secure freedom to the black man. You tell me, some of you, I know, that it is so prosecuted because this is the only way to restore the Union; but others openly and candidly confess that the purpose of the prosecution of the war is to abolish slavery. And thus, sir, it is that the freedom of the negro is to be purchased, under this bill, at the sacrifice of every right of the white men of the United States. . . .

The Constitution declares that:

"The enumeration in the Constitution of certain rights shall not be construed to deny or disparage others retained by the people."

And again:

"The powers not delegated to the United States by the Constitution, nor prohibited by it to the States, are reserved to the States respectively or to the people."

And yet, under the monstrous doctrine that in war the Constitution is suspended, and that the President as Commander-in-Chief, not of the military forces only, but of the whole people of the United States, may, under "the war power," do whatever he shall think necessary and proper to be done, in any State or part of any State, however remote from the scene of warfare, every right of the people is violated or threatened, and every power of the States usurped. Their last bulwark, the militia, belonging solely to the States when not called as such into the actual service of the United States, you now deliberately propose, by this bill, to sweep away, and to constitute the President supreme military dictator, with a standing army of three millions and more at his command. And for what purpose are the militia to be thus taken from the power and custody of the States? Sir, the opponents of the Constitution, anticipated all this, and were denounced as raving incendiaries or distempered enthusiasts."

"The Federal Government"—

Said Patrick Henry, in the Virginia Convention,

"squints towards monarchy. Your President may easily become a king."[28]

Despite the heated debate, the House on March 3, the same date of the Indemnity Act, passed the Enrollment or Conscription bill 115-49, all of the nay votes cast by Democrats. Lincoln welcomed the bill by signing it into law.

General William T. Sherman on March 14 wrote to his brother, the senator from Ohio, to say that the measure was not only welcome but also necessary. Writing from his camp before Vicksburg, Sherman enthused:

The Conscript Bill is all even I could ask, it is the first real step toward war. And if Mr. Lincoln will now use the power thus conferred, ignore popular clamor and do as near right as he can, we may at last have an army somewhat approximating the vast undertaking which was begun in utter, blind, willful ignorance of the difficulties and dangers that we were forced to encounter.[29]

Senator John Sherman responded in detail:

I am at length at home with sufficient leisure to think, but still somewhat jaded from a very laborious session. When I went into the Senate I antici-pated quiet and dignified leisure with ample time to read, reflect and study such grave questions of politics as I chose to turn my attention to. Such thus far has not been my experience. The vast and complicated legislature required by war, demands of Senators an amount of labor in committees never before given. The Senate has become a laborious committee where bills are drawn as well as discussed. It has so happened that although a junior yet I have had to carry the most important financial bills, such as the Bank Loan and Tax Bills, subjects full of difficulty and detail. . . .

The laws passed at the last session will be a monument of evil or of good. They cover such vast sums, delegate and regulate such vast powers, and are so far-reaching in their effects, that generations will be affected well or ill by them. These measures are distinguished as much by what were omitted as by what were adopted. The negro was not legislated upon. The laws of confiscation, emancipation, &c., were left precisely upon the basis of previous laws, the proclamations of the President and ultimate decisions of the courts. The arming and employment of negroes is left upon the old law and mainly to the discretion of the President. There was but little speech-making and that mainly to the matter in hand. The Union or rather Republican members made scarcely a political speech in either house. They felt too constantly the pressure of practical measures demanding action. On the whole, the recent Congress may fairly appeal to their constituents for a favorable judgment upon the general aggregate of their acts. For myself, I do not reproach myself with any glaring fault.

I opposed arbitrary arrests, general confiscation, the destruction of State lines and other extreme measures, and thereby have lost the confidence of some of my old friends. On the other hand, I have taken my full share in framing and supporting other great measures that have proved a success, and think I may fairly claim credit for many of the most valuable features of our financial system, which has been wonderfully sustained under enormous expenditure. I can also claim the paternity of the Bank Law yet to be tested by experience, and for the main features of the Conscription Law.[30]

When the Thirty-seventh Congress closed on March 4 it had taken long strides in strengthening Lincoln's authority, in raising an army and money, sanctioning suspension of habeas corpus, and adding a free state to the Union. What was striking, however, was the antipathy in Congress toward the president described by Riddle and corroborated by Thaddeus Stevens.

Richard Henry Dana, remembered for his book *Two Years before the Mast,* was an antislavery Massachusetts lawyer. He successfully argued the administration's case that it had the authority to blockade the Confederate coast. While in Washington for the hearing, on March 9 he wrote to Charles Francis Adams:

As to the politics of Washington, the most striking thing is the absence of personal loyalty to the President. It does not exist. He has no admirers, no enthusiastic supporters, none to bet on his head. If a Republican convention were to be held to-morrow, he would not get the vote of a State. He does not act or talk or feel like the ruler of a great empire in a great crisis. This is felt by all, and has got down through all the layers of society. It has a disastrous effect on all departments and classes of officials, as well as on the public. He seems to me to be fonder of details than of principles, of tithing the mint, anise and cumin of patronage, and personal questions, than of the weightier matters of empire. He likes rather to talk and tell stories with all sorts of persons who come to him for all sorts of purposes than to give his mind to the noble and manly duties of this great post. It is not difficult to detect that this is the feeling of his cabinet. He has a kind of shrewdness and common sense, mother wit, and slipshod, low leveled honesty, that made him a good western jury lawyer. But he is an unutterable calamity to us where he is. Only the army can save us.[31]

CHAPTER TWENTY-ONE

THE SUPREME COURT AND
LINCOLN'S WAR POWERS

As spring beckoned, Lincoln had little to look forward to. If Congress seemed alienated from the president, particularly over his claims to the war power, what was the attitude of the third branch of government? While Congress was concluding its session, the Supreme Court was considering that question, one on which much of Lincoln's presidency rested. His call for militia in 1861, his appropriation of money, his suspension of habeas corpus, his blockade of the Confederate ports, his codification of rules and regulations for the conduct of armies in the field, his emancipation of slaves, and his control over reconstruction—all these executive policies involving the manner in which he ran the war—raised questions of encroachment on the constitutional authority of Congress.

The Supreme Court in early 1863 was still headed by eighty-three-year-old Roger B. Taney, not only the principal author of the Dred Scott decision but also author of *ex parte Merryman,* in which he charged that the president had failed to "take care that the laws be faithfully executed."

By March 1863 the composition of the court had changed. Lincoln in 1862 had appointed three of the sitting justices. Attorney General Edward Bates delayed hearings on a series of cases, called the Prize Cases, involving the constitutionality of Lincoln's proclamation of a blockade, until the appointments had been made. The third of these, in December 1862, was Lincoln's old friend and leader of the Illinois delegation that helped swing the presidential nomination for him, the portly David Davis. The appointments changed the composition of the court from its heavily Democratic and pro-southern character to a more balanced body.

In May and June 1861, before the special session of Congress that validated many of Lincoln's actions, naval cruisers had captured vessels violating the blockade and carrying property belonging to rebels. Owners brought suit to recover their property taken as prize, claiming that the president did not possess authority to proclaim a blockade; nor, they said, did Congress, because the lawmakers had never declared war. The strife was called a rebellion. The cases were brought together before the Supreme Court in the Prize Cases.

Three men figured importantly in the court proceedings. Richard Henry Dana had earlier litigated the case of the *Amy Warwick,* brought into Boston as a prize. An auditor of his Supreme Court argument remembered "that luminous and exquisite presentation of the status which armed the Executive with power to use the methods and process of war to suppress the great rebellion." Anticipating the proceedings, Dana wrote Charles Francis Adams:

> Contemplate, my dear sir, the possibility of a Supreme Court deciding that this blockade is illegal! What a position it would put us in before the world whose commerce we have unlawfully subjected to a cotton famine and domestic dangers and distress for two years! It would end the war, and where it would leave us with neutral powers it is fearful to contemplate! Yet such an event is legally possible,—I do not think it probable, hardly possible, in fact. But last year I think there was danger of such a result, when the blockade was new, and before the three new judges were appointed. The bare contemplation of such a possibility makes us pause in our boastful assertion that our written Constitution is clearly the best adapted to all exigencies, the last, best gift to man.[1]

Justice Robert Grier, a northern Democrat who had concurred in the Dred Scott case and was now a Unionist, possessed an imposing tall, stout body and an ability to write opinions marked by clarity and conciseness. Justice Samuel Nelson was a northern Democrat who had narrowed his opinion in the Dred Scott case to the statement that Scott, not a citizen, could not sue in a federal court. He had favored compromise during the secession crisis and watched with alarm the growth of Lincoln's executive authority.

Dana argued that "the rule of coercion by capture is applied to private property at sea. *If the power with which you are at war has such an interest in its transit, arrival or existence, as to make its capture one of the fair modes of coercion, you may take it. The reason why you may capture it is that it is a justifiable mode of coercing the power with which you are at war. The fact which makes it a justifiable mode of coercing that power is that the owner is residing under his jurisdiction and control. . . .* In case of civil war, the President may, in the absence of an applicable act of Congress, meet the war by the exercise of belligerent maritime capture. . . . Since the capture, Congress has recognized the validity of these acts of the President."[2]

Justice Grier, a Democrat who acknowledged he had been won over to the administration side by Dana's eloquent argument, spoke for the majority:

That a blockade *de facto* actually existed, and was formally declared and notified, by the President the 27th and 30th of April, 1861, is an admitted fact in these cases.

That the President, as the Executive Chief of the Government and Commander-in-chief of the Army and Navy, was the proper person to make such notification, has not been, and cannot be disputed.

The right of prize and capture has its origin in the "*jus belli*," and is governed and, adjudged under the law of nations. To legitimate the capture of a neutral vessel or property on the high seas, a war must exist *de facto,* and the neutral must have a knowledge or notice of the intention of one of the parties belligerent to use this mode of coercion against a port, city, or territory, in possession of the other.

Let us enquire whether, at the time this blockade was instituted, a state of war existed which would justify a resort to these means of subduing the hostile force.

War has been well defined to be, "That state, in which a nation prosecutes its right by force."

The parties belligerent in a public war are independent nations. But it is not necessary to constitute war, that both parties should be acknowledged as independent nations or sovereign States. A war may exist where one of the belligerents, claims sovereign rights as against the other.

Insurrection against a government may or may not culminate in an organized rebellion, but a civil war always begins by insurrection against the lawful authority of the Government. A civil war is never solemnly declared; it becomes such by its accidents—the number, power, and organization of the persons who originate and carry it on. When the party in rebellion occupy and hold in a hostile manner a certain portion of territory; have declared their independence; have cast off their allegiance; have organized armies; have commenced hostilities against their former sovereign, the world acknowledges them as belligerents and the contest a *war*. *They* claim to be in arms to establish their liberty and independence, in order to become a sovereign State, while the sovereign party treats them as insurgents and rebels who owe allegiance, and who should be punished with death for their treason.

The laws of war, as established among nations, have their foundation in reason, and all tend to mitigate the cruelties and misery produced by the scourge of war. Hence the parties to a civil war usually concede to each other belligerent rights. They exchange prisoners, and adopt the other courtesies and rules common to public or national wars.

"A civil war," says Vattel, "breaks the bands of society and government, or at least suspends their force and effect; it produces in the nation two independent parties, who consider each other as enemies, and acknowledge no common judge. Those two parties, therefore, must necessarily be considered as constituting, at least for a time, two separate bodies, two distinct societies. Having no common superior to judge between them, they stand in precisely the same predicament as two nations who engage in a contest and have recourse to arms.

"This being the case, it is very evident that the common laws of war—those maxims of humanity, moderation, and honor—ought to be observed by both parties in every civil war. Should the sovereign conceive he has a right to hang up his prisoners as rebels, the opposite party will make reprisals, &c., &c.; the war will become cruel, horrible, and every day more destructive to the nation."

As a civil war is never publicly proclaimed, *eo nomine* against insurgents, its actual existence is a fact in our domestic history which the Court is bound to notice and to know.

The true test of its existence, as found in the writing of the sages of the common law, may be thus summarily stated: "When the regular course of justice is interrupted by revolt, rebellion, or insurrection, so that the Courts of Justice cannot be kept open, *civil war* exists and hostilities may be prosecuted on the same footing as if those opposing the Government were foreign enemies invading the land."

By the Constitution, Congress alone has the power to declare a national or foreign war. It cannot declare war against a State, or any number of States, by virtue of any clause in the Constitution. The Constitution confers on the President the whole Executive power. He is bound to take care that the laws be faithfully executed. He is Commander-in-chief of the Army and Navy of the United States, and of the militia of the several States when called into the actual service of the United States. He has no power to initiate or declare a war either against a foreign nation or a domestic State. But by the Acts of Congress of February 28th, 1795, and 3d of March, 1807, he is authorized to called out the militia and use the military and naval forces of the United States in case of invasion by foreign nations, and to suppress insurrection against the government of a State or of the United States. . . .

This greatest of civil wars was not gradually developed by popular commotion, tumultuous assemblies, or local unorganized insurrection. However long may have been its previous conception, it nevertheless sprung forth suddenly from the parent brain, a Minerva in the fully panoply of *war*. The President was bound to meet it in the shape it presented itself, without waiting for Congress to baptize it with a name; and no name given to it by him or them could change the fact.

It is not the less a civil war, with belligerent parties in hostile array, because it may be called an "insurrection" by one side, and the insurgents be considered as rebels or traitors. It is not necessary that the independence of the revolted province or State be acknowledged in order to constitute it a party belligerent in a war according to the law of nations. Foreign nations acknowledge it as war by a declaration of neutrality. The condition of neutrality cannot exist unless there be two belligerent parties. In the case of the *Santissima Trinidad,* (7 Wheaton, 337,) this Court say: "The Government of the United States has recognized the existence of a civil war between Spain and her colonies, and has avowed her determination to remain neutral between the parties. Each party is therefore deemed by us a belligerent nation, having, so far as concerns us, the sovereign rights of war." (See also 3 Binn., 252.)

As soon as the news of the attack on Fort Sumter, and the organization of a government by the seceding States, assuming to act as belligerents, could become known in Europe, to wit, on the 13th of May, 1861, the Queen of England issued her proclamation of neutrality, "recognizing hostilities as existing between the Government of the United States of America and *certain States* styling themselves the Confederate States of America." This was immediately followed by similar declarations or silent acquiescence by other nations.

After such an official recognition by the sovereign, a citizen of a foreign State is estopped to deny the existence of a war with all its consequences as regards neutrals.[3]

Justice Nelson in dissent said:

In the case of a rebellion or resistance of a portion of the people of a country against the established government, there is no doubt, if in its progress and enlargement the government thus sought to be overthrown sees fit, it may by the competent power recognize or declare the existence of a state of civil war, which will draw after it all the consequences and rights of war between the contending parties as in the case of a public war. Mr. Wheaton observes, speaking of civil war, "But the general usage of nations regards such a war as entitling both the contending parties to all the rights of war as against each other, and even as respects neutral nations." It is not to be denied, therefore, that if a civil war existed between that portion of the people in organized insurrection to overthrow this Government at the time this vessel and cargo were seized, and if she was guilty of a violation of the blockade, she would be lawful prize of war. But before this insurrection against the established Government can be dealt with on the footing of a civil war, within the meaning of the law of nations and the Constitution of the United States, and which will draw after it belligerent rights, it must be recognized or declared by the war-making power of the Government. No power short of this can change the legal status of the Government or the relations of its citizens from that of peace to a state of war, or bring into existence all those duties and obligations of neutral third parties growing out of a state of war. . . .

So the war carried on by the President against the insurrectionary districts in the Southern States, as in the case of the King of Great Britain in the American Revolution, was a personal war against those in rebellion, and with encouragement and support of loyal citizens with a view to their co-operation and aid in suppressing the insurgents, with this difference, as the war-making power belonged to the King, he might have recognized or declared the war at the beginning to be a civil war which would draw after it all the rights of a belligerent, but in the case of the President no such power existed: the war therefore from necessity was a personal war, until Congress assembled and acted upon this state of things. . . .

Congress assembled on the call for an extra session the 4th of July, 1861, and among the first acts passed was one in which the President was authorized by proclamation to interdict all trade and intercourse between all the inhabitants of States in insurrection and the rest of the United States, subjecting vessel and cargo to capture and condemnation as prize, and also to direct the capture of any ship or vessel belonging in whole or in part to any inhabitant of a State whose inhabitants are declared by the proclamation to be in a state of insurrection, found at sea or in any part of the rest of the United States. Act of Congress of 13th of July, 1861, secs. 5, 6. The 4th section also authorized the President to close any port in a Collection District obstructed so that the revenue could not be collected and provided for the capture and condemnation of any vessel attempting to enter. . . .

This Act of Congress, we think, recognized a state of civil war between the Government and the Confederate States, and made it territorial. . . .

Upon the whole, after the most careful consideration of this case which the pressure of other duties has admitted, I am compelled to the conclusion that no civil war existed between this Government and the States in insurrection till recognized by the Act of Congress 13th of July, 1861; that the President does not possess the power under the Constitution to declare war or recognize its existence within the meaning of the law of nations, which carries with it belligerent rights, and thus change the country and all its citizens from a state of peace to a state of war; that this power belongs exclusively to the Congress of the United States, and, consequently, that the President had no power to set on foot a blockade under the law of nations, and that the capture of the vessel and cargo in this case, and in all cases before us in which the capture occurred before the 13th of July, 1861, for breach of blockade, or as enemies' property, are illegal and void, and that the decrees of condemnation should be reversed and the vessel and cargo restored.[4]

The high court divided five to four; the three justices appointed by Lincoln were joined by two he had not appointed, Grier and James Wayne, a seventy-one-year-old Georgian who sided with the Union. Taney of course joined in dissent. The decision failed to curtail Lincoln's conduct of the war. He continued to wield broad executive authority, prevailing over Congress's effort to take control over Reconstruction. Not until after his death would the Supreme Court strike down some of his actions.

What the Court did decide was:

That in case of domestic war, the Government of the United States may, at its option, use the powers and rights, known to the international laws of war as blockade, and capture of enemy's property at sea.

That to determine whether property found at sea is "enemy's property," within the meaning of the law of Prize, the same tests may be applied in domestic as in international wars.

One of these tests is that the owner of the property so found has his domicile and residence in a place of which the enemy (whether rebel or foreign enemy) has a certain kind and degree of possession, with the exercise of a *de facto* jurisdiction.

Richmond, Virginia, was, at the time of the capture and condemnation of those vessels, under such possession and control of the enemy as to render it indisputably "enemy's territory" within the strictest definitions known to the laws of war.[5]

The *New York Times* saw another dimension to the Prize Cases. It charged that from 1861 "Copperheads had used the civil courts to embarrass and weaken the Government. . . . [T]he hope of the 'Copperheads' to cast a vast burden upon the Treasury, by annulling the blockade proclaimed by the President before the meeting of Congress, is dashed."[6] The Times editorial argued:

Among the many methods employed to embarrass and weaken the Government, appealing to the civil Courts has figured largely. It began at the very opening of the conflict, in the memorable applications to Chief Justice TANEY for the discharge of MERRIMAN and the other bridge-burners . . . We censured the Journal's language, at the time, as involving an utterly baseless and fatal heresy. It however was fast becoming the predominant copperhead idea. The resolutions of the late Copperhead Convention in Connecticut, which nominated SEYMOUR for Governor, were mainly shaped by it. It is well, just at this time, that the Supreme Court has found occasion to reaffirm the true principle. Said Justice GRIER in rendering the decision of the Court, in the blockade question, "We are of opinion that the President has a right, *jure belli,* to proclaim a blockade, which neutrals were bound to observe. The destruction of property is a consequence of war. Money, wealth, the product of agriculture, are said to be the sinews of war. The laws of nations authorize the cutting of these sinews by capturing property on the high seas. Under our very peculiar Constitution, citizens *not only owe allegiance to the United States,* but to the States in which we live." This principle of concurrent allegiance crushes at once the so-called right of secession. It is the corner-stone of loyalty, and we are glad to see it again solemnly authenticated.

It will also be observed that the Court in the language just quoted, distinctly recognizes the *just belli,* the war power, against which so much passionate declamation has been expended. It is said that the President may exert this power by proclamation, and that all the sinews of war may thus be cut. It is difficult to see why the very broad language of the Court in respect to the Proclamation of the blockade does not involve the constitutional validity of the Proclamation against slave property.

Again, it is said in another part of the decision, that "Congress had approved and ratified the acts of the President, *as if they were legally done previous to their legalization.*" This is recognized as confirming the original validity of the blockade proclamation.[7]

The war ground on, entering its third year in the spring of 1863. Lincoln would use his war powers again.

CHAPTER TWENTY-TWO

HOOKER AND CHANCELLORSVILLE

After the disastrous "mud march" and the failures of Burnside at Fredericksburg, the Army of the Potomac passed into the hands of "Fighting Joe" Hooker, an outspoken critic of his predecessor and equipped with a reputation for popularity among his men and an ability to command. Twenty-ninth in the fifty-member class of 1837 at the United States Military Academy, he had displayed his skill as a division commander in 1862 during McClellan's Peninsula Campaign. Rosy-cheeked and well-proportioned, erect in the saddle of his white horse, Hooker looked the part of a soldier who, when asked what the highest form of enjoyment was, replied, "Campaigning in an enemy's country."

Recognizing that the appointment was controversial, Lincoln wrote Hooker a letter remarkable for its candor and ambivalence:

> General:—I have placed you at the head of the Army of the Potomac. Of course I have done this upon what appear to me to be sufficient reasons, and yet I think it best for you to know that there are some things in regard to which I am not quite satisfied with you. I believe you to be a brave and skilful soldier, which of course I like. I also believe you do not mix politics with your profession, in which you are right. You have confidence in yourself, which is a valuable if not an indispensable quality. You are ambitious, which within reasonable bounds does good rather than harm; but I think that during General Burnside's command of the army you have taken counsel of your ambition and thwarted him as much as you could, in which you did a great wrong to the country and to a most meritorious and honorable brother officer. I have heard, in such a way as to believe it, of your recently

saying that both the army and the government needed a dictator. Of course it was not for this, but in spite of it, that I have given you the command. Only those generals who gain successes can set up dictators. What I now ask of you is military success, and I will risk the dictatorship. The government will support you to the utmost of its ability, which is neither more nor less than it has done and will do for all commanders. I much fear that the spirit that you have aided to infuse into the army, of criticizing their commander and withholding confidence from him, will now turn upon you. I shall assist you as far as I can to put it down. Neither you nor Napoleon, if he were alive again, could get any good out of an army while such a spirit prevails in it. And now beware of rashness. Beware of rashness, but with energy and sleepless vigilance go forward and give us victories.[1]

Taking charge of an army demoralized by Burnside's reverses, afflicted with soldiers' opposition to the Emancipation Proclamation, and weakened by daily desertions in the hundreds, Hooker reorganized his army and worked to restore morale.

On April 5, accompanied by his wife and son Tad and the journalist Noah Brooks, Lincoln arrived at Hooker's camp. There were grand reviews, hospital visits, and many discussions. Excessively proud of his troops, Hooker boasted he had the finest army on the planet. Brooks wrote: "I recall with sadness the easy confidence and nonchalance which Hooker showed in all his conversations with the President and his little party. The general seemed to regard the whole business of command as if it were a larger sort of picnic. . . . One of his most frequent expressions when talking with the President was, 'When I get to Richmond,' or 'After we have taken Richmond,' etc. The president, noting this, said to me confidentially and with a sigh: 'That is the most depressing thing about Hooker. It seems to me that he is overconfident.'" Hooker one night read Lincoln's appointment letter to Brooks. After reading it aloud, he remarked, "That is just such a letter as a father might write to his son. It is a beautiful letter, and, although I think he was harder on me than I deserved, I will say I love the man who wrote it." Before departing, Lincoln said to Hooker and his senior corps commander, "Gentlemen, in your next battle *put in all your men.*"[2]

By mid-April Hooker was able to communicate his plan of operations to the president: "I am apprehensive that he [the enemy] will retire from before me the moment I should succeed in crossing the river, and over the shortest line to Richmond, and thus escape being seriously crippled."[3]

On the day that Hooker wrote, Lincoln penned a memorandum disclosing his own strategic concepts:

> My opinion is that, now, with the enemy directly ahead of us, there is *no* eligible route for us into Richmond; and consequently a question of preference between the Rappahannock route and the James River route is a contest about nothing. Hence our prime object is the enemy's army in front of us, and is not with or about Richmond at all, unless it be incidental to the main object.
>
> What then? The two armies are face to face with a narrow river between them. Our communications are shorter and safer than are those of the enemy. For this reason we can, with equal powers, fret him more than he can us. I do not think that by raids towards Washington he can derange the Army of the Potomac at all. He has no distant operations which can call any of the Army of the Potomac away; we have such operations which may call him away, at least in part. While he remains intact, I do not think we should take the disadvantage of attacking him in his intrenchments; but we should continually harass and menace him, so that he shall have no leisure nor safety in sending away detachments. If he weakens himself, then pitch into him.[4]

Outnumbering Lee by two to one, Hooker began his move, writing on April 27 to Lincoln:

> I fully appreciate the anxiety weighing upon your mind, and hasten to relieve you from so much of it as lies in my power. You know that nothing would give me more pleasure than to keep you fully advised of every movement and every intended movement made and to be made by this Army, as is my duty to do. But the country is so full of traitors, and there are so many whose desire it is to see this Army meet with no success, that it almost makes me tremble to disclose a thing concerning it to anyone except yourself. Not that there are not many as true to the cause as yourself; but all have friends and their fidelity I am not so sure of. The following is what I have done and what I propose to do. . . .
>
> The only element which gives me apprehension with regard to the success of this plan is the weather. How much will depend upon it. The details will readily suggest themselves to you.

After crossing the Rapidan I can hear from the column descending the rivers, by the troops now at Bank's Ford, where I shall throw over two bridges as soon as the development of the battle will permit.

I write in great haste as I leave for Kelley's Ford tomorrow morning and am busy in making the necessary preparations.

I send you the Richmond papers last received. The remarkable feature in them is that they write from Fredericksburg that in their opinion we are quitting this line.[5]

Lincoln responded the next day:

The maps, newspapers, and letter of yesterday are received, for all which I thank you. While I am anxious, please do not suppose I am impatient, or waste a moment's thought on me, to your own hindrance, or discomfort.[6]

Hooker's initial operation was nearly a stunning success. His army probed west of Fredericksburg, crossed the Rappahannock and the Rapidan rivers and began moving east toward Lee's army. The armies under Hooker and Lee clashed at Chancellorsville, Virginia, on May 2. The next morning at 8:50 Lincoln learned from Hooker's chief of staff, General Butterfield, "a battle is in progress." Lincoln anxiously responded, "Where is Gen. Hooker? Where is Sedgwick? [W]here is Stoneman?"

The battle unfolded over nearly three days and covered more than twenty-five square miles. Lee divided his forces to meet Hooker and then divided them again to drive Hooker back across the rivers. Hooker himself was strangely inert while Lee's forces hammered away at the Union army. At midnight May 4–5 Hooker took counsel of his commanders, with the result that he ordered a retreat. On May 7 Lincoln wrote to Hooker:

The recent movement of your army is ended without effecting its object, except perhaps some important breakings of the enemies communications. What next? If possible I would be very glad of another movement early enough to give us some benefit from the fact of the enemies communications being broken, but neither for this reason or any other, do I wish anything done in desperation or rashness. An early movement would also help to supersede the bad moral effect of the recent one, which is sure to be considerably injurious. Have you already in your mind a plan wholly, or partially formed? If you have, prosecute it without interference from me.

If you have not, please inform me, so that I, incompetent as I may be, can try [to] assist in the formation of some plan for the Army.[7]

Hooker replied:

I have the honor to acknowledge your communication of this date, and in answer to state that I do not deem it expedient to suspend operations on this line from the reverse we have experienced in endeavoring to extricate the army from its present position. If in the first effort we failed it was not from want of strength or conduct of the small number of the troops actually engaged, but from a cause which could not be foreseen, and could not be provided against. After its occurrence the chances of success were so much lessened that I felt another plan might be adopted in place of that we were engaged in, which would be more certain in its results. At all events, a failure would not involve disaster, while in the other case it was certain to follow the absence of success. I may add that this consideration almost wholly determined me in ordering the army to return to its old camp.

As to the best time for renewing our advance upon the enemy, I can only decide after an opportunity has been afforded to learn the feeling of the troops. They should not be discouraged or depressed, for it is no fault of theirs—if I may except one Corps—that our last efforts were not crowned with glorious victory. I suppose details are not wanted of me at this time.

I have decided in my own mind the plan to be adopted in our next effort,—if it should be your wish to have one made. It has this to recommend it—It will be one in which the operations of all the Corps, unless it be a part of the Cavalry, will be within my personal supervision.[8]

On May 13 Hooker wrote:

My movements have been a little delayed by the withdrawal of many of the two-years' and nine-months' regiments, and those whose time is not already up it will be expedient to leave on this side of the river. This reduction imposes upon me the necessity of partial reorganization. My marching force of infantry is cut down to about 80,000, while I have artillery for an army of more than double that number. It has always been out of proportion, considering the character of the country we have to campaign in, and I shall be more efficient by leaving at least one-half of it in depot. In addition, Stoneman's cavalry returned to camp day before

Yesterday, and will require a day or two more to be in readiness to resume operations.

I know that you are impatient, and I know that I am, but my impatience must not be indulged at the expense of dearest interests.

I am informed that the bulk of Longstreet's force is in Richmond. With the facilities at hand, he can readily transfer it to Lee's army, and no doubt will do so if Lee should fight and fall back, as he will try to do.

The enemy's camps are reported to me as being more numerous than before our last movement, but of this I have no positive information. They probably have about the same number of troops as before the last battle, but with these and Longstreet's they are much my superior, besides having the advantage of acting on the defensive, which, in this country, can scarcely be estimated.

I hear nothing of Peck's movements and of the force at West Point, which is too small to be of much importance in the general movement. If it is expected that Peck will be able to keep Longstreet's force in and about Richmond, I should be informed of it, and if not, a reserve infantry force of 25,000 should be placed at my disposal in this vicinity. I merely state this for your information, not that I know even that you have such a force, or, if you have, that you would be disposed to make use of it in this way, I only desire that you should be informed of my views. In my opinion, the major part of the troops on the Upper Potomac, in and around Washington and Baltimore, are out of position, and if great results are expected from the approaching movement, every man and vessel at the disposal of the Government should be assigned their posts. I hope to be able to commence my movement to-morrow, but this must not be spoken of to any one.[9]

A week later, Lincoln replied yet again to Hooker:

When I wrote you on the 7th. I had an impression that possibly, by an early movement, you could get some advantage from the supposed facts that the enemies communications, were disturbed and that he was somewhat deranged in position. That idea has now passed away, the enemy having re-established his communications, regained his positions and actually received re-inforcements. It does not now appear probable to me that you can gain any thing by an early renewal of the attempt to cross the Rappahannock. I therefore shall not complain, if you do no more, for a time, than to keep the enemy at bay, and out of other mischief, by menaces and occasional cavalry raids, if practicable; and to put your own army in good condition again. Still, if in your own clear judgment, you can renew the attack successfully, I do not mean to restrain you, Bearing upon this last point, I must tell you I have some painful intimations that some of your corps and Division Commanders are not giving you their entire confidence. This would be ruinous, if true; and you should therefore, first of all, ascertain the real facts beyond all possibility of doubt.[10]

With new information that Lee might be moving north toward Maryland and possibly Pennsylvania, Hooker on June 5 informed the president:

Yesterday morning appearances indicated that during the night the Enemy had broken up a few of his camps and abandoned them. These changes were observed on the right of his line in the vicinity of Hamilton Crossing. So far as I was enabled to judge from all my means of information it was impossible for me to determine satisfactorily whether this movement had been merely a change of camps—the Enemy had moved in the direction of Richmond, or up the river, but taken in connection with the fact that some deserters came in from the divisions of [John B.] Hood and [George] Pickett I conclude that those divisions had been brought to the front from their late positions at Gordonsville and Taylorville and that this could be for no other purpose but to enable the Enemy to move up the river with a view to the execution of a movement similar to that of Lee's last year. He must either have it in mind to cross the Upper Potomac or to throw his army between mine and Washington. In case I am correct in my conjecture, to accomplish either he must have been greatly reinforced and, if making this movement, the fair presumption is that he has been by the troops from Charleston. . . .

In the event the Enemy should move, as I almost anticipate he will[,] the head of his column will probably be headed towards the Potomac via Gordonsville or Culpepper while the rear will rest on Fredericksburg. After giving the subject my best reflections I am of opinion that it is my duty to pitch into his rear although in so doing the head of his column may reach Warrenton before I can return. Will it be within the spirit of my instructions to do so? In view of these contemplated movements of the Enemy I cannot too forcibly impress upon the mind of His Excellency The President the necessity of having one commander for all of the troops whose operations can have influence on those of Lee's army. Under the present system all independent commanders are in ignorance of the movements of the others at least such is my situation.

I trust that I may not be considered in the way to this arrangement as it is a position I do not desire and only suggest it as I feel the necessity for concerted as well as vigorous action. It is necessary for me to say this much that my motive may not be misunderstood.[11]

Wary that Lee might seize this chance to invade the North, Lincoln on June 5 with colorful language presented the general with "but one idea":

Yours of to-day was received an hour ago. So much of professional military skill is requisite to answer it, that I have turned the task over to Gen. Halleck. He promises to perform it with his utmost care. I have but one idea which I think worth suggesting to you, and that is in case you find Lee coming to the North of the Rappahannock, I would by no means cross to the South of it. If he should leave a rear force at Fredericksburg, tempting you to fall upon it, it would fight in intrenchments, and have you at disadvantage, and so, man for man, worst you at that point, while his main force would in some way be getting an advantage of you Northward. In one word, I would not take any risk of being entangled upon the river, like an ox jumped half over a fence, and liable to be torn by dogs, front and rear, without a fair chance to gore one way or kick the other. If Lee would come to my side of the river, I would keep on the same side & fight him, or act on the defence, according as might be my estimate of his strength relatively to my own. But these are mere suggestions which I desire to be controlled by the judgment of yourself and Gen. Halleck.[12]

Five days later Hooker told Lincoln:

I shall leave the cavalry . . . where they are, near Bealeton, with instructions to resist the passage of the river by the enemy's forces. If to effect this he should bring up a considerable force of infantry, that will so much weaken him in my front that I have good reason to believe that I can throw a sufficient force over the river to compel the enemy to abandon his present position. If it should be the intention to send a heavy column of infantry to accompany the cavalry on the proposed raid, he can leave nothing behind to interpose any serious obstacle to my rapid advance on Richmond. I am not satisfied of his intention in this respect, but from certain movements in their corps I cannot regard it as altogether improbable. If it should be found to be the case, will it not promote the true interest of the cause for me to march to Richmond at once?[13]

To this Lincoln responded with excellent military advice, not to march to Richmond but instead to find Lee's army and destroy it. The next day Halleck told Hooker, "I agree with him."[14]

During many of these stressful days Lincoln kept a virtually round-the-clock vigil. Telegrams flew back and forth at late hours. At 8:30 p.m. on June 15 Lincoln wired Hooker:

> The facts are now known here that Winchester and Martinsburg were both besieged yesterday; the troops from Martinsburg have got into Harper's Ferry without loss; those from Winchester, are also in, having lost, in killed, wounded and missing, about one third of their number. Of course the enemy holds both places; and I think the report is authentic that he is crossing the Potomac at Williamsburg. We have not heard of his yet appearing at Harper's Ferry, or on the river anywhere below. I would like to hear from you.[15]

At 10:00 Hooker responded:

> With regard to the enemy, your dispatch is more conclusive than any I have received. I now feel that invasion is his settled purpose. . . . It is an act of desperation on his part, no matter in what force he moves. It will kill copperheadism in the North. I do not know that my opinion as to the duty of this army in the case is wanted; if it should be, you know that I will be happy to give it. I have heard nothing of the movements of the enemy to-day. . . . I have only heard that all of A.P. Hill's forces moved up the river this morning, in the direction of Culpeper. If it should be determined for me to make a movement in pursuit, which I am not prepared to recommend at this time, I may possibly be able to move some corps to-morrow, and can reach the point of the enemy's crossing in advance of A.P. Hill. . . . If they are moving toward Maryland, I can better fight them there than make a running fight. If they come up in front of Washington, I can threaten and cut their communications, and Dix can be re-enforced from the south to act on their rear.[16]

That same day Lincoln called for 100,000 militia for six months' service from Pennsylvania, Ohio, and the new state of West Virginia. The response was tepid.

As Lee's army moved north, Hooker on June 16 informed Lincoln that he believed he did not enjoy the confidence of general in chief Halleck. On the same day Lincoln said:

I send you this by the hand of Captain Dahlgren. Your dispatch of 11:30 A.M. to-day is just received. When you say I have long been aware that you do not enjoy the confidence of the major-general commanding, you state the case much too strongly.

You do not lack his confidence in any degree to do you any harm. On seeing him, after telegraphing you this morning, I found him more nearly agreeing with you than I was myself. Surely you do not mean to understand that I am withholding my confidence from you when I happen to express an opinion (certainly never discourteously) differing from one of your own.

I believe Halleck is dissatisfied with you to this extent only, that he knows that you write and telegraph ("report," as he calls it) to me. I think he is wrong to find fault with this; but I do not think he withholds any support from you on account of it. If you and he would use the same frankness to one another, and to me, that I use to both of you, there would be no difficulty. I need and must have the professional skill of both, and yet these suspicions tend to deprive me of both.

I believe you are aware that since you took command of the army I have not believed you had any chance to effect anything till now. As it looks to me, Lee's now returning toward Harper's Ferry gives you back the chance that I thought McClellan lost last fall. Quite possibly I was wrong both then and now; but, in the great responsibility resting upon me, I cannot be entirely silent. Now, all I ask is that you will be in such mood that we can get into our action the best cordial judgment of yourself and General Halleck, with my poor mite added, if indeed he and you shall think it entitled to any consideration at all.[17]

Lincoln had long carried on a correspondence directly with his commanders in the field. He had at times bypassed Halleck, and now with his telegram sought to restore the normal relationship between the general in chief and the general in the field.

Meanwhile Lee was continuing his northward march; and friction between Hooker and Halleck persisted. On June 27 at this moment of enemy invasion, Hooker abruptly submitted his resignation. The following day, a Sunday, Gideon Welles described the cabinet's reception of the news:

After disposing of this subject, the President drew from his pocket a telegram from General Hooker asking to be relieved. The President said he had, for several days as the conflict became imminent, observed in Hooker the same failings that were witnessed in McClellan after the Battle of Antietam. A want of alacrity to obey, and a greedy call for more troops which could not, and ought not to be taken from other points. He would, said the President, strip Washington bare, had demanded the force at Harper's Ferry, which Halleck said could not be complied with—he (Halleck) was opposed to abandoning our position at Harper's Ferry. Hooker had taken umbrage at the refusal, or at all events had thought it best to give up the command.

Some discussion followed, chiefly in regard to a successor. The names of Meade, Sedgwick and Couch were introduced. I soon saw this review of names was merely a feeler to get an expression of opinion—a committal—or to make it appear that all were consulted and it shortly became obvious that the matter had already been settled, and the President finally remarked, he supposed General Halleck had issued the orders. He asked Stanton if it was not so. Stanton replied affirmatively, that Hooker had been ordered to Baltimore and Meade succeeded him.

Chase was disturbed more than he cared should appear. Seward and Stanton were obviously cognizant of the fact before the meeting took place,—had been consulted—perhaps advised proceedings, but, doubtful of results, wished the rest to confirm their act. . . .

Instead of being disturbed, like Chase, I experienced a feeling of relief, and only regretted that Hooker had not been relieved immediately after the Battle of Chancellorsville. No explanation has ever been made of the sudden paralysis which befell the army at that time.[18]

From the beginning of Hooker's appointment, there had been doubts. Lincoln's frank letter suggested to some biographers that Lincoln had made a mistake. The Battle of Chancellorsville and subsequent events sustained this unfavorable outlook. Hooker's departure from his command forced Lincoln to renew his search for a winning general.

CHAPTER TWENTY-THREE

VALLANDIGHAM AND CIVIL LIBERTIES

Following his failure at Fredericksburg, his much ridiculed "mud march," and his unsuccessful effort to purge his staff, General Ambrose Burnside was sent west to command the Department of the Ohio, which included, among other states, Ohio and Illinois. Though predominantly loyal to the Union, the department included many elements who criticized Lincoln and his policies and favored peace over continuing the war. Learning that his command incorporated many disloyal persons, who were aiding the Confederate cause, on April 13 he issued a sweeping order decreeing military arrest and death, if convicted, of persons committing acts for the benefit of enemies.

The leading western Copperhead, so-called, was Clement L. Vallandigham, who even before Lincoln's inauguration had become an acute critic of Lincoln. Three days after Congress adjourned in March 1863 he delivered a long speech entitled "Peace—Liberty—The Constitution." Among other things, to the accompaniment of cheers from a New York City audience, he said, "I am for peace, and would be, even if the Union could not be restored . . . without peace, permitting this Administration for two years to exercise its tremendous powers, the war will not have one remnant of civil liberty left. . . . The existence of this war, is utterly incompatible with the stability of the Constitution and of constitutional liberty."[1]

Back home in Ohio on May 1 Vallandigham gave a speech heard by some of Burnside's men, wearing plain clothes. Three days later, just before midnight, he was awakened by soldiers, arrested, and placed in a military prison in Cincinnati. The next day he published an address to Ohio Democrats:

I am here in a military bastile for no other offence than my political opinions, and the defence of them, and of the rights of the people, and of your constitutional liberties. Speeches made in the hearing of thousands of you in denunciation of the usurpations of power, infractions of the Constitution and laws, and of military despotism, were the sole cause of my arrest and imprisonment. I am a Democrat—for the Constitution, for law, for the Union, for liberty—this is my only "crime." For no disobedience to the Constitution; for no violation of law; for no word, sign, or gesture of sympathy with the men of the South, who are for disunion and Southern independence, but in obedience to their demand as well as the demand of Northern abolition disunionists and traitors, I am here in bonds to-day; but
"Time, at last, sets all things even!"
Meanwhile, Democrats of Ohio, of the Northwest, of the United States, be firm, be true to your principles, to the Constitution, to the Union, and all will yet be well. As for myself, I adhere to every principle, and will make good, through imprisonment and life itself, every pledge and declaration which I have ever made, uttered, or maintained, from the beginning. To you, to the whole people, to TIME, I again appeal. Stand firm! Falter not an instant![2]

Four days later he faced a military commission where the judge advocate read the charge and the specifications. Included in the specifications was Vallandigham's assertion that "the men in power are attempting to establish a despotism in this country." When the testimony was all over, Vallandigham offered his protest:

Arrested without due "process of law," without warrant, from any judicial officer, and now in a military prison, I have been served with a "charge and specification," as in a court-martial or military commission.

I am not in either "the land or naval forces of the United States nor in the militia in the actual service of the United States," and therefore am not triable for any cause by any such court, but am subject, by the express terms of the Constitution, to arrest only by due process of law, judicial warrant, regularly issued upon affidavit and by some officer or court of competent jurisdiction for the trial of citizens, and am now entitled to be tried on an indictment or presentment of a grand jury of such court, to speedy and public trial by an impartial jury of the State of Ohio, to be confronted with witnesses against me, to have compulsory process for witnesses in my behalf, the assistance of counsel for my defence, and evidence and argument according to the common laws and the ways of judicial courts. And all these I here demand as my right as a citizen of the United States, and under the Constitution of the United States.

But the alleged "offence" itself is not known to the Constitution of the United States, nor to any law thereof. It is words spoken to the people of Ohio in an open and public political meeting, lawfully and peacefully assembled under the Constitution and upon full notice. It is words of criticism of the public policy of the public servants of the people, by which policy it was alleged that the welfare of the country was not promoted. It was an appeal to the people to change that policy, not by force, but by free elections and the ballot box. It is not pretended that I counselled disobedience to the Constitution or resistance to laws and lawful authority. I never have. Beyond this protest, I have nothing further to submit.[3]

The court found him guilty of the charge and sentenced him to imprisonment during the war. The day after the sentencing Burnside wired a reply to a telegram from Lincoln that has been lost: "Your dispatch just rec'd. I thank you for your kind assurance of support & beg to say that every possible effort will be made on my part to sustain the Govt. of the United States in its fullest authority."

"No act of the Government has been so strongly criticized, and none having relation to the rights of an individual created a feeling so deep and so widespread," acknowledged Lincoln's private secretaries.

The *Louisville Journal* vigorously opposed the arrest and trial:

It is a great mistake, it is indeed an inexcusable mistake, to suppose that the all but universal feeling, which the arrest and trial of Vallandigham by the military power has awakened, arises in any degree from sympathy with his peculiar views; on the contrary, it arises in spite of a decided antipathy to those views, as is shown conclusively by the fact that the feeling is shared by such Republican champions as the New York "Tribune," the New York "Evening Post," the New York "Commercial Advertiser," the Albany "Statesman," the Boston "Advertiser," the Boston 'Traveller," the Springfield "Republican," and, in short, by the ablest and most influential champions of the Republican party, backed, as the New York "Evening Post" avows, by at least three-fourths of the Republican party itself.

The feeling under notice arises clearly not in consequence of Vallandigham's peculiar views . . . but in lite of them; it arises in spite of them and in spite of many other things, from an irrepressible sense of the value and sacredness of the rights which have been violated in his person. In other words, it arises from a rooted and solemn conviction of the truth of the principle which the General Assembly of Kentucky declares that the power which has recently been assumed by the President of the United States, whereby under the guise of military necessity he has proclaimed and extended martial law over the State where war does not exist, and has suspended the writ of *habeas corpus,* is unwarranted by the constitution, and its tendency is to subordinate civil to military authority, and to subvert constitutional and free government." This declaration a few weeks afterward was adopted by the Union State Convention of Kentucky, and has since been adopted in like manner by the Democracy of Pennsylvania and of New York. The principle itself formed a conspicuous part of the platform on which the conservatives of the north won their great triumph at the ballot box last fall. It is a principle dear as life to the whole people. It is one they never will surrender—one they never can surrender without ceasing to be freemen. And the all but universal protest against the arrest and trial of Vallandigham by the military power is simply the expression of his vital devotion.

... It is impossible that the President can deliberately set at defiance the voice of the whole people thus unequivocally and impressively uttered in behalf of what he must own up to be the right. There is not at present on the face of the globe a monarch who would even dream of defying such monitions as President Lincoln is now receiving in this grave matter from the free and loyal people whose Chief Magistrate he is. Let him at once respect these monitions, if he would serve and not freshly imperil his country, to say nothing of his own future renown.[4]

Secretary of War Edwin Stanton, noting the northern furor over the arrest and trial, feared that a court might ignore Lincoln's blanket suspension of habeas corpus. He prepared an order specifically suspending habeas corpus in Vallandigham's case. Apprised of Stanton's proposal, Lincoln wrote to him:

Since parting with you I have seen the Secretaries of State and the Treasury, and they both think we better not issue the special suspension of the Writ of Habeas Corpus spoken of. Gov. Chase thinks the case is not before Judge Swaine, that it is before Judge Levett, that the writ will probably not issue, whichever the application may be before; and that, in no event, will

Swaine commit an imprudence. His chief reason for thinking the writ will not issue, is that he has seen in a newspaper that Judge Levett stated that Judge Swaine & he refused a similar application last year.[5]

Six days later, at the behest of the president, Stanton ordered Burnside to "send C. L. Vallandigham under secure guard to the headquarters of General Rosecrans to be put by him beyond our military lines and in case of his return within our lines he be arrested and kept in close custody for the term specified in his sentence."

Toward the end of the month a worried Burnside telegraphed Lincoln:

A messenger from Govr. Morton came to me this morning in reference to the arrest, by the military authorities of a citizen of Indiana. I understood from him that my action . . . was not approved by a single member of your Cabinet.

This, taken in connection with your dispatch to me . . . approving of my course convinces me that my action here has been a source of embarrassment to you. . . . I should be glad to be relieved if the interest of the public service requires it, but at the same time I am willing to remain & assume the responsibility of carrying out the policy which has been inaugurated if it is approved.[6]

In response Lincoln assured him:

Your dispatch of to-day received. When I shall wish to supersede you I will let you know. All the cabinet regretted the necessity of arresting, for instance, Vallandigham, some perhaps, doubting, that there was a real necessity for it—but, being done, all were for seeing you through with it.[7]

On the day that Lincoln sent Vallandigham into exile, the bumbling Burnside aggravated the crisis in civil liberties further by issuing an order that read in part: "On account of the repeated expression of disloyal and incendiary sentiments, the publishing of the newspaper known as the Chicago 'Times' is hereby suppressed."

Burnside's violation of freedom of the press provoked an uproar in Illinois. The state House of Representatives by a vote of 47-13 passed resolutions denouncing the suppression, deeming it "the establishment of a military despotism." More serious was the gathering of some twenty thousand citizens of Chicago, who listened to speakers of both parties and dispatched force-ful resolutions to the president:

> Twenty thousand loyal citizens of Illinois, assembled this evening to consult upon their interests, do resolve,
>
> 1. That law is the bulwark of liberty; the abrogation of law is the death of liberty; the constitution guarantees the freedom of speech and of the press and the right of the people peaceably to assemble and to petition the Government for the redress of grievances. An infringement of these rights is a blow at the Constitution; an abrogation of these Rights is the overthrow [of] the Constitution. He who seeks to abridge or destroy these rights is a traitor to law and liberty. The people of Illinois will forever demand and insist upon these rights. They will obey the laws themselves and insist upon alike obedi-ence by all men. They will seek redress for grievances through the forms of law and the tribunals of justice. They will demand and insist upon the trial by jury, of men not in the military or naval service, who are charged with crime; they will demand and insist upon the right to speak and print their opinions of men in power, and the measures of those men; they will demand and insist upon the judgment of the civil tribunals upon men or newspapers charged with the expression of "disloyal and incendiary sentiments."
>
> 2. The military power is and must remain subordinate to the civil power. Military, like civil functionaries, derive all their powers from the law. So far as they act under the law they must be obeyed. When they exceed the law their orders and decrees are void.
>
> 3. General Order No. 84, promulgated by General Burnside, by which the publication of the Chicago "Times" is declared to be suppressed, is without warrant of law, and should, as we have an abiding belief that it will forthwith be rescinded by the President. If the "Times" or any other public journal has exceeded the limits of lawful discussion or criticism, the civil tribunals, and they alone, are the competent and lawful judges of its crime. To the courts of law it appeals; let the courts, and the courts alone, decide its fate.
>
> 4. The people of Illinois are devoted, with their lives and their fortunes to the glorious Union of the States under the Constitution made by our fathers; they will sacrifice life and fortune and all but liberty to preserve that Union; they will cordially sustain the authorities in all honest and lawful efforts to preserve that Union; but they will not sacrifice their liberties, though life and fortune go together. Peaceably, soberly, loyally, they will maintain their liberties, so long as they can thus be maintained, but they will have them at every hazard by some means.[8]

On June 4 Burnside informed the editor of the pro-Vallandigham, anti-Lincoln *Chicago Times:* "By direction of the President of the United States, my order suppressing the circulation of your paper is revoked. You are at liberty to resume its publication."

If the *Chicago Times* affair was a brief squall, the Vallandigham case was a long storm. On the day Lincoln ordered Vallandigham sent beyond Union lines, earnest Albany Democrats, prompted by a letter from New York Governor Horatio Seymour, adopted a series of resolutions. These were transmitted to the president under a cover letter signed by Erastus Corning, president of the Albany meeting, a Democratic member of Congress and president of the New York Central Railroad. He was reported to have offered Lincoln the post of general counsel for the railroad at a salary of ten thousand dollars when Lincoln was in New York to deliver his Cooper Union address in February 1860. The resolutions read:

> *Resolved,* That as Democrats we are determined to maintain this patriotic attitude, and, despite of adverse and disheartening circumstances, to devote all our energies to sustain the cause of the Union, to secure peace through victory, and to bring back the restoration of all the States under the safeguards of the Constitution.
>
> *Resolved,* That while we will not consent to be misapprehended upon these points, we are determined not to be misunderstood in regard to others not less essential. We demand that the Administration shall be true to the Constitution; shall recognize and maintain the rights of the States and the liberties of the citizen; shall everywhere, outside of the lines of necessary military occupation and the scenes of insurrection, exert all its powers to maintain the supremacy of the civil over military law.
>
> *Resolved,* That in view of these principles we denounce the recent assumption of a military commander to seize and try a citizen of Ohio, Clement L. Vallandigham, for no other reason than words addressed to a public meeting, in criticism of the course of the Administration, and in condemnation of the military orders of that General.[9]

On June 12 Lincoln made a thoughtful reply, offering his interpretation of the Constitution; explaining why Vallandigham was arrested; making an emotional plea about protecting "a simple-minded soldier boy" from "a wily agitator"; strengthening his argument by referring to Union Democrats, a

precedent set by the Democratic Andrew Jackson; and candidly acknowledging his own uncertainty that he would have ordered Vallandigham's
arrest. His letter read:

> The resolutions, as I understand them, are resolvable into two propositions—
> first, the expression of a purpose to sustain the cause of the Union, to
> secure peace through victory, and to support the Administration in every
> constitutional, and lawful measure to suppress the rebellion; and secondly,
> a declaration of censure upon the Administration for supposed unconsti-
> tutional action, such as the making of military arrests. . . .
>
> [U]nder cover of "liberty of the press," and *habeas corpus,* [Confederate
> sympathizers] hoped to keep on foot amongst us a most efficient corps
> of spies, informers, suppliers, and aiders and abettors of their cause in a
> thousand ways. They knew that in times such as they were inaugurating
> by the Constitution itself, the *habeas corpus* might be suspended; but they
> also knew they had friends who would make a question as to who was to
> suspend it; meanwhile their spies and others might remain at large to help
> on their cause. . . . [T]horoughly imbued with a reverence for the guaran-
> teed rights of individuals, I was slow to adopt the strong measures which
> by degrees I have been forced to regard as being within the exceptions of
> the Constitution and as indispensable to the public safety. . . .
>
> In view of these and similar cases, I think the time not unlikely to come
> when I shall be blamed for having made too few arrests rather than too
> many. . . .
>
> It is asserted, in substance, that Mr. Vallandigham was, by a military
> commander, seized and tried "for no other reason than words addressed
> to a public meeting, in criticism of the course of the Administration, and
> in condemnation of the military orders of the general." Now, if there be no
> mistake about this—if this assertion is the truth and the whole truth—if
> there was no other reason for the arrest, then I concede that the arrest
> was wrong. But the arrest, as I understand, was made for a very different
> reason. Mr. Vallandigham avows his hostility to the war on the part of the
> Union; and his arrest was made because he was laboring, with some effect,
> to prevent the raising of troops, to encourage desertions from the army, and
> to leave the rebellion without an adequate military force to suppress it. He
> was not arrested because he was damaging the political prospects of the
> Administration, or the personal interests of the commanding general, but
> because he was damaging the army, upon the existence and vigor of which
> the life of the nation depends. He was warring upon the military, and this

gave the military constitutional jurisdiction to lay hands upon him. If Mr. Vallandigham was not damaging the military power of the country, then his arrest was made on mistake of fact, which I would be glad to correct on reasonably satisfactory evidence.

I understand the meeting, whose resolutions I am considering, to be in favor of suppressing the rebellion by military force—by armies. Long experience has shown that armies can not be maintained unless desertion shall be punished by the severe penalty of death. The case requires, and the law and the Constitution, sanction this punishment. Must I shoot a simple-minded soldier boy who deserts, while I must not touch a hair of a wily agitator who induces him to desert? This is none the less injurious when effected by getting a father or brother or friend into a public meeting, and there working upon his feelings, till he is persuaded to write the soldier boy that he is fighting in a bad cause, for a wicked administration of a contemptible government, too weak to arrest and punish him if he shall desert. I think that in such a case to silence the agitator and save the boy is not only constitutional, but withal a great mercy.

If I be wrong on this question of constitutional power, my error lies in believing that certain proceedings are constitutional when, in cases of rebellion or invasion, the public safety requires them, which would not be constitutional when, in absence of rebellion or invasion, the public safety does not require them. In other words, that the Constitution is not in its application in all respects the same, in cases of rebellion or invasion involving the public safety, as it is in times of profound peace and public security. The constitution itself makes the distinction; and I can no more be persuaded that the government can constitutionally take no strong measures in time of rebellion, because it can be shown that the same could not be lawfully taken in time of peace, than I can be persuaded that a particular drug is not good medicine for a sick man, because it can be shown to not be good food for a well one. Nor am I able to appreciate the danger apprehended by the meeting that the American people will, by means of military arrests during the rebellion, lose the right of public discussion, the liberty of speech and the press, law of evidence, trial by jury and *habeas corpus,* throughout the indefinite peaceful future, which I trust lies before them. . . .

[L]et me say that in my own discretion, I do not know whether I would have ordered the arrest of Mr. Vallandigham. While I can not shift the responsibility from myself, I hold that, as a general rule, the commander in the field is the better judge of the necessity in any particular case. Of course I must practice a general directory and revisory power in the matter.

One of the resolutions expresses the opinion of the meeting that arbitrary arrests will have the effect to divide and distract those who should be united in suppressing the rebellion, and I am specifically called on to discharge Mr. Vallandigham. I regard this as, at least, a fair appeal to me, on the expediency of exercising a constitutional power which I think exists. In response . . . it gave me pain when I learned that Mr. Vallandigham had been arrested,—that is, I was pained that there should have seemed to be a necessity for arresting him—and that it will afford me great pleasure to discharge him so soon as I can, by any means, believe the public safety will not suffer by it.[10]

To this on June 30 the Albany Democrats made an extended and spirited reply, which included a charge that the exile of Vallandigham "asserts the principles of a supreme despotism."

In Vallandigham's home state of Ohio the Democrats in convention nominated their martyred hero in exile for governor. They also drew up a set of resolutions that were carried to Washington by a committee. Meeting the members, Lincoln reheard their resolutions and commented on them point by point. In the course of his remarks he invoked his power not as president but as commander in chief of the army and navy.[11]

Ex-president Franklin Pierce, whose ineptitude had contributed to the coming of the Civil War, speaking to a Democratic mass meeting in Concord, New Hampshire, defended "that noble martyr of free speech, Mr. Vallandigham," and assailed "the mailed hand of military usurpation."[12]

Lincoln would return to the Vallandigham matter later in a notable letter to Springfield Republicans. In 1864 the Supreme Court of the United States declined to rule on an appeal, holding that the court did not have jurisdiction over a military commission such as the one that sentenced Vallandigham.

CHAPTER TWENTY-FOUR

ARMING BLACK SOLDIERS

The matter of putting guns in the hands of African Americans became a public issue early in the war, largely because of the advocacy of leading black abolitionists. On May 1, 1861, Frederick Douglass wrote: "A lenient war is a lengthy war. . . . Let us stop it. . . . This can be done at once, by *'carrying the war into Africa.' Let the slaves and colored people be called into service, and formed into a liberating army,* to march into the South and raise the banner of Emancipation among the slaves."[1]

As in the case of emancipation, the army and the Congress were ahead of the president. General Ben Butler, who had helped save Maryland for the Union and was now on duty in Virginia at Fort Monroe, faced the problem of receiving great numbers of slaves taking refuge within his lines. Ignoring the obligation of returning fugitives under the fugitive slave law, he cleverly called the blacks "contraband," gave them protection and shelter, and used them to support military services.

Through the first Confiscation Act, in July 1861, Congress sought among other goals to weaken the Confederacy by confiscating slaves used for military purposes. The act thus recognized the value of black labor in winning the war. In December Secretary of War Simon Cameron advocated freeing and arming blacks. Acting without regard to Lincoln's conservative policy, he placed his plans to do so in his annual report to Congress. Largely because of his malfeasance and corruption, Cameron was dispatched to Russia and replaced with a Pennsylvania Democrat, Edwin Stanton.

In its second session the Thirty-seventh Congress passed two measures in July 1862 that advanced the participation of blacks in military service. The Militia Act contained this provision:

That the President be, and he is here authorized to receive into the service of the United States, for purposes of constructing entrenchments, or performing camp service, or any other labor, or any military or naval service for which they may be found competent, persons of African descent; and such persons shall be enrolled and organized under such regulations, not inconsistent with the Constitution and laws as the President may prescribe.

The second Confiscation Act read in part:

That the President of the United States is authorized to employ as many persons of African descent as he may deem necessary and proper for the suppression of this rebellion, and for this purpose he may organize and use them in such manner as he may judge best for the public welfare.[2]

Lincoln remained reluctant to give guns to African Americans. In his proposed veto of the second confiscation bill he wrote: "I am ready to say now, I think it is proper for our military commanders to employ, as laborers, as many persons of African descent as can be used to advantage." At the cabinet meeting where the preliminary emancipation was discussed Bates recorded in his diary: "The question of arming slaves was then brought up and I advocated it warmly. The President was unwilling to adopt this measure, but proposed to issue a Proclamation, on the basis of the Confiscation Bill, calling upon the States to return to their allegiance." In an interview with Lincoln prior to passage of the bill Senator James Harlan of Iowa, former Free Soiler, urged the president to arm slaves belonging to both disloyal and loyal owners. Lincoln answered that the policy would threaten the loyalty of the Border States.

Lincoln publicly revealed his reluctance to arming blacks in early August 1862 when a deputation from Indiana came to offer two black regiments. The *New York Tribune* reported:

A deputation of Western gentlemen waited upon the President this morning to offer two colored regiments from the State of Indiana. Two members of Congress were of the party. The President received them courteously, but stated to them that he was not prepared to go the length of enlisting negroes as soldiers. He would employ all colored men offered as laborers, but would not promise to make soldiers of them.

The deputation came away satisfied that it is the determination of the Government not to arm negroes unless some new and more pressing emergency arises. The President argued that the nation could not afford to lose Kentucky at this crisis, and gave it as his opinion that to arm the negroes would turn 50,000 bayonets from the loyal Border States against us that were for us.

Upon the policy of using negroes as laborers, the confiscation of Rebel property, and the feeding the National troops upon the granaries of the enemy, the President said there was no division of sentiment. He did not explain, however, why it is that the Army of the Potomac and the Army of Virginia carry out this policy so differently. The President promised that the war should be prosecuted with all the rigor he could command, but he could not promise to arm slaves or to attempt slave insurrections in the Rebel States. The recent enactments of Congress on emancipation and confiscation he expects to carry out.[3]

The *Tribune* lamely endorsed the president's position, but the *Chicago Tribune* on its front page sharply criticized the president:

Assuredly, the most rejoicing, . . . will not be among loyal men at the decision of the President against arming the negroes. Lukewarm patriots, "fire in the rear" sympathizers with the rebellion, men who love slavery more than the Union, will openly exult at the evidence that the Government is not yet ready to use every loyal arm in the restoration of its power and destruction of its enemies. There would, of course, be those who could not hail the policy statement with joy. With men who have no wish but that the country shall be saved, and who believe of all its evils slavery is the worst, the regret will be sincere, that our national trials thus far have not sufficed to do away with the prejudice which will consult hues and complexion when what is wanted are laborers at the fire. . . . [T]he band on our national dial is steadily moving to the end that must come, too resistless to be stayed by old time prejudices, or held back by President or Congress. Destiny has forced it. The people will it.[4]

A little more than a month later, responding to a memorial from Chicago Christians urging emancipating as well as arming blacks, Lincoln not only reiterated his reluctance to place guns in black hands but also voiced a concern: "If we were to arm them, I fear that in a few weeks the arms would be in the hands of the rebels; and indeed thus far we have not had arms enough to equip our white troops."[5]

Meanwhile Generals David Hunter and Jim Lane had been experimenting with black troops; and the governor of Wisconsin on the day of Lincoln's interview with the Hoosiers inquired about policy. Stanton wired back: "The President declines to receive Indians or negroes as troops." Shortly thereafter Stanton told Lane that "regiments of African descent can only be raised upon express and special authority of the President."[6]

Despite all this, on August 25 in a communication that "should never see daylight," Stanton authorized General Rufus Saxton to raise as many as five thousand black troops in the area of Port Royal, South Carolina.

In October Lincoln had an interview with Daniel Ullmann, a former Know Nothing and commander of the 78th New York Volunteers in the Peninsula campaign. Lincoln suggested ambivalence in his outlook on black enlistment. Ullmann entreated Lincoln: "You arm the Blacks, and enlist them into the Armies of the United States." Lincoln broke in, saying it "would drive many of our friends from us. The people are not prepared for it." Ullmann persisted with his plea until Lincoln again interrupted with him a surprising question: "Ullmann, would you be willing to command black soldiers?"[7]

In his second annual message Lincoln affirmed, "I strongly favor colonization." Yet a month later in the formal Emancipation Proclamation he announced of the freedmen, "I further declare and make known that such persons, of suitable condition, will be received into the armed service of the United States to garrison forts, positions, stations, and other places, and to man vessels of all sorts in said service."[8] The president may have been influenced by the opinion of his attorney general in a case involving detention by a U.S. revenue cutter of a schooner because it was commanded by a black man. The liberal secretary of the treasury Salmon P. Chase asked the attorney general for a ruling on whether colored men could be citizens. In a long opinion the conservative attorney general Edward Bates, having consulted with Columbia law professor Francis Lieber, concluded that the *Dred Scott* decision had no authority beyond its specific facts:

> I give it as my opinion that the *free man of color,* mentioned in your letter, if born in the United States, is a citizen of the United States, and, if otherwise

qualified, is competent, according to the acts of Congress, to be master of a vessel engaged in the coasting trade.[9]

A fortnight following his great proclamation Lincoln wrote a "Private & confidential" letter to General John A. Dix, an eminent Union Democrat commanding at Fort Monroe, Virginia. Lincoln discreetly inquired about employing black troops at Dix's command:

> The proclamation has been issued. We were not succeeding—at best, were progressing too slowly—without it. Now, that we have it, and bear all the disadvantage of it, (as we do bear some in certain quarters) we must also take some benefit from it, if practicable. I therefore will thank you for your well considered opinion whether Fortress-Monroe, and York-town, one or both, could not, in whole or in part, be garrisoned by colored troops, leaving the white forces now necessary at those places, to be employed elsewhere.[10]

Dix unenthusiastically responded:

> I regard this Fortress . . . as second to no other in the Union. It is the key to the Chesapeake Bay. . . . In a political point of view . . . the tranquility . . . of Maryland may depend on the possession of this Fortress. . . .
>
> Under these circumstances I think this post should be held by the best and most reliable troops the country can furnish. . . .
>
> The question of employing colored troops at Yorktown may be determined by a totally different class of considerations. The position is of little practical importance. . . .
>
> If it be decided to employ colored troops any where, I know no place where they could be used with less objection. The proper garrison is 4000 half of that number at least should be white troops. . . .[11]

From mid-January until the session's close Congress at intervals debated the issue of black enrollment. A lively debate involving Lincoln's views on race relations occurred on January 29. The Ohio peace Democrat S. S. Cox, known as "Sunset Cox," complained that "the pending law, as the gentleman correctly observed, is intended to place the African soldier upon a perfect equality in every regard with the white soldier, and that is the gist of our objection."

The "gentleman" Cox disparaged was Representative Thaddeus Stevens, radical Republican, who retorted, "I have not said so. I said the object was to put them on an equality as to the protection which the President could afford them. I do not mean to say that they are to be put upon a social and political equality. . . . I intend merely to put them on an equality, in rights as soldiers in being protected and punished by the Executive."[12]

Congressman Horace Maynard from eastern Tennessee, who had campaigned for the Constitutional Unionist presidential candidate in 1860, spoke of his fear that the president might appoint a black general commanding troops.

> If they are to be officered indiscriminately, either by white or by black persons—as officered by somebody they must be—we shall have not only brigadier generals but major generals of the African race, if under the powers conferred by this bill the President should choose to confer that high authority upon men of that race; and when they are brought into the same field with white troops officered by white men who are outranked by such colored officers, the consequence will be that the white officers must yield military obedience to them.[13]

And Senator John Jordan Crittenden, the Kentucky conciliator who had failed to prevent the war, stoutly opposed black enrollment.[14]

On the same day "Sunset" Cox moved to insert the word "white" in order to restrict enrollment to white males. Owen Lovejoy, Illinois abolitionist and brother of the martyred editor of an abolitionist newspaper, called for a vote. Cox's amendment lost 52-85. In objecting to the final bill Cox said:

> I believe the object of gentlemen, in forcing this bill here, is to bring about—or, rather to make final and forever—the dissolution of the Union. . . . Every man along the border [Ohio] will tell you the Union is for ever rendered hopeless if you pursue this policy of taking the slaves from the master and arming them in this civil strife.[15]

Lincoln in subsequent letters would flatly contradict this view of the relationship between black enlistment and saving the Union.

The Enrollment Act of March 3, 1863, embraced all able-bodied male citizens of the United States. Though the act did not mention blacks, the War Department construed the phrase "all male citizens" to embrace free blacks. Fortified with this measure Lincoln began to throw his energies into enrolling African American soldiers.

Before the month was out he wrote to Andrew Johnson, military governor of Tennessee:

> I am told you have at least *thought* of raising a negro military force. In my opinion the country now needs no specific thing so much as some man of your ability, and position, to go to this work. When I speak of your position, I mean that of an eminent citizen of a slave-state, and himself a slave-holder. The colored population is the great *available* and yet *unavailed* of, force for restoring the Union. The bare sight of fifty thousand armed, and drilled black soldiers on the banks of the Mississippi, would end the rebellion at once. And who doubts that we can present that sight, if we but take hold in earnest? If you *have* been thinking of it please do not dismiss the thought.[16]

Three days later Lincoln wrote to General Nathaniel P. Banks, who had been assigned to hold New Orleans and assist Grant in opening the Mississippi River, to help Daniel Ullmann, now a brigadier general, in raising black troops:

> Hon. Daniel Ullmann, with a commission of Brigadier General, and two or three hundred other gentlemen as officers, goes to your department and reports to you, for the purpose of raising a colored brigade. To now avail ourselves of this element of force, is very important, if not indispensable. I therefore will thank you to help Gen. Ullmann forward with his undertaking, as much, and as rapidly, as you can; and also to carry the general object beyond his particular organization if you find it practicable. The necessity of this is palpable if, as I understand, you are now unable to effect anything with your present force; and which force is soon to be greatly diminished by the expiration of terms of service, as well as by ordinary causes. I shall be very glad if you will take hold of the matter in earnest.
>
> You will receive from the Department a regular order upon this subject.[17]

Another three days later Lincoln wrote to General David Hunter, whose early emancipation proclamation in South Carolina he had countermanded, now commending him for the positive accounts circulating about the general's use of black troops in Florida:

My dear Sir: I am glad to see the accounts of your colored force at Jacksonville, Florida. I see the enemy are driving at them fiercely, as is to be expected. It is important to the enemy that such a force shall not take shape, and grow, and thrive, in the South; and in precisely the same proportion, it is important to us that it *shall*. Hence the utmost caution and vigilance is necessary on our part. The enemy will make extra efforts to destroy them; and we should do the same to preserve and increase them.[18]

The following day in this fast-moving enlistment effort Stanton sent none other than the adjutant general of the army, Lorenzo Thomas, to the Mississippi Valley to promote raising black troops. In mid-April from Grant's headquarters at Milliken's Bend, where Grant was preparing his Vicksburg campaign, Thomas telegraphed:

The policy respecting the negroes having been adopted, commanding officers are perfectly willing and ready to afford every aid in carrying it out to a successful issue. . . . I shall find no difficulty in organizing negro troops to the extent of 20,000, if necessary. The prejudice in this army respecting arming the negroes is fast dying out.[19]

Blacks proved their valor on the battlefield by mid-1863 and, in so doing, put down race prejudice. Referring to black fighting at Port Hudson, Louisiana, Lincoln in 1864 declared, "There have been men who have proposed to me to return to slavery the black warriors of Port Hudson & Olustee [Florida] to their masters to conciliate the south. I should be damned in time & eternity for so doing." Following the battle of Milliken's Bend, Louisiana, Charles A. Dana, assistant secretary of war, who was with Grant at the time, wrote, "The bravery of the blacks in the battle of Milliken's Bend completely revolutionized the sentiment of the army with regard to the employment of black troops." The courageous assault of a black regiment on Fort Wagner in South Carolina caused the *Atlantic Monthly* to observe, "Through the cannon smoke of that dark night the manhood of the colored race shines before many eyes that would not see."[20]

Lincoln's newfound zeal for black enlistments marked a note to Stanton following the Union victories at Vicksburg and Gettysburg:

I desire that a renewed and vigorous effort be made to raise colored forces along the shores of the Mississippi.

Please consult the General-in-Chief; and if it is perceived that any acceleration of the matter can be effected, let it be done.

I think the evidence is nearly conclusive that Gen. Thomas is one of the best, if not the very best, instruments for this service.[21]

In 1862–63 threats against black soldiers and white commanders of black troops emanated from the Confederacy. Northerners were concerned about the Confederate threats to execute white officers of black soldiers and to sell black soldiers into slavery. Hannah Johnson, mother of a black soldier in the 54th Massachusetts, appealed to Lincoln for fair treatment of black soldiers—"Now Mr. Lincoln dont you think you ought to stop this thing and make them do the same by the colored men."[22] On July 30, 1863, after the Confederacy had threatened captured Union officers and men of black regiments with death or enslavement, Lincoln issued a stern retaliatory order:

It is the duty of every Government to give protection to its citizens, of whatever class, color, or condition, and especially to those who are duly organized as soldiers in the public service. The law of nations, and the usages and customs of war, as carried on by civilized powers, permit no distinction as to color in the treatment of prisoners of war as public enemies. To sell or enslave any captured person, on account of his color, and for no offence against the laws of war, is a relapse into barbarism, and a crime against the civilization of the age.

The Government of the United States will give the same protection to all its soldiers; and if the enemy shall sell or enslave anyone because of his color, the offense shall be punished by retaliation upon the enemy's prisoners in our possession.

It is therefore ordered, that for every soldier of the United States killed in violation of the laws of war, a rebel soldier shall be executed; and for every one enslaved by the enemy or sold into slavery, a rebel soldier shall be placed at hard labor on the public works, and continued at such labor until the other shall be released and receive the treatment due to a prisoner of war.[23]

On August 9 Lincoln wrote to General Grant:

Gen. Thomas has gone again to the Mississippi Valley, with the view of raising colored troops. I have no reason to doubt that you are doing what you reasonably can upon the same subject. I believe it is a resource which, if vigorously applied now, will soon close the contest. It works doubly, weakening the enemy and strengthening us. We were not fully ripe for it until the river was opened. Now, I think at least a hundred thousand can, and ought to be rapidly organized along its shores, relieving all the white troops to serve elsewhere.

Mr. Dana understands you as believing that the emancipation proclamation has helped some in your military operations. I am very glad if this is so. Did you receive a short letter from me dated the 13th. of July?[24]

Responding to a letter inviting him to a mass meeting of unconditional Union men in Springfield, Lincoln penned a public letter defending his policies on continuing the war and emancipating and enlisting blacks. Behind his letter stood many factors. His home state had turned against him. Democrats controlled the state legislature, which had condemned the Emancipation Proclamation. They also controlled a constitutional convention that banned black immigration into the state but failed to win ratification; and they held a state rally where they adopted a resolution "in favor of peace upon the basis of a restoration of the Union." Lincoln's letter spoke to these concerns:

There are those who are dissatisfied with me. To such I would say: You desire peace; and you blame me that we do not have it. But how can we attain it? There are but three conceivable ways. First, to suppress the rebellion by force of arms. This, I am trying to do. Are you for it? If you are, so far we are agreed. If you are not for it, a second way is, to give up the Union. I am against this. Are you for it? If you are, you should say so plainly. If you are not for *force,* nor yet for *dissolution,* there only remains some imaginable *compromise.* I do not believe any compromise, embracing the maintenance of the Union, is now possible. . . .

But, to be plain, you are dissatisfied with me about the negro. Quite likely there is a difference of opinion between you and myself upon that subject. I certainly wish that all men could be free, while I suppose you do not. Yet I have neither adopted, nor proposed any measure, Which is not consistent with even your view, provided you are for the Union. I suggested compensated emancipation; to which you replied you wished not to be taxed to buy negroes.

But I had not asked you to be taxed to buy negroes, except in such way, as to save you from greater taxation to save the Union exclusively by other means.

You dislike the emancipation proclamation; and, perhaps, would have it retracted. You say it is unconstitutional—I think differently. I think the constitution invests its commander-in-chief, with the law of war, in time of war. The most that can be said, if so much, is, that slaves are property. Is there—has there ever been—any question that by the law of war, property, both of enemies and friends, may be taken when needed? . . .

I know as fully as one can know the opinions of others, that some of the commanders of our armies in the field who have given us our most important successes, believe the emancipation policy, and the use of colored troops, constitute the heaviest blow yet dealt to the rebellion; and that, at least one of those important successes, could not have been achieved when it was, but for the aid of black soldiers. Among the commanders holding these views are some who have never had any affinity with what is called abolitionism, or with republican party politics; but who hold them purely as military opinions. I submit these opinions as being entitled to some weight against the objections, often urged, that emancipation, and arming the blacks, are unwise as military measures, and were not adopted, as such, in good faith.

You say you will not fight to free negroes. Some of them seem willing to fight for you; but, no matter. Fight you, then, exclusively to save the Union. I issued the proclamation on purpose to aid you in saving the Union. Whenever you shall have conquered all resistance to the Union, if I shall urge you to continue fighting, it will be an apt time, then, for you to declare you will not fight to free negroes.

I thought that in your struggle for the Union, to whatever extent the negroes should cease helping the enemy, to that extent it weakened the enemy in his resistance to you. Do you think differently?

I thought that whatever negroes can be got to do as soldiers, leaves just so much less for white soldiers to do, in saving the Union. Does it appear otherwise to you? But negroes, like other people, act upon motives. Why should they do any thing for us, if we will do nothing for them? If they stake their lives for us, they must be prompted by the strongest motive—even the promise of freedom. And the promise being made, must be kept. . . .

Peace does not appear so distant as it did. I hope it will come soon, and come to stay; and so come as to be worth the keeping in all future time. It will then have been proved that, among free men, there can be no successful appeal from the ballot to the bullet; and that they who take such appeal are sure to lose their case, and pay the cost. And then, there will be some black men who can remember that, with silent tongue, and clenched teeth, and steady eye, and well-poised bayonet, they have helped mankind

367

on to this great consummation; while, I fear, there will be some white ones, unable to forget that, with malignant heart, and deceitful speech, they have strove to hinder it.

Still let us not be over-sanguine of a speedy final triumph. Let us be quite sober. Let us diligently apply the means, never doubting that a just God, in his own good time, will give us the rightful result.[25]

Lincoln received numerous letters about the Springfield address. Charles Sumner wrote, "It is a historical document." Henry Wilson, his fellow Illinoisan, told him, "It will be on the lips and in the hearts of hundreds of thousands this day."[26] A letter from ninety-one-year-old Josiah Quincy, former president of Harvard, Lincoln particularly liked. Quincy said:

Old age has its privileges, which I hope this letter will not exceed; but I cannot refrain from expressing to you my gratification and my gratitude for your letter to the Illinois Convention—happy, timely, conclusive, and effective. What you say concerning emancipation, your proclamation, and your course of proceeding in relation to it was due to truth and to your own character, shamefully assailed as it has been. The development is an imperishable monument of wisdom and virtue.[27]

Lincoln responded, "Allow me to express the personal gratification I feel at the receipt of your very kind letter of the 7th of September, and to thank you most cordially for its wise and earnest words of counsel."[28]

Recruitment of black soldiers, of course, mainly took place in southern states, where most blacks lived. Efforts to recruit blacks in the border slave states encountered resistance from governors who objected to arming blacks, enlisting by out-of-state recruiters to help fill their states' quotas, and losing black workers.

Frederick Douglass throughout the war was concerned about black enlistment, commissioning black men in the officer corps, and equal pay for black and white soldiers; at Lincoln's invitation he had an interview with Lincoln on August 10. He recounted their meeting in his autobiography:

My efforts to secure just and fair treatment for the colored soldiers did not stop at letters and speeches. . . . I was induced to go to Washington and lay the complaints of my people before President Lincoln and the Secretary of War and to urge upon them such action as should secure to the colored troops then fighting for the country a reasonable degree of fair play. I need not say that at the time I undertook this mission it required much more nerve than a similar one would require now. The distance then between the black man and the white American citizen was immeasurable. I was an ex-slave, identified with a despised race, and yet I was to meet the most exalted person in this great republic. It was altogether an unwelcome duty, and one from which I would gladly have been excused. I could not know what kind of a reception would be accorded me. I might be told to go home and mind my business. . . .

I shall never forget my first interview with this great man. . . . The room in which he received visitors was the one now used by the President's secretaries. I entered it with a moderate estimate of my own consequence, and yet there I was to talk with, and even to advise, the head man of a great nation. Happily for me, there was no vain pomp and ceremony about him. I was never more quickly or more completely put at ease in the presence of a great man than in that of Abraham Lincoln. He was seated, when I entered, in a low armchair with his feet extended on the floor, surrounded by a large number of documents and several busy secretaries. The room bore the marks of business, and the persons in it, the President included, appeared to be much overworked and tired. Long lines of care were already deeply written on Mr. Lincoln's brow, and his strong face, full of earnestness, lighted up as soon as my name was mentioned. As I approached and was introduced to him he arose and extended his hand, and bade me welcome. I at once felt myself in the presence of an honest man—one whom I could love, honor, and trust without reserve or doubt. Proceeding to tell him who I was and what I was doing, he promptly, but kindly, stopped me, saying: "I know who you are, Mr. Douglass; Mr. Seward has told me all about you. Sit down. I am glad to see you." I then told him the object of my visit—that I was assisting to raise colored troops—that several months before I had been very successful in getting men to enlist, but that now it was not easy to induce the colored men to enter the service, because there was a feeling among them that the government did not, in several respects, deal fairly with them. Mr. Lincoln asked me to state particulars. I replied that there were three particulars which I wished to bring to his attention. First, that colored soldiers ought to receive the same wages as those paid to white soldiers. Second, that colored soldiers ought to receive the same protection when taken prisoners, and be exchanged as readily and on the same terms as any other prisoners, and if Jefferson Davis should shoot or hang colored soldiers in cold blood the United States government should, without delay, retaliate in kind and degree upon Confederate prisoners in its hands. Third, when colored soldiers, seeking "the bubble reputation at the cannon's mouth," performed great and uncommon service on the battlefield, they should be rewarded by distinction and promotion precisely as white soldiers are rewarded for like services.

Mr. Lincoln listened with patience and silence to all I had to say. He was serious and even troubled by what I had said and by what he himself had evidently before thought upon the same points. He, by his silent listening not less than by his earnest reply to my words, impressed me with the solid gravity of his character.

He began by saying that the employment of colored troops at all was a great gain to the colored people—that the measure could not have been successfully adopted at the beginning of the war—that the wisdom of making colored men soldiers was still doubted—that their enlistment was a serious offense to popular prejudice—that they had larger motives for being soldiers than white men—that they ought to be willing to enter the service upon any condition—that the fact that they were not to receive the same pay as white soldiers seemed a necessary concession to smooth the way to their employment at all as soldiers, but that ultimately they would receive the same. On the second point, in respect to equal protection, he said the case was more difficult. Retaliation was a terrible remedy, and one which it was very difficult to apply—that, if once begun, there was no telling where it would end—that if he could get hold of the Confederate soldiers who had been guilty of treating colored soldiers as felons he could easily retaliate, but the thought of hanging men for a crime perpetrated by others was revolting to his feelings. He thought that the rebels themselves would stop such barbarous warfare—that less evil would be done if retaliation were not resorted to and that he had already received information that colored soldiers were being treated as prisoners of war. In all this I saw the tender heart of the man rather than the stern warrior and commander-in-chief of the American army and navy, and, while I could not agree with him, I could but respect his human spirit.

On the third point he appeared to have less difficulty, though he did not absolutely commit himself. He simply said that he would sign any commission to colored soldiers whom his Secretary of War should commend to him. Though I was not entirely satisfied with his views, I was so well satisfied with the man and with the educating tendency of the conflict that I determined to go on with the recruiting.[29]

Summing up the year's experience with enlisting blacks, Lincoln told the Congress in his annual message:

Of those who were slaves at the beginning of the rebellion, full one hundred thousand are now in the United States military service, about one-half of which number actually bear arms in the ranks; thus giving the double advantage of taking so much labor from the insurgent cause, and supplying the places which otherwise must be filled with so many white men. So far as tested, it is difficult to say they are not as good soldiers as any. No servile insurrection, or tendency to violence or cruelty, has marked the measures of emancipation and arming the blacks. These measures have been much discussed in foreign countries, and contemporary with such discussion the tone of public sentiment there is much improved. At home the same measures have been fully discussed, supported, criticized, and denounced, and the annual elections following are highly encouraging to those whose official duty it is to bear the country through this great trial. Thus we have the new reckoning. The crisis which threatened to divide the friends of the Union is past.[30]

At the war's start Lincoln opposed enlisting blacks. Generals and the Congress took the lead. Needs of the service, a shift of public opinion, and demonstrated loyalty of the border slave states made black enlistment desirable and feasible.

Once committed to enlisting blacks, however, Lincoln took up the matter with energy, urging governors and generals to employ black troops. He dispatched a highly placed federal official to encourage enlistment. He ignored the protests of Democrats in Congress. In the end, about two hundred thousand blacks served in the Union forces, counting those in the naval service (often omitted in estimates, perhaps 10 percent of the whole).

Black participation in battle added momentum to the movement both to win the war and to abolish slavery. In an eloquent public letter the president praised black troops and challenged critics of the new policy. But the problem of equal pay, nettling Frederick Douglass and others, persisted.

CHAPTER TWENTY-FIVE

GIBRALTAR OF THE WEST

Vicksburg, perched two hundred feet above the Mississippi River, controlled the great artery linking North and South and separating three Confederate states from the other eight. From west of the river came beef in large quantity, and grain and sugar moved eastward as well as munitions imported into Mexico and thence to the Confederacy.

Protected on the west by its elevation and the wide river, Vicksburg enjoyed further geographical protection by the hills, streams, forests, and ravines on the north. Under the command of Confederate General John C. Pemberton, a Pennsylvanian, Vicksburg had a garrison of 50,000 men.

Late in 1862 Grant prepared to move southward into Mississippi, and to order Sherman, accompanying him, to take Vicksburg. When Halleck directed him to muster 25,000 troops at Memphis for the attack on Vicksburg, Grant asked on December 8, 1862, "Do you want me to command the expedition on Vicksburg, or shall I send Sherman?" He took Halleck's words, "You will move your troops as you may deem best to accomplish the great object in view," to mean he had full charge. But he had not reckoned on John McClernand, a prominent Illinois Democrat whom Lincoln had made a political general. He had wrung from the president an order to organize troops, which under his command, were to move against Vicksburg and to clear the Mississippi River and open navigation to New Orleans.

An ambitious and angry John McClernand conducted a virtually insubordinate correspondence with Lincoln over his status that ended on May 5 with Stanton's order: "General Grant has full and absolute authority to enforce his own commands, and to remove any person who, by ignorance, inaction, or any cause, interferes with or delays his operations. He has the

372

full confidence of the Government."[1] Friction continued until June 17, when Grant, after reading in a newspaper that McClernand had issued a Congratulatory Address claiming most of the credit for the success thus far achieved, relieved the presumptuous general from command.

Though influential friends, including the governor of Illinois, appealed to Lincoln on behalf of the general, Lincoln replied, "Better to leave it where the law of the case has placed it." McClernand directly asked Lincoln for a court of inquiry; and Stanton on behalf of the president denied the request. Early in January 1864 McClernand sent Lincoln his letter of resignation.

Topography made taking Vicksburg a daunting task. Though Lincoln told a reporter that he considered Grant to be the rising general of the war, he heard reports that Grant was incompetent and a drunkard. Chase sent him two such letters. One was from Murat Halstead, forthright Cincinnati journalist, who wrote, among other aspersions, that Grant was "a jackass in the original package . . . most of the time more than half drunk and much of the time idiotically drunk." Chase himself believed Grant should be replaced by Sherman because "he is certainly an abler and better and more reliable Commander." Lincoln is supposed to have said about Grant, "If I knew what brand of whisky he drinks, I would send a barrel or so to some other generals."[2]

In the case of his generals in the eastern theater Lincoln visited them in the field, talked to them in the White House, and conducted much correspondence with them. Grant was too distant for presidential visits, and as Lincoln remarked, "Gen. Grant is a copious worker, and fighter, but a very meagre writer."[3] Wanting to know the truth about the unfavorable rumors as well as the progress of the campaign, Lincoln in March dispatched Assistant Secretary of War Charles Dana to Grant's headquarters to report. In his recollections of the war, Dana wrote:

> Living at headquarters as I did throughout the siege of Vicksburg, I soon became intimate with General Grant, not only knowing every operation while it was still but an idea, but studying its execution on the spot. Grant was an uncommon fellow—the most modest, the most disinterested, and the most honest man I ever knew, with a temper that nothing could disturb,

and a judgment that was judicial in its comprehensiveness and wisdom. Not a great man, except morally; not an original or brilliant man, but sincere, thoughtful, deep, and gifted with courage that never faltered, when the time came to risk all, he went in like a simple-hearted, unaffected, unpretending hero, whom no ill omens could deject and no triumph unduly exalt. A social, friendly man, too, fond of a pleasant joke and also ready with one; but liking above all a long chat of an evening, and ready to sit up with you all night, talking in the cool breeze in front of his tent. Not a man of sentimentality, not demonstrative in friendship, but always holding to his friends, and just even to the enemies he hated.[4]

Lincoln also kept a sharp eye on War Department dispatches that Dana sent to Stanton. He cast about for news, writing to Major General Dix on May 11, "Do the Richmond papers have anything to say about Grand Gulf [Mississippi] or Vicksburg?"[5] Dix returned a negative answer.

In late April Grant executed a remarkable feat. He moved his army west across the river, marched it below Vicksburg, recrossed the river, and then laid siege to the town. The stress on Lincoln in the weeks before the long-besieged Vicksburg fell and the great clash of Confederate and Union forces at Gettysburg is suggested in correspondence between Lincoln and his friend Isaac N. Arnold, the Illinois congressman.

Arnold on May 18, 1863, wrote to the president:

I desire as one of your old and true friends to respectfully suggest whether in view of the condition of military affairs of our country, the office of *General in Chief* should not either be discontinued, or filled by a person other than Halleck. Whatever may be his merits, I can assure you from personal knowledge that Gen. Halleck has lost the confidence of the people. The people generally believe that it is his personal hostility and prejudice that has driven from the public services, & keeps out of employment such men as Butler, Fremont, & Sigil.

Whatever of disaster or want of success has befallen our arms, the people to a very considerable extent attribute to him.

Whether this opinion is right or wrong a change is needed to inspire confidence.

I write this from no feeling of hostility to Gen. Halleck, but from a sense of duty to the country. You I know have no wish but to crush the rebellion, maintain the integrity of the Union, & preserve our liberties.[6]

Lincoln replied in a "Private & confidential" letter, concerning the public's false beliefs about what he had done about some of his generals, describing his dilemmas in dealing with them, and heaping praise on Grant and his Vicksburg campaign.

On the Fourth of July Pemberton surrendered to Grant. Welles recorded how the news arrived in Washington and how Lincoln behaved:

> When I returned [to his office] from the Cabinet council . . . I was handed a dispatch from Admiral Porter, communicating the fall of Vicksburg on the fourth of July. Excusing myself to the delegation I immediately returned to the Executive Mansion. The President was detailing certain points . . . on the map to Chase and two or three others, when I gave him the tidings. Putting down the map, he said we would drop these topics, and I myself will telegraph this news to General Meade. He rose and seized his hat, but suddenly stopped, his countenance beaming with joy—he caught my hand and throwing his arm around me, exclaimed: "What can we do for the Secretary of the Navy for this glorious intelligence—He is always giving us good news. I cannot, in words, tell you my joy over this result. It is great, Mr. Welles, it is great!"
>
> We walked across the lawn together. This, said he, will relieve Banks. It will inspire Meade. The opportunity I thought a good one to request him to insist upon his own views, to enforce them, not only on Meade but on Halleck.[7]

Four days after Vicksburg surrendered, Port Hudson, the remaining Confederate stronghold on the river, long besieged, surrendered to General N. P. Banks. Lincoln later said in his picturesque language, "the Father of Waters again goes unvexed to the sea."[8]

Lincoln wrote to Grant on July 13 praising him for the victory and at the same acknowledging he had been wrong in wanting Grant to go down the Mississippi to join General Banks:

> I do not remember that you and I ever met personally. I write this now as a grateful acknowledgment for the almost inestimable service you have done the country. I wish to say a word further. When you first reached the vicinity of Vicksburg, I thought you should do, what you finally did—march the troops across the neck, run the batteries with the transports: and thus go below; and I never had any faith, except a general hope that you knew better

than I, that the Yazoo Pass expedition, and the like, could succeed. When you got below, and took Port-Gibson, Grand Gulf, and vicinity, I though you should go down the river and join Gen. Banks; and when you turned Northward East of the Big Black, I feared it was a mistake. I now wish to make the personal acknowledgment that you were right, and I was wrong.[9]

Simultaneously, Union forces scored a meaningful victory in the eastern theater. They repulsed Lee's second, more significant attempt to invade the North. Gettysburg was a massive battle of huge armies and huge casualties. Together the twin victories formed a turning point in the great struggle. The battles differed in character. Vicksburg ended in an undoubted Union success: capture of the Confederate fortress and 30,000 enemy soldiers, control of the mighty river, and the opening of opportunity to advance. An aggressive general grew in stature. Gettysburg, as we shall see, marked a repulse of invaders, but for months the Union failed to follow up with an advance in the eastern theater.

CHAPTER TWENTY-SIX

GETTYSBURG

George Gordon Meade graduated from West Point in 1835, nineteenth in his class of fifty-six. He served in the Mexican War, held various assignments as a topographical engineer; and in August 1861, through the influence of Governor Curtin of Pennsylvania, he became a brigadier general of volunteers. A man of courage, he was gaunt and grizzled, with a short temper that earned him the nickname "the old snapping turtle."

For his outstanding service in a roster of battles—including the Peninsula Campaign, where he was badly wounded, Second Bull Run, Antietam, Fredericksburg, and Chancellorsville—he won appointment as Hooker's successor to command the Army of the Potomac. News of this came in dramatic circumstances. Early in the morning of June 28 a messenger from Lincoln awakened him to inform him of his appointment. Lee was already in Pennsylvania, and four days later the men in gray and blue clashed at Gettysburg.

David Homer Bates, who managed the military telegraph office in the War Department building, related Lincoln's activity during the dreadful days:

> Lee's invasion of Maryland in June had greatly increased the anxiety felt by the President, especially as communication with our army was frequently interrupted. All the news we received dribbled over a single line of wire via Hagerstown; and when Meade's headquarters were pushed beyond that place through the necessity of following Lee's advance, we lost telegraphic connection altogether, only regaining it by the Hanover Junction route, a day or two later. From that point to Hanover there was a railroad wire. Thence to Gettysburg the line was on the turnpike, and the service was poor and desultory. Lincoln was in the telegraph office hour after hour

during those anxious days and nights, until, on the morning of July 4, he penned his welcome announcement to the country that Meade had won a notable victory.[1]

Radical Republican Senator Zach Chandler recalled:

I shall never forget the painful anxiety of those few days when the fate of the nation seemed to hang in the balance; nor the restless solicitude of Mr. Lincoln, as he paced up and down the room, reading dispatches, soliloquizing, and often stopping to trace the map which hung on the wall; nor the relief we all felt when the fact was established that victory, though gained at such fearful cost, was indeed on the side of the Union.[2]

On the Fourth of July as the great battle ended, Meade addressed his troops, remarking, "Our task is not yet accomplished, and the commanding general looks to the army for greater efforts to drive from our soil every vestige of the presence of the invader."[3]

Lincoln, in despair that yet another general had a weak grasp of strategy and failed to follow victory with pursuit, wrote to Halleck:

I left the telegraph office a good deal dissatisfied. You know I did not like the phrase, in Orders, No. 68, I believe, "Drive the invaders from our soil." Since that, I see a dispatch from General French, saying the enemy is crossing his wounded over the river in flats, without saying why he does not stop it, or even intimating a thought that it ought to be stopped. Still later, another dispatch from General Pleasonton, by direction of General Meade, to General French, stating that the main army is halted because it is believed the rebels are concentrating "on the road toward Hagerstown, beyond Fairfield," and is not to move until it is ascertained that the rebels intend to evacuate Cumberland Valley.

These things all appear to me to be connected with a purpose to cover Baltimore and Washington, and to get the enemy across the river again without a further collision, and they do not appear connected with a purpose to prevent his crossing and to destroy him. I do fear the former purpose is acted upon and the latter is rejected.

If you are satisfied the latter purpose is entertained, and is judiciously pursued, I am content. If you are not so satisfied, please look to it.[4]

Observers of the president, his cabinet officers, generals, and War Department secretaries during these difficult days recalled:

Between 3 July, when the fighting ended, and 14 July, when Lee safely returned to Virginia, Lincoln's "anxiety seemed as great as it had been during the battle itself," according to an officer in the Washington telegraph office. The president, he recalled, "walked up and down the floor, his face grave and anxious, wringing his hands and showing every sign of deep solicitude. As the telegrams came in, he traced the positions of the two armies on the maps, and several times called me up to point out their location, seeming to feel the need of talking to some one. Finally, a telegram came from Meade saying that under such and such circumstances he would engage the enemy at such and such a time. "Yes," said the President bitterly, "he will be ready to fight a magnificent battle when there is no enemy there to fight!"[5]

On July 5, visiting the wounded General Daniel Sickles, whose leg was amputated during the Battle of Gettysburg, Lincoln explained to Sickles the sources of his confidence during the three days of battle:

When Lee crossed the Potomac and entered Pennsylvania, followed by our army, I felt that the great crisis had come. I knew that defeat in a great battle on northern soil involved the loss of Washington, to be followed perhaps by the intervention of England and France in favor of the Southern Confederacy. I went to my room and got down on my knees in prayer. Never before had I prayed with so much earnestness. I wish I could repeat my prayer. I felt I must put all my trust in Almighty God. He gave our people the best country ever given to man. He alone could save it from destruction. I had tried my best to do my duty and had found myself unequal to the task. The burden was more than I could bear. I asked Him to help us and give us victory now. I was sure my prayer was answered. I had no misgivings about the result at Gettysburg.

When he rose to go, Lincoln said: Sickles, I have been told, as you have been told perhaps, your condition is serious. I am in a prophetic mood today. You will get well.[6]

Three days after Gettysburg ended, Welles wrote in his diary:

The President said this morning with a countenance indicating sadness and despondency, that Meade still lingered at Gettysburg when he should have been at Hagerstown or near the Potomac, to cut off the retreating army of Lee. While unwilling to complain, and willing and anxious to give all praise to the general and army for the great battle and victory, he feared the old idea of driving the Rebels out of Pennsylvania and Maryland instead of capturing them was still prevalent among the officers. He hoped this was not so, said he had spoken to Halleck and urged that the right tone and spirit should be infused into officers and men, and General Meade specially reminded of his wishes and expectations. But General Halleck gave him a short and curt reply, showing that he did not participate and sympathize in this feeling, and, said the President, "I drop the subject."

This is the President's error. His own convictions and conclusions are infinitely superior to Halleck's more sensible and more correct always but yet he says it being strictly a military question, it is proper I should defer to Halleck whom I have called here to counsel, advise and direct me in these matters, where he is an expert. I question whether he should be considered an expert. I look upon him as a pretty good critic of other men's deeds and acts, but as incapable to originating or directing military operations.[7]

The next day Lincoln sent a note to Halleck, who telegraphed it to Meade, adding a word:

We have certain information that Vicksburg surrendered to General Grant on the 4th of July. Now, if General Meade can complete his work, so gloriously prosecuted thus far, by the literal or substantial destruction of Lee's army, the rebellion will be over.[8]

As Meade's inertia persisted, on July 8 Welles wrote:

The Potomac is swollen by the late heavy rains and the passage of the Rebel army rendered impossible for several days. In the mean time our generals should not lose their opportunity. I trust they will not. Providence favors them. Want of celerity however had been one of the infirmities of some of our generals in this war. Stanton and Halleck should stimulate the officers to press forward at such a time as this, but I fear that in smaller matters they will be more unmindful of these which are more important. Halleck's policy consists in stopping the enemy's advance, or in driving the enemy back,—never to capture. Enough has been said to S. and H. to make them aware of the urgency of the President and Cabinet, and I trust it may have a good effect, but I do not learn that anything extra is being done. The President says he is rebuffed when he undertakes to push matters.[9]

Although Vicksburg and Gettysburg were triumphs, the aftermath of these battles proved frustrating. July 14 was a dark day for Lincoln. Meade had telegraphed that five of six generals were unqualifiedly opposed to making an attack. John Hay recorded in his diary:

> This morning the Prest. seemed depressed by Meade's despatches of last night. They were so cautiously & almost timidly worded—talked about reconnoitering to find the enemy's weak place and other such. He said he feared he would do nothing.
>
> About noon came the despatch stating that our worst fears were true. The enemy had gotten away unhurt. The Prest was deeply grieved. ["]We had them within our grasp" he said. "We had only to stretch forth our hands & they were ours. And nothing I could say or do could make the Army move."
>
> Several days ago he sent a despatch to Meade which must have cut like a scourge but Meade returned so reasonable and earnest a reply that the Prest concluded he knew best what he was doing & reconciled to the apparent inaction which he hoped was merely apparent.
>
> Every day he has watched the progress of the Army with agonizing impatience, hopes struggling with fear. He has never been easy in his own mind about Gen Meade since Meades General Order in which he called on his troops to drive the invader from our soil. The Prest. says "This is a dreadful reminiscence of McClellan. The same spirit that moved McC. to claim a great victory because Pa & Md were safe. The hearts of 10 million people sank within them when McClellan raised that shout last fall. Will our Generals never get that idea out of their heads? The whole country is *our* soil."[10]

The mood only darkened as Lee's army slipped back into Virginia. "The cabinet was not full today," wrote Welles. He continued:

> The President said he did not believe we could take up anything in Cabinet to-day. Probably none of us were in a right frame of mind for deliberation—he was not. He wanted to see General Halleck at once. Stanton left abruptly. I retired slowly. The President hurried and overtook me. We walked together across the lawn and stopped and conversed a few moments at the gate. He said with a voice and countenance which I shall never forget, that he had dreaded yet expected this—that there has seemed to him for a full week, a determination that Lee should escape with his force and plunder,—and that, my God is the last of this Army of the Potomac. There is bad faith somewhere. Meade had been pressed and urged but only one of his generals was for an immediate attack, was ready to pounce on Lee—the rest held back. What does it mean, Mr. Welles? Great God, what does it mean? I asked what orders had gone from him, while our troops had been

quiet with a defeated and broken army in front, and an impassable river to prevent their escape. He could not say that anything positive had been done, but both Stanton and Halleck professed to agree with him and he thought Stanton did. Halleck was all the time wanting to hear from Meade. Why, I said, he is within four hours of Meade—is it not strange that he has not been up there to advise and encourage him. I stated I had observed the inertness, if not incapacity, of the General in Chief and had hoped that he, who had better and more correct views would issue peremptory orders. The President immediately softened his tone and said Halleck knew better than he what to do—he was a military man, had a military education, he had brought him here to give the President military advice. His views and mine are widely different. It is better that I who am not a military man should defer to him, rather than he to me. I told the President I did not profess to be a military man, but there were some things on which I could form perhaps as correct an opinion as General Halleck, and I believed that he, the President could more correctly direct military movements than Halleck, who it appeared to me could originate nothing, and was as now, all the time waiting to hear from Meade or whoever was in command.

I can see that the shadows which have crossed my mind have clouded the President's also. On only one or two occasions have I ever seen the President so troubled, so dejected and discouraged.[11]

At 1:00 p.m. on July 14 Halleck wired Meade:

The enemy should be pursued and cut up, wherever he may have gone. This pursuit may or may not be upon the rear or flank, as circumstances may require. The inner flank toward Washington presents the greatest advantages. Supply yourself from the country as far as possible. I cannot advise details, as I do not know where Lee's army is, nor where your pontoon bridges are. I need hardly say to you that the escape of Lee's army without another battle had created great dissatisfaction in the mind of the President, and it will require an active and energetic pursuit on your part to remove the impression that it had not been sufficiently active heretofore.[12]

An hour and a half later Meade responded:

Having performed my duty conscientiously and to the best of my ability, the censure of the President conveyed in your last dispatch of 1 p.m. this day, is, in my judgment, so undeserved that I feel compelled most respectfully to ask to be immediately relieved from the command of this army.[13]

On reading Meade's response Lincoln wrote a lengthy letter to the general, penning on the envelope, "To Gen. Meade, never sent, or signed." What he forebore to tell Meade was his gratitude for winning at Gettysburg, his "deep distress," and the meaning for the war's duration of letting Lee escape:

> I have just seen your dispatch to Gen. Halleck, asking to be relieved of your command, because of a supposed censure of mine. I am very—*very*—grateful to you for the magnificent success you gave the cause of this country at Gettysburg; and I am sorry now to be the author of the slightest pain to you. But I was in such deep distress myself that I could not restrain some expression of it. I had been oppressed nearly ever since the battles at Gettysburg, by what appeared to be evidences that yourself, and Gen. Couch, and Gen. Smith, were not seeking a collision with the enemy, but were trying to get him to cross the river without another battle. What these evidences were, if you please, I hope to tell you at some time, when we shall both feel better. The case, summarily stated, is this: You fought and beat the enemy at Gettysburg; and, of course, to say the least, his loss was as great as yours. He retreated; and you did not, as it seemed to me, pressingly pursue him; but a flood in the river detained him, till, by slow degrees, you were again upon him. You had at least twenty thousand veteran troops directly with you, and as many more raw ones within supporting distance, all in addition to those who fought with you at Gettysburg; while it was not possible that he had received a single recruit; and yet you stood and let the flood run down, bridges be built, and the enemy move away at his leisure, without attacking him. . . .
>
> Again, my dear general, I do not believe you appreciate the magnitude of the misfortune involved in Lee's escape. He was within your easy grasp, and to have closed upon him would, in connection with our other late successes, have ended the war. As it is, the war will be prolonged indefinitely. If you could not safely attack Lee last monday, how can you possibly do so South of the river, when you can take with you very few more than two thirds of the force you then had in hand? It would be unreasonable to expect, and I do not expect you can now effect much. Your golden opportunity is gone, and I am distressed immeasurably because of it.
>
> I beg you will not consider this a prossecution, or persecution of yourself. As you had learned that I was dissatisfied, I have thought it best to kindly tell you why.[14]

The depth of Lincoln's disappointment was recorded by Noah Brooks, who after a visit to Meade's camp, reported to the commander in chief on what he had seen and heard. "His grief and anger were something sorrowful to behold." The lost opportunity warped Lincoln's normal generosity toward others. Responding to a letter from Simon Cameron, former secretary of war, he said: "I would give much to be relieved of the impression that Meade, Couch, Smith, and all, since the battle of Gettysburg, have striven only to get Lee over the river without another fight."[15]

Long after the event, Robert Todd Lincoln confided to a golfing companion that his father had wept on learning that Lee had crossed the Potomac. The account reads:

> Entering my father's room right after the Battle of Gettysburg, I found him in tears, with head bowed upon his arms resting on the table at which he sat. "Why, what is the matter, father," I asked. For a brief interval he remained silent, then raised his head, and the explanation of his grief was forthcoming. "My boy," said he, "when I heard that the bridge at Williamsport had been swept away, I sent for General Haupt and asked him how soon he could replace the same. He replied, 'If I were uninterrupted I could build a bridge with the material there within twenty-four hours and, Mr. President, General Lee has engineers as skillful as I am'. Upon hearing this I at once wrote Meade to attack without delay, and if successful to destroy my letter, but in case of failure to preserve it for his vindication. I have just learned that at a Council of War, of Meade and his Generals, it had been determined not to pursue Lee, and now the opportune chance of ending this bitter struggle is lost."[16]

Both Meade's failure to pursue Lee and the advice of his commanders became the subjects of newspaper comment. General Oliver O. Howard, one of those commanders, wrote to Lincoln:

> Having noticed in the newspapers certain statements bearing upon the battles [*sic*] of Gettysburg and subsequent operations which I deem calculated to convey a wrong impression to your mind, I wish to submit a few statements. The successful issue of the battle of Gettysburg was due mainly to the energetic operations of our present commanding General prior to the engagement and to the manner in which he handled his troops on the field. The reserves have never before during the war been thrown in at just the right moment.... Moreover I have never seen a more hearty co-operation on the part of General officers as since General Meade took the command.

As to not attacking the enemy prior to leaving his stronghold beyond the Antietam it is by no means certain that the repulse of Gettysburg might not have been turned upon us; at any rate the Commanding General was in favor of an immediate attack but with the evident difficulties in our way, the uncertainty of a success and the strong conviction of our best military minds against the risk, I must say, that I think the General acted wisely.

As to my request to make a reconnaissance on the morning of the 14th which the papers state was refused; the facts are, that the General had required me to reconnoiter the evening before and give my opinion as to the practicability of making a lodgement on the enemy's left, and his answer to my subsequent request was, that the movements he had already ordered would subserve the same purpose.

We have, if I may be allowed to say it, a Commanding General in whom all the officers, with whom I have come in contact, express complete confidence. I have said this much because of the censure and of the misrepresentations which have grown out of the escape of Lee's army.[17]

Lincoln's response on July 21 disclosed both his mortification and his generosity toward Meade:

Your letter of the 18th. is received. I was deeply mortified by the escape of Lee across the Potomac, because the substantial destruction of his army would have ended the war, and because I believed, such destruction was perfectly easy—believed that Gen. Meade and his noble army had expended all the skill, and toil, and blood, up to the ripe harvest, and then let the crop go to waste. Perhaps my mortification was heightened because I had always believed—making my belief a hobby possibly—that the main rebel army going North of the Potomac, could never return, if well attended to; and because I was so greatly flattered in this belief, by the operations at Gettysburg. A few days having passed, I am now profoundly grateful for what was done, without criticism for what was not done. Gen. Meade has my confidence as a brave and skillful officer, and a true man.[18]

On July 29 a defensive Meade telegraphed Halleck, "I am making every effort to prepare this army for an advance." Halleck helped in easing Meade's relationship with Lincoln. On the same day Halleck wrote to the general:

I take this method of writing you a few words which I could not communicate in any other way. Your fight at Gettysburg met with universal approbation of all military men here. You handled your troops in that battle as well, if not better, than any general has handled his army during the war. You brought all your forces into action at the right time and place, which no commander of the Army of the Potomac has done before. You may well be proud of that battle. The President's order of proclamation of July 4th showed how much he appreciated your success. And now a few words in regard to subsequent events. You should not have been surprised or vexed at the President's disappointment at the escape of Lee's army. He had examined into all the details of sending you reinforcements to satisfy himself that every man who could possibly be spared from other places had been sent to your army. He thought that Lee's defeat was so certain that he felt no little impatience at his unexpected escape. I have no doubt, General, that you felt the disappointment as keenly as any one else. Such things sometimes occur to us without any fault of our own. Take it all together, your short campaign has proved your superior generalship, and you merit, as you will receive, the confidence of the Government and the gratitude of the country. I need not assure you, General, that I have lost none of the confidence which I felt in you when I recommended you for the command.[19]

Meade continued in command of the Army of the Potomac, but there was little action to show for it. In late September Welles took occasion to ask what Meade had been doing in recent weeks. Lincoln's reply was sour.

I asked what Meade was doing with his immense army and Lee's skeleton and depleted show in front. He said he could not learn that Meade was doing anything, or wanted to do anything. It is, said he, the same old story of this Army of the Potomac. Imbecility, inefficiency—don't want to *do*—is defending the Capital. I inquired of Meade, said he, what force was in front. Meade replied he thought there were 40,000 infantry. I replied he might add 50,000 and if Lee with 60,000 could defend their capital against our 90,000,—and if defense i[s] all our armies are to do,—we might, I thought, detach 50,000 from his command, and leave him with 40,000 to defend us. Oh, groaned the President, it is terrible, terrible, this weakness, this indifference of our Potomac generals, with such armies of good and brave men.

Why said I not rid yourself of Meade who may be a good man and good officer, but is not a great general, certainly is not the man for the position he occupies. The escape of Lee with his army across the Potomac has distressed me almost beyond any occurrence of the War. And the impression made upon me in the personal interview shortly after was not [as] I wished, had inspired no confidence.

The President assented to all I said, but "What can I do, he asked, with such generals as we have? To sweep away the whole of them from the chief command would cause a shock, and be likely to lead to combinations and troubles greater than we now have. I see all the difficulties as you do. They oppress me."[20]

Three days before this conversation, a hesitant Meade had telegraphed Halleck: "I have reached such a position that I do not feel justified in making a further advance without some more positive authority than was contained in your last letter enclosing one from the President." Halleck turned the dispatch over to the president, who urged the general to take advantage of his numerical superiority and "make Lee's army, and not Richmond [your army's] objective point." The military authority Colonel Trevor Nevitt Dupuy, a century later, judged that the letter "may be the most remarkable military document ever written by a civilian. It reveals the thinking processes of a highly logical mind—a mind clearly unmilitary, but equally clearly familiar with the fundamentals of strategy and with the best principles of war."[21]

In mid-October Lincoln pursued the matter of getting Meade to move. In a letter to Halleck, Lincoln urged Meade to attack Lee, adding that Meade would get the honor for success, but Lincoln would get the blame for failure:

> I do not believe Lee can have over sixty thousand effective men. Longstreet's corps would not be sent away, to bring an equal force back upon the same road; and there is no other direction for them to have come from. Doubtless, in making the present movement Lee gathered in all available scraps, and added them to Hills & Ewell's corps; but that is all. And he made the movement in the belief that *four* corps had left Gen. Meade; and Gen. Meade's apparently avoiding a collision with him has confirmed him in that belief. If Gen. Meade can now attack him on a field no worse than equal for us, and will do so with all the skill and courage, which he, his officers and men posses, the honor will be his if he succeeds, and the blame may be mine if he fails.[22]

Halleck sent the letter to Meade, who acknowledged receipt, replying "that it has been my intention to attack the enemy, if I can find him on a field no more than equal for us." Later, at a cabinet meeting attended by Meade, Lincoln said, "Do you know, general, what your attack towards Lee for a week after the battle reminded me of?"

"No, Mr. President, what is it?"

"I'll be hanged if I could think of anything else than an old woman trying to shoo her geese across a creek."[23]

No significant action transpired, and Meade went into winter quarters. Early in 1864 he became involved in a storm of controversy over what he did at Gettysburg. The Joint Committee on the Conduct of the War summoned him for investigation. What he described as "assaults upon my reputation," particularly a pseudonymous piece in the *New York Herald,* caused him to ask for a court of inquiry.

Lincoln refused, saying it was unnecessary, and charitably remarked that it would be better for Meade to be engaged in doing more good service to the country.

CHAPTER TWENTY-SEVEN

LINCOLN VS. SEYMOUR

Horatio Seymour, elected Democratic governor of New York in 1862 in part in an anti-Lincoln campaign, had previously served as governor in the early 1850s. A Douglas Democrat, he had urged compromise during the secession winter. A soft-spoken, smiling man, tall, thin, and swarthy, he disarmed and charmed people, his manner not suggesting his strong convictions: dislike of abolitionists, conscription, and suspension of habeas corpus. In late 1862 he cooperated with Republican governor Edwin D. Morgan in furnishing troops for the Union army. But as governor of New York Seymour oversaw one of the largest, wealthiest, and most significant states in the Union, a position that, given his views, brought him into immediate and sustained conflict with Lincoln.

On the first day of January 1863, in his inaugural speech, Seymour stressed his loyalty to the Union and to states' rights under the Constitution. A week later he sent his annual message to the legislature. Only about one-third of its forty pages pertained to state affairs. He attacked arbitrary arrests, abolition, and suspension of habeas corpus and pointed out that Lincoln was a minority president. Yet he recognized the need to support the Union Army and rejected division of the Union.[1]

William Cullen Bryant, poet and editor, responded in an editorial headed "The Perversions and Errors of Governor Seymour's Message":

> The message of Governor Seymour deserves the consideration which it receives, not because of its originality or profundity, but because of the importance which attaches to it as a political manifesto from a partisan Governor of the great State of New York, bent upon opposing the Administration of the general government in this time of rebellion and war. . . .

Governor Seymour is a politician; not an inexperienced politician, with his position yet to select, his lessons yet to learn—but a trained politician, too far advanced to willingly change his theories or practices. He has "learned the ropes" of the system as it is, or, rather, as it was while he was undergoing his political education. Had the Charleston Convention compromised its difficulties, no man in the land was so likely to be its nominee for President as Horatio Seymour of New York . . .

He is doubtless perfectly sincere in desiring the Union to be preserved, especially if he can share largely in the honor of preserving it. Besides, its preservation is essential to his political purposes. Another thing, also, is essential to them—very essential—and that is *slavery*.[2]

Seymour at times seemed lax in corresponding with Lincoln. On one occasion, however, he had an account from his older brother, John, of an exchange of views with the president. John on January 9 wrote to Horatio saying Lincoln had remarked that he and the governor had the same stake in the nation's existence, and if the Union were destroyed there would be no next president.

John reported his own response to Lincoln:

To this I replied . . . that you had no aspirations for the Presidency; that when you were here with me several years ago you said you did not envy the occupant of the White House; that there was too much trouble and responsibility, and no peace there; that you, and those who believed with you, were determined to sustain and maintain this Government and keep the country unbroken, and considered the ballot box the only remedy for evils; that you contended for respect for those in authority, and that while holding him responsible, you would sustain him against any unconstitutional attempts against his administration from any quarter; that these were the doctrines of your message. He said he would read it. I also said that although you did not indulge in loud denunciation of the rebellion as that was not your manner, yet it was a very great grief to you; that you were especially vexed at some of the Republican party who claimed to have a patent right for all the patriotism. That our all was at stake, and if you and the Democratic party differed with him respecting military arrests, it was with the same view, and that was the benefit of the country.[3]

In an unusual letter, which he could have written only to a Democratic governor of New York, Lincoln on March 23 explained:

You and I are substantially strangers; and I write this chiefly that we may become better acquainted. I, for the time being, am at the head of a nation which is in great peril; and you are at the head of the greatest State of that nation. As to maintaining the nation's life, and integrity, I assume, and believe, there can not be a difference of *purpose* between you and me. If we should differ as to the *means,* it is important that such difference should be as small as possible—that it should not be enhanced by unjust suspicions on one side or the other. In the performance of my duty, the cooperation of your State, as that of others, is needed—in fact, is indispensable. This alone is a sufficient reason why I should wish to be at a good understanding with you.

Please write me at least as long a letter as this—of course, saying in it, just what you think fit.[4]

Three weeks later Seymour replied, rejecting the smallness of the differences between them, and claiming he spoke for half of the northern people:

I have delayed answering your letter for some days with a view of preparing a paper in which I wished to state clearly the aspect of public affairs from the stand point I occupy. . . . I have been prevented from giving my views in the manner I intended by a pressure of official duties. . . . In the mean while I assure you that no political resentments, or no personal objects will turn me aside from the pathway I have marked out for myself—I intend to show to those charged with the administration of public affairs a due deference and respect and to yield them a just and generous support in all measures they may adopt within the scope of their constitutional powers. For the preservation of this Union I am ready to make every sacrifice. . . .[5]

Seymour never sent the promised letter.

Following the arrest of Clement Vallandigham, the Democratic Copperhead in Ohio who publicly spoke out and opposed the war, Seymour sharply criticized the event in a public letter widely distributed throughout the North:

I cannot attend the meeting at the capitol this evening, but I wish to state my opinion in regard to the arrest of Mr. Vallandigham. It is an act which has brought dishonor upon our country. It is full of danger to our persons and our homes. It bears upon its front a conscious violation of law and justice.

Acting upon the evidence of detailed informers, shrinking from the light of day, in the darkness of night, armed men violated the home of an American citizen, and furtively bore him away to military trial, conducted without those safeguards known in the proceedings of our judicial tribunals. The transaction involved a series of offenses against our most sacred rights.

It interfered with the freedom of speech; it violated our rights to be secure in our homes against unreasonable searches and seizures; it pronounced sentence without trial, save one which was a mockery, which insulted as well as wronged. The perpetrators now seek to impose punishment, not for an offense against law, but for the disregard of an invalid order put forth in the utter disregard of the principles of civil liberty.

If this proceeding is approved by the government, and sanctioned by the people, it is not merely a step toward revolution, it is revolution; it will not only lead to military despotism, it establishes military despotism. In this aspect it must be accepted, or in this aspect rejected. If it is upheld, our liberties are overthrown; the safety of our persons, security of our property will hereafter depend upon the arbitrary will of such military rulers as may be placed over us; while our Constitutional guarantees will be broken down.

Even now, the governors and courts of some of the great Western States have sunk into insignificance before the despotic powers claimed and exercised by military men who have been sent into their borders. It is a fearful thing to increase the danger which now overhangs us, by treating the law, the judiciary, and the State authorities with contempt.

The people of this country now wait with the deepest anxiety the decisions of the administration upon these acts. Having given it a generous support in the conduct of the war, we pause to see what kind of government it is for which we are asked to pour out our blood and our treasures.

The action of the administration will determine in the minds of more than one half of the people of the loyal States, whether the war is waged to put down rebellion at the South or destroy free institutions at the North. We look for its decision with most solemn solicitude.[6]

Seymour carried on a three-pronged dispute with Lincoln over arbitrary arrest, conscription, and emancipation. And Seymour refused to enlist blacks in New York regiments. After the Union League Club of New York was organized, its members asked Seymour for permission to form a black regiment. He claimed he had no authority to give permission. Eventually an appeal was made to Secretary of War Edwin Stanton, and he gave permission. A black regiment was organized, private funds of $18,000 were contributed; the black regiment paraded on Broadway, and in January 1864, it marched off to duty.

Despite his differences with Lincoln, Seymour loyally and with alacrity supplied troops to the administration. As Lee was crossing the Potomac in 1863, the administration called for additional militia. Seymour rushed to dispatch New York troops. Stanton on June 18 telegraphed Seymour: "The President directs me to return thanks to His Excellency Governor Seymour, and his staff, for their energetic and prompt action."

Lee's northward advance caused many voices to clamor for restoration of McClellan to command. Pressure on the president to restore McClellan came from Philadelphia, New York, New Jersey, and elsewhere. On June 18 the *National Intelligencer* in Washington, under the heading "A Calm Appeal," urged:

> After much reflection and with a full sense of the responsibility which it involves, we feel it our solemn duty at this juncture to avow the deliberate but earnest conviction that the President cannot by any one act do so much to restore the confidence of the nation as by the recall of General McClellan to the army of the Potomac.[7]

This view provoked a tart reply by Bryant's *New York Evening Post:* "The utter rout and annihilation of the Army of the Potomac by the rebel forces under Lee in a pitched battle would not be a severer blow to the hopes of the friends of the Union than such an act of folly on the part of Lincoln."[8]

If Seymour had refrained from asking that his fellow Democrat General McClellan be restored to command, on the Fourth of July, last day of the Union's great victory at Gettysburg, he lashed out at the Lincoln administration, asserting that it looked upon members of the Democratic organization as "men of treasonable purposes and enemies to our country."[9]

Alexander McClure, an influential Pennsylvanian and Republican, on the morning of June 30 had telegraphed Lincoln:

> Have been twenty-four hours hoping to hasten the organization of troops. It seems impossible to do so to an extent at all commensurate with the emergency. Our people are paralyzed—for want of confidence and leadership, and, unless they can be inspired with hope, we shall fail to do anything worthy

of our State or Government. I am fully persuaded that to call McClellan to a command here would be the best thing that could be done. He could rally troops from Pennsylvania, and I am well assured that New York and New Jersey would also respond to his call with great alacrity. With his efficiency in organizing men, and the confidence he would inspire, early and effective relief might be afforded us, and great service rendered to the Army of the Potomac.

Unless we are in some way rescued from the hopelessness now prevailing, we shall have practically an inefficient conscription, and be powerless to help either ourselves or the National Government.

After free consultation with trusted friends of the Administration, I hesitate not to urge that McClellan be called here. He can render us and you the best service, and in the present crisis no other consideration should prevail. Without military success we can have no political success, no matter who commands. In this request I reflect what seems to be an imperative necessity rather than any preference of my own.[10]

Lincoln briefly responded: "Do we gain anything by opening one leak to stop another? Do we gain any thing by quieting one clamor, merely to open another, and probably a larger one?"[11]

On the same day Lincoln responded to a telegram from New Jersey's governor Joel Parker. Parker wrote:

The people of New Jersey are apprehensive that the invasion of the enemy may extend to her soil. We think that the enemy should be driven from Pennsylvania. There is now certainly great apathy under such fearful circumstances. That apathy should be removed. The people of New Jersey want McClellan at the head of the Army of the Potomac. If that cannot be done, then we ask that he may be put at the head of the New Jersey, New York, and Pennsylvania troops now in Pennsylvania, defending these Middle States from invasion. If either appointment be made, the people would rise en masse.

I feel it my duty, respectfully, to *communicate* this state of feeling to you.[12]

Lincoln wrote:

Your despatch of yesterday received. I really think the attitude of the enemies' army in Pennsylvania, presents us the best opportunity we have had since the war began. I think you will not see the foe in New-Jersey. I beg you to

394

be assured that no one out of my position can know so well as if he were in it, the difficulties and involvements of replacing Gen. McClellan in command—and this aside from any imputations upon him.

Please accept my sincere thanks for what you have done, and are doing to get troops forward.[13]

Drafting, authorized in March by Congress, began in New York City in mid-July. On Monday, July 13, anti-draft riots erupted as enraged white workers feared black competition, Confederate sympathizers, and the foreign born, among others. Some of the rioters shouted, "How are you, Old Abe?" and hundreds joined in the violence—looting, killing, and arson. Seymour was in New Jersey until the morning of Tuesday, July 14. Returning to town he sought to soothe the rioters. Standing on the steps of City Hall he addressed a crowd of rioters, supposedly as "My friends," doing lasting injustice to his historical reputation. Provost Marshal James B. Fry on Wednesday suspended drafting. Federal troops arrived to restore order.

Major General John A. Dix, a Union Democrat, one of the best of Lincoln's political generals and no friend of Seymour, was assigned to the Department of the East after the draft riots. On July 30 he asked Seymour whether state forces would be available in case of resistance:

[W]hether the military power of the State may be relied on to enforce the execution of the [draft] law in case of forcible resistance to it. I am very anxious that there should be perfect harmony between the Federal Government and that of the State of New York, and if, under your authority to see the laws faithfully executed, I can feel assured . . . I need not ask the War Department to put at my disposal . . . troops in the service of the United States. . . .[14]

Instead of replying to Dix, Seymour on August 1 wired Provost Marshal General Fry in Washington, saying he had information from Nelson J. Waterbury, judge advocate general of New York:

Mr. Waterbury told me on his return from Washington that the Draft would not be made in New York and Brooklyn without some notice being given to me. I see it is stated in some of the Journals that it will [be] made at once. I trust this is not so. I have in preparation a letter to the President which will reach him next week probably on Tuesday next [.][15]

Seymour turned to Lincoln for help, writing him a long letter. Seymour complained that the quotas assigned to New York and Kings County were unjust; he asked that the draft be suspended until the results of recruiting were known and that the courts should judge the constitutionality of the draft law.

Lincoln replied on August 7, noting disparities in district quotas and presenting the arithmetic for some options in addressing these, but also insisting that the draft proceed forthwith because time was of the essence; his full reply is in chapter 20.[16] The epistolary dispute continued. Seymour answered Lincoln:

I regret your refusal to comply with my request to have the draft in this State suspended until it can be ascertained if the enrollments are made in accordance with the laws. . . . I now send you a full report, made to me by Judge-Advocate-General [Nelson J.] Waterbury. . . . You will see by the report . . . that there is no theory which can explain or justify the enrollments in this State.[17]

Lincoln replied:

Yours of the 8th. with Judge Advocate General Waterbury's report, was received to-day. Asking you to remember that I consider *time* as being very important, both to the general cause of the country, and to the soldiers already in the field, I beg to remind you that I waited, at your request, from the 1st till the 6th. Inst. to receive your communication dated the 3rd. In view of its great length, and the known time, and apparant care, taken in its preparation, I did not doubt that it contained your full case as you desired to present it. It contained figures for twelve Districts, omitting the other nineteen, as I supposed, because you found nothing to complain of, as to them. I answered accordingly. In doing so, I laid down the principle to which I purpose adhering—which is, to proceed with the draft, at the same time employing infallible means to avoid any great wrongs. With the communication received to-day, you send figures for twenty eight Districts, including the twelve sent before, and still omitting three, from which I suppose the enrolments are not yet received. In looking over this fuller list of twenty eight Districts, I find that the quotas for sixteen of them are above 2000 and below 2700, while, of the rest, six are above 2700 and six are below 2000. Applying the principle to these new facts, the 5th. and

7th. Districts must be added to the four in which the quotas have already been reduced to 2200 for the first draft; and, with these, four others must be added to those to be re-enrolled.

The correct case will then stand:

The quotas of the 2nd. 4th. 5th. 6th. 7th. & 8th. Districts fixed at 2200 for the first draft.

The Provost-Marshal-General informs me that the drawing is already completed in 16th. 17th. 18th. 22nd. 24th. 26th. 27th. 28th. 29th. & 30th. Districts.

In the others, except the three outstanding, the drawing will be made upon the quotas as now fixed.

After the first draft, the 2nd. 4th. 5th. 6th. 7th. 8th. 16th. 17th. 21st. 25th. 29th & 31st. Districts will be re-enrolled for the purpose, and in the manner stated in my letter of the 7th. Inst. The same principle will be applied to the now outstanding Districts when they shall come in. No part of my former letter is repudiated, by reason of not being restated in this, or for any other cause.[18]

He later explained to Stanton what he done about the New York draft:

In my correspondence with Gov. Seymour in relation to the draft, I have said to him, substantially, that credits shall be given for volunteers up to the latest moment, before drawing in any district, that can be done without producing confusion or delay. In order to do this, let our mustering officers in New-York, and elsewhere, be at once instructed that whenever they muster into our service any number of volunteers, to at once make return to the War Department, both by telegraph and mail, the date of the muster, the number mustered, and the Congressional or enrolment District, or Districts, of their residences, giving the number separately for each District. Keep these returns diligently posted, and by them give full credit on the quotas, if possible, on the last day before the draft begins in any District.

Again, I have informed Governor Seymour that he shall be notified of the time when the draft is to commence in each District in his State. This is equally proper for all the States. In order to carry it out, I propose that so soon as the day for commencing the draft in any District is definitely determined, the Governor of the State, including the District, be notified thereof, both by telegraph and mail, in form, about as follows:

. . . .

. . . . 1863

Governor of . . . .

. . . .

You are notified that the draft will commence in the . . . . District, at . . . . on the day of . . . . 1863, at . . . . . . A.M. of said day. Please acknowledge receipt of this, by telegraph and mail.

. . . .

. . . .

This notice may be given by the Provost-Marshall-General here, the sub-Provost-Marshall-Generals in the States, or perhaps by the District Provost-Marshalls.

Whenever we shall have so far proceeded in New York as to make the re-enrolments specially promised there, practicable, I wish that also to go forward; and I wish Governor Seymour notified of it; so that, if he choose, he can place agents of his, with ours, to see the work fairly done.[19]

In December Lincoln named a commission to study the draft in New York. Late in February of the next year he described to Stanton what the commission had done and his view of the report:

You ask some instruction from me in relation to the Report of Special Commission constituted by an order of the War Department, dated Dec. 5 1863, "to revise the enrolment & quotas of the City & State of New-York, & report whether there be any & what errors, or irregularities therein, and what corrections, if any should be made." [The aspect of this case, as presented by this order and report, is entirely new to me, I having personally known nothing of the order, commission, or report, until now presented for my consideration.] In the correspondence between the Governor of New-York and myself last summer, I understood him to complain that the enrolments in several of the Districts of that State had been neither accurately nor honestly made; and, in view of this I for the draft then immediately ensuing, ordered an arbitrary reduction of the quotas in several of the Districts, wherein they seemed too large, [for the draft then immediately ensuing,] and said "After this drawing these four Districts and also the seventeenth and twenty-ninth shall be carefully re-enrolled, and, if you please, agents of yours may witness every step of the process." In a subsequent letter I believe some additional Districts were put to the list of those to be re-enrolled. My idea was to do the work over, according to the law, in presence of the complaining party, and thereby to correct anything which might be found amiss. The Commission, whose work I am considering, seem to have proceeded upon a totally different idea. Not going forth to find men at all, they have proceeded altogether upon paper examinations and mental processes. One of their conclusions, as I understand is, that as the law stands, and attempting to follow it, the e[n]rolling officers could not have made the enrolments much more accurately than they did. The report, on this point, might be useful to Congress.

The Commission conclude that the quotas for the draft should be based upon entire population, and they proceed upon this basis to give a table for the State of New-York, in which some districts are reduced, and some increased. For the now ensuing draft, let the quotas stand as made by the enrolling officers, in the Districts wherein this table requires them to be increased; and let them be reduced according to the table, in the others. This to be no precedent for subsequent action; but as I think this report may, on full consideration, be shown to have much that is valuable in it, I suggest that such consideration be given it; and that it be especially considered whether its suggestions can be conformed to without an alteration of the law.[20]

Not hearing from Seymour on so important a matter under his responsibility, Dix, anticipating resumption of the draft, on August 12 appealed to Lincoln. He asked for 10,000 Federal troops and inquired whether the president should call out the state militia.

Lincoln acted swiftly. John Hay recorded in his diary:

The preparations for the draft still continue in New York. Dix is getting ready rather slowly. Fry goes to N.Y. tonight, armed with various powers. He carries a paper to be used in certain contingencies calling the militia of the State into the service of the general Government, and calling upon rioters to disperse. . . . Dix has already authority to declare martial law when it appears necessary. The devil of treason is pretty well muzzled there. We must tear out its fangs if it takes off the muzzle. Seymour is half lunatic, half demagogue. He is a delicate soul, without courage or honesty, fallen on evil times. His reason, never the most robust, is giving way under its overwork.[21]

The paper, written by Stanton and hand-carried by Colonel Fry to Dix August 14, read:

Enclosed herewith I send you by the hands of Colonel Fry—

1. A Proclamation by the President to be used by you in case of any necessity arising for the employment of military force to overcome unlawful combinations against the authority of the General Government in executing the Act of Congress to enroll and call out the National force. Of this necessity you are authorized to be judge, and if it arises, you will fill up the blanks and promulgate the Proclamation. The original with the Great Seal remains with the Archives of the Government in the State Department.

2. A call upon the Governor of New York by the President, notifying him to issue orders to Major General Sanford (Charles W.) (*sic*). The use of this paper is left to your discretion. It has occurred to the President that it may be proper and serviceable to put upon Governor Seymour a call for assistance, and let him render it or shoulder the responsibility of refusing. It is not supposed that this call is essential to the authority of the President, or that the assent or obedience of Governor Seymour affects the right or power of the President to issue an order to General Sanford directly. But it may be an expedient courtesy of which you are to judge and which you should have the means of employing if you think proper.

A blank is left for you to fill up with the State of New York, or any specific districts, as the case may require, and also a blank for date to be filled.

3. An order by the President upon General Sanford to report to you.

The date and also the blank for state or specific districts are to be filled up.

You will be apprised by the Provost Marshal General what reinforcements will be sent forward. He will confer with you. Any further aid or direction you may require, will on notice, be given you if in the power of the Government.[22]

The proclamation was not made.

Lincoln directly addressed Seymour in a letter dated August 15, provisionally calling forth the state militia, leaving a blank space to be filled in concerning state or districts to be called upon and date. At 9:30 the next morning Seymour wired Lincoln, asking that volunteers already recruited be substitutes for draftees in their districts:

In view of the uncertainty as to the quotas which may be required from the several Congressional districts . . . there is a doubt by many as to whether volunteers now recruited will be available to reduce the quotas as they may be ultimately adjusted. This doubt interferes with the recruiting of volunteers. I therefore request that volunteers heretofore recruited and mustered . . . shall be accepted as substitutes for such conscripts residing in the same Congressional districts, whether now drawn or heretofore drawn, as may be designated by the State authorities. I am satisfied that such an arrangement will secure immediately a large number of volunteers.[23]

A perplexed president replied:

Your despatch of this morning is just received; and, I fear I do not perfectly understand it.

My view of, the principle is that every soldier obtained voluntarily, leaves one less to be obtained by draft. The only difficulty is, in applying the principle properly. Looking to *time,* as heretofore I am unwilling to give up a drafted man *now,* even for the *certainty,* much less for the mere *chance,* of getting a volunteer *hereafter.*

Again, *after* the draft in any District would it not make trouble to take any drafted man out and put a volunteer in; for how shall it be determined, which drafted men is to have, the previlege of thus going out, to the exclusion of all the others?

And even *before* the draft in any District the quota must be fixed; and the draft might be postponed indefinitely; if every time a volunteer is offered the officers must stop and reconstruct the quota. At least I fear there might be this difficulty; but, at all events let credits for volunteers be given up to the last moment, which will not produce confusion or delay.

That, the principle of giving credits for volunteers shall be applied by Districts seems fair and proper, though I do not know how far, by present statistics, it is practicable. When, for any cause, a fair credit is given at one time, it should be given as soon thereafter is practicable.

My purpose is to be fair and just; and yet to not lose time.[24]

On August 19, with 10,000 Federal infantrymen and three batteries of artillery and the First Division of the New York State National Guard in place, and Seymour by proclamation urging compliance with the draft law, drafting without violence resumed. Two days later, however, Seymour again objected to the draft.[25]

Lincoln on August 26 explained to Stanton what he had done responding to Seymour's complaints. Concerned about the constitutionality of the draft law, about mid-September Lincoln penned a long opinion on the draft law, invoking the constitutional power of Congress to raise and support armies:

> We are prone . . . to find false arguments with which to excuse ourselves for opposing such disagreeable things. In this case those who desire the rebellion to succeed, and others who seek reward in a different way, are very active in accommodating us with this class of arguments. They tell us the law is unconstitutional. It is the first instance, I believe, in which the power of congress to do a thing has ever been questioned, in a case when the power is given by the constitution in express terms. Whether a power can be implied, when it is not expressed, has often been the subject of controversy; but this is the first case in which the degree of effrontery has been ventured upon, of denying a power which is plainly and distinctly written down in the constitution. The constitution declares that "The congress shall have power . . . To raise and support armies; but no appropriation of money to that use shall be for a longer term than two years." The whole scope of the conscription act is "to raise and support armies." There is nothing else in it. It makes no appropriation of money; and hence the money clause just quoted, is not touched by it. The case simply is the constitution provides that the congress shall have power to raise and support armies; and, by this act, the congress has exercised the power to raise and support armies. This is the whole of it. It is a law made in litteral pursuance of this part of the United States Constitution; and another part of the same constitution declares that "This constitution, and the laws made in pursuance thereof . . . shall be the supreme law of the land, and the judges in every state shall be bound thereby, anything in the constitution or laws of any state to the contrary notwithstanding."[26]

His opinion was never published.

Chief Justice Taney also wrote an opinion, "Thoughts on the Conscription Law in the United States." He branded the law unconstitutional. Referring to the federal structure of the American government, he asserted that the federal law encroached on state sovereignty. Through the law state militia might be taken under the federal government, destroying state militias. Pushing this line of thought to an extreme, he declared that all the civil officers of the state except for the governor might be taken into the federal government. Taney's opinion remained in manuscript, and Lincoln's public views prevailed.

By the fall of 1863 matters had not gone well for Seymour. His cooperation in raising troops, on the one hand, and his resistance to the draft, on the other, combined with his veto of a bill to allow soldiers to vote, embittered him.

Invited by Milwaukee Democrats to speak, he instead sent a letter attacking the Lincoln administration:

> In the gloomy night which overshadows the nation, there is no hope but in the restoration to power of the democratic conservative party. The fanatical leaders who precipitated this bloody conflict by underrating the South, its resources and military ability, who scoffed at the Crittenden compromises and all other efforts to avert civil war—who rejected the measures of the Peace Convention, and who, after war was forced upon us, have persistently created obstacles to its vigorous and successful prosecution, by perverting it from its original purpose, the restoration of the Union, as solemnly avowed in our National Congress, into a hopeless Emancipation crusade, and by driving from the army through abolition intrigues, General McClellan and other officers of military capacity, to make place for political adventurers— have, by their entire policy exhibited alike their incapacity to carry on war or inaugurate peace.
>
> Failing to crush the southern rebellion, their entire energies seem now directed to the destruction of popular rights and personal freedom throughout the North. Safeguards of Liberty wrested from despotism after a struggle of centuries, are by them ignored or swept away. The substitution of an irresponsible military tyranny in place of law, the suppression of free speech—the muzzling of the press, the mid-night seizure, mock trial and illegal banishment of a distinguished citizen of Ohio, and that too in a loyal district, where the civil law is in unobstructed operation,—are among the mad acts, by which all constitutional government and every principle dear to freedom, are sought to be crushed and destroyed.
>
> While we will freely expend blood and treasure to overcome southern traitors, we must with equal spirit and similar sacrifices resist such treasonable usurpation at the North. The latter formidable and dangerous, because secret and insidious in its advance, must be expelled at all hazards.[27]

Republican losses in the elections of 1862 encouraged a peace movement in the northern states. Democratic voters had won the governorship of New York and New Jersey; increased their party's numbers in the House of

Representatives, especially from Pennsylvania, Ohio, Illinois, and Indiana; and attained control of the state legislatures of Illinois and Indiana.

As if foreseeing this setback, Lincoln made a rare foray into state politics in July 1862. In a letter to Indiana senator Joseph A. Wright, who had succeeded Jesse D. Bright, expelled for treason after twenty days of debate, Lincoln wrote:

> Our mutual friends, R. W. Thompson, and John P. Usher, assure me that they believe you, more certainly than any other man, can carry the Terre-Haute District for the Union cause. Please try. The effort shall not go unappreciated, so far as I am concerned.[28]

He was hoping to replace the Peace Democrat Daniel W. Voorhees, a constant critic of the administration. Nothing came of this attempt; Voorhees was returned to Congress, where he continued to heap opprobrium on what he branded a tyrannical government. At the opening of Congress in December 1862 Senator Garrett Davis of Kentucky offered a resolution for a peace convention; Vallandigham offered another for "an immediate cessation of hostilities" and settlement of the controversies that had brought on the war.

Fernando Wood, as mayor of New York, in January 1861 had recommended secession of the city. Together with his brother Benjamin and James Brooks in the 1862 elections, he had been swept into the House of Representatives by New York voters, forming a peace triumvirate from the North's largest city. In a letter to the state's Democratic leaders, praising "the triumphant revolutionary party of New York," George Sanders, a Kentuckian who became a Confederate agent, cried: "Get rid of the Baboon, (or What is it!) Abraham Lincoln, pacifically if you can, but by the blood of his followers if necessary."[29]

Wood in December 1862 entered into a correspondence with Lincoln. Writing on December 8 he said:

> On the 25th of November last I was advised by an authority, which I deemed likely to be well informed as well a reliable and truthful, that the Southern States would send Representatives to the next Congress, provided that a full and general amnesty should permit them to do so. No guarantee or terms

were asked for other than the amnesty referred to. Deeming this information of great value, it well founded, I communicated it in substance to the Hon. George Opdyke, the mayor of this city, whom I knew to hold confidential relations to members of your Administration, and proposing, through him, that if the Government would permit the correspondence, under its own inspection, I would undertake to procure something definite and positive from persons connected with the so-called Confederate authorities. Mr. Opdyke stated in reply that several Senators from New England States were then in this city on their way to Washington, to whom he would at once communicate the proposition, and advise me of the answer. Knowing that these gentlemen were your friends, and supposing that they would immediately center with you on their arrival at the capital, and supposing that I should be speedily informed of the result, I have delayed until now making a communication direct to you.

I now learn, however, from Mr. Opdyke this day, that he failed to see these Senators when in New York, and that he had not made the proposition, and that therefore you are not in possession of it as coming from myself.

As an humble but loyal citizen, deeply impressed with the great necessity of restoring the Union of these States, I ask your immediate attention to this subject. The magnitude of the interests at stake warrant some executive action predicated upon this information, if it be only to ascertain if it be grounded upon even probable foundation. If it shall prove groundless no harm shall have been done, provided the inquiry be made, as it can be, without compromising the Government or injury to the cause in which it is now engaged. If, however, it shall prove well founded, there is no estimate too high to place upon its national value.

Now, therefore, Mr. President, I suggest that gentlemen whose former political and social relations with the leaders of the Southern revolt may be allowed to hold unofficial correspondence with them on this subject—the correspondence to be submitted to you. It may be thus ascertained what, if any, credence may be given to these statements, and also whether a peaceful solution of the present struggle may not be attainable. I am sure nothing that I can say can add to your own well known desire to produce this result. Your exalted position, the embarrassments and responsibilities which surround you upon all sides, the bleeding condition of the country, becoming exhausted, not only in the impoverishment of its best life blood, of industrial production, but in the deterioration and consequent destruction of our political institutions—all call upon you, as our chief ruler, to take one step upon the road of peaceful effort, by which to ascertain whether the time has not arrived when other methods than brute fighting may not accomplish what military force has failed to do.

In the origin of this struggle, you foresaw, that such a time would come. Your inaugural address delivered near two years ago, pointed with prophetic vision the certain results of the impending conflict of arms. Your language then was, "Suppose you go to war, you cannot fight always, and when, after much loss on both sides, and no gain or either, you cease fighting, the identical questions as to terms of intercourse are again upon you." You saw that after a bloody and terrible struggle "the still small voice of reason" would intervene and settle the controversy. You know that since the establishment of Christian civilization negotiation and compromise have, sooner or later, determined every military conquest. It cannot be otherwise here. Has not the time arrived when, to quote your own language, we should "cease fighting," at least long enough to ascertain whether "the identical questions" about which we began the fight may not be amicably and honorably adjusted, and the "terms of intercourse" be once more peaceably established? It is to this end that I now address you—with confidence in your patriotism, and with no desire to interfere with your legitimate constitutional prerogatives.[30]

A dubious Lincoln responded, asking for information and mentioning the date for his formal Emancipation Proclamation:

Your letter of the 8th, with the accompanying note of some date, was received yesterday.

The most important paragraph in the letter, as I consider, is in these words: "On the 26th of November last I was advised by an authority which I deemed likely to be well informed as well as reliable and truthful, that the Southern States would send representatives to the next Congress, provided that a full and general amnesty should permit them to do so. No guarantee or terms were asked for other than the amnesty referred to."

I strongly suspect your information will prove to be groundless; nevertheless, I thank you for communicating it to me. Understanding the phrase in the paragraph above quoted—"the Southern States would send representatives to the next Congress"—to be substantially the same as that "the people of the Southern States would cease resistance, and would reinaugurate, submit to, and maintain the national authority within the limits of such States, under the Constitution of the United States," I say that in such case the war would cease on the part of the United States; and that if within a reasonable time "a full and general amnesty" were necessary to such end, it would not be withheld.

I do not think it would be proper now to communicate this, formally or informally, to the people of the Southern States. My belief is that they already know it; and when they choose, if ever, they can communicate with me unequivocally. Nor do I think it proper now to suspend military operations to try any experiment of negotiation.

I should nevertheless receive, with great pleasure, the exact information you now have, and also such other as you may in any way obtain. Such information might be more valuable before the 1st of January than afterward.

While there is nothing in this letter which I shall dread to see in history, it is, perhaps, better for the present that its existence should not become public. I therefore have to request that you will regard it as confidential.[31]

The day after Lincoln wrote, the Union disaster at Fredericksburg occurred. Wood seized the opportunity to scold the chief executive, asserting that he was following an unconstitutional policy and urging an amnesty and peace negotiations. Lincoln did not respond to this letter.[32]

Throughout the year Union casualties mounted: killed, wounded, and missing at the major battles of Murfreesboro, Chancellorsville, Vicksburg, Gettysburg, Chickamauga, and Chattanooga. The ardor of the peacemakers abated after the twin victories of Vicksburg and Gettysburg, but in mid-December 1863 Wood introduced a peace resolution that was tabled by a vote of 98 to 59.

New Hampshire was the first state to hold an election in 1863. Though its vote revealed a gain in Democratic ballots, voters reelected the Republican governor and retained a Republican legislature. New Hampshire senator Daniel Clark, who had been criticized in 1861 for believing reconciliation possible, uneasily told Lincoln about the outcome:

Scarcely a Democrat supported the Administration. Almost every one who had heretofore avowed himself for the Union and the country turned in for peace and party. Yet we have beaten them. They have retired from the field. The two houses in convention will choose a Republican governor, and Frank Pierce in retirement will not have beaten Abraham Lincoln in office.[33]

Events in the North, including an immense peace meeting in New York City and the Ohio Democrats' nomination of the peace advocate Vallandigham for governor, encouraged the vice president of the Confederacy, Alexander H. Stephens, to undertake a peace mission to Washington. He secured two letters from Jefferson Davis, both addressed to Lincoln, one not as president of the United States but as commander in chief of the army and navy of the United States. If that letter should be refused, he would present the other letter, identical in content but addressed to Lincoln as president. Davis signed himself in like fashion. Stephens requested a pass through the Union blockade maintained by Rear Admiral Samuel P. Lee. At a lively cabinet meeting where the request was discussed, Lincoln startled Seward and Stanton when he remarked that though Stephens should not come to Washington, he himself might go to Fort Monroe to meet Stephens. The outcome was Lincoln's telegram to Lee advising that "the request of A. H. Stephens is inadmissible. The customary agents and channels are adequate for all needful communication and conference between the United States forces and the insurgents."[34]

Voting in key states held special interest. Pennsylvania, the Keystone State, witnessed a contest between the incumbent governor, Curtin, who had loyally supported the Union, and Justice George Woodward of the state's supreme court, who had ruled that the draft law was unconstitutional. Woodward in 1861 had declared, "If the Union is to be divided, I want the line of separation run north of Pennsylvania." To the consternation of many, General George B. McClellan, still in federal service, wrote a letter published on election day, saying he agreed with Woodward "in the opinion that the *sole* objects of this war are the restoration of the unity of this nation, the preservation of the Constitution, & the supremacy of the laws of the country."[35] He omitted mention of the draft, which he had urged as early as 1861. As the voting proceeded Lincoln sent two telegrams, one asking Curtin, "How does it stand?" and a later wire asking, "How does it stand now?" He was relieved to receive a reply that Curtin had been reelected by at least 20,000 votes.

Ohio Democrats nominated for governor the exiled Vallandigham, now living in Canada. Vallandigham loyalists declared that if he should win election, a large force of armed men would escort him to the Ohio State House. Ohio Republicans nominated John Brough, a Union Democrat. Lincoln watched the contest with unusual interest. Waiting in the War Department telegraph office on the day of these critical state elections, Lincoln twice wired Brough about the results. When at midnight Brough reported that he led by over 50,000 and the next morning by over 100,000, Lincoln exulted, "Glory to God in the highest. Ohio has saved the nation."[36]

New York held its election for minor state offices. In 1862 Seymour had prevailed by 10,000 votes; in 1863 after the draft riots, Republican candidates prevailed by nearly 30,000.

Indiana and Illinois, where in 1862 voters had elected Democratic legislators who proceeded to send Democratic senators to Washington, now in 1863 in effect repudiated the lawmakers by electing Republicans to local offices. In sum, except for New Jersey, Unionists carried the free states as well as the border slave states of Delaware, Maryland, and Kentucky. Undaunted by these reversals, Fernando Wood insistently called for peace overtures. In December as the new Thirty-Eighth Congress convened, he urged Lincoln to declare an amnesty for Vallandigham and other northerners sympathetic with the rebels. When Lincoln declined, Wood the next day appeared at the White House, only to have the president refuse to see him. He then introduced a resolution in the House of Representatives to open negotiations to end the war; the resolution was tabled. Kentucky's senator Green Clay Smith offered a resolution opposing peace propositions until the last rebel had put down arms, which comfortably passed. However the peace movement flared up more conspicuously the next year—1864, a presidential election year.

CHAPTER TWENTY-EIGHT

THE EMERGENCE OF GRANT

Grant in 1863 sought to strengthen his command by dismissing an unsatis-
factory general and elevating capable ones. Among many political generals,
Lincoln had commissioned John A. McClernand as a brigadier. A Union
Democrat in Congress in 1861, he loyally supported legislation to raise
men and money. He was an influential and popular Illinois politician and
had been a militia colonel. But he was not a very effective general, mainly
because he consistently went around his superiors.

Ambitious for authority and fame, and maintaining a close connection
with Lincoln (as Grant did not), McClernand was a thorn in Grant's flesh.
Grant suffered the discomfort until June 18, when he removed McClernand from command. McClernand, without the authorization required by
regulations, had given the press a copy of his order congratulating his corps,
identifying his men as heroes of the Vicksburg campaign, and insinuating
that his and their failure to reduce Vicksburg on May 22 was through lack
of support from generals Sherman and McPherson.

Grant explained the removal to Adjutant General Lorenzo Thomas:

Inclosed I respectfully transmit the letters of Maj. Gen. W. T. Sherman,
commanding Fifteenth Army Corps, and Maj. Gen. J. B. McPherson, commanding Seventeenth Army Corps, of date, respectively the 17th and 18th
instant, relative to the congratulatory order of Maj. Gen. John A. McClernand to his troops, a copy of which order is also herewith transmitted,
together with copies of the correspondence relating thereto, and my order
relieving General McClernand from the command of the Thirteenth Army
Corps and assigning Maj. Gen. E.O.C. Ord to the command thereof, subject
to the approval of the President.

A disposition and earnest desire on my part to do the most I could with the means at my command, without interference with the assignments to command which the President alone was authorized to make, made me tolerate General McClernand long after I thought the good of the service demanded his removal. It was only when almost the entire army under my command seemed to demand it that he was relieved.

The inclosed letters show the feelings of the army corps serving in the field with the Thirteenth Corps. The removal of General McClernand from the command of the Thirteenth Army Corps has given general satisfaction, the Thirteenth Army Corps sharing, perhaps, equally in that feeling with the other corps of the army. My action in the relieving of Maj. Gen. John A. McClernand from the command of the Thirteenth Army Corps and the assignment of Maj. Gen. E.O.C. Ord to that command I trust will meet the approval of the President.[1]

An uneasy Grant sent his principal staff officer, John A. Rawlins, carrying his report on Vicksburg to Washington to ascertain the effect of his removal order. Rawlins spoke with the president and his cabinet for nearly two hours. Welles in his diary gave an insider's account of Rawlins's interview:

I met at the President's and was introduced by him to Colonel Rawlins of General Grant's staff. He arrived yesterday with the official report of the capture of Vicksburg and Pemberton's army. Was much pleased with him, his frank intelligent and interesting description of men and of army operations. His interview with the President and Cabinet was of nearly two hours' duration, and all, I think, were entertained and instructed by him. His unpretending and unassuming manners pleased me—the absence of pretension and I may say the unpolished and unrefined deportment of this earnest and sincere patriot and soldier interested me more than that of almost any officer whom I have met. He was never at West Point and has had few educational advantages, yet he is a solider, and has a mind which has served his general and his country well.[2]

Rawlins was a convincing emissary, and McClernand's removal was sealed. Grant's victory at Vicksburg was not only a military but also a political triumph. An angry McClernand on August 3 appealed to his friend, the president:

According to news-paper account it is the purpose of my enemy's, at this late day, to attempt to gloss the more than mortal injury they have done me, by bringing me before a court martial. If so; let me, as an American . . . more jealous of my honor than of my life, appeal to you to see that I am fairly dealt by—that I am not held up before the country for months in the character of an alleged culprit, as an excuse for withholding from me a command.[3]

Lincoln on August 10 turned to his Secretary of War Edwin Stanton for information, asking, "I have not heard of any charges being filed against Gen. J. A. McClernand. Are there any?" Stanton replied, "There are no formal charges against Major Genl McClernand. Genl Grant has reported his reasons for removing him from command."[4]

Two days later Lincoln wrote to McClernand:

Our friend, William G. Greene, has just presented a kind letter in regard to yourself, addressed to me by our other friends, Yates, Hatch, and Dubois. I doubt whether your present position is more painful to you than to myself. Grateful for the patriotic stand so early taken by you in this life- and-death struggle of the nation, I have done whatever has appeared practicable to advance you and the public interest together. No charges, with a view to a trial, have been preferred against you by any one; nor do I suppose any will be. All there is, so far as I have heard, is Gen. Grant's statement of his reasons for relieving you. And even this I have not seen or sought to see; because it is a case, as appears to me, in which I could do nothing without doing harm. Gen. Grant and yourself have been conspicuous in our most important successes; and for me to interfere, and thus magnify a breach between you, could not but be of evil effect. Better leave it where the law of the case has placed it. For me to force you back upon Gen. Grant, would be forcing him to resign. I can not give you a new command, because we have no forces except such as already have commanders. I am constantly pressed by those who *scold* before they *think,* or without thinking at all, to give commands respectively to Fremont, McClellan, Butler, Sigel, Curtis, Hunter, Hooker, and perhaps others; when, all else out of the way, I have no commands to give them. This is now your case, which, as I have before said, pains me, not less than it does you.

My belief is that the permanent estimate of what a general does in the field, is fixed by the "cloud of witnesses" who have been with him in the field; and that relying on these, he who has the right needs not to fear.[5]

McClernand replied:

Your kind favor, by the hand of Mr. Green, is received. Please accept my grateful acknowledgments for the friendly assurances it contains. If my humble efforts in behalf of the country have in any degree, met your approbation I am rejoiced. I only regret that I am debarred the privilege of continuing them in the same form.

Feeling that I have done my duty I shrink from no charges that Genl. Grant may prefer. On the contrary . . . I challenged investigation both of his and my conduct. . . . I only ask . . . for an impartial court. Such investigation would bring to light . . . many things, both military and personal, which are unwritten or unheeded.[6]

The persevering McClernand appealed to Stanton for a court of inquiry. Stanton responded in September:

Your letter of the 5th instant has been submitted to the President, who directs me to say that a court of inquiry embracing any one of the subjects specified in that letter would necessarily withdraw from the field many officers whose presence with their commands is absolutely indispensable to the service, and whose absence might cause irreparable injury to the success of operations now in active progress. For these reasons he declines at present your applications, but if hereafter it can be done without prejudice to the service, he will, in view of your anxiety upon the subject, order a court.[7]

After Lincoln's refusal to call a court of inquiry McClernand reacted by warning he would publish an attack on Grant:

Failing to be restored to my command (now, as I understand, passed from General Grant's control), or to any command, and failing also to obtain a court of inquiry, no other mode of self-vindication is left to me than an official and responsible statement by myself of my own case. The accompanying paper is that statement, which I send to you for your perusal as a matter rightfully claiming your attention, and which, in justice to myself, my children, and my friends, I propose to publish.[8]

Given little to do, McClernand submitted his resignation. The next month Lincoln restored him to command in New Orleans, where he coped with bad weather and illness. He resigned the post in November.

While ridding himself of the troublesome McClernand, Grant was seeking promotion in the regular army of Major Generals W. T. Sherman and J. B. McPherson, two generals whom McClernand had blamed for his lack of success. A letter from General in Chief Henry W. Halleck a week after Gettysburg encouraged Grant to recommend promotion of the two commanders who did so much to win Vicksburg. Halleck wrote:

> There is still one vacant Brig Generalcy & I hope that Harney, Anderson & Cook will soon be retired, making three more vacancies. The most prominent candidates at present for Brig Genls in regular army are W. T. Sherman, McPherson, G. H. Thomas, Sedgwick & Hancock. I am of opinion that Sherman & McPherson have rendered the best service & should come in first. If you think so, write an official letter to that effect, urging their appointment to the first vacancies.[9]

Grant, seizing on this on July 22, 1863, wrote to Lincoln:

> I would most respectfully but urgently recommend the promotion of Maj. Gen. Wm. T. Sherman, now commanding the 15th Army Corps, and Maj. Gen. J. B. McPherson, commanding the 17th Army Corps to the positions of Brig. Gen. in the regular Army.
>
> The first reason for this is their great fitness for any command that it may ever become necessary to intrust to them. Second, their great purity of character and disinterestedness in everything except the faithful performance of their duty and the success of every one engaged in the great battle for the preservation of the Union. Third they have honorably won this distinction upon many well fought battle fields. I will only mention some of their services since serving under my command.
>
> To Gen. Sherman I was greatly indebted for his promptness in forwarding to me, during the siege of Fort Donelson, reinforcements and supplies from Paducah. At the battle of Shiloh on the first day he held, with raw troops, the key point to the landing. To his individual efforts I am indebted for the success of that battle. Twice hit and several, I think three, horses shot on that day he maintained his position with his raw troops. It is no disparagement to any other officer to say that I do not believe there was another Division commander on the field who had the skill or experience to have done it. . . . The siege of Vicksburg and last capture of Jackson, and dispersion of Johnston's Army, entitle Gen. Sherman to more credit than it usually falls to the lot of one man to earn.
>
> Gen. McPherson has been with me in every battle since the com-

mencement of the rebellion except Belmont. . . . In the advance through Central Mississippi last November & December Gen. McPherson commanded one Wing of the Army with all the ability possible to show, he having the lead on the advance and the rear returning. . . .

In the assault of the 22d of June on the fortifications of Vicksburg and during the entire siege, Gen. McPherson and his command won unfading laurels. He is one of our ablest Engineers and most skilfull Generals. The promotion of such men as Sherman and McPherson always add strength to our Arms.[10]

Within a fortnight he heard from Halleck that the two generals had been appointed.

Soon after the victory at Vicksburg Grant had received word from Halleck that he was "exceedingly anxious about General Banks' command" in New Orleans. Grant on July 24 responded:

My troops are very much exhausted, and entirely unfit for any present duty requiring much marching. But, by selecting, any duty of immediate pressing importance could be done. It seems to me that Mobile is the point deserving the most immediate attention. It could not be taken from here at this season of the year. The country through which an army would have to pass is poor and water scarce. The only present route, it seems to me, would be from some point in Lake Ponchartrain. I have not studied this matter, however, it being out of my department. . . .

Should my course not be sustained, all the surplus men can be transferred to other organizations. The negro troops are easier to preserve discipline among than our white troops, and I doubt not will prove equally good for garrison duty. All that have been tried have fought bravely.

Before raising any new regiments of colored troops, I think it advisable to fill those already organized. General Herron's trip to Yazoo City gave us a great many recruits, and General Ransom's expedition to Natchez has given and will give several thousand. The absence of General Hawkins has been a great drawback to the perfect organization of the black troops. I have no one to fully take his place.[11]

After reading Grant's letter, Lincoln wrote to him on August 9 (a portion of this letter also appears on pp. 365–66):

I see by a despatch of yours that you incline quite strongly towards an expedition against Mobile. This would appear tempting to me also, were it not that in view of recent events in Mexico, I am greatly impressed with the importance of re-establishing the national authority in Western Texas as soon as possible. I am not making an order, however. That I leave, for the present at least, to the General-in-Chief.

A word upon another subject. Gen. Thomas has gone again to the Mississippi Valley, with the view of raising colored troops. I have no reason to doubt that you are doing what you reasonably can upon the same subject. I believe it is a resource which, if vigorously applied now, will soon close the contest. It works doubly, weakening the enemy and strengthening us. We were not fully ripe for it until the river was opened. Now, I think at least a hundred thousand can, and ought to be rapidly organized along its shores, relieving all the white troops to serve elsewhere.

Mr. Dana understands you as believing that the emancipation proclamation has helped some in your military operations. I am very glad if this is so. Did you receive a short letter from me, dated the 13th. of July?[12]

Responding to Lincoln's query about the effectiveness of the Emancipation Proclamation as a military measure, Grant on August 23 replied:

Your letter of the 9th inst. reached me at Vicksburg just as I was about starting for this place. Your letter of the 13th of July was also duly received.

After the fall of Vicksburg I did incline very much to an immediate move on Mobile. I believed then the place could be taken with but little effort, and with the rivers debouching there, in our possession, we would have such a base to operate from on the very center of the Confederacy as would make them abandon entirely the states bound West by the Miss. I see however the importance of a movement into Texas just at this time.

I have reinforced Gen. Banks with the 13th Army Corps comprising ten Brigades of Infantry with a full proportion of Artillery.

I have given the subject of arming the negro my hearty support. This, with the emancipation of the negro, is the heavyest blow yet given the Confederacy. The South rave a great deel about it and profess to be very angry. But they were united in their action before and with the negro under subjection could spare their entire white population for the field. Now they complain that nothing can be got out of their negroes.

There has been great difficulty in getting able bodied negroes to fill up the colored regiments in consequence of the rebel cavalry running off all that class to Georgia and Texas. This is especially the case for a distance of fifteen or twenty miles on each side of the river. I am now however sending two expeditions into Louisiana, one from Natchez to Harrisonburg and one from Goodriche's Landing to Monroe, that I expect will bring back a large number. I have ordered recruiting officers to accompany these expeditions. I am also moving a Brigade of Calvary from Tennessee to Vicksburg which will enable me to move troops to a greater distance into the interior and will facilitate materially the *recruiting service.*

Gen. Thomas is now with me and you may rely on it I will give him all the aid in my power. I would do this whether the arming the negro seemed to me a wise policy or not, because it is an order that I am bound to obey and do not feel that in my position I have a right to question any policy of the Government. In this particular instance there is no objection however to my expressing an honest conviction. That is, by arming the negro we have added a powerful ally. They will make good soldiers and taking them from the enemy weaken him in the same proportion they strengthen us. I am therefore most decidedly in favor of pushing this policy to the enlistment of a force sufficient to hold all the South falling into our hands and to aid in capturing more.[13]

Instead of going to Mobile or Texas, Grant was placed in charge of Rosecrans's faltering campaign in southeast Tennessee. Proceeding to Chattanooga, he smashed General Braxton Bragg's army, forcing him to retreat into Georgia. All the while Sherman, Grant's valued colleague, forced Confederate General Longstreet to retire from northeast Tennessee. The two men had arrived at a goal long desired by Lincoln, the liberation of eastern Tennessee. He wrote to Grant:

Understanding that your lodgment at Chattanooga and Knoxville is now secure, I wish to tender you, and all under your command, my more than thanks—my profoundest gratitude—for the skill, courage, and perseverance, with which you and they, over so great difficulties, have effected that important object. God bless you all.[14]

Grant's star was rising.

Yet Lincoln's concern about securing the loyalty of eastern Tennessee had not entirely vanished. Grant informed Halleck that he was withdrawing much of Sherman's force from the region. Halleck responded: "The force to be retained in East Tennessee must, of course, be limited by your means of supplying it. I only wish to convey to you the anxiety of the President that the enemy should, if possible, be prevented from laying waste that country and gathering up its products for his own subsistence during the winter."

Talk of Grant for president in 1864 spread following news of his victories in Tennessee. His friend and benefactor Congressman Elihu Washburne introduced a bill in the House to elevate Grant to the rank of lieutenant general, the first since George Washington, the revered commander who became president. Lincoln had some cause to worry whether he might be replaced by the popular general.

Reassurances to the contrary filtered into Washington. Assistant Secretary of the Navy Gustavus V. Fox learned in early January that "Grant could not be kicked into the presidency, he would not have it at 40,000 per year." A few days before Lincoln signed the bill into law, a correspondent informed Major General Francis P. Blair Jr., brother of the postmaster general: "I have just heard that Haw (How) put the question to Grant . . . whether he would consent to be a candidate for the Presidency. He answered that under no circumstances would he be a candidate in opposition to Lincoln."[15]

A little more than a month later a scruffy looking soldier arrived in the capital city. Hearing that a reception was occurring at the White House, Grant walked a short distance and entered the reception room. A "stir and buzz" alerted Lincoln to Grant's presence. The president walked over to him, hand extended, remarking, "Why here is General Grant. Well, this is a great pleasure." The next day Lincoln commissioned Grant lieutenant general of the U.S. Army.

CHAPTER TWENTY-NINE

THIRTY-EIGHTH CONGRESS, FIRST SESSION

The Thirty-Eighth Congress assembled in December 1863, and its Republican membership, shrunken in numbers by the 1862 elections, faced an immediate crisis. Rumors circulated that a conspiracy existed to gain Democratic control of the House of Representatives. Emerson Etheridge, the disgruntled House clerk, plotted to exclude some Republican members-elect from the roll call, thereby placing the Democrats in power. Appraised of the plot, Lincoln counseled Republicans, "The main thing . . . is to be sure to have all our men there. Then if Mr. Etheridge undertakes revolutionary proceedings," the frontier president continued, sanctioning force, "let him be carried out on a chip [log], and let our men organize the House." When Etheridge brazenly attempted to exclude nineteen names from the roll call, Republicans, who had their men there, defeated the attempt, and won control of the House.[1]

Under a newly completed Capitol dome, surmounted by a bronze figure of freedom, lawmakers heard Lincoln's Annual Message to Congress. Sounding an affirmative note and observing "the improved condition of our national affairs," he suggested a number of measures to the legislative body, including measures involving banks, conscription, homesteads for veterans, immigrant labor, and a transatlantic telegraph. Congress transformed all of them into law.[2]

Most striking, Lincoln presented an accompanying presidential Proclamation of Amnesty and Reconstruction, virtually an executive law that lasted throughout his administration. Behind this grasp of power lay Lincoln's

419

fundamental purpose in the war—to restore national unity. His inaugural address, his resort to arms, his suspension of habeas corpus, his emancipation policies—all looked to saving the Union, which increasingly he was calling the "nation." He had never accepted the claim of the right to secede, that the states had lost their identity or sovereignty, or that Congress alone held the power to reconstruct.

Formidable opposition faced his views. Two years earlier radical Republican Thaddeus Stevens, congressman from Pennsylvania, objecting to seating members-elect from West Virginia and Tennessee, had argued that "we know that their States are, so far as they can be, out of the Union." Sometimes deemed dictator of the House, Stevens continued voicing his view that rebel states had forfeited their status as states.

A year and a half later, speaking to his constituents in Lancaster, Pennsylvania, Stevens branded the rebel states, when defeated, as "conquered provinces." He said:

> Early after the commencement of the rebellion, as soon as the traitors had formed a separate government and maintained their independence *de facto* by force of arms, and were acknowledged as a belligerent power, I expressed the opinion that the Constitution and laws of the United States had no longer any valid effect to restrain our action in the rebel States, or to afford them protection; although when peace should be restored the traitors might be dealt with under those revived laws for the treason they committed in their transition state, from insurgents to belligerents. That we were restrained by nothing but the law of nations. That we might seize all their territory, and hold and appropriate it as conquered provinces, and apply both their real and personal estate in fee simple to defray the expenses of the war. And in addition to all this, as when conquered, they would not be protected by their belligerent rights—they might be tried and executed as traitors.[3]

Even more vociferous in denying rights to rebel states was Senator Charles Sumner of Massachusetts. Long before Lincoln's amnesty proclamation Sumner had introduced resolutions arguing that rebel states by seceding had committed suicide. He further claimed that after the suicide, Congress, not the president, assumed complete jurisdiction:

Whereas certain States, rightfully belonging to the Union of the United States, have through their respective governments wickedly undertaken to abjure all those duties by which their connection with the Union was maintained; to renounce all allegiance to the Constitution; to levy war upon the national Government; and, for the consummation, of this treason, have unconstitutionally and unlawfully confederated together, with the declared purpose of putting an end by force to the supremacy of the Constitution within their respective limits; ... and whereas the extensive territory thus usurped by these pretended governments and organized into a hostile confederation, belongs to the United States as an inseparable part thereof, under the sanctions of the Constitution, to be held in trust for the inhabitants in the present and future generations, and is so completely interlinked with the Union that it is forever dependent thereupon; and whereas the Constitution, which is the supreme law of the land, cannot be displaced in its rightful operation within this territory, but must ever continue the supreme law thereof, notwithstanding the doings of any pretended governments acting singly or in confederation, in order to put an end to its supremacy:

Therefore–

1. *Resolved,* That any vote of secession or other act by which any State may undertake to put an end to the supremacy of the Constitution within its territory is inoperative and void against the Constitution, and when sustained by force it becomes a practical *abdication* by the State of all rights under the Constitution, while the treason which it involves still further works an instant *forfeiture* of all those functions and powers essential to the continued existence of the State as a body politic, so that from that time forward the territory falls under the exclusive jurisdiction of Congress as other territory, and the State being, according to the language of the law, *felo-de-se,* ceases to exist.[4]

Still another outlook gained adherents as early as 1862—the idea that territorialization was the best avenue of reconstructing the rebel states. Though holding diverse ideas about future policy on reconstruction, Congress accepted the idea that the president might appoint military governors of conquered states. Adroitly acting through the secretary of war, thus avoiding a charge that he was overreaching, Lincoln named Andrew Johnson military governor of Tennessee. In defiance of his home state, which had

seceded, Johnson had remained the senator from Tennessee and cospon-
sored the resolution defining the purposes of the war as maintaining the
Constitution and the Union.

Lincoln granted him broad powers to reconstruct Tennessee:

> You are hereby appointed Military Governor of the State of Tennessee,
> with authority to exercise and perform, *within the limits of that state,* all
> and singular, the powers, duties and functions pertaining to the office of
> Military Governor (including the *power* to *establish all necessary offices and
> tribunals,* and *suspend* the *writ of Habeas Corpus*) during the pleasure of the
> President, or until the loyal inhabitants of that state shall organize a civil
> government in conformity with the Constitution of the United States.[5]

The Senate the following day confirmed Johnson's appointment as brigadier general, ushering in a series of presidential appointments of military
governors. Though Congress approved Lincoln's establishment of military
governments, the president did not escape congressional criticism for establishing them. Radical Republican Owen Lovejoy of Illinois asked, "If these
revolted States are in the Union, what right, [has] the President . . . to place
Governors over them, as in the case of Tennessee?" New York congressman
Charles B. Sedgwick said of the seceded states, "They are authorized to
require of us the guarantee of a Republican form of government; and yet
the President of the United States, as Commander-in-Chief of the Army,
without any warrant of constitutional authority, by the military power,
gives them instead a tyrannical, despotic military government."[6]

On Wednesday, December 9, 1863, when the Etheridge conspiracy had
been thwarted and Republican speaker Schuyler Colfax had been installed,
John Hay carried the president's message with its proclamation to Congress.
He recorded in his diary:

> Wednesday we went up with the document and it was read. We watched
> the effect with great anxiety.
>
> Whatever may be the results or the verdict of history the immediate
> effect of this paper is something wonderful. I never have seen such an effect
> produced by a public document. Men acted as if the Millennium had come.
> Chandler was delighted, Sumner was beaming, while at the other political
> pole Dixon & Reverdy Johnson said it was highly satisfactory. Forney said

"We only wanted a leader to speak the bold word. It is done and all can follow. I shall speak in my two papers tomorrow in a way to make these Presidential aspirants squirm." Henry Wilson came to me and laying his broad palms on my shoulders said "The President has struck another great blow. Tell him from me God Bless him."

In the House the effect was the same. Boutwell was looking over it quietly & saying, It is a very able and shrewd paper. It has great points of popularity: & it is right." Lovejoy seemed to see on the mountains the feet of one bringing good tidings.[7]

In the document Lincoln further stretched his executive power, claiming he had the right to reconstruct the nation under the Constitution's grant of power "to grant reprieves and pardons." The Proclamation of Amnesty and Reconstruction read:

Whereas, in and by the Constitution of the United States, it is provided that the President "shall have power to grant reprieves and pardons for offences against the United States, except in cases of impeachment;" and

Whereas a rebellion now exists whereby the loyal State governments of several States have for a long time been subverted, and many persons have committed and are now guilty of treason against the United States; and

Whereas, with reference to said rebellion and treason, laws have been enacted by Congress declaring forfeitures and confiscation of property and liberation of slaves, all upon terms and conditions therein stated, and also declaring that the President was thereby authorized at any time thereafter, by proclamation, to extend to persons who may have participated in the existing rebellion, in any State or part thereof, pardon and amnesty, with such exceptions and at such times and on such conditions as he may deem expedient for the public welfare; and

Whereas the congressional declaration for limited and conditional pardon accords with well-established judicial exposition of the pardoning power; and

Whereas, with reference to said rebellion, the President of the United States has issued several proclamations, with provisions in regard to the liberation of slaves; and

Whereas it is now desired by some persons heretofore engaged in said rebellion to resume their allegiance to the United States, and to reinaugurate loyal State governments within and for their respective States; therefore,

I, Abraham Lincoln, President of the United States, do proclaim, declare, and make known to all persons who have, directly or by implication, participated in the existing rebellion, except as hereinafter excepted, that a full pardon is hereby granted to them and each of them, with restoration of all rights of property, except as to slaves, and in property cases where rights of third parties shall have intervened, and upon the condition that every such person shall take and subscribe an oath, and thenceforward keep and maintain said oath inviolate; and which oath shall be registered for permanent preservation, and shall be of the tenor and effect following, to wit:

"I, ___, do solemnly swear, in presence of Almighty God, that I will henceforth faithfully support, protect and defend the Constitution of the United States, and the union of the States thereunder; and that I will, in like manner, abide by and faithfully support all acts of Congress passed during the existing rebellion with reference to slaves, so long and so far as not repealed, modified or held void by Congress, or by decision of the Supreme Court; and that I will, in like manner, abide by and faithfully support all proclamations of the President made during the existing rebellion having reference to slaves, so long and so far as not modified or declared void by decision of the Supreme Court. So help me God."

The persons excepted from the benefits of the foregoing provisions are all who are, or shall have been, civil or diplomatic officers or agents of the so-called confederate government; all who have left judicial stations under the United States to aid the rebellion; all who are, or shall have been, military or naval officers of said so-called confederate government above the rank of colonel in the army, or of lieutenant in the navy; all who left seats in the United States Congress to aid the rebellion; and all who resigned commissions in the army or navy of the United States, and afterwards aided the rebellion; and all who have engaged in any way in treating colored persons or white persons, in charge of such, otherwise than lawfully as prisoners of war, and which persons may have been found in the United States service, as soldiers, seamen, or in any other capacity.

And I do further proclaim, declare, and make known, that whenever, in any of the States of Arkansas, Texas, Louisiana, Mississippi, Tennessee, Alabama, Georgia, Florida, South Carolina, and North Carolina, a number of persons, not less than one tenth in number of the votes cast in such State at the Presidential election of the year of our Lord one thousand eight hundred and sixty, each having taken the oath aforesaid and not having since violated it, and being a qualified voter by the election law of the State existing immediately before the so-called act of secession, and excluding all others, shall re-establish a State government which shall be republican, and in no wise contravening said oath, such shall be recognized as the true government of the State, and the State shall receive thereunder the benefits of the constitutional provision which declares that "The United States shall guaranty to every State in this union a republican form of government, and shall protect each of them against invasion; and, on application of the legislature, or the executive, (when the legislature cannot be convened,) against domestic violence."

And I do further proclaim, declare, and make known that any provision which may be adopted by such State government in relation to the freed people of such State, which shall recognize and declare their permanent freedom, provide for their education, and which may yet be consistent, as a temporary arrangement, with their present condition as a laboring, landless, and homeless class, will not be objected to by the national Executive. And it is suggested as not improper, that, in constructing a loyal State government in any State, the name of the State, the boundary, the subdivisions, the constitution, and the general code of laws, as before the rebellion, be maintained, subject only to the modifications made necessary by the conditions hereinbefore stated, and such others, if any, not contravening said conditions, and which may be deemed expedient by those framing the new State government.

To avoid misunderstanding, it may be proper to say that this proclamation, so far as it relates to State governments, has no reference to States wherein loyal State governments have all the while been maintained. And for the same reason, it may be proper to further say that whether members sent to Congress from any State shall be admitted to seats, constitutionally rests exclusively with the respective Houses, and not to any extent with the Executive. And still further, that this proclamation is intended to present the people of the States wherein the national authority has been suspended, and loyal State governments have been subverted, a mode in and by which the national authority and loyal State governments may be re-established within said States, or in any of them; and, while the mode presented is the best the Executive can suggest, with his present impressions, it must not be understood that no other possible mode would be acceptable.[8]

CHAPTER THIRTY

RECONSTRUCTION

Although historians have often dated reconstruction from Lincoln's amnesty proclamation of December 1863, the process of reconstructing the Union began in April 1861 when Lincoln called out the militia to put down the rebellion. He subsequently sought to entice states to return to the Union with his emancipation policies, including state-compensated emancipation and avoidance of his formal emancipation proclamation by voluntary return to the Union. His veto of the Wade-Davis Bill held out the possibility of other formulas being acceptable to him. Meanwhile he continued with his own policy of carrying out reconstruction through appointing military governors and encouraging state action.

A major difference between Lincoln and the radical Republicans was over black suffrage, which he believed was beyond the power of Congress to confer. Abolitionists, notably Wendell Phillips, blasted him for his stand on black suffrage. An exception was William Lloyd Garrison, who in correspondence with British professor Francis Newman of London University, wrote in defense of Lincoln:

> By what political precedent or administrative policy, in any country, could he have been justified if he had attempted to do this? When was it ever known that liberation from bondage was accompanied by a recognition of political equality? Chattels personal may be instantly translated from the auction-block into freemen; but when were they ever taken at the same time to the ballot-box, and invested with all political rights and immunities? According to the laws of development and progress, it is not practicable. To denounce or complain of President Lincoln for not disregarding public sentiment, and not flying in the face of these laws, is hardly just. Besides, I

doubt whether he has the constitutional right to decide this matter. Ever since this government was organized, the right of suffrage has been determined by each State in the Union for itself, so that there is no uniformity in regard to it. In some free States, colored citizens are allowed to vote; in others, they are not. It is always a State, never a national, matter. In honestly seeking to preserve the Union, it is not for President Lincoln to seek, by a special edict applied to a particular State or locality, to do violence to a universal rule, accepted and acted upon from the beginning till now by the States in their individual sovereignty. Under the war power, he had the constitutional right to emancipate the slaves in every rebel State, and also to insist that, in any plan of reconstruction that might be agreed upon, slavery should be admitted to be dead, beyond power of resurrection. That being accomplished, I question whether he could safely or advantageously—to say the least—enforce a rule, ab initio, touching the ballot, which abolishes complexional distinctions; any more than he could safely or advantageously decree that all women (whose title is equally good) should enjoy the electoral right, and help form the State. Nor, if the freed blacks were admitted to the polls by Presidential fiat, do I see any permanent advantage likely to be secured by it; for, submitted to as a necessity at the outset, as soon as the State was organized and left to manage its own affairs, the white population, with their superior intelligence, wealth, and power, would unquestionably alter the franchise in accordance with their prejudices, and exclude those thus summarily brought to the polls. Coercion would gain nothing.[1]

In his annual message of 1864 Lincoln pointed out: "A year ago general pardon and amnesty, upon specified terms, were offered to all, except certain designated classes. . . . Thus, practically, the door has been, for a full year, open to all, except such as were not in condition to make free choice." He warned, however, "But the time may come—probably will come—when public duty shall demand that it be closed."[2]

At the same time he offered a conciliatory hand to Congress. He declared, "The Executive power itself would be greatly diminished by the cessation of actual war." Further, he noted, some questions "would be beyond the Executive power to adjust; as, for instance, the admission of members to Congress." In this language he adroitly combined the present existence of presidential power, its future diminution, and the continuing existence of congressional power over seating members.

Louisiana, recovered to Union control under Lincoln's policy, had become the center of the reconstruction controversy between Congress, pressing for black suffrage, and Lincoln, willing to extend suffrage to "the very intelligent, and especially those who have fought gallantly in our ranks."[3]

On January 15, 1865, James Ashley of Ohio, a former Free Soiler and now a member of the Joint Committee on Reconstruction, introduced a compromise measure that recognized, on one hand, Lincoln's Louisiana government and, on the other hand, black political equality. Three days later Lincoln discussed Ashley's measure with Montgomery Blair and General Nathaniel P. Banks, who had been given military control over Louisiana. Lincoln was exerting his influence on Congress through keeping the general, the first Republican speaker of the House, in Washington during the session. John Hay, Lincoln's secretary and the auditor of many Lincoln conversations, recorded the exchange:

> When the President came in, he called Blair and Banks into his office meeting them in the hall.
>
> They immediately began to talk about Ashleys Bill in regard to states in insurrection. The President had been reading it carefully & said that he liked it with the exception of one or two things which he thought rather calculated to conceal a feature which might be objectionable to some. The first was that under the provisions of that bill negroes would be made jurors & voters under the temporary governments. "Yes, said Banks, that is to be stricken out and the qualification white male citizens of the U.S. is to be restored. What you refer to would be a fatal objection to the Bill. It would simply throw the Government into the hands of the blacks, as the white people under that arrangement would refuse to vote."
>
> The second said the President is the declaration that all persons heretofore held in slavery are declared free. This is explained by some to be not a prohibition of slavery by Congress but a mere assurance of freedom to persons actually then [free] in accordance with the proclamation of Emancipation. In that point of view it is not objectionable though I think it would have been preferable to so express it.
>
> The President and General Banks spoke very favorably, with these qualifications of Ashley's bill. Banks is especially anxious that the Bill may pass and receive the approval of the President. He regards it as merely concurring in the Presidents own action in the one important case of Louisiana and

recommending an observance of the same policy in other cases. He does not regard it, nor does the President, as laying down any cast iron policy in the matter. Louisiana being admitted & this bill passed, the President is not estopped by it from recognizing and urging Congress to recognize another state of the South coming in with constitution & conditions entirely dissimilar. Banks thinks that the object of Congress in passing the Bill at all is merely to assert their conviction that they have a right to pass such a law in concurrence with the executive action. They want a hand in the reconstruction. It is unquestionably the prerogative of Congress to decide as to qualifications of its own members: that branch of the subject is exclusively their own. It does not seem wise therefore to make a fight upon a question purely immaterial, that is, whether this bill is a necessary one or not, and thereby lose the positive gain of this endorsement of the President's policy in the admission of Louisiana, and the assistance of that state in carrying the constitutional amendment prohibiting slavery.

Blair talked more than both Lincoln and Banks, and somewhat vehemently attacked the radicals in the house and senate who are at work upon this measure accusing them of interested motives and hostility to Lincoln. The President said "It is much better not to be led from the region of reason into that of hot blood, by imputing to public men motives which they do not avow."[4]

As extensive legislative debate ensued, the expectation of agreement increased. During the Christmas recess Senator Charles Sumner had written to Francis Lieber: "I have presented to the president the duty of harmony between Congress and the Executive. He is agreed. It is proposed to admit Louisiana (which ought not to be done), and" [over-optimistically adding] "at the same time pass the reconstruction bill for all the other states, giving the electoral franchise to 'all citizens' without distinction of color."[5]

When Congress resumed, Ashley introduced amendments that substantially expanded his bill, requiring every southern state to guarantee equality to all persons and providing for congressional recognition of both Louisiana and Arkansas, subject to conditions that raised doubt about the Lincoln governments in those states.

As debate continued, the Republican delegation in the House splintered, in contrast to the general unity that passed the Wade-Davis Bill. A forcible objection came from Henry L. Dawes of Massachusetts, who opposed a uniform method of reorganization for all states. When the roll was called on February 21 the House voted 91 to 64 to table the bill.

Ashley announced, "[I]t is very clear to my mind that no bill providing for the reorganization of loyal State governments in the rebel States can pass this Congress. On this great question, a question of more magnitude and importance to the people of this country than any other, the majority of the House, I regret to acknowledge, are utterly unable to agree." Dawes in a combination of glee and rue, wrote to his wife, "We killed the Bill dead—and Fernando Wood [the Copperhead Democrat from New York, who as mayor had wanted his city to secede] killed me dead by complimenting me."[6]

While in Washington Banks testified before the Senate Judiciary Committee, where he made a long statement about Louisiana affairs. Senator Lyman Trumbull, chairman of the Judiciary Committee, on January 9 asked Lincoln for a copy of Banks's statement, which Lincoln supplied the same day with a letter. The Senate was considering seating two senators-elect from Louisiana. Lincoln succinctly suggested the question to be asked in considering seating the men:

> The paper, relating to Louisiana, submitted to the Judiciary Committee of the Senate, by Gen. Banks, is herewith returned. The whole of it is in accordance with my general impression, and I *believe* it to be true; but much the larger part is beyond my absolute *knowledge,* as in its nature it must be. All the statements which lie within the range of my knowledge are strictly true; and I think of nothing material which has been omitted. Even before Gen. Banks went to Louisiana I was anxious for the loyal people there to move for re-organization and restoration of proper practical relations with the Union, and when he, at last, expressed his decided conviction that the thing was practicable, I directed him to give his official co-operation to effect it. On the subject, I have sent and received many letters to and from Gen. Banks and many other persons. These letters, as you remember, were shown to you yesterday, as they will be again, if you desire.
>
> If I shall neither take sides nor argue, will it be out of place for me to make what I think is the true statement of your question as to the proposed Louisiana Senators?
>
> "Can Louisiana be brought into proper practical relations with the Union, sooner, by *admitting* or by *rejecting* the proposed Senators?"[7]

Lincoln had earlier endorsed the Louisiana constitution. But he had expressed concerns that military commanders such as General Edward R. S. Canby and General Stephen A. Hurlbut in New Orleans "were opposed to new state government and that they had not adequately protected the state convention. Moreover, they had asserted that the civil government in Louisiana was 'subject to military revision and control.'" In a letter to Hurlbut, commanding the Department of the Gulf, he had written:

> Few things, since I have been here, have impressed me more painfully than what, for four or five months past, has appeared as bitter military opposition to the new State Government of Louisiana. I still indulged some hope that I was mistaken in the fact; but copies of a correspondence on the subject, between Gen. Canby and yourself, and shown me to-day, dispel that hope. A very fair proportion of the people of Louisiana have inaugurated a new State Government, making an excellent new constitution—better for the poor black man than we have in Illinois. This was done under military protection, directed by me, in the belief, still sincerely entertained, that with such a nucleous around which to build, we could get the State into position again sooner than otherwise. In this belief a general promise of protection and support, applicable alike to Louisiana and other states, was given in the last annual message. During the formation of the new government and constitution, they were supported by nearly every loyal person and opposed by every secessionist. And this support, and this opposition, from the respective stand points of the parties, was perfectly consistent and logical. Every Unionist ought to wish the new government to succeed; and every disunionist must desire it to fail. Its failure would gladden the heart of Slidell in Europe, and of every enemy of the old flag in the world. Every advocate of slavery naturally desires to see blasted, and crushed, the liberty promised the black man by the new constitution. But why Gen. Canby and Gen. Hurlbut should join on the same side is to me incomprehensible.
>
> Of course, in the condition of things at New-orleans, the military must not be thwarted by the civil authority; but when the constitutional convention, for what it deems a breach of privilege, arrests an editor, in no way connected with the military, the military necessity for insulting the Convention, and forcibly discharging the editor, is difficult to perceive. Neither is the military necessity for protecting the people against paying large salaries, fixed by a Legislature of their own choosing, very apparant.

Equally difficult to perceive is the military necessity for forcibly interposing to prevent a bank from loaning its own money to the State. These things, if they have occurred, are, at the best, no better than gratuitous hostility. I wish I could hope that they may be shown to not have occurred. To make assurance against misunderstanding, I repeat that in the existing condition of things in Louisiana, the military must not be thwarted by the civil authority; and I add that on points of difference the commanding general must be judge and master. But I also add that in the exercise of this judgment and control, a purpose, obvious, and scarcely unavowed, to transcend all military necessity, in order to crush out the civil government, will not be overlooked.[8]

Debate began on the Trumbull committee resolution on February 24. The report recognized the Lincoln government of Louisiana as the "legitimate government." Trumbull's advocacy of recognition encountered Sumner's opposition. When Sumner said of the resolution, "I shall regard its passage as a national calamity," Trumbull retorted that Sumner wanted "to browbeat the Senate."[9]

Sumner proposed a proviso to the resolution: "that this shall not take effect except on the fundamental condition that within the State there shall be no denial of the electoral franchise, or of any other rights on account of color or race, but all persons shall be equal before the law."[10] These words carried his central purpose.

Sumner had the support of other radical Republicans. Maryland's Henry Winter bitterly assailed the president, saying:

> Sir, when I came into Congress ten years ago this was a Government of law. I have lived to see it a Government of personal will. Congress has dwindled from a power to dictate law and the policy of the Government to a commission to audit accounts and to appropriate moneys to enable the Executive to execute his will and not ours. I would stop at the boundaries of law.[11]

Discussion lagged until the Congress adjourned on March 4, 1865. Lincoln's Louisiana government and its counterparts in Arkansas and Virginia remained in place, Lincoln's plans for reconstruction undeterred. Using the republican guarantee clause in the Constitution, Lincoln had established a "mode" for the states to restore their "practical" position in the Union. He left open the possibility that Congress might propose other modes that would be acceptable. Congress could not agree in 1864 and 1865 on whether the states could be forced to extend the ballot to black freedmen, and yet Lincoln's efforts to persuade these states to approve voting for black soldiers and the well-educated fell on deaf ears.

CHAPTER THIRTY-ONE

GRANT MOVES SOUTH

While Congress wrangled over reconstruction, General U. S. Grant was active in his new role as general in chief. His letter of April 9, 1864, to General Meade, commanding the Army of the Potomac, explained his confidential plans:

> So far as practicable all the armies are to move together, and towards one common centre. . . . Sherman will move at the same time you do, or two or three days in advance, Joe Johnston's army being his objective point, and the heart of Georgia his ultimate aim. If successful he will secure the line from Chattanooga to Mobile with the aid of Banks. . . . Lee's army will be your objective point. Wherever Lee goes, there you will go also. . . . There will be naval co-operation on the James River, and transports and ferries will be provided that should Lee fall back into his intrenchments at Richmond, Butler's force and yours will be a unit, or at least can be made to act as such.[1]

On April 21, 1864, the governors of five midwestern states meeting in Washington offered Lincoln 85,000 infantry troops for one hundred days. Secretary of War Edwin Stanton informed Grant of the offer and asked for advice about accepting it with its particulars. With reservations Grant agreed to accept the offer. Lincoln, having gained the approval of Stanton and Grant, on April 23 formally accepted the governors' "proposition," as he called it. The final coordinated push to conquer the South demanded the additional manpower, even if these men were largely untrained and only in service for three months.[2]

Toward the end of April John Hay wrote in his diary:

> The President has been strongly reminded by General Grant's present plan of his, the President's, old suggestion, so constantly made, and as constantly

434

neglected, to Buell, Halleck, *et al.,* to move at once upon the enemy's whole line, so as to bring into action to our advantage our great superiority of numbers. Otherwise, by use of interior lines, and control of the interior railroad system, the enemy can shift their men rapidly from one position to another as they may be required. In this concerted movement, however, great superiority of numbers must tell, as the enemy, however successful where he concentrates, must necessarily weaken other portions of his line and lose important positions. This idea of his own the President recognized with special pleasure when Grant said it was his intention to make all the line useful, "those not fighting could help the fighting." "Those not skinning can hold a leg," added the President.[3]

On the last day of the month Lincoln wrote to Grant, assuring him he had Lincoln's confidence:

Not expecting to see you again before the Spring campaign opens, I wish to express, in this way, my entire satisfaction with what you have done up to this time, so far as I understand it. The particulars of your plans I neither know, or seek to know. You are vigilant and self-reliant; and, pleased with this, I wish not to obtrude any constraints or restraints upon you. While I am very anxious that any great disaster, or the capture of our men in great numbers, shall be avoided, I know these points are less likely to escape your attention than they would be mine—If there is anything wanting which is within my power to give, do not fail to let me know it. And now with a brave Army, and a just cause, may God sustain you.[4]

The next day Grant graciously replied:

Your very kind letter of yesterday is just received. The confidence you express for the future, and satisfaction with the past, in my Military administration is acknowledged with pride. It will be my earnest endeavor that you, and the country, shall not be disappointed.

From my first entrance into the volunteer service of the country, to the present day, I have never had cause of complaint, have never expressed or implied a complaint, against the Administration, or the Sec. of War, for throwing any embarassment in the way of my vigerously prosecuting what appeared to me my duty. Indeed since the promotion which placed me in command of all the Armies, and in view of the great responsibility, and importance of success, I have been astonished at the readiness with which every thin[g] asked for has been yielded without even an explaination being asked. Should my success be less than I desire, and expect, the least I can say is, the fault is not with you.[5]

In spite of Lincoln's disclaimer that he neither knew nor sought to know the particulars of Grant's plans, he did keep an eye on Grant. When Grant requested that General N. P. Banks be superseded by another general, the reply from Henry W. Halleck, now serving in a subordinate role as chief of staff of the army, said Secretary of War Edwin Stanton had copies of all Grant's telegrams, "and I believe they have all been read by the President," Halleck chided.

By May 4 Grant had crossed the Rapidan River in Virginia, and on the fifth and sixth the disastrous slaughter known as the Battle of the Wilderness occurred. Grant suffered about 18,000 casualties, Lee about 10,000.

On the night of the sixth Henry Wing, a nineteen-year-old reporter for the *New York Tribune* who had been at the battlefield, wired the War Department for permission to use its wires to file his report to his paper. Stanton demanded that Wing first give him the report. Fearing censorship, Wing refused unless assured he could send his report. Stanton was threatening to arrest him when Lincoln entered the scene. Lincoln directed the telegraph operator: "Ask him if he will talk to the President." On the condition he could send one hundred words to his paper, the reporter promised to tell the president all he knew. Lincoln agreed, and Stanton dispatched a special locomotive to bring the reporter to Washington.

Sometime after 2:00 a.m. Wing arrived at the White House, where Lincoln and cabinet members were gathered. Wing told of heavy slaughter on both sides and said when he had left at the close of the first day, the outcome was in doubt. Directly addressing Lincoln, he said Grant had sent a message. "He told me to tell you, Mr. President, that there would be no turning back." Lincoln embraced the young man and kissed him.[6]

On the ninth the first dispatches from Grant arrived. Hay wrote: "The president thinks very highly of what Grant has done. He was talking about it today with me and said, 'How near we have been to this thing before and failed. I believe if any other general had been at the head of that army it would have now been on this side of the Rapidan. It is the dogged pertinacity of Grant that wins.'" After a Marine Band concert Lincoln spoke to the audience: "Ladies and Gentlemen, you, no doubt, desire to have a speech from me. In lieu of a speech, I propose that we give three cheers for Major General Grant and all the armies under his command."[7]

"Dogged pertinacity" correctly characterized Grant. Following the Wilderness fight, on May 7 Grant formed his men to move. Not knowing whether they were to retreat or go forward, when they heard the order to march toward Richmond, they cheered. Their immediate objective was Spotsylvania Court House, where again a blood bath occurred. On May 11 Grant wired Washington: "We have now entered the sixth day of very hard fighting. Our losses have been heavy as have those of the enemy. . . . I propose to fight it out on this line if it takes all summer."[8]

The pertinacious Grant continued to move south until he was nearly in sight of the Confederate capital's spires. Reaching Lee's well entrenched forces, he almost recklessly assailed his enemy at Cold Harbor. In a few minutes he lost thousands of men, and in all suffered about 7,000 casualties. From May 4 to June 12, Grant's losses numbered about 55,000 men. Grant "the Butcher" became a familiar term of opprobrium, but Lincoln sustained him.

Famed as an aggressive warrior who could not be spared because he fought, Grant moved his army south of the James River and entered into a long siege of Petersburg. On June 14 Grant wired Halleck: "Our forces will commence crossing the James to-day. The enemy show no signs yet of having brought troops to the south side of Richmond. I will have Petersburg secured, if possible, before they get there in much force. Our movement from Cold Harbor to the James River has been made with great celerity and so far without loss or accident."[9]

Lincoln replied: "Have just read your despatch of 1 P.M. yesterday. I begin to see it. You will succeed. God bless you all." For months Grant engaged in a war of attrition, eventually surrounding Petersburg. He attempted repeatedly to cut off Lee's supply lines by making flanking attacks. In July Grant launched a massive direct assault on the Petersburg trenches by exploding an underground mineshaft packed with gunpowder under the Confederate line. The Confederates held on at each point, and the siege lasted until the next April. Meanwhile, Lincoln waited, his confidence in Grant unshaken but his patience, like that of the northern public, strained.

CHAPTER THIRTY-TWO

PRESIDENTIAL

NOMINATION SAGA

To the astonishment of many Europeans the United States conducted a presidential election in the midst of civil war. And to the astonishment of many Americans of later generations, Lincoln's reelection long lay in doubt. Abolitionists divided over whether to support Lincoln, despite his Emancipation Proclamation. A member of his cabinet aspired to the office, and two of his generals headed parties opposed to him. Though renominated, Lincoln encountered within his party a movement for peace and a bid to substitute a different candidate. All the while Grant was failing to defeat Lee, and Sherman was failing to attain "the heart of Georgia." August was the cruelest month, when Lincoln sincerely believed he could not be reelected.

Two prominent abolitionists parted company with the president over his amnesty and emancipation policies. At the annual meeting of the Massachusetts Anti-Slavery Society the eloquent Wendell Phillips introduced a resolution reading:

> That, in our opinion, the Government, in its haste, is ready to sacrifice the interest and honor of the North to secure a sham peace, thereby risking the introduction into Congress of a strong Confederate minority to embarrass legislation, and leaving the freedmen and the Southern States under the control of the late slaveholders, embittered by their defeat in war, and entailing on the country intestine feuds for another dozen years; and we listen in vain, either from the leaders of the Republican party or from its journals, for any such protest as would arrest national attention, or create a public opinion definite enough to avert the sacrifice.[1]

438

William Lloyd Garrison, suffering under the personal strain of his wife's crippling malady, which had taken a turn for the worse, nevertheless delivered a spirited reply:

> Mr. President, in consequence of a severe domestic affliction and of bodily debility, I am not mentally or physically in a condition to make a speech; and, therefore, I shall not attempt to make one. But I wish to propose an amendment to the resolution which was submitted to the meeting by my friend Mr. Phillips this forenoon, and which he advocated with his usual ability and eloquence. As it now stands, it reads thus:
>
> Resolved, That, in our opinion, the Government, in its haste, *is ready to sacrifice the interest and honor of the North to secure a sham peace,* etc.
>
> I am not prepared to bring this charge, nor to cast this imputation. I believe that there is only one party at the North that is ready to make such a sacrifice for such an object, and that is the party of Copperheads. I would therefore propose that the resolution be amended as follows:
>
> Resolved, That, in our opinion, the Government, *in its haste, is in danger of sacrificing,* etc.
>
> This, Mr. President, is what I am willing to admit, and what I believe; but I would always rather err on the side of charitable judgment than of excessive condemnation. The resolution, as offered, is an impeachment of motives, not of ability or vigilance. It commits us to the assertion, that we believe the Government—meaning Mr. Lincoln in particular—is ready to do a most infamous act, namely, "to sacrifice the interest and honor of the North to secure a sham peace," whereby the President's Emancipation Proclamation shall be rendered null and void, and the slave oligarchy restored to their original supremacy. Now, sir, I do not believe a word of it, and therefore I cannot vote for it. To be ready to do a base thing for a base end implies both will and purpose; it means something more than liability: it amounts to perfidy. There was a time when I had little confidence in Abraham Lincoln, and very little respect for him: it was when, for almost eighteen months after secession had taken place, he was evidently averse to seeing that slavery had any vital connection with the rebellion, and so refused to strike a blow at its existence. . . . But the time came at last when the President, unless he was determined to be wilfully and wickedly blind, was compelled to see that slavery and the rebellion were indissolubly bound up together. Then came the proclamation of unconditional and everlasting emancipation to three million three hundred thousand slaves, leaving not one to clank his fetters in any

rebel State; and then, all that is vile and seditious in the Copperhead, pro-slavery, rebel-sympathizing element in the North burst forth against him, and to this hour continues to pour every vial of its wrath upon his head. Since that event, and in view of what has followed in the enrolment of tens of thousands of colored soldiers, I have changed my opinion of Abraham Lincoln. In proportion as he has fallen in the estimation of the disloyal portion of the North, he has risen in my own. True, he is open to criticism for his slowness, and needs spurring on to yet more decisive action; but I am not willing to believe that he is "ready to sacrifice the interest and honor of the North to secure a sham peace" with the rebels. That is a very grave charge.[2]

The third-party movement to replace Lincoln centered on a convention to meet in Cleveland. Radicals in turbulent St. Louis, many of them German Americans, and admirers in New York of 1856 Republican presidential candidate John C. Frémont, united in bringing about the convention. The Call signed by many New Yorkers read:

> Whereas a Convention has been called by certain parties favorable to changing the present Administration, and for the purpose of "counseling concerning the approaching Presidential election," on Tuesday the 31st of the present month; and whereas we are glad to learn that such a convention is to assemble, and having confidence that the objects of those issuing the call are in unison with those of the radical men of the country;
>
> Therefore, the undersigned, having been appointed by the Central Fremont Club of the city of New York, for that purpose, do hereby invite their radical fellow-citizens in every State, county, and town throughout the country to meet them in the above-named Convention, on the said Tuesday, the 31st of this month, in order, then and there to recommend the nomination of John C. Fremont for the Presidency of the United States, and to assist in Organizing for his election.
>
> The imbecile and vacillating policy of the present Administration in the conduct of the war, being just weak enough to waste its men and means to provoke the enemy, but not strong enough to conquer the rebellion—and its treachery to justice, freedom, and genuine democratic principles in its plan of reconstruction, whereby the honor and dignity of the nation have been sacrificed to conciliate the still existing and arrogant slave power, and to further the ends of an unscrupulous partisan ambition—call in thunder tones upon the lovers of justice and their country to come to the rescue of

the imperiled nationality and the cause of impartial and universal freedom, threatened with betrayal and overthrow.

The way to victory and salvation is plain. Justice must be throned in the seats of national legislation, and guide the executive will. The things demanded, and which we ask you to join us to render sure, are, *the immediate extinction of slavery throughout the whole United States by Congressional action, the absolute equality of all men before the law, without regard to race or color,* and such a plan of reconstruction as shall *conform entirely to the policy of freedom for all,* placing the political power *alone in the hands of the loyal,* and *executing with vigor the law for confiscating the property of the rebels.*

Come, then, in formidable numbers, and let us take counsel together, in this crisis of the nation's calamity, and, with one united effort, endeavor to redeem the country from slavery and war, that it may be consecrated to FREEDOM and PEACE FOREVER MORE. Men of God! Men of humanity! Lovers of justice! Patriots and freemen! One and all, rally!![3]

The Call struck a chord with many who had long desired a more aggressive and punishing program for reconstructing the southern states. Elizabeth Cady Stanton, the suffragette, responded:

To your call "to the radical men of the nation," taking it for granted you use "men" in, its largest sense, I desire to append my name, and for the following reasons:

  1. This is the only call ever issued for a political convention, demanding the right of suffrage for the black man—that safeguard of civil liberty, without which emancipation is a mockery.

  2. When a body of men thus consecrate themselves to "freedom and peace" and declare their high resolve to found a republic on the eternal principles of justice, they have lifted politics into the sphere of morals and religion, and made it the duty of all true men and women to unite with them in building up the *New Nation.*[4]

Wendell Phillips sent a vigorous letter denouncing Lincoln's reconstruction plan and branding his policy "a civil and military failure." Frederick Douglass lent his name to the Call, supposing the group intended "the complete abolition of every vestige of . . . slavery . . . perfect equality for the black man [in voting, jury service, and on the battlefield]."[5]

The Cleveland delegates resolved:

First. That the Federal Union shall be preserved.

Second. That the Constitution and laws of the United States must be observed and obeyed.

Third. That the rebellion must be suppressed by force of arms, and without compromise.

Fourth. That the rights of free speech, free press, and the habeas corpus be held inviolate, save in districts where martial law has been proclaimed.

Fifth. That the rebellion has destroyed slavery, and the Federal Constitution should be amended to prohibit its reestablishment, and to secure to all men absolute equality before the law.

Sixth. That integrity and economy are demanded at all times in the administration of the Government; and that in time of war the want of them is criminal.

Seventh. That the right of asylum, except for crime and subject to law, is a recognized principle of American liberty; that any violation of it cannot be overlooked, and must not go unrebuked.

Eighth. That the national policy known as the "Monroe doctrine" has become a recognized principle, and that the establishment of an anti-republican Government on this continent by any foreign power cannot be tolerated.

Ninth. That the gratitude and support of the nation are due to the faithful soldiers and the earnest leaders of the Union army and navy for their heroic achievements and deathless valor in defence of our imperiled country and of civil liberty.

Tenth. That the one-term policy for the Presidency, adopted by the people, is strengthened by the force of the existing crisis, and should be maintained by constitutional amendments.

Eleventh. That the Constitution should be so amended that the President and Vice President shall be elected by a direct vote of the people.

Twelfth. That the question of the reconstruction of the rebellious States belongs to the people, through their representatives in Congress, and not to the Executive.

Thirteenth. That the confiscation of the lands of the rebels, and their distribution among the soldiers and actual settlers, is a measure of justice.[6]

Like all third party movements, the Cleveland convention provided a platform for both sensible and strange ideas. The Monroe Doctrine *did* appear to be unenforced as Napoleon III invaded Mexico. The concept of a one-term presidency, on the other hand, has rarely been discussed seriously. Friends of Lincoln told him that rather than thousands gathering in Cleveland to displace and denounce him, fewer than four hundred had come. The number struck a familiar chord with the president, and as he commonly did, he picked up the Bible, always on his desk. Then he read aloud from 1 Samuel 22:2: "And every one that was in distress, and every one that was in debt, and every one that was discontented, gathered themselves unto him; and he became a captain over them: and there were with him about four hundred men."

Promptly accepting the nomination of this convention, John C. Frémont wrote:

> In answer to the letter which I have had the honor to receive from you, on the part of the representatives of the people assembled at Cleveland, the 31st of May, I desire to express my thanks for the confidence which led them to offer me the honorable and difficult position of their candidate in the approaching Presidential election. . . .
>
> Had Mr. Lincoln remained faithful to the principles he was elected to defend, no schism could have been created, and no contest could have been possible. This is not an ordinary election. It is a contest for the right even to have candidates, and not merely, as usual, for the choice among them. Now, for the first time since '76, the question of constitutional liberty has been brought directly before the people for their serious consideration and vote. The ordinary rights secured under the Constitution and the laws of the country have been violated and extraordinary powers have been usurped by the Executive. It is directly before the people now to say whether or not the principles established by the Revolution are worth maintaining. . . .
>
> To-day we have in the country the abuses of a military dictation without its unity of action and vigor of execution—an Administration marked at home by disregard of constitutional rights, by its violation of personal liberty and the liberty of the press, and as a crowning shame, by its abandon of the right of asylum, a right especially dear to all free nations abroad. Its course has been characterized by a feebleness and want of principle which has misled European powers and driven them to a belief that only commercial interests and personal aims are concerned, and that no great principles are involved in the issue. . . .
>
> Against this disastrous condition of affairs the Cleveland Convention was a protest.

The principles which form the basis of its platform have my unqualified and cordial approbation, but I cannot so heartily concur in all the measures which you propose. *I do not believe that confiscation extended to the property of all rebels, is practicable,* and if it wore so, I do not think it a measure of sound policy. It is, in fact, a question belonging to the people themselves to decide, and is a proper occasion for the exercise of their original and sovereign authority. As a war measure, in the beginning of a revolt which might be quelled by prompt severity, I understand the policy of confiscation, but not as a final measure of reconstruction after the suppression of an insurrection.

In the adjustments which are to follow peace no considerations of vengeance can consistently be admitted.

The object of the war is to make permanently secure the peace and happiness of the whole country, and there was but a single element in the way of its attainment. This element of *slavery may be considered practically destroyed* in the country, and it needs only your proposed amendment of the Constitution, to make its extinction complete.

With this extinction of slavery the party divisions created by it have also disappeared.... *[I]f Mr. Lincoln should be nominated*—as I believe *it would be fatal to the country* to indorse a policy and renew a power which has cost us the lives of thousands of men, and needlessly put the country on the road to bankruptcy—there will remain no other alternative but to organize against him every element of conscientious opposition with the view to prevent the misfortune of his re-election.[7]

William Lloyd Garrison, who had separated from Wendell Phillips on the issue of whether Lincoln should be renominated, called on the president on June 11. Arriving in Washington, Garrison had an interview with Lincoln, which he described as very satisfactory.

In his interview with the President, Mr. Garrison said to him: "Mr. Lincoln, I want to tell you frankly that for every word I have every spoken in your favor, I have spoken ten in favor of General Frémont"; and he went on to explain how difficult he had found it to commend the President when the latter was revoking the proclamations of Frémont and Hunter, and reiterating his purpose to save the Union, if he could, without destroying slavery; "but, Mr. president," he continued, "from the hour that you issued the Emancipation Proclamation, and showed your purpose to stand by it, I have given you my hearty support and confidence." Mr. Lincoln received this good-naturedly, set forth the difficulties under which he had labored, and expressed his anxiety to secure the adoption of the Constitutional Amendment, that the question might be forever settled and not hazarded by his possible death or failure of reelection.[8]

Salmon P. Chase, secretary of the treasury, possessed an inordinate appetite for the presidency, a desire spanning many years. Defeated for the nomination in 1860, he settled for a cabinet post with a large patronage, a position he exploited to broaden his base of followers. Lincoln was quite aware of the secretary's maneuvers:

"I have determined to shut my eyes, so far as possible, to everything of the sort," he told John Hay. "Mr. Chase makes a good Secretary, and I shall keep him where he is. If he becomes President, all right. I hope we may never have a worse man. I have observed with regret his plan of strengthening himself. Whenever he sees that an important matter is troubling me, if I am impelled to decide in a way to give offense to a man of some influence, he always ranges himself in opposition to me and persuades the victim that he has been hardly dealt with, and that he would arrange it differently. . . . I am entirely indifferent as to his success or failure in these schemes so long as he does his duty at the head of the Treasury Department."[9]

Chase wrote in late January sharp criticisms of the Lincoln administration:

Had there been here an Administration in the true sense of the word—a President conferring with his Cabinet and taking their united judgments, and with their aid enforcing activity, economy, and energy in all departments of public service—we could have spoken boldly and defied the world. But our condition here has always been very different. . . . How, under such circumstances, can anybody announce a policy which can only be made respectable by union, wisdom, and courage? . . .

The Administration cannot be continued as it is. There is, in fact, no Administration, properly speaking. There are departments and there is a President. The latter leaves administration substantially to the heads of the former, deciding himself comparatively few questions. These heads act with almost absolute independence of each other.[10]

Days later Attorney General Edward Bates, no friend of Chase, quietly told Lincoln of the scheming to elect Chase:

Called on the President and had a private conversation, of some ½ hour, chiefly about the presidential election. He is fully apprehensive of the schemes of the Radical leaders. When I suggested some of their plots, he said they were almost *fiendish*. He is also fully aware that they would strike him at once, if they durst; but they fear that the blow would be ineffectual, and so, they would fall under his power, as *beaten enemies;* and, for that only reason the hypocrit[e]s try to occupy equivocal ground so that, when they fall, as *enemies,* they may still pretend to be *friends.*

He told me (what I partly knew before) that the extremists (Chase men?) had called several caucuses in the hope of finding it safe to take open ground ag[ain]st L[incoln]'s re-nomination, but had never found one in three of the M. [embers of] C[ongres]s that would go against him—<I tried to impress upon him the important fact, that they need him quite as much as he does them—that they are cunning and unscrupulous, and when they find that they dare not openly oppose him, their effort will *then* be to commit him to as many as possible, of their extreme measures, so as to drive off his other friends, until he is weakened down to their level, and it becomes *safe to cast him off*—I think he sees it plainly[.]>

He told me also, that the Editor of the Mo. Democrat ([ ]) sometime ago, wrote a letter to Jim Lane, . . . declaring that *Lincoln* must be *defeated, at all hazards*—But that it is not *prudent yet, to declare openly against him*!![11]

The underground movement to nominate Chase broke through to the surface on Washington's birthday, 1864, when a secretly distributed document called the Pomeroy Circular was published in a Washington newspaper and then taken up by the national press. Samuel C. Pomeroy, to whom authorship was attributed, was a radical Republican senator from Kansas. His election in 1861 had been clouded by suspicions of bargaining, and his reelection in 1867 would fail when a senator announced that Pomeroy had bargained for his vote for eight thousand dollars. The Pomeroy Circular assailed Lincoln with a series of charges, and praised Chase, and declared that an organization had been established to make him president.[12]

Smoked out of concealment, Chase immediately wrote to Lincoln, suppressing his efforts to get the nomination and offering his resignation. Lincoln responded the next day, acknowledging the letter and promising to write more fully. On February 29 he wrote:

Now, on consideration, I find there is really very little to say. My knowledge of Mr. Pomeroy's letter having been made public came to me only the day you wrote; but I had, in spite of myself, known of its *existence* several days before. I have not yet read it, and I think I shall not. I was not shocked, or surprised by the appearance of the letter, because I had had knowledge of Mr. Pomeroy's Committee, and of secret issues which I supposed came from it, and of secret agents who I supposed were sent out by it, for several weeks. I have known just as little of these things as my own friends have allowed me to know. They bring the documents to me, but I do not read them—they tell me what they think fit to tell me, but I do not inquire for more. I fully concur with you that neither of us can be justly held responsible for what our respective friends may do without our instigation or countenance; and I assure you, as you have assured me, that no assault has been made upon you by my instigation, or with my countenance.

Whether you shall remain at the head of the Treasury Department is a question which I will not allow myself to consider from any stand-point other than my judgment of the public service; and, in that view, I do not perceive occasion for a change.[13]

In between these two letters the legislature of Chase's home state, Ohio, destroyed his aspiration for the highest office by nominating Lincoln for reelection.

With the Frémont movement having attracted so few and the Chase boom having collapsed, Lincoln's candidacy sped forward. As early as the first week in January states had begun to endorse Lincoln's reelection. Did Lincoln want to be reelected? In October 1863, writing to Congressman Elihu B. Washburne, sponsor of Grant's military rise, Lincoln in language characteristic of politicians had said, "A second term would be a great honor and a great labor, which together perhaps I would not decline if tendered." Grant's name for the presidency was on many tongues. Asked by various persons about Grant's nomination, Lincoln responded, "If he takes Richmond, let him have it." The exception to state endorsement was faction-ridden Missouri, where the assembly, by a vote of 45 to 37, tabled a resolution in favor of renominating Lincoln.[14]

In late March upon hearing of the date for the nominating convention, William Cullen Bryant, poet and editor of the *New York Evening Post,* headed the list of petitioners to have the date postponed. The petition to the national committee in part said:

The undersigned, friends of the Government and supporters of the present Administration, respectfully suggest to you the propriety of reconsidering your recent action calling a convention of the Union and republican parties at Baltimore, on the 7th day of June next, to nominate a candidate for President of the United States for the ensuing term.

In the opinion of the undersigned, the country is not now in a position to enter into a Presidential contest. It is very important that all parties friendly to the Government shall be united in support of a single candidate, and that, when a selection shall be made, it shall be acquiesced in by all loyal sections of the country, and by all branches of the loyal party. It is equally clear that such unanimity cannot at present be obtained, and it is not believed that it can be reached as early as the day named by you for the national convention. . . .

In the opinion of the undersigned, whatever will tend to lessen the duration and allay the acrimony of the Presidential strife, which is always exciting and disturbing in proportion to the length of the canvass, will be an advantage to the country.

In periods of war and great civil revulsions, time is reckoned by events, and months are as years in the periods of peace.

With a pure and patriotic desire to serve the best interests of the country, and in the belief that they will be best served by a postponement of a political convention to the latest day possible, we respectfully ask that you will reconsider your action, and name a day for the assembling of the national convention not earlier than the first day of September next.[15]

Senator Edwin D. Morgan, completing eight years as national chairman of the Republican Party and keenly aware of the factions within the party, told veteran political boss Thurlow Weed, "There would be a really strong opposition to the re-nomination of Mr. Lincoln if those against him knew in what manner to organize their party. They are not by any means unanimous for Mr. Chase, but would take Grant, Fremont, Banks or Butler more readily than Mr. Lincoln." To another correspondent he said, "I now say, that, not withstanding my preference as indicated for Mr. Lincoln that if Genl. Grant should take Richmond before the 7th of June, there will be such a furor for him that nobody but himself will be able to resist his nomination for the Presidency."[16]

On June 7, Richmond having eluded Grant's grasp, Morgan opened the convention in Baltimore. In a brief address Morgan told the delegates that "you, gentlemen . . . will fall far short of accomplishing its [the convention's] great mission, unless among its other resolves it shall declare for such an amendment of the Constitution as will positively prohibit African slavery in the United States."[17] Morgan's declaration met with three cheers and lengthy applause.

A New York newspaper a few days after the convention reported a group's meeting with Lincoln. "When one of us mentioned the great enthusiasm at the Convention, after Senator E. D. Morgan's proposition to amend the Constitution, abolishing slavery, Mr. Lincoln instantly said, 'It was I who suggested to Mr. Morgan that he should put that idea into his opening speech.'"[18]

The convention readily adopted the platform, in which the radical Republicans had inserted two veiled thrusts at Lincoln, one aimed at the conservative Postmaster General Blair and the other at the administration's management of the French occupation presence in Mexico.

What remained was the nomination. Missouri was represented by two sets of delegates. The convention in a rebuke to Lincoln approved the more radical anti-Blair delegates by a vote of 440 to 4, who, as instructed, cast 22 votes for Grant. Immediately after the total count was announced, the Missourians switched their votes to Lincoln, making the nomination unanimous.

Lincoln responded to his renomination in three letters, each emphasizing a separate matter: one speaking of the commitment to a constitutional amendment to abolish slavery; a second using a rural analogy about keeping him in office while the war continued; and the third praising the resolute Grant.

> I will neither conceal my gratification, nor restrain the expression of my gratitude, that the Union people, through their convention, in their continued effort to save, and advance the nation, have deemed me not unworthy to remain in my present position.
>
> I know no reason to doubt that I shall accept the nomination tendered; and yet perhaps I should not declare definitely before reading and considering what is called the Platform.

I will say now, however, [that] I approve the declaration in favor of so amending the Constitution as to prohibit slavery throughout the nation. When the people in revolt, with a hundred days of explicit notice, that they could, within those days, resume their allegiance, without the overthrow of their institution, and that they could not so resume it afterwards, elected to stand out, such [an] amendment of the Constitution as [is] now proposed, became a fitting, and necessary conclusion to the final success of the Union cause. Such alone can meet and cover all cavils. Now, the unconditional Union men, North and South, perceive its importance, and embrace it. In the joint names of Liberty and Union, let us labor to give it legal form, and practical effect.

I can only say, in response to the kind remarks of your chairman, as I suppose, that I am very grateful for the renewed confidence which has been accorded to me. . . . I am not insensible at all to the personal compliment there is in this; yet I do not allow myself to believe that any but a small portion of it is to be appropriated as a personal compliment. The convention and the nation, I am assured, are alike animated by a higher view of the interests of the country for the present and the great future, . . . entitled to appropriate as a compliment is only that part which I may lay hold of as being the opinion . . . that I am not entirely unworthy to be instructed with the place I have occupied for the last three years. I have not permitted myself, gentlemen, to conclude that I am the best man in the country; but I am reminded, in this connection, of a story of an old Dutch farmer, who remarked to a companion once that "it was not best to swap horses when crossing streams."

What we want, still more than Baltimore conventions or presidential elections, is success under Gen. Grant. (Cries of "Good," and applause.) I propose that you constantly bear in mind that the support you owe to the brave officers and soldiers in the field is of the very first importance, and we should therefore bend all our energies to that point. Now, without detaining you any longer, I propose that you help me to close up what I am now saying with three rousing cheers for Gen. Grant and the officers and soldiers under his command.[19]

During the summer while Grant fruitlessly persisted in his siege of Petersburg, a peace movement stronger than that of 1863 surged, led principally by the mercurial *New York Tribune* editor Horace Greeley. On July 7 Greeley sent Lincoln an impassioned appeal to negotiate a peace, enclosing materials from two adventurers. Greeley had been in communication with one of them, W. C. Jewett, called Colorado Jewett, for at least a year and a half. Jewett had frequently written letters to Lincoln, which the president did not read. The second, a Kentuckian named George N. Sanders, was a Confederate now in Canada. The Jewett note in Greeley's packet read:

Dear Mr. Greeley:—In reply to your note, I have to advise having just left Hon. George N. Sanders on the Canada side. *I am authorized to state to you, for our use only, not the public, that two ambassadors of Davis & Co. are now in Canada, with full and complete powers for a peace,* and Mr. Sanders requests that you come on immediately to me, at Cataract House, to have a private interview, or if you will send the President's protection *for him and two friends,* they will come and meet you. He says the whole matter can be consummated by me, you, them, and President Lincoln. Telegraph me in such form that I may know if you come here, or they to come on with me. Yours, W. C. Jewett[20]

Two days later Lincoln responded, stipulating that the person must bear a written proposition of peace from the Confederate president, accepting return to the Union and abandonment of slavery. The president also imposed on the gullible Greeley the obligation to bring the negotiators to him:

Your letter of the 7th., with inclosures, received. If you can find, any person anywhere professing to have any proposition of Jefferson Davis in writing, for peace, embracing the restoration of the Union and abandonment of slavery, what ever else it embraces, say to him he may come to me with you, and that if he really brings such proposition, he shall, at the least, have safe conduct, with the paper (and without publicity, if he choose) to the point where you shall have met him. The same, if there be two or more persons.[21]

As if trapped by Lincoln's stipulations, and embarrassed by his scant knowledge of Jewett and Sanders, Greeley on the 13th wrote to Lincoln saying he now had information he could rely on and naming two eminent Confederate political leaders empowered to negotiate:

I have now information on which I can rely that two persons duly commissioned and empowered to negotiate for peace are at this moment not far from Niagara Falls, in Canada, and are desirous of conferring with yourself, or with such persons as you may appoint and empower to treat with them. Their names (only given in confidence) are Hon. Clement C. Clay, of Alabama, and Hon. Jacob Thompson, of Mississippi. If you should prefer to meet them in person, they require safe-conducts for themselves, and for George N. Sanders, who will accompany them. Should you choose to empower one or more persons to treat with them in Canada, they will of course need no safe-conduct; but they cannot be expected to exhibit credentials save to commissioners empowered as they are. In negotiating directly with yourself, all grounds of cavil would be avoided, and you would be enabled at all times to act upon the freshest advices of the military situation. You will of course understand that I know nothing and have proposed nothing as to terms, and that nothing is conceded or taken for granted by the meeting of persons empowered to negotiate for peace. All that is assumed is a mutual desire to terminate this wholesale slaughter, if a basis of adjustment can be mutually agreed on, and it seems to me high time that an effort to this end should be made. I am of course quite other than sanguine that a peace can now be made, but I am quite sure that a frank, earnest, anxious effort to terminate the war on honorable terms would immensely strengthen the Government in case of its failure, and would help us in the eyes of the civilized world, which now accuses us of obstinacy, and indisposition even to seek a peaceful solution of our sanguinary, devastating conflict. Hoping to hear that you have resolved to act in the premises, and to act so promptly that a good influence may even yet be exerted on the North Carolina election next month.[22]

Lincoln on July 15 replied with two sharply worded epistles, one a telegram, the other a letter carried to New York by John Hay and handed to Greeley the following morning:

Any proposition which embraces the restoration of peace, the integrity of the whole Union, and the abandonment of slavery, and which comes by and with an authority that can control the armies now at war against the United States, will be received and considered by the executive government of the United States, and will be met by liberal terms on substantial and collateral points, and the bearer or bearers thereof shall have safe conduct both ways.[23]

Greeley reluctantly made the journey to Niagara Falls. He quickly discovered that the men he was to meet were not accredited from Richmond. Learning of this fiasco from Greeley, Lincoln advised that he was sending

Greeley a statement at Niagara Falls, brought by Hay. The statement reaffirmed the stipulations for peace negotiations made in his letter of July 9 to Greeley.

Together Greeley and Hay delivered Lincoln's statement to the Confederate commissioners—Sanders, whom Hay described as "a seedy-looking Rebel, with grizzled whiskers," and J. P. Holcombe, whom he described as "tall, solemn, spare, false-looking man, with false teeth, false eyes, and false hair." Greeley quickly discerned that negotiations were fruitless and left for New York City.[24]

The commissioners wrote Greeley a long letter, blaming Lincoln for "this sudden and entire change in views," and saying they left it to others to "fathom the caprice of his imperial will." Jewett distributed the letter to the press, a boon to Lincoln's enemies, who were made to believe he had rejected an opportunity to negotiate peace.

The *Washington Chronicle* came to Lincoln's defense in a piece that read:

> As an irresponsible person named Jewett, who has recently been acting as an agent and messenger for the Rebel emissaries in Canada, is assiduously laboring, and apparently with some success, to create the impression that he acts by virtue of a certain implied understanding or connection with the Executive Mansion we deem it not improper to state that he has never received from the President the slightest recognition; and that Maj. Hay, at Niagara, expressly declined to meet him, and that the only letter he has ever received from the Executive Office in answer to his voluminous communications is the follow[ing]: . . .

> Sir: In the exercise of my duty as Secretary in charge of the President's correspondence, it is necessary for me to use a certain discretion in the choice of letters to be submitted to the personal attention of the President. In order to avoid a further waste of time on your part, I have to inform you that your letters are never so submitted. My proceeding in this matter has the sanction of the President.[25]

In a private letter to Abram Wakeman, postmaster of New York, Lincoln saw the affair as a political maneuver:

> I feel that the subject which you pressed upon my attention in our recent conversation is an important one. The men of the South, recently (and

perhaps still) at Niagara Falls, tell us distinctly that they *are* in the confidential employment of the rebellion; and they tell us as distinctly that they are *not* empowered to offer terms of peace. Does any one doubt that what they *are* empowered to do, is to assist in selecting and arranging a candidate and a platform for the Chicago convention? Who could have given them this confidential employment but he who only a week since declared to Jaquess and Gilmore that he had no terms of peace but the independence of the South—the dissolution of the Union? Thus the present presidential contest will almost certainly be no other than a contest between a Union and a Disunion candidate, disunion certainly following the success of the latter. The issue is a mighty one for all people and all time; and whoever aids the right, will be appreciated and remembered.[26]

Though marked private, Lincoln's letter itself was a political maneuver. It was apparently intended to be shown to the editor of the *New York Herald,* James Gordon Bennett, with the offer of a political office for him in return for the paper's support. Wakeman told Lincoln he had read it to Bennett. The *Herald,* often close to copperheadism in tone, swung over to support Lincoln's reelection, and months later Lincoln offered Bennett the post of minister to France.

Senator Harlan of Iowa said to the president: "Some of us think, Mr. Lincoln, that you didn't send a very good ambassador to Niagara." "Well, I'll tell you about that, Harlan," Lincoln replied, "Greeley kept abusing me for not entering into peace negotiations. He said he believed we could have peace if I would do my part and when he began to urge that I send an ambassador to Niagara to meet the Confederate emissaries, I just thought I would let him go up and crack that nut for himself."[27]

Following the collapse of his trial balloon for the presidential nomination, Chase became increasingly embittered toward Lincoln and persistently demanded that Lincoln accept his preferences for office in his department. Writing to Governor John Brough of Ohio, Chase indicted the nominating convention and the lagging progress of the war:

> The terrible rains have arrested the progress of Grant & have given the rebels an opportunity to mass a large force against Butler & force him back to his entrenchments. . . .

It has become quite apparent now that the importunity of Mr. Lincoln's special friends for an Early Convention in order to make his nomination sure was a mistake both for him & for the country. The Convention will not be regarded as an Union Convention; but simply as a Blair-Lincoln Convention, by a great body of citizens whose support is essential to success. Few except those already committed to Mr. Lincoln will consider themselves bound by a predetermined nomination. Very many, who may ultimately vote for Mr. Lincoln, will wait the course of events, hoping that some popular movement for Grant or some other successful general will offer a better hope of saving the country. Others, and the number seems to be increasing, will not support his nomination in any event; believing that our ill success, thus far, in the suppression of the rebellion is due mainly to his course of action & inaction; & that no change can be for the worse.[28]

Relations between Lincoln and Chase rose to a crisis over patronage. Chase had grown accustomed to having his nominees approved by the president, more than once threatening to resign if he did not get his way. The assistant treasurer of New York City resigned his office, and the position held much financial and political significance. Senator Morgan of New York was eager to have an appointee from his wing of the party. At first Chase seemed compliant, but after two men had declined, he determined to name his own man.

Morgan strenuously took exception, believing the man lacked the status in New York requisite for the work as well as adherence to Morgan's wing of the Union party. Lincoln wrote to Chase:

Yours inclosing a blank nomination for Maunsell B. Field to be Assistant Treasurer at New-York was received yesterday. I can not, without much embarrassment, make this appointment, principally because of Senator Morgan's very firm opposition to it. Senator Harris has not spoken to me on the subject, though I understand he is not averse to the appointment of Mr. Field; nor yet to any one of the three named by Senator Morgan, rather preferring, of them, however, Mr. Hillhouse. Gov. Morgan tells me he has mentioned the three names to you, to wit, R. M. Blatchford, Dudley S. Gregory, and Thomas Hillhouse. It will really oblige me if you will make choice among these three, or any other man that Senators Morgan and Harris will be satisfied with, and send me a nomination for him.[29]

Chase in reply told Lincoln: "I shall be glad to have a conversation with you on the subject of Mr. Cisco's successor at any time & place convenient to you."[30] In answer Lincoln said:

> When I received your note this forenoon suggesting a verbal conversation in relation to the appointment of a successor to Mr. Cisco, I hesitated because the difficulty does not, in the main part, lie within the range of a conversation between you and me. As the proverb goes, no man knows so well where the shoe pinches as he who wears it. I do not think Mr. Field a very proper man for the place, but I would trust your judgment, and forego this, were the greater difficulty out of the way. Much as I personally like Mr. Barney, it has been a great burden to me to retain him in his place, when nearly all our friends in New-York, were directly or indirectly, urging his removal. Then the appointment of Judge Hogeboom to be general Appraiser, brought me to and has ever since kept me at, the verge of open revolt. Now, the appointment of Mr. Field would precipitate me in it, unless Senator Morgan and those feeling as he does, could be brought to concur in it. Strained as I already am at this point I do not think I can make this appointment in the direction of still greater strain.
>
> The testimonials of Mr. Field, with your accompanying notes, were duly received and I am now waiting to see your answer from Mr. Cisco.[31]

By the next day Chase had contrived to secure Cisco's withdrawal of his resignation. He sent the withdrawal to Lincoln together with his own resignation, which read:

> I have just received your note and have read it with great attention. I was not aware of the extent of the embarrassment to which you refer. In recommendations for office I have sincerely sought to get the best men for the places to be filled without reference to any other classification than supporters and opponents of your administration. Of the latter I have recommended none; among the former I have desired to know no distinction except degrees of fitness.
>
> The withdrawal of Mr. Cisco's resignation, which I enclose, relieves the present difficulty; but I cannot help feeling that my position here is not altogether agreeable to you; and it is certainly too full of embarrassment and difficulty and painful responsibility to allow in me the least desire to retain it.
>
> I think it my duty therefore to enclose to you my resignation. I shall regard it as a real relief if you think proper to accept it; and will most

cheerfully tender to my successor for any aid he may find useful in entering upon his duties.[32]

Lincoln's patience snapped. "Mr. Chase has resigned and I have accepted his resignation. I thought I could not stand it any longer," he told John Hay. He wrote to Chase:

Your resignation of the office of Secretary of the Treasury, sent me yesterday, is accepted. Of all I have said in commendation of your ability and fidelity, I have nothing to unsay; and yet you and I have reached a point of mutual embarrassment in our official relation which it seems can not be overcome, or longer sustained, consistently with the public service.[33]

Chase, still not without ambition, spent the remainder of the summer traveling and talking with people discontented with Lincoln. The editor of the *Springfield Republican,* Samuel Bowles, observed: "Chase is going around peddling his griefs in private ears and sowing dissatisfaction about Lincoln."[34]

The months of June through August formed a summer of discontent. Grant failed to capture Petersburg; Sherman progressed slowly toward Atlanta; and Confederate general Jubal A. Early menaced Washington. On the political front the Union's dark military position clouded over the election. Influential Republicans lost faith in Lincoln's capacity to lead.

Adding to all this was the question, what would the Democrats do? They had postponed their nominating convention until late August, leaving Republicans without platform or candidate at which to take aim. As the summer progressed, matters would get worse before they got better.

In mid-June the exiled Vallandigham returned to Ohio without hindrance from Lincoln. Speaking to the Democratic convention at Hamilton, after referring to charges that there was a conspiracy in the Northwest, he continued, reidentifying himself with the Democratic Party:

A powerful, widely-spread and very dangerous secret, oath-bound combination among the friends of the Administration, known as the "Loyal Union League," exists in every State. Yet the very men who control it charge persistently upon the members of the Democratic party, that they have organized—especially in the Northwest—[one or another] secret society, treasonable or "disloyal" in its character, affiliated with the South, and for the purpose of armed resistance to the authorities of the Federal and State Government. Whether any such ever existed, I do not know; but the charge that organizations of that sort, or having any such purpose, do now exist among members of that party in Ohio or other nonslaveholding States, is totally and positively false. That lawful political or party associations have been established, having as their object the organizing and strengthening of the Democratic party and its success in the coming Presidential election, and designed as a counter-movement to the so-called "Union Leagues," and, therefore, secret in their proceedings is very probable; and however objectionable hitherto, and in ordinary times, I recognize, to the fullest extent, not the lawfulness only, but the propriety and necessity of such organizations now, for "when bad men combine, good men must associate." But they are no conspiracy against the Government, and their members are not conspirators, but patriots. . . . There is, indeed a "conspiracy" very powerful, very ancient, and I trust that before long I may add, strongly consolidated also, upon sound principles, and destined yet to be triumphant—a conspiracy known as the Democratic party, the present object of which is the overthrow of the Administration in November next, not by force but through *the ballot box,* and the election of a President who shall be true to his oath, to Liberty, and to the Constitution. This is the sole conspiracy of which I know anything; and I am proud to be one of the conspirators. If any other exist, looking to unlawful armed resistance to the Federal or State authorities anywhere, in the exercise of their legal and constitutional rights, I admonish all persons concerned, that the act is treason and the penalty death. But I warn also the men in power, that there is a vast multitude, a host whom they cannot number, bound together by the strongest and holiest ties, to defend, by whatever means the exigencies of the times shall demand, their natural and constitutional rights as freemen, at all hazards and to the last extremity.

Three years have now passed, Men of Ohio, and the great issue of Constitutional Liberty and Free Popular Government is still before you. To you I again commit it, confident that in this the time of their greatest peril, you will be found worthy of the ancestors who for so many ages in England and America, on the field, in prison, and upon the scaffold, defended them against tyrants and usurpers whether in council or in arms.[35]

Meanwhile, General Early, though stooped with rheumatism contracted in the Mexican War, led his Confederate warriors down the Shenandoah

Valley, crossing the Potomac River and threatening Washington. As Early approached the capital Grant telegraphed:

> Forces enough to defeat all that Early has with him should get in his rear south of him, and follow him up sharply, leaving him to go north, defending depots, towns, &c., with small garrisons and the militia. If the President thinks it advisable that I should go to Washington in person I can start in an hour after receiving notice, leaving everything here on the defensive.[36]

The next day Lincoln responded:

> Your despatch to Gen. Halleck, referring to what I may think in the present emergency, is shown me. Gen. Halleck says we have absolutely no force here fit to go to the field. He thinks that with the hundred-day men, and invalids we have here, we can defend Washington, and scarcely Baltimore. . . . Now what I think is that you should provide to retain your hold where you are certainly, and bring the rest with you personally, and make a vigorous effort to destroy the enemie's force in this vicinity. I think there is really a fair chance to do this if the movement is prompt. This is what I think, upon your suggestion, and is not an order.[37]

A Baltimore committee appointed by the mayor wired: "Baltimore is in danger," and inquired about sending large reinforcements. Lincoln answered:

> Yours of last night received. I have not a single soldier but whom is being disposed by the Military for the best protection of all. By latest account the enemy is moving on Washington. They can not fly to either place. Let us be vigilant but keep cool. I hope neither Baltimore or Washington will be sacked.[38]

Lincoln's life seemed in danger. The secretary of war sent a note saying "come into town tonight," insisting that the president come back to the city from the Soldiers' Home, his summer residence. The navy prepared a vessel for his evacuation in the event of necessity. The next morning Lincoln read a reassuring telegram received the previous night from Grant:

> I have sent from here a whole corps commanded by an excellent officer, besides over three thousand other troops. One Division of the Nineteenth Corps, six thousand strong is now on its way to Washington. One Steamer loaded with these troops having passed Ft. Monroe today. They will probably

reach Washington tomorrow night. This force under [Horatio G.] Wright will be able to compete with the whole force with [Richard S.] Ewell.

Before more troops can be sent from here [David] Hunter will be able to join Wright in rear of the Enemy, with at least ten thousand men, besides a force sufficient to hold Maryland Heights.

I think on reflection it would have a bad effect for me to leave here, and with Genl [Edward O. C.] Ord at Baltimore and Hunter and Wright with the forces following the enemy up, could do no good

I have great faith that the enemy will never be able to get back with much of his force.[39]

Lincoln replied:

Yours of 10:30 P.M. yesterday received, and very satisfactory. The enemy will learn of Wright's arrival, and then the difficulty will be to unite Wright and Hunter, South of the enemy before he will recross the Potomac. Some firing between Rockville and here now.[40]

Learning that the enemy was at nearby Fort Stevens, Lincoln, accompanied by his wife, rode to the fort, where he watched the first shot fired. Oblivious of danger he stood tall upon the parapet. Hay reported, "A soldier roughly ordered him to get down or he would have his head knocked off." The following day, again with Mary, he observed the firing until an officer three feet from him fell mortally wounded. When General Wright told Lincoln to get out of danger, Lincoln did not move. Then Oliver Wendell Holmes Jr. shouted, "Get down you fool!" and the commander in chief obeyed the lieutenant.[41]

The evening of July 11, munching a piece of army bread in place of dinner, he went down to the wharf to greet the troops sent by Grant. When he saw them his face lit up. "It is the old Sixth Corps," he remarked. "The danger is over."

Three days later the president faced a challenge to his authority over his cabinet. Secretary of War Stanton sent him a letter from Major General Halleck virtually demanding dismissal of Postmaster General Blair. The Halleck letter that Stanton sent Lincoln read:

I am informed by an officer of rank and standing in the military service that the Hon. M. Blair, Post Master Genl, in speaking of the burning of his house in Maryland, this morning, said, in effect, that "the officers in command about Washington are poltroons; that there were not more than five hundred rebels on the Silver Spring road and we had a million of men in arms; that it was a disgrace; that General Wallace was in comparison with them far better as he would at least fight."

As there have been for the last few days a large number of officers on duty in and about Washington who have devoted their time and energies night and day, and have periled their lives, in the support of the Government, it is due to them as well as to the War Department that it should be known whether such wholesale denouncement & accusation by a member of the cabinet receives the sanction and approbation of the President. . . . If so the names of the officers accused should be stricken from the rolls of the Army; if not, it is due to the honor of the accused that the slanderer should be dismissed from the cabinet.[42]

In a blunt memorandum affirming his authority, Lincoln told his cabinet:

I must myself be the judge, how long to retain in, and when to remove any of you from, his position. It would greatly pain me to discover any of you endeavoring to procure anothers removal, or, in any way to prejudice him before the public. Such endeavor would be a wrong to me; and much worse, a wrong to the country. My wish is that on this subject, no remark be made, nor question asked, by any of you, here or elsewhere, now or hereafter.[43]

The grave military situation forced Lincoln to make an unpopular move in an election year. On July 18 he called for half a million volunteers and stipulated that if the figure was not met by volunteering, he would resort to drafting after September, shortly before the voting season would begin.

Unaware of the call for more troops, Grant, in cipher, telegraphed the president:

In my opinion there ought to be an immediate call for say 300.000 men to be put in the field in the shortest possible time. The presence of this number of reinforcements would save the annoyance[e] of raids and would enable us to drive the enemy back from his present front, particularly from Richmond, without attacking fortifications. The enemy now have their last man in the field. Every depletion of their Army is an irreparable loss. Desertions from it are now rapid. With the prospect of large additions to our force these desertions would increase. The greater number of men we have the shorter and less sanguinary will be the war.

I give this entirely as my view and not in any spirit of dictation, always holding myself in readiness to use the material given me to the best advantage I know how.[44]

On August 5 Secretary of State William H. Seward, now one of Lincoln's most trusted cabinet officials, read aloud to Lincoln the shrill "manifesto" written by radical Republican Ohio senator Benjamin Wade and Maryland congressman Henry Winter Davis. Lincoln had pocket vetoed their more radical approach to Reconstruction (the Wade-Davis bill), and they in turn accused him of subverting and defying Congress, indeed of acting in a "dictatorial" manner. Lincoln responded, "I would like to know whether these men intend openly to oppose my election—the document looks that way." He told a friend, "To be wounded in the house of one's friends is perhaps the most grievous affliction that can befall a man." That day brightened, however, with news of Admiral Farragut's victory in Mobile Bay.

But early in August a movement within the Republican Party to replace Lincoln as its nominee gathered some strength. A Cincinnati correspondent wrote to Chase on August 10:

> About Presidential matters. I learned reliably in Washington that a secret movement is being made by leading war democrats in favor of Brough / They think McClellan is neither fish nor flesh. If the war democrats get the control of the Convention at Chicago, it will be a struggle probably between McC. & Brough. If this grows vindictive, who is so likely to be agreed to by both as you? If democrats there are as smart as democrats have heretofore been, I can hardly doubt the result.—There is also talk of a compromise ticket with McClellan and Pendleton, as the nominees. I don't believe any body can prognosticate upon any reliable basis.
>
> The dissatisfaction with Mr. Lincoln grows to abhorrence. I don't believe he can be elected. Every day satisfies the public more and more, that instead of the "Honest old Abe" they believed him to be, he has been a cunning trickster unscrupulously devising for *himself*—that instead of administering his office with fidelity to the country, individuality rather than nationality has influenced his action. His treatment of you and retaining Blair, has contributed largely to this eye-opening process. Have you seen the paper of Ben. Wade and Winter Davis? Every one who had read it whom I have heard express an opinion of it, says "Amen." I understand the meaning of

the call for a convention on the 22nd Sept. to be, that if a peace man is nominated at Chicago and the dissatisfaction with Mr. Lincoln continues, a new candidate combining the war democrats, the Freemont men, and the dissatisfied republicans may be put into the field. So far as I can learn no *individual* has been named. What a day it would be for the Country, if at last the real patriots and true men of all parties, should select you as the man of the nation. It seems to me that if God directs human affairs and has decreed success to our cause, this may be the means through which it is to be accomplished.[45]

And on August 12 Thurlow Weed, long experienced in politics, confided to Seward, "I told Mr. Lincoln that his re-election was an impossibility, I also told him that the information would come to him through other channels." Ten days later the National Executive Committee of what was now called the Union party, headed by the editor of the *New York Times,* Henry J. Raymond, met to consider the party's plight. The committee wrote a gloomy letter to the president:

I feel compelled to drop you a line concerning the political condition of the country as it strikes me. I am in active correspondence with your stanchest friends in every State and from them all I hear but one report. The tide is setting strongly against us. Hon. E. B. Washburne writes that "were an election to be held now in Illinois we should be beaten." Mr. Cameron writes that Pennsylvania is against us. Governor Morton writes that nothing but the most strenuous efforts can carry Indiana. This State, according to the best information I can get, would go 50,000 against us to-morrow. And so of the rest. Nothing but the most resolute and decided action, on the part of the Government and its friends, can save the country from falling into hostile hands. Two special causes are assigned for this great reaction in public sentiment,—the want of military successes, and the impression in some minds, the fear and suspicion in others, that we are not to have peace in any event under this Administration until slavery is abandoned. In some way or other the suspicion is widely diffused that we can have peace with Union if we would. It is idle to reason with this belief—still more idle to denounce it. It can only be expelled by some authoritative act, at once bold enough to fix attention and distinct enough to defy incredulity and challenge respect.

Why would it not be wise, under these circumstances, to appoint a commission, in due form, to make distinct proffers of peace to Davis, as the head of the rebel armies, on the sole condition of acknowledging the supremacy of the Constitution—all other questions to be settled in a convention of the people of all the States?[46]

The following morning, virtually abandoning hope of reelection, Lincoln penned a remarkable secret memorandum:

> This morning, as for some days past, it seems exceedingly probable that this Administration will not be re-elected. Then it will be my duty to so co-operate with the President elect, as to save the Union between the election and the inauguration; as he will have secured his election on such ground that he can not possibly save it afterwards.[47]

Without revealing its contents, he asked each cabinet member to sign the sealed paper.

Pessimism lay in Lincoln's memorandum, as gloom lay in much of the North; fighting showed feeble progress by both Grant and Sherman, the leading Union generals; and a peace movement was gathering strength in all quarters. All these factors plunged the president and the Union cause to the lowest level of the war. What would the months before the voters spoke hold? Lincoln's reelection seemed unlikely.

CHAPTER THIRTY-THREE

THE ELECTION OF 1864

Peace, military success, the Democratic Party nomination of a presidential candidate, and emancipation all hung in the balance as the election season approached in 1864.

Replying to a letter saying Lincoln should withdraw from the race, Frémont on August 25 said friends of Lincoln and Frémont should unite to hold a new convention where they could coalesce and name a man who would "receive the support of the patriotic masses of the people."[1] The *National Intelligencer* had published an article the day before titled, "Peace breaking and Peace making," adding to the pressure to end the war by negotiating with the Confederates.[2]

Henry Jarvis Raymond, chair of the National Executive Committee of the Republican Party, appeared with members of the committee at the White House to urge an overture of peace to the Confederacy. Their purpose was explicitly political, driven by fears that the Republicans and the administration would lose the election if they did not see military success soon. Lincoln's secretary John George Nicolay in August made a record of the interview:

> The President and the stronger half of the Cabinet, Seward, Stanton, and Fessenden, held a consultation with him [Raymond] and showed him that they had thoroughly considered and discussed the proposition of his letter of the 22d; and on giving him their reasons he very readily concurred with them in the opinion that to follow his plan of sending a commission to Richmond would be worse than losing the Presidential contest—it would be ignominiously surrendering it in advance. Nevertheless the visit of himself and committee here did great good. They found the President and Cabinet

much better informed than themselves, and went home encouraged and cheered. Events, political and military, which occurred and came to public knowledge very few days afterwards, silenced the preposterous clamor of "peace" fanatics.[3]

Though few African Americans held the franchise in 1864, thousands were fighting in the U.S. Colored Troops, and thousands more paid attention to the political contest and its significance. But black attitudes toward Lincoln diverged. Leonard Pennington, a black abolitionist, explained why blacks should prefer Lincoln as president:

> The prospect of having HIS EXCELLENCY ABRAHAM LINCOLN for our next President should awaken in the inmost soul of every American of African descent emotions of the most profound and patriotic enthusiasm. There was a kind and wise Providence in bringing Mr. Lincoln into the Presidential chair, and I believe that the same all-wise Providence has directed him in everything he has done as our President. I say OUR President, because he is the only American President who has ever given any attention to colored men as citizens. I believe that his renomination by the Convention is not only sound policy, but that it is equivalent to reelection, and especially if colored men will do their duty at the ballot box next November.
>
> It lies with colored men now to decide this great issue. The wisest, the safest, and the soundest policy for colored Americans is to exert all our influence to keep our present Chief Magistrate where he is for four years from next March.
>
> There are many reasons why we, as colored men, should prefer Mr. Lincoln for our next President. Among the many I may say: 1. He is an honest President. 2. He is faithful to the whole nation. 3. He commands the respect of the world. 4. He is more cordially hated by the Copperheads of the North and the rebels of the South than any other living man. 5. His reelection will be the best security that the present well-begun work of negro freedom and African redemption will be fully completed. May God grant us four long years more of the judicious administration of that excellent man, ABRAHAM LINCOLN, and when I speak thus I believe I speak the sentiments of nine-tenths of my colored fellow-citizens. What say you, Mr. Editor?[4]

Yet a black soldier from Massachusetts, where black males could vote, explained his preference for Frémont:

Many of our intelligent colored men believe in Mr. Lincoln; but we, who have studied him thoroughly, know him better, and as we desire to conglomerate in the land of our nativity, and not be severed from the ties we hold most dear, we hail the nomination of one of liberty's most radical sons—John C. Fremont. Mr. Lincoln's policy in regard to the elevation and inseparability of the negro race has always been one of a fickle minded man—one who, holding anti-slavery principles in one hand and colonization in the other, always gave concessions to slavery when the *Union* could be preserved without touching the peculiar institution. Such a man is not again worthy the votes of the voting portion of the colored race, when the intrepid Frémont, explorer of the Mariposa Valley, the well-known freedom-cherishing, negro-equalizing patriot, is the competitor. The press, like Mr. Lincoln, has always been, and will ever be, in favor of negro colonization; for, like him, they fear competition, and it is not extraordinary if the press should now uphold Mr. Lincoln though dissatisfied with his vacillating administration, to keep John C. Fremont from occupying the presidential chair. The loyal and truehearted people of the North will, no doubt, weigh the two men now before the public, and choose the one not found wanting. We are within ourselves satisfied that the Cleveland Convention will carry its object—that of electing Freedom's son—while the Baltimore Convention, with its nominee for reelection, will return to the plowshare.

While we thank Mr. Lincoln for what the exigencies of the times forced him to do, we also censure him for the non-accomplishment of the real good this accursed rebellion gave him the power to do, and which if he had done, instead of bartering human sinews and human rights with slaveholding Kentucky, the world would have looked upon him as the magnanimous regenerator of American institutions, and the benevolent protector of human freedom.[5]

In late August Leonard Swett, longtime friend of Lincoln, writing to his wife from New York, described "the fearful things" occurring about the election:

The fearful things in relation to the country have induced me to stay a week here. I go to Washington to-night, and can't see how I can get away from there before the last of the week.

Swett summarized the movements against Lincoln as follows:

The malicious foes of Lincoln are calling or getting up a Buffalo convention to supplant him. They are Sumner, Wade, Henry Winter Davis, Chase, Frémont, Wilson, etc.

The Democrats are conspiring to resist the draft. We seized this morning three thousand pistols going to Indiana for distribution. The war Democrats are trying to make the Chicago nominee a loyal man. The peace Democrats are trying to get control of the Government, and through alliance with Jefferson Davis, to get control of both armies and make universal revolution necessary.

The most fearful things are probable.

I am acting with Thurlow Weed, Raymond, etc., to try to avert. There is not much hope.

Unless material changes can be wrought, Lincoln's election is beyond any possible hope. It is probably clean gone now.[6]

During this anxious August, General Grant, though failing to produce victories, significantly contributed to Lincoln's limp candidacy. In mid-month he penned a widely read letter to his friend and patron, Congressman E. B. Washburne, depicting the rebels' waning in strength, waiting for the election, hoping for a counterrevolution. Perhaps most striking was his remark about the rebels, "They have robbed alike the cradle and the grave."[7]

Anticipating the Democratic convention, Lincoln presciently remarked to Noah Brooks, a close friend and reporter who was about to depart to cover the convention, "They must nominate a Peace Democrat on a war platform, or a War Democrat on a peace platform; and I personally can't say that I care much what they do."[8]

As the day approached for the Democratic convention Daniel S. Dickinson, a Union Democrat who had won 108 votes for the vice presidency in the Baltimore convention, pondered:

I cannot believe that Mr. Lincoln, if fully advised of the public mind, would desire to enter upon a canvass. If the necessities of the shoddy contractors and longing office-holders had been less, the Union convention would have been postponed to September, and the true popular sentiment might be consulted and obeyed. . . . The war has been protracted beyond popular expectation. Men and money have been given freely. The helm has not been held with a firm and steady grasp, and there is a cry of change, which, no matter whether wise or ill-founded, should be both heard and heeded.[9]

The Democrats during the long summer of Republican frustration had delayed as long as possible to hold their convention. They met in Chicago in late August. At the convention the party's national chairman August Belmont, American agent of the Rothschild family of European bankers, opened the proceedings with a vituperative speech castigating the Lincoln administration:

> We are assembled here to-day, at the National Democratic Convention, for the purpose of nominating candidates for the Presidency and Vice Presidency of the United States. This task, at all times a most important and arduous one, has, by the sad events of our civil war, assumed an importance and responsibility of the most fearful nature. Never, since the formation of our government, has there been an assemblage, the proceedings of which were fraught with more momentous and vital results, than those which must flow from your action. Towards you, gentlemen, are directed at this moment the anxious fears and doubts, not only of millions of American citizens, but also of every lover of civil liberty throughout the world. [Cheers.] In your hands rests, under the ruling of an all-wise Providence, the future of this Republic. Four years of misrule by a sectional, fanatical and corrupt party, have brought our country to the very verge of ruin. The past and present are sufficient warnings of the disastrous consequences which would befall us if Mr. Lincoln's re-election should be made possible by our want of patriotism and unity. The inevitable results of such a calamity must be the utter disintegration of our whole political and social system amidst bloodshed and anarchy, with the great problems of liberal progress and self-government jeopardized for generations to come.
>
> The American people have at last awakened to the conviction that a change of policy and administration can alone stay our downward course; and they will rush to the support of your candidate and platform, provided you will offer to their suffrage a tried patriot, who has proved his devotion to the Union and the Constitution, and provided that you pledge him and yourselves to maintain that hallowed inheritance by every effort and sacrifice in your power. [Loud applause.] Let us, at the very outset of our proceedings, bear in mind that the dissensions of the last democratic convention were one of the principal causes which gave the reins of government into the hands of our opponents; and let us beware not to fall again into the same fatal error. We must bring at the altar of our country the sacrifice of our prejudices, opinions and convictions—however dear

and long cherished they may be—from the moment they threaten the harmony and unity of action so indispensable to our success. We are here not as war democrats, nor as peace democrats, but as citizens of the great Republic, which we will strive to bring back to its former greatness and prosperity, without one single star taken from the brilliant constellation that once encircled its youthful brow. [Cheers.] Let peace and disinterested patriotism, tempered by moderation and forbearance, preside over our deliberations; and, under the blessings of the Almighty, the sacred cause of the Union, the constitution and the laws, must prevail against fanaticism and treason. [Cheering.][10]

The Democratic Party delegates elected Governor Horatio Seymour of New York as permanent chairman of the convention. And on taking the chair Seymour said:

I have not language to tell with what anxious solicitude the people of this country watch our proceedings. The prayers of men and women in ten thousand homes to up to heaven that we may be so guided in our deliberations that our action many conduce to the restoration of our Union, to the return of peace, and the maintenance of liberty in this land. [Cheers] . . .

There is no man here who does not love the Union. [Cheers] There is no man here who does not desire peace. [Cheers] There is no man here who is not resolved to uphold the great principles of constitutional freedom. [Applause] . . .

This administration cannot now save this Union if it would. It has, by its proclamations, by vindictive legislation, by displays of hate and passion, placed obstacles in its own pathway which it cannot overcome, and has hampered its own freedom of action by unconstitutional acts.

But if the administration cannot save this Union, we can. [Loud applause] Mr. Lincoln values many things above the Union; we put it first of all. [Continued cheering] He thinks a proclamation worth more than peace; we think the blood of our people more precious than the edicts of the President. [Cheers] There are no hindrances in our pathways to Union and to peace. We demand no conditions for the restoration of our Union; we are shackled with no hates, no prejudices, no passions. We wish for fraternal relationship with the people of the South. [Applause] We demand for them what we demand for ourselves—the full recognition of the rights of States. We mean that every star on our nation's banner shall shine with an equal luster.[11]

The delegates' spirit was often intemperate, as members of the convention took aim at Lincoln personally and disparaged nearly every action he had taken in office. The Rev. Henry Clay Dean of Iowa unsparingly assailed Lincoln:

> For over three years, Lincoln had been calling for men, and they had been given. But, with all the vast armies placed at his command, he had failed! *failed!!* FAILED!!! *FAILED!!!!* Such a failure had never been known. Such destruction of human life had never been seen since the destruction of Sennacherib by the breath of the Almighty. And still the monster usurper wanted more men for his slaughter-pens. . . . Ever since the usurper, traitor, and tyrant, had occupied the Presidential chair, the Republican party had shouted "War to the knife, and the knife to the hilt!" Blood had flowed in torrents; and yet the thirst of the old monster was not quenched. His cry was for more blood.[12]

The Democratic message of Lincoln's failure continued. Vallandigham became a member of the platform committee and was thought to draft the notorious plank on the prosecution of the war. The platform was read while Vallandigham rubbed his hands "with unrestrained glee":

> *Resolved,* That this Convention does explicitly declare, as the sense of the American people, that, after four years of failure to restore the Union by the experiment of war, during which, under the pretense of a military necessity of a war power higher than the Constitution, the Constitution itself has been disregarded in every part, and public liberty and private right alike trodden down, and the material prosperity of the country essentially impaired, justice, humanity, liberty, and the public welfare demand that immediate efforts be made for a cessation of hostilities, with a view to an ultimate Convention of all the States, or other peaceable means, to the end that, at the earliest practicable moment, peace may, be restored on the basis of the Federal Union of the States. . . .
>
> *Resolved,* That the aim and object of the Democratic party is to preserve the Federal Union and the rights of the States unimpaired; and they hereby declare that they consider the Administrative usurpation of extraordinary and dangerous powers not granted by the Constitution, the subversion of the civil by military law in States not in insurrection, the arbitrary military arrest, imprisonment, trial, and sentence, of American citizens in States where civil law exists in full force, the suppression of freedom of speech

and of the press, the denial of the right of asylum, the open and avowed disregard of State rights, the employment of unusual test-oaths and the interference with and denial of the right of the people to bear arms, as calculated to prevent a restoration of the Union and the perpetuation of a government deriving its just powers from the consent of the governed.

Resolved, That the shameful disregard of the Administration to its duty, in respect to our fellow-citizens who now and long have been prisoners of war in a suffering condition, deserve the severest reprobation, on the score alike of public interest and common humanity.[13]

After the platform came the Democratic nomination. George B. McClellan easily became the party's candidate. Popular as a general at the head of the Army of the Potomac, McClellan had seen service in the war that included victories in western Virginia, the stalled campaign for Richmond in the summer of 1862, and the bloody victory at Antietam. On nearly every issue he stood in contrast to Lincoln. He waged a war of conciliation and opposed national conscription, emancipation, and Lincoln's policy of suspension of habeas corpus. Before he could respond to word of his nomination, however, news flashed across the country: "Sherman has taken Atlanta." At long last, an augury of eventual Union victory appeared in the war. The northern mood changed from despondency to exhilaration.

McClellan the warrior campaigned uncomfortably on a war failure and peace platform. He labored over his acceptance letter. The final draft read:

It is unnecessary for me to say to you that this nomination comes to me unsought. I am happy to know that when the nomination was made, the record of my public life was kept in view. . . .

The Union was originally formed by the exercise of a spirit of conciliation and compromise. To restore and preserve it the same spirit must prevail in our councils and in the hearts of the people. The reestablishment of the Union in all its integrity is and must continue to be the indispensable condition in any settlement. So soon as it is clear, or even probable, that our present adversaries are ready for peace, upon the basis of the Union, we should exhaust all the resources of statesmanship practiced by civilized nations and taught by the traditions of the American people, consistent with the honor and interests of the country, to secure such peace, re-establish the Union, and guarantee for the future the constitutional rights of every state. The Union is the one condition of peace—we ask no more.

I could not look in the face of my gallant comrades of the army and navy, who have survived so many bloody battles, and tell them that their labors and the sacrifice of so many of our slain and wounded brethren had been in vain; that we had abandoned that Union for which we have so often periled our lives. A vast majority of our people, whether in the army and navy or at home, would, as I would, hail with unbounded joy the permanent restoration of peace, on the basis of the Union under the Constitution, without the effusion of another drop of blood. But no peace can be permanent without Union.

As to the other subjects presented in the resolutions of the Convention, I need only say that I should seek, in the Constitution of the United States, and the laws framed in accordance therewith, the rule of my duty and the limitations of executive power; endeavor to restore economy in public expenditure, re-establish the supremacy of law, and, by the operation of a more vigorous nationality, resume our commanding position among the nations of the earth.[14]

Custom prescribed that presidential candidates participate little in the campaign. Lincoln, however, contrived to keep his views known by dint of his public letters and speeches. In March a committee of workingmen came to honor him and secure his views. The *New York Tribune* reported the event:

A Committee on behalf of the New-York Workingmen's Democratic Republican Association today waited on the President to inform him that their association had elected him an honorary member. The object of the organization is to advance the workingmen of America in morals, position and loyalty; it binds them together in support of the Union, and induces them at all sacrifices to sustain it. They requested Mr. Lincoln to give his views on the subject matter of which their address treated.[15]

Lincoln seized the opportunity to describe his outlook on labor and capital, citing his first annual message and stressing the importance of the war to working people:

The honorary membership in your Association, as generously tendered, is gratefully accepted.

You comprehend, as your address shows, that the existing rebellion, means more, and tends to more, than the perpetuation of African Slavery—that

473

it is, in fact, a war upon the rights of all working people. . . . None are so
deeply interested to resist the present rebellion as the working people. Let
them beware of prejudice, working division and hostility among themselves.
The most notable feature of a disturbance in your city last summer, was the
hanging of some working people by other working people. It should never
be so. The strongest bond of human sympathy, outside of the family relation, should be one uniting all working people, of all nations, and tongues,
and kindred. Nor should this lead to a war upon property, or the owners
of property. Property is the fruit of labor—property is desirable—is a positive good in the world. That some should be rich, shows that others may
become rich, and hence is just encouragement to industry and enterprise.
Let not him who is houseless pull down the house of another; but let him
labor diligently and build one for himself, thus by example assuring that
his own shall be safe from violence when built.[16]

In late March two influential Kentuckians called on Lincoln, and he
turned the occasion into a defense of his slavery policy. His close friend
O. H. Browning described the meeting:

The President told me that a few days before Govr Bramlett of KY: Hon
Archibald Dixon & Mr Hodges of the same state had called upon him in
regard to the enlistment of slaves as soldiers in Ky, in reference to which
there has been much dissatisfaction in that State, and that everything had
been amicably adjusted between them, and that they had gone home satisfied. He said when they were discussing the matter he asked them to let
him make a little speech to them, which he did and with which they were
much pleased.[17]

Lincoln wrote out his remarks:

"You ask me to put in writing the substance of what I verbally said the
other day, in your presence, to Governor Bramlette and Senator Dixon. It
was about as follows:

"I am naturally anti-slavery. If slavery is not wrong, nothing is wrong. I
can not remember when I did not so think, and feel. And yet I have never
understood that the Presidency conferred upon me an unrestricted right
to act officially upon this judgment and feeling. It was in the oath I took
that I would, to the best of my ability, preserve, protect, and defend the
Constitution of the United States. I could not take the office without taking the oath. Nor was it my view that I might take an oath to get power,

and break the oath in using the power. I understood, too, that in ordinary civil administration this oath even forbade me to practically indulge my primary abstract judgment on the moral question of slavery. I had publicly declared this many times, and in many ways. And I aver that, to this day, I have done no official act in mere deference to my abstract judgment and feeling on slavery. I did understand however, that my oath to preserve the constitution to the best of my ability, imposed upon me the duty of preserving, by every indispensable means, that government—that nation—of which that constitution was the organic law. Was it possible to lose the nation, and yet preserve the constitution? By general law life and limb must be protected; yet often a limb must be amputated to save a life; but a life is never wisely given to save a limb. I felt that measures, otherwise unconstitutional, might become lawful, by becoming indispensable to the preservation of the constitution, through the preservation of the nation. Right or wrong, I assumed this ground, and now avow it. I could not feel that, to the best of my ability, I had even tried to preserve the constitution, if, to save slavery, or any minor matter, I should permit the wreck of government, country, and Constitution all together. When, early in the war, Gen. Fremont attempted military emancipation, I forbade it, because I did not then think it an indispensable necessity. When a little later, Gen. Cameron, then Secretary of War, suggested the arming of the blacks, I objected, because I did not yet think it an indispensable necessity. When, still later, Gen. Hunter attempted military emancipation, I again forbade it, because I did not yet think the indispensable necessity had come. When, in March, and May, and July 1862 I made earnest, and successive appeals to the border states to favor compensated emancipation, I believed the indispensable necessity for military emancipation, and arming the blacks would come, unless averted by that measure. They declined the proposition; and I was, in my best judgment, driven to the alternative of either surrendering the Union, and with it, the Constitution, or of laying strong hand upon the colored element. I chose the latter. In choosing it, I hoped for greater gain than loss; but of this, I was not entirely confident. More than a year of trial now shows no loss by it in our foreign relations, none in our home popular sentiment, none in our white military force,—no loss by it any how or any where. On the contrary, it shows a gain of quite a hundred and thirty thousand soldiers, seamen, and laborers. These are palpable facts, about which, as facts, there can be no cavilling. We have the men; and we could not have had them without the measure.

["]And now let any Union man who complains of the measure, test himself by writing down in one line that he is for subduing the rebellion by force of arms; and in the next, that he is for taking these hundred and thirty thousand men from the Union side, and placing them where they would be but for the measure he condemns. If he can not face his case so stated, it is only because he can not face the truth.["]

I add a word which was not in the verbal conversation. In telling this tale I attempt no compliment to my own sagacity. I claim not to have controlled events, but confess plainly that events have controlled me. Now, at the end of three years struggle the nation's condition is not what either party, or any man devised, or expected. God alone can claim it. Whither it is tending seems plain. If God now wills the removal of a great wrong, and wills also that we of the North as well as you of the South, shall pay fairly for our complicity in that wrong, impartial history will find therein new cause to attest and revere the justice and goodness of God.[18]

Later in the month, invited to speak to the Sanitary Fair in Baltimore, Lincoln used the occasion to dwell on the meaning of liberty and the stakes in the war:

Calling to mind that we are in Baltimore, we can not fail to note that the world moves. Looking upon these many people, assembled here, to serve, as they best may, the soldiers of the Union, it occurs at once that three years ago, the same soldiers could not so much as pass through Baltimore. The change from then till now, is both great, and gratifying. Blessings on the brave men who have wrought the change, and the fair women who strive to reward them for it.

But Baltimore suggests more than could happen within Baltimore. The change within Baltimore is part only of a far wider change. When the war began, three years ago, neither party, nor any man, expected it would last till now. Each looked for the end, in some way, long ere to-day. Neither did any anticipate that domestic slavery would be much affected by the war. But here we are; the war has not ended, and slavery has been much affected, how much needs not now to be recounted. So true is it that man proposes, and God disposes.

But we can see the past, though we may not claim to have directed it; and seeing it, in this case, we feel more hopeful and confident for the future.

The world has never had a good definition of the word liberty, and the American people, just now, are much in want of one. We all declare for

476

liberty; but in using the same *word* we do not all mean the same *thing*. With some the word liberty may mean for each man to do as he pleases with himself, and the product of his labor; while with others the same word may mean for some men to do as they please with other men, and the product of other men's labor. Here are two, not only different, but incompatable things, called by the same name—liberty. And it follows that each of the things is, by the respective parties, called by two different and incompatable names—liberty and tyranny.

The shepherd drives the wolf from the sheep's throat, for which the sheep thanks the shepherd as a *liberator,* while the wolf denounces him for the same act as the destroyer of liberty, especially as the sheep was a black one. Plainly the sheep and the wolf are not agreed upon a definition of the word liberty; and precisely the same difference prevails to-day among us human creatures, even in the North, and all professing to love liberty. Hence we behold the processes by which thousands are daily passing from under the yoke of bondage, hailed by some as the advance of liberty, and bewailed by others as the destruction of all liberty. Recently, as it seems, the people of Maryland have been doing something to define liberty; and thanks to them that, in what they have done, the wolf's dictionary, has been repudiated.

... A painful rumor, true I fear, has reached us of the massacre, by the rebel forces, at Fort Pillow, in ... Tennessee ... of some three hundred colored soldiers and white officers, who had just been overpowered by their assailants. There seems to be some anxiety in the public mind whether the government is doing its duty to the colored soldier, and to the service, at this point. At the beginning of the war, and for some time, the use of colored troops was not contemplated. . . . Upon a clear conviction of duty I resolved to turn that element of strength to account; and I am responsible for it to the American people, to the christian world, to history, and on my final account to God. Having determined to use the negro as a soldier, there is no way but to give him all the protection given to any other soldier. . . . We are having the Fort-Pillow affair thoroughly investigated; and such investigation will probably show conclusively how the truth is. If, after all that has been said, it shall turn out that there has been no massacre at Fort-Pillow, it will be almost safe to say there has been none, and will be none elsewhere. If there has been the massacre of three hundred there, or even the tenth part of three hundred, it will be conclusively proved; and be being so proved, the retribution shall as surely come. It will be matter of grave consideration in what exact course to apply the retribution; but in the supposed case, it must come.[19]

Toasted while at the Sanitary Fair in Philadelphia, Lincoln used the occasion to respond in praise of voluntary contributions to the war effort:

I supposed that this toast was intended to open the way for me to say something. [Laughter.] War, at the best, is terrible, and this war of ours, in its magnitude and in its duration, is one of the most terrible. It has deranged business, totally in many localities, and partially in all localities. It has destroyed property, and ruined homes; it has produced a national debt and taxation unprecedented, at least in this country. It has carried mourning to almost every home, until it can almost be said that the "heavens are hung in black." Yet it continues, and several relieving coincidents [*coincidences*] have accompanied it from the very beginning, which have not been known, as I understood [*understand*], or have any knowledge of, in any former wars in the history of the world. The Sanitary Commission, with all its benevolent labors, the Christian Commission, with all its Christian and benevolent labors, and the various places, arrangements, so to speak, and institutions, have contributed to the comfort and relief of the soldiers. You have two of these places in this city—the Cooper-Shop and Union Volunteer Refreshment Saloons. [Great applause and cheers.] And lastly, these fairs, which, I believe, began only in last August, if I mistake not, in Chicago; then at Boston, at Cincinnati, Brooklyn, New York, at Baltimore, and those at present held at St. Louis, Pittsburg, and Philadelphia. The motive and object that lie at the bottom of all these are most worthy; for, say what you will, after all the most is due to the soldier, who takes his life in his hands and goes to fight the battles of his country. [Cheers.] In what is contributed to his comfort when he passes to and fro [*from city to city*], and in what is contributed to him when he is sick and wounded, in whatever shape it comes, whether from the fair and tender hand of woman, or from any other source, is much, very much; but, I think there is still that which has as much value to him [*in the continual reminders he sees in the newspapers, that while he is absent he is yet remembered by the loves ones at home.*]—he is not forgotten. [Cheers.] Another view of these various institutions is worthy of consideration, I think; they are voluntary contributions, given freely, zealously, and earnestly, on top of all the disturbances of business, [*of all the disorders,*] the taxation and burdens that the war has imposed upon us, giving proof that the national resources are not at all exhausted, [cheers;] that the national spirit of patriotism is even [*firmer and*] stronger than at the commencement of the rebellion [*war*].

It is a pertinent question often asked in the mind privately, and from one to the other, when is the war to end? Surely I feel as deep [*great*] an interest in this question as any other can, but I do not wish to name a day, or month, or a year when it is to end. I do not wish to run any risk of seeing the time come, without our being ready for the end, and for fear of disappointment, because the time had come and not the end. [*We accepted this war; we did not begin it.*] We accepted this war for an object, a worthy object, and the war will end when that object is attained. Under God, I hope it never will until that time. [Great cheering.] . . . I have never been in the habit of making predictions in regard to the war, but I am almost tempted to make one. [*(Do it—do it!)*] If I were to hazard it, it is this: That Grant is this evening, with General Meade and General Hancock, of Pennsylvania, and the brave officers and soldiers with him, in a position from whence he will never be dislodged until Richmond is taken [loud cheering], and I have but one single proposition to put now, and, perhaps, I can best put it in form of an interrogative [*interragatory*]. If I shall discover that General Grant and the noble officers and men under him can be greatly facilitated in their work by a sudden pouring forward [*forth*] of men and assistance, will you give them to me? [Cries of "yes."]. Then, I say, stand ready for I am watching for the chance. [Laughter and cheers.] I thank you, gentlemen.[20]

Troops passing through Washington often marched to the White House to pay their respects to their commander in chief. Responding to a visit from the 166th Ohio Regiment, Lincoln emphasized the value of a free society offering equal opportunity to all:

I suppose you are going home to see your families and friends. For the service you have done in this great struggle in which we are engaged I present you sincere thanks for myself and the country. I almost always feel inclined, when I happen to say anything to soldiers, to impress upon them in a few brief remarks the importance of success in this contest. It is not merely for to-day, but for all time to come that we should perpetuate for our children's children this great and free government, which we have enjoyed all our lives. I beg you to remember this, not merely for my sake, but for yours. I happen temporarily to occupy this big White House. I am a living witness that any one of your children may look to come here as my father's child has. It is in order that each of you may have through this free government which we have enjoyed, an open field and a fair chance for your industry, enterprise and intelligence; that you may all have equal privileges in the

race of life, with all its desirable human aspirations. It is for this the struggle
should be maintained, that we may not lose our birthright—not only for
one, but for two or three years. The nation is worth fighting for, to secure
such an inestimable jewel.[21]

Responding to Maryland serenaders, whose state in contrast to its attitude in 1861 had emancipated its slaves in 1864, Lincoln on October 19
congratulated them on their achievement and reassured them of the constancy of his purpose to save the country and its liberties:

> I am notified that this is a compliment paid me by the loyal Marylanders,
> resident in this District. I infer that the adoption of the new constitution for
> the State, furnishes the occasion; and that, in your view, the extirpation of
> slavery constitutes the chief merit of the new constitution. Most heartily do
> I congratulate you, and Maryland, and the nation, and the world, upon the
> event. I regret that it did not occur two years sooner, which I am sure would
> have saved to the nation more money than would have met all the private
> loss incident to the measure. But it has come at last, and I sincerely hope
> its friends may fully realize all their anticipations of good from it; and that
> its opponents may, by its effects, be agreeably and profitably, disappointed.
>   A word upon another subject.
>   Something said by the Secretary of State in his recent speech at Auburn,
> has been construed by some into a threat that, if I shall be beaten at the
> election, I will, between then and the end of my constitutional term, do
> what I may be able, to ruin the government.
>   Others regard the fact that the Chicago Convention adjourned, not
> *sine die,* but to meet again, if called to do so by a particular individual,
> as the intimation of a purpose that if their nominee shall be elected, he
> will at once seize control of the government. I hope the good people will
> permit themselves to suffer no uneasiness on either point. I am struggling
> to maintain government, not to overthrow it. I am struggling especially to
> prevent others from overthrowing it. I therefore say, that if I shall live, I shall
> remain President until the fourth of next March; and that whoever shall
> be constitutionally elected therefor in November, shall be duly installed
> as President on the fourth of March; and that in the interval I shall do my
> utmost that whoever is to hold the helm for the next voyage, shall start
> with the best possible chance to save the ship.
>   This is due to the people both on principle, and under the constitution.
> Their will, constitutionally expressed, is the ultimate law for all. If they

should deliberately resolve to have immediate peace even at the loss of their country, and their liberty, I know not the power or the right to resist them. It is their own business, and they must do as they please with their own. I believe, however, they are still resolved to preserve their country and their liberty; and in this, in office or out of it, I am resolved to stand by them.

I may add that in this purpose to save the country and its liberties, no classes of people seem so nearly unanimous as the soldiers in the field and the seamen afloat. Do they not have the hardest of it? Who should quail while they do not?

God bless the soldiers and seamen, with all their brave commanders.[22]

By September 3 Lincoln had learned of two victories helpful both in securing victory in the war and in retaining his high office. Rear Admiral David Farragut conducted successful operations in Mobile Bay, and General William Sherman occupied long-desired Atlanta on September 2. Lincoln made note of these events, issuing an order to celebrate the victories as well as orders of thanks to Farragut and Sherman. On September 3 he proclaimed a day of Thanksgiving. The first of these orders, which all were made public, read:

First,—That on Monday, the 5th. day of September, commencing at the hour of twelve o'clock noon, there shall be given a salute of one hundred guns at the Arsenal and Navy Yard at Washington, and on Tuesday September 6th., or on the day after the receipt of this order, at each Arsenal and Navy Yard in the United States, for the recent brilliant achievements of the fleet and land forces of the United States in the harbor of Mobile and in the reduction of Fort Powell, Fort Gaines, and Fort Morgan. The Secretary of War and Secretary of the Navy will issue the necessary directions in their respective Departments for the execution of this order.

Second.—That on Wednesday, the 7th. day of September, commencing at the hour of twelve o'clock noon, there shall be fired a salute of one hundred guns at the Arsenal at Washington, and at New York, Boston, Philadelphia, Baltimore, Pittsburg, Newport, Ky. and St. Louis, and at New Orleans, Mobile, Pensacola, Hilton Head & Newberne, the day after the receipt of this order, for the brilliant achievements of the army under the command of Major General Sherman, in the State of Georgia, and the capture of Atlanta. The Secretary of War will issue directions for the execution of this order.[23]

Prompted by a letter from Sara Josepha Hale, editor of the *Lady's Book,* Lincoln established the custom of annual national observance of Thanksgiving. Mrs. Hale wrote to Secretary of State William H. Seward:

Enclosed is an article (or proof) on the National Thanksgiving. As you were, last year, kindly interested in this subject, I venture to request your good offices again.

My article will appear in the *November* number of the "Lady's Book"; but before its publication I trust that *President Lincoln* will have issued his *proclamation appointing the last Thursday in November as the Day.*

I sent a copy of the *proof* for the President. You will greatly oblige me by handing this to him and acquainting him with the contents of this letter. I do not like to trouble him with a note. Should the president see fit to issue his proclamation at once, the important paper would have time to reach the knowledge of American citizens in Europe and Asia, as well as throughout our wide land. If the President should recommend that all American ministers and consuls etc—should observe the day in their respective offices in Foreign countries would it not have a good effect on our citizens abroad? And if, on land and sea, wherever the American Flag floats over an American citizen all should be invited and unite in this National Thanksgiving, would it not be a glorious Festival?[24]

Lincoln's Proclamation of Thanksgiving read:

It has pleased Almighty God to prolong our national life another year, defending us with his guardian care against unfriendly designs from abroad, and vouchsafing to us in His mercy many and signal victories over the enemy, who is of our own household. It has also pleased our Heavenly Father to favor as well our citizens in their homes as our soldiers in their camps and our sailors on the rivers and seas with unusual health. He has largely augmented our free population by emancipation and by immigration, while he has opened to us new sources of wealth, and has crowned the labor of our working men in every department of industry with abundant rewards. Moreover, He has been pleased to animate and inspire our minds and hearts with fortitude, courage and resolution sufficient for the great trial of civil war into which we have been brought by our adherence as a nation to the cause of Freedom and Humanity, and to afford to us reasonable hopes of an ultimate and happy deliverance from all our dangers and afflictions.

Now, therefore, I, Abraham Lincoln, President of the United States, do, hereby, appoint and set apart the last Thursday in November next as a day, which I desire to be observed by all my fellow-citizens wherever they may then be as a day of Thanksgiving and Praise to Almighty God the beneficent Creator and Ruler of the Universe. And I do farther recommend to my fellow-citizens aforesaid that on that occasion they do reverently humble themselves in the dust and from thence offer up penitent and fervent prayers and supplications to the Great Disposer of events for a return of the inestimable blessings of Peace, Union and Harmony throughout the land, which it has pleased him to assign as a dwelling place for ourselves and for our posterity throughout all generations.[25]

Meanwhile, Lincoln's aloofness from campaigning did not seal him off from quietly seeking votes. Governor Oliver Perry Morton of Indiana and Indiana Republican members of Congress, aware of the uncertain vote in their state election, appealed to Secretary of War Stanton:

[W]e express it as our profound conviction that upon the issue of the election that occurs within a month from this date may depend the question as to whether the secession element shall be effectually crushed or whether it shall acquire strength enough, we do not say to take the state out of the Union, but practically to sever her from the general government, so far as future military aid is concerned.

We further express the gravest doubts as to whether it will be possible for us to secure success at the polls on the 11th of October unless we can receive aid—

1. By delay of the draft until the election has passed.
2. By the return, before election day, of fifteen thousand Indiana soldiers.[26]

Lincoln on September 19 wrote to Sherman:

The State election of Indiana occurs on the 11th. of October, and the loss of it to the friends of the Government would go far towards losing the whole Union cause. The bad effect upon the November election, and especially the giving the State Government to those who will oppose the war in every possible way, are too much to risk, if it can possibly be avoided. The draft proceeds, notwithstanding its strong tendency to lose us the State. Indiana is the only important State, voting in October, whose soldiers cannot vote in the field. Any thing you can safely do to let her soldiers, or any part of them, go home and vote at the State election, will be greatly in point. They need not remain for the Presidential election, but may return to you at once. This is, in no sense, an order, but is merely intended to impress you with the importance, to the army itself, of your doing all you safely can, yourself being the judge of what you can safely do.[27]

The bearer of the letter, William Mitchell, a former congressman from Indiana, on October 7 wired Lincoln, "I have succeeded very well."

Party unity was essential to Lincoln's reelection. Senator Zachariah Chandler claimed that he arranged Frémont's withdrawal in exchange for Blair's dismissal from the cabinet. Frémont, nominee of some radical Republicans, withdrew on September 17 in a letter that scored Lincoln:

> Mr. Lincoln says he does not lead, but follows the will of the people. It remains, then for the people, in the event of his re-election, vigilantly to require the following at his hands, and, further to require that, in the execution of his duties, he keeps scrupulously within the Constitution and the laws; to make him recognize that he holds his place and his power, not as belonging to himself, but as a really faithful servant of the people.[28]

Postmaster General Blair, a conservative and former Democrat, had incurred the strong dislike of radical Republicans. Obliquely criticized in the party platform, he stood as an obstacle to party unity. "Blair every one hates," Senator Henry Wilson, influential chairman of the Committee on Military Affairs, told Lincoln. Less than a week after Frémont's withdrawal Lincoln wrote to Blair:

> You have generously said to me more than once, that whenever Your resignation could be a relief to me, it was at my disposal. The time has come. You very well know that this proceeds from no dissatisfaction of mine with you personally or officially. Your uniform kindness has been unsurpassed by that of any friend; and, while it is true that the war does not so greatly add to the difficulties of your Department, as to those of some others, it is yet much to say, as I most truly can, that in the three years and a half during which you have administered the General Post-Office, I remember no single complaint against you in connection therewith.[29]

The Blair family, seasoned in politics, took the blow well. Frank Jr. alternately congressman and general, replied to a letter from his father:

> I received yours and my sisters letter yesterday giving an account of late transactions in Washington. I feel in regard to the matter precisely as you

do. Indeed before I received your letter my instincts told me that my brother had acted his part for the good of the country and for the re-election of Mr. Lincoln in which the safety of the country is involved. I believe that a failure to re-elect Mr. Lincoln would be the greatest disaster that could befall the country and the sacrifice made by the Judge to avert this is so incomparably small that I felt it would not cost him a penny to make. Indeed the only sacrifice involved in it appears to be the triumph which it gives to our enemies & the enemies of the Presidents. It is somewhat mortifying to reflect that this triumph has been given to those who are equally the enemies of the President & "the Blairs" but at the same time the Judge leaves the cabinet with an untarnished name and the reputation of having administered the Dept with the greatest ability & success and that as far as worldly considerations go, it is far better for him to go out than to remain in the cabinet. This is rather a contrast to the position of Chase, Fremont & all the rest of the enemies & persecutors of the "Blairs."[30]

Montgomery Blair, the dismissed cabinet member, was soon loyally campaigning on behalf of the president, although after the war he returned to the Democratic Party.

In his public letters, speeches, and proclamations, Lincoln had reached out to laborers, abolitionists, friends of liberty, volunteers, persons believing in constancy of purpose, and observers of Thanksgiving. He had promoted his presidential candidacy by arranging for soldiers to vote and dismissing an unpopular cabinet officer. Though refraining from campaigning, he had been skillfully electioneering.

On election day, looking back over the embittered campaign Lincoln observed to Hay: "It is a little singular that I who am not a vindictive man, should have always been before the people for election in canvasses marked for their bitterness: always but once: When I came to Congress it was a quiet time: But always besides that the contests in which I have been prominent have been marked with great rancor."[31]

In November voters overwhelmingly maintained Lincoln in the presidency. Contrasting with his less than 40 percent of the votes in the four-way election of 1860, voters awarded him about 60 percent of their votes. Soldiers who had cheered "Little Mac" in 1861–62 voted in 1864 by a ratio of over three to one to give their vote to their commander in chief, not McClellan.

General Grant telegraphed Stanton, "Enough now seems to be known to say who is to hold the reins of Government for the next four years. Congratulate the President for me for the double victory. The election having passed off quietly, no bloodshed or riot throughout the land, is a victory worth more to the country than a battle won. Rebeldom and Europe will so construe it."[32]

Two nights after the victory Lincoln, standing at a window, spoke to a throng that appeared before the White House. In a philosophical mood he discussed the significance to a free government of holding elections in wartime:

> It has long been a grave question whether any government, not *too* strong for the liberties of its people, can be strong *enough* to maintain its own existence, in great emergencies.
>
> On this point the present rebellion brought our republic to a severe test; and a presidential election occurring in regular course during the rebellion added not a little to the strain. If the loyal people, *united,* were put to the utmost of their strength by the rebellion, must they not fail when *divided,* and partially paralyzed, by a political war among themselves?
>
> But the election was a necessity.
>
> We can not have free government without elections; and if the rebellion could force us to forego, or postpone a national election, it might fairly claim to have already conquered and ruined us. The strife of the election is but human-nature practically applied to the facts of the case. What has occurred in this case, must ever recur in similar cases. Human-nature will not change. In any future great national trial, compared with the men of this, we shall have as weak, and as strong; as silly and as wise; as bad and good. Let us, therefore, study the incidents of this, as philosophy to learn wisdom from, and none of them as wrongs to be revenged.
>
> But the election, along with its incidental, and undesirable strife, has done good too. It has demonstrated that a people's government can sustain a national election, in the midst of a great civil war. Until now it has not been known to the world that this was a possibility. It shows also how *sound,* and how *strong* we still are. It shows that, even among candidates of the same party, he who is most devoted to the Union, and most opposed to treason, can receive most of the people's votes. It shows also, to the extent yet known, that we have more men now, than we had when the war began. Gold is good in its place; but living, brave, patriotic men, are better than gold.

But the rebellion continues; and now that the election is over, may not all, having a common interest, re-unite in a common effort, to save our common country? For my own part I have striven, and shall strive to avoid placing any obstacle in the way. So long as I have been here I have not willingly planted a thorn in any man's bosom.

While I am deeply sensible to the high compliment of a re-election; and duly grateful, as I trust, to Almighty God for having directed my countrymen to a right conclusion, as I think, for their own good, it adds nothing to my satisfaction that any other man may be disappointed or pained by the result.

May I ask those who have not differed with me, to join with me, in this same spirit towards those who have?

And now, let me close by asking three hearty cheers for our brave soldiers and seamen and their gallant and skillful commanders.[33]

A month later in his annual message he amplified the theme:

The most reliable indication of public purpose in this country is derived through our popular elections. Judging by the recent canvass and its result, the purpose of the people, within the loyal States, to maintain the integrity of the Union, was never more firm, nor more nearly unanimous, than now. The extraordinary calmness and good order with which the millions of voters met and mingled at the polls, give strong assurance of this. Not only all those who supported the Union ticket, so called, but a great majority of the opposing party also, may be fairly claimed to entertain, and to be actuated by, the same purpose. It is an unanswerable argument to this effect, that no candidate for any office whatever, high or low, has ventured to seek votes on the avowal that he was for giving up the Union. There have been much impugning of motives, and much heated controversy as to the proper means and best mode of advancing the Union cause; but on the distinct issue of Union or no Union, the politicians have shown their instinctive knowledge that there is no diversity among the people. In affording the people the fair opportunity of showing, one to another and to the world, this firmness and unanimity of purpose, the election has been of vast value to the national cause.[34]

The cabinet met on November 11; John Hay described the session:

At the meeting of the Cabinet today, the President took out a paper from his desk and said, "Gentlemen do you remember last summer I asked you all to sign your names to the back of a paper of which I did not show you the inside? This is it. Now, Mr Hay, see if you can get this open without tearing it!" He had pasted it up in so singular style that it required some cutting to get it open. He then read as follows:

Executive Mansion
Washington
Aug. 23, 1864.

This morning, as for some days past, it seems exceedingly probable that this Administration will not be re-elected. Then it will be my duty to so cooperate with the President elect, as to save the Union between the election and the inauguration; as he will have secured his election on such ground that he cannot possibly save it afterwards.
 A Lincoln.

The President said "you will remember that this was written at a time (6 days before the Chicago nominating convention) when as yet we had no adversary, and seemed to have no friends. I then solemnly resolved on the course of action indicated above. I resolved, in case of the election of General McClellan being certain that he would be the Candidate, that I would see him and talk matters over with him. I would say, 'General, the election has demonstrated that you are stronger, have more influence with the American people than I. Now let us together, you with your influence and I with all the executive power of the Government, try to save the country. You raise as many troops as you possibly can for this final trial, and I will devote all my energies to assisting and finishing the war.'"

Seward said, "And the General would answer you 'Yes, Yes'; and the next day when you saw him again & pressed these views upon him he would say 'Yes—yes' & so on forever and would have done nothing at all."

"At least" added Lincoln "I should have done my duty and have stood clear before my own conscience."[35]

After the election McClellan resigned from the army on November 8; he told a friend, "I have abandoned public life forever." His friend Samuel Barlow had written:

For your want of success I am sorry. I believed that in your election lay the only hope of peace with Union. Under Mr. Lincoln, I see little prospect of anything, but fruitless war, disgraceful peace, & ruinous bankruptcy. But I cannot resist the feeling . . . that if you had been triumphantly chosen, you would be today more pitied, than envied. The fearful responsibility to be assumed by a president next March, with an empty treasury, a wasted army, and a defiant and apparently united people in rebellion, is enough to appal anyone.[36]

The election marked the passing of a great trial for the Republican administration. And the passing of Chief Justice Roger B. Taney, aged eighty-seven, on October 12 seemed to mark the passing of an era. His enemies had long waited for the event. Radical senator Benjamin F. Wade had earlier remarked, "No man ever prayed as I did that Taney might outlive James Buchanan's term, and now I am afraid I have overdone it."

Taney had figured importantly in Lincoln's life. His notorious pro-slavery *Dred Scott* decision had loomed large in Lincoln's argument in the Lincoln-Douglas debates. As chief justice Taney had sworn Lincoln into the presidency, administering the oath to "preserve, protect and defend the Constitution." Acting as circuit court justice he had rejected Lincoln's authority to suspend habeas corpus and charged the president to fulfill his constitutional obligation to execute the laws faithfully. In the Prize Cases Taney had joined the minority in stating, "The president does not possess power under the Constitution to declare war or recognize its existence."

Chase's fellow Ohioan Albert G. Riddle, strongly antislavery, recalled his role in seeking Chase's appointment to the court to succeed Taney:

The request of his appointment came from all parts of the Union States. The old anti-slavery men were very urgent, nor was there any other. . . . Mr. Lincoln was slow to act and Mr. Chase desired that I should interview the President on this grave matter. I undertook it reluctantly, but his wish was law.

Mr. Lincoln—"Do you expect that Chase will relinquish his desire to become President?"

Mr. Riddle.—"Mr. Chase's ambition springs from a consciousness of great ability to serve. It is said that a man once bitten of the Presidency dies of it."

Mr. Lincoln.—"I should deplore seeing a man trying to swap the Chief-Justiceship for the Presidency."

Mr. Riddle.—"Mr. President, you are fully aware that Mr. Chase is a man of the most elevated character, and that personal dignity in him rises to grandeur. A traffic such as you suggest would be impossible.

"There is a consideration which I beg to suggest. The weighty matters involved in this war have been thoroughly discussed by Congress and the President. They are undergoing the arbitrament of battle. They will next inevitably be submitted to the Supreme Court for the last and final human decision. Do you know a man in the world to whom you would sooner submit them?"

Mr. Lincoln.—"Would you have me pack the Supreme Court, Mr. Riddle?"

Mr. Riddle.—"Would you appoint a man with no preconceived notions of law? There is not a man at our bar whom you or I would call a lawyer, who has not convictions on these questions."

Mr. Lincoln.—"This is a matter for reflection." And I took leave.[37]

Chase had for some time aspired to the chief justiceship, and his friends, particularly radicals, promoted his ambition. Senator Charles Sumner told Lincoln, "A chief-justice is needed whose position on the slavery question is already fixed and will not need argument of counsel to convert him." Not one to hide his light under a bushel, Chase promoted himself, telling Sumner on October 19, "It is perhaps not exactly *en regle* to say what a man will do in regard to an appointment not tendered to him; but it is certainly not wrong to say to you that I should accept."[38]

Chase's correspondence about becoming chief justice is full of interest. From the time of Taney's death in early October to December 6, the letters that Chase wrote and received included discussions of his candidacy. The extracts are in chronological sequence.

[Chase to Stanton]: Your telegram, announcing the death of the Chief justice was received this morning. As a lawyer he leaves a name behind him which any lawyer might be proud of; as a man I have rarely known one more kind & genial. I differed widely from him on political questions—let the veil drop upon the differences.

Within the last three or four months I have been assured that it was the Presidents intention, to offer the place to me in case of a vacancy. I think I should accept it if offered: for I am weary of political life & work. What do you think.[39]

[Greeley to Chase]: As to the Chief Justiceship, I hear but one voice; yet there are whispers that [Mrs.] L. is committed to Ira Harris, while I have

heard (but do not believe) that Gov. Dennison favors Noah H. Swayne. Gov. Morgan went on to Washington on Monday night to urge your appointment. And I can hear of no counter movement in this quarter.

I think you ought not only to accept the appointment if tendered, but to change your residence to Maryland, on some pleasant farm near Baltimore, so as to exert the influence of your character and position over the destinies of that new born State. I cannot feel that our Anti-Slavery work is half done so long as the Blacks remain politically under the feet of the Whites. I look for a great anti-negro reaction the moment the War is over—an uprising of all that is [ruffianly] under the direction of all that is rascally in the land to revenge on the poor negroes the humiliation and [discomfiture] of the slaveholders. This brutality will have to be resisted every where, but we especially need genius as well as character on the Bench to administer the proper legal discipline to its contrivers as well as their tools. I pray you to consider this. Maryland is destined to bear a leading, unenviable part in this predestined rebound of the Rebellion; and the Baltimore roughs will need the promptest and sternest judicial discipline to convince them that the good old days, when negroes might be knocked down, maimed or ravished with impunity exist no longer. You should not only be Chief justice, but be living where you can [inspire] and direct the judicial [*illeg.*] needed to bring these miscreants to order.[40]

[*Chase to Dennison*]: Perhaps you know that it is supposed by many that Mr. Lincoln will offer me the seat vacated by the death of Judge Taney. I should have gone to Washington this week had I not been unwilling even to seem to seek the appointment. I expect now to go as soon as the question is decided. Katie & Nettie will spend the winter there. I am not at all sanguine that the vacant seat will be offered me. I should like the offer better than the seat. I think I should take it, but am afraid I should not much relish the transfer from the active responsibilities of life to the quiet work of the bench.[41]

[*Chase to Sumner*]: As yet nothing has reached touching the *decision* of the President as to the vacant seat; though what I have heard indicates that his purpose of offering it to me is unchanged.

Quite recently it has been told me that, last spring, when it was so probable that the vacancy would immediately occur, a paper was drawn up & signed by the other Judges—whether the new or all was not said recommending the appointment of Judge Swayne. I do not know how this may be but I do know that just before the adjt. of the Court, Judge Field expressed a very strong wish for my appointment & that Judge Miller has recently expressed the same. However this may be the paper, if prepared, must have been in the Presidents hands at the time of his conversations with you before & other Senators since my resignation and it will certainly no more affect his intention now than then.

I have heard from others before I read it in your note that the President told the Senate Committee that he & I could not get along together in the cabinet. Doubtless there was a difference of temperament and, on some points, of judgment. I may have been too earnest & Eager while I thought him not earnest enough & too slow. On some occasions indeed I found it was so. But I never desired anything else than his complete success & never indulged a personal wish incompatible with absolute fidelity to his Admn.[42]

[Hooper to Chase]: Ten days since I expressed in a note to Mr Fessenden my anxiety in consequence of certain reports—lest Mr Lincoln may not keep the promise he made to him as well as to myself & others. In reply Mr Fessenden assures me *"there is no danger about Mr Chase"*. While I was in Washington & within a week after the death of Judge Taney—Mr Fessenden repeated to me what the President had said to him,—that he should fulfill the promise he made in regard to filling the vacancy if the Chief Justice died—and Mr Fessenden, affecting not to understand him, asked what he referred to— when the President repeated the promise, and added, that he should make the appointment after the elections were over. As the rumors refer now to Mr. Stanton,—and Mr Fessenden has said we may not be disturbed by any rumors concerning himself or Mr Stanton,—my faith in the promise of the President is not shaken. At the same time I shall be better satisfied when the appointment is announced. Colfax is here—and says the West, so far as he knows it, is unanimous in your favor, and that he had so written to the President. Here your appointment will give great satisfaction.[43]

[Colfax to Chase]: Friday night I had a long talk with the President. He told me of various objections he had heard, which he added, did not influence him, *but he repeated them*. Some were sinister ones, whose paternity I think I can recognize, & which, I told Mr. Lincoln, were unworthy of their author. Another was that your ambition was the Presidency, & that a Presl. candidate should not be C.J. to use it as a stepping stone, impairing the strength & impartiality of the judiciary. I asked Mr. Lincoln if you had not yourself once told him your preference to be C.J. rather than President. He replied yes; & I added that, if appointed, I felt certain you would dedicate the remainder of your life to the Bench. I did not say it to the President,

but I may say it here frankly, that I never did fancy C.J. McLean being a candidate for President.

I have been urging M.C.s to day to go up & see the President. Mr Sumner saw him Sat night, I hear, & found him, as I did undecided. Gen Wilson told me last night he would go specially. And Grinnell, Wilson, & others told me they would go to day or to night.

I neglected to add one thing to the President, which struck me after I left the White House might have influenced him, if his mind was evenly balanced—to ask him if, with all this overwhelming public sentiment in your favor, he appd. some one else, History might not say that he did so because you had dared to be a candidate for the Presl. nomination against him. It would have touched him on a point of honor & magnanimity. I asked Garfield yesterday to hint it to him to day.[44]

When Senator Henry Wilson heard Montgomery Blair's opinion that Chase would not be nominated, he hastened to the president, gave arguments in favor of Chase, and suggested Lincoln could overlook the harsh language Chase had been using about him.

"Oh! as to that, I care nothing," Lincoln answered. "Of Mr. Chase's ability and of his soundness on the general issues of the war there is, of course, no question. I have only one doubt about his appointment. He is a man of unbounded ambition, and has been working all his life to become President. That he can never be; and I fear that if I make him chief-justice he will simply become more restless and uneasy and neglect the place in his strife and intrigue to make himself President. If I were sure that he would go on the bench and give up his aspirations and do nothing but make himself a great judge, I would not hesitate a moment."[45]

The Supreme Court was scheduled to open the first Monday in December, the fifth, without a chief justice. Speculation remained rife. Welles thought Blair would be the man. So did the *New York Times*. The *New York Herald* anticipated that Swayne would secure the appointment. On December 6 Lincoln sent the Senate Chase's nomination, which won unanimous approval.[46] The cabinet had not been consulted. The *New York Tribune* exclaimed, "Five years ago, had any one suggested Salmon P. Chase as the probable successor of Roger B. Taney, he would have been regarded as in need of a straight jacket."[47]

Widespread disappointment met the appointment; Lincoln himself seems to have been unhappy about what he did. According to Welles, the president told Chandler of New Hampshire, who remonstrated against such selections, "that he would rather have swallowed his buckthorn chair than to have nominated Chase."[48]

On the same day that Lincoln sent his annual message to Congress he sent a nomination to the Senate: "I nominate Salmon P. Chase of Ohio, to be Chief Justice of the Supreme Court of the United States vice Roger B. Taney, deceased." That night when Chase arrived at his home, his daughter Kate greeted him by his new title. A grateful Chase immediately sat down and penned a note to the president: "Before I sleep I must thank you for this mark of your confidence, and especially for the manner in which the nomination was made. I will never forget either, and trust you will never forget either. Be assured that I prize your confidence, and good-will more than any nomination to office."[49] On the day Chase took his oath of office, the irreverent Wade—his prayer answered, and feeling giddy with the elevation of his fellow radical—said another: "Lord, now lettest thou thy servant depart in peace, for my eyes have seen thy salvation." To Wade and other radicals the change in the chief justiceship from Taney to Chase seemed divinely ordained, even miraculous.

Welles recorded in his diary the manner in which the nomination was made and his own estimate of his former fellow cabinet member:

> Shortly after leaving the Cabinet I heard that Chase had been nominated to, and confirmed by the Senate as Chief Justice. Not a word was interchanged in the Cabinet respecting it. Stanton who came in late and just as we were leaving, professed to have come over merely to learn if the message had been received, and how. It is possible he was in the secret but no other one who was present, and his knowledge is perhaps doubtful. The President had said to us before Stanton came in that he had sent up yesterday the nominations of Dennison and Speed but no others. I am sorry he should have withheld the fact, which we all knew in less than one hour, that he had to-day sent in Chase for Chief Justice.
>
> Dennison informs me that he went to the theater with the President last evening and parted with him after 11 o'clock, and not a word was said to him on the subject.

THE ELECTION OF 1864

I hope the selection may prove a good one. I would not have advised it, because I have apprehensions on that subject. Chase has mental power and resources, but he is ambitious and restless, prone to intrigue and subtle management. If he applies himself strictly and faithfully to his duties he may succeed although his mind is not I fear so much judicial as ministerial.[50]

Lincoln had been reelected during a civil war, vindicating democratic government. McClellan had been defeated as a politician as well as rejected as a general. Lincoln faced the necessity to appoint a chief justice of the Supreme Court, replacing a man whose decisions had done so much to sustain Lincoln's opponents. The election settled the war policy, which had been in doubt for months. The Lincoln administration would fight the war to the end.

CHAPTER THIRTY-FOUR

THE LAST CIVIL
WAR CONGRESS

When members of the Thirty-Eighth Congress gathered on December 2, 1864, for their final session, gone was the dark mood marking the days of their July adjournment and summer of discontent. The complexion of the war had changed since then: they had seen Farragut's victory in Mobile Bay, Sherman's capture of Atlanta, Sheridan's laying waste to the Shenandoah Valley, Lincoln's triumphant reelection, and Grant's bulldog grip on Petersburg. All contributed to an amiable atmosphere among Republicans, at least for the moment.

John George Nicolay, Lincoln's senior secretary, carried to Congress the president's annual message, required by the Constitution. Much of the message dealt with matters of the executive departments. Portrayal of his own role appeared toward the message's end. "The war continues," he reminded the Congress. Movements toward state emancipation were going forward, and Maryland, which had hovered on the brink of secession in 1861, had now decided on emancipation.

Lincoln urged this session to approve the resolution to send the emancipation amendment to the states for ratification. During the war the national resources in men and material resources had grown, he observed. After the war, he declared, his power would diminish:

> Again the blessings of health and abundant harvests claim our profoundest gratitude to Almighty God.
> The condition of our foreign affairs is reasonably satisfactory. . . .
> I regard our emigrants as one of the principal replenishing streams which

are appointed by Providence to repair the ravages of internal war, and its wastes of national strength and health. All that is necessary is to secure the glow of that stream in its present fullness, and to that end the government must, in every way, make it manifest that it neither needs nor designs to impose involuntary military service upon those who come from other lands to cast their lot in our country. . . .

The national banking system is proving to be acceptable to capitalists and the people. On the twenty-fifth day of November five hundred and eighty-four national banks had been organized, a considerable number of which were conversions from State banks. Changes from State systems to the nation system are rapidly taking place, and it is hoped that, very soon, there will be in the United States, no banks of issue not authorized by Congress, and no bank-note circulation not secured by the government. That the government and the people will derive great benefit from this change in the banking systems of the country can hardly be questions. The national system will create a reliable and permanent influence in support of the national credit, and protect the people against losses in the use of paper money. Whether or not any further legislation is advisable for the suppression of State bank issues, it will be for Congress to determine. It seems quite clear that the treasury cannot be satisfactorily conducted unless the government can exercise a restraining power over the bank-note circulation of the country. . . .

The quantity of public land disposed of during the five quarters ending on the 30th of September last was 4,221,243 acres, of which 1,538,614 acres were entered under the homestead law. The remainder was located with military land warrants, agricultural scrip certified to States to railroads, and sold for cash. The cash received from sales and location fees was $1,019,446. . . .

The great enterprise of connecting the Atlantic with the Pacific States by railways and telegraph lines had been entered upon with a vigor that gives assurance of success, notwithstanding the embarrassments arising from the prevailing high prices of materials and labor. The route of the main line of the road has been definitely located for one hundred miles westward from the initial point at Omaha City, Nebraska, and a preliminary location of the Pacific railroad of California has been made from Sacramento eastward to the great bend of the Truckee river in Nevada. . . .

It was recommended in my last annual message that our Indian system be remodeled. Congress, at its last session, acting upon the recommendation, did provide for reorganizing the system in California, and it is believed that under the present organization the management of the Indians there will be attended with reasonable success. Much yet remains to be done to provide for the proper government of the Indians in other parts of the country to render it secure for the advancing settler, and to provide for the welfare of the Indian. The Secretary reiterates his recommendations, and to them the attention of Congress is invited. . . .

The war continues. Since the last annual message all the important lines and positions then occupied by our forces have been maintained, and our arms have steadily advanced; thus liberating the regions left in rear, so that Missouri, Kentucky, Tennessee and parts of other States have again produced reasonably fair crops.

The most remarkable feature in the military operations of the year is General Sherman's attempted march of three hundred miles directly through the insurgent region. It tends to show a great increase of our relative strength that our General-in-Chief should feel able to confront and hold in check every active force of the enemy, and yet to detach a well-appointed large army to move on such an expedition. The result not yet being known, conjecture in regard to it is not here indulged.

Important movements have also occurred during the year to the effect of moulding society for durability in the Union. Although short of complete success, it is much in the right direction, that twelve thousand citizens in each of the States of Arkansas and Louisiana have organized loyal State governments with free constitutions, and are earnestly struggling to maintain and administer them. The movements in the same direction, more extensive, though less definite in Missouri, Kentucky and Tennessee, should not be overlooked. But Maryland presents the example of complete success. Maryland is secure to Liberty and Union for all the future. The genius of rebellion will no more claim Maryland. Like another foul spirit, being driven out, it may seek to tear her, but it will woo her no more.

At the last session of Congress a proposed amendment of the Constitution abolishing slavery throughout the United States, passed the Senate, but failed for lack of the requisite two-thirds vote in the House of Representatives. Although the present is the same Congress, and nearly the same members, and without questioning the wisdom or patriotism of those who stood in opposition, I venture to recommend the reconsideration and passage of the measure at the present session. Of course the abstract question is not changed; but an intervening election shows, almost certainly, that the next Congress will pass the measure if this does not. Hence there is only a question of *time* as to when the proposed amendment will go to the States for their action. And as it is to so go, at all events, may we not agree that the sooner the better? It is not claimed that the election has imposed a duty on members to change their views or their votes, any further than, as an additional element to be considered, their judgment may be affected by it. It is the voice of the people now, for the first time, heard upon the question. In a great national crisis, like ours, unanimity of action among those seeking a common end is very desirable—almost indispensable. And yet no approach to such unanimity is attainable, unless some deference shall be paid to the will of the majority, simply because it is the will of the majority. In this case the common end is the maintenance of the Union; and, among the means to secure that end, such will, through the election, is most clearly declared in favor of such constitutional amendment. . . .

The public purpose to re-establish and maintain the national authority is unchanged, and, as we believe, unchangeable. The manner of continuing the effort remains to choose. On careful consideration of all the evidence accessible it seems to me that no attempt at negotiation with the insurgent leader could result in any good. He would accept nothing short of severance of the Union—precisely what we will not and cannot give. His declarations to this effect are explicit and oft-repeated. He affords us no excuse to deceive ourselves. He cannot voluntarily reaccept the Union; we cannot voluntarily yield it. Between him and us the issue is distinct, simple, and inflexible. It is an issue which can only be tried by war, and decided by victory. If we yield, we are beaten; if the Southern people fail him, he is beaten. Either way, it would be the victory and defeat following war. What is true, however, of him who heads the insurgent cause, is not necessarily true of those who follow. Although he cannot reaccept the Union, they can. Some of them, we know, already desire peace and reunion. The number of such may increase. They can, at any moment, have peace simply by laying down their arms and submitting to the national authority under the Constitution. After so much, the government could not, if it would, maintain war against them. The loyal people would not sustain or allow it. If questions should remain, we would adjust them by the peaceful means of legislation, conference, courts, and votes, operating only in constitutional and lawful channels. Some certain, and other possible, questions are, and would be, beyond the Executive power to adjust; as, for instance, the admission of members into Congress, and whatever might require the appropriation of money. The Executive power itself would be greatly diminished by the cessation of actual war. Pardons and remissions of forfeitures, however, would still be within Executive control. In what spirit and temper this control would be exercised can be fairly judged of by the past. . . .

In presenting the abandonment of armed resistance to the national authority on the part of the insurgents, as the only indispensable condition to ending the war on the part of the government, I retract nothing heretofore said as to slavery. I repeat the declaration made a year ago, that "while I remain in my present position I shall not attempt to retract or modify the emancipation proclamation, nor shall I return to slavery any person who is free by the terms of that proclamation, or by any of the Acts of Congress. If the people should, by whatever mode or means, make it an Executive duty to re-enslave such persons, another, and not I, must be their instrument to perform it.

In stating a single condition of peace, I mean simply to say that the war will cease on the part of the government, whenever it shall have ceased on the part of those who began it.[1]

Events in the ensuing month afforded further reason to believe peace would come by force and not by negotiation. On December 15 General George H. Thomas at Nashville virtually destroyed the Confederate army of General John B. Hood. Four days later Lincoln called for 300,000 volunteers, strengthening the Union forces. On Christmas Day Lincoln received word from Sherman: "I beg to present you as a Christmas gift the city of Savannah with 150 heavy guns & plenty of ammunition & also about 25,000 bales of cotton."

The next day, happy with the twin successes of Thomas and Sherman, Lincoln wired Sherman, revealing his anxiety about the march to the sea from Atlanta and inquiring about the next move:

Many, many, thanks for your Christmas-gift—the capture of Savannah.

When you were about leaving Atlanta for the Atlantic coast, I was *anxious,* if not fearful; but feeling that you were the better judge, and remembering that "nothing risked, nothing gained" I did not interfere. Now, the undertaking being a success, the honor is all yours; for I believe none of us went farther than to acquiesce. And, taking the work of Gen. Thomas into the count, as it should be taken, it is indeed a great success. Not only does it afford the obvious and immediate military advantages; but, in showing to the world that your army could be divided, putting the stronger part to an important new service, and yet leaving enough to vanquish the old opposing force of the whole—Hood's army—it brings those who sat in darkness, to see a great light. But what next? I suppose it will be safer if I leave Gen. Grant and yourself to decide.

Please make my grateful acknowledgments to your whole army, officers and men.[2]

Within days Lincoln read a dispatch from Sherman to Halleck. Upon seeing it he urged Secretary of War Stanton to press on Sherman the importance of time, as the enemy wavered:

Since parting with you, it has occurred to me to say that while Gen. Sherman's *"get a good ready"* is appreciated, and is not to be overlooked, *time,* now that the enemy is wavering, is more important than ever before. Being on the downhill, & some what confused, keeping him going. Please say so much to Genl. S.[3]

While some northerners thought the war should be halted and unilateral moves made toward peace, Congressman Amos Myers of Pennsylvania told his congressional colleagues:

We are told if we must have an armistice, negotiation, must exhaust all the arts of statesmanship and have a national convention. Sir, we *have* peace Commissioners. They are Grant, Sherman, Sheridan, Thomas, and Farragut. We have our national convention, and the delegates to it are the invincible soldiers and sailors of the Union, clothed in the royal purple of the nation, the Union blues; and they are now debating that question. . . .[4]

Despite the battlefield successes of the Union Army and the tough-minded support of Republican congressmen, Lincoln's suggestion that the Thirteenth Amendment should be taken up by Congress met with considerable resistance. Congressman James Ashley of Ohio, a former Free Soiler and now an ardent champion of emancipation, on January 6 moved to reconsider the vote that had failed to approve state ratification of the Thirteenth Amendment. A major opponent of the measure had been George H. Pendleton, who had become the Democratic Party's nominee for the vice presidency in 1864 and continued to view the amendment as largely beyond the constitutional power of Congress.

Pendleton in June had argued:

The experience of seventy-five years had confirmed the wisdom of the fathers. The States administering their own internal affairs, the Federal Government regulating their international and inter-State relations, have each fulfilled their respective duties and exercised in harmony their respective powers. We have had peace and prosperity; we have had liberty and social order; we have had variety of institutions in the parts, and unity and vigor in the whole; we have solved the problem of large confederations; we have reconciled the liberty of the citizen with the expansion of empire; individuals have been free; communities have been self-governing; minorities have been protected. The theory of State sovereignty, the theory of State rights, has done this. I beg gentlemen not to depart from it.[5]

Ashley in reintroducing the bill responded to Pendleton's argument, defending Lincoln's desire to have the Thirteenth Amendment passed:

My colleague from the first district (Mr. Pendleton), in a speech which he made at the last session against the passage of this amendment, raised the question as to the constitutional power of Congress to propose, and three-fourths of the Legislatures of the States to adopt, an amendment of the character of the one now under consideration. He claimed that, though Congress passed the proposed amendment by the requisite two-thirds, and three-fourths of the Legislatures of the several States adopted it, or, indeed, all the States save one, it would not legally become a part of the national Constitution. These are his words:

But neither three-fourths of the States, nor all the States save one, can abolish slavery in that dissenting State, because it lies within the domain reserved entirely to each State for itself, and upon it the other States cannot enter.

Is this position defensible? If I read the Constitution aright and understand the force of language, the section which I have just quoted is to-day free from all limitations and conditions save two, one of which provides that the suffrage of the several States in the Senate shall be equal, and that no State shall lose this equality by any amendment of the Constitution without its consent; the other relates to taxation. These are the only conditions and limitations.[6]

Heated debate over the measure so dearly wanted by the anxious president waxed through the month. He had once said to Senator E. D. Morgan, "We are like whalers who have been long on a chase: we have at last got the harpoon into the monster, but we must now look how we steer, or with one 'flop' of his tail he will send us all into eternity."

Rumors abounded that Lincoln quietly exerted extraordinary influence on doubtful congressmen to gain their support. A surprising obstacle arose in the person of the foremost senatorial champion of black freedom, Senator Charles Sumner of Massachusetts. Nicolay made a memorandum about the incident:

> I went to the President this afternoon at the request of Mr. Ashley, on a matter connecting itself with the pending amendment of the Constitution. The Camden and Amboy Railroad interest promised Mr. Ashley that if he would help postpone the Raritan railroad bill over this session they would in return make the New Jersey Democrats help about the amendment, either by their votes or absence. Sumner being the Senate champion of the Raritan bill, Ashley went to him to ask him to drop it for this session. Sumner, however, showed reluctance to adopt Mr. Ashley's suggestion, saying that he hoped the amendment would pass anyhow, etc. Ashley thought veiled in Sumner's manner two reasons: (1) That if the present Senate resolution were not adopted by the House, the Senate would send them another in which they would most likely adopt Sumner's own phraseology and thereby gratify his ambition; and (2) that Sumner thinks the defeat of the Camden and Amboy monopoly would establish a principle by legislative enactment which would effectually crush out the last lingering relics of the States rights dogma. Ashley therefore desired the President to send for Sumner, and urge him to be practical and secure the passage of the amendment in the manner suggested by Mr. Ashley. I stated these points to the President, who replied at once: "I can do nothing with Mr. Sumner in these matters. While Mr. Sumner is very cordial with me, he is making his history in an issue with me on this very point. He hopes to succeed in beating the President so as to change this Government from its original form and make it a strong centralized power." Then calling Mr. Ashley into the room, the president said to him, "I think I understand Mr. Sumner; and I think he would be all the more resolute in his persistence on the points which Mr. Nicolay has mentioned to me if he supposed I were at all watching his course on this matter."[7]

Congressman James S. Rollins of slaveholding Missouri, himself a slave owner, had been elected as a conservative Unionist. He enjoyed Lincoln's confidence and left a record of his relationship with Lincoln and abolition of slavery through the Thirteenth Amendment:

> The President had several times in my presence expressed his deep anxiety in favor of the passage of this great measure. He and others had repeatedly counted votes in order to ascertain as far as they could the strength of the measure upon a second trial in the House. He, was doubtful about its passage, and some ten days or two weeks before it came up for consideration in the House, I received a note from him written in pencil on a card, while sitting at my desk in the House, stating he wished to see me, and asking that I call on him at the White House. I responded that I would be there the next morning at nine o'clock. I was prompt in calling upon him, and found him alone in his office. He received me in the most cordial manner: and said in his usual familiar way: "Rollins, I have been wanting to talk to you for some time about the 13th amendment proposed to the Constitution of the United States, which will have to be voted on now before a great while." I said: "Well, I am here, and ready to talk upon that subject." He said: "You and I were old Whigs, both of us followers of that great statesman, Henry Clay, and I tell you I never had an opinion upon the subject of slavery in my life that I did not get from him. I am very anxious that the war should be brought to a close, at the earliest possible date, and I don't believe this can be accomplished as long as those fellows down South can rely upon the Border States to help them; but if the members from the Border States would unite, at least enough of them to pass the 13th amendment to the Constitution, they would soon see they could not expect much help from that quarter, and be willing to give up their opposition, and quit their war upon the Government; this is my chief hope and main reliance, to bring the war to a speedy close, and I have sent for you, as an old Whig friend, to come and see me, that I might make an appeal to you to vote for this amendment. It is going to be very close; a few votes one way or the other will decide it." To this I responded, "Mr. President, so far as I am concerned you need not have sent for me to ascertain my views on this subject, for although I represent perhaps the strongest slave district in Missouri, and have the misfortune to be one of the largest slave-owners in the country where I reside, I had already determined to vote for the 13th amendment." Then he arose from his chair, and grasping me by the hand, gave it a hearty shake, and said, "I am most delighted to hear that." . . . He said: "I would like you to talk to all the Border State men whom you can approach properly, and tell them of my anxiety to have the measure pass; and let me know the prospect of the Border State vote," which I promised

to do. He again said: "The passage of this amendment will clinch the whole subject: it will bring the war, I have no doubt, rapidly to a close." I have never seen any one evince deeper interest and anxiety upon any subject than did Mr. Lincoln upon the passage of this amendment. . . . I conversed with most of the Border State men who could be approached, upon the question; told them of the President's deep anxiety in regard to it, and I have ever believed that the interviews had some influence in strengthening the final vote for the 13th amendment. It will be remembered that when the vote in the House was taken, the amendment was carried by a small *majority.* . . .[8]

Speaking to his colleagues in the divided House of Representatives on January 13, 1865, the Missourian Rollins said:

I adopt precisely the sentiment so felicitously expressed by the President of the United States in a letter which he addressed to Mr. Greeley wrote more than two years ago; and, in order to refresh the minds of these gentlemen who are pleased to give me their attention, I desire to read one or two sentences from that letter. It expresses the correct views, as I think, that all men who aim at the preservation of the Government should adhere to. The President said:

My paramount object in this struggle *is* to save the Union, and is *not* either to save or to destroy slavery. If I could save the Union without freeing *any* slave I would do it; and if I could save it by freeing *all* slaves I would do it; and if I could save it by freeing some and leaving others alone, I would also do that. What I do about slavery and the colored race, I do because I believe it helps to save this Union; and what I forbear, I forbear because I do *not* believe it would help to save the Union. I shall do *less* whenever I shall believe what I am doing hurts the cause, and I shall do *more* whenever I shall believe doing more will help the cause.

That was the disposition of the President two years ago. That was my position two years ago; that is my position now. And what I propose to do now in the vote which I shall give upon this proposition, is simply because I believe that ultimately it will tend to save the Union; and to do that I am willing to do more now than I have heretofore done. . . .

Is this amendment constitutional? How are we to get light upon this subject? My answer is, by referring to the instrument itself; and I have yet to meet the first gentleman on either side of the House who will deny the proposition that in accordance with *the letter of the Constitution* this amendment may be proposed to the States for their adoption or rejection.[9]

A two-thirds majority was needed in the House of Representatives. The historic moment came on the last day of January at four in the afternoon, when sufficient Democrats either joined the Republicans or did not vote, dispatching the Thirteenth Amendment to the states for ratification.

The next night, marching to the sound of music, serenaders paraded to the executive mansion and called the president to appear. That day the governor of his home state had informed him Illinois was the first state to ratify the amendment. Lincoln spoke to the serenaders:

> The President said he supposed the passage through Congress of the Constitutional amendment for the abolishment of Slavery throughout the United States, was the occasion to which he was indebted for the honor of this call. [Applause.] The occasion was one of congratulation to the country and to the whole world. But there is a task yet before us—to go forward and consummate by the votes of the States that which Congress so nobly began yesterday. [Applause and cries—"They will do it," &c.] He had the honor to inform those present that Illinois had already to-day done the work. [Applause.] Maryland was about half through; but he felt proud that, Illinois was a little ahead. He thought this measure was a very fitting if not an indispensable adjunct to the winding up of the great difficulty. He wished the reunion of all the States perfected and so effected as to remove all causes of disturbance in the future; and to attain this end it was necessary that the original disturbing cause should, if possible, be rooted out. He thought all would bear him witness that he had never shrunk from the doing all that he could to eradicate Slavery by issuing an emancipation proclamation. [Applause.] But that proclamation falls far short of what the amendment will be when fully consummated. A question might be raised whether the proclamation was legally valid. It might be added that it only aided those who came into our lines and that it was inoperative as to those who did not give themselves up, or that it would have no effect upon the children of the slaves born hereafter. In fact it would be urged that it did not meet the evil. But this amendment is a King's cure for all the evils. [Applause.] It winds the whole thing up. He would repeat that it was the fitting if not indispensable adjunct to the consummation of the great game we are playing. He could not but congratulate all present, himself, the country and the whole world upon this great moral victory.[10]

CHAPTER THIRTY-FIVE

THE HAMPTON ROADS
PEACE CONFERENCE

On February 3, 1865, peace commissioners met at Hampton Roads, Virginia, in the United States vessel called the *River Queen*. Peace settlement had been an elusive and yet to some an attractive option since hostilities had begun. In 1862 Great Britain and France came close to attempting to mediate an armistice and a peace. Then in 1863 as resistance to the draft and other war measures spiked, Clement Vallandigham more than any other politician gave voice to peace sentiments, concluding a speech in New York city with the cry, "stop this war." Peace had been a leading theme in 1864 among Democrats, whose platform called for "a cessation of hostilities." And as we have seen, in 1864 the egregiously misled *New York Tribune* editor Horace Greeley spurred a movement that bore a very different character from that of 1865. The gullible editor had listened to persons who without position or authority spoke of bringing peace. Lincoln quite properly was skeptical, distancing himself and sending his junior secretary to accompany Greeley on a fruitless inquiry to Canada. Empty of substance, the peace initiative collapsed.

In his annual message of 1864 the president spoke of the dim prospect of negotiation and mentioned terms: his administration would settle only for the abandonment of fighting, return to the Union, and adherence to emancipation. He had said much the same thing in July. Late in the year Francis P. Blair Sr. hinted to Lincoln that he would like to mediate between Confederacy and Union. The president put him off with the remark, "Come to me after Savannah falls."

"The master Spirit . . . of the party . . . in power at Washington," as
Alexander H. Stephens characterized Blair, reappeared within a week after
Savannah fell in late December 1864. Lincoln refused to authorize Blair to
discuss peace but handed him a card reading, "Allow the bearer, F. P. Blair,
Sr. to pass our lines, go South, and return." Once a friend of Davis, well
known in the South, and a former close adviser to the southern Democrat
President Andrew Jackson, Blair enjoyed a cordial reception from Davis.
He was therefore an appropriate figure to attempt to open a conversation.

Working well beyond his brief while closeted with the Confederate
president, Blair dwelt at length on the opportunity for Davis to drive the
French-installed puppet Maximilian from Mexico. The premise of this idea
was that such a move would be preceded by preliminaries for an armistice.
Such maneuvers would allow Davis to shift armies to Texas. By upholding
the Monroe Doctrine, forcing a foreign monarchy from the Americas, Davis
would win favor from Lincoln and the South and North as the negotiation
went forward. The Proclamation of Amnesty and Reconstruction, Blair
suggested, had opened the way for reconcilement.

When Davis asked, "What do you think of Mr. Seward?" Blair replied:

Mr. Seward is a very pleasant companion; he has good social qualities, but
I have no doubt that where his ambition is concerned his selfish feelings
prevail over all principle. I have no doubt he would betray any man, no
matter what his obligations to him, if he stood in the way of his selfish and
ambitious schemes. But, I said, this matter, if entered upon at all, must be
with Mr. Lincoln himself.[1]

Davis gave Blair a letter to carry to Lincoln:

I have deemed it proper and probably desirable to you to give you in this
form the substance of remarks made by me to be repeated by you to Presdt.
Lincoln &c &c

I have no disposition to find obstacles in forms, and am willing now
as heretofore to enter into negociations for the restoration of Peace; am
ready to send a commission whenever I have reason to suppose it will be
received, or to receive a commission if the U.S. Govt. shall choose to send
one. That notwithstanding the rejection of our former offers, I would if
you could promise, that a Commissioner, Minister or other Agent would

be received, appoint one immediately and renew the effort to enter into conference with a view to secure peace to the two countries.[2]

Blair shuttled the message back to the president. Lincoln took exception to Davis's words "the two countries." In reply Lincoln gave Blair a letter welcoming any agent Davis might send to secure peace to "our one common country."[3]

Swiftly acting on this, Davis dispatched three agents as peace commissioners. Unaware of these proceedings, both the army in the field under Grant and the secretary of war felt unable to admit the agents. Lincoln instructed the secretary of war to tell the agents he was sending a messenger to the agents. He was Major T. T. Eckert, carrying documents given him by the president. The next day Lincoln ordered Secretary of State William H. Seward to go to Fort Monroe, not Washington as the agents desired, in a letter reading:

> You will proceed to Fortress-Monroe, Virginia, there to meet, and informally confer with Messrs. Stephens, Hunter, and Campbell, on the basis of my letter to F. P. Blair, Esq. of Jan. 18, 1865, a copy of which you have.
>
> You will make known to them that three things are indispensable, to wit:
>
> 1. The restoration of the National authority throughout all the States.
>
> 2. No receding by the Executive of the United States, on the Slavery question, from the position assumed thereon, in the late Annual Message to Congress, and on preceding documents.
>
> 3. No cessation of hostilities short of an end of the war, and the disbanding of all forces hostile to the government.[4]

Apprised of Lincoln's inflexible terms, the agents were told by Eckert they could not proceed unless they complied with these. The conference seemed aborted until General Grant, who usually refrained from politics, intervened. It is said he was influenced by his wife Julia, southern born and, like Grant, once a slaveholder. Probably also motivated by a desire to see the war end, as the agents sensed, Grant telegraphed Lincoln:

> Now that the interview between Maj. Eckert, under his written instructions, and Mr Stevens & party, has ended I will state confidentially, but not officially to become a matter of record, that I am convinced, upon conversation with Messrs Stevens & Hunter that their intentions are

good and their desire sincere to restore peace and union. I have not felt myself at liberty to express even views of my own or to account for my reticency. This has placed me in an awkard position which I could have avoided by not seeing them in the first instance. I fear now their going back without any expression from any one in authority will have a bad influence. At the same time I recognize the difficulties in the way of receiving these informal commissioners at this time and do not know what to recommend. I am sorry however that Mr Lincoln cannot have an interview with the two named in this despatch if not all three now within our lines. Their letter to me was all that the Presidents instructions contemplated, to secure their safe conduct if they had used the same language to Maj Eckert.[5]

On reading Grant's wire Lincoln at once replied he would meet the commissioners at Fort Monroe. When the cabinet learned of this decision, Secretary of the Navy Gideon Welles entered in his diary:

> The President and Mr. Seward have gone to Hampton Roads to have an interview with the Rebel commissioners, Stephens, Hunter, and Campbell. None of the Cabinet were advised of this move, and, without exception I think it struck them unfavorably that the Chief Magistrate should have gone on such a mission.[6]

The next morning, February 3, Lincoln and Seward and Alexander H. Stephens, R.M.T. Hunter, and John A. Campbell gathered in a large cabin of the *River Queen*. The experienced Old Man Blair, as he was sometimes called, had initiated the discussion; and here was the president himself, with his secretary of state. Representing the Confederacy were its vice president, Stephens; the former Confederate secretary of state, Hunter; and the Confederate assistant secretary of war, Campbell, once a justice of the U.S. Supreme Court.

After amenities, Stephens and Lincoln recalling old times when they had been fellow Whig congressmen, Stephens opened the formal discussion. By agreement no one took notes. After the conference the three southerners published accounts. The best of these—the fullest—is Stephens's, which Lincoln's secretaries, Nicolay and Hay, followed closely in their massive account of the life of the president.

Stephens apparently was overimpressed by what Blair had said to Davis about joining together to enforce the Monroe Doctrine and driving the French puppet government out of Mexico. Stephens related the account in the first person:

> I said in substance: Well, Mr. President, is there no way of putting an end to the present trouble, and bringing about a restoration of the general good feeling and harmony *then* existing between the different States and Sections of the country? . . .
>
> Mr. Lincoln in reply said, in substance, that there was but one way that he knew of, and that was, for those who were resisting the laws of the Union to cease that resistance. All the trouble came from an armed resistance against the National Authority.
>
> But, said I, is there no other question that might divert the attention of both Parties, for a time, from the questions involved in their present strife, until the passions on both sides might cool, when they would be in better temper to come to an amicable and proper adjustment of those points of difference out of which the present lamentable collision of arms has arisen? Is there no Continental question, said I, which might thus temporarily engage their attention? We have been induced to believe that there is.[7]

Lincoln said in substance:

> I suppose you refer to something that Mr. Blair has said. Now it is proper to state at the beginning, that whatever he said was of his own and without the least authority from me. When he applied for a passport to go to Richmond, with certain ideas which he wished to make known to me, I told him flatly that I did not want to hear them. If he desired to go to Richmond of his own accord, I would give him a passport; but he had no authority to speak for me in any way whatever. When he returned and brought me Mr. Davis's letter, I gave him the one to which you alluded in your application for leave to cross the lines. I was always willing to hear propositions for peace on the conditions of this letter and on no other. The restoration of the Union is a *sine qua non* with me, and hence my instructions that no conference was to be held except upon that basis.[8]

The persistent Stephens pressed the gambit further, asserting that both North and South did not want a French empire, and he raised the possibility of stopping the war and jointly enforcing the Monroe Doctrine:

Could not both Parties then, said I, in our contest, come to an understanding and agreement to postpone their present strife, by a suspension of hostilities between themselves, until this principle [against control by any European power] is maintained in behalf of Mexico; and might it not, when successfully sustained there, naturally, and would it not almost inevitably, lead to a peaceful and harmonious solution of their own difficulties? Could any pledge now given, make a permanent restoration or re-organization of the Union more probable, or even so probable, as such a result would?

Mr. Lincoln replied with considerable earnestness, that he could entertain no proposition for ceasing active military operations, which was not based upon a pledge first given, for the ultimate restoration of the Union. He had considered the question of an Armistice fully, and he could not give his consent to any proposition of that sort, on the basis suggested.[9]

Campbell and Lincoln had a brief exchange:

Judge Campbell now renewed his inquiry how restoration was to take place, supposing that the Confederate States were consenting to it?

Mr. Lincoln replied; By disbanding their armies and permitting the National Authorities to resume their functions.

Mr. Seward interposed and said, that Mr. Lincoln could not express himself more clearly or forcibly in reference to this question, than he had done in his message to Congress in December before, and referred specially to that portion in these words:

In presenting the abandonment of armed resistance to the National Authority, on the part of the insurgents, as the only indispensable condition to ending the war on the part of the Government, I retract nothing heretofore said as to Slavery. I repeat the declaration made a year ago, that, while I remain in my present position, I shall not attempt to retract or modify the Emancipation Proclamation, nor shall I return to slavery any person who is free by the terms of that Proclamation, or by any of the Acts of Congress. If the people should, by whatever mode or means, make it an Executive duty to re-enslave such persons, another, and not I, must be their instrument to perform it.

In stating a single condition of peace, I mean simply to say that the war will cease on the part of the Government whenever it shall have ceased on the part of those who began it. . . .

I asked Mr. Lincoln what would be the *status* of that portion of the Slave population in the Confederate States, which had not then become free under his Proclamation; or in other words, what effect that Proclamation would have upon the entire Black population? Would it be held to emancipate the whole, or only those who had, at the time the war ended, become actually free under it?

Mr. Lincoln said, that was a judicial question. How the Courts would decide it, he did not know, and could give no answer. His own opinion was, that as the Proclamation was a war measure, and would have effect only from its being an exercise of the war power, as soon as the war ceased, it would be inoperative for the future. . . .

Mr. Seward said there were only about two hundred thousand slaves, who, up to that time, had come under the actual operation of the Proclamation, and who were then in the enjoyment of their freedom under it; so, if the war should then cease, the *status* of much the larger portion of the slaves would be subject to judicial construction. Mr. Lincoln sustained Mr. Seward as to the number of slaves who were then in the actual enjoyment of their freedom under the Proclamation. Mr. Seward also said, it might be proper to state to us, that Congress, a day or two before, had proposed a Constitutional Amendment for the immediate abolition of slavery throughout the United States, which he produced and read to us from a newspaper. He said this was done as a *war measure.* If the war were then to cease, it would probably not be adopted by a number of States, sufficient to make it a part of the Constitution; but presented the case in such light as clearly showed his object to be, to impress upon the minds of the Commissioners that, if the war should not cease, this, as a war measure, would be adopted by a sufficient number of States to become a part of the Constitution, and without saying it in direct words, left the inference very clearly to be perceived by the Commissioners that his opinion was, if the Confederate States would then abandon the war, they could of themselves defeat this amendment, by voting it down as members of the Union. The whole number of States, it was said, being thirty-six, any ten of them could defeat this proposed amendment.

I inquired how this matter could be adjusted, without some understanding as to what position the Confederate States would occupy towards the others, if they were then to abandon the war. Would they be admitted to representation in Congress?

Mr. Lincoln very promptly replied, that his own individual opinion was, they ought to be. He also thought they would be; but he could not enter into any stipulation upon the subject. His own opinion was, that when the resistance ceased and the National Authority was recognized, the States would be immediately restored to their practical relations to the Union. This was a form of expression repeatedly used by him during the conversation, in speaking of the restoration of the Union. He spoke of it as a "restoration of the States to their practical relations to the Union." . . .

Mr. Hunter interposed, and in illustration of the propriety of the Executive entering into agreements with persons in arms against the acknowledged rightful public authority, referred to repeated instances of this character between Charles I, of England, and the people in arms against him.

Mr. Lincoln in reply to this said: I do not profess to be posted in history. On all such matters I will turn you over to Seward. All I distinctly recollect about the case of Charles I, is, that he lost his head in the end. . . .

I insisted that if he could, as a war measure, issue his Proclamation for Emancipation, which he did not venture to justify under the Constitution on any other grounds, he could certainly, as a like war measure, or as a measure for putting an end to the war rather, enter into some stipulation on this subject.

He then went into a prolonged course of remarks about the Proclamation. He said it was not his intention in the beginning to interfere with Slavery in the States; that he never would have done it, if he had not been compelled by necessity to do it, to maintain the Union; that the subject presented many difficult and perplexing questions to him; that he had hesitated for some time, and had resorted to this measure, only when driven to it by public necessity; that he had been in favor of the General Government prohibiting the extension of Slavery into the Territories, but did not think that that Government possessed power over the subject in the States, except as a war measure; and that he had always himself been in favor of emancipation, but not immediate emancipation, even by the States. Many evils attending this appeared to him.

After pausing for some time, his head rather bent down, as if in deep reflection, while all were silent, he rose up and used these words, almost, if not, quite identical:

Stephens, if I were in Georgia, and entertained the sentiments I do— though, I suppose, I should not be permitted to stay there long with them; but if I resided in Georgia, with my present sentiments, I'll tell you what I would do, if I were in your place: I would go home and get the Governor of the State to call the Legislature together, and get them to recall all the State troops from the war; elect Senators and Members to Congress, and ratify this Constitutional Amendment prospectively, so as to take effect—say in five years. Such a ratification would be valid in my opinion. I have looked into the subject, and think such a prospective ratification would be valid. Whatever may have been the views of your people before the war, they must be convinced now, that Slavery is doomed. It cannot last long in any event, and the best course, it seems to me, for your public men to pursue, would be to adopt such a policy as will avoid, as far as possible, the evils of immediate emancipation. This would be my course, if I were in your place. . . .

Mr. Lincoln said that so far as the Confiscation Acts, and other penal acts, were concerned, their enforcement was left entirely with him, and on that point he was perfectly willing to be full and explicit, and on his assurance perfect reliance might be placed. He should exercise the power of the Executive with the utmost liberality. He went on to say that he would be willing to be taxed to remunerate the Southern people for their slaves. He believed the people of the North were as responsible for slavery as the people of the South, and if the war should then cease, with the voluntary abolition of slavery by the States, he should be in favor, individually, of the Government paying a fair indemnity for the loss to the owners. He said he believed this feeling had an extensive existence at the North. He knew some who were in favor of an appropriation as high as Four Hundred Millions of Dollars for this purpose. I could mention persons, said he, whose names would astonish you, who are willing to do this, if the war shall now cease without further expense, and with the abolition of slavery as stated. But on this subject he said he could give no assurance—enter into no stipulation. He barely expressed his own feelings and views, and what he believed to be the views of others upon the subject. . . .

After thus going through with all these matters, in a conversation of about four hours, of which I have given you only the prominent leading points, and these in substance leading only, there was a pause, [a]s if all felt that the interview should close. . . .

The two parties then took formal and friendly leave, of each other, Mr. Lincoln and Mr. Seward withdrawing first from the saloon together.[10]

The chief matters of the long conversation included Stephen's persistent proposal to have the two warring parties joining in forcing France from Mexico, to which he added cessation of hostilities between South and North. They also embraced Lincoln's unyielding terms for reunion, the status of slaves and his emancipation proclamation, exchange of prisoners, and Lincoln's statement that he favored compensation to slave states for the slaves made free.

Not long later Hunter complained about the terms of the discussion and Lincoln's intransigence:

It would seem possible that Lincoln might have offered something to a people with two hundred thousand soldiers, and such soldiers, under arms. Could it be probable to him that we could go into the United States Government as rebels, assuming the responsibility of all the blood that has been shed, confessing that we have kept up a wicked and needless war, submitting to laws confiscating our property, and taking the lives of our people? It is true, he said that these laws would be administered by him in a spirit of kindness; but when did men ever give to one man the power over their lives and property, and all that they hold dear, trusting to his spirit of kindness, and divesting themselves of the power to resist his tyranny? And it is to be remembered that whenever we go into the Union as a conquered people, we give up the laws of the United States, and must take such as they choose to make for us; and we go in without representation in making those laws; for Mr. Lincoln told us, told me, that while we could send representatives to the Yankee Congress, yet it rested with that Congress to say whether they would receive them or not. Thus we would cast every thing away, and go to them as a subdued, subjugated, and degraded people, to be held in subjection by their soldiery. Nor is all told yet. More than three million slaves are to be let loose, and one billion five hundred thousand dollars' worth of property destroyed at one fell swoop. These slaves are to wander about and become the lazzaroni of the land. The Congress would be continually interfering between the white and black man; the laws would be made by a Congress hostile to us, and any attempt to make these thriftless wanderers useful would be interfered with. If, under the old Government, they interfered with our domestic institutions, what would become of us if we were helpless in their hands, and those hands holding the power to arbitrate in all questions concerning us?[11]

Lincoln's secretaries recorded President Jefferson Davis's angry response to the conference:

"Sooner than we should ever be united again," he said, "he would be willing to yield up everything he had on earth—if it were possible he would sacrifice a thousand lives"; and yet "compel the Yankees, in less than twelve months, to petition us for peace on our own terms." He denounced President Lincoln as "His Majesty Abraham the First," and said "before the campaign was over he and Seward might find 'they had been speaking to their masters.'"[12]

Secretary of the Navy Gideon Welles, who had disapproved of Lincoln's going to the conference, penned in his diary:

> There was a Cabinet meeting last evening. The President had matured a scheme which he hoped would be successful in promoting peace. It was a proposition for paying the expense of the war for two hundred days, or four millions to the Rebel States to be for the extinguishment of slavery, or as the States were disposed. This in few words was the scheme. It did not meet with favor, but was dropped. The earnest desire of the President to conciliate and effect peace was manifest, but there may be such a thing as so overdoing as to cause a distrust or adverse feeling. In the present temper of Congress the proposed measure, if a wise one, could not be carried through successfully.[13]

Schuyler Colfax, speaker of the House, wrote to Lincoln:

> The Senate have been hesitating for two days about Mr. Sumner's resolution, asking for information as to the recent Conference at Hampton Roads. . . . I stated . . . to Mr. [Thaddeus] Stevens this morning that I understood from you that you had no objection to communicating the information, & a resolution has been passed unanimously, asking for it. . . . Under the circumstances, even if the Senate pass the resolution today, I hope you will reply to the House Resolution, in duplicate, if you feel required to answer the delayed Senate Resolution to that Body. I know the answer cannot fail to increase the confidence of the American people in you.[14]

Lincoln sent the Congress correspondence concerning the conference.[15]

The high level conference had been unproductive of results, but it underscored the persistence of Lincoln's aims: abandonment of fighting, returning to the Union, and acceptance of his emancipation policies.

CHAPTER THIRTY-SIX

DEATH OF LINCOLN

Though immersed in politics and peace discussions in early 1865, Lincoln kept a constant watch on military affairs, and he faced difficult personal decisions as well. As the success of Union arms rose, he became increasingly close to General Grant. And he turned to Grant when Robert Todd Lincoln, his eldest son, graduated from Harvard College in 1864. As the commander in chief's son, Robert incurred criticism for being a civilian. His mother, who had lost two sons in their childhood, became hysterical when Robert announced he wanted to enlist, to "see something of the war before it ends."

Wanting to please Robert and placate Mary, Lincoln appealed to Grant:

Please read and answer this letter as though I was not President, but only a friend. My son, now in his twenty second year, having graduated at Harvard, wishes to see something of the war before it ends. I do not wish to put him in the ranks, nor yet to give him a commission, to which those who have already served long, are better entitled, and better qualified to hold. Could he, without embarrassment to you, or detriment to the service, go into your Military family with some nominal rank, I, and not the public, furnishing his necessary means? If no, say so without the least hesitation, because I am as anxious, and as deeply interested, that you shall not be encumbered as you can be yourself.[1]

Grant promptly responded:

Your favor of this date in relation to your son serving in some Military capacity is received. I will be most happy to have him in my Military family in the manner you propose. The nominal rank given him is immaterial but I would suggest that of Capt. as I have three Staff officers now, of conciderable service, in no higher grade. Indeed I have one officer with only the rank of Lieut. who has been in the service from the begining of the war. This however will make no difference and I would still say give the rank of Capt.—Please excuse my writing on a half sheet. I had no resource but to take the blank half of your letter.[2]

On the eve of the Hampton Roads conference Lincoln had instructed Grant: "Let nothing which is transpiring, change, hinder, or delay your Military movements or plans." He incorporated the general's reassuring response in his report to the House of Representatives on the conference.

The day after Lincoln's monitory letter to Grant, Lee proposed to Grant that they meet to discuss "the controversy between belligerents." Lee's letter read:

General: Lieut Genl Longstreet has informed me that in a recent conversation between himself and Maj Genl Ord as to the possibility of arriving at a satisfactory adjustment of the present unhappy difficulties, by means of a military convention, Genl Ord stated that if I desired to have an interview with you on the subject you would not decline, provided I had authority to act. Sincerely desiring to leave nothing untried which may put an end to the calamities of war, I propose to meet you at such convenient time and place as you may designate with the hope that upon an interchange of views it may be found practicable to submit the subjects of controversy between belligerents to a convention of the kind mentioned.

In such event I am authorized to do whatever the result of the proposed interview may render necessary or advisable. Should you accede to this proposition, I would suggest if agreeable to you, we meet at the place selected by Genls Ord and Longstreet for their interview at 11 AM on Monday next.[3]

Grant sent the letter to Stanton together with a brief explanation:

Genl Ord met Genl Longstreet a few days since at the request of the latter to arrange for the exchange of citizen prisoners. . . .

He had my authority to do so and to arrange definitely for such as were confined in his Dept. arrangements for all others to be submitted for approval.

A general conversation ensued on the subject of the war and it has induced the above letter. I have not returned any reply but promised to do so at noon tomorrow. I respectfully request instructions.[4]

Secretary of War Edwin Stanton was at the Capitol with Seward and Lincoln, who was signing legislative bills, as the session was ending. Lincoln read the communication and picked up a pen. Reserving political matters to himself, he wrote his response without consulting either of his major advisers. He then showed the response to Seward and handed it to Stanton to be dispatched:

> The President directs me to say to you that he wishes you to have no conference with General Lee unless it be for the capitulation of Gen. Lee's army, or on some minor, and purely, military matter. He instructs me to say that you are not to decide, discuss, or confer upon any political question. Such questions the President holds in his own hands; and will submit them to no military conferences or conventions. Meantime you are to press to the utmost, your military advantages.[5]

The Confederacy was reaching a breaking point. Conscription in 1864 had been extended to the ages of seventeen and fifty. The larger manpower pool of the North continued to feed its armies, while large-scale desertions in the South made it difficult to meet the Confederacy's needs. Confederate officials considered enrolling blacks and began debating a "Negro Soldier" Bill. In early March the measure passed the Confederate Congress. All these developments formed the background to a speech Lincoln made to the 140th Indiana Regiment in March, the month the Confederate Congress authorized calling up as many as 300,000 slaves for military duty. Presenting to the Indiana governor a flag captured by the regiment in North Carolina, Lincoln said:

> *Fellow Citizens.* A few words only. I was born in Kentucky, raised in Indiana, reside in Illinois, and now here, it is my duty to care equally for the good people of all the States. I am to-day glad of seeing it in the power of an Indiana regiment to present this captured flag to the good governor of their State. And yet I would not wish to compliment Indiana above other states, remembering that all have done so well. There are but few aspects of this great war on which I have not already expressed my views by speaking or writing. There is one—the recent effort of our erring brethren, sometimes so-called, to employ the slaves in their armies. The great question with them has been; "will the negro fight for them?" They ought to know better than we; and, doubtless, do know better than we. . . . I have always

thought that all men should be free; but if any should be slaves it should be first those who desire it for *themselves,* and secondly those who *desire* it for *others.* Whenever [I] hear any one, arguing for slavery I feel a strong impulse to see it tried on him personally.

There is one thing about the negroes fighting for the rebels which we can know as well [as] they can; and that is that they can not, at [the] same time fight in their armies, and stay at home and make bread for them. And this being known and remembered we can have but little concern whether they become soldiers or not. . . . We have to reach the bottom of the insurgent resources; and that they employ, or seriously think of employing, the slaves as soldiers, gives us glimpses of the bottom. Therefore I am glad of what we learn on this subject.[6]

Grant, saying, "I think the rest would do you good," invited Lincoln to visit him for a day or two at City Pont, Virginia, where he had his headquarters. Remarking that he had already thought of visiting, Lincoln accepted, saying he intended to bring Mrs. Lincoln and a few others. One of the attractions was to see his son, now Captain Lincoln, on Grant's staff. He was also concerned that Lee might slip away from Grant and Joseph E. Johnston from Sherman. Lincoln told Sherman at City Point that Johnston "will get away if he can, and you will never catch him until after miles of travel and many bloody battles." Grant shared the same worry; he acknowledged in his *Memoirs,* "I was afraid every morning that I would awake from my sleep to hear that Lee had gone, and that nothing was left but a picket line." Lincoln further wanted to manage peace negotiations, should they start, and assure the South of reconciliation. It was more than a recreational visit. Lincoln stayed for two weeks.[7]

At City Point Lincoln spent time inspecting troops, visiting a battlefield, making trips up the James River to visit Rear Admiral Horace Porter, and at the camp telegraph exchanging news with Stanton.

On board the president's steamer, *River Queen,* he brought together Grant, Porter, and Sherman, who had now reached North Carolina. At Sherman's request, the following year Porter wrote his recollections of the conference, the accuracy of which has been doubted:

The day of General Sherman's arrival at City Point (I think the 27th of March, 1865), I accompanied him and General Grant on board the President's flag-ship, the Queen, where the President received us in the upper saloon, no one but ourselves being present.

The President was in an exceedingly pleasant mood, and delighted to meet General Sherman, whom he cordially greeted.

It seems that this was the first time he had met Sherman, to remember him, since the beginning of the war, and did not remember when he had seen him before, until the general reminded him of the circumstances of their first meeting.

This was rather singular on the part of Mr. Lincoln, who was, I think, remarkable for remembering people, having that kingly quality in an eminent degree. Indeed, such was the power of his memory, that he seemed never to forget the most minute circumstance.

The conversation soon turned on the events of Sherman's campaign through the South, with every movement of which the President seemed familiar.

He laughed over some of the stories Sherman told of his "bummers," and told others in return, which illustrated in a striking manner the ideas he wanted to convey. For example, he would often express his wishes by telling an apt story, which was quite a habit with him, and one that I think he adopted to prevent his committing himself seriously.

The interview between the two generals and the President lasted about an hour and a half, and, as it was a remarkable one, I jotted down what I remembered of the conversation, as I have made a practice of doing during the rebellion, when any thing interesting occurred.

I don't regret having done so, as circumstances afterward occurred (Stanton's ill-conduct toward Sherman) which tended to cast odium on General Sherman for allowing such liberal terms to Jos. Johnston.

Could the conversation that occurred on board the Queen, between the President and General Sherman, have been known, Sherman would not, and could not, have been censured. Mr. Lincoln, had he lived, would have acquitted the general of any blame, for he was only carrying out the President's wishes.

My opinion is, that Mr. Lincoln came down to City Point with the most liberal views toward the rebels. He felt confident that we would be successful, and was willing that the enemy should capitulate on the most favorable terms.

I don't know what the President would have done had he been left to himself, and had our army been unsuccessful, but he was then wrought up to a high state of excitement. He wanted peace on almost any terms, and there is no knowing what proposals he might have been willing to listen to. His heart was tenderness throughout, and, as long as the rebels laid down their arms, he did not care how it was done. I do not know how far he was influenced by General Grant, but I presume, from their long conferences, that they must have understood each other perfectly, and that the terms given to Lee after his surrender were authorized by Mr. Lincoln. I know that the latter was delighted when he heard that they had been given, and exclaimed, a dozen times, "Good!" "All right!" "Exactly the thing!" and other similar expressions. Indeed, the President more than once told me what he supposed the terms would be: if Lee and Johnston surrendered, he considered the war ended, and that all the other rebel forces would lay down their arms at once.

In this he proved to be right. Grant and Sherman were both of the same opinion, and so was every one else who knew anything about the matter.

What signified *the terms* to them, so long as we obtained the actual surrender of people who only wanted a good opportunity to give up gracefully? The rebels had fought "to the last ditch," and all that they had left them was the hope of being handed down in history as having received honorable terms.

After hearing General Sherman's account of his own position, and that of Johnston, at that time, the President expressed fears that the rebel general would escape south again by the railroads, and that General Sherman would have to chase him anew, over the same ground; but the general pronounced this to be impracticable. He remarked: "I have him where he cannot move without breaking up his army, which, once disbanded, can never again be got together; and I have destroyed the Southern railroads, so that they cannot be used again for a long time." General Grant remarked, "What is to prevent their laying the rails again?" "Why," said General Sherman, "my 'bummers' don't do things by halves. Every rail, after having been placed over a hot fire, has been twisted as crooked as a ram's-horn, and they never can be used again."

This was the only remark made by General Grant during the interview, as he sat smoking a short distance from the President, intent, no doubt, on his own plans, which were being brought to a successful termination.

The conversation between the President and General Sherman, about the terms of surrender to be allowed Jos. Johnston, continued. Sherman energetically insisted that he could command his own terms, and that Johnston would have to yield to his demands; but the President was very decided about the matter, and insisted that the surrender of Johnston's army must be obtained on any terms.

General Grant was evidently of the same way of thinking, for, although he did not join in the conversation to any extent, yet he made no objections, and I presume had made up his mind to allow the best terms himself.

He was also anxious that Johnston should not be driven into Richmond, to reënforce the rebels there, who, from behind their strong intrenchments, would have given us incalculable trouble.

Sherman, as a subordinate officer, yielded his views to those of the President, and the terms of capitulation between himself and Johnston were exactly in accordance with Mr. Lincoln's wishes. He could not have done any thing which would have pleased the President better.

Mr. Lincoln did, in fact, arrange the (so considered) liberal terms offered General Jos. Johnston, and, whatever may have been General Sherman's private views, I feel sure that he yielded to the wishes of the President in every respect. It was Mr. Lincoln's policy that was carried out, and, had he lived long enough, he would have been but too glad to have acknowledged it. Had Mr. Lincoln lived, Secretary Stanton would have issued no false telegraphic dispatches, in the hope of killing off another general in the regular army, one who by his success had placed himself in the way of his own succession.

The disbanding of Jos. Johnston's army was so complete, that the pens and inks used in the discussion of the matter were all wasted.

It was asserted, by the rabid ones, that General Sherman had given up all that we had been fighting for, had conceded every thing to Jos. Johnston, and had, as the boys say, "knocked the fat into the fire;" but sober reflection soon overruled these harsh expressions, and, with those who knew General Sherman, and appreciated him, he was still the great soldier, patriot, and gentleman. In future times this matter will be looked at more calmly and dispassionately. The bitter animosities that have been engendered during the rebellion will have died out for want of food on which to live, and the very course Grant, Sherman, and others pursued, in granting liberal terms to the defeated rebels, will be applauded. The fact is, they met an old beggar in the road, whose crutches had broken from under him: they let him have only the broken crutches to get home with!

I sent General Sherman back to Newbern, North Carolina, in the steamer Bat.

While he was absent from his command he was losing no time, for he was getting his army fully equipped with stores and clothing; and, when he returned, he had a rested and regenerated army, ready to swallow up Jos. Johnston and all his ragamuffins.

Johnston was cornered, could not move without leaving every thing behind him, and could not go to Richmond without bringing on a famine in that destitute city.

I was with Mr. Lincoln all the time he was at City Point, and until he left for Washington. He was more than delighted with the surrender of Lee, and with the terms Grant gave the rebel general; and would have given Jos. Johnston twice as much, had the latter asked for it, and could he have been certain that the rebel would have surrendered without a fight. I again repeat that, had Mr. Lincoln lived, he would have shouldered all the responsibility.

One thing is certain: had Jos. Johnston escaped and got into Richmond, and caused a larger list of killed and wounded than we had, General Sherman would have been blamed. Then why not give him the full credit of capturing on the best terms the enemy's last important army and its best general, and putting an end to the rebellion?

It was a finale worthy of Sherman's great march through the swamps and deserts of the South, a march not excelled by any thing we read of in modern military history.[8]

At eight in the morning on April 3 Lincoln telegraphed Stanton: "This morning Gen. Grant reports Petersburg evacuated; and he is confident Richmond also is. He is pushing forward to cut off if possible, the retreating army. I start to him in a few minutes." A worried Stanton replied:

I congratulate you and the nation on the glorious news in your telegram just recd. Allow me respectfully to ask you to consider whether you ought to expose the nation to the consequence of any disaster to yourself in the pursuit of a treacherous and dangerous enemy like the rebel army. If it was a question concerning yourself only I should not presume to say a word. Commanding Generals are in the line of their duty in running such risks. But is the political head of a nation in the same condition?[9]

To this Lincoln responded:

Yours received. Thanks for your caution; but I have already been to Petersburg, staid with Gen. Grant an hour & a half and returned here. It is certain now that Richmond is in our hands, and I think I will go there to-morrow. I will take care of myself.[10]

Met by Grant on a deserted square in Petersburg, Lincoln told him, "I had a sort of sneaking feeling all along that you intended to do something like this, but I thought some time ago that you would so maneuver as to have Sherman come up and be near enough to cooperate with you." Grant replied, "I had a feeling that it would be better to let Lee's old antagonists give his army the final blow and finish the job." The Army of the Potomac, long suffering, once the object of scorn, would under Grant have the honor of taking the surrender of its bitter foe, Lee's now shrunken Army of Northern Virginia.

The following day Lincoln paid a visit to Richmond, now evacuated by Jefferson Davis and the Confederate government. When his barge reached its landing, black workmen recognized the president as a liberator. "Bless the Lord, there is the great Messiah," shouted one . . . Glory, Hallelujah!" In biblical fashion some men dropped to their knees and tried to kiss Lincoln's feet.

"Don't kneel to me," he said. "That is not right. You must kneel to God only, and thank Him for the liberty you will hereafter enjoy." Told during the day that he was in danger, he replied, "I cannot bring myself to believe that any human being lives who would do me any harm." Under armed escort he visited the Confederate White House, sat in Jefferson Davis's study chair, and then lunched with General Godfrey Weitzel, commanding the city.[11]

While he was in the Confederate White House Lincoln had an interview with John A. Campbell, the former U.S. Supreme Court justice whom he had recently seen at Hampton Roads. Campbell related the discussion:

> I was conducted to a small room in that building, where I met President Lincoln and General Weitzel. . . . His manner indicated that he expected some special and, perhaps, authorized communication to him from the Confederate Government. I disabused his mind of this by saying that I had no commission to see him. . . . I then told Mr. Lincoln that the war was over, and all that remained to be done was to compose the country. . . . I spoke to him particularly for Virginia, and urged him to consult and counsel with her public men and her citizens as to the restoration of peace, civil order, and the renewal of her relations as a member of the Union. I urged that, although there had been passion, petulance, and animosity in the secession movements, there were also serious differences of opinion as to constitutional obligations and responsibilities, upon which there was a ground for opposing opinions. I informed him that efforts for peace had been made

during the winter and that the most prominent men of the State were ready to aid in the work of pacification, and that if he would call them together the work would be nearly done; that "when leniency and cruelty play for the conquest of a kingdom, the gentlest player will be the soonest winner."[12]

They arranged to meet the next day. Campbell continued his narrative:

The President was prepared for the visit and spoke with freedom and apparent decision. . . . In the course of the conversation, he produced a paper written by himself, but not signed or addressed to any one. This paper he read over, and then commented upon each clause at some length and handed the paper to me. I did not perceive any material difference between the terms expressed in this paper and those announced by the President at Hampton Roads. . . . My answer to the President was that I did not believe that there would be any opposition to his terms. . . . Mr. Lincoln told me that he had been meditating a plan, but that he had not fixed upon it, and if he adopted it, would write to General Weitzel from City Point. This was to call the Virginia Legislature together, "the very Legislature which had been sitting up yonder," pointing to the Capitol, "to vote the restoration of Virginia to the Union." He said he had a government in Virginia—the Pierpont Government—but it "had a very small margin," and he was not "disposed to increase it."[13]

The paper Campbell referred to stated:

As to peace, I have said before, and now repeat, that three things are indispensable.

1. The restoration of the national authority throughout all the States.

2. No receding by the Executive of the United States on the slavery question, from the position assumed thereon, in the late Annual Message to Congress, and in preceding documents.

3. No cessation of hostilities short of an end of the war, and the disbanding of all force hostile to the government.

That all propositions coming from those now in hostility to the government; and not inconsistent with the foregoing, will be respectfully considered, and passed upon in a spirit of sincere liberality.

I now add that it seems useless for me to be more specific with those who will not say they are ready for the indispensable terms, even on conditions to be named by themselves. If there be any who are ready for those indispensable terms, on any conditions whatever, let them say so, and state their conditions, so that such conditions can be distinctly known, and considered.

It is further added that, the remission of confiscations being within the executive power, if the war be now further persisted in, by those opposing the government, the making of confiscated property at the least to bear the additional cost, will be insisted on; but that confiscations (except in cases of third party intervening interests) will be remitted to the people of any State which shall now promptly, and in good faith, withdraw its troops and other support, from further resistance to the government.

What is now said as to remission of confiscations has no reference to supposed property in slaves.[14]

In the late afternoon Assistant Secretary of War Charles A. Dana wired Stanton:

> Judge Campbell . . . had an interview with the President here this morning to consider how Virginia can be brought back to the Union. All they ask is an amnesty and a military convention to cover appearances. Slavery they admit to be defunct. General Weitzel, who was present, tells me that the President did not promise the amnesty, but told them he had the pardoning power, and would save any repentant sinner from hanging. They . . . are sure if amnesty could be offered the rebel army would dissolve and all the States return. The President went to City Point this morning, and I have not been able to see him. . . .
>
> Meeting of five members of the Virginia legislature held here to-day upon the President's propositions to Judge Campbell. The President showed me the papers confidentially to-day. They are two in number, one without address [*supra*], the other . . . to General Weitzel [April 6, *infra*]. The one states *sine qua non* of reunion, and does not differ essentially from previous statements. The second authorizes Weitzel to allow members of the body claiming to be legislature of Virginia to meet here for purpose of recalling Virginia soldiers from rebel armies, with safe conduct to them; so long as they do and say nothing hostile to the United States. Judge Campbell laid these papers before the five men. . . . The President told me this morning that Sheridan seemed to be getting Virginia soldiers out of the war faster than this legislature could think.[15]

Lincoln informed Grant of the impending meeting, and of plans to protect the legislators, and ordered that if necessary they should be arrested.

On the same day, April 6, he notified General Weitzel of the development, cautiously referring to the legislators as "the gentlemen who have acted as the Legislature of Virginia."[16]

Shortly before midnight Lincoln received a telegram from Sheridan forwarded by Grant:

> Lieutenant-General Grant: I have the honor to report that the enemy made a stand at the intersection of the Burke's Station road with the road upon which they were retreating. I attacked two divisions of the Sixth Army Corps and routed them handsomely, making a connection with the cavalry. I am still pressing on with both cavalry and infantry. Up to the present time we have captured Generals Ewell, Kershaw, Barton, Corse, DuBose, and Custis Lee, several thousand prisoners, 14 pieces of artillery with caissons and a large number of wagons. If the thing is pressed I think Lee will surrender.[17]

The next morning Lincoln telegraphed Grant: "Gen. Sheridan says 'If the thing is pressed I think that Lee will surrender.' Let the *thing* be pressed."[18]

Following his meetings with Lincoln, Campbell wrote to Weitzel:

> The events of the war have placed under the military control of the United States the natural and artificial channels of communication of the Confederate States, their emporiums of commerce and intercourse, and all the places that have any special importance in a military point of view. The armies of the Confederacy are diminished in point of numbers, and debilitated from the want of adequate equipments, transportation, and supplies. . . . All the powers of negotiation are in the hands of the [President], and he is not willing to employ them for such [a] result. . . . I [think] that an armistice would obviate much of this difficulty, nor [do] I believe that there would be any danger of a [delay] in securing peace by this temporary cessation of hostilities. The [disbanding] of the armies would be the probable, I may say the [certain], result of such a measure.
>
> The legislature of Virginia [will or should] be immediately convened. The legislature of South Carolina will meet according [to] adjournment in May.
>
> The President of the United States in his memorandum left with [me] states three indispensable conditions to peace, which when examined are [all] included in the single one of the restoration of the Union by [the] consent of the seceding States. If his proclamation upon the subject of slavery have the force of law I suppose that it became operative when it

was issued, and that rights were vested under it. I do not presume that his revocation of that proclamation could destroy the rights thus acquired.

The acceptance of the Union involves acceptance of his proclamation, if it be valid as a law. In Virginia the question of limits is one of great concern and interest, and in both States the averages of taxes, the confiscation acts, the bills of pains and penalties, the oaths of allegiance, the right to representation in Congress, and the condition of the slave population, are subjects of importance. I do not very well see how these matters can be adjusted without a very grave, important, and patient inquiry between the parties; that is, the United States and the authorities of the States. I have stated that the regular session of the legislature of South Carolina will be held in May. I would recommend that all the facilities offered in Virginia to the assembling of their legislature be extended to that State, and that it be invited to send commissioners to adjust the questions that are supposed to require adjustment.

I have made a statement of the practical difficulties that exist in order to encourage you to persevere in the course of patience, moderation, forbearance, and conciliation that has marked your conduct since you entered Richmond. Many of the difficulties will be removed or lessened by such a course, and I do not know of any that will not be aggravated by the adoption of the opposite.[19]

Lincoln's willingness to allow the rebel Virginia legislature to meet encountered some serious opposition from his cabinet members. Twice on the twelfth, supported by the attorney general, Stanton argued that giving authority to the legislature "would be giving away the scepter of the conquerer," would endanger the blacks, and would fail to gain support in Congress. Stanton argued that only federal authority could reorganize the seceded southern states. To allow Virginia to reorganize itself would defeat the very purpose of the war.

Secretary of the Navy Welles agreed, penning in his diary:

The President asked me what views I took of Weitzel's calling the Virginia legislature together. Said Stanton and others were dissatisfied. Told him I doubted the policy of convening a Rebel legislature. It was a recognition of them, and once convened, they would with their hostile feelings be inclined perhaps to conspire against us. He said he had no fear of that. They were too badly beaten, too much exhausted. His idea was, that the members of the legislature, being the prominent and influential men of their respective counties, had better come together and undo their own work. He felt assured they would do this, and the movement he believed a good one. Civil government must be reestablished, he said, as soon as possible—there must be courts, and law, and order, or society would be broken up, the disbanded armies would turn into robber bands and guerrillas, which we must strive to prevent. These were the reasons why he wished them to come together and turn themselves and their neighbors into good Union men. But as we all took a different view he had perhaps made a mistake, and was ready to correct it if he had.

I remarked, in the course of conversation, that if the so called legislature came together, they would be likely to propose terms which might seem reasonable, but which we could not accept,—that I had not great faith in negotiating with large bodies of men,—each would encourage the other in asking and doing what no one of them would do alone—that he could make an arrangement with any one—the worst of them—than with all—that he might be embarrassed by recognizing and treating with them, when we were now in a condition to prescribe what should be done.[20]

Lincoln that day ordered Weitzel not to allow the meeting:

I have just seen Judge Campbell's letter to you of the 7th. He assumes as appears to me that I have called the insurgent Legislature of Virginia together, as the rightful Legislature of the State, to settle all differences with the United States. I have done no such thing. I spoke of them not as a Legislature, but as "the gentlemen who have *acted* as the Legislature of Virginia in support of the rebellion." I did this on purpose to exclude the assumption that I was recognizing them as a *rightful* body. I dealt with them as men having power *de facto* to do a specific thing, to wit, "to withdraw the Virginia troops, and other support from resistance to the General Government," for which in the paper handed Judge Campbell I promised a specific equivalent, to wit, a remission to the people of the State, except in certain cases, the confiscation of their property. I meant this and no more. In as much however as Judge Campbell misconstrues this, and is still pressing for an armistice, contrary to the explicit statement of the paper I gave him; and particularly as Gen. Grant has since captured the Virginia troops, so that giving a consideration for their withdrawal is no longer applicable, let my letter to you, and the paper to Judge Campbell both be withdrawn or, countermanded, and he be notified of it. Do not now allow them to assemble; but if any have come, allow them safe-return to their homes.[21]

On Sunday April 9 Lincoln and his party steamed back toward Washington. Lincoln, tired but cheerful, spent much of the day reading. To his companions, he recited from *Macbeth*:

> Duncan is in his grave;
> After life's fitful fever he sleeps well;
> Treason has done his worst; nor steel, nor poison,
> Malice domestic, foreign levy, nothing,
> Can touch him further.[22]

On reaching Washington he learned cheering news—culmination of four years of strain and storm: Lee had surrendered to Grant at Appomattox. After visiting Seward, who had been injured in a carriage accident, Lincoln went to the White House. There a crowd gathered. The *National Intelligencer* described the event:

> The procession proceeded along Pennsylvania avenue gaining accessions at every step, despite the mud and rain, and when it turned up Fifteenth street it is estimated that there were over three thousand persons in the crowd. The procession proper—that is, those who had come from the Navy Yard—and a portion of the crowd proceeded to the residence of Secretary Welles, while the other portion kept along Pennsylvania avenue to the White House and the War Department. At the latter place the band of the Quartermaster's regiment, Capt. Tompkins, under the leadership of Prof. Blish, and the band of the Fourteenth regiment V.R.C., were stationed, and their excellent music attracted an immense concourse of people, who called again loudly for Secretary Stanton, but failing to get him out, the crowd, preceded by the Quartermaster's band, moved toward the White House, and in a few moments an immense number of people were assembled, and completely filled the portico, the carriageway, and pavements on either side, while many were forced to content themselves with a stand-up place in the mud. The bands played, the howitzers belched forth their thunder, and the people cheered. Call after call was made for the President, and his failure to appear only made the people cry out the louder. Master Tad Lincoln, who was at the window, appeared to hugely enjoy the shouting, cheering, and swaying to and fro of the crowd, who evinced a determination not to depart until the Chief Magistrate acknowledged their greeting by his presence. At length, after persistent

effort, the presence of Mr. Lincoln was secured. Three loud and hearty cheers were given.[23]

Lincoln spoke "pleasantly and briefly," one writer said:

Fellow Citizens: I am very greatly rejoiced to find that an occasion has occurred so pleasurable that the people cannot restrain themselves. [Cheers.] I suppose that arrangements are being made for some sort of a formal demonstration, this, or perhaps, to-morrow night. [Cries of "We can't wait," "We want it now," &c.] If there should be such a demonstration, I, of course, will be called upon to respond, and I shall have nothing to say if you dribble it all out of me before. [Laughter and applause.] I see you have a band of music with you, [Voices, "We have two or three."] I propose closing up this interview by the band performing a particular tune which I will name. Before this is done, however, I wish to mention one or two little circumstances connected with it. I have always thought "Dixie" one of the best tunes I have ever heard. Our adversaries over the way attempted to appropriate it, but I insisted yesterday that we fairly captured it. [Applause.] I presented the question to the Attorney General, and he gave it as his legal opinion that it is our lawful prize. [Laughter and applause.] I now request the band to favor me with its performance.[24]

He had achieved a fine light touch.

In accordance with the request, the band struck up "Dixie," and at its conclusion played "Yankee Doodle," the President remaining at the window meanwhile.

The President then said: "Now give three good hearty cheers for General Grant and all under his command." These were given with a will, after which Mr. Lincoln requested "three more cheers for our gallant Navy," which request was also readily granted.

The President then disappeared from the window, amid the cheers of those below. The crowd then moved back to the War Department, and loud calls were again made for Secretary Stanton.[25]

Lincoln promptly told Mary of the surrender. The next morning she wrote to Senator Charles Sumner: "Mr. L. told me the news, last night at ten o'clock, that Lee & and his Army were in our hands, in the midst of the bands playing, they break forth into singing."

On April 11 Salmon P. Chase, still concerning himself about politics although now chief justice, wrote to Lincoln about reconstruction, especially about affairs in Virginia, Louisiana, and Arkansas:

> When all mankind are congratulating you, one voice, heard or not, is of little account; but I add mine.
>
> I am very anxious about the future: and most about the principles which are to govern reconstruction: for as these principles are sound or unsound so will be the work & its results. . . .
>
> And first as to Virginia.
>
> By the action of every branch of the Government we are committed to the recognition & maintenance of the State organization of which Governor Pierpont is the head. . . . There will be a pressure for the recognition of the rebel organization on condition of profession of loyalty. It will be far easier and wiser, in my judgment, to stand by the loyal organization already recognized.
>
> And next as to the other rebel States:
>
> The easiest & safest way seems to me to be the enrollment of the loyal citizens, without regard to complexion, and encouragement & support to them in the reorganization of State Governments under constitutions securing suffrage to all citizens of proper age & unconvicted of crime. . . .
>
> This way is recommended by its simplicity, facility &, above all, justice. It will be, hereafter, counted equally a crime & a folly if the colored loyalists of the rebel states shall be left to the control of restored rebels, not likely in that case to be either wise or just, until taught both wisdom and justice by new calamities.
>
> The application of this principle to Louisiana is made somewhat difficult by the organization which has already taken place: but happily the Constitution enables the Legislature to extend the right of suffrage; and it is not to be doubted that, on a suggestion from the National Authorities that its extension to colored citizens on equal terms with white citizen is believed to be necessary to the future tranquility of the country as well as just in itself, the Legislature will act promptly in the desired direction. . . .
>
> The same result can be secured in Arkansas by an amendment of the State Constitution; or what would be better, I think, by a new Convention the Members of which should be elected by the loyal citizens without distinction of color. To all the other states the general principle may be easily applied.[26]

That night, as he had intimated he would, Lincoln made a public address; his last, as it turned out. He first disclaimed what may have been a victory speech, but gave a discourse on reconstruction, especially for Louisiana. He twice avowed what he thought to be the heart of the Louisiana question: "Can Louisiana be brought into proper practical relation with the Union *sooner* by *sustaining* or by *discarding* her new State Government?"[27]

After reading the speech the next morning in the *Washington American,* Chase again wrote to Lincoln pressing for the vote for all blacks. He now told Lincoln:

> The American of this morning contains your speech of last evening. Seeing that you say something on the subject of my letter to you yesterday—reconstruction—, & refer, though without naming me, to the suggestions I made in relation to the Amnesty Proclamation, when you brought it before the Heads of Departments, I will ask your permission to add . . . to what I have already written. . . .
>
> Ever since questions of reconstruction have been talked about, it has been my opinion that the colored loyalists ought to be allowed to participate in it: and it was because of this opinion that I was anxious to have this question left open. I did not however say much about the restriction. I was the only one who expressed a wish for its omission: & I did not desire to seem pertinacious.[28]

For some time the ardent abolitionist William Lloyd Garrison, having split with his fellow abolitionist Wendell Phillips, had been a supporter of Lincoln's Louisiana policy. Responding to Professor Francis H. Newman's criticism of Lincoln's unwillingness to enfranchise all black men in Louisiana, Garrison wrote:

> By what political precedent or administrative policy, in any country, could he have been justified if he had attempted to do this? When was it ever known that liberation from bondage was accompanied by a recognition of political equality? . . . To denounce or complain of President Lincoln for not disregarding public sentiment, and not flying in the face of these laws, is hardly just. Besides, I doubt whether he has the constitutional right to decide this matter. Ever since this government was organized, the right of suffrage has been determined by each State in the Union for itself, so that there is no uniformity in regard to it. In some free States, colored citizens are allowed to vote; in others, they are not. It is always a State, never a national, matter. In honestly seeking to preserve the Union, it is not for President

Lincoln to seek, by a special edict applied to a particular State or locality, to do violence to a universal rule. . . . Under the war power, he had the constitutional right to emancipate the slaves in every rebel State, and also to insist that, in any plan of reconstruction that might be agreed upon, slavery should be admitted to be dead, beyond power of resurrection. That being accomplished, I question whether he could safely or advantageously—to say the least—enforce a rule, *ab initio,* touching the ballot, which abolishes complexional distinctions. . . . Nor, if the freed blacks were admitted to the polls by Presidential fiat, do I see any permanent advantage likely to be secured by it; for, submitted to as a necessity at the outset, as soon as the State was organized and left to manage its own affairs, the white population, with their superior intelligence, wealth, and power, would unquestionably alter the franchise in accordance with their prejudices, and exclude those thus summarily brought to the polls. Coercion would gain nothing. In other words,—as in your own country,—universal suffrage will be hard to win and to hold without a general preparation of feeling and sentiment. But it will come, both at the South and with you; yet only by a struggle *on the part of the disfranchised,* and a growing conviction of its justice, "in the good time coming." With the abolition of slavery in the South, prejudice or "colorphobia," the natural product of the system, will gradually disappear—as in the case of your West India colonies—and black men will win their way to wealth, distinction, eminence, and official station. I ask only a charitable judgment for President Lincoln respecting this matter, whether in Louisiana or any other State.[29]

Disappointed in the April 11 speech, Sumner wrote to Francis Lieber: "The president's speech and other things augur confusion and uncertainty in the future, with hot controversy. Alas! Alas!"[30]

On the last full day of his life, after breakfasting with his son Robert, who had been present at Appomattox, Lincoln held a three-hour cabinet meeting. Gideon Welles, writing seven years later, described the discussion of reconstruction, especially the Louisiana and Virginia problems:

When I went to the Cabinet meeting on Friday, the 14th of April, General Grant, who had just arrived from Appomattox, was with the President, and one or two members were already there. Congratulations were interchanged, and earnest inquiry was made whether any information had been received from General Sherman. The Secretary of War came late to the meeting, and the telegraph office from which we obtained earliest news was in the

War Department. General Grant, who was invited to remain, said he was expecting hourly to hear from Sherman, and had a good deal of anxiety on the subject.

The President remarked that the news would come soon and come favorably, he had no doubt, for he had last night his usual dream which had preceded nearly every important event of the war. I inquired the particulars of this remarkable dream. He said it was in my department—it related to the water; that he seemed to be in a singular and indescribable vessel, but always the same, and that he was moving with great rapidity toward a dark and indefinite shore; that he had had this singular dream preceding the firing on Sumter, the battles of Bull Run, Antietam, Gettysburg, Stone River, Vicksburg, Wilmington, etc. General Grant remarked with some emphasis and asperity that Stone River was no victory—that a few such victories would have ruined the country, and he knew of no important results from it. The President said that perhaps he should not altogether agree with him but whatever might be the facts, his singular dream preceded that fight. Victory did not always follow his dream, but the event and results were important. He had no doubt that a battle had taken place or was about being fought, "and Johnston will be beaten, for I had this strange dream again last night. It must relate to Sherman; my thoughts are in that direction, and I know of no other very important event which is likely just now to occur."

Great events did indeed follow. Within a few hours the good and gentle as well as truly great man who narrated his dream was assassinated, and the murder which closed forever his earthly career affected for years and perhaps forever, the welfare of his country.

The session of the Cabinet on that eventful day, the last of President Lincoln's life, was chiefly occupied on the subject of our relations with the rebels—the communications, the trade, etc. . . . It was generally agreed that commercial intercourse with the rebel States should be speedily established. . . . .

In regard to opening the ports to trade, Mr. Stanton thought it should be attended with restrictions, and that traffic should not extend beyond the military lines. I proposed opening the whole coast to every one who wished to trade, was entitled to coast license, and should obtain a regular clearance. I wished the reestablishment of unrestricted commercial and social intercourse with the Southern people with as little delay as possible, from a conviction that it would conduce to a more speedy establishment of friendly relations. General Grant concurred with me, and recommended that there should be no restrictions east of the Mississippi. The President referred the whole subject to the Secretaries of the Treasury, War, and Navy, and said he should be satisfied with any conclusions to which they might arrive, or on which they could agree.

At the close of the session Mr. Stanton made some remarks on the general condition of affairs and the new phase and duties upon which we were about to enter. He alluded to the great solicitude which the President felt on this subject, his frequent recurrence to the necessity of establishing civil governments and preserving order in the rebel States. Like the rest of the Cabinet, doubtless, he had given this subject much consideration, and with a view of having something practical on which to base action, he had drawn up a rough plan or ordinance which he had handed to the President.

The President said he proposed to bring forward that subject, although he had not had time as yet to give much attention to the details of the paper which the Secretary of War had given him only the day before; but that it was substantially, in its general scope, the plan which we had sometimes talked over in Cabinet meetings. We should probably make some modifications, proscribe further details; there were some suggestions which he should wish to make, and he desired all to bring their minds to the question, for no greater or more important one could come before us, or any future Cabinet. He thought it providential that this great rebellion was crushed just as Congress had adjourned, and there were none of the disturbing elements of that body to hinder and embarrass us. If we were wise and discreet, we should reanimate the States and get their governments in successful operation, with order prevailing and the Union reestablished, before Congress came together in December. This he thought important. We could do better; accomplish more without than with them. There were men in Congress who, if their motives were good, were nevertheless impracticable, and who possessed feelings of hate and vindictiveness in which he did not sympathize and could not participate. He hoped there would be no persecution, no bloody work, after the war was over. . . . Louisiana, he said, had framed and presented one of the best constitutions that had ever been formed. He wished they had permitted negroes who had property, or could read, to vote; but this was a question which they must decide for themselves. Yet some, a very few of our friends, were not willing to let the people of the States determine those questions, but, in violation of first and fundamental principles, would exercise arbitrary power over them. These humanitarians break down all State rights and constitutional rights.

Had the Louisianians inserted the negro in their Constitution, and had that instrument been in all other respects the same, Mr. Sumner, he said, would never have excepted to that Constitution. The delegation would have been admitted, and the State all right. Each House of Congress, he said, had the undoubted right to receive or reject members; the Executive had no control in this matter. But Congress had nothing to do with the State governments, which the President could recognize, and under existing laws treat as other States, give them the same mail facilities, collect taxes, appoint judges, marshals, collectors, etc., subject, of course, to confirmation. There were men who objected to these views, but they were not here, and we must make haste to do our duty before they came here.

Mr. Stanton read his project for reorganizing, reestablishing, or reconstructing governments. It was a military or executive order, and by it the War Department was designated to reorganize those States whose individuality it assumed was sacrificed. Divested of its military features, it was in form and outline essentially the same as the plan ultimately adopted. This document proposed establishing a military department to be composed of Virginia and North Carolina, with a military governor. After reading this paper, Mr. Stanton made some additional remarks in furtherance of the views of the president and the importance of prompt measures....

The President directed Mr. Stanton to take the document and have separate plans presented for the two States. They required different treatment. "We must not," said he, "stultify ourselves as regards Virginia, but we must help her." North Carolina was in a different condition. He requested the secretary of War to have copies of the two plans for the two States made and furnished each member of the Cabinet by the following Tuesday—the next regular Meeting. He impressed upon each and all the importance of deliberating upon and carefully considering the subject before us, remarking that this was the great question pending, and that we must now begin to act in the interest of peace. He again declared his thankfulness that Congress was not in session to embarrass us.

The President was assassinated that evening, and I am not aware that he exchanged a word with any one after the Cabinet meeting of that day on the subject of a resumption of the national authority in the States where it had been suspended, or of reestablishing the Union.[31]

After the meeting the president and first lady had a late lunch. That afternoon they went for a drive, as they often had. Putting aside affairs of state, they talked of themselves and their future:

When asked by Mrs. Lincoln if he would like any one to accompany them, he replied, "No; I prefer to ride by ourselves to-day." Mrs. Lincoln subsequently said that she never saw him seem so supremely happy as on this occasion. In reply to a remark to this effect, the president said: "And well I may feel so, Mary, for I consider this day the war has come to a close." And then added: "We must both be more cheerful in the future; between the war and the loss of our darling Willie, we have been very miserable."[32]

That fateful Friday, ironically Good Friday, Abraham and Mary Todd Lincoln attended the theater. Though she had a headache, Mary deferred to her husband's insistence on going. She said later, "His mind was fixed upon having some relaxation and bent on the theater." The play was *Our American Cousin*, advertised as the "celebrated eccentric comedy," suitable both for the president's sense of humor and his need for relaxation.

In the theater (but not performing in the play) was John Wilkes Booth, a prominent actor whom Lincoln had seen a number of times on the stage. Sympathetic with the South and slavery, he wrote to a friend that slavery was "one of the greatest blessings (both for themselves [the slaves] and us) that God ever bestowed upon a favoured nation." Opposed to the war against the South, he had been in the crowd when Lincoln gave his April 11 speech with its plea for reconstruction of Louisiana and suggestion that some blacks be given the vote. In a low voice Booth had said to a friend, "That is the last speech he will ever make."

Lincoln responded on that Friday to a letter of warning. The editor of his works, observing that the cautionary letter has not been found, quoted his source: "General Van Alen wrote Lincoln, requesting him, for the sake of his friends and the nation, to guard his life and not expose it to assassination as he had by going to Richmond."

Lincoln replied, "My dear Sir: I intend to adopt the advice of my friends and use due precaution. . . . I thank you for the assurance you give me that I shall be supported by conservative men like yourself, in the efforts I may make to restore the Union, so as to make it, to use your language, a Union of hearts and hands as well as of States."[33] At about eight-thirty in the evening to the sound of "Hail to the Chief," Abraham and Mary Lincoln, accompanied by Miss Clara Harris and Major Henry R. Rathbone, took their seats in Ford's Theater. During the third act she nestled close to her husband and looked up in his face. Aware of their guests' presence, she asked, "What will Miss Harris think of my hanging to you so?"

"She won't think anything about it," her husband reassured her. They were his last words.

The door to their box was closed but not locked. The stealthy Booth, entering, fired a shot into the back of Lincoln's head. Mortally wounded, the president was carried to a house across the street. He lingered until the next morning. At 7:22 a.m. on April 15 Lincoln died.

To Stanton—once contemptuous of the prairie lawyer, and a severe critic before accepting appointment as his secretary of war—is ascribed Lincoln's epitaph: "Now he belongs to the ages."

NOTES

ABBREVIATIONS

AL Abraham Lincoln.

Beale, *Welles Diary* Gideon Welles, *Diary of Gideon Welles, Secretary of the Navy under Lincoln and Johnson,* 3 vols., ed. Howard Beale and Alan Brownsword (New York: W. W. Norton, 1960).

Burlingame, *Hay Diary* John Hay, *Inside Lincoln's White House: The Complete Civil War Diary of John Hay,* ed. Michael Burlingame and John Ettlinger (Carbondale: Southern Illinois University Press, 1997).

CG *Congressional Globe,* debates of Congress, 1833–73.

CW *The Collected Works of Abraham Lincoln,* ed. Roy P. Basler, 9 vols., 2 supplements (New Brunswick NJ: Rutgers University Press, 1953).

Cyclopaedia *The American Annual Cyclopaedia and Register of Important Events,* 42 vols. (New York: D. Appleton, 1862–1903).

GBM George B. McClellan.

McClellan, *Own Story* George B. McClellan, *McClellan's Own Story: The War for the Union, the Soldiers Who Fought It, the Civilians Who Directed It, and His Relations to It and to Them* (New York: Charles Webster and Company, 1887).

Niven, *Chase Papers* Salmon P. Chase, *The Salmon P. Chase Papers,* 5 vols., ed. John Niven (Kent OH: Kent State University Press, 1993–98).

OR U.S. War Department, *The War of the Rebellion: A Compilation of the Official Records of the Union and Confederate Armies,* 128 vols. (Washington DC: Government Printing Office, 1880–1901).

Sears, *Selected Correspondence* George McClellan, *The Civil War Papers of George B. McClellan: Selected Correspondence, 1860–65,* ed. Stephen Sears (New York: Ticknor and Fields, 1989).

1. LINCOLN IS NOMINATED

1. Frederic Bancroft, *The Life of William H. Seward,* 2 vols. (New York: Harper and Brothers, 1900), 1: 530–31.

2. Abraham Lincoln to Lyman Trumbull, Springfield, Illinois, 29 April 1860, in *The Collected Works of Abraham Lincoln,* ed. Roy P. Basler, 9 vols., 2 supplements (New Brunswick NJ: Rutgers University Press, 1953), 4: 45–46 (*Collected Works* hereafter cited as *CW; Abraham Lincoln* hereafter cited as AL).

3. AL to Richard Corwine, Springfield, Illinois, 2 May 1860, *CW,* 4: 47–48.

4. Remarks to Republican State Convention, Decatur, Illinois, 9 May 1860, *CW,* 4: 48.

5. Henry Commager, ed., *Documents of American History,* 8th ed. (New York: Appleton-Century-Crofts, 1968), 363–65.

6. Albert B. Hart, ed., *American History Told by Contemporaries,* 5 vols. (New York: Macmillan, 1897–1929), 4: 155–59, bracketed aside [the third] present in the original.

7. AL to George Ashmun, Springfield, Illinois, 23 May 1860, *CW,* 4: 52.

8. Edward Bates, *The Diary of Edward Bates, 1859–1866,* ed. Howard Beale (1933; repr., New York: Da Capo Press, 1971), 128–29.

9. "Nomination of Lincoln," *New York Herald, 22 May 1860; see also "Our Michigan Correspondence," New York Herald, 22 May 1860, and "Lincoln's Radicalism Proved— His Obedience to the Abolition Idea," 6 September 1860.*

10. Wendell Phillips, "Speech at the New England Anti-Slavery Convention," *Liberator,* 8 June 1860, 89.

2. THE CAMPAIGN OF 1860

1. Wendell Phillips, "Abraham Lincoln the Slave-Hound of Illinois," *Liberator,* vol. 30, 22 June 1860, 99.

2. H. Ford Douglas, "Speech of H. Ford Douglas," *Liberator,* vol. 30, 13 July 1860, 109–10.

3. R. B. Rhett, "The Presidential Election and Union Savers," *Charleston Mercury,* 4 August 1860, in Dwight Dumond, ed., *Southern Editorials on Secession* (Gloucester MA: Peter Smith, 1964), 157–59.

4. Samuel Bowles, *Springfield Republican,* in Allan Nevins, *American Press Opinion, Washington to Coolidge: A Documentary Record of Editorial Leadership and Criticism, 1785–1927,* 2 vols. (1928; reprint, Port Washington NY: Kennikat Press, 1969), 1: 242–43.

5. John Auer, ed., *Antislavery and Disunion, 1858–1861: Studies in the Rhetoric of Compromise and Conflict* (New York: Harper and Row, 1963), 264.

6. *Liberator,* 7 September 1860, 142.

7. "The Danger a Reality," *Washington Constitution,* 6 September 1860, in Howard Perkins, ed., *Northern Editorials on Secession* (Gloucester MA: Peter Smith, 1964), 1: 34–35.

8. George D. Prentice to Lincoln, 26 October 1860, Robert Todd Lincoln Papers, Library of Congress.

9. AL to George D. Prentice, Springfield, Illinois, 29 October 1860, *CW,* 4: 134–35.

10. *New York Herald,* 6 November 1860.

11. *New York Herald,* 8 November 1860.

3. INTERREGNUM

1. Gideon Welles to AL, Hartford, 12 November 1860, Gideon Welles Papers, H. E. Huntington Library, San Marino CA.

2. "Southern Desperation," *Liberator,* vol. 30, 16 November 1860.

3. Cobb, in *Confederate Records of the State of Georgia* (C. P. Byrd: Atlanta, 1919), 1:157–82; Beecher, *New York Tribune,* 30 November 1860; Douglass, in Philip S. Foner, *The Life and Writings of Frederick Douglass: Pre-Civil War Decade, 1850–1860* (International Publishers, 1950), 536.

4. AL to Nathaniel P. Paschall, Springfield, Illinois, 16 November 1860, *CW,* 4: 139–40.

5. Edward McPherson, *The Political History of the United States of America during the Great Rebellion,* 2d ed. (Washington DC: Philp and Solomons, 1865), 51–52.

6. James D. Richardson, ed., *A Compilation of the Messages and Papers of the Presidents, 1789–1908,* 11 vols. (n.p.: Bureau of National Literature and Art, 1908), 5: 634–36.

7. AL to Nicolay, 15 November 1860, in Early Miers, ed., *Lincoln Day by Day: A Chronology, 1809–1865,* 3 vols. (Washington DC: Lincoln Sesquicentennial Association, 1980), 2: 297.

8. AL to Lyman Trumbull, Springfield, Illinois, 10 December 1860, *CW,* 4: 149–50.

9. AL to Alexander H. Stephens, Springfield, Illinois, 22 December 1860, *CW,* 4: 160–61.

10. Alexander Stephens to AL, *CW,* 4:160–61n.

11. AL to William Kellogg, Springfield, Illinois, 11 December 1860, *CW,* 4: 150.

12. AL to Elihu B. Washburne, Springfield, Illinois, 13 December 1860, *CW,* 4: 151.

13. David C. Mearns, ed. *The Lincoln Papers,* 2 vols. (Garden City NY: Doubleday and Company, 1948), 2: 344–45.

14. Winfield Scott, *Memoirs of Lieut.-General Scott LL.D. Written by Himself, 2 vols.* (New York: Sheldon, 1864), 2: 614–15.

15. AL to Elihu B. Washburne, Springfield, Illinois, 21 December 1860, *CW,* 4: 159n.

16. AL to Duff Green, Springfield, Illinois, 28 December 1860, *CW,* 4: 162–63.

17. AL, Resolutions Drawn up for Republican Members of Senate Committee of Thirteen (20 December 1860), *CW,* 4: 156–67. Lincoln used "it's," as was fairly common at the time; such apostrophes have been dropped throughout this volume.

18. Bancroft, *Life of William H. Seward,* 2: 10.

19. AL to William H. Seward, Springfield, Illinois, 1 February 1861, *CW,* 4: 183.

4. FROM SPRINGFIELD TO WASHINGTON

1. AL, Farewell Address at Springfield, Illinois, 11 February 1861, *CW,* 4: 190.

2. AL, Speech from the Balcony of the Bates House at Indianapolis, Indiana, 11 February 1861, *CW,* 4: 195–96.

3. *Congressional Globe,* 36th Cong., 893 (hereafter cited as *CG).*

4. AL, Address in Cincinnati, 11 February 1861, *CW,* 4: 199.

5. AL, Address in Columbus, 11 February 1861, *CW,* 4: 204.

6. Editorial, "Mr. Lincoln's Speeches," *Daily Missouri Republican,* 15 February 1861, in Dumond, *Southern Editorials,* 460–61.

7. Grace Bedell to AL, Westfield, New York, 15 October 1860, *CW,* 4: 130n.

8. AL to Grace Bedell, Springfield, Illinois, 19 October 1860, *CW,* 4: 129.

9. AL, Remarks at Westfield, New York, 16 February 1861, *CW,* 4: 219. Whether it was Lincoln or the reporter who got her name wrong we cannot know.

10. AL, Speech in Independence Hall, Philadelphia, Pennsylvania, 22 February 1861, *CW,* 4: 240–41.

11. AL, Address to the Pennsylvania General Assembly at Harrisburg, 22 February 1861, *CW,* 4: 244–45.

12. John G. Nicolay and John Hay, *Abraham Lincoln: A History,* 10 vols. (New York: Century Company, 1909), 3: 311–12.

13. Frank Moore, ed., *The Rebellion Record: A Diary of American Events, with Documents, Narratives, Illustrative Incidents, Poetry, Etc.,* 11 vols. (New York: G. P. Putnam, 1861–63; D. Van Nostrand, 1864–68), 1: 34.

14. Benson Lossing, *Pictorial History of the Civil War,* 3 vols. (Philadelphia: George W. Childs, 1866–68), 1: 279–80.

5. LINCOLN FRAMES A CABINET

1. Thurlow Weed, *Life of Thurlow Weed including His Autobiography and a Memoir,* ed. Harriet Weed and Thurlow Weed Barnes, 2 vols. (Boston: Houghton Mifflin, 1883–84), 1: 605–8; for Lincoln's remark on leaving the telegraph office see Nicolay and Hay, *Abraham Lincoln,* 3: 347.

2. AL to William Seward, Springfield, Illinois, 8 December 1860, *CW,* 4: 148, 148–49.

3. AL to Lyman Trumbull, Springfield, Illinois, 8 December 1860, *CW,* 4: 149.

4. William Seward to AL, Washington, 13 December 1860, in Nicolay and Hay, *Abraham Lincoln,* 3: 350–51.

5. William Bryant, *The Letters of William Cullen Bryant,* ed. William Bryant II and Thomas Voss, 6 vols. (New York: Fordham, 1975), 4: 187–88.

6. AL to William C. Bryant, Springfield, Illinois, 29 December 1860, *CW,* 4: 163.

7. AL to William H. Seward, Executive Mansion, 12 January 1861, *CW,* 4: 173.

8. AL to William H. Seward, Executive Mansion, 4 March 1861, *CW,* 4: 273.

9. AL to William H. Seward, Executive Mansion, 4 March 1861, *CW,* 4: 273.

10. Bates, *Diary,* 164–66.

11. AL to Edward Bates, Springfield, Illinois, 18 December 1860, *CW,* 4: 154. The *St. Louis Daily Missouri Democrat* was a Republican newspaper associated with the radical wing of the party.

12. Salmon Chase to AL, Columbus, Ohio, 7 November 1860, in Robert Warden, *An Account of the Private Life and Public Services of Salmon Portland Chase* (Cincinnati: Wilstach and Baldwin, 1874), 364.

13. AL to Simon Cameron, and AL to Salmon Chase, 31 December 1860, *CW,* 4: 168.

14. Salmon Chase to John Trowbridge, Columbus, 7 November 1860, in Warden, *Account of the Private Life*, 364–65.

15. Salmon Chase to Abraham Lincoln, Columbus, Ohio, 11 January 1861, in Salmon Chase, *The Salmon Chase Papers,* ed. John Niven, 5 vols. (Kent OH: Kent State University Press, 1993–1998), 3: 48–49 (hereafter cited as Niven, *Chase Papers).*

16. John Niven, *Salmon P. Chase: A Biography* (New York: Oxford University Press, 1995), 230.

17. AL to Simon Cameron, Springfield, Illinois, 3 January 1861, *CW,* 4: 169–70.

18. AL, "Remarks to a Pennsylvania Delegation," Springfield, Illinois, *CW,* 4: 179–81.

19. Burton Hendrick, *Lincoln's War Cabinet* (Boston: Little, Brown and Company, 1946), 78.

20. AL to Hannibal Hamlin, 14 December 1860, *The Papers and Writings of Abraham Lincoln,* 7 vols., ed. Arthur Brooks Lapsley, commentators Theodore Roosevelt, Carl Schurz, and Joseph Choate (Project Gutenberg eBook 3253, www.gutenberg.org, 2009, updated 2012), vol. 5; *CW,* 4: 161.

21. Weed, *Life of Thurlow Weed*, 606; Edward Morgan to Gideon Welles, 19 February 1861, Abraham Lincoln Presidential Library, Manuscripts Collection SC 1637.

6. THE FIRST INAUGURAL

1. Scott, *Memoirs*, 2: 612.

2. Charles Francis Adams, Jr., in *Proceedings of the Massachusetts Historical Society* (Boston: Massachusetts Historical Society, 1879), vol. 42: 148–49.

3. *CW,* 4: 262–71.

4. Perkins, *Northern Editorials,* 2: 628–29.

5. Perkins, *Northern Editorials,* 2: 629.

6. Reprinted in Nevins, *American Press Opinion,* 1: 249–51.

7. Moore, *Rebellion Record,* 1: 40.

8. Frederick Douglass, *The Life and Writings of Frederick Douglass,* ed. Philip Foner, 5 vols. (New York: International Publishers, 1950), April 1861, 3: 71–80.

9. L. Q. Washington to General L. Pope Walker, 5 March 1861, in U.S. War Department, *The War of the Rebellion: A Compilation of the Official Records of the Union and Confederate Armies,* 128 vols. (Washington DC: Government Printing Office, 1880–1901), ser. 1, 1: 263 (hereafter cited as *OR).*

10. Dumond, *Southern Editorials,* 474–75.

11. H. D. Faulkner to AL, 5 March 1861, in Harold Holzer, *The Lincoln Mailbag* (Carbondale: Southern Illinois University Press, 1998), 7, 8n.

12. *CG,* 37th Cong., special sess., 1436.

13. *CG,* 37th Cong., special sess., 1436.

7. FORT SUMTER CRISIS

1. Mearns, *Lincoln Papers,* 2: 465.

2. Winfield Scott to AL, Washington, 11 March 1861, in Mearns, *Lincoln Papers,* 2: 477–78.

3. Winfield Scott to Major Robert Anderson, Washington, 11 March 1861, in Mearns, *Lincoln Papers,* 2: 476.

4. Nicolay and Hay, *Abraham Lincoln,* 3: 387.

5. Salmon Chase to AL, Washington, 16 March 1861, in Niven, *Chase Papers,* 3: 53–54.

6. Samuel W. Crawford, *The Genesis of the Civil War: The Story of Sumter, 1860–1861,* (New York: n.p., 1887), 331.

7. Perkins, *Northern Editorials,* 1: 363; Douglas, *CG,* pt. 2, 36th Cong., 2nd sess., 1459–60.

8. William Seward, "Some Thoughts for the President's Consideration," 1 April 1861, *CW,* 4: 317–18.

9. AL to William Seward, Executive Mansion, 1 April 1861, *CW,* 4: 316–17.

10. Simon Cameron to Robert Anderson, Washington, 4 April 1861, *CW,* 4: 321–22.

11. *New York Herald,* 9 April 1861.

12. *New York Times,* 13 April 1861.

13. "Proclamation Calling Militia and Convening Congress," Washington, 15 April 1861, *CW,* 4: 331–32; Lincoln's "yet belonging" is also from *CW* 4.

14. Henry Tappan to AL, Ann Arbor, Michigan, 19 April 1861, in Mearns, *Lincoln Papers,* 2: 572–73.

15. Edward McPherson, *Political History,* 114.

16. James Vallandigham, *A Life of Clement L. Vallandigham by His Brother, Rev. James L. Vallandigham* (Baltimore: Turnbull Brothers, 1872), 161–63.

17. Edward McPherson, *Political History,* 155–58.

18. Moore, *Rebellion Record,* 2: 185–93.

19. Moore, *Rebellion Record,* 1: 64.

20. *Lyrics of Loyalty,* ed. Frank Moore (New York: n.p., 1864), 325–26.

8. THE FIRST CIVIL WAR CONGRESS

1. Orville Browning, *The Diary of Orville Hickman Browning,* 2 vols., ed. Theodore Calvin Pease and James G. Randall (Springfield: Trustees of the Illinois State Historical Library, 1925–33), 1: 475, 3 July 1861.

2. AL, Message to Congress in Special Session, Washington, 4 July 1861, *CW,* 4: 421–41.

3. *CG,* 37th Cong., 1st sess., 10 July 1861, 40.

4. *CG,* 37th Cong., 1st sess., 10 July 1861, 44–45.

5. *CG,* 37th Cong., 1st sess., 16 July 1861, 139–40.

6. *CG,* 37th Cong., 1st sess., 16 July 1861, 152.

7. *CG,* 37th Cong., 1st sess., 2 August 1861, 393.

8. *CG,* 37th Cong., 1st sess., 2 August 1861, 393.

9. LOYALTY QUESTION IN BORDER SLAVE STATES

1. AL, Reply to the Frontier Guard, Executive Mansion, 26 April 1861, *CW,* 4: 345; and see Hicks, *Journal of the State Convention* (Jackson MI, 1861) 182–83; Wise, in John

G. Nicolay and John Hay, "The National Uprising," *Century* 35 (1888), 906; Cameron, *OR, SER. 2, 1: 564.*

2. George William Brown, *Baltimore and the Nineteenth of April, 1861: A Study of the War* (Baltimore: N. Murray, Johns Hopkins University, 1887), 57; Nicolay and Hay, *Abraham Lincoln,* 4: 119.

3. Nicolay and Hay, *Abraham Lincoln,* 4: 124.

4. AL to Thomas H. Hicks and George W. Brown, Washington, 20 April 1861, *CW,* 4: 340.

5. Nicolay and Hay, *Abraham Lincoln,* 4: 120.

6. AL, Reply to Baltimore Committee, 22 April 1861, *CW,* 4: 341–42.

7. AL to Reverdy Johnson, Executive Mansion, 24 April 1861, *CW,* 4: 342–43; for Lincoln's anxious remarks see William Roscoe Thayer, *The Life and Letters of John Hay* (Boston: Houghton Mifflin, 1915); 1: 106; Johnson, *CW,* 4: 343 .

8. AL to Winfield Scott, Washington, 25 April 1861, *CW,* 4: 344.

9. AL to Gideon Welles, Executive Mansion, 29 April 1861, *CW,* 4: 348.

10. AL to Otho Scott, Robert M. McLane, and William J. Ross, Washington DC, 6 May 1861, *CW,* 4: 358; resolution in *Journal of the Proceedings of the Senate of the State of Maryland,* 106.

11. James Randall and David Donald, *The Civil War and Reconstruction,* 2d ed. (Lexington MA: Heath, 1969), 232.

12. Reverdy Johnson, "The Power of the President to Suspend the Writ of Habeas Corpus," *National Intelligencer,* 20 June 1861; John Pendleton Kennedy, *The Great Drama: An Appeal to Maryland* (Baltimore: John D. Toy), 1861.

13. Resolution of the House of Representatives and Reply of the President, 24 July 1861, *OR,* ser. 1, 2: 156.

14. Resolution and Reply, 24 July 1861, *OR,* ser. 1, 2: 156

15. *The American Annual Cyclopaedia and Register of Important Events,* 42 vols. (New York: D. Appleton, 1862–1903), 1: 448 (hereafter cited as *Cyclopaedia*).

16. AL to Reverdy Johnson, Executive Mansion, 26 July 1862, *CW,* 5: 342–43.

17. AL, Reply to Delegation of Baltimore Citizens, 15 November 1861, *CW,* 5: 24.

18. AL to the Senate and House of Representatives, 26 May 1862, *CW,* 5: 240–43.

19. *Louisville Democrat,* in Moore, *Rebellion Record,* 1: 66; Magoffin's response, *OR,* ser. 3, vol. 5, pt. 1, 886.

20. Archibald Dixon, Speech, *Louisville Journal,* 21 April 1861, in Moore, *Rebellion Record,* 1: 76.

21. *Cyclopaedia,* 1: 397.

22. AL, Order to Robert Anderson, 7 May 1861, *CW,* 4: 359.

23. AL to Robert Anderson, Washington DC, 14 May 1861, *CW,* 4: 368–69.

24. AL to Simon B. Buckner, 10 July 1861, *CW,* 4: 444.

25. AL to the Kentucky Delegation in Congress, Executive Mansion, 29 July 1861, *CW,* 4: 464.

26. *Cyclopaedia,* 1: 398.

27. AL to Beriah Magoffin, Washington DC, 24 August 1861, *CW,* 4: 497.

10. MISSOURI, AN UNRULY UNION PARTNER

1. *Cyclopaedia,* 1: 488.

2. C. Gibson to Edward Bates, Saint Louis, 22 April 1861, *OR,* ser. 1, 1: 672–73.

3. Nicolay and Hay, *Abraham Lincoln,* 4: 212.

4. Claiborne Jackson to Leroy Walker, Jefferson City, Missouri, 5 May 1861, *OR,* ser. 1, 1: 690.

5. Lorenzo Thomas to W. S. Harney, Washington, 27 May 1861, *OR,* ser. 1, 3: 376.

6. AL to Francis Blair Jr., Washington DC, 18 May 1861, *CW,* 4: 372–73.

7. Nicolay and Hay, *Abraham Lincoln,* 4: 222.

8. Nicolay and Hay, *Abraham Lincoln,* 4: 223n.

9. In Memoriam, Hamilton R. Gamble, Governor of Missouri (St. Louis: George Knapp Printers, 1864), 8.

10. Lincoln to Cameron, 6 September 1861, *CW,* 4: 511.

11. *Cyclopaedia,* 1: 136.

12. First Message to Congress, 3 December 1861, *CW,* 5: 49.

11. FRÉMONT PROCLAIMS FREEDOM IN MISSOURI

1. Julian Hawthorne, *Nathaniel Hawthorne and His Wife* (Boston: Houghton Mifflin, 1884), 2: 294.

2. Nicolay and Hay, *Abraham Lincoln,* 4: 416–17.

3. AL to John C. Fremont, Washington DC, 2 September 1861, *CW,* 4: 506.

4. Nicolay and Hay, *Abraham Lincoln,* 4: 418–19.

5. AL to John C. Fremont, Washington DC, 11 September 1861, *CW,* 4: 517–18.

6. Jessie Benton Fremont, *The Letters of Jessie Benton Fremont,* ed. Pamela Herr and Mary Lee Spence (Urbana: University of Illinois Press, 1993), 264–67.

7. AL to Mrs. General Fremont, 12 September 1861, *CW,* 4: 519.

8. Moore, *Rebellion Record,* 3: 126–27.

9. AL to Joseph Holt, Executive Mansion, 12 September 1861, *CW,* 4: 520.

10. Moore, *Rebellion Record,* 3: 127–29.

11. William Salter, *The Life of James W. Grimes, Governor of Iowa, 1854–1858* (New York: D. Appleton and Company, 1876), 153.

12. Maurice Baxter, *Orville H. Browning, Lincoln's Friend and Critic* (Bloomington: Indiana University Press, 1957), 131.

13. AL to Orville H. Browning, Executive Mansion, 22 September 1861, *CW,* 4: 531–32.

14. AL to Samuel R. Curtis, Washington DC, 7 October 1861, *CW,* 4: 549.

15. Quoted from Chase Papers MS., in James Ford Rhodes, *History of the United States from the Compromise of 1850 to the Final Restoration of Home Rule at the South in 1877,* 8 vols. (New York: Macmillan, 1904–19), 3: 370–71.

12. FIRST BULL RUN

1. *Papers and Writings of Abraham Lincoln* (eBook 3253), 2: 38.
2. Collin R. Ballard, *The Military Genius of Abraham Lincoln: An Essay* (Cleveland: World Publishing Company, 1952), 3.
3. Nicolay and Hay, *Abraham Lincoln,* 4: 305.
4. John Adams Dix, *Memoirs of John Adams Dix,* ed. Morgan Dix, 2 vols. (New York: Harper and Brothers, 1883), 2: 19.
5. AL to Heads of Bureaus, Washington, 22 June 1861, *CW,* 4: 415.
6. *OR,* ser. 3, 1: 177–78.
7. *OR,* ser. 3, 1: 250.
8. *OR,* ser. 3, 1: 178.
9. U.S. Congress, *Report on the Conduct of the War,* 37th Cong., 3rd sess., 26 December 1861.
10. *CG,* 37th Cong., 1st sess., 246.
11. *CG,* 37th Cong., 1st sess., 246, 387.
12. AL, Memoranda of Military Policy Suggested by the Bull Run Defeat, 23 and 27 July 1861, *CW,* 4: 457–58.
13. Nicolay and Hay, *Abraham Lincoln,* 4: 365–66.
14. John Hay, *Inside Lincoln's White House: The Complete Civil War Diary of John Hay,* ed. Michael Burlingame and John Ettlinger (Carbondale: Southern Illinois University Press, 1997), 193 (hereafter cited as Burlingame, *Hay Diary*).

13. ENTER MCCLELLAN

1. George B. McClellan, *McClellan's Own Story: The War for the Union, the Soldiers Who Fought It, the Civilians Who Directed It, and His Relations to It and to Them* (New York: Charles Webster and Company, 1887), 82–85.
2. George McClellan, *The Civil War Papers of George B. McClellan: Selected Correspondence, 1860–65,* ed. Stephen Sears (New York: Ticknor and Fields, 1989), 85–86, 106, 135 (hereafter cited as Sears, *Selected Correspondence*).
3. Burlingame, *Hay Diary,* 32.
4. William Russell, *My Diary North and South* (Boston: TOHP Burnham, 1863), 552.
5. Sears, *Selected Correspondence,* 171.
6. AL, Order Retiring Winfield Scott from Command, Executive Mansion, 1 November 1861, *CW,* 5: 10.
7. AL to George B. McClellan, Executive Mansion, 1 November 1861, *CW,* 5: 9–10.
8. Burlingame, *Hay Diary,* 29.
9. Burlingame, *Hay Diary,* 30.
10. Bruce Tap, *Over Lincoln's Shoulder: The Committee on the Conduct of the War* (Lawrence: University of Kansas Press, 1998), 104.

11. AL to George B. McClellan, Executive Mansion, 1 and 9 January 1862, *CW*, 5: 88, 94.

12. Bates, *Diary*, 218–19.

13. "General M. C. Meigs on the Conduct of the Civil War," *American Historical Review* 26 (October 1920): 292.

14. Michael Burlingame, *The Inner World of Abraham Lincoln* (Champaign: University of Illinois Press, 1994), 183.

15. Burlingame, *The Inner World*, 292–93.

16. AL to Simon Cameron, Executive Mansion, 11 January 1862, *CW*, 5: 96.

17. AL to Simon Cameron, Executive Mansion, 11 January 1862, *CW*, 5: 96–97.

18. Cameron to AL, 11 January 1862, *CW*, 5: 97.

19. AL, President's General War Order No.1, Executive Mansion, 27 January 1862, *CW*, 5: 111–12; AL, President's Special War Order No. 1, Executive Mansion, 31 January 1862, *CW*, 5: 115.

20. Sears, *Selected Correspondence*, 162–70.

21. AL to George B. McClellan, Executive Mansion, 3 February 1862, *CW*, 5: 118–19.

22. AL, President's General War Order No. 3, Executive Mansion, 8 March 1862, *CW*, 5: 151.

23. George B. McClellan to AL and Edwin Stanton, 9 March 1862; Sears, *Selected Correspondence*, 200.

24. AL, President's War Order No. 3, Executive Mansion, 11 March 1862, *CW*, 5: 155.

14. THIRTY-SEVENTH CONGRESS

1. *CW*, Annual Message to Congress, 5: 35–53.

2. *CG*, 37th Cong., 2nd sess., 2 January 1862, 436–37.

3. *CG*, 37th Cong., 2nd sess., 2 January 1862, 506–20.

4. Bates, *Diary*, 227.

5. T. Harry Williams, *Lincoln and the Radicals* (Madison: University of Wisconsin Press, 1965), 54.

6. David Herbert Donald, *Lincoln* (New York: Simon and Schuster, 1995), 342.

7. *CG*, 37th Cong., 2nd sess., 22 January 1862, 440.

8. *CG*, 37th Cong., 2nd sess., 10 March 1862, 1136.

9. *CG*, 37th Cong., 2nd sess., 10 March 1862, 1136.

10. *CG*, 37th Cong., 2nd sess., 25 June 1862, 2195–96.

11. *CG*, 37th Cong., 2nd sess., 25 June 1862, 2918–20.

12. *CG*, 37th Cong., 2nd sess., 27 June 1862, 2929.

13. *CG*, 37th Cong., 2nd sess., 2930.

14. *CG*, 37th Cong., 2nd sess., 27 June 1862, 2964.

15. AL to the Senate and House of Representatives, 17 July 1862, *CW*, 5: 328–31.

16. William Whiting, *The War Powers of the President, and the Legislative Powers of Congress, in Relation to Rebellion, Treason and Slavery* (Boston: John L. Shorey, 1863), 82–83.

15. GRANT AND THE WAR IN THE WEST

1. AL to Oliver Morton, Washington DC, 29 September 1861, *CW*, 4: 541.

2. AL, Memorandum for a Plan of Campaign, (ca. 1 October 1861), *CW*, 4: 544–45.

3. AL to Henry W. Halleck and Don C. Buell, Washington DC, 31 December 1861, *CW*, 5: 84.

4. D. C. Buell to Abraham Lincoln, Louisville, Kentucky, 1 January 1862, *OR*, ser. 1, 7: 526; H. W. Halleck to AL, Saint Louis, Missouri, 1 January 1862, *OR*, ser. 1, 7: 526.

5. AL to Don Buell, Washington City, 1 January 1862, *CW*, 5: 86; AL to Henry W. Halleck, Washington DC, 1 January 1861 (1862), *CW*, 5: 87.

6. AL to Henry W. Halleck, Executive Mansion, 1 January 1862, *CW*, 5: 87.

7. H. W. Halleck to AL, 6 January 1862, *CW*, 5: 87.

8. AL to Don C. Buell, Washington DC, 4 January 1862, *CW*, 5: 90.

9. Don C. Buell to AL, 5 January 1862, *CW*, 5: 90n.

10. *OR*, ser. 1, 7: 533.

11. *OR*, ser. 1, 7: 533.

12. AL to Don C. Buell, Executive Mansion, 6 January 1862, *CW*, 5: 91.

13. AL to Don C. Buell, Washington DC, 7 January 1862, *CW*, 5: 91–92.

14. Don C. Buell to AL, *CW*, 5: 94.

15. AL to Simon Cameron, 10 January 1862, *CW*, 5: 95.

16. AL to Don C. Buell, Executive Mansion, 13 January 1862, *CW*, 5: 98–99.

17. Stephen Ambrose, *Halleck: Lincoln's Chief of Staff* (Baton Rouge: Louisiana State University Press, 1962), 32.

18. James McPherson, *Ordeal by Fire: The Civil War and Reconstruction,* 3rd ed. (Boston: McGraw Hill, 2001), 250.

19. *CG*, 37th Cong., 2nd sess., 2036.

20. *Century Magazine* 45, no. 3 (January 1893): 429.

21. Alexander McClure, *Abraham Lincoln and Men of War-times,* 4th ed. (1892; repr. with introduction by James A. Rawley, Lincoln: University of Nebraska Press, 1996), 193–96.

22. Francis F. Browne, *The Everyday Life of Abraham Lincoln* (New York: N. D. Thompson Publishing Company, 1886; repr., Lincoln: University of Nebraska Press, 1995), 600.

23. Halleck to AL, 26 April 1862, *OR*, ser. 1, vol. 10, pt. 2, 129.

24. AL to Henry W. Halleck, Washington City DC, 24 May 1862, *CW*, 5: 231.

25. Nicolay and Hay, *Abraham Lincoln,* 5: 340.

26. Stanton to Halleck, 28 June 1862, *OR*, ser. 1, vol. 11, pt. 3, 271.

27. AL to Henry W. Halleck, Washington DC, 30 June 1862, *CW*, 5: 295.

16. EXIT MCCLELLAN, ENTER POPE

1. George McClellan to AL, Yorktown, 5 April 1862, Sears, *Selected Correspondence*, 228 (George McClellan hereafter cited as GBM).

2. GBM to Mary Ellen McClellan, Yorktown, 6 April (1862), Sears, *Selected Correspondence*, 230.

3. GBM to AL, Head Quarters Army of the Potomac, 6 April 1862, Sears, *Selected Correspondence*, 231.

4. AL to GBM, Washington, 6 April 1862, *CW*, 5: 182.

5. GBM to Mary Ellen McClellan, Yorktown, 8 April (1862), Sears, *Selected Correspondence*, 234.

6. AL to GBM, Washington, 9 April 1862, *CW*, 5: 184-85.

7. GBM to AL, (Camp Winfield Scott), 23 April 1862, Sears, *Selected Correspondence*, 246-47.

8. AL to GBM, Executive Mansion, 1 May 1862, *CW*, 5: 203-4.

9. McClellan, *Own Story*, 343-44.

10. AL to GBM, Washington City DC, 15 May 1862, *CW*, 5: 216.

11. McClellan, *Own Story*, 350-51.

12. AL to GBM, Washington City DC, 24 May 1862, *CW*, 5: 232.

13. McClellan, *Own Story*, 313, 316-17.

14. AL to GBM, Washington DC, 25 May 1862, *CW*, 5: 235-36.

15. GBM to Mary Ellen McClellan, Coal Harbor, 25 May (1862), Sears, *Selected Correspondence*, 275-76.

16. GBM to Mary Ellen McClellan, Coal Harbor, 25 May (1862), Sears, *Selected Correspondence*, 275-76.

17. GBM to Edwin M. Stanton, Camp Lincoln, 25 June (1862), Sears, *Selected Correspondence*, 309-10.

18. AL to GBM, Washington, 26 June 1862, *CW*, 5: 286.

19. GBM to Edwin M. Stanton, Savage Station, 28 June (1862), Sears, *Selected Correspondence*, 322-23.

20. AL to GBM, Washington City DC, 28 June 1862, *CW*, 5: 289-90.

21. AL to William H. Seward, Executive Mansion, 28 June 1862, *CW*, 5: 291-92.

22. *OR*, ser. 3, vol. 2, pt. 1, 181-82.

23. *CW*, 6: 298.

24. *CW*, 6: 323.

25. McClellan, *Own Story*, 495, 498.

26. Report of the Joint Committee on the Conduct of the War, pt. III (Washington: Government Printing Office, 1863), 278-83.

27. John Hay, *Lincoln and the Civil War in the Diaries and Letters of John Hay*, ed. Tyler Dennett (New York: Dodd, Mead and Company, 1939; repr. New York: Da Capo Press, 1988), 43.

28. GBM to AL, *CW*, 5: 399n.

29. Burlingame, *Hay Diary*, 37.

30. Burlingame, *Hay Diary*, 37-38.

31. Gideon Welles, *Diary of Gideon Welles, Secretary of the Navy under Lincoln and*

Johnson, 3 vols., ed. Howard Beale and Alan Brownsword (New York: W. W. Norton, 1960), 1: 116 (hereafter cited as Beale, *Welles Diary).*

32. Wendell Phillips and Theodore Pease, *Speeches, Lectures, and Letters, by Wendell Phillips,* 2 vols. (Boston: Lee and Shepard, 1892), 449–55.

17. ANTIETAM AND ANOTHER MCCLELLAN EXIT

1. Beale, *Welles Diary,* 104–5.
2. Don E. Fehrenbacher and Virginia Fehrenbacher, *Recollected Words of Abraham Lincoln* (Stanford: Stanford University Press, 1996), 209.
3. Niven, *Chase Papers,* 1: 375.
4. Gary W. Gallagher, ed., *Antietam: Essays on the 1862 Maryland Campaign* (Kent OH: Kent State University Press, 1989), 12.
5. McClellan, *Own Story,* 627–28.
6. McClellan, *Own Story,* 628.
7. GBM to AL, *CW,* 5: 474n.
8. AL to GBM, Washington City DC, 24 (25) October 1862, *CW,* 5: 474.
9. Sears, *Selected Correspondence,* 511.
10. Burlingame, *Hay Diary,* 51.
11. Burlingame, *Hay Diary,* 218–19.
12. Sears, *Selected Correspondence,* 529–31.

18. EMANCIPATION

1. AL, Protest in Illinois Legislature on Slavery, 3 March 1837, *CW,* 1: 74–75.
2. George Bancroft to AL, 15 November 1861, *CW,* 5: 26n.
3. AL to George Bancroft, 18 November 1861, *CW,* 5: 25–26.
4. AL, Drafts of a Bill for Compensated Emancipation in Delaware, (26? November 1861), *CW,* 5: 29–30.
5. AL to Henry J. Raymond, Executive Mansion, 9 March 1862, *CW,* 5: 152–53.
6. Edward McPherson, *Political History,* 210–11.
7. AL to James A. McDougall, Executive Mansion, 14 March 1862, *CW,* 5: 160–61.
8. AL, Message to Congress, 16 April 1862, *CW,* 5: 192.
9. *Papers and Writings of Abraham Lincoln* (eBook 3253), 6: 2.
10. AL, Proclamation Revoking General Hunter's Order of Military Emancipation of May 9, 1862, 19 May 1862, *CW,* 5: 222–24.
11. Niven, *Chase Papers,* 3: 202.
12. AL, Appeal to Border State Representatives to Favor Compensated Emancipation, 12 July 1862, *CW,* 5: 317–19.
13. Edward McPherson, *Political History,* 217–20.
14. AL, *Emancipation Proclamation—First Draft,* 22 July 1862, *CW,* 5: 336–38.
15. AL, Address on Colonization to a Deputation of Negroes, 14 August 1862, *CW,* 5: 370–75.

16. Horace Greeley, "The Prayer for Twenty Millions," *New York Tribune,* 19 August 1862.

17. AL to Horace Greeley, Executive Mansion, 22 August 1862, *CW,* 5: 388–89.

18. Lydia Maria Child, *A Lydia Maria Child Reader,* ed. Carolyn Karcher (Durham NC: Duke University Press, 1997), 254–61.

19. AL, Reply to Emancipation Memorial Presented by Chicago Christians of All Denominations, 13 September 1862, *CW,* 5: 419–25.

20. Niven, *Chase Papers,* 1: 393–95.

21. AL, Preliminary Emancipation Proclamation, 22 September 1862, *CW,* 5: 433–36.

22. Edward McPherson, *Political History,* 232–33.

23. Robert Harper, *Lincoln and the Press* (New York: McGraw-Hill Book Company, 1951), 177.

24. Harper, *Lincoln and the Press,* 178.

25. AL to Hannibal Hamlin, Executive Mansion, 28 September 1862, *CW,* 5: 444.

26. McClellan, *Own Story,* 34.

19. THE FALL OF 1862

1. H. W. Halleck to Major-General Buell, Corinth, 8 July 1862, *OR,* ser. 1, vol. 16, pt. 2, 104.

2. H. W. Halleck to Maj. Gen. Horatio G. Wright, Washington, 25 August 1862, *OR,* ser. 1, vol. 16, pt. 2, 421.

3. AL to Jeremiah T. Boyle, Washington City DC, 7 September 1862, *CW,* 5: 408.

4. Jeremiah T. Boyle to AL, Washington City DC, 7 September 1862, *CW,* 5: 409.

5. AL to Don C. Buell, Washington City DC, 7 September 1862, *CW,* 5: 409.

6. H. W. Halleck to Major-General Buell, Washington, 19 October 1862, *OR,* ser. 1, vol. 16, pt. 2, 626–27.

7. AL to Henry W. Halleck, Executive Mansion, Washington, 8 December 1862, *CW,* 5: 545.

8. AL to William S. Rosecrans, Executive Mansion, Washington, 5 January 186(3), *CW,* 6: 39.

9. AL to Carl Schurz, Executive Mansion, 24 November 1862, *CW,* 5: 509–10.

10. AL to Henry W. Halleck, Steamer Baltimore Off Aquia Creek, Va., 27 November 1862, *CW,* 5: 514–15.

11. William Osborn Stoddard, *Inside the White House in War Times,* (New York: C. L. Webster and Company, 1890), 178–79.

12. Nicolay and Hay, *Abraham Lincoln,* 6: 210–11.

13. AL, Congratulations to the Army of the Potomac, Executive Mansion, 22 December 1862, *CW,* 6: 13.

14. Benjamin French, *Witness to the Young Republic: A Yankee's Journal, 1828–1870,* ed. by Donald Cole and John McDonough (Hanover NH: University Press of New England, 1989), 415.

15. *CW,* 6: 15–16, 22.

16. AL to Henry W. Halleck, Executive Mansion, 1 January 1863, *CW,* 6: 31–32.

17. AL to Ambrose E. Burnside, 8 January 1863, *CW,* 6: 46.

18. "Extracts from the Journal of Henry J. Raymond," edited by his son, *Scribner's Monthly* 19 (March 1880): 705.

20. A WINTER OF DISCONTENT

1. Russell Weigley, *A Great Civil War: A Military and Political History, 1861–1865* (Bloomington: Indiana University Press, 2000), 214.

2. Rhodes, *History of the United States*, 4: 169.

3. AL, Annual Message to Congress, 1 December 1862, *CW*, 5: 518–37.

4. *CG*, 37th Cong., 3rd sess., 39–41.

5. Edward McPherson, *Political History*, 229.

6. Edward McPherson, *Political History*, 229.

7. James Fessenden, ed., *Life and Public Service of William Pitt Fessenden*, 2 vols. (Boston: Houghton Mifflin, 1907), 1: 231–32.

8. Beale, *Welles Diary*, 1: 194–204, passim.

9. Nicolay and Hay, *Abraham Lincoln*, 6: 271.

10. Nicolay and Hay, *Abraham Lincoln*, 6: 297–313.

11. AL, Opinion on the Admission of West Virginia into the Union, (31 December 1862), *CW*, 6: 26–28.

12. Douglass, *Life and Writings*, 3: 306–7.

13. Moore, *Rebellion Record*, 6: 35.

14. Browning, *Diary*, 1: 606–7.

15. *CW*, 6: 28–30.

16. Moore, *Rebellion Record*, 6: 344; AL to the Workingmen of Manchester, England, Executive Mansion, 19 January 1863, *CW*, 6: 63–65.

17. Commager, *Documents of American History*, 421–22.

18. *CW*, 6: 61.

19. *CG*, 37th Cong., 3rd sess., 869–70

20. James McPherson, *Battle Cry of Freedom* (New York: Oxford University Press, 1988), 594; Chester G. Hearn, *Lincoln, the Cabinet, and the Generals* (Baton Rouge: Louisiana State University Press, 2010), 144.

21. *Cyclopaedia*, 3: 242.

22. *CG*, 37th Cong., 3rd sess., 1057–63.

23. *CG*, 37th Cong., 3rd sess., 1063.

24. Albert Gallatin Riddle, *Recollections of War Times: Reminiscences of Men and Events in Washington, 1860–1865* (New York: G. P. Putnam's Sons, 1895), 218n; *CG*, 37 Cong., 3rd sess., 1399.

25. AL to Horatio Seymour, Executive Mansion, 7 August 1863, *CW*, 6: 369–70.

26. *CG*, 37th Cong., 3rd sess., 976–78.

27. *CG*, 37th Cong., 3rd sess., 1214–15.

28. *CG*, 37th Cong., 3rd sess., 1288–99.

29. William T. Sherman and John Sherman, *The Sherman Letters: Correspondence between*

General and Senator Sherman from 1837 to 1891, ed. Rachel Thorndike (New York: Scribner's Sons, 1894), 193.

30. Sherman and Sherman, *Sherman Letters,* 194–95.

31. Charles Francis Adams, *Richard Henry Dana: A Biography,* 2 vols. (Boston: Houghton, Mifflin and Company, 1890), 2: 264–65.

21. SUPREME COURT AND LINCOLN'S WAR POWERS

1. Adams, *Richard Henry Dana,* 2: 267.

2. U.S. Supreme Court, *Prize Cases,* 2 Black 635 (1863), 653, 660–61.

3. *Prize Cases,* 666–69.

4. *Prize Cases,* 688, 694–95, 698–99.

5. Carl B. Swisher, *History of the Supreme Court of the United States,* vol. 5: *The Taney Period, 1836–64* (New York: Macmillan, 1974), 5: 897.

6. *New York Times,* 13 March 1863.

7. *New York Times,* 13 March 1863.

22. HOOKER AND CHANCELLORSVILLE

1. AL to Joseph Hooker, Executive Mansion, 26 January 1863, *CW,* 78–79.

2. Noah Brooks, *Washington, D.C., in Lincoln's Time,* ed. Herbert Mitgang (New York: Rinehart, 1958), 51ff.

3. Nicolay and Hay, *Abraham Lincoln,* 7: 89–90.

4. Nicolay and Hay, *Abraham Lincoln,* 7: 90.

5. Hooker to AL, 27 April 1863, *CW,* 6: 190.

6. AL to Joseph Hooker, 27 April 1863, *CW,* 6: 189–90.

7. AL to Joseph Hooker, 7 May 1863, *CW,* 6: 201.

8. Joseph Hooker to AL, *CW,* 6: 201n.

9. *CW,* 6: 217–18n.

10. AL to Joseph Hooker, Executive Mansion, 14 May 1863, *CW,* 6: 217.

11. Joseph Hooker to AL, Washington DC, 5 June 1863, *CW,* 6: 249–50n.

12. AL to Joseph Hooker, Washington DC, 5 June 1863, *CW,* 6: 249, and see Hooker, 249n, and Halleck to Hooker, 250–51n.

13. Joseph Hooker to AL, 10 June 1863, *CW,* 6: 257n1.

14. AL to Joseph Hooker, Washington DC, 10 June 1863, *CW,* 6: 257.

15. AL to Joseph Hooker, Washington City, 15 June 1863, *CW,* 6: 276.

16. *OR,* ser. 1, vol. 27, pt. 1, 43–44.

17. AL to Joseph Hooker, Executive Mansion, 16 June 1863, *CW,* 6: 281–82.

18. Beale, *Welles Diary,* 1: 348.

23. VALLANDIGHAM AND CIVIL LIBERTIES

1. Clement Vallandigham, *Speeches, Arguments, Addresses, and Letters of Clement L. Vallandigham* (New York: J. Walter, 1864), 494–95.

2. Clement Vallandigham to the Democracy of Ohio, Military Prison, Cincinnati, 5 May 1863, in *Cyclopaedia*, 3: 474.

3. *Cyclopaedia,* 3: 480.

4. *Cyclopaedia,* 3: 483.

5. AL to Edwin M. Stanton, Executive Mansion, 13 May 1863, *CW* ,6: 215.

6. Burnside to AL, *CW,* 6: 237n1.

7. AL to Ambrose E. Burnside, Washington DC, 29 May 1863, *CW,* 6: 237.

8. *Cyclopaedia,* 3: 424.

9. Moore, *Rebellion Record,* 7: 298–99.

10. AL to Erastus Corning and Others, Executive Mansion, 12 June 1863, *CW,* 6: 260–69.

11. AL to Matthew Birchard and Others, Washington DC, 29 June 1863, *CW,* 6: 300–306.

12. *Great Debates in American History: The Civil War Volume 6,* ed. Marion Mills Miller (New York: Current Literature Publishing Company, 1913): 325.

24. ARMING BLACK SOLDIERS

1. Douglass, *Life and Writings,* 3: 94.

2. Edward McPherson, *Political History,* 274, 196.

3. AL, Remarks to Deputation of Western Gentlemen, 4 August 1862, *CW,* 5: 356–57.

4. Dudley Cornish, *The Sable Arm: Negro Troops in the Union Army, 1861–1865* (New York: Longmans, Green, 1956), 51–52.

5. AL to Chicago Christians, *CW,* 5: 423.

6. Cornish, *The Sable Arm,* 73–74.

7. John T. Hubbell, "Abraham Lincoln and the Recruitment of Black Soldiers," *Journal of the Abraham Lincoln Association* 2, no. 1 (1980).

8. Edward McPherson, *Political History,* 384.

9. *Official Opinions of the Attorneys General of the United States,* 12 vols. (Washington DC: R. Farnham, 1852–70), 10: 382–413.

10. AL to John A. Dix, *Executive Mansion,* 14 January 1863, *CW,* 6: 56.

11. AL to John A. Dix, *Executive Mansion,* 14 January 1863, *CW,* 6: 56.

12. *CG,* 37th Cong., 3rd sess., 599.

13. *CG,* 37th Cong., 3rd sess., 599.

14. *CG,* 37th Cong., 3rd sess., 1290.

15. Horace Greeley, *The American Conflict,* 2 vols. (Hartford CT: O.D. Case and Company, 1865–67), 2: 526.

16. AL to Andrew Johnson, Executive Mansion, 26 March 1863, *CW,* 6: 149–50.

17. AL to Nathaniel P. Banks, Executive Mansion, 29 March 1863, *CW,* 6: 154.

18. AL to David Hunter, Executive Mansion, 1 April 1863, *CW,* 6: 158.

19. Nicolay and Hay, *Abraham Lincoln,* 6: 460–61.

20. James McPherson, *Ordeal by Fire,* 352, 358.

21. AL to Edwin Stanton, Executive Mansion, 21 July 1863, *CW,* 6: 342.

22. Ira Berlin, Barbara J. Fields, Thavolia Glymph, Joseph P. Reidy, and Leslie S. Rowland, eds. *Freedom: A Documentary History of Black Emancipation, 1861–1867* (Cambridge: Cambridge University Press, 1982), 233, 582–83.

23. *OR,* ser. 1, vol. 33, 866.

24. AL to Ulysses S. Grant, Executive Mansion, 9 August 1863 CW, 6: 374–75.

25. AL to James C. Conkling, Executive Mansion, 26 August 1863, *CW,* 6: 406–410.

26. Nicolay and Hay, *Abraham Lincoln,* 7: 385, 6n.

27. Nicolay and Hay, *Abraham Lincoln,* 7: 387.

28. AL to Josiah Quincy, *CW,* 6: 443.

29. Frederick Douglass, *The Life and Times of Frederick Douglass* (1892; repr., New York: Collier Books, 1962), 346–49.

30. AL, Annual Message to Congress, 8 December 1863, *CW,* 7: 49–50.

25. GIBRALTAR OF THE WEST

1. Nicolay and Hay, *Abraham Lincoln,* 7: 143.

2. Frederick Blue, *Salmon P. Chase: A Life in Politics* (Kent OH: Kent State University Press, 1987), 212. Rhodes, *History of the United States,* 4: 302.

3. *Century Magazine* 53 (1897): 157.

4. Charles Dana, *Recollections of the Civil War: With the Leaders at Washington and in the Field in the Sixties* (New York: D. Appleton and Company, 1898 [1908 printing]), 73.

5. *Papers and Writings of Abraham Lincoln* (eBook 3253), 6: 235.

6. Isaac N. Arnold to AL, Chicago, 18 May 1863, Robert Todd Lincoln Papers, Library of Congress.

7. Beale, *Welles Diary,* 1: 364–65.

8. *CW,* 7: 47.

9. AL to Ulysses S. Grant, Executive Mansion, 13 July 1863, *CW,* 6: 326.

26. GETTYSBURG

1. David Bates, *Lincoln in the Telegraph Office: Recollections of the United States Military Telegraph Corps during the Civil War* (Lincoln: University of Nebraska Press, 1995), 155–56.

2. Browne, *Everyday Life of Abraham Lincoln,* 597–98.

3. General Orders No. 68, July 4, 1863, in *OR,* ser. 1, vol. 27, pt. 3, 519.

4. AL to Henry W. Halleck, Soldiers' Home, 6 July 1863, *CW,* 6: 318.

5. Burlingame, *Hay Diary,* 302–3.

6. Fehrenbacher and Fehrenbacher, *Recollected Words of Abraham Lincoln,* 406.

7. Beale, *Welles Diary,* 1: 363–64.

8. AL to Henry W. Halleck, (7 July 1863), *CW,* 6: 319.

9. Beale, *Welles Diary,* 365–66.

10. Burlingame, *Hay Diary,* 62.

11. Beale, *Welles Diary,* 1: 369–71.

12. Halleck to Meade, 14 July 1863, *OR,* ser. 1, vol. 27, pt. 1, 92.

13. Halleck to Meade, 14 July 1863, *OR,* ser. 1, vol. 27, pt. 1, 93.

14. AL to George G. Meade, Executive Mansion, 14 July 1863, *CW,* 6: 327–28.

15. Michael Burlingame, *The Inner World of Abraham Lincoln* (Champaign: University of Illinois Press, 1997), 189.

16. *American Historical Review,* 32: 282–83.

17. Howard to AL, 18 July 1863, *CW,* 6: 341–42n.

18. AL to Oliver O. Howard, Executive Mansion, 21 July 1863, *CW,* 6: 341.

19. George Gordon Meade, *The Life and Letters of George Gordon Meade,* ed. George Meade and George Gordon Meade, 2 vols. (New York: Charles Scribner's Sons, 1913), 2: 138–39.

20. Beale, *Welles Diary,* 439–40.

21. *CW,* 6: 466–67; Trevor Nevitt Dupuy, *The Military Life of Abraham Lincoln,* (New York: F. Watts, 1969), 139.

22. AL to Henry W. Halleck, Executive Mansion, 16 October 1863, *CW,* 6: 518.

23. T. Harry Williams, *Lincoln and His Generals* (New York: Alfred Knopf, 1952), 270–71.

27. LINCOLN VS. SEYMOUR

1. Horatio Seymour, *Public Record,* ed. Thomas Cook and Thomas Knox (New York: I. W. England, 1868), 45–58.

2. William Cullen Bryant, in Stewart Mitchell, *Horatio Seymour of New York* (Cambridge MA: Harvard University Press, 1938), 269.

3. Mitchell, *Horatio Seymour,* 276–77.

4. AL to Horatio Seymour, Executive Mansion, 23 March 1863, *CW,* 6: 145–46.

5. *CW,* 6: 146n1 (Seymour to AL).

6. Mitchell, *Horatio Seymour,* 293–94.

7. *National Intelligencer,* 18 June 1863.

8. *New York Evening Post,* 23 June 1863.

9. Horatio Seymour, Speech to the Academy of Music, July 4, 1863, *Public Record: Including Speeches, Messages, Proclamations, Official Correspondence, and Other Public Utterances of Horatio Seymour* (New York: I. W. England, 1868).

10. Alexander McClure to AL, 30 June 1863, *CW,* 6: 311n.

11. AL to Alexander K. McClure, Washington City, 30 June 1863, *CW,* 6: 311.

12. Governor Joel Parker to AL, 29 June 1863, *CW,* 6: 312n.

13. AL to Joel Parker, Executive Mansion, 30 June 1863, *CW,* 6: 311–12.

14. Major General John A. Dix to Governor Seymour, 30 July 1863, *CW,* 6: 390n.

15. Governor Seymour to Provost Marshal General James B. Fry, 1 August 1863, *CW,* 6: 361–62n.

16. AL to Horatio Seymour, Executive Mansion, 7 August 1863, *CW,* 6: 369–70.

17. Horatio Seymour to AL, 8 August 1863, *CW,* 6: 382n.

18. AL to Horatio Seymour, Executive Mansion, 11 August 1863, *CW,* 6: 381–82.

19. AL to Edwin M. Stanton, Executive Mansion, 26 August 1863, *CW,* 6:412–13.

20. AL to Edwin M. Stanton, Executive Mansion, 27 February 1864, *CW,* 7: 210–11.

21. Hay, *Lincoln and the Civil War,* 81.

22. Edwin Stanton to John Dix, 14 August 1863, *CW,* 6: 390–91n.

23. Governor Seymour to AL, 16 August 1863, *CW,* 6: 392n.

24. AL to Horatio Seymour, Executive Mansion, 16 August 1863, *CW,* 6: 391.

25. *CW,* 6: 392, from *OR,* ser. 3, 3: 703.

26. AL, Opinion on the Draft, (14 September) 1863, *CW,* 6: 444–49.

27. Mitchell, *Horatio Seymour,* 352–53.

28. AL to Joseph A. Wright, Executive Mansion, 31 July 1863, *CW,* 5: 351–52.

29. R. Guy McClellan, *Republicanism in America* (Philadelphia: J. M. Stoddart, 1868), 268.

30. Fernando Wood to AL, 8 December 1862, *CW,* 5: 554n.

31. AL to Fernando Wood, Executive Mansion, 12 December 1862, *CW,* 5: 553–54.

32. Edward McPherson, *Political History,* 296–97.

33. Daniel Clark to AL, 13 March 1863, Nicolay and Hay, *Abraham Lincoln,* 7: 375.

34. *OR,* ser. 2, vol. 6, pt. 1, 84 (6 July 1863).

35. "The Pennsylvania Election: General McClellan Declares for the Democratic Candidate," *New York Times,* 13 October 1862.

36. James A. Rawley, *The Politics of Union: Northern Politics during the Civil War* (Lincoln: University of Nebraska Press, 1980), 132.

28. THE EMERGENCE OF GRANT

1. Ulysses S. Grant to Brig. Gen. Lorenzo Thomas, in Camp near Vicksburg, 26 June 1863, *OR,* ser. 1, vol. 24, pt. 1, 158–59.

2. Beale, *Welles Diary,* 1: 386–87.

3. John McClernand to AL, 3 August 1863, *CW,* 6: 380n.

4. AL to Edwin M. Stanton, Executive Mansion, 10 August 1863, *CW,* 6: 380n.

5. AL to John A. McClernand, Executive Mansion, 12 August 1863, *CW,* 6: 383–84.

6. John McClernand to AL, 24 August 1863, *CW,* 6: 384n.

7. Edwin Stanton to John McClernand, 14 September 1863, *CW,* 6: 384n.

8. John A. McClernand to AL, Springfield, Illinois, 28 September 1863, *OR,* ser. 1, vol. 36, pt. 1, 169.

9. Ulysses S. Grant, *The Papers of Ulysses S. Grant,* ed. John Simon, 24 vols. (Carbondale: Southern Illinois University Press, 1967–), 9: 99.

10. Grant, *Papers,* 9: 96–99.

11. Ulysses S. Grant to Maj. Gen. H. W. Halleck, Vicksburg, Mississippi, 24 July 1863, *OR,* ser. 1, vol. 24, pt. 3, 546–47.

12. AL to Ulysses S. Grant, Executive Mansion, 9 August 1863, *CW,* 6: 374.

13. U.S. Grant to AL, Cairo, Illinois, 23 August 1863, in Grant, *Papers,* 9: 195–97.

14. AL to Ulysses S. Grant, Executive Mansion, 8 December 1863, *CW*, 7: 53.

15. Bruce Catton, *Grant Takes Command* (Boston: Little, Brown and Company, 1969), 110; Grant, *Papers*, 10: 167.

29. THIRTY-EIGHTH CONGRESS

1. Herman Belz, "The Etheridge Conspiracy of 1863: A Projected Conservative Coup," *Journal of Southern History* 36 (1970): 549–67.

2. AL, Annual Message to Congress, 8 December 1863, *CW*, 7: 36–53.

3. Thaddeus Stevens, *The Selected Papers of Thaddeus Stevens*, ed. Beverly Palmer and Holly Ochoa, 2 vols. (Pittsburgh PA: University of Pittsburgh Press, 1997), 1: 385–90.

4. Edward McPherson, *Political History*, 322–23.

5. Andrew Johnson, *The Papers of Andrew Johnson*, ed. LeRoy Graf and Ralph Haskins, 15 vols. (Knoxville: University of Tennessee Press, 1967–), 177.

6. *CG*, 37th Cong., 2nd sess., 1796, 2325.

7. Burlingame, *Hay Diary*, 121–22.

8. AL, Proclamation of Amnesty and Reconstruction, 8 December 1863, *CW*, 7: 53–56.

30. RECONSTRUCTION

1. Wendell Garrison and Francis Garrison, *William Lloyd Garrison, 1805–1879: The Story of His Life Told by His Children*, 4 vols. (New York: Century Company, 1885–89), 4: 123–24.

2. *CW*, 8: 152.

3. AL to Gov. Michael Hahn, 13 March 1864, *CW*, 7: 243.

4. Burlingame, *Hay Diary*, 253–54.

5. Charles Sumner, *Memoir and Letters of Charles Sumner*, ed. Edward Pierce, 4 vols. (Boston: Roberts Brothers, 1877 93), 4: 205.

6. *CG*, 38th Cong., 2nd sess., 969.

7. AL to Lyman Trumbull, Executive Mansion, 9 January 1865, *CW*, 8: 206–7.

8. AL to Stephen A. Hurlbut, Executive Mansion, 14 November 1864, *CW*, 8: 106–7.

9. *CG* 38th Cong., 2nd sess., 1108.

10. *CG* 38th Cong., 2nd sess., 1099.

11. *CG* 38th Cong., 2nd sess., 970.

31. GRANT MOVES SOUTH

1. Ulysses S. Grant, *Personal Memoirs of Ulysses S. Grant*, 2 vols. (New York: C. L. Webster and Company, 1885–86), 2: 134–37.

2. AL to Edwin M. Stanton, 23 April 1864, *CW*, 7: 312–13.

3. Nicolay and Hay, *Abraham Lincoln*, 8: 348n.

4. Grant, *Papers*, 10: 380.

5. Grant, *Papers*, 10: 380.

6. Ida M. Tarbell, *A Reporter for Lincoln: The Story of Henry E. Wing, Soldier and Newspaperman* (Curtis Publishers, 1928), 13; Henry E. Wing, *When Lincoln Kissed Me: A Story of the Wilderness Campaign* (New York: Abingdon Press, 1913).

7. Hay, *Lincoln and the Civil War*, 180.

8. Grant, *Papers*, 10: 422.

9. Grant, *Papers*, 11: 45.

32. PRESIDENTIAL NOMINATION SAGA

1. William Lloyd Garrison, *The Letters of William Lloyd Garrision,* ed. Walter Merrill and Louis Ruchames, 6 vols. (Cambridge MA: Harvard University Press, 1971–), 4: 94.

2. Garrison, *Letters*, 4: 95–96.

3. Edward McPherson, *Political History,* 410.

4. Edward McPherson, *Political History*, 411.

5. Edward McPherson, *Political History*, 413.

6. Edward McPherson, *Political History*, 413.

7. Edward McPherson, *Political History*, 413–14.

8. Garrison, *Letters,* 4: 117.

9. Nicolay and Hay, *Abraham Lincoln*, 8: 316–17.

10. Nicolay and Hay, *Abraham Lincoln*, 8: 312–13.

11. Bates, *Diary,* 333.

12. Nicolay and Hay, *Abraham Lincoln*, 8: 321.

13. AL to Salmon P. Chase, Executive Mansion, 29 February 1864, *CW,* 7: 212–13.

14. *Papers and Writings of Abraham Lincoln* (eBook 3253), 6: 141; James Ford Rhodes, *History of the Civil War, 1861–1865* (New York: Macmillan, 1917), 320, and *Century Illustrated Monthly Magazine* 38 (1889): 408.

15. *Cyclopaedia,* 1864, 785.

16. *Abraham Lincoln Quarterly* 6, no. 5; James A. Rawley, *Edwin D. Morgan, 1811–1883: Merchant in Politics* (New York: Columbia University Press, 1955), 197–99.

17. Rawley, *Edwin D. Morgan,* 197–99.

18. Nicolay and Hay, *Abraham Lincoln*, 10: 79.

19. AL, Reply to Committee Notifying Lincoln of His Renomination; AL, Reply to Delegation from the National Union League; AL, Response to a Serenade by the Ohio Delegation, 9 June 1864, *CW,* 7: 380–84.

20. Henry Raymond, *The Life and Public Services of Abraham Lincoln* (New York: Derby and Miller, 1865), 571.

21. AL to Horace Greeley, Washington DC, 9 July 1864, *CW,* 7: 435.

22. Harlan Horner, *Lincoln and Greeley* (Urbana: University of Illinois Press, 1953), 301–2.

23. Horner, *Lincoln and Greeley,* 309.

24. Burlingame, *Hay Diary,* 226.

25. Horner, *Lincoln and Greeley,* 314–15.

26. AL to Abram Wakeman, Executive Mansion, 25 July 1864, *CW,* 7: 461.

27. Ida Tarbell, *The Life of Abraham Lincoln,* 2 vols. (New York: McClure, Phillips and Company, 1908), 2: 199.

28. Niven, *Chase Papers,* 4: 384–85.

29. AL to Salmon P. Chase, Executive Mansion, 28 June 1864, *CW,* 7: 412–13.

30. Niven, *Chase Papers,* 4: 408.

31. AL to Salmon P. Chase, Executive Mansion, 28 June 1864, *CW,* 7: 413–14.

32. Salmon P. Chase to AL, *CW,* 7: 414n.

33. AL to Salmon P. Chase, Executive Mansion, 30 June 1864, *CW,* 7: 419.

34. Rhodes, *History of the United States,* 4: 528.

35. Vallandigham, *Speeches,* 531.

36. Ulysses S. Grant to H. W. Halleck, 9 July 1864, *CW,* 7: 437n.

37. AL to Ulysses S. Grant, Washington City, 10 July 1864, *CW,* 7: 437.

38. AL to Thomas Swann and Others, Washington DC, 10 July 1864, *CW,* 7: 437–38.

39. Ulysses S. Grant to AL, 10 July 1864, *CW,* 7: 438n.

40. AL to Ulysses S. Grant, Washington, 11 July 1864, *CW,* 7: 438.

41. This story is not documented. See Burlingame, *Hay Diary,* footnote 512, p. 672.

42. H. W. Halleck to Edwin M. Stanton, 14 July 1864, *CW,* 7: 440n.

43. AL to Cabinet, 14 July 1864, *CW,* 7: 439.

44. *CW,* 7: 453.

45. Niven, *Chase Papers,* 4: 421.

46. Henry Raymond to AL, 22 August 1864, in Nicolay and Hay, *Abraham Lincoln,* 9: 218–19.

47. AL, Memorandum Concerning His Probable Failure of Re-Election, Executive Mansion, 23 August 1864, *CW,* 7: 514.

33. THE ELECTION OF 1864

1. *Cyclopaedia,* 1864, 791–92.

2. Bates, *Diary,* 402.

3. Nicolay and Hay, *Abraham Lincoln,* 9: 221.

4. C. Peter Ripley, ed., *The Black Abolitionist Papers,* 5 vols. (Chapel Hill: University of North Carolina Press, 1985–), 5: 276–77.

5. Ripley, *Black Abolitionist Papers,* 277–78.

6. Tarbell, *Life of Abraham Lincoln,* 2: 200.

7. Grant, *Papers,* vol. 12, August 16–November 15, 1864, 16.

8. *Century Illustrated Monthly Magazine* 49, no. 5 (March 1885): 732.

9. Rhodes, *History of the United States,* 4: 518n4.

10. Edward McPherson, *Political History,* 417.

11. Edward McPherson, *Political History,* 418–19.

12. Greeley, *American Conflict,* 2: 667.

13. Greeley, *American Conflict,* 2: 668.

14. George B. McClellan, Letter Accepting the Nomination, Orange, New Jersey, 8 September 1864, in Edward McPherson, *Political History,* 421.

15. *New York Tribune,* 22 March 1864, as found in *CW,* 7: 260n.

16. AL, Reply to New York Workingmen's Democratic Republican Association, 21 March 1864, *CW,* 7: 259–60.

17. Browning, *Diary,* 1: 664–65.

18. AL to Albert G. Hodges, Executive Mansion, 4 April 1864, *CW,* 7: 281–82.

19. AL, Address at Sanitary Fair, Baltimore, Maryland, 18 April 1864, *CW,* 7: 301–2.

20. AL, Speech at Great Central Sanitary Fair, Philadelphia, Pennsylvania, 16 June 1864, *CW,* 7: 394–96.

21. AL, Speech to 166th Ohio Regiment, 22 August 1864, *CW,* 7: 512.

22. AL, Response to a Serenade, 19 October 1864, *CW,* 8: 52–53.

23. AL, Order for Celebration of Victories at Atlanta, Georgia, and Mobile, Alabama, 3 September 1864, *CW,* 7: 532.

24. Hale to Seward, 9 October 1864, *CW,* 8: 56n.

25. AL, Proclamation of Thanksgiving, 20 October 1864, *CW,* 8: 55–56.

26. Oliver Morton to Edwin M. Stanton, 12 September 1864, *CW,* 8: 11n.

27. AL to William T. Sherman, Executive Mansion, 19 September 1864, *CW,* 8: 11.

28. Edward McPherson, *Political History,* 426.

29. AL to Montgomery Blair, Executive Mansion, 23 September 1864, *CW,* 8: 18.

30. Francis P. Blair Jr. to Montgomery Blair, 30 September 1864, *CW,* 8: 18–19.

31. Burlingame, *Hay Diary,* 238.

32. "From Gen. Grant; He Congratulates the President on His Double Victory," *New York Times,* 13 November 1864.

33. AL, Response to a Serenade, 10 November 1864, *CW,* 8: 100–101.

34. AL, Annual Message to Congress, 6 December 1864, *CW,* 8: 149–51.

35. Burlingame, *Hay Diary,* 247–48.

36. Sears, *Selected Correspondence,* 619.

37. Riddle, *Recollections of War Times,* 312–13.

38. Salmon Chase, *Inside Lincoln's Cabinet: The Civil War Diaries of Salmon P. Chase,* ed. David Donald (New York: Longmans, Green, 1954), 240.

39. Chase to Stanton, 13 October 1864, Niven, *Chase Papers,* 6: 434–35.

40. Horace Greeley to Chase, 19 October 1864, Niven, *Chase Papers,* 6: 435–36.

41. Chase to George S. Dennison, 11 November 1864, Niven, *Chase Papers,* 6: 437–38.

42. Chase to Charles Sumner, 12 November 1864, Niven, *Chase Papers,* 6: 439.

43. Samuel Hooper to Chase, 20 November 1864, Niven, *Chase Papers,* 6: 443.

44. Schuyler Colfax to Chase, 5 December 1864, Niven, *Chase Papers,* 6: 444.

45. The source for Lincoln's answer to Wilson has not been found; a reviewer indicated it as Nicolay, "Personal Memorandum." The John G. Nicolay Papers include various notes and memoranda and are housed at the Library of Congress, along with some correspondence by his daughter and literary executor Helen Nicolay.—William G.

Thomas, ed. See also John G. Nicolay, *A Short Life of Abraham Lincoln* (New York: Century Company, 1902), 490; and John G. Nicolay and John Hay, "Abraham Lincoln: A History," *Century Illustrated Monthly Magazine* 38, no. 5 (September 1889): 704.

46. Beale, *Welles Diary,* 2: 192–93.

47. James G. Randall and Richard N. Current, *Lincoln, the President,* vol. 4: *Last Full Measure* (New York: Dodd Mead, 1955; repr. Urbana: University of Illinois Press, 1999), 4: 273.

48. Beale, *Welles Diary,* 2: 196.

49. Chase to Lincoln, 6 December 1864, Niven, *Chase Papers,* 6: 445.

50. Beale, *Welles Diary,* 2: 192–93.

34. THE LAST CIVIL WAR CONGRESS

1. AL, Annual Message to Congress, 6 December 1864, *CW,* 8: 136–52.

2. AL to William T. Sherman, Executive Mansion, 26 December 1864, *CW,* 8: 181–82.

3. AL to Edwin M. Stanton, Executive Mansion, 5 January 1865, *CW,* 8: 201.

4. Allan Nevins, *The War for the Union,* vol. 4: *The Organized War to Victory 1864–1865* (New York: Scribner, 1971; vol. 8 in the series The Ordeal of War), 4: 211–12.

5. *CG,* 38th Cong., 1st sess., 2292–94.

6. *Cyclopaedia,* 1865, 206–7.

7. Nicolay and Hay, *Abraham Lincoln,* 10: 84–85.

8. Osborn Oldroyd, *The Lincoln Memorial: Album-immomtelles* (Boston: D. L. Guernsey, [1882]), 490–93.

9. *CG,* 38th Cong., 1st sess., 258.

10. AL, *CW,* 8: 254–55.

35. HAMPTON ROADS PEACE CONFERENCE

1. Nicolay and Hay, *Abraham Lincoln,* 10: 103–5.

2. *CW,* 8: 275.

3. *CW,* 8: 275–76.

4. *CW,* 8: 279.

5. *CW,* 8: 282.

6. Beale, *Welles Diary,* 2: 235.

7. Alexander H. Stephens, *A Constitutional View of the Late War between the States,* 2 vols. (Philadelphia: National Publishing Company, 1868), 2: 599–600.

8. Stephens, *Constitutional View,* 600–601.

9. Stephens, *Constitutional View,* 602.

10. Stephens, *Constitutional View,* 609–18.

11. *Cyclopaedia,* 1865, 191.

12. Nicholas and Hay, *Abraham Lincoln,* 10: 130–31.

13. Beale, *Welles Diary,* 2: 237.

14. *CW,* 8: 274–75n.

15. *CW,* 8: 274–85.

36. DEATH OF LINCOLN

1. AL to Ulysses S. Grant, Executive Mansion, 19 January 1865, *CW,* 8: 223.

2. Grant, *Papers,* 13: 281.

3. Robert E. Lee to Ulysses S. Grant, 2 March 1865, *CW,* 8: 331n.

4. Ulysses D. Grant to Edwin M. Stanton, 2 March 1865, *CW,* 8: 331n.

5. AL to Ulysses S. Grant, 3 March 1865, *CW,* 8: 330–31.

6. AL, Speech to One Hundred Fortieth Indiana Regiment, 17 March 1865, *CW,* 8: 360–61.

7. Grant, *Personal Memoirs,* 2: 424.

8. Porter's account is in William T. Sherman, *Memoirs of General W. T. Sherman,* 2 vols. (New York: D. Appleton and Company, 1875), 2: 328–31.

9. Edwin M. Stanton to AL, 3 April 1865, *CW,* 8: 384–85.

10. AL to Edwin M. Stanton, City Point, 3 April 1865, *CW,* 8: 385.

11. Donald, *Lincoln,* 576–77.

12. Henry Connor, *John Archibald Campbell, Associate Justice of the United States Supreme Court, 1853–1861* (1920; repr., New York: Da Capo Press, 1971), 175–76.

13. Connor, *John Archibald Campbell,* 177.

14. AL to John A. Campbell, (5 April 1865), *CW,* 8: 386–87.

15. R. H. Dana to Edwin M. Stanton, (5 April 1865), *CW,* 8: 387n.

16. AL to Godfrey Weitzel, City Point, 6 April 1865, *CW,* 8: 389.

17. AL to Edwin M. Stanton, City Point, 7 April 1865, *CW,* 8: 389.

18. AL to Ulysses S. Grant, City Point, 7 April 1865, *CW,* 8: 392.

19. Judge Campbell to Weitzel, 6 April 1865, *CW,* 8: 407–8.

20. Beale, *Welles Diary,* 2: 279–80.

21. AL to Godfrey Weitzel, Washington DC, 12 April 1865, *CW,* 8: 406–7n.

22. Nevins, *War for the Union,* vol. 4: *Organized War to Victory,* 316.

23. *CW,* 8: 393.

24. *CW,* 8: 393.

25. *CW,* 8: 393–94.

26. Niven, *Chase Papers,* 5: 15–16.

27. *Cyclopaedia,* 5: 799.

28. Niven, *Chase Papers,* 5: 17–19.

29. Garrison, *Letters,* 4: 123–24.

30. Sumner, *Memoir and Letters,* 4: 236.

31. Gideon Welles, "Lincoln and Johnson," *Galaxy* 16, no. 4 (April 1872): 525–27.

32. Francis Carpenter, *The Inner Life of Abraham Lincoln: Six Months at the White House* (1866; originally *Six Months at the White House with Abraham Lincoln;* repr. of 1866 edition, Lincoln: University of Nebraska Press, 1995), 293.

33. AL to James H. Van Alen, Washington, 14 April 1865, *CW,* 8: 413.

INDEX